☆☆☆☆☆☆☆☆☆☆☆☆☆☆☆☆

*ZEB VANCE: Champion of Personal Freedom*

☆☆☆☆☆☆☆☆☆☆☆☆☆☆☆☆

*A modern interpretation and a striking likeness of **Zeb Vance** when governor of North Carolina at age 32. By Mrs. Margaret Reed of Brevard, N.C.*

Glenn Tucker

# ZEB VANCE

*Champion of Personal Freedom*

*The Bobbs-Merrill Company, Inc.*
*A Sudsidiary of Howard W. Sams & Co., Inc., Publishers*
*Indianapolis · Kansas City · New York*

The author acknowledges with appreciation permission from the University of North Carolina Press to quote from Kemp Plummer Battle, *Memories of an Old-Time Tar Heel,* Chapel Hill, 1945; from E.P. Dutton & Co., Publishers, New York, for permission to quote extracts from David Macrae, *The Americans at Home* (American edition, E.P. Dutton, 1952); from Harry H. Hall, Nashville, Tennessee, for permission to quote from his book *A Johnny Reb Band from Salem: The Pride of Tarheelia,* Raleigh, 1963; from Wilma Dykeman for permission to quote from her book, *The French Broad,* New York, 1955; from Christopher Crittenden, editor in chief, for permission to quote and use material from The North Carolina *Historical Review;* and from Bill Sharpe, editor of *The State,* Raleigh, North Carolina, for permission to use material from issues of that magazine.

*Library of Congress catalog card number 65-26513*
*Copyright © 1965 by Glenn Tucker*
*All rights reserved*
*First printing, 1965*
*Printed in the United States of America*
*Designed by The Etheredges*

BOOKS BY GLENN TUCKER

Poltroons and Patriots, 2 vols.
*(A History of the War of 1812)*

Tecumseh
*Vision of Glory*

High Tide at Gettysburg
*The Campaign in Pennsylvania*

Hancock the Superb

Chickamauga
*Bloody Battle in the West*

Front Rank
*A Story of North Carolina in the Civil War*

Dawn Like Thunder
*The Barbary Wars and the Birth of the U. S. Navy*

Zeb Vance
*Champion of Personal Freedom*

# Contents

☆☆☆☆☆☆☆☆☆☆☆☆☆☆☆☆☆

# Chapter One

# The Senator Reflects

☆☆☆☆☆☆☆☆☆☆☆☆☆☆☆☆☆

Old Zeb sat in the evening light reminiscing with his son Charlie. Spring had come at last to Washington, touching the marshlands along the Potomac flats with a clean green and alerting the daffodils and pansies through the Mall and in the gardens. The elms showed leaflets and the maples along Massachusetts Avenue where Zeb lived were in the russet of mid-bud. The ride to the Capitol each morning for the business of the Senate was glorious and invigorating.[1]

Old Zeb, four times elected United States senator from North Carolina and three times governor of his state, might reflect with satisfaction on the achievements of the present. By hard toil and driving study he had elevated himself to become almost by common agreement, in the spring of 1894, the leading Southern spokesman on Capitol Hill. He had mastered the intricacies of such inherently wearisome subjects as the tariff and the monetary system, though he was not by inclination a student of trade and finance.[2]

Only his infernal sense of humor—an inability to pass over a chance for a good joke, such as always seemed to pop into his mind to illustrate a point—had retarded his progress toward the pinnacle of greatness. Jocundity, while relished, was not the attendant of sober influence or pretentious responsibility. That was particularly true with one whose fre-

*1*

quent yarns and drollery, though apt and penetrating, too often carried with them a whiff of the North Carolina barnyard. They made him more the central figure of the cloakroom huddle than a model of weighty decorum in the Senate pit.[3]

Yet Old Zeb, in his fourteen years in the Senate, despite this zestful human impediment, had gradually asserted his power. Voorhees of Indiana, "the Tall Sycamore of the Wabash," one of the convincing orators of his day, saw that the North Carolinian was not all mirth and anecdote: "He is good natured, but a dangerous antagonist when aroused."[4] And McDill of Iowa found him "sweet as summer, but terrible if rubbed the wrong way."[5] The North Carolina press analyzed the Senate membership and adjudged him the leader of the delegations from the old South.

Some regarded him as clearly of presidential stature, debarred from that high office only by the circumstance that he came from a Southern state involved in the Late Unpleasantness. At least one New York journalist looked behind his humor and found the firm outline of the statesman. "If the state of New York had Zeb Vance of North Carolina, there is no telling what he might become within the next four years."[6] Another scribe wrote: "The answer is not difficult to those who have watched the growth of this remarkable man."[7]

Who were the Southern statesmen and spokesmen who sat with Vance in the 1880s and early 1890s? Lucius Quintus Cincinnatus Lamar had in Mississippi, as had Vance in North Carolina, outlasted the Radicals and carpetbaggers in their spendthrift domination of his state, to become first a representative and then in 1877 a senator. Rated as "brilliant and brave and a great orator," he was looked on nevertheless as "a man of moods,"[8] which meant that none could harness him with the straps of party or sectional regularity. Like Vance, he had served in Lee's army on the Peninsula. But from the Senate he had gone ahead to become a member of President Cleveland's cabinet, and then, at length, had stepped across to decorate the United States Supreme Court with more than a normal admixture of learning, prudence and courage. Unhappily, on the high bench his inspiring oratory on pressing public questions was stilled, and he was restricted to the languid chanting of passionless legalistic phraseology.

Wade Hampton, the intrepid South Carolina planter who had risen to the command of Lee's cavalry and a lieutenant general's rank after the death of Jeb Stuart, was accounted "a man of much heroic metal," but more at home in the saddle than a Senate chair. In a body that was presumed to be sedate he "sometimes needed ballast for his daring."[9] None could dispute that the ever-embattled Joseph Emerson Brown of Georgia, who appears from time to time in the Zeb Vance story, was a powerful natural force. As governor of his state during the Civil War, he was prepared—even eager, it appeared on occasions—to join in simultaneous combat with the Richmond and Washington governments, and any other comers.

Brown, the darling of Alexander Hamilton Stephens, had been even more repugnant to the Jefferson Davis government than had Vance. As a post-bellum United States senator, he was commonly recognized to be shrewd, but adjudged by some capricious and self-centered, traits which had seemed to appear during the stormy course of his four terms in the Georgia governor's chair. Vance's companion as a war governor, Brown was a farmboy from Pickens County, the "dark corner of South Carolina," who had migrated to Georgia after the rough edges had been knocked off at Yale. Like Vance, he had been in political eclipse during the reconstruction years, then, again like Vance, had emerged from the arena of combat and action of the war years to sit in the august forum of contemplation and delay.[10]

Who then but Vance was the spokesman for the South? John Tyler Morgan of Alabama was as strong a legislator as he had been bold a soldier; a private in 1861, without military training, he was a brigadier general in 1863, with such grueling combats as Manassas, Murfreesboro and Chickamauga behind him. But Morgan showed more ability to arrest and challenge than versatility to argue and persuade.[11] Though he had served for a time under Nathan Bedford Forrest, his approach was obvious, lacking in the cunning and strategy which flared in his chief at Brice's Cross Roads and Bogler's Creek and on many other fields. Bate of Tennessee, who had miraculously survived the penetration of the Union center at Chickamauga, was still a newcomer, having more lingering military than tyro-parliamentary recognition.

Vance's friends might call the roll: Coke of Texas, capable but without flair; sturdy, Scotch-plucky Beck of Kentucky; steady and durable Jones of Arkansas—none could equal Vance when it came to crossing swords with the flamboyant spokesmen of the North in an era when the bloody shirt was frequently waved over the Senate debates. None but Vance could stand resolutely against the vitriol of the bitter but sonorous Kansan John J. Ingalls, "the keenest and most venomous mind in the whole body."[12] Only Vance seemed willing, during the embittered debates of the 1880s, to test lances with this magnificent, stormy man, a master of sarcasm and invective. Vance alone, because of his early studies of the classics and assiduous, lifelong reading of the Bible and noted works, among them Dickens, Motley, and Sir Walter Scott (reading was a pursuit he never abandoned), could match the magnetic Kansan in forensic outbursts and rolling words of Greek derivation, as well as in penetration of thought. Had not Jeb Stuart long before called him the greatest orator who ever lived?[13] That judgment was confirmed by Congressman Sam S. ("Sunset") Cox, Speaker pro tempore of the House, who declared that Vance was the greatest stump speaker in America.[14]

None but Vance could meet head on the cool reasoning, ready eloquence, and statistical information of Allison of Iowa, Hoar of Massachusetts, John Sherman of Ohio. Vance was not innately as organized a scholar as some of his Northern colleagues and might be cornered at times by facts and figures. But he could always extricate himself. When driven to the protection of an anecdote from the North Carolina hills, he would convulse the Senate and send the debate off on a tangent where the point at issue might be forgotten until the Senators read the *Record* the next morning.

Now, on April 13, 1894, with the forsythia in full bloom and the congenial Washington spring at hand, Old Zeb sat reflecting not so much on the present as on the long ago days in North Carolina. One by one his earlier Senate companions were dropping away. Ingalls had gone from public life, to become a farmer and mere scribbler, remembered more for his poem "Opportunity" (Theodore Roosevelt always kept it before him on his desk) than for having dominated the Senate with the mastery of his rhetoric for eighteen years. Blaine was resting in his fresh grave overlooking Rock Creek, missed as much by those who sat under the shade trees of Lafayette Park as he was in the executive branch or on the Senate floor, where he would no longer dazzle and disappoint.[15] The gifted Dan Voorhees, who had succeeded the less personable radical Hoosier Oliver P. Morton, was closing out his last term. John B. Gordon of Georgia was soon to retire. Hampton had been ousted from his Senate seat by the rise in South Carolina of the Pitchfork Ben Tillman machine. Henry L. Dawes of Massachusetts was quitting after eighteen industrious years in the House and eighteen distinguished years in the Senate, while the learned New York lawyer William Evarts, grandson of Roger Sherman and chief counsel for President Johnson during the impeachment trial, was voluntarily dropping from public life.

Jefferson Davis, one of the long surviving and notable representatives of the ante-bellum Senate, had died a little more than four years before in New Orleans and his body already had been reinterred in Richmond amid the Confederate great. Of all who had sat in the United States Senate in the years immediately before the Civil War, in the Senate of 1860, sometimes accounted the greatest ever assembled even though it had failed to avert a desperate and costly conflict, only one Southern member lived. He was the ancient and decaying Thomas Lanier Clingman of North Carolina, once brilliant as a legislator, courageous to rash as a Confederate general, and persistent as a mountain explorer. He was often Zeb Vance's adversary, at times his friend.[16] Those who had debated the momentous issue of slavery and disunion could be met with chiefly in the history books. Vance, who had entered as a youngster at the age of twenty-eight, remained with one or two others of the ante-bellum House.

The era of the giants was drawing to a close. True, there were some who awarded Vance no more than mediocre stature. "His chief fame in Washington," said the Chicago *Daily News,* "rests upon his success as a relater of tales which would hardly bear repetition in polite society."[17] The North Carolina rejoinder was to call on President Cleveland to put Vance in the cabinet. But the New York *Times* correspondent shared the Chicago view about Vance's inelegance. The *Times* story forecast that he would speak soon on the Civil Service bill, then: "When that happens, the next number of the [Congressional] Record will be interesting reading. It will contain much vulgarity and much that a Senator of this generation ought to be ashamed of, but it will not be dull."[18]

Vance's North Carolina friends held, to the contrary, that their spokesman had gradually won his way to a position of respect acknowledged throughout the country. Although it was true that at the beginning he often dexterously hid his ignorance behind a sly tale, he had worked his way to the top by diligent study. None in the Senate could present a record of greater industry. Going to that body without familiarity with national politics and affairs, he had read assiduously, as was the custom begun in his boyhood in the log cabin on Reems Creek. Progressively he had mastered the pressing issues before the country and assumed a forward position in the debates. Never was it announced in advance that Vance would speak but that the galleries were crowded and Representatives deserted the House floor to stand in the Senate corridors.

As an orator, he won by his sincerity and deep conviction. Said his colleague Senator Matt Ransom: "He believed what he said. . . . This was the secret of his popularity, fame, and success. . . . He studied his speeches with the greatest care, deliberated, meditated upon them constantly, arranged the order of his topics with consummate discretion, introduced authorities from history, and very often sacred history."[19]

As old soldier Ransom put it, "He did not skirmish; he marched into the battle, charged the center of the lines, and never failed to draw the blood of the enemy."[20] He appears to have been as much a master of pathos as of humor and understood how closely the two were allied.

Vance was something of an anomaly—an admixture of courtly Southern charm with ribald spontaneity. Along with his gentility and dazzling flashes of brilliant rhetoric was the earthy quality which tied him to the common run of people of the mountain coves.

What Billy Herndon said of Lincoln might be said of Vance. Herndon had seen Lincoln at times surrounded by a crowd of two to three hundred persons, all eagerly listening and awaiting the point of the story. Then when they had it, they would rush forth to repeat it in every grocery store and lounging place of the neighborhood.

Vance never visited a village but a crowd assembled. For three generations in the North Carolina mountains, rarely was a for-men-only story related without being prefaced by the remark, "Zeb Vance told this one, so I guess I can."

Big, bull-necked, combative, but still exuding joy, confidence and utter sincerity, and ever ready with a nimble-witted illustration, he stalked down from his back-country home to become rated the greatest force that ever came out of the Blue Ridge. He has been called "a magnet among steel shavings." At few times in American history has a man so endeared himself for so long to the people of his native state—Henry Clay undoubtedly; John C. Calhoun and Daniel Webster; William E. Borah and Robert A. Taft of later days perhaps; Huey Long for a briefer time. As a lawyer Vance was devastating before a jury. The tradition was that if Zeb could get a man past the judge and before the jury, acquittal was as certain as tomorrow's sunrise.

In his fourteen Senate years, Old Zeb, by the warmth of his personality, had won the admiration and respect, if not the love, of most of his colleagues and the Capitol staff. A Cleveland *Leader* correspondent who interviewed him found him "possessed of great common sense" and summed him up: "He is now one of the brightest and brainiest Democrats in the United States Senate," and he is "indeed one of the most popular men in Washington." He saw Vance ". . . a tall man, with well-padded frame, and a big round head covered with short gray hair." His forehead was high, complexion florid, eyes blue, mouth pleasant, teeth white. He wore a short, silvery mustache. "He talks easily, bursting into a laugh now and then as he tells some funny anecdote or makes some ridiculous comparison."[21]

"He is the only man in American history except Mr. Lincoln," said the State *Chronicle*, "who could combine incessant jocularity with determined seriousness and receive credit for his seriousness. A jocular reputation is the worst possible handicap of a strong man. Yet he has so asserted his serious power that not only his wit, but even his vulgar wit has taken its proper place in his life and in men's estimate of it— as a mere incident."[22]

Incident it might be. But while interest in the tariff and the civil service and free silver was as dead as secession in the North Carolina back country, the story ran like a forest fire through the coves and valleys of how Old Zeb had turned the tables on the Yankees when he went to Massachusetts to deliver a lecture. The Bay Staters, knowing his droll manner and practical jokes, baited him by hanging Robert E. Lee's picture in the men's outhouse. When Vance returned from it he disappointed them by remaining silent. Finally they were compelled to query him.

"Senator, did you see General Lee's picture hanging in the privy?" someone asked.

"Yes," Vance replied indifferently.

"Well, what did you think of it?" they prodded.

"I thought it was very appropriate," he responded. "That is a good place for General Lee's picture. If ever a man lived who could scare the dung out of the Yankees, that man was Robert E. Lee!"[23]

Men's room humor indeed, but telling rebuttal. Again, when the Senate was considering an appropriation for his own French Broad River, the stream of his boyhood, which rises near the South Carolina border and meanders northward and westward, cleaving through high mountains on either side and bounding over boulders and shelvings until it joins the Tennessee River opposite Knoxville, he became annoyed at Yankee criticism. The obstacle to the dredging appropriation was a Senator from Rhode Island who, according to the version which reached the North Carolina mountains, made the mistake of belittling the beautiful French Broad, the pride of every western North Carolinian. It was a small stream indeed alongside such navigable rivers as the Hudson and the Delaware, but scarcely the trickle the New Englander claimed when he said he could stand on one bank and spit halfway across it. Vance in truth had not favored the appropriation, or others of the pork barrel type. It had been introduced in the House by his brother Robert, a Congressman representing the western North Carolina district. But Zeb was unwilling to have his beloved French Broad degraded by anyone and went to its defense. He rose half in drollery, but with a touch of irritation, to take advantage of the opening.

"The gentleman who makes that remark about the French Broad comes from the puny little state of Rhode Island," he declared. "Why, I could stand on one border of Rhode Island and piss halfway across that state!"

"Order! Order!" shouted the presiding officer. "The gentleman from North Carolina is out of order!"

"Yes," Vance blandly continued, "and if I wasn't out of order I could piss clear across the whole durned state!"[24]

Punster, wag, raconteur, he was at the same time rugged, dominant, dynamic. He could tell a story which Chauncey Depew would declare was the funniest he ever heard delivered on the Senate floor, and none was better qualified to judge witticisms.[25]

Sometimes his illustrations, like Lincoln's, were double edged and had to be examined to see where the cut was finest. One day Senator George Graham Vest of Missouri was talking about conditions in Indian Territory (now Oklahoma) and Jones of Arkansas tore him to shreds on his facts. The slaughter of the old veteran of the legislative halls of two governments and of Sterling Price's army was so utter that the carnage was discussed in the cloakrooms. Senator Faulkner of West Virginia, another former Confederate who had served with the Virginia Military Institute cadets in the battle of New Market, ventured that the debate had stripped Vest of his outer garments down to his shirt sleeves, as far as his reputation for veracity was concerned.

Vance took over with the remark that Vest's predicament reminded him of a story about Jack Plunkett back in the North Carolina mountains. Jack was a simple, honest fellow who owned only one shirt. When it became sufficiently ripe he would have to go to bed while his wife scrubbed it in the tub. Once she had laundered it and hung it on the clothesline to dry when the calf came along and chewed it up. The wife went weeping to her husband's bed and told him his only shirt was gone.

"Don't cry, my dear," said Jack Plunkett philosophically. "Them what's got must lose."[26]

Like Jack Plunkett, Vest's loss was complete, but still meager.

Vance had been ill of late and unable to attend to his correspondence, but the letters continued to come in. The superintendent of the Wilmington, North Carolina, schools wanted his picture, to buy it and not as a gift. The children were buying the pictures of "eminent Southern gentlemen" to hang in their assembly hall. They already had Washington, Lee, Davis, and Stonewall Jackson, and, above any others, now voted preference to Vance.[27]

From Kingsland, Texas, came the affectionate missive from an old soldier, A. M. Luckey, who had left Randolph County, North Carolina, after the war to become a Texas ranger and later principal of a high school. He and his wife had been unable to name their boy baby, now eight months old. They stood him on the table the night before when they had company, "whereupon the lad began to play such pranks as to excite everyone present with laughter." The father exclaimed to his guests, "He puts me in mind of Zeb Vance."

"Name him Vance, then," said the mother, and thus the boy joined the hundreds, possibly thousands, of others bearing the name.[28]

Though Grover Cleveland was the first Democratic President after the Civil War, Vance, a devoted Democrat, heartily disliked him. Cleveland, in turn, stripped Vance of his last penny's worth of patronage. But Vance, as those in North Carolina noticed, did not need patronage.[29] He never built a personal organization or political machine. He brought to mind the statement that "Insects swarm; the lion forages alone."[30]

Other Democrats had the same trouble with Cleveland and talked about it at the Senate. One senator said the President was so inattentive he was actually disrespectful. Vance declared he dealt with everybody that way.

"I went to see him a few days ago," said Vance, "and he treated me so indifferently that I was reminded of a case I had in court up in Buncombe County soon after I began to practice law. An old man had died, leaving a small estate, mostly of land in the mountains. His two sons, Bill and Jim, the only heirs, employed me to settle up the estate, pay off the debts and divide the balance of the money between them."

To summarize the tale, there were numerous delays. Creditors made disturbances and the settlement had to be deferred through several terms of the court, with the boys growing more and more impatient. Just when it looked as if a settlement were at hand there was more wrangling and another continuance. Bill, the elder brother, not wishing to blame his lawyer, said he was satisfied with the turn of events.

"Well I am not," declared Jim. "I know our lawyer is not to blame, but I'll tell you what's a fact. There's been so much bother about this case, so many disputes and continuances, and I'm so disgusted with the whole business that I'm durned if I ain't almost sorry the old man died."[31]

In those days, members who later became known as "rubber stamps" on Capitol Hill were termed "cuckoo Senators,"[32] who merely echoed the President's mandates. As Vance did not warm to Cleveland during the New Yorker's first term, he opposed him thereafter for renomination. When Cleveland was re-elected, Vance still held aloof. As someone said, "he paid no court to the King."[33] He would not be a "cuckoo Senator." Still, he was intense in his party loyalty.

"We have our differences and dissensions in the Democratic party, of course," he explained, "but we will settle them inside the church, and without calling on the ungodly."[34] His definition of a mugwump, the party swapper of the 1880s, was "a man who fought now and then on either side but lied very steadily on all."[35] He seemed to look on splinter parties with more odium than normal Republican opposition. Once after he attended a Populist meeting he was quoted as saying he "felt like a grain of wheat in a bushel of rat turds."[36]

Though Benjamin Harrison was a Republican, he was an old soldier and Vance found him more approachable. When Aunt Abby House of Franklin, North Carolina, famed for her care of wounded Confederates on the battlefields and whom Vance had once sent off with a letter to General Lee, wanted to see about her Mexican War pension, Vance wrote for her a remarkable transportation ticket. It stated merely: "To all railroad and steamboat captains: Please pass Aunt Abby to and from Washington, D.C., on official business." None dreamed of rejecting her when she presented it over Vance's signature.

In Washington Vance arranged to have her received at the White House. His colleague Matt Ransom took her down. President Harrison listened politely as the senator described her mission, then told her to leave the pension application and supporting papers so they might be processed. "No, Sir!" said Aunt Abby, firmly. "I am not going to leave any valuable documents in the hands of a Republican!"

Harrison's laughter resounded into the White House grounds. He was delighted with Aunt Abby and told her not to worry, her request was granted. Assuaged, and again bearing Vance's *carte blanche* for transportation, she returned to North Carolina with much the same attention on the railroads as would have been accorded Vance or any traveling dignitary.[37]

Harrison's reception of the North Carolina heroine rather belied the notion that "if you pricked him he would bleed ice water."[38]

As Zeb sat in the twilight, he was not thinking of Senate debates, lectures in Massachusetts, of Cleveland, Harrison, or even the burgeoning beauty of the spring that was erupting over Washington. His mind, according to his son Charlie, had of late been dwelling on earlier times, and that meant the stirring events of the war years and youthful days in Buncombe County, North Carolina.[39]

There was the boyhood walk he had taken through the mountain woods, holding the hand of the great John C. Calhoun, which had sparked his ambition and sent him off on the long quest for accomplishment and eminence. There was the journey in homespun to college at Chapel Hill, and the curious looks of the sophisticates when he appeared, a gawky, friendless rustic. There was the lasting and stimulating acquaintance with noble David L. Swain, at times president of North Carolina University and governor of the state—his mother's early schoolmate and beau, who had fancied him and counseled him as student, legislator and finally as war governor, the youngest of the Southern war governors, but able enough to win for himself the title of "The War Governor of the South."[40] There was the even closer friendship and association with lovable old Professor Elisha Mitchell, truly an inspiring man. He possessed the vast learning and rich personality to influence any student of serious intent. How untiring had been Vance's search for the professor's body on a shelf of the Black Dome, the highest mountain east of the Mississippi, which now bears Mitchell's name, and on its summit, beside a tower erected in his honor, his remains.

Then there were the boisterous youthful years in the crude western North Carolina courts; the whirlwind campaign of the young Whig for Congress, and the surprise of the complacent politicians when he was sent to Washington at the early age of twenty-eight. In the House the flaming orator from the hills had participated boldly in the prolonged speakership fight which foreshadowed the desperate war. Bitter as was the struggle between the factions, Zeb managed to inject some wit into the debate and the transcripts of his remarks are sprinkled with the parenthetical word "Laughter."

Then came secession. In the argument which raged throughout North Carolina, Zeb Vance was a stanch defender of the Union. His campaign to keep the state loyal to the old government was spirited and dramatic. It gave him stature as a character who did not shun a bitter fight. But he capitulated in an instant when Lincoln called on North Carolina for volunteers to subdue her sister Southern states.

These could not have been the arresting years for Old Zeb as he sat in reverie. Before him in memory he could see the long gray column of marching men, upwards of 185,000, possibly upwards of 200,000, from his own sparsely populated state,[41] which possessed no large cities; a greater percentage of available manpower than was offered by any sister commonwealth. If they could march past his Massachusetts Avenue window, it would require more than three days for him to review them, as he had reviewed many of them in 1864 on the plain near Orange Court House, riding alongside General Lee.[42] He had recruited a great portion of them, clothed them by his own energies, fed them largely provisions sent up to the army quartermasters from the rich lowlands of his own state, supplied them with medicine, equipment, shoes, and much else brought in by the fleet of blockade-runners he had bought or chartered through his personal influence and effort.

He had set up manufacturers aplenty and combed the South and the markets of Europe for machinery, raw materials and supplies. He had stimulated textile manufacturing, which ever since has remained one of the leading industries of his state. He had refused adamantly to surrender to Richmond the right North Carolina had reserved to clothe her own men, though the Confederate authorities frequently and urgently importuned him to turn over his contracts and plants. Had he been selfish in this respect? Other governors or the central government might have followed his pattern and introduced textile manufacturing and blockade-running on their own account. And he did, indeed, provide large quantities of uniforms and overcoats to other than North Carolina troops.

He had marshaled public sentiment, restricted the acreage of cotton and tobacco, and given preference to growing food. He had organized his state for war mainly by enlisting the voluntary co-operation of the people, who had rallied behind him and awarded to him their confidence, most of them as eager as he was to see the South succeed.[43]

He had jealously guarded the rights of his soldiers, visited their camps, cared for their distressed parents, and fed the homefolks left in privation.

Forty-one thousand of these gray-clad North Carolina soldiers had not come back. Their bodies had been left on the Manassas plain, along Antietam Creek, across the Peninsula, up the Pennsylvania hillside, and in the thickets of the Wilderness. Among the lost leaders of these phantom battalions were brown-eyed, boyish Dodson Ramseur, a major general at twenty-seven, shot through the lungs at Cedar Creek; hard-hitting Major General Dorsey Pender, who fell at the age of twenty-nine at a critical hour at Gettysburg; brilliant Johnston Pettigrew, dead at thirty-five, whose grades remained the highest ever scored at the University of North Carolina at Chapel Hill; blond, much-loved William Henry Chase Whiting, who like Pettigrew at North Carolina had achieved at West Point the highest scholastic record ever made, to his time—a bit free with his liquor, perhaps, but brilliant nevertheless and Vance's friend—mortally wounded at Fort Fisher. These were a few, but by no means all, of the top leaders whom Vance had cherished, and lost in the forward line of battle.

So it had gone during four years of costly, needless war. North Carolina had suffered one fourth of the losses of Lee's army at Chancellorsville, one third at Fredericksburg, one fifth at Gettysburg. Two of the three brigades which had sustained the heaviest casualties at Gettysburg were Pettigrew's and Daniel's, composed entirely of North Carolina troops. The third, Davis's, held the glorious old 55th regiment, credited in North Carolina history with making the farthest advance in the disastrous July 3 assault on Cemetery Ridge. "First at Bethel, farthest at Gettysburg"—so a portion of the North Carolina story went. Zeb's own regiment, the 26th, the boys he had trained and loved before being elected governor, had displayed his own indomitable spirit at Gettysburg. They had slugged it out with the enemy until the casualties reached 83.5 per cent, perhaps the highest loss suffered by any regiment of either army in any battle of the war.[44]

But these matters of North Carolina's war history were not Vance's main achievement. Under the old Union, in the Confederacy, and in Congress after the reconstruction, he might well be regarded as a foremost champion of local self-government and personal rights. None gave the Confederacy more loyal and industrious service, yet none battled with its army and civilian officers alike, from Jefferson Davis down, with more determination to safeguard the element of freedom in the Southern cause than did Vance. If the Southern states seceded because they detected a growing centralization of power in Washington, and feared a despotism, he would not permit his people to become creatures of a new despotism in Richmond.

Alone of all the governors, North and South, he refused to allow the writ of *habeas corpus* to be suspended in his state. And while he fought for freedom, he demonstrated the fallacy of an old belief, a misconception that is a heritage of Roman times, that personal liberty and civil law must inevitably be the first wartime casualties. Vance showed that concentration camps are not the earmarks of a strong cause. A free, unrestrained people, under inspiring leadership, will fight with perseverance and fury for what they believe to be right. If, as has been claimed often, the South lost because it had too much democracy,[45] this was not evidenced in a state where civilians had access to independent courts, lived by the civil law and constitutional guarantees, and were shielded in the possession of their basic rights by their resolute and high-principled governor; yet at the same time served their cause with an ardor and self-sacrifice never surpassed in the history of modern war.

True, there were defections in some of the western counties of the state, which sent upwards of 3,000 men into the Northern armies, and where the war became a matter of family against family and often brother against brother. All Southern states except Mississippi had organized units fighting in the armies of the North. But even with these pockets of Northern sympathy and the loss of manpower they involved, North Carolina still sent far in excess of her normal military population into the Confederate service.

Many of Vance's quarrels with President Davis were due to the appointment of Virginians or citizens of other states to supervise conscription and tax collection in North Carolina. The controversy, as it will be unfolded, was deep-seated and prolonged.

So it would be that Old Zeb reflected about the past, on the balmy spring evening in Washington, as he chatted with his son Charlie. He had but recently taken a sea voyage for his health, on which, as he remarked, he "threw up everything except his Senate seat."[46] Then he had visited Florida to avoid the midwinter in the North. Now he seemed improving, and would go to the Senate in the morning to talk on the free silver question, about which all Washington would be concerned until the next general election.

But Old Zeb would never make the trip down Massachusetts Avenue to the Senate chamber again.

Early on the next morning, after the Senate barber had shaved him at his home, a stroke of apoplexy overcame him. Soon the muffled drum-beat called. That evening he had gone to join Pettigrew and Branch, Whiting, Ramseur and Pender, and the long gray column of North Carolina troops that had marched through some of the most stirring pages of American history.

## Chapter Two

## *A Spark Is Struck in the Mountains*

An event of high influence on the life of Zeb Vance occurred two and a half years before he was born: it was the duel between his uncle Dr. Robert Brank Vance of Asheville and Congressman Samuel P. Carson of Morganton. It chanced to give Zeb books, and books more than his sturdy legs, or horse or stagecoach or any other propulsion, wrested him out of his mountain cove on Reems Creek, lifted him over the crest of the Blue Ridge, and precipitated him into the world of struggle and achievement beyond.

The duel was fought November 6, 1827, at Saluda Gap, just over the South Carolina line, where the old pioneer road from Greenville to Asheville crosses the Saluda Mountain range, and like most duels of that day had no more behind it than jealousy and a sudden burst of temper.[1]

Because of the play of coincidence involved in this affair of high emotions and disastrous consequences to both participants, and its indirect but profound bearing on the life of the lad yet unborn and on all he came to influence, the duel is an essential part of the Zeb Vance story.

Zeb's uncle Dr. Vance was the youngest of the three sons of Colonel David Vance, a veteran of Valley Forge, Brandywine, Germantown,

King's Mountain, and other hard-fought battles of the Revolutionary
War on northern and southern fronts. Zeb's father, David, was the
second son. The eldest, Samuel, served for a time as sheriff of Bun-
combe County, North Carolina; then, with three of Zeb's aunts, Jean,
Sarah and Priscilla, he moved to Tennessee and passed out of North
Carolina history.

Robert, born in 1793 in Buncombe County, suffered an early illness
which was diagnosed as one of the group of ailments called "white
risin' " or "white swelling." The aftereffects make it appear much
like poliomyelitis. When the ailment had passed, one of Robert's legs
was shortened six inches and his body was bent. He stood five feet five
and walked with a limp. But his countenance was attractive and his
intelligence so marked that, after he attended Newton Academy on the
southern fringe of Asheville, he went off to medical school, then returned to Asheville in 1818 to practice medicine.

Scarcely had Dr. Vance opened his office before he won $5,000 in a
lottery. The source of the windfall was not recorded for posterity by
the doctor, but lotteries were then in great vogue and through them
much of the early development of the capital city of Washington and
real estate ventures elsewhere were conducted. The doctor's father,
Colonel Vance, had died in 1813, and had left a substantial part of
his estate to his youngest son. Such affluence led Dr. Vance to purchase
a library that was unusually splendid by mountain standards, containing
about five hundred volumes.

Otherwise his sudden wealth served him poorly. He quit the practice
of medicine and looked for enterprises that, viewed from a doctor's
chair at the bedside, would seem more exciting.

Samuel P. Carson, his young Morganton friend, four years his junior,
who represented the western North Carolina district in the state legislature, was handsome, eloquent, and in all respects so personable that
he was pointed toward a public career. Carson, back home from Raleigh,
urged Dr. Vance to run for Congress against Felix Walker, who had
been famous as one of Daniel Boone's companions in the journey to
Kentucky and the settlement of Boonesboro in 1775. After Revolutionary War service Walker had tried other areas, then moved to
the Asheville neighborhood and eventually gained election to Congress
in 1816. His popularity had taken a sudden plunge in his second term
and he had become the butt of much ridicule after his notorious speech
in the House, which had put a new word, "buncombe," into the English

language. The word was soon contracted to "bunkum" and ultimately to "bunk."[2]

The origin came when the House was discussing the Missouri Compromise of 1820. The members were anxious to vote but Walker, when he gained the floor, preferred to declaim tediously on unrelated subjects he thought would interest his home people or reflect to them his diligence. The members began to drift toward the corridors. He generously told those who remained that they might go, too, if they wished, because he was "only speaking for Buncombe."[3]

Something in the freak manner by which new words are adopted clicked in the halls of Congress that day. The name of Buncombe County became synonymous with vaporing and empty talk, or irrelevance, insincerity, or even falsehood, no part of which could have pleased the good citizens of the county for whom Felix Walker thought he was performing amiably.

Little, rich Dr. Vance was not popular. When he ran against the derided Felix Walker in 1823 he was elected by a single vote. The only event worth recording during his tenure in Washington was that he gained the notice of John Randolph of Roanoke on his arrival because of his small, drawn stature. The Virginian commented, "Surely that little man has come to apply for a pension."[4] Randolph did not seem to recall that when he had first arrived at the House, he, too, was looked on curiously, and was so boyish in appearance that the suspicious doorman questioned whether he was old enough to serve as a Congressman. (The inquiry was one Randolph haughtily declined to answer, declaring it should be addressed not to him, but to his constituents.)[5]

Carson now decided that he wanted to go to Congress himself, so he quit the state legislature, made the race, and ousted the doctor after the single term. In Washington, Carson voted for an appropriation for $25,000 for the relief of sufferers from the fire which had destroyed much of Alexandria, Virginia, then a part of the District of Columbia and looked on as a federal responsibility. But watching over public money was regarded as almost a sacred duty in those days, so the doctor, proclaiming that Carson had "sent a benevolent hand into some other man's pocket,"[6] and that he was a demagogue as well, opposed him again for the House seat. The erstwhile warm friends had now become bitter political enemies.

Carson declared in an Asheville debate that he would hold his opponent accountable for the charge of demagogy except for the doctor's small stature, whereupon the doctor rebuked him, saying, "You are a coward and fear to do it." He added the warning, "If I am lame in the foot I am not in the arm."[7] Carson had declined earlier a challenge from a young man on the ground that the common drunkenness of the challenger deprived him of the right of gentlemanly consideration, and this the doctor mistakenly construed as lack of courage.

Dueling had been illegal in North Carolina since the drastic law of 1803, passed a year before Aaron Burr killed Alexander Hamilton. It resulted from a famous duel between former Governor Richard Dobbs Spaight and Congressman John Stanly, a Princeton graduate, who charged that Spaight, when in Congress, had ducked a vote on the Alien and Sedition Act by feigning poor health. A handbill followed, then a challenge and duel in which Spaight was wounded mortally. Dueling was continued despite the law, covertly and usually across a state line.[8]

The crowd intervened at the Asheville debate and Vance was saved from the fists of Carson's five brothers, but the diminutive doctor, misunderstanding his opponent's tolerance, called a council of his friends and informed them that he was going to center his fire on Carson's aged father on the ground of an unproved tradition that after the defeat of Gates's army at Camden, in the Revolutionary War, Carson had applied to Lord Cornwallis for the protection of his property.

Vance launched his attack when the debate was resumed at Carson's home town of Morganton: "In the time of the Revolutionary War, my father, Colonel Vance, stood up to fight, while my competitor's father, Colonel Carson, skulked and took British protection."

Colonel Carson wanted to challenge at once, but his six sons decreed that they wait until after the election. In it Dr. Vance was snowed under three to one by a constituency which then, like most constituencies today, did not relish personal attacks on a candidate's family.

Soon after the balloting, General Alney Burgin arrived in Asheville with the challenge from Congressman Carson. General Franklin Patton was Vance's second—what post-Revolutionary War planter or distinguished citizen was not a general or a colonel? Dr. Vance before leaving made his will and according to a close acquaintance courted death. He was chagrined by the election returns. Defeat was an interloper he apparently could not dwell with. His nephew Zeb did not like defeat either, but learned to tolerate it.

At Saluda Gap, amid a sprinkling of seconds, a group of generals, and friends of the two principals, a noted character appeared, Davy Crockett. He was one of Carson's Congressional associates who, according to one of the versions of the affair, had been coaching Carson in the use of the pistol, the selected weapon.[9] Davy had married a girl from the banks of the Swannanoa and lived across the Tennessee line.

On the proper signal, Carson sent a ball into the doctor's side an inch and a half above the hipbone, a wound which, in those days, was quite obviously fatal.

Carson, in deep sorrow, wanted to speak to the doctor but his friends hurried him away, which Vance regretted when he learned of it, for he also desired a reconciliation before death. He uttered some heroics about, "It is the way I have wished to die, on the field of honor," and expired. The site of it all is now marked on the Greenville highway, thirty-odd miles south of Asheville.

The important circumstance for Zeb Vance was in the disposition of the doctor's property. Politics had siphoned off most of the lottery cash but the library remained intact. Since the eldest brother had gone to Tennessee, the books fell to Captain David Vance, Zeb's father, and became an extraordinary accession to his farm establishment on Reems Creek. Unfortunately no one seems to have recorded all of the titles, or those of a smattering of books he had received from his father, Colonel David Vance. The fact that Zeb, who read them in his boyhood years, was enraptured through his life with the campaigns of Alexander, Hannibal, Cyrus the Great, and Julius Caesar, and with the great constitutional principles of Anglo-Saxon government, suggests that they included a good store of ancient history and English political and constitutional history as well. Vance had also a lifelong devotion to Sir Walter Scott, who had completed much of his great writing at the time Dr. Vance collected the library, and ended his performance on a rising note two years after Zeb's birth. A reasonable deduction is that Scott, a novelist and poet at top fame around 1820, would have been well represented in the doctor's library. Zeb was a great admirer of Burke, who surely was there.

As courses and characters are most often charted in the early years, something seized Zeb in his boyhood and veered him from becoming an ordinary farmer and storekeeper as his father had been. He became a man who knew the use and power of words. Words were his tools. Words sent him off to leadership and greatness. They made him an orator, and where could they have sprung from except these books?[10]

Carson meantime finished his term in Congress. Deeply affected, he emigrated to Texas and never returned. Sam Houston, who had served in Congress with him, appointed him secretary of state of Texas. Many stories drifted back: that he was in love with Andrew Jackson's niece, the beautiful Miss Donelson;[11] that he was haunted by the specter of Dr. Vance as he appeared on the ground just after he pitched over from the pistol ball, with his eyes speaking mutely and kindly to his foe; that this vision drove him to the bottle and he rarely sobered. These rumors were doubted; the members of his family gave them no credence. Dr. Vance's name suffered no obloquy. Those killed in duels are rarely condemned, usually extolled. People still talk in rapt terms about the duel, as they pass the marker where it occurred.

Another incident of significance to the career and advancement of Zeb Vance was the visit of John C. Calhoun to the mountains, and to a lesser extent, perhaps, visits of another South Carolina senator, William C. Preston, the polished and urbane Philadelphian who had drifted South by way of attending Washington College at Lexington, Virginia.[12] After study of law in Edinburgh, Scotland, much travel abroad, and eventual residence in Columbia, Preston, an ardent Calhoun nullifier, went to the Senate, and, after voluntary retirement, became president of South Carolina University. Both he and Calhoun were occasional visitors in Vance's home.

Calhoun, according to the pioneer mountain impression, was a restless man who often sought escape from his frustration over the loss of the Presidency, an elusive prize which evaded him as frequently and beguilingly as it did his famous colleagues Clay and Webster. Mountain journeys gave him relief, and while the incidents occurring on them did not work their way into much Calhoun biography, the knowledge of them is still handed down in North Carolina family lore and mountain history.

Sometime around the 1842-1843 period, while Calhoun was presumed to be in retirement or was looking toward it, he visited the Vance homestead in Lapland, where Captain Vance had moved his family in 1837 from Reems Creek.

On his overnight stay at Zeb's home he was attracted by the vivacity and quickness of the boy and "amused at the sprightliness of his manner." On the next morning Calhoun invited the lad to take a walk and spent some time talking with him. The result, as offered in the formal phrases of an early account, was that Calhoun "so impressed the young man's mind by the picture he drew of what might be accomplished if he would only cultivate his mind and apply himself to study," that he made a profound mark on the "imaginative boy."[13] Unassuming in his greatness; of easy, gracious manners; frank in the expression of his views; natural and without a trace of pose in his actions and gestures, Calhoun was the very type who could win the confidence of the boy Zeb on a jaunt, and leave him inspired to unusual effort.

The result of this tramp over the mountain trails with the leading statesman of the South was that young Vance prevailed upon his father to send him to Washington College—an imposing name for what was no more than an academy of high school level—near Jonesboro, Tennessee. "The spark kindled by the great Calhoun," said a newspaper version, "was fanned into an ardent flame."[14]

Books and Calhoun! Still a third coincidence entered into the formative process. Sometime probably before the Calhoun visit Zeb had an illness which was diagnosed as "white swelling."[15] One guess is as good as another as to what it might have been, but it was sufficiently serious that Dr. William Lucius McRee, an eminent physician of Morganton and a graduate of the University of South Carolina Medical College at Charleston, came all the way up the mountains to Lapland, a distance of about seventy-five miles, to give treatment. At another time, Zeb fell from a tree and was ruptured and once more Dr. McRee administered, either in Lapland or Morganton.[16]

Zeb's most serious mishap was breaking his thigh bone by still another fall from a tree, this one a horse apple about a mile from his home. His elder brother, Robert, carried him home on his shoulders and Dr. J. F. E. Hardy, who had been a friend of Zeb's uncle, the dueling Dr. Vance, set the fracture. As was then the custom, he put the leg in a box. This meant that Zeb was confined for a stretch, and during the period his uncle's books became much closer companions. Scarcely is it to be credited that one of his lively imagination would have passed his time merely playing with the pebbles collected out of the French Broad River, as has sometimes been averred, but he certainly gave rocks his attention. When he came to study geology later under Dr. Elisha Mitchell at the University of North Carolina he had a good background understanding of rocks—geological structures as well as pebbles. More likely it would have come from a book on geology in his uncle's library than from examining river pebbles without a guide.

Western North Carolina was a newer country than parts of Kentucky, Tennessee, Ohio, and Indiana, mainly because it had been inhabited during and before the Revolutionary War by the warlike Cherokee, a branch of the Iroquois family that was settled, curiously, in the South, far removed from the Five Nations of New York State and Canada. The area, both for reason of the Indians and the lack of adequate roadways, remained sparsely populated until after the Civil War. But after the colonies had won their independence, settlers began to push over the Blue Ridge. The circumstance that the Cherokee had sided with the British gave the United States some pretext to enforce on them a series of treaties pushing them farther into the mountains and opening the Swannanoa and the upper French Broad valleys to colonization.

Here and there Tory families who had fled the vengeance of patriot forces had settled in the coves, where they remained undisturbed in their possession. Some of the hardy families still residing in the area are sprung from this strong stock. The bulk of the new population was Ulster Presbyterian and Pennsylvania Dutch, who had worked down the mountain valleys through Maryland and Virginia, with a heavy intermixture of Carolinians of English descent who eased over the Blue Ridge from the piedmont. The Swannanoa valley, so closely associated with the life of Zeb Vance, had its first settlers in 1784, and Asheville, nearby the Swannanoa, in Buncombe County, was founded in 1791, well after the frontier had been pushed out into the Cumberland, Tennessee, and Ohio River valleys.

Buncombe County, which originally embraced a mountain empire, now cut into about fifteen counties, was named in honor of Colonel Edward Buncombe, English-born but ardently imbued during the Revolutionary War with the cause of the colonies against the mother country. At the age of twenty-five he moved, a total stranger, to North Carolina, and soon became a leader. He appeared in American history as commander of the 5th North Carolina regiment of Continental troops during the attack on Charleston by the British fleet in 1776. He then led the regiment on the long march northward to join Washington in front of Philadelphia, where he fought at Brandywine. At Germantown he was wounded and captured. He died from his wound in captivity at the age of thirty-five. In 1792 the North Carolina legislature as a fitting tribute gave his name to the new county being formed in the western part of the state. Colonel David Vance, Zeb's grandfather, who had served in another regiment of North Carolina Continental troops, and fought alongside Buncombe at Brandywine and German-town, represented the western section in the legislature and helped in selecting the name.

Between the time of settlement beyond the Blue Ridge and the coming of the Civil War, the greatest excitement provided was from reports current in Zeb's youth that the railroad which was being built from Raleigh through Salisbury would be extended to Asheville. Though it reached close to Morganton before the Civil War, Asheville, because of the setback of the war and reconstruction, was without a railroad until 1881 and without telegraphic connection with the world until 1877. Even after Civil War days, when the currency had been stabilized, it cost forty dollars and required ten days to travel from Asheville to Raleigh.[17]

Among the first comers to the Asheville neighborhood were the Vances. The tide of English, German, and Scotch-Irish immigration which reached the mountains later had inundated the piedmont in the 1740s and 1750s and with it came David Vance, Scotch-Irish, native of Frederick County, Virginia, son of Irish-born Samuel Vance. David, born in 1745 near Winchester, moved southward with his father. The father tarried near Abington, Virginia, but David continued into Rowan County, North Carolina, of which Salisbury is the seat. When Burke County was organized his homestead fell into Burke. There he found Priscilla Brank living on the bank of the Catawba River. Her family had been part of the German immigration which had added to the sturdy, industrious character of the North Carolina piedmont.[18]

Scarcely were they married in 1775 before David, who had been teaching and surveying, was called off to serve as an ensign in the 2nd North Carolina regiment of Continental troops, and with it he, like Colonel Buncombe of the 5th North Carolina, marched to Philadelphia to fight, then suffer through the hardships and despair of Valley Forge.

After the battle of Monmouth, he returned home to organize a militia company, which he led at Ramseur's Mill, King's Mountain, and Cowpens. At the end of the war he had attained the rank of lieutenant colonel. Until his death in 1813, he was called "colonel" and did, in fact, serve as colonel of the militia, being elected by his neighbors. His second son, Zeb's father, was David who became a captain of militia in the War of 1812, which permits an easy identification of the two. Colonel David Vance was Zeb's grandfather, Captain David Vance his father. The captain did not get into action in the 1812-1815 conflict. Word about the war had scarcely reached the back country before it was over.

After the Revolutionary War Colonel Vance represented Burke County in the legislature, then moved from his Catawba River farm near the present town of Morganton, across the Blue Ridge to a tract of about nine hundred acres he acquired out of the old Cherokee lands, on Reems Creek, a tributary of the French Broad River, twelve miles north of the site where Asheville later was settled. He resumed work as a surveyor, and after Buncombe County was formed, became clerk of the court. His family consisted of three sons and five daughters. He built a house of pine logs which was to stand for a hundred years and in which, on May 13, 1830, Zebulon Baird Vance was born.[19]

That the martial spirit permeated the colonel's entire family could be seen from a story told about one of his daughters, Celia. The colonel had conducted a militia muster, which involved drill in the manual of arms. Miss Celia, inspired by the display, returned home and got down the old family shotgun, which bore the name of "Old Billy Craig." The barrel was six and a half feet long, but she handled it nearly as well as the militiamen, and gave the orders, even to the final command of "Ready. Aim. Fire." She had not known the gun was loaded. The kick of it knocked her down, and the shot blasted a hole in the corner of the room large enough for a man to put his arm through. Eighty years later visitors at the old house were still shown the hole in the partition between the two rooms that had never been repaired, remaining as evidence of Celia's military prowess.[20]

One of Colonel Vance's early assignments was to serve on the commission to survey and establish the North Carolina-Tennessee border line, which was supposed to run along the crest of the Unakas, of which the Great Smoky Mountains are a part. Anyone can notice from the map that the line winds along the top ridge until it nears the Hiawassee River a dozen miles or so from the Georgia line. The old tradition, often denied but still more often repeated, is that the surveying party, after meandering along the summits from White Top Mountain where the two states touch Virginia, and being nearly exhausted when they finally approached the Hiawassee, learned that there was a good corn liquor still just over the Georgia line. They at once stopped their wandering course and drew the border line straight for Georgia. The official records will not sustain the tale, which may have an element of truth nonetheless, for it is a part of the folklore involving the Vance family which the mountaineers cherish.

This surveying party produced another result, perhaps as lasting as the boundary: an intimate, eyewitness account of the Battle of King's Mountain, which found its way into the Lyman C. Draper manuscript collection, where it has been used often and perhaps by all serious latter-day students of the battle. The other North Carolina commissioners serving with Colonel Vance were General Joseph McDowell and Massentine Matthews, while the party included also two surveyors, John Strother and Robert Henry, and chain bearers and pack horsemen. They had little to do as they sat around the fires at night except to relate tales. When Colonel Vance talked about King's Mountain, and McDowell, who had commanded a patriot detachment, offered his version of how the British Colonel Patrick Ferguson suffered death and crushing defeat, Henry took it all down in his surveyor's book. He gave these notes to Colonel Vance, who dressed them up properly at a spring by the side of what was known as the Bald Ground on Yellow Mountain.

"Taking the whole campaign, including the battle," said Vance, "I know of no parallel to it in the annals of ancient or modern warfare; the nearest was that of the Grecian Leonidas and his army at the battle of Thermopylae with the great Xerxes. Leonidas and his army were formed, victualed and clothed at public expense; each individual of our army had to find his own expens." He considered Ferguson's defeat the turning point of the Revolutionary War.[21]

Zeb's name came from his maternal grandfather, Zebulon Baird (pronounced Beard),[22] a Scottish peddler and merchant who came south from New Jersey, stopped for a time in Augusta, Georgia, then in 1795 drove the first four-wheel wagon up the mountain to Buncombe County. Of an entrepreneur type, he cleared the land on which the city of Asheville now stands, built and conducted the first store, and became noted above all else, it seems, for bringing the first jew's-harp ever seen in that pioneer neighborhood, where the square dance and mountain music ever since have flourished. Once settled on his huge tract of fourteen square miles, reaching as far north as the mouth of Beaver Dam, he not only set up his emporium and dispensed merchandise, which he hauled overland from Augusta, to the incoming settlers, but also built the first log courthouse and log jail. The first name of the

town was Morristown, possibly in honor of Robert Morris of Philadelphia, the patriot financier who for a time owned much western
North Carolina land.[23]

Zebulon Baird was easily the first citizen of Morristown, as Colonel
David Vance was of the Reems Creek territory farther north, which
in later years acquired the name of Vanceville, with a post office in the
house he had built. Baird represented the Buncombe County area in the
state legislature for a number of terms.

Morristown, or Asheville, was incorporated by action of the state
legislature and given five commissioners, of whom Zebulon Baird was
one. The settlement then was named for Samuel Ashe, governor at the
time. The post office was opened in 1801. Not until the coming of the
Buncombe turnpike, completed in 1827 from Saluda Gap on the South
Carolina border to the Tennessee line, was the country readily accessible
to trade and travelers. Asheville was then launched on its way to
becoming a tourist center. Especially in the summer the area became
a residential refuge for coastal residents seeking to avoid yellow fever,
a disease known to occur in the lowlands and swamplands but not in
the mountains, though none suspected that the absence of the infectious
mosquito in the uplands was what gave security from the devastating
plague.

The question was and is asked at times why families like the Vances
and Bairds and many others of attainment would have settled in a
lean, rugged country offering few agricultural advantages, broken by
mountain ranges, difficult of access, and from which it was almost impossible to transport products to an acceptable market. At that time
there was an overabundance of invitingly fertile land in the vast open
stretches of Ohio, Indiana, Illinois, and Wisconsin, and unbroken
expanses becoming available for settlement beyond the Mississippi after
the Louisiana Purchase.

The answer, or at least a partial answer, on behalf of the mountain
pioneers, is that they liked the country for the same reasons people do
today—because it possesses invigorating mountain air and as favorable
a year-round climate (its residents maintain) as can be experienced
anywhere in the world. Zeb Vance after his boyhood found it difficult
to become adjusted to the lowlands, and spoke longingly of the mountains. "The weather," he wrote from Chapel Hill, "has been warmer
here than I ever felt it in my life before."[24]

Settlers in the Blue Ridge and Unakas soon took the mountains for granted, but they were a source of delight to newcomers arriving either from the North or South. Marie Louise Pool, who came up from Spartanburg, South Carolina, later in the century found the weather "a continued, glorified kind of Indian summer.[25]

"The air was thrillingly sweet, while it was also stimulating. We had recalled all the descriptions of these North Carolina mountains, and had agreed as to the supreme folly of them all. They are as far beyond words as that benignly vivid sky is beyond a painter's power."

She was enchanted by "the silently rolling French Broad, with giants clustering their tall wooded heads everywhere."

The marriage of Captain David Vance and Mira Margaret Baird, daughter of Zebulon Baird, joined the offspring of two rugged settlers of the leader and doer type. Zeb was the third of their eight children. The closest to him throughout life was his elder brother, Robert Brank Vance, named after the dueling uncle. Traditionally Zeb's wit and vivacity were inherited from his mother,[26] but much of it seemed to well up from clear springs of unfathomed depth and unknown source out of which most genius is whimsically born.

Mira Margaret's brothers were men of ready wit. Mira Margaret herself was educated ahead of the frontier standards of her day. But it is an obvious mistake to attribute to her, as has at times been done, the scholarly guidance and book instruction which made Zeb progress rapidly in his educational and character development.

Mothers are conventionally credited with supplying the incentives and possessing the characteristics that go to make strong sons. This has been the case with Zeb's mother, who is alleged to have been a prodigious reader and to have instructed Zeb a great deal in literature and lore during his childhood. One is not likely to read assiduously without acquiring an understanding of good English. Conversationally a frontier woman might fall into the colloquialisms of the neighborhood, and errors of spelling might creep into her writing, but she would ordinarily be responsive to good literature and reflect the depth of her education and reading in her correspondence. While there is a natural hesitancy in criticizing a mother's letter to her son, Mira Margaret's correspondence to Zeb while he was at Washington College in Tennessee, though a scant example appears to have been preserved, does not suggest a woman of much education or extensive reading.

She did attend school, for it has been handed down that two of her schoolmates became governors. These were David Lowry Swain,

governor of North Carolina for three one-year terms, from 1832 to
1835; and Benjamin F. Perry, governor of South Carolina after the
Civil War. They would have been Mira Margaret's schoolmates only
in the elementary grades, for they went on to the Newton Academy
south of the town, located on a hill overlooking the Swannanoa River,
opposite the site where George Vanderbilt, nearly a century later, established his fabulous Biltmore mansion and estate. Academies in those
days were not coeducational and there is no suggestion that Mira
Margaret attended there. Phrases such as "we was" and "you was" and
"we herd last Knight that," which occur in her correspondence, are
not those of a well-read woman.[27]

But she was a stimulus and an inspiration. Her request that "we hope
that you will improve your time so as to make a great & good man" met
a response in the prankishly disposed, jesting lad.[28]

She must have been attractive because Swain in later reminiscences
referred to her a little wistfully as his early sweetheart, an avowal he
would not likely have made except of one he remembered as comely.
Zeb himself in later years spoke of her in terms of great affection and
admiration.

Handed down to the present day in some older Asheville families
is the story of how when Zeb was a baby his mother would bring him
to town and sit with him at the center of the city in the square that is
now dominated by the tall shaft of his monument. When mealtime
came she would open her dress and feed him with natural directness,
and it was commented that "the table cloth was not very clean."[29]

Asheville became the market for the western North Carolina counties,
the center of folk entertainment and such cultural advantages as the
pioneer settlers enjoyed. Zeb in his early years was a frequent visitor in
town, which was easily reached down the French Broad from Lapland.
Holidays brought in the country people.

Christmas in the mountains, which had not changed much in some
respects since Zeb Vance's childhood, especially insofar as some of the
types are concerned, was aptly described by a writer later in the last
century. When the Christmas season came on, all went into Asheville.

"On the path which circles below us we saw, about sunrise, several
carts moving toward the town; they came from farms even more remote
than ours, and were going to the state road by the nearest ways, bump-
ing and sidling about among the deep ruts. On the bottom of each cart
were seated the women with their babies. They were chewing snuff and

calling to each other in flat, nasal voices . . . I have not seen a fat mountain woman. Evidently this region and this way of life are not favorable to the secretion of adipose tissue."[30]

Zeb had his first formal schooling when he was six years old, at the Flat Creek school twelve miles from his home on the road to Burnsville, a distance he and his brother Robert sometimes covered on foot. But mainly they boarded with "Uncle Miah" and "Aunt Leeky" Blackstock, who, with their son, Robert Vance Blackstock (apparently named in honor of the dueling Dr. Vance), were good observers and passed down some of the boyhood stories preserved about Zeb and his brother. These stories are a little flat and are not treasured bits of North Carolina folk-lore, as may be understood from an example. Squire Blackstock told Zeb that if he did anything bad, a black spot would appear in the squire's book. Zeb had a fight at school one day and that evening shrank from going into the squire's room. Finally he felt bold enough to make the confrontation and inquired, "Is it there, Uncle Miah?"

"Yes," the elder said, "it is very large and black today. What have you done?"

"I whipped another boy," said Zeb frankly.

"What for, Zeb?" asked the squire.

"Well, Uncle Miah, he was so cussed ugly I couldn't help it."[31]

The Flat Creek school, conducted by Matthew Woodson, was held in the building that served as the church of the Reverend Stephen Morgan, the Baptist preacher who had married Zeb's mother and father at the Baird home north of Asheville. Woodson moved his school to near Lapland when Zeb was seven, and the same year the Vance family moved from the Reems Creek farm to a house overlooking the French Broad River in Lapland. Zeb had a hit-and-miss schooling for a time, until he met Calhoun and induced his father to allow him to go to Washington College.

Some of the stories about Zeb's precociousness and pranks come from sources other than "Uncle Miah." He showed a surprising turn in an early addiction to profanity. He dropped the cursing tendency to an extent in later life, when the imagery of his language did not require an oath in a struggle for emphasis. Anecdotes, even those of the dung-heap variety, served better. As a boy his vocabulary became so shameful that his chagrined elders attributed his oaths to the slaves who worked on the Vance farm, though the common language of the mountain whites was in most instances far from elegant.

Matthew Woodson, his early teacher on Flat Creek, vowed to break his bad habit. He made Zeb sit in the corner of the schoolroom in front of a mousehole, holding a pair of tongs. He told the boy not to open his mouth under any circumstances until he had caught the mouse. Zeb took his station and the other pupils resumed their classwork. They became so absorbed in a spelling round that everyone forgot Zeb until the class was suddenly jerked up by an excited shout. "Damned if I haven't got him," exclaimed Zeb. There, in front of the class, he held up the mouse pinched between the tongs.[32]

Zeb's father understood his son's disposition toward practical jokes, for his instructions to the boy while at Washington College were "do mind your Books and be careful of giving offense to your School Mates."[33]

Jonesboro, where Washington College was situated, was rich with the associations of Andrew Jackson, who in the early days of his law practice was in such constant attendance at the courts there and in Nashville as to make twenty-two trips on horseback between the two towns. It has been calculated that these journeys involved a distance of 4,400 miles and 750 hours in the saddle. Here Jackson had his altercation with his fellow attorney Waightstill Avery, against whose grandson Vance was to make his first race for Congress, and win.

The Avery family ties in so closely to the Zeb Vance story, and is so much a part of an account of North Carolina affairs during the Civil War, that the incident involving the Avery patriarch and the fiery future President of the United States may be properly mentioned here. Waightstill Avery, mellow and learned, of Burke County, North Carolina, was an ornament to the frontier bar. A Connecticut Yankee, he had roomed at Princeton with Oliver Ellsworth, later to be Chief Justice of the United States. Graduated in 1766, he moved down through Virginia, settled in North Carolina, became active and influential in public affairs, heartily espoused the patriot cause and became a leader of it, and when North Carolina became an independent state, he was the first attorney general. He moved farther west, to the wilderness of Burke County, to escape malaria, and soon became a large landowner and an active attorney on the mountain circuit extending into present Tennessee. Like Zeb Vance at a later time, Avery mixed a sense of humor with his serious law work, which came near proving fatal when he encountered belligerent young Andrew Jackson in Jonesboro.

Jackson, according to the mountain tradition (which does not accord

in all respects with the stripped down biographies of the great man),
was devoted particularly to one lawbook, Bacon's *Abridgement*, a copy
of which he carried, carefully wrapped in brown grocer's paper, in his
saddlebag. In court, when the issue narrowed, it was his custom to pull
out Bacon, the unwrapping of which was studied and ritualistic. Then
he would announce to the court, "We will now see what Bacon says
about this."

Waggish Avery determined, before the court meeting in 1788, when
Jackson was twenty-one years old, to break the habit of showmanship, so
he slipped the book from the young man's saddlebag and wrapped and
tied a slab of real bacon of the same dimensions in the brown paper.
Court met and Jackson at the end of an emotional plea reached the
critical point. He slowly untied the package, folded back the paper
gravely, looked at the judge, held up the object and declared triumphantly, "Let's see what Bacon says." The crowd burst out laughing
and Jackson saw too late that the bacon he held was cut from a hog's
back. Furious, he challenged Avery, of course, and no intercessions
could cool his anger. Avery, a Presbyterian who opposed dueling, was
compelled to accept. Jackson fired and his well-aimed bullet clipped
Avery's ear. The older man might then have killed young Jackson, who
stood unflinching, but instead he smiled pleasantly, fired into the air,
and advanced and shook hands to close the incident and allow the
impetuous young man to go on to military fame and political fortune.[34]

At Jonesboro Jackson had rescued his horse from the burning livery
stable, wearing in his haste nothing except his shirt. More than that,
he had quieted the panic and, with the help of a jailbreaker who was a
veteran of King's Mountain, had used wet blankets and water and in
fact saved the town, and thereby Zeb's opportunity for further intellectual awakening there.

Washington College prided itself as being the first college established
west of the Appalachians. In Vance's day it was conducted by the
Reverend Dr. Alexander Doak, who had eighty young students. Zeb
went there in 1843, when he was thirteen years old. His year was cut
short by word from Lapland that his father was grievously ill. Washington College contributed much to Zeb's advancement. It opened for
him the fascinating world of public speaking and debate, in which, from
the very beginning, he could somehow hold his own with all comers.
He worked hard over his lessons.

Long afterwards one of Zeb's schoolmates at Washington College, a doctor named Esnor, from Bristol, Tennessee, told how the two had been designated to deliver speeches at a formal occasion and went together to the fields to practice. Vance spoke, then listened to Esnor, lying on the grass to get the full import and criticize. When they finished, he rolled over and said: "Esnor, I feel it from the top of my head to the ends of my fingers and toes, that I am to be governor of North Carolina."[35]

The spark that had been struck by Calhoun was beginning to mount into a flame.

Zeb reached Lapland just before his father died, on January 14, 1844. Captain Vance left a large family, virtually no money and little convertible property, but a resolute, devoted widow, strong enough to advance the family's fortunes and intent on seeing that her boys were educated. Chiefly to get them near a better school, but also as an economy, she sold her home in Lapland and bought a house in Asheville, which thereafter was Zeb's home. He and his brother Robert studied some at Newton Academy, but Zeb was forced to help his mother and the only income opportunity that opened was at the hotel down the French Broad River beyond Lapland, at the Warm Springs resort which, in the 1840s, enjoyed a thriving tourist trade[36] in its mountain seclusion.

Zeb was early familiar with Warm Springs (now Hot Springs), North Carolina, situated where the French Broad River cleaves through Bald Mountain eighteen miles northwest of Lapland. Far up in the heights, without rail or telegraph communication until long after the Civil War, reached only by long coach rides from Asheville or Knoxville, Tennessee, Warm Springs nevertheless drew visitors from cities as far distant as New York. Before 1820 an inn for invalids was on the site, while in the 1830s a hotel accommodating 250 guests was built.[37]

The story is still told in the Hot Springs community of how Zeb Vance, when a mere child, would come to the hotel from Lapland to sell flowers to guests. He had competitors and noticed one day that the guests bought flowers more readily from the little girls. On the next day he appeared with his flowers but wearing a girl's dress.[38] The struggle for business advancement has its heroes also. The hotel burned about 1840, before Vance was ten, so it is clear his merchandising efforts were begun early. It was replaced by a much larger hotel accommodating 1,000 persons.

Zeb, short of money after his interrupted schooling at Washington College, returned to the hotel to work as a clerk and obtain his first contact with business and affairs. This hotel, which had thirteen white columns representing the thirteen original colonies, stood for about forty years, became a popular vacation center after the Civil War, and burned in 1884.

Zeb's leg fracture never healed properly. Possibly other complications, such as the "white swelling," had more consequences to his health than his family in those early days recognized. His leg remained somewhat shortened for the rest of his life. In his youthful years it gave him a slight limp, or, more exactly, a sort of ambling gait, but in later life he corrected the handicap by wearing a thicker heel on the shoe of the short leg. His difficulty was not nearly so marked as that of his uncle had been, for he stood erect and in his adolescence passed six feet.

In describing the influence on Governor Swain of the remote area and humble circumstances in which Swain was born, Vance might well have been referring to himself when he said: "For a child to be born amid such surroundings, and with such blood in his veins as coursed through those of young Swain, constitute the very highest advantages which could surround the birth and bringing up of a young man who had to fight his way in a country like ours. The surest elements of success were found in a freedom from indulgences."[39]

☆☆☆☆☆☆☆☆☆☆☆☆☆☆☆☆☆

## Chapter Three

## Enlivening Chapel Hill

☆☆☆☆☆☆☆☆☆☆☆☆☆☆☆☆☆

Dwight W. Morrow, Wall Street tycoon, United States senator and ambassador to Mexico in the 1920s and 1930s, and general adviser to Presidents, nearly shook down the ancient ivy-clad halls at Amherst College when a student there, by voting that, of his class of 1895, the taciturn, self-effacing Calvin Coolidge from the Vermont hills would be the one most likely to succeed.

Morrow went so far, according to the story told in Washington, as to mention to classmates that there was a chance that "Cooley," as he was known to those who watched him dart furtively about the campus in silence and seeming abstraction, might someday become President of the United States.[1]

Kemp Plummer Battle, onetime president of the University of North Carolina and its diligent historian, had a slightly more lustrous but still unpolished stone to work with when he saw the gleam of future greatness in Zeb Vance.

Kemp's father, William Horn Battle, long a professor of law at the university and at the same time an associate justice of the North Carolina Supreme Court, was in the 1840s a judge of the superior court on the western North Carolina circuit. That required him to make the rounds of the raw little courthouse towns by stagecoach, and to conduct the term of the court in one of the largest of them, Asheville. Kemp, the eldest son, frequently went on the trip to give his father company.

One summer night in 1848, in Asheville, Kemp was sitting in the moonlight on a pile of lumber which had been brought to the square for the erection of a new courthouse, to replace the structure built by Zebulon Baird, which had burned. He was talking with Newton Coleman, nephew of President David Lowry Swain of the university, and the Buncombe County representative in the lower house of the state assembly, a man who, according to young Battle, possessed a brain "large enough to place him among the mountain giants."[2]

Just then a youth of about eighteen passed with rolling gait. Coleman called him over to introduce him to the young visitor, the judge's son. Kemp Plummer Battle went on to become college president, author, eminent professor of history, and to achieve much else, but the memory of that meeting with young Zeb Vance while sitting in the moonlight on the lumber pile in Asheville never left him. More than once he wrote the story of it. Let him tell it as he recalled it half a century later:

"My new acquaintance impressed me at once as a youth of peculiar attractiveness of manner and gifts of mind. I thought I knew something of Shakespeare, but his familiarity with the characters and words of the Titan poet put me to shame. I claimed to be in a measure intimate with the personages of the romances of my favorite, Scott, but he had evidently lived with him as with home folks. I had been from childhood, not always a willing, but certainly a regular attendant on Sunday school and church services, and I thought I had at least a familiarity with the Bible, but his mind seemed to be stored with Scriptural texts as fully as a theological student preparing for his examination."

Battle noticed that the Biblical references were employed more often for "conversational risibility" than pious discourse. They were used as the backdrop for a wit which "sparkled like the wavelets of the ocean." About him there was no jesting at the expense of others, "no acridity,"[3] no venom, no malice, but a welling up of humor out of a great reservoir of sunny gaiety and fondness for life and people. Still he was a mountaineer with a good many rough edges, and it required some discernment to see he was destined to leadership and greatness.

When Kemp Battle returned to Chapel Hill with his father he carried sharp memories of the mountain country, memories of "pellucid waters and tumbling cascades, green laurel and gray crags, the dark summits and graceful outline of sleeping Pisgah and frowning

Mitchell," but the most agreeable and abiding recollection was of his genial, well-read new friend, Zeb Vance. He poetically told those at the college that out on the Blue Ridge "a light was kindling which would one day illuminate our state" and send its rays afar.[4]

That talk in the moonlight was one of the most consequential events in the life of young Zeb. Three years sped by and Kemp Battle became an instructor in mathematics at the university, which entitled him to attend faculty meetings. One day President Swain produced a letter and said smilingly that it was from a young man named Zeb Vance, son of an old sweetheart of his, who applied for a loan of three hundred dollars to cover his costs at the university for a course in law and special studies. The tone of the letter was forthright. Zeb said he had some small property not then productive, but would repay the loan (which he did, not long afterwards, with interest). Swain was favorable. Young Battle's recommendation was influential. The loan was approved promptly without a dissent.[5]

Zeb was gawky when he reached Chapel Hill in homespun, with trousers that missed his shoetops by plenty of bare space. He had no wardrobe, but had a good grounding in Latin gained partly from the Newton Academy, and a passion for public speaking which had been pent up like a river log jam since his Washington College days. The years between the college at Jonesboro and his arrival at Chapel Hill had not been wasted. When not clerking at Warm Springs, he had studied under the Reverend Mr. Newton and Long Billy Smith, and had lived with his uncle's books, as his conversation with Kemp Battle readily disclosed.

When in 1851 he jumped from the western stage in front of Miss Nancy Hilliard's boardinghouse, he was on his own, without a single acquaintance in the village or at the university. The summer heat hung over the town. The stage carried other, older students returning for the new term, and when they alighted, there was much rushing about, shouted greetings, and handshaking. Zeb, apparently in mimicry, in which he excelled even more than in Latin or Greek, rushed over to an old-time Negro standing by as an onlooker and began to lavish on him exuberant salutations. The others, attracted, then amused, came over and took him into their crowd, and such was his proficiency in making friends that within five minutes, as some of them related, he knew every young man in the company, and within a very short time, every person in the village and university.[6]

"I well remember Vance's first appearance at the Hill," wrote Major James W. Wilson forty-odd years later, "—home-made shoes and clothes, about three inches between pants and shoes, showing his sturdy ankles; quick and rough at repartee, and mostly remarkable for his jokes." That affliction of his innate humor, if it can be accounted a misfortune, was already with him. Being "mostly remarkable for his jokes," it was quite natural that none would remember him as much of a student, yet he gained so much good grounding in that one year at the university that he rated it as the most important year of his life. "The thing that has been of the most benefit to me," he said long after, "is the fact that I was a student at the University of North Carolina."[7]

Kemp Battle, discussing his arrival, said few could help but be impressed with the newcomer, just as he had been in their moonlight talk in Asheville. What Zeb had was "a brain large and active; a memory tenacious, a nature overflowing with joyous love of fun, and to a surprising degree accurate information on many subjects and many authors."

The University of North Carolina at the time of Zeb's arrival, though it had only about two hundred students, was already a great institution, with an able faculty, and a highly distinguished alumni list. This first of the state universities to open its gates to students, in 1795 (the University of Georgia at Athens had been chartered in 1785 but did not open until later), had supplied one President, James K. Polk, who stood first in his class of 1818; the senator from Missouri Thomas Hart Benton, who studied for a time there; another able legislator and diplomat soon to become Vice President, William Rufus de Vane King, a graduate in 1803; other distinguished senators and cabinet officers; jurists, and a host of governors of North Carolina and other states. The list was ever growing.

Among the more attractive was the handsome James Johnston Pettigrew, valedictorian of the class of 1847,[8] and not the least renowned was Senator Willie Person Mangum, long in Congress, president pro tempore of the Senate for many years, and mentioned so enthusiastically for the Presidency that he received a goodly number of votes in the electoral college in 1837. Added to these were numerous college presidents and professors and men of distinction throughout the state and the South. Among the controversial alumni was Senator John H. Eaton of Tennessee, Secretary of War under President Jackson, whose marriage to Peggy O'Neill, a comely barmaid, had disrupted the Jackson cabinet.

Destined to become one of Vance's close friends was senator, governor and cabinet member William A. Graham, a graduate in 1824, who was serving as Secretary of the Navy under President Fillmore at the time Zeb was a student at Chapel Hill. He would become Zeb's principal adviser, with the scholarly President Swain a close second, during the trying years of war and the bitter months of defeat.

Despite the great names in its past, the university in Zeb's period had an unbridled side in the high jinks of some of the students, extending to drunkenness and rank insubordination, as was reported graphically in some of the contemporary literature. Knifings and gunplay were accepted as the natural manifestations of spirited youth. Neither the dormitory halls nor the campus had lighting; card games flourished by day and the penalty seems to have been that when they were detected the deck was confiscated. Corn liquor was briefly hidden from sight when the inspectors made their rounds. A good picture of life at the mid-century was provided by the publication of the well-edited diary of Thomas Miles Garrett, of the class of 1851, with supporting documents.[9]

Possibly the castigations were too severe, but enough was noted down by historians, commentators, diarists, and preceptors of that period to show that campus rules had their pockets of rude rebellion and rough mutiny.

Diarist Garrett, like so many other Chapel Hill students of his era, was killed in the war. He fell at Spotsylvania in 1864. As a member of the 5th North Carolina of Iverson's Brigade, he had been lucky to survive Gettysburg. He did well in the university despite the unruly distractions, being second in scholarship and deportment. The bulk of his ample diary, covering the period from June, 1849, to November, 1850, shows that despite the upheavals, life at the university in Vance's time was reasonably placid.

Vance himself gave one of the most satisfying accounts of his mentor, the mountain scholar and statesman President David Lowry Swain.

The Swain family was generously endowed with initiative and the instincts of builders. The father, George Swain, had come down from Roxboro, Massachusetts, to Georgia in 1763. In 1795, because of poor health, he had moved to Buncombe County and settled in what Vance termed a "mountain-cradled dale," shaded in the morning by the Craggies and not far from the great form of the Black Dome, later Mount Mitchell. Beaver Dam, a bold, clear brook, gushed down through the cove to join the French Broad River.[10]

Near the head of the valley George Swain set out an orchard and

built a double log cabin, which he shared with his brother-in-law Jesse
Lane. Jesse's brother, Joel, had founded a plantation in Wake County
which grew to become the capital of the state and take the name of
Raleigh. George Swain, after reaching North Carolina from Georgia,
tarried understandably for a time in Wake County, where the Lanes
lived. There he married the widow Caroline Lowry, who had been a
Lane and was a sister of Joel and Jesse.

A striking coincidence was that in the double log cabin in the cove,
shared by the families of George Swain and Jesse Lane, two future
governors were born in the same year, 1801. They were David Lowry
Swain, who became governor of North Carolina, and Joseph Lane, who
became governor of Oregon, a general, and later United States senator.
At Buena Vista in the Mexican War, Lane distinguished himself by
holding the line with his regiment until Captain Braxton Bragg could
bring up his guns and, in response to Zachary Taylor's orders, "give
them a little more grape." He ran as a candidate for Vice President on
the Breckinridge ticket in 1860.

George Swain's health improved in the mountains to the extent that
he could not only farm his Beaver Dam land, but also re-establish himself as a hatter and serve as postmaster of Asheville. More important
than his hats—though they became known for their good quality
throughout western North Carolina—was his apple orchard, set out
from cuttings brought from Massachusetts. His was undoubtedly the
first in what is now one of the largest orchard regions of the eastern
United States. Because of its elevation it is also the southernmost area
where apples, a temperate zone fruit, are grown on an extensive scale.
Vance said that some of the names he gave his apples still obtained in
the 1870s. They probably do today, but Vance did not designate them.
Another phase of George Swain's effort was the strong support he gave
to education in that pioneer region.

Such was the father who influenced the man who, in turn, exercised
perhaps the strongest and most enduring influence on Zeb Vance.
George's son David, Vance's teacher and friend, the scholar and governor, was born in the double log cabin at the head of the valley, under
the shadow of the Craggies, January 4, 1801. He was twenty-nine years
Vance's senior.

More than half a century later, when Vance visited the cabin in 1852
in company with Swain, Zeb recalled that it was here he first saw a
wagon, "this wondrous vehicle," which belonged to his grandfather

and uncle, Zebulon and Bedent Baird. Because there was no roadway, it had to come up the valley by way of the creek bed, rumbling over the rocks "frighteningly," according to Zeb. This was the same wagon that Zebulon Baird had brought up from Augusta and the first to cross the North Carolina Blue Ridge. It had been well made, for it had proved its durability.

David Lowry Swain was thoroughly educated but largely self-educated. Although he held no diploma, he came to be looked on as one of the great presidents in the history of the university and he guided to their graduation a host of men who became distinguished. He had studied at Newton Academy under the Reverend George Newton and Long Billy Smith, Newton's successor. In 1821, he entered the University of North Carolina in the junior class, but his money gave out in four months and he had to abandon the thought of graduation.

He read law in Raleigh, then returned to Buncombe County with great ambition and all the zest of the mountain brook that bounded past his boyhood cabin. He went to the legislature, became the leading authority in the state on taxation and finance; he put through the Buncombe turnpike which opened the mountains to the piedmont and gave good road contact at last with Tennessee and Kentucky; he became judge of the Superior Court, and to cap it all, three days before his thirty-first birthday, he was sworn in as governor. He was the governor who built North Carolina's striking capitol, for which he laid the cornerstone in 1833, and which still stands.

After his third term, when the way to the United States Senate was opened invitingly to him, or when he might have returned to the dignity of the bench, he preferred a less spectacular but perhaps more satisfying and influential role, and accepted the presidency of the state university. By that time he had become as diligent a student of constitutional principles as, during his legislative career, he had been an expert on taxation and finance. Through the next three decades he was looked on as one of the most learned and benign men of the state. Vance, in observing that few had risen more rapidly than Swain, and in dealing with his great capacity, gave an indication of how he, himself, happened to become aligned with the Whig party. Swain's influence was apparent. Swain was as devoted to Clay and Webster as he had been to John Quincy Adams. He corresponded on constitutional questions with John C. Hamilton, son of Alexander Hamilton. Like his father, the younger Hamilton was a student of constitutional matters. He became interested in the North Carolina constitution of 1835, to which Swain had made substantial contributions. Vance's opinion of this document was that, in view of its purpose, a more excellent constitution "was never framed by an English speaking people."

Heartfelt was Vance's tribute in later years to this guiding spirit of his younger days. Swain's personality and erudition were better portals to learning than the textbooks, especially on those occasions when he would, as Vance said, "give his whole soul to the stirring up of those generous and emulous sentiments in the hearts of his pupils."

Vance supplied an example. On his first day in class President Swain, who taught constitutional, international, and moral law, and history, asked a question or so, then launched into a discourse on Chancellor James Kent, the Columbia College professor and chief justice of the New York Supreme Court, whose *Commentaries on American Law,* in four volumes, was then as now judged the foundation of equity juris-prudence. The class was studying Kent's treatise. Let Vance continue the story:

"From Kent he went to Story, from Story to Marshall, repeating anecdotes of the great Americans who had framed and interpreted our organic law; and touching on the debate between Hayne and Webster. From these, he went back and back to the men and times when the great seminal principles of Anglo-Saxon liberty were eliminated from feudal chaos, and placed one by one as stones polished by the genius of the wise, and cemented by the blood of the brave, in the walls of the temple of human freedom."

Swain could not have told it with quite the same flair for lan-guage, but these diversions from the formal recitations were what made his courses, and many of his students, great. Vance continued his reminiscence:

"He told us of the eloquence of Burke, of the genius of Chatham; he took us into the prison of Eliott and went with us to the death-bed of Hampden; into the closet with Coke and Seargent Maynard; and to the forum where Somers spoke; to the deck of the *Brill* where William, the deliverer, stood as he gazed upon the shores of England; to the scaffolds of Sydney and our own glorious Raleigh."

The professor would warm to his subject. He used no lecture notes. He spoke from the vast store of learning he had accumulated out of reading history and law, when reduced circumstances deprived him of the desired college years. His recitation room was the college library, housed in the building known as "Old South." There he would walk back and forth, "with long and awkward strides," as Vance remembered them, "heaving those heavy passionate sighs," always the sign of his deep emotion. At times he would reach to the library shelf and grasp tenderly the book of some great poet. "With trembling voice" he would read the grand and thrilling words that held the class captive. The students discovered that the hour had gone "almost before we knew it had begun."

Zeb found in Swain kindred characteristics. The President enjoyed anecdotes and repartee, and he took especial delight when a student could thrust as readily as stand on guard. "Like a true humorist and story teller he enjoyed the taking as well as the giving."

The picture of this remarkable man, who helped to mold Zeb Vance as a student and counseled with him when he became legislator and governor, would not be complete without brief reference to his extra-curricular activities. He planted shrubbery and trees, great elms that came to give the Chapel Hill campus the beauty it still enjoys. He took over supervision of the Chapel Hill streets, provided a drainage system, laid out the stone culverts. He enclosed the college grounds with the stone wall and employed the first college gardener. He founded the university magazine and contributed articles regularly, and organized the Historical Society of North Carolina, which flourishes today.

Vance in delivering the memorial oration in Swain's honor in 1877 told that though "thirty-three years of his best days, and the sincerest labors of his existence were spent here in the training of young men," he had no monument at Chapel Hill. "In very truth," said Vance, "the University may be looked on as his monument."[11]

The University of North Carolina had other stimulating professors, some of whose names are treasured among the Chapel Hill great. Judge William Horn Battle taught law inspiringly when not on the bench, at first on the circuit, then, after 1852, on the North Carolina Supreme Court. His two sons became Zeb's close friends. The elder, Kemp Plummer Battle, who had stood first in the class of 1849 at Chapel Hill though only seventeen years old, served his state notably in numerous capacities, and for years was president and for sixteen years professor of history at the university. The youngest of the family, Richard H. Battle, of "remarkable gifts" and "very independent mind," served as confidant and executive secretary when Vance was governor, and left an excellent appraisal of the governor's character and work.[12]

Another admired teacher was James Phillips, professor of mathematics, but seemingly more distinguished on account of his talented daughter Cornelia than his mastery of logarithms.

Dr. James Phillips in 1850 was made a Visitor at West Point, which was tantamount to membership on the board of directors, though a bit more advisory than the normal college board. The appointment required his attendance at times and the broadening nature of such trips might be seen from his journey to the Military Academy in 1850, on which he took his son Charles and Kemp Battle, both then young tutors. They stopped in New York to hear in Tripler Hall the incomparable singing of Jenny Lind. The professors did have some cultural opportunities away from the campus.[13]

Vance became well acquainted with the family and admired Cornelia, whom he later termed the greatest woman North Carolina ever produced. She married James M. Spencer, and established a literary career. After the Civil War, at Vance's suggestion, she wrote and published in 1866 the fascinating account of *The Last Ninety Days of the War in North Carolina*, which is prized as a source record of the period it covers. Vance said to her, as he was about to enter the United States Senate, "I have often thanked God for leading my steps to Chapel Hill."

Professor James Phillips gave his years and his life to the university. Two years after the war, when its fortunes and finances were low and it was soon to close its doors during the poverty of the reconstruction years, he died, probably as he would have desired. He was conducting morning prayers for the students when he suddenly sank down on the rostrum and quietly expired.

But above all the other professors, measured in terms of the deep attachment which springs up between student and teacher, was Zeb's love of the university's great seer, geologist, scientist, philosopher, and mountain explorer, Dr. Elisha Mitchell.

Vance recorded much later his lasting impressions of Dr. Mitchell, who served the University of North Carolina for nearly forty years "with zeal, fidelity and ability scarcely surpassed in the history of literary men." There was nothing moderate in Vance's estimate of this beloved professor, whose deepest devotion was to the natural sciences. But Mitchell seemed to know substantially everything.

"So great and accurate were his attainments," wrote Vance, "that he was the referee of all knotty or disputed points which arose in the other departments; and it was said of him that at a moment's notice, in case of absence or sickness, he could fill the chair of any other professor in the university."[14]

Another revealing observation by Vance was that "if you wanted to know *what anything was,* you went to Dr. Mitchell; if you wanted to know *who anybody was,* you went to Governor Swain." Mitchell was loaded with information about everything. Swain knew everybody. "With a very little help indeed," said Vance, "he could have supplied a 'Doomsday Book' of North Carolina by far more accurate than that of the Conqueror."[15]

Mitchell made an intensive study of the geology of North Carolina and conducted field trips and surveys in every direction out of Chapel Hill. "Scarcely a stream, valley, mountain, coal-bed, gold field, or mineral deposit in the State, but was visited and inspected by him," Vance continued. "He it was who first determined by barometric measurement what had often been conjectured, that the peaks of Black Mountain were higher than those of the White Mountains in New Hampshire . . ."

When it came vacation time at Chapel Hill, Mitchell did not relax. He devoted these periods of freedom to scientific excursions. At times, as one who liked to commune with nature, he made explorations alone.

Said Thomas Miles Garrett, the student diarist, in his entry of July 22, 1849: "Dr. Mitchell is a verry humerous old man, and certainly a man who never spoke without displaying some learning. I am confident I never heard such an entertaining lecture, in my life. He brought in every sciance to illustrate some point, and seemed perfectly acquainted with each of them."[16]

Mitchell, a graduate at the head of his Yale class of 1813, had been born in Washington, Connecticut, but he became one of the most respected of North Carolinians and one of the great men in the history of the state. He was a direct descendant of John Eliot, the English divine who settled in Boston and Roxboro, translated portions of the Bible into the Indian tongue, and became the "Apostle" who introduced the divine word to the red men. Although he had this heritage, or perhaps because of it, Dr. Mitchell was persuaded to leave his native state, he said, because of "a desire to escape those theological disputes which are filling every village of New England with bitterness." He remained a devout Christian and preached when needed in the college chapel. "My mathematical recitations," he explained, "have no bearing on the subject of religion." Sometimes he boldly held these recitations on Sunday.[17]

One of Vance's schoolmates wrote years later of his first encounter with Zeb on the campus. Just after the term opened, he was passing, on a depressingly humid day, along the walk leading from "East Building toward Miss Nancy's," the Chapel Hill boardinghouse. He stopped to cool himself under the big poplar tree, the "Davie poplar" which all of that generation knew familiarly, and which still stands. There, under its branches, was another youth, about whom he used the adjectives "raw," "gawky," "awkward," "onery," and "ganglin'." At a glance one could tell that the lad had not been long in the more cultivated society of central Carolina. But Zeb glanced around and remarked to the newcomer, "This seems to be a very *pop'lar* resort."[18]

The anonymous writer who described the incident became Zeb's friend. His first thought was "Who in the devil are you, anyway?" for he saw before him a figure that had arresting qualities. These were not in the fact that his breeches were too short and his coat far from the mode of the smart set at Chapel Hill. "His eyes were grayish, deep set and expressive. They 'meant business.' His hair was as black as a quarter past twelve at night, when there is no moon." The writer went on to say that he could not call Zeb handsome.

"One day soon afterwards," he continued, "that great, good, noble man, Professor Elisha Mitchell, said to me, in that gloomy and dismal laboratory in the South Building, says he,

" 'Where were you and Vance going Saturday afternoon? I saw you pass my house and the direction in which you traveled is rather suspicious.' "

The more carefree element would steal off at times to a corn liquor still in the country.

"We only went to Merritt's mill, doctor, for a walk—and came back like two good little boys," he answered.

" 'Yes, yes,' " said Mitchell. " 'Humph! Well, what do you think of that fellow from the mountains, anyhow? Remember what I say now. There's something in him. He will make a man of whom this state will be proud. I may not live to see it, but you are young and may recall my prediction.' "[19]

Vance's schoolmate—the writer of the letter—went on to describe Vance's later rise, through the state legislature and Congress to the governor's chair, and then to the Senate. Being in Washington and hearing that Vance would speak, he went to the Senate gallery and heard what he described as "one of the greatest speeches of my life." The galleries were crowded. As he sat there, he thought back over the meeting beneath the *pop'lar* tree and of what Dr. Mitchell had said so long ago.[20]

Another of the law professors, Samuel F. Phillips, who became a successful Raleigh attorney and later Solicitor General of the United States, thought Zeb's good standing was due more to a mental alertness and innate ability than to diligent study of the texts. But President Swain, even in those student days, accepted Kemp Battle's view that Zeb was cut out for leadership and predicted that he would be governor.

How his quick mind could serve as a substitute for hard study in an emergency was evidenced by the story of his classmate Dr. Richard H. Lewis of Kinston. Lewis had the seat next to him during President Swain's course in international law and Swain, departing from his fascinating discourses, was demanding recitations on the touchy subject of contraband in wartime. The textbook was irritatingly loaded with from thirty to forty examples of contraband articles and cases and the class was expected to know them all. Lewis with foresight had listed them with a lead pencil on his boot and leg, but it was Vance whom the professor called on to recite.

"Lewis, lend me your leg," said Zeb softly, as he jerked the left member into his own lap and recited the list flawlessly. President Swain smelled a whiff of humbuggery and called on Zeb to come to the front of the room. Knowing Zeb's proclivity to pun, he pleased himself to the extent of a smile by using one himself. "Mr. Vance, advance to the front," he said, not suspecting that the term *Ad-Vance* would one day become famous as the name of a blockade-runner on which much of the comfort of General Lee's army and North Carolina would depend.

Zeb went to the front, to be greeted with the professor's request, "Now, cite the cases bearing on this point."

Zeb went down the list without a miss and with the tolerant, half-bored attitude of one who had been called on for the most elementary of tasks. Swain, outwitted, could not utter a word, but Zeb, when he resumed his seat, put his elbow into his companion's ribs and said jibingly, "Lewis, why don't you study your lesson, you lazy fellow."[21]

He rarely repressed his efforts at humor. Punning was the salient part at this stage, when college students were devoted to the British literary luminary Thomas Hood, who had died only a few years before, and whose "Faithless Nelly Gray" and "Faithless Sally Brown" were more to be cherished than Milton's "Lycidas" or "Il Penseroso." When President Swain switched from international law and put on his political-economy cap, he dwelt for a time on the State of Franklin, the unrecognized political and geographical entity which John Sevier and other frontiersmen had set up out of the counties of western North Carolina and east Tennessee. He told that the state had no currency but used coonskins for the purpose. Shrewd traders began to sew the tails of coons to possum skins, and pass off the spurious pelts on the unwary.

"What kind of a currency would you call that, Mr. Vance?" the professor inquired.

"A retail currency," Zeb shot back quickly.[22]

Again, when out on a geological excursion with Professor Mitchell, the group passed a run-down, dilapidated millhouse that had long been out of service. Turning to the professor, Zeb inquired gravely, "Doctor, do you think that old millhouse is worth a dam?"[23]

Some of his jests obviously were not too successful—they would today be called "corny"—but they bubbled up from a genial, cordial spirit and the bad ones seemed to create as much merriment as the good. Zeb had a manner in the telling.

Dubrutz Cutlar, one of his schoolmates, had a reaction similar to that of Kemp Battle: "I was always astonished then, and always afterwards, at the quantity and variety of things he knew from books." Something of that view was reflected by Richard H. Lewis, whose room at the college was a meeting place for gab sessions. Lewis noticed that "when a question was under discussion in the class-room, it was wonderful to see how much he would get out of it by short, pithy suggestions."[24] Zeb, more wily than most students, endeared himself at times to the others when the going got rough in Dr. Mitchell's chemistry class and the learned professor was steering toward difficult questions. By a beguiling inquiry Zeb would send the old doctor off into recollections of experiences in the Black Mountain chain or the Blue Ridge, and other tangential remarks which consumed the balance of the hour.

Alexander McIver, a brilliant scholar who became superintendent of public instruction in North Carolina in later years, belonged to Vance's fraternity. While his view might be slightly partisan, he wrote that

Zeb had a "surprising amount of general culture"—which must have meant it had to be detected and was not too evident—and good habits and honorable views, which is what a good fraternity man ought to find in his brother.[25]

The word "surprising," used frequently in comments about Zeb's learning and mental traits, was probably employed not so much because his appearance belied those attributes, but because his answers and rejoinders invariably were arresting, never the ordinary and expected. Richard H. Lewis, who was a senior with much status, decided on Zeb's arrival to make a call and knocked at Zeb's door. Invited in, he introduced himself, then noticed a pipe nearby in a box on the table. Pointing to the box he asked, "Is this tobacco or what?" "It's what," said Zeb. "Help yourself."[26] Never the obvious answer! The young man's mind was not grooved. He was not given to pattern thinking, except insofar as it might involve his miserable puns.

Before going to Chapel Hill, Zeb had read law for a time in the office of John W. Woodfin, a wealthy landowner and talented attorney of Asheville, in whose office Augustus S. Merrimon, later United States senator and chief justice of the state Supreme Court and one of the outstanding men of his generation, was also beginning the study of law. As Zeb was engaged in his studies, Merrimon stopped by Chapel Hill en route to Raleigh to take his examination for a license to practice. He tarried long enough to take a trial examination under Professor Phillips, who found that he was not clear enough on Blackstone to sustain the rigors of the Raleigh test. Seeing how distressed he was when he left the professor, Zeb whispered to another student, "He came in a Merry mon. He goes out a sorry mon." Merrimon must have boned up on Blackstone because he went on to Raleigh, passed the examination, and displayed a strong, clear intellect throughout a distinguished career.[27]

Merrimon was a serious type who the year before Zeb went to the university judged him to be both talented and lively, but appeared to be thinking of him when he commented that he could not understand why "some men can drink and loaf around the street."[28] Zeb's human understanding, like that of the Bard of Avon he quoted so much, resulted from his association with people and not from his reading in Woodfin's law office or his uncle's library. While he was not abstemious, he never appeared to have much trouble with liquor. Back when he was fourteen he had written of his "Whig zeal" in the Clay campaign of 1844, when James K. Polk, the North Carolina-born President, was elected. Zeb claimed to have headed the muleback procession through what is now at times known as "bloody" Madison County, and to have been filled with "patriotism and hard cider," and to have either been in or instigated "fifteen separate and distinct fights."[29] But hard cider on an election procession was different from hard drinking. Zeb was termed "an orderly student and respectful of his superiors." The reason was partly an appreciation of the opportunity opened to him by the college loan.

James J. Slade, a classmate who became mayor of Columbus, Georgia, dealt with this point: "Naturally a sensitive and honorable man, being a college beneficiary . . . he was more prudent than many of us wished him to be on student and faculty differences. This prudence at first was misinterpreted, but a word from his friend, Leon F. Siler, who was himself a prudent and very honorable man, set our minds right as to Vance."[30]

Gratitude was not the sole inducement to his seemly attitude. Zeb was inherently a respecter of age and authority. While he could delight his friends by mimicking the professors, he preserved a decorum and an esteem for them personally. Siler, incidentally, profited by his attention to duty and became valedictorian of his class, embarked on a career as writer and minister, but died young.

In one year's time Zeb established himself as a campus leader, known by every student for his frank geniality and quick repartee, and by all the faculty as fresh but not impudent, irrepressible but not obtrusive, mimicking but not annoying, and in all respects one who made Chapel Hill a more exciting place for every student, faculty member and townsman. The staff of Negro attendants and workers came to know and enjoy him, and after reconstruction days, when they belonged to the Republican Party, gave him, a Democrat, their votes.

An impetus to his extempore speaking was provided by the Dialectic Society, which the large part of the student body attended and where the rules for orderly conduct were so scrupulously enforced that the group was compared favorably in this respect with both the national Congress and state legislature. Vance was an active participant. Said Kemp Battle: "In readiness, tact, wit, aptness of illustration, and occasional flashes of eloquence, he had no superiors, nor was he deficient in knowledge of the subject under debate."[31]

Battle, the young instructor who watched him carefully because of his prediction after the moonlight meeting in Asheville, went on to compliment Zeb on still another score: "Notwithstanding his rollicksome gaiety, he was really a hard student. He possessed great power of concentrating all his faculties at will, and was accustomed to turn from his gay companions and make rapid progress by desperate exertions. His memory was strong and accurate, and his perfect self command and easy flow of words, made him a formidable adversary of the ablest debater in the University."[32]

Another element which impressed Kemp Battle was Zeb's utter lack of timidity or stage fright. "He was at ease anywhere and in any company. He was never known to show the least evidence of fear or abashment." This assuredness did not extend to effrontery. Continued Battle: "He had a degree of self-confidence rare among students, but it arose from a proper estimate of his powers. He was never accused of self-conceit or presumption, or what is well expressed in the slang word, cheekiness." When initiated to a bogus fraternity, "the Mystic Circle," which involved a good deal of student horseplay in which the awkward neophytes were supposed to become confused, he provided full half of the merriment by his sharp, laughable answers to the august tribunal before which he was supposed to quake.[33]

His friends conceded that Vance suffered the fate of all punsters—that while he hit a high note at times, at others he dropped to the atrocious. His anecdotes appeared to be strikingly apt. His mind, like Lincoln's, was stored with them. Kemp Battle noticed that he had collected them from mountain hunters, horse and hog drivers who moved along the French Broad turnpike, commercial travelers he had met at the Warm Springs hotel, lawyers and their clients, anyone who had a good, humorous story to relate. Sometimes—again much like Lincoln—he made jocular use of Biblical subjects in a manner which shocked many and gave him a reputation for impiety, which, just as in the case of Lincoln, notably in Lincoln's later years, was a faulty conclusion.

One of his lows in punning was in a letter from Chapel Hill to his girl cousin "Matt": "Do make everybody *write* and then everybody will *do right*. Aint that *rite* funny? *Write soon*."[34]

Zeb never forgot the liberal tendencies of college students he met and was not impatient with their mental adventuring and skepticism in his mature years. When he spoke in 1872 to the students of Wake Forest

College, a reverent Baptist institution, he ventured that "there is doubtless some infidelity among you." All of it seemed matter of course to him:

"When young minds are thoroughly imbued with the Pagan classics, and come first to exercise their powers of reason, the desire is to test them upon every subject, and especially upon the received creeds of religion, attacking them with almost a savage delight. A spell of skepticism comes upon the young Senior and the young graduate as naturally as the spell of love ere long, or as the measles in childhood. He reads and perforce admires Hume, Bolingbroke, Gibbon, Voltaire, and thoughts present themselves which he imagines never before, since the world began, entered the mind of man. He has thus made a discovery—it seems clear to him; and he wonders at the hypocrisy or stupidity of preaching and priestcraft. He wants the world to know that *he*, at least, is not to be deluded with cunningly devised fables of Hebrews—Jews—and old wives' tales. . . . He is strongly tempted by the glittering fallacies of materialism to forsake the simple faith of the fathers . . ."[35]

But he went on to tell them not to be deceived, that the greatest intellects of the world have had those same doubts which the student treated as his own discoveries; that "they have sounded all the depths and shallows of human skepticism, and have found it worse than folly." Defeated as he often had been, and prostrate as was his country about him in those years, he proclaimed that "none can escape the conviction of the existence of a beneficent God" and that "there is no book so God-like as the Bible."[36]

That book was something more for Zeb, it proved, than "conversational risibility."

Zeb became a good writer by practice. His first letters from Chapel Hill are devoid of the eloquence which became characteristic of his later rhetoric, and the grammar was not flawless, but he managed to crowd a good many letters into his busy college days, and quite apparently some of them were to test his powers of expression. He wrote to his cousins, rather frequently to Martha E. Weaver, his cousin Matt, one of the Baird family, and to his cousin John M. Davidson, whose mother was a Vance, and Cousin Kate, who was Kate Erwin Smith, another of the Bairds. To Matt he gave, not long after his arrival, a description of Chapel Hill:

"This is a beautiful place indeed. The main college buildings are 3 in number each 3 story high coulored yellow and surrounded with neat terraces of earth thrown up and platted with grass. They are very large buildings. [One is struck by this, considering how they are dwarfed on the great University of North Carolina campus today.] In addition to these are 3 other buildings, the ball room, Chapel and recitation hall large and tasty. They are all situated in a large oak & poplar grove, checkered off with splendid white gravel walks, set out in shrubbery, and the whole, I suppose about 20 or more acres surrounded with a stone wall neatly put up. The elevation is likewise high and I presume healthy, though one of our fellow students named Watters is laying near unto death at this time." (Watters survived his illness and the Confederate Army and died at the age of seventy-nine in 1912.)

Zeb mentioned his courses. He studied botany, "the science of flowers," he termed it, "a Ladies' science in particular." He gave his schedule: "I rise at 5 and go to bed at 10 and I give you my word I don't lose more than two hours during that time, and that is necessary for recreation." He was pleased with his progress. "I think I am establishing the character of a well-behaved student, in the eyes of the Faculty." He asked about a number of girls of his acquaintance, which he would scarcely have done if he had entertained genuinely sentimental affection for Matt. Already he was amorously disposed toward Harriette Espy of Quaker Meadows, in Burke County near Morganton, who was to become the wife Hattie of his triumphal years and his years of misfortune.[37]

To Cousin John, on September 14, 1851, he gave a better account of his studies: he took the full senior class course except French and Greek, plus law. The seniors during their first term had chemistry and mineralogy, political economy, moral philosophy and the two language courses which Zeb omitted. In the second term the course was again chemistry and geology, national and constitutional law (separate from the law course), and Latin. The law course covered Blackstone, Kent, Stephen on Pleading, Greenleaf on Evidence, Chitty on Contracts, Williams on Executors, and Cruise's Digest of Real Property, plus municipal laws and legislative enactments.

"I am taking a severe course of studies," he wrote to John, "which occupy more than half my time from Law, and yet I am reading Law

faster and learning more than when I was reading at home [in Woodfin's office] with nothing else to do. You know I had to loaf . . . and
play marbles . . . But the scales have fallen from my eyes, John, and I
have taken to real hard confinement & study."[38]

His next letter to Matt was a bit baffling. He told how safe he was
from falling in love with the pretty ladies he met because he was unable
to decide between them, but more especially because "I *thought of
somebody's bright eyes,* way up in the mountains, and that kept me away
from danger." Clearly he was referring to her and not Hattie Espy. But
it was not a very good lover's letter to Cousin Matt, because he went
on to gloat over his feminine society: "There are not a great many
ladies here, but they are very select, and the most intelligent ones I have
ever met with in my life. It allmost scares me to venture into conversation with them. There are some here on a visit all the time, from
every direction, but principally from St. Marys School in Raleigh and
Edgeworth Seminary in Greensboro." Then he added reassuringly, "But
my heart is in the mountains without a doubt."[39] Quaker Meadows,
where Hattie Espy lived, was not in the mountains. If he had dreams of
Matt, they did not materialize, because she married a Methodist preacher
in 1853 and moved to Tennessee, while Zeb, on August 3 of that year,
after he had set himself up as an Asheville lawyer, married Hattie.

Writing again to Matt on February 8, 1852, Zeb talked much about
the ladies and showed that perhaps he did not entertain serious hopes
about his cousin when he said, "Sometimes I am trembling all over for
fear I shall hear of my own sweetheart getting married without asking
me to the wedding." He had moments of homesickness that winter:
"How are my friends on Rims Creek? . . . The fact is I want to see
everybody, or in other words, Cousin Matt, I want to see *home, home,*
that sweetest of all places especially when you are away from it. Home is
like health, we never properly appreciate its blessings until we are away
from it."[40]

Zeb at that time was projecting a walking trip from Chapel Hill to
the mountains—one not infrequent among students in that day—with
Albert W. Siler, the student from Cherokee County at the far western
tip of the state, but as the day approached the coach looked better,
or more speedy. Sometime prior to April 25, 1852—the spring when he
was writing to Cousin Matt about her bright eyes burning into his
memory—he was writing to Charles McDowell of Quaker Meadows

for the hand of his niece, Hattie, a demure and pious girl. At the age of two, she had been left an orphan by the death of her father, Thomas Espy, a Presbyterian preacher and graduate of Princeton Theological Seminary, and her mother, Sarah Tate Espy, soon after. Her uncle answered Zeb on April 25, when he was still at Chapel Hill, giving his consent, and making the sensible observation: ", . . . you say your patrimony is all gone to Secure you an education poverty under Sutch Circumstances is I think a blessing it shows that you are determined to Relye on your Resorses for a living may you be successful is my Cincear wish you have been represented to me as an ennerJetick Sober young man I have a high Regard for your family there four I give my Consent . . ."[41]

During Christmas vacation Zeb had gone to Raleigh and obtained his license to practice law. That was something of a triumph because Samuel M. McDowell, who like him had read in Woodfin's office in Asheville, had been rejected on his first try. Zeb had heard of other rejections and was fearful. But he told his cousin John hopefully that Judge Battle, his head professor, predicted "I shall have them like a deer in a walk."[42]

Vance joined the Phi Gamma Delta fraternity at Chapel Hill. His joining had repercussions in Indiana many years later. Thomas R. Marshall, Vice President in the Woodrow Wilson administration, said that when he went to "a small Presbyterian college in Indiana" (Wabash, now a larger and a more important school), the inducement held out by the Phi Gams when they invited him to join was that among his brothers would be Lew Wallace, the Hoosier author of *Ben Hur,* and the great North Carolinian Zeb Vance. Tom Marshall decided it would be good to belong to an organization that had a war governor of the South and a Union general of the North, so for forty years, he said, he had enjoyed referring at fraternity banquets to "Brother Zeb Vance" and "Brother Lew Wallace."[43] None ever knew what impelled silent "Cooley" at Amherst to join this same group. When invited he said merely one word, "Yes."[44]

Vice President Marshall by coincidence had the privilege of presenting Indiana's monument of Lew Wallace to the Hall of Fame in the Capitol in Washington, and of accepting on behalf of the government for the Hall of Fame the monument of Zebulon B. Vance presented by North Carolina.

Such was the career of Zeb Vance at Chapel Hill. One of the students in the group which saw him off in front of Miss Nancy's heard but could not quite understand his pun, which had something to do with the wheel as he put his foot on it, to mount to the seat beside the driver. The crowd told him to keep plugging, he was bound to amount to something in time, and he shot back another pun as the coach sped away. The recorder of the incident said he never met Vance to speak to him again, but saw him as they passed on the slope of Malvern Hill.[15]

☆☆☆☆☆☆☆☆☆☆☆☆☆☆☆☆☆

# Chapter Four

## Searching for Dr. Mitchell's Body

☆☆☆☆☆☆☆☆☆☆☆☆☆☆☆☆☆

By the autumn of 1854 Zeb's letters, like that to his cousin Kate on September 12, were showing improvement in spelling and ease of expression. They were more graceful and natural than the abrupt missives he had written two years before from Chapel Hill.

Kate had become a teacher in Tazewell, Tennessee, and Zeb was now the one who had to supply home information. Letter-writing was a part of his discipline and training. Meantime he began his first flirtation with politics and public office. Even before he had qualified to practice law, but in anticipation that he would pass the examination easily, he had been elected solicitor of Buncombe County, beating the more studious and orderly minded Merrimon, his only rival for the post. The election was by the Buncombe County magistrates and he won eleven to eight. Then in 1854 he triumphed in a hot fight for a seat in the House of Commons of the state legislature.

Vance gave his own, and the most picturesque, version of the contest in his letter to Cousin Kate. "The canvass lasted three months and was warm in a great many respects beside the weather I can tell you." He ran "as a regular built, old fashioned Whig . . . and had to run against the Democratic party and the Southern Rights party too, who combined, as they always do in this country, have a majority of six hundred voters.

"That prospect was rather 'blue' wasn't it?" he continued. "But I put in with unparalleled impudence, fought the race through, and beat my competitor [the elderly Colonel Daniel Reynolds] one hundred and ten votes. I hope you will not think me vain in saying that my friends all agree . . . it was the greatest triumph that has been accomplished in this country for many years—Consequently I am something of a *lion* at present, among grocery [store] men and Crossroads politicians in particular."[1]

Just before the election a blue-eyed boy weighing ten pounds was born to Hattie and Zeb—"one of the brightest, sweetest little fellows that you ever beheld in the world."[2] This first child died in infancy, to the great grief of the Vances, but Hattie, to console herself, thought he was "better fitted to dwell with the angels . . . than with us on earth."[3]

That Zeb continued to excite puns, as well as coin them, was seen in the letter of his friend Henry R. Dickson, a native of Charleston, South Carolina, and a Yale graduate who had moved to Asheville because of his health. He wrote while on a visit to Charleston in October, 1852, saying he had been quarantined there, could not go outdoors and was about to die of *room*atism. Zeb had deprecated his own style in an earlier letter, but Dickson made a cogent observation: "I must protest against criticism of composition . . . For my humble self it is my way in epistolary scribblings, to send my notations to my correspondence . . . in a wild & careless manner, as a matter of purpose . . . If I have any notion of letter-writing at all, it is that it is conversation in ink, on paper,—as when a couple of good fellows meet and tell each other of matters and things . . . You know, my dear fellow, what a humbug the conversation of friends would soon become, if two men were to carry into each others company, when they met, note-books to take down each others sayings to *criticise* them."

He did show a misery something like Zeb's when away from the mountains. "Nostalgia-home-sickness-hankering after the hills and their dear blue scenery—my sunny home among the sparkling water and all that sort of thing—it would seem that I'd die of thirst, and panting to be with you in that Switzerland of America. The doctors say that to an absent Mountaineer in this sort of Indian Summer weather, home-sickness is the most common and natural thing in the world."[4]

Zeb at about this time bought a five-acre lot—"I can now walk around my extensive plantation"—in the middle of Asheville, at College and Spruce streets. He paid $2,300, which came as his wife's dowry.[5]

Scarcely was Zeb Vance launched on his law career before he had to discharge the sad task of searching for the body of his old professor, Dr. Elisha Mitchell, lost on the Black Dome. He had sided strongly with Mitchell and President Swain in helping to resolve the dispute between Mitchell and Congressman Thomas Lanier Clingman about who had first explored and measured the highest peak of the Appalachian range, the peak that now bears Mitchell's name. The highest peak of the Great Smokies is Clingman's Dome.

Dr. Mitchell went to the Blacks in 1857 and ascended the Black Dome, accompanied this time by his son, Charles A. Mitchell, his daughter, Margaret Elliott Mitchell, and a servant boy.

About 2:30 P.M. Saturday, June 27, Mitchell announced that he was going over the mountain to the Caney River settlement, where dwelt Big Tom Wilson, a guide he had employed. He told his son Charles he would rejoin the party at the Halfway House on the following Monday, June 29. He was never seen alive again.

Zeb Vance entered into the search the moment word came down that Dr. Mitchell was missing on the slopes of the Black Dome. By coincidence Zeb was visiting in the neighborhood and went up with the first search party. The story as told by Charles Mitchell was that no apprehension had been felt when the professor failed to appear on Monday, nor was there much concern on Tuesday, because many factors might account for the delay. But when he failed to arrive by Wednesday night, July 1, his son grew apprehensive and with John Stepp, son of the farmer at the foot of the mountain, crossed the mountain to the Caney River settlement, where they learned from Big Tom Wilson that Professor Mitchell had never reached there.[6]

The searchers divided into two groups, Vance's being headed by a mountain hunter, Fred Burnett, and the other by Jesse Stepp. Moving at dawn around the waist and over the summit of the Black Dome in a heavy, chilling rain, both detachments headed toward Sugar Camp Creek on the far side. On reaching the summit without discovering a trace of the professor's trail, Vance's party scattered into small details. They now pressed ahead rapidly for several miles over what Vance described as "inconceivably rough and dangerous gound," until compelled to halt by fatigue and darkness. Vance's party and that of Jesse Stepp, having covered other areas fruitlessly, returned that night, exhausted, to the Halfway House. Though it was July, the temperature was 44 degrees at noon and most of the time the mountains were wrapped in heavy fog. "It seemed as if the genii of those vast mountain solitudes," wrote Vance, "were angered at our unwonted intrusion, and had invoked the Storm-God to enshroud in deeper gloom the sad and mysterious fate of their noble victim."[7]

Vance told of the search in a graphic story he wrote for the Asheville *Spectator* a few days later, which disclosed how far he had advanced in his rhetorical powers since his early days at Chapel Hill. He had procured a half interest in the *Spectator,* a Whig organ for the mountain area, in 1855, and the reporting he mixed with his law practice was gradually giving him the writing assurance that could come only from experience and the discipline required in meeting deadlines. His account, published in the *Spectator* in July, 1857, is the best extant of the search and perhaps the most frequently consulted source.

Undoubtedly the heavy rain which continued through Sunday and obscured the mountain had dulled the trail. The gloom, according to Zeb, proved contagious and the conclusion became general that the professor was dead. "It could not be possible, we thought, that he was alive, for cold, and hunger, and fatigue, if nothing worse had happened to him, would ere this have destroyed him."[8]

By this time Asheville residents were arriving to assist and by Monday, July 6, eighty men were combing the mountain.

Vance was with a detachment working down a mountain stream when they heard shots and the blast of a horn telling that the distressing search was about finished. Still, it was not until after midnight that information was received that the body had been found. The dextrous mountaineers had followed the trail down Sugar Camp Creek and had detected evidences of Mitchell's passing. Finally they came to a cataract which spilled downward for forty feet, now called Mitchell Falls. Members of the party picked their way carefully down the precipice to the pool which the cataract had cut out of the solid rock and made into a basin of crystal clear water fourteen feet deep. At the bottom they could see in the last light the professor's body, his arms outstretched. According to Vance's news story, he was lying in quiet repose, "the good, the great, the wise, the simple minded, the pure of heart, the instructor of youth, the disciple of knowledge and the preacher of Christianity."[9]

Big Tom Wilson lived in fame for half a century thereafter as the man who had found Dr. Mitchell's body. He came to be known as the greatest of the hunter-guides of the southern Appalachians. He died

February 1, 1908, in his Yancey County fastness on Cane River, where Mitchell had been going to find him when he slipped and fell.[10]

Reporter Vance described the tragedy of such an event in so wild a setting: "Oh what friend to science and virtue, what young among all the thousands that have listened to his teachings, what friend that has ever taken him by the hand, can think of this wild and awful scene unmoved by the humanity of tears! can think of those gigantic pyramidal firs, whose interlocking branches shut out the light of heaven, the many hued rhododendrons that freight the air with their perfume and lean weepingly over the waters, that crystal stream leaping down the great granites and hastening from the majestic presence of the mighty peak above, whilst in the deep pool below, where the weary waters rest but a single moment, lies the inanimate body of his dear friend and perceptor, apparently listening to the mighty requiem of the cataract!"[11]

Zeb the reporter, now twenty-seven years old, was learning to play with words. He summoned forth his best decorative phrases in his eulogistic outpouring for his old professor.

Less than a year passed before Mitchell's body was exhumed from the Presbyterian Church cemetery in Asheville, and on June 14, 1858, it was reburied atop the present Mount Mitchell, the loftiest of the Black Mountain peaks, where it remains today. The family yielded to an almost universal request that the professor be so honored. The body was drawn to the summit by oxen pulling a sled, but in places where mud or the steepness of the slope made the trail impassable for the beasts, the mountaineers put the casket on their shoulders and continued the ascent. Dr. Swain was among the speakers and expressed satisfaction with the place of burial. In 1888 the Mitchell monument was completed on the summit and bolted to the bedrock of the mountain. It was constructed of a white bronze that is almost pure zinc, sandblasted to give it the appearance of granite. Probably it will endure as long as the stone beneath it. There Mitchell rests, as someone said, "alone with God."[12]

## Chapter Five

## Mountain Politician and Congressman

Much as the pioneer settlers of the Middle West used strong drink as a protection from the cold and many other ills, both severe and fancied, so the mountaineers distilled freely and drank at times excessively, though they, like the adventurers who crossed the Ohio, could not be rated as drunkards.

A good picture is offered by attorney Augustus S. Merrimon of the convening of the Madison County court in 1853 by Judge David F. Caldwell, at Jewell Hill, the first county seat of Madison County, situated a few miles north of the present county seat of Marshall. The court met in what lawyer Merrimon termed "a verry bad house," having no seats fit for use, open to the weather, and with no bench for the judge. But Judge Caldwell went ahead and charged the grand jury and then began to clear the docket of the unimportant cases. By adjournment time late in the day the crowd was "getting in a weaving way," and most of the twenty to thirty women present were in varying degrees of inebriation.

Merrimon blamed it on the locality. "I do not know of any rival for this place in regard to drunkenness, ignorance, superstition and almost brutal debauchery. I regret that it is so, yet it is true. Scores of women attend this court for the sole purpose of drinking and pandering to the lustful passions of dirty men."[1]

Next day the judge ordered the whisky wagon removed from the scene and better order was preserved until darkness, but Merrimon said that after court "as I passed along to my lodgins I saw several persons so drunk they could not walk." They were being dragged home by friends. This was the locality in which Zeb Vance spent his youth at Lapland. As if to contrast the weakness of mankind with the glory of nature, young Merrimon exulted over the scene as he passed along: "The night is cool and the moon shines down on the river and the cliffs along its side, in majestic splendor. O, it is a pleasing sight to see the French Broad rolling over the rocks in the moonlight."[2]

Such were the conditions of human frailty and natural grandeur under which Merrimon and Vance conducted their early practice in the mountain counties of western North Carolina.

Vance a little later was trying a case against his old adversary Merrimon, and though they were both young, Merrimon was exhibiting his studious qualities, Vance his nimble wit. Vance buttressed his case with a decision by Chief Justice Thomas Ruffin of the North Carolina Supreme Court and was filled with confidence until Merrimon rose holding a volume of statutes enacted by the last state legislature. The act which he read repealed the law on which Chief Justice Ruffin had based his decision. Vance was cornered. The means he took to extricate himself were probably not those he would have pursued in later more prudent years. He had the last summation. He turned to the jury in his gravest attitude and said:

"Gentlemen, are you not amazed at the assurance of my friend, Mr. Merrimon, in citing an act of the Legislature, passed by such good men as your neighbor, John Smith, who knows no more law than you do, and Bill Jones of Yancey, who knows less, against the decision of our Supreme Court, constituted by such men as Ruffin, Gaston and Daniel?"[3]

There is scarcely any reason why the lawyers should have been surprised, but it is related that they were, nevertheless, when the jury came in with a decision for the Supreme Court of Ruffin, Gaston and Daniel over the Legislature of John Smith and Bill Jones. Richard H. Battle, Zeb's secretary during the war years, excused him for taking advantage of the jury by saying the wronged litigant might easily win surcease by an appeal to the Supreme Court. But Battle explained what all later came to know, that Zeb's usual method was to win the confidence of the jury by a fair statement of the law, and not to mislead it.[4]

Zeb's older brother, Robert, told of an incident which showed that

Zeb in his early practice was as ready to fight with fists as lawbooks. When he was in his first office, county solicitor, he got into an altercation with another young lawyer back of the courtroom, only thirty feet from where the honorable justices were hearing a case. Robert did not say who began the fracas, but it grew so heated and boisterous that the justices had to adjourn court. They came rushing to the back lot.

Zeb and the other lawyer were facing each other belligerently and Zeb held a wisp of hair in his hand which he had yanked from his adversary's scalp. The justices by severe injunctions restored tranquillity, but did not heal either the raging spirits or physical wounds of the two young barristers. Vance had apparently given the other lawyer rough handling. The man was bloody, had a bloodshot eye and was shorn of a forelock. A duel seemed inevitable.

The other lawyers sought conciliation and Vance was ready to forget. The other maintained that a gentleman would not resort to gouging in a fight and declared he must have satisfaction. When it was reported that the gouging of the eye remained the inexcusable point of honor in the affair, Zeb said frankly that he had not intended to assail his adversary's eye, but had merely poked his long finger into it when he had been trying to draw the man to him and pinion him to check his fisticuffs. The gouging was in truth accidental. The explanation was accepted, the duel averted, and Zeb practiced law thereafter by the books.[5]

Robert told also of Zeb's retort when queried in his first race for the legislature. The only issue raised against him was his age. When his adversary adverted to it—Zeb was then twenty-four—he rose solemnly and apologized to the big gathering for his youth.

"Fellow citizens," he said, "I must admit I am young, but it is not my fault. My parents did not consult me as to the time when I should be born. All I can do is to promise to try to do better next time."[6]

Robert said the uproar which followed was such that Zeb's opponent got angry and said that while he liked to see a smart boy, this one was "entirely too smart." Robert thought this little retort was what sent Zeb to the legislature and started him on his political career.

When he ran next term for state senator he had stiffer opposition in David Coleman, later commander of the celebrated 39th North Carolina and, after the wounding of the brigade commander, of McNair's "star brigade" of Bushrod Johnson's Division which pierced the center

of the Federal Army at Chickamauga.[7] Meantime Thomas Lanier Clingman, foreseeing the demise of the Whig party to which he had adhered
when elected to Congress in 1842, had become a Democrat in 1846
and had recovered his old seat in the House, from which he had been
ousted in the election of 1844. Being the outstanding political leader
of the mountain area, well versed in national affairs and the most
penetrating and astute debater, he had gradually led a substantial segment of the traditional but confused Whigs into the Democratic party.
The general weakening of the Whigs rather than any disappointment
in Vance's service in the House of Commons in Raleigh accounted
for his defeat. Coleman, about seven years older than Vance, was not
only well educated. His manners were pleasant and according to Merrimon he was a young man "of some sprightliness."[8] He possessed a
much broader experience than the other fledglings of the western
North Carolina bar because he had served in the navy and knew the
world beyond the Blue Ridge. He and Vance were to meet in a later
campaign under conditions of much greater stress.

Vance at the age of twenty-eight launched his campaign for Congress
in one of these court gatherings, which customarily drew litigants, the
principal lawyers from the mountain area, and crowds who came down
from the hills for the spectacles of the trials or for the conviviality of
the liquor wagon.

On May 6, 1858, Clingman, who had served seven terms in the
House, one as a Whig and six as a Democrat, was appointed to the
United States Senate to fill the vacancy caused by the resignation of
Senator Asa Biggs of Williamston, whom President Buchanan appointed federal judge for the North Carolina district. Though Zeb
had been defeated by Coleman for the State Senate, he decided to
plunge into the race for the House seat with all the vigor he could
command, realizing that he had three handicaps which allowed him
no more than an outside chance.

One was his youth—"he was a mere stripling," commented an Asheville resident who saw him on the day he left for the race.[9] Another
was his Whiggery. Clingman during his fourteen years in the House
had built a strong Democratic organization in the mountain area and
few believed it could be challenged successfully in 1858. Zeb analyzed
the situation carefully but confided his intention to very few friends
until he was prepared to make his announcement.

"I saw him the morning he left Asheville for Cherokee to enter the campaign," wrote an acquaintance. "I do not think that more than half a dozen people knew that he had any intention of running for Congress."[10]

The third and most imposing obstacle was the standing of his Democratic opponent, William Waightstill Avery of the distinguished Morganton family, whose grandfather, the first attorney general of North Carolina, had had the audacity to put the slab of bacon in Andrew Jackson's saddlebag. Coleman had announced along with Avery, but withdrew and left the Democratic nomination uncontested.

Avery had led his class of 1837 at the University of North Carolina and been valedictorian, then had read law under the famed William Gaston of the North Carolina Supreme Court. Gaston, a graduate of Princeton and a Federalist Congressman during the War of 1812 years, was looked on during the 1830s as the leading lawyer and jurist of the state, and Avery had entered into practice in 1837 with the prestige not only of his Burke County family but of association with one of the great names of the North Carolina bench and bar. He went to the legislature in 1842 at the early age of twenty-six and about the same time became a trustee of the University of North Carolina. As a devoted Calhoun state-rights Democrat he had won repeated elections to the house of commons and had been elected Speaker in 1856, a year in which he also headed, as a chairman with secessionist sentiments, the North State delegation to the Democratic National Convention. Scarcely was there an abler or more distinguished man in the state than Avery for Vance to select as a political adversary, and even the long-haired orator's most devoted friends would not have counted his chances worthy of comment.[11]

But Avery had one scar on his record, and just how deep it remained as a blemish was a matter for the voters to determine. He had risen abruptly in the courtroom, in the very presence of the judge, had drawn a pistol concealed in his coat, and had shot a Yancey County politician, Samuel Fleming, a fellow member of the house of commons, dead.[12]

Fleming, "a big rugged mountain man" who was "blatant and boastful, truculent but proud," had been angered by Avery's sharp language in litigation in the Marion court over collection of a debt, and when they met on the street after adjournment had challenged Avery to repeat his words. The lawyer declined, saying he was not accountable to Fleming for remarks he made on behalf of his client in court. He declined also Fleming's challenge to a fist battle, whereupon Fleming brought out a cowhide whip he had concealed in his coat and lashed the small, studious lawyer until the blood gushed from his lacerated face. He was treated by a good physician, who not only stanched his bleeding and ministered to his wounds, but also handed him a pistol, which he carried when the Superior Court met next in Morganton. There Fleming imprudently appeared and stamped brazenly down to the clerk's desk in front of the bench, and within five feet of the distraught Avery. The lawyer's bullet went through Fleming's heart, spun him around and dropped him before he could speak.

Opinion seemed so preponderantly on Avery's side that he was acquitted that same week by a jury which deliberated only ten minutes.

Judge William H. Battle was on the bench when the brooding Avery shot Fleming, and presided at the trial in which Avery was acquitted. The judge confided to his son Kemp that the jury would have found the judge and every lawyer at the bar guilty before it would have convicted Avery for his offense. The defense was temporary insanity. As Kemp Battle averred, it was *ipso facto* in those days that when a man had been horsewhipped he would be insane and the death of his attacker would be merited retribution. Kemp thought that the slaying of Fleming made Avery more popular.[13]

Dr. Edward W. Phifer, historian of the Avery family and a North Carolina physician qualified to diagnose, concluded that while Avery's professional and political standing seemed unimpaired by the affair, he suffered a profound emotional reaction. He became preoccupied and a brooder and walked the streets at night because he was plagued by insomnia. Being sensitive and proud, he bore emotionally the scars of the incident long after the whip marks had faded from his face.[14] That may have affected his manner when campaigning.

Cherokee County, where Zeb planned to make his announcement for Congress, is the far southwestern county of the state, bordering on Tennessee and Georgia, with Murphy the county seat. Zeb rode the one hundred and thirty miles on horseback over the weekend and reached Murphy exhausted on the Monday of court week. The custom in campaign years was to set aside Tuesday afternoon of court week for the political candidates to make their presentations. The Tuesday crowds were always large.[15]

Avery had gone to Murphy several days earlier and was not only well rested, but had ample time to prepare his speech. Smiling, pleasant, dignified, possessing not the vaguest notion that he woud have opposition in the campaign from the disorganized Whigs, he spoke for no more than an hour. A careful observer noticed that Zeb kept a sheet of paper in his hand and took notes freely. Avery won hearty applause. After quiet was restored to the courtroom, to the surprise of nearly everyone young Zeb Vance stood up, carried his saddlebags down to the front of the room, pulled out some documents and announced that he was a candidate for Congress on the Whig ticket from the western district of North Carolina.

The only report which seems to be available of Vance's first speech for Congress rated it as unimpressive.[16] His brother Robert does not refer to it in discussing Zeb's political career. But Zeb grew stronger with each appearance and by time the court reached Waynesville he was eliciting such responses to his droll yarns and bitter denunciation of the Democrats that he wrote to Asheville in clear elation. "Say to my Whig friends to go to work," he entreated. "I have Mr. A. under hack, and if my Whig friends will work I will carry the district from three to four thousand."[17]

Much as he had been trapped in his law case opposing Merrimon, Vance was caught at times by Avery and had to extricate himself by wile. Avery turned on the Whigs and said even the sons of the party's leaders and founders were deserting it, and mentioned specifically the sons of Clay and Webster. Zeb declared that Daniel Webster had no sons, that all his children were daughters, which prompted Avery to say contemptuously, "You do not remember Colonel Fletcher Webster of the Mexican War?" (Webster's last son, Fletcher, then surviving, would fall at the head of his regiment in the Civil War.) Zeb recalled him belatedly. "Oh, no," he said, "that was Noah Webster's son—the spelling book man's son." The crowd rejected Avery's, accepted Zeb's version. In any event, it was understandable that one would confuse two Yankees like Daniel and Noah. Avery that night confronted Zeb with the accusation that he had pulled a mean one. Vance agreed, but stated simply, "I had to wiggle out somehow."[18]

Zeb's political perspicacity was a better gauge than the "scientific" methods of modern political pollsters, for when the votes were counted he led by 3,700 and had upset a Democratic plurality of 5,000 in the last Congressional election won by Clingman.

In the reconciliation which followed the campaign, Vance and Avery met on an Asheville platform. Zeb, whom most had expected to be cooked up brown by Avery's debating skill, pointed out that exactly the opposite had happened, then compared himself to the possum a Caldwell County mountaineer had told him about: "I stretched that possum's neck tell I thought he was dead. I skinned him and boiled him fur three hours, but . . . when I took the lid off'n the pot, the cussed little devil was sittin' up thar on its hind legs, and had licked up the gravy."[19]

Such prominence as Zeb enjoyed before the race was due to his editorship of the robust Asheville *Spectator,* which couched its political utterances in terms violent even for that era of sturdy partisan journalism. That could be understood from one of its effusions of the mid 1850s about the national campaign of 1852: "Gen. Pierce was elected President by one of the vilest, most damnable and infamous coalitions between abolitionists, freesoilers, democrats, locofocos, secessionists, disunionists, land-reformers, anti-renters, woman-righters, bloomers, thimble-riggers, villains, cut-throat scoundrels, renegade whigs—in a word, by the most corrupt combination that was ever witnessed in the operation of government."[20]

Pierce, of whom it has been said "his smile was sweet, his manners winning,"[21] was essentially a kindly, generous-hearted and cultivated man who relished more the companionship of the gentle Nathaniel Hawthorne or the visiting William Makepeace Thackeray than the sharp ring of the political invective. He could not have dreamed that he was put into office by such an aggregation of rascals, but embattled Zeb Vance with his militant Whiggery never would have doubted it. He had admired Clay as sincerely as Abraham Lincoln ever had, and now, after the passing of Clay, that devotion had been transferred into an intense loyalty to the Union, which dominated most of his utterances.

Vance retired as joint editor of the *Spectator* after a year—the financial returns were far from substantial. His co-editor, John D. Hyman, remained his friend, and the newspaper was such a devoted supporter that the opposition *News* felt called on to observe a little later: "If Mr. Vance does not have reason to exclaim, 'save me from my friends,' let him be grateful, for he will certainly be fortunate. If he survives the embarrassment of the Asheville *Spectator,* he need not fear what his enemies can do. Mr. Vance is the *Spectator's speciality,* and at every mention of his name it sputters and snaps and snarls like a cat with its tail in a steel trap. To question the correctness of his views on a public question, the *Spectator* seems to regard as little short of treason. That sheet had as well understand now, if it has not learned it before, that we shall criticise Mr. Vance's public acts at our own discretion, and the *organ,* and all concerned, can help themselves in any way they prefer. We snap our fingers at the whole caboodle."[22]

Vance's political thinking at this time is best reflected by his letter of February 19, 1858, to David F. Caldwell, Whig leader of Greensboro with whom he had served in the house of commons.[23] They were close friends then but were estranged at a later period, mainly, it appears, because Vance when governor would not give Caldwell a commission in the Senior Reserves. For reasons that are not apparent, Caldwell was forced to serve as a private at the age of fifty.

Vance wrote that his own politics were not like the almanac, which had to be changed with each new year. He said the definition of where he stood "would answer as well for my grave stone as it does now."[24] Nothing more clearly indicates than this statement the caprices of politics and the futility of prediction, for no partisan alignment ever underwent more abrupt change than Vance's. Similarly his Asheville friend, who watched him depart for Cherokee to announce his candidacy, referred to his own party steadfastness and years later wrote: "I was so strong a Whig in those days that I had serious doubt whether a man who would vote the Democratic ticket could enjoy religion. I am as strong a Democrat now, as Whig then. Times change, and men change with them. Don't they?"[25]

Zeb recalled that he had learned the alphabet at his father's knee from the head letters of the *National Intelligencer* and the Raleigh *Register.* Both were Seaton and Gales publications. Vance said that "from their pages I drank in an early and earnest love for the *conservative,* a sincere admiration for our state and federal constitutions, and a lasting veneration for the wise and true men who formed them." The *National Intelligencer* under Joseph Gales, Jr., had at first been ardently Jeffersonian and the mouthpiece of Madison and his successors until controversy with Andrew Jackson threw it to the Whigs at the time when Jackson was calling Francis P. Blair to Washington to edit a more subservient Democratic organ, the *Globe.* Before he became proprietor of the *National Intelligencer* in 1810, Joe Gales, a political refugee with his father from Sheffield, England, in 1795, established the *Register* with his father in Raleigh and later took his brother-in-law, William W. Seaton, into partnership with him.[26] The transfer to Whiggery from Jeffersonian Republicanism was not difficult in an age which looked on Clay more than on Jackson as a political descendant of Jefferson, in view of Jefferson's well-known intense dislike of Jackson. Lincoln, who has been termed by one of his eminent biographers "a Jeffersonian liberal,"[27] was campaigning this same year against Stephen A. Douglas for the Senate in Illinois, with vigor equal to Vance's against Avery, with a good deal of similar drollery in his remarks, but with words much less cutting than Zeb's invectives.

Although Vance did concede there was some good in the Democratic party, he declared it "combines so many elements of death and destruction, that it has not only brought us to our present dangerous pass, but will eventually overthrow us entirely and irredeemably." He lamented that the Democrats had swept out of power in North Carolina and Washington such "great and conservative statesmen" as Senators Willie Person Mangum, William Alexander Graham, and George E. Badger— they, like statesmen elsewhere, were being replaced by "half-brained fire-eaters,"—but also had caused the fall from the cabinet of John J. Crittenden of Kentucky and John Bell of Tennessee, along with the retirement from Congress of Edward Everett and Rufus Choate. They "went down for their conservatism," he declared, then added that Webster "was dead before he died," while "the great and glorious Millard Fillmore" was brought low by foes who to serve their party "covered him with slanderous and blackguardish vituperation."

Recognizing that the Whig party was withering away and that political fortune was to be found with the Democrats, he nevertheless avowed his opposition to the Democratic party "until it amends or I grow corrupt." But he felt some satisfaction: "Though I am completely shut off from advancement, by these opinions, which to a young man endowed with considerable ambition, is a gloomy enough prospect, yet I can say it with a clear conscience before God & man, that the very fact of my standing almost alone in defense of what I believe to be the *right*, in the face of overwhelming odds, affords me a gratification— an inner feeling of moral rectitude—which I would not surrender for a seat in the senate of the United States, were I old enough to be allowed one!"[28]

Zeb's service in Washington was as undistinguished as the second session of the Thirty-fifth Congress in which it fell. The session was devoted mainly to the appropriations, and expired, according to the law then prevailing, on March 3, 1859. Zeb's term of active duty on the floor was consequently less than three months. The Speaker was the Southern Rights Democrat James L. Orr of Anderson County, South

Carolina, who did not seem to fancy the job, for he retired voluntarily from Congress after a single term in the chair; he was a secessionist and Confederate States senator and soldier who reversed Vance's procedure and turned Republican after the war.

Vance's first participation in the discussion, aside from a casual question or so, was his healthy opposition to an ever recurring indulgence in Congresses before and after his time—the increase in fringe benefits to the members. He focused his attention on a miscellaneous item of $40,000 in the Congressional appropriation bill and by his calculations concluded that his successor in Congress, whoever he might be, would receive $10,000 more for the term than he did, or an increase of 25 per cent in emoluments, though he did not believe this person would be 25 per cent greater than he was.

"I do not think that he is entitled to $10,000 more for miscellaneous items than I am myself. . . . This whole bill reminds me very much of the bills I have seen of fast young men at fashionable hotels: For two days board, $5; sundries, $50. [Laughter.] It is like a comet, a very small body with an exceedingly great tail."[29]

He went on to say the comparison with the tail was not quite pertinent because with a good telescope one could see through the tail of a comet, but "what glasses will enable us to see through this miscellaneous item? [Laughter.] I should like to know what it is for, what it is intended for."

His only pretentious address was delivered on the combined issues of the tariff, public lands, and the question of pensions for soldiers of the War of 1812. In it he showed, at the age of twenty-eight, the control of words that would make him a leading orator of his times. They reflected also his constant hope for the Union. He called attention to the fury over the slavery issue which had but recently shaken the Thirty-fifth Congress and the contrasting quietude of the second session. The Kansas question of the first session had provoked fierce sectional debates. Said Vance:

"The late fury of the political heavens having spent itself in the fierce and bitter contests which raged in these halls, we have now a comparative quiet. But whether the winds merely pause to gather more wrath, whether it is merely a truce to enable the combatants to recruit and bury their dead, we cannot tell . . . I, for one, am determined to interpret the omens for good. I think they are full of hope and peace and promise for the Republic. I hope, sir, that the lull is not a treacherous stillness, heralding the deadly simoon, but it is Halcyon herself, who comes to brood upon the dark and restless deep. Eight weeks of this session have gone by; grave and important questions have been discussed and passed upon; and yet harmony and good feeling have prevailed. Zeal there has been, but without fanaticism; warmth and spirit, but without bitterness and rancor . . . Too long, already, has the country suffered from this all-absorbing excitement, which has so much hindered practical legislation."

He deplored the recurring Treasury deficit. Brushing aside charts and figures, he extracted the simple fact: "As we are in debt, and spending more than our income, and as our income is derived principally from the tariff, we have to do one of three things; either raise that income, lower our expenses, or walk into the insolvent court and file our schedule. I do not think there is, or ever was, a political economist on earth who could deny these propositions."[30]

He opposed a tariff for protection, thought a policy of free trade equally absurd, but felt the rates should be hiked for revenue purposes. He could see no wrong in the incidental protection which might be afforded industry, but opposed a schedule that would "build up Northern manufacturers at the expense of Southern agriculturalists." Though calling for retrenchment, he defended his vote for the old soldiers' bill.

"I do not wish to begin to economize in the wrong place," he declared. "I do not wish, sir, to let the first stroke fall on the best, the noblest, the most useful part of the whole nation, the gallant soldiers of the War of 1812. What would be thought, sir, of the man who would begin to reform his household expenses, by giving a half feed to his horse, his ox, and his plowman . . . We might profitably decapitate some thousands of that class of hungry hangers-on, who swarm in the land with the numbers and rapacity of the Egyptian locust . . . I contend, sir, that the citizen soldier is at once the pride and glory, the stay and the surety of the nation; and no government is wise which refuses to contribute, in this way, to the fostering of that warlike spirit in its militia."

Zeb's vote for these pensions became a sharp issue against him, but he took pleasure in it. Answering the contention of an Ohio Congressman that it would insult the veterans to put their service on a dollar basis and that "patriotism is its own reward," he told of a custom in Catholic countries of having a priest pass over the fields in spring and bless the expected crop. On one occasion a priest who was an agriculturalist perceived that the land was lean and sterile. "Here, my friends," he said, "blessings will do no good. This field must have manure." The old soldiers prized their glory, but wanted something with which they could buy a leg of mutton. The pension amounted to eight dollars a month, and since recognition had been delayed until nearly half a century after the date of that conflict, not a great number remained. Vance objected to the expenditure of lavish sums on other projects, such as advocacy of using millions to corrupt Spanish authorities, and turning the weather-beaten veteran away.[31]

That, in fact, became a leading issue in the campaign for re-election he waged in 1859 against his old adversary who had trounced him for the state senate, David Coleman. Vance dealt with it lightly and triumphantly by arousing much nationalistic fervor over the rallying of the country after the British had burned Washington in 1812, then in one of his emotional outbursts he portrayed the old soldier on crutches, destitute and heavy with years, asking eight dollars a month to ease his passage to the grave. Veterans and pensions were more popular in those days when getting into wars was less of a habit. Ever since the Battle of King's Mountain it had been easy to stir patriotism in the North Carolina hill country. Honor was due anyone who had fought against the redcoats in any way. Zeb surely was in time with home sentiment in this appeal, even to his quotation of Robert Burns:

> *The poor old soldier ne'er despise*
> *Nor count him as a stranger;*
> *Remember he is his country's stay*
> *In the day and hour of danger.*

Zeb's brother Robert described one of his talks in Asheville on the pension question: "The effect of this effort will never be forgotten by those who heard it. Strong men wept throughout the court room, and the old men in the place became as little children when they remembered what the soldiers had done for our country and how little a return had been made them."[32]

Among Zeb's political companions in the House were the young Ohioan John Sherman, seven years older than Vance, who had entered Congress in 1855 as a Whig. He had turned Republican and in 1855 served as president at the first Republican state convention ever held in Ohio.[33]

Another was the Vermonter Justin Smith Morrill, who like Vance had been elected as a Whig. Though the Whig party was dying, word of the demise had not resounded through the back country of Vermont or the North Carolina mountains and the political corpse was still sending vigorous new members to the House. There is little significance to Vance's early political compatibility with these two men except that in later decades he would serve alongside both as their most spirited adversary in the postwar Senate. Vance stood out in the House not only because of his rollicking good humor, but also because he was the youngest member of the Thirty-fifth Congress. Having been elected for a partial term, he took his seat December 7, 1858. Partly through John Sherman and partly through his drollery, Vance won the acquaintance of Thomas Corwin, an old-line Ohio Whig, representative, senator, governor of Ohio, and Secretary of the Treasury under Millard Fillmore. Now, in Vance's time, he had returned to be a member of the House. "Cello-voiced, witty"[34] Tom Corwin had been a frequent visitor in earlier years at the home of the Sherman boys, John and Tecumseh, in New Lancaster, Ohio, and had been a sharp influence on them during their formative years. He found in Zeb a congenial spirit and the friendship bore fruit for Zeb when he was languishing in prison after the war.

Samuel S. (Sunset) Cox, new like Vance in the Thirty-fifth Congress, but destined to long service from Ohio and New York and eventually to rise to the Speakership, found Vance "strong in integrity, wondrous in vitality." Cox had points in common with Vance, notably his use of adjectives. His writings about the glories of Ohio—he had edited a Columbus newspaper—were comparable to Zeb's about the French Broad and Swannanoa valleys. Cox had already won his nickname of "Sunset," not from his initials, but by the florid article he had written in 1853 entitled "A Great Old Sunset," which had more to do with the majesty of an Ohio storm than the luster of the sun's last rays.[35] Writing in later years, Cox recalled that Vance's voice "was never heard at Washington for disunion."[36]

Zeb's correspondence as a Congressman from the mountain district could not have been heavy but he resisted it. He commented, a touch complainingly, in a letter to his cousin Jane L. Smith, of Baird family connection, that "two or three letters are at my elbow to be answered," but he did say that if he put aside a letter for future attention it got lost in the heap and he never got back to it. His impression of Washington was far from complimentary. "Although I neither drink, gamble nor do anything else *very* bad," he told Jane, "yet a young man is always in danger when amid temptations, and I really believe, in point of wickedness and vice, that the cities at the bottom of the Dead Sea were holy places, compared to this."[37]

He had opportunities to meet the nation's great. He dined with President Buchanan and swung on his arm at the dance the charming Harriet Lane, the President's niece and hostess and one of the most delightful ladies ever to preside over the White House. He wrote about "supping with Judge Douglas & his magnificent wife," née Adele Cutts, who was a collateral descendant of the inimitable Dolley Madison,[38] the North Carolina Quaker girl whose vibrancy and grace were still well remembered in the capital city. Adele Cutts was the "Little Giant's" second wife and, because she possessed much of the radiance of her great-aunt Dolley, was as sought after in Washington social circles of the late 1850s as were Mrs. Jefferson Davis and the pleasant Mrs. Joseph E. Johnston, a ruler of the army set.

Whiggery was fading more slowly in the Southern mountains than it was elsewhere because it was quite apparent that the Republican party, largely sectional and directed against slavery, into which the Northern Whigs were moving, would not be a vehicle for political advancement in the slave states. Zeb's victory in overturning the big Democratic majority and restoring the western Carolina district to the Whigs seemed illusively to breathe new life into the faltering party. It won him the attention of the eastern Tennessee Whigs. After his return from Washington he was invited to address a giant Whig rally in Knoxville. Zeb's brother Robert apparently accompanied him, for he told the story of it with details. The issue at the moment was the renewed talk in Buchanan administration circles of the purchase of Cuba—a sort of revival of the old Golden Circle scheme to extend American dominion around the Gulf of Mexico and Caribbean Sea. The press had carried stories about the possibility that Congress might appropriate $100,000,000—a vast sum in those frugal times—for bribing Spanish officials and buying Cuba. That figure had been used by President Polk in his covert effort to buy Cuba in 1848, without consulting Congress.[39]

Vance, long-haired and, as was usual with him in those days, a bit unkempt, was a source of curiosity to a distinguished Presbyterian clergyman who shared the platform with him in Knoxville and studied him carefully. The young orator denounced Buchanan severely on the score of the hundred million dollars and then quoted, as applicable to the President, the phrase which appeared at Belshazzar's feast, *"Mene, mene, tekel, upharsin."* After an oratorical pause during which he surveyed the full sweep of the audience, he continued: "I don't know whether a single one of my hearers knows the literal meaning of that awful Scripture or not."

The Presbyterian divine, being quite sure that he did, waited confidently. "It means," Zeb continued, "Jeems, Jeems, you stole that money."

The poke at Buchanan caused the crowd to roar, but not the minister, who was awaiting the translation "thou art weighed in the balances, and art found wanting." The surprise at Zeb's remark literally upset the good man, who had been leaning forward in anticipation. He plunged headlong from the platform and fell on the floor while the merriment continued.[40]

David Coleman, Zeb's adversary in the campaign for the Thirty-sixth Congress, destined to greatness in western North Carolina history because of his later intrepid leadership of one of the best known of the North Carolina regiments, was a formidable antagonist even before the war. He was an easy, persuasive talker. He had the backing of Clingman's Democratic organization that, before the appearance of Vance, dominated the mountain district. Coleman, the former midshipman, later the distinguished colonel, campaigned jointly with Vance in the courthouses on Tuesday mornings, and both did much personal handshaking through the back country.

Coleman tried to drive home two points against Vance: first, that he had been associated with the American party, the infamous "Know-Nothings" who had appeared in the early 1840s in Pennsylvania and reached their maximum power at about the time Zeb was entering politics; and second, that Vance's first term in Congress had been undistinguished—that he had done nothing except fill his seat.

Zeb had always been a Whig, but he was a strong supporter of President Millard Fillmore who, when denied the Whig nomination of 1852, had run as the candidate of the American party in 1856. The Know-Nothing party was the outgrowth of antiforeign agitation at a time when heavy immigration, especially from Ireland and Germany, was depressing wages, jamming the cities, creating slums, and fostering bossism in city politics. The Democrats were more successful in forming the immigrants into city machines, and Know-Nothingism rode along with the Whigs, then latched itself onto Fillmore's American party. Fillmore was out of the presidential picture before Vance entered

national politics but Vance often expressed his admiration of the
New Yorker whose ability has had more recognition in history than
in his own times. Fillmore lost the Whig nomination in 1852, which
went to General Winfield Scott because of Fillmore's approval of the
Compromise of 1850 and resultant unpopularity in many Northern
states. Vance had an affiliation, largely technical, with the Know-Nothings of the mountains.

But as he soon detected, Know-Nothingism was wearing thin as an
issue in 1859. Vance himself poked fun at the Know-Nothings during
his campaign in 1858. When Coleman began, in the words of Robert
Vance, to draw "frightful pictures of the Know-Nothings, with their
secret meetings, their oaths, etc., which once had been potent and
effective to talk about"—the so-called "raw head and bloody bones"
stories of the politics of the 1850s—the bored audiences could no
longer be stirred to apprehension. Zeb summed up the flatness of the
issue by telling how Coleman had stopped a man plowing in the field
and asked if he had heard the dreadful news.

"What in the world is it?" the plowman inquired.

"The Know-Nothings are rising," Coleman exclaimed.

"Can that be possible?" the farmer replied ironically. "If so, just
let 'em rise." Then he went on with his plowing.[41] Zeb joked so much
about the Know-Nothings that many voters thought Coleman was
their candidate.

Coleman made the mistake in debate of quoting from Scripture,
where Zeb, as Kemp Battle had learned long before, excelled. Coleman
compared his opponent's first term in Congress with the barren fruit
tree, then shouted: "And now, fellow citizens, cut him down." Vance's
followers were low-spirited after this telling speech, but Zeb jerked
them up when he challenged his opponent's understanding of the
good book.

"The facts are," said Zeb, "that the Lord went into the garden with
his gardener, and seeing no fruit on the fig tree he said to the gardener,
'Cut it down'; but the gardener answered, 'Not so, Lord, but let it
stand another year, and I will dig about it . . . and then if it bears no
fruit cut it down.' Now gentlemen, all things according to Scripture."
He said his competitor Coleman was digging about him, that he should
go back to Congress again, and "if I then do not bear fruit, cut me
down."[42] His sportive good nature, his ready admission that he had
not done much during his first term, the readiness of his repartee
provoked a wave of laughter, then a shout. This was the closing meet-

ing of the campaign and Zeb ended on a high note. He won by the impressive plurality of 1,695 votes. The election showed a rapport between Vance and Wilkes County that was enduring. He was at Traphill in Wilkes on election day and stirred such enthusiasm that he got an almost solid vote.

Zeb's abrupt, blunt language in the campaign caused Coleman to meditate moodily over his defeat. He had beaten Vance for the state senate and had expected victory again. In a letter dated August 15, 1859, he demanded from Vance an accounting.[43] A reading of the correspondence which passed between them leaves one with the impression that Coleman was reaching for a complaint. Finding no clear-cut affront he harkened back to remarks which went unchallenged at the time they were uttered. He explained his silence by saying he had determined during the canvass to demand reparation for the indignity, but did not want to interrupt the campaign by a personal conflict. He did not cite his adversary's precise words, but alleged that Vance at Waynesville had questioned him "in an extremely offensive manner" and in one case had declared he was asking the question "in order to pronounce my answer *false,* in the contingency of my replying in a certain way." The other offense was that Vance had "given countenance" at Lenoir in Caldwell County on election day to a report that Coleman had been drunk at a time when the two were stopping at the Suddereth home north of Lenoir. Vance was not charged with spreading the report. His offense, as alleged, was that when he was questioned about it, he stated merely that he was a candidate and had nothing to say. He had, in fact, been in adjoining Wilkes, not Caldwell County, on election day.

Vance expressed surprise in his reply, said he thought the Waynesville incident was cleared satisfactorily at the time and that "the general language of your note does not permit me to know specifically wherein my offense consists." He asked more particulars. As to the second point, he positively denied that he had "given countenance" to any report that Coleman had been drunk, but to the contrary had contradicted it often in conversation and also publicly at Burnsville, without solicitation, as Coleman full well knew.

The correspondence grew protracted. Coleman's letters were lengthy and must have consumed much of Vance's time. He was compelled to write that he had assumed Coleman wanted an amicable adjustment, but now it was apparent that the object of the worsted man was merely to seek a difficulty in order to take away some of the sting of defeat.

Therefore, said Zeb, "I beg leave to recall anything of a conciliatory character" which his earlier letters contained. Coleman replied with a challenge, and a duel appeared imminent.

Much as his uncle's adversary, Carson, had been coached by Davy Crockett, Zeb was now taken into the woods near Arden by Samuel Brown, his close friend who died while serving in his company "the Rough and Ready Guards" during the war.

Samuel's brother, William Caleb Brown, had become Vance's law partner in 1858. Later he would serve as first lieutenant of Vance's company.

Samuel Brown was Vance's second and John D. Hyman, the recent co-editor of the Asheville *Spectator* with Vance, conducted the arrangements. He specified that the duel should be fought at 8 A.M., August 30, 1859, at Waddell's cabin just over the line in Cocke County, Tennessee. Rarely was a duel in prospect over matters so trivial, concerning which the party who was supposed to have committed the offense was disposed to be conciliatory.

At this juncture Dr. James F. E. Hardy, the Asheville physician and friend of Zeb's father who had set Zeb's leg when he fell from the apple tree, and lawyer John W. Woodfin, in whose office Zeb had begun to read law, intervened and asked of both contestants permission to read the correspondence that had been exchanged. Vance readily consented in case Coleman agreed first He explained that his notes were based on and were in reply to those addressed to him and that withdrawal of his should properly follow withdrawal of Coleman's. But Coleman declined to withdraw his letters unless—and here again he seemed vague—Vance should make an adjustment "on the basis of my former notes."

Finally Messrs. Woodfin and Hardy, as friends of both parties, were able to effect a "mutual and simultaneous" withdrawal of the correspondence and a restoration of the two individuals to the "grounds which they occupied before Mr. Coleman's first note to Mr. Vance." A further exchange showed Coleman still disturbed, but Vance stating "in entire sincerity" that he had no purpose to give offense, though he stood much of his ground and was in no manner apologetic. Coleman accepted his note on August 29 as "full, frank and satisfactory." Zeb would survive to attend the exciting Thirty-sixth Congress, which convened December 5, 1859.

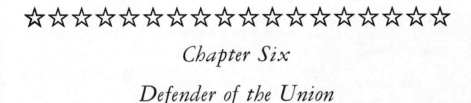

## Chapter Six

## Defender of the Union

Zeb Vance's most trying political year came in 1860, when he fought a tough, determined, but gradually losing battle against secession of the Southern states, and after that movement was under way, another desperate but still losing struggle to keep his own state fom joining the trend and parting company with the old government.

Both in Washington, where the Thirty-sixth Congress was in session until near the end of June and when it met again in December, and in North Carolina, where he spoke frequently and wrote much, all of his qualities of industry, forthrightness and aggressiveness were brought into full play. But he was opposing an inexorable sweep of events.

On the floor of the House he and the other members were plunged headlong into the embittered wrangle over almost every aspect of the relation of the states with the central government. In his own participation, he tried to deal with issues with the lightness and good humor he fervently wished he could impart into the remarks of others. His main object during this year of discord and decision was to gain time. Time, he believed, would allow the heat to cool and the good judgment of the more conservative elements of both sections of the country to assert itself. He could see clearly that a ghastly civil war was impending and wanted to spare no effort to avert it.[1]

Vance was on hand for the convening December 5, 1859, of the first session of the Thirty-sixth Congress, the first to meet in the spacious marble chambers which had been added as wings to each side of the old Capitol and gave to that building the imposing grandeur it now enjoys.

Contention and conflict were in the very atmosphere which hung over the city. Three days before the session opened, John Brown's body had dangled from the noose at nearby Charleston, Virginia. The slavery question came surging forward with the arrival of the new Congress. In both Houses the Republican memberships had been largely augmented by the last election, though not sufficiently to give them a majority in either.

Perhaps there was never a more memorable Congress or one sprinkled so heavily with illustrious names. On the Senate side Sumner was back after long absence from his foreign travels, taken for his health and possibly for reasons of engendering sympathy as well. Sam Houston's old seat was filled by the turbulent Texan disunionist Louis T. Wigfall. Judah P. Benjamin, who had represented Louisiana brilliantly as a Whig, was back for a second term, this time as a Democrat. Jefferson Davis of Mississippi retained his full measure of prestige and power. Among those of note were fiery Robert Toombs of Georgia, James A. Bayard of Delaware, Stephen R. Mallory of Florida, Stephen A. Douglas of Illinois. The roll call has worked almost intact into the history books. Others were James Harlan of Iowa, William H. Seward of New York, James M. Mason and Robert M. T. Hunter of Virginia; Clingman and Thomas Bragg of North Carolina; Ben Wade of Ohio, Edward D. Baker of Oregon.

On the House side were men equally celebrated, or in some instances notorious: Dan Sickles was there, and Roscoe Conklin from New York; Morrill came from Vermont. The three Washburn brothers represented different states: Elihu B. of Galena, Illinois, Cadwallader C. of La Crosse, Wisconsin, and a little later, after Hannibal Hamlin was sworn in as Vice President, Israel Washburn, Jr., of Maine. Elihu distinguished himself from his brothers by adding an e to his name and becoming Washburne.[2]

Scowling Thad Stevens, of Vermont birth but enjoying Pennsylvania tolerance, was on hand after an absence of six years, having changed from Whig to Republican. Some of the others were Sherman and Vallandigham of Ohio, Colfax and English of Indiana, and William

Pennington of New Jersey, a former governor who would serve but a single term in Congress, and during that would rule in the exalted position of Speaker. Henry L. Dawes, Charles Francis Adams and Columbus Delano were accompanied from Massachusetts by Anson Burlingame, perhaps the most flowery and impassioned of them all.

Georgia had in Martin Jenkins Crawford another of that famous name, while big, blond William Barksdale, who would fall at the head of his brigade at Gettysburg, and the former professor of mathematics who would become one of the country's great jurists, Lucius Quintus Cincinnatus Lamar, were ornaments of the Mississippi delegation. John A. McClernand and "Blackjack" John A. Logan, both to rise to high command in the Union armies, were a part of the Douglas coterie from Illinois. In this era of stress, most states endeavored to send their ablest and best. Of the North Carolina delegation, distinguished names other than Vance's were Thomas Ruffin of Goldsboro, who would fall mortally wounded at Bristoe Station while commanding the 1st North Carolina Cavalry; and John Adams Gilmer, a Vance associate in the Whig-American party.

Washington Irving, dean of American literature, died in Tarrytown, New York, and Thomas Babington Macaulay in Kensington, England, little noticed amid the turmoil and sudden publicity given in 1859 to a new book written by Hinton R. Helper, an obscure and impoverished bookstore clerk and wanderer of Mocksville, North Carolina, entitled *The Impending Crisis in the South: How to Meet It*. It dwelt on the economic disaster inherent in the system of slavery and recommended that the Negro slaves be deported.

Scarcely could it be expected that this volume, which possessed much sound but long-range thinking and called for the industrial development of the South, which happily has been reached in many sections a century later, would set off the most prolonged and frenzied battle over the Speakership in the whole history of the House of Representatives, unapproached in duration even to the present day. Charles Darwin's *Origin of Species* appeared at about the same time, but was not to be compared with Helper's sensation. Helper's book was generally banned in the South and copies were burned publicly in North Carolina. A good many Northerners endorsed it, among them the imprudent John Sherman of Ohio. He acknowledged when the matter became pressing that he, like many later commentators about books, had not read it when he evaluated it. The Speakership fight, which ensued because

Sherman had given the book his sanction, plunged Vance into the middle of the House debate, but he was a temperate moderator somewhat bewildered by the antics of that turbulent and often capricious and emotional body.

Sherman was put forward for Speaker by the Republicans, who had a plurality but not a majority in the House. The division was Republicans, 113; Administration Democrats, 93; Anti-Lecompton Democrats, 8; Southern Americans (or Whigs), 23. The last group included Vance. In advance of the voting, Representative John B. Clark of Missouri, a native of Kentucky who adhered to his state-rights principles in the House, maintained that anyone who had endorsed the Helper book was not qualified to be Speaker, while Representative John S. Millson of Virginia wondered if such a person ought not to be snuffed out altogether, or felt at least that he was not a fit candidate for living. Clark put his ideas into a resolution and Gilmer of North Carolina introduced a companion resolution the next day. The debate and balloting consumed an inordinate amount of time because the presiding officer declined to rule on points of order and they consequently had to be submitted to the full House for debate.

For nearly two months the turmoil seethed. At his highest point Sherman got 110 of 231 votes cast, or six short of the necessary majority. The Democrats brought several members forward and Sherman withdrew when Smith of North Carolina passed him. Smith came within one vote of victory and Keitt of South Carolina contended he actually was elected, then some members changed their votes before the tally could be announced. The Democrats concentrated on McClernand of Illinois for a time. On the forty-fifth ballot William Pennington, the first-term former governor of New Jersey, inexperienced in legislative practices, was elected Speaker by a bare margin of 117 out of 233 votes cast.[3]

Vance began by supporting Alexander R. Boteler, a new American party Congressman from Virginia, later a member of Stonewall Jackson's staff and Confederate Congressman, who got fourteen votes. He surveyed the proceedings with an amused tolerance, his object being more to suppress the excitement and inject some lightness into the proceedings than to advance the cause of a candidate. His fear was of aroused passions, which would thwart all efforts at compromise between the sections. Midway in the proceedings, on December 29, 1859, he advised the House about the pattern of his voting: "I have voted for a Lecompton Democrat. I have voted for those who did not approve the Lecompton bill. I have voted for an administration Democrat. And if there is any other member of that great, prolific Democratic family that I have neglected, I hope they will trot him out and give me an opportunity to vote for him [Laughter]." He made quite a point of his vote for McClernand because that Illinois Democrat had voted for his fellow North Carolinian Smith.[4]

Some of Zeb's jests through the session seemed more humorous on the floor than in the record. Delano of Massachusetts was in the House restaurant when the signal came for a vote. He hurried up and arrived before the roll call ended. He asked permission to vote and the Speaker asked if he were in the bar of the House when the vote was called. He explained he was in the bar of the restaurant and added: "I was engaged in the great work of self protection." Vance interposed: "I thought perhaps the gentleman might have been engaged in the matter of *internal improvement.*" The remark was greeted by a wave of laughter.[5]

On some matters, conditions then were not vastly different from those of the present. Complaints were voiced about the high cost of repairs being made on the Capitol. When the appropriation bill was considered Vance offered an amendment, "Provided, that there shall not be expended for labor and material upon the capitol extension more than twice as much as the same could be obtained for by private individuals." That also provoked laughter. When Ethridge of Tennessee, a fellow Whig, asked to be excused from the floor for half an hour, Zeb suspected that he was going for a drink of liquor. "I move to amend by asking the gentleman to take me along with him," he said, to the general amusement. Another exchange which sounded more humorous to the members than in the report of the session occurred when Zeb was aroused from his bed by the sergeant-at-arms and brought to the House for a quorum call. The House decorum was stricter in those days and he was required to offer an excuse.

"Well, sir," he said, "I am rather afraid to undertake to render an excuse, as it seems that any excuse having a reason in it is not in order in the House [Laughter]." He said the demands of food and sleep took him home. "I was disagreeably disturbed at a few minutes past two o'clock this morning, while I was wrapped in the arms of Morpheus and dreaming pleasant dreams which I need not detain this House to relate."

Soon the Speaker stole off himself. Zeb took delight in calling his absence to the attention of the House and asking that the sergeant-at-arms be sent to fetch him. Someone said the Speaker rated a committee; that to send the sergeant-at-arms would be unbecoming. "I do not wish to be wanting in courtesy," Vance continued, "but there was some courtesy due my slumbers, so rudely broken at half past two o'clock this morning." The Speaker was brought in and Vance airily wished him the top of the morning.[6]

Attention was called to the absence of Representative Lansing Stout of Oregon, and a Maryland colleague explained that he was not in good health. Zeb saw the opportunity for a pun. "I am happy to inform the gentleman from Maryland that the member from Oregon is quite Stout." Vance must have been mistaken about the robustness of the Oregonian, who died at the age of forty-three. Vance was paired with Stout during Stout's attendance of the Democratic convention in Baltimore and created laughter when he announced that Stout had gone "to witness the riot."[7]

One of the outstanding events of the year 1860 in North Carolina was the Whig convention at Salisbury and the high point of the convention was the stirring address for the Union delivered by the spectacular young Congressman from the mountains, Zebulon B. Vance.

For nearly a generation prior to 1856 the Whig party had dominated North Carolina politics. Many of the great names of statesmen from the Old North State were those of Whigs. Few better examples of political perseverance can be found than that of the North Carolina Whigs, who, after their party had succumbed as a national influence and was not even contemplating entering a national ticket in the 1860 election, determined to maintain their party solidarity and their stand for the preservation of the Union.

Many North Carolina Whigs, it is true, had been drifting into the Democratic party, but neither the leaders nor the body of the rank and file was prepared to amalgamate with their old and bitter enemies. Nor could the Democrats offer such oratorical prowess or distinguished names as those which ornamented the leadership of the Whigs. The tacit affiliation between the Whigs and Know-Nothings had driven voters to Buchanan in 1856 when they could neither support the new Republican party under John C. Fremont nor vote for Fillmore under the merged and blurred American and Know-Nothing party labels. Kemp Battle recorded that the Know-Nothing alliance behind Fillmore so disgusted him that "without losing my dislike of the Democrats I gave my first presidential vote for Buchanan."[8]

The Republican National Convention of 1856, which put the first Republican ticket into a national campaign, was an amalgamation of Northern Whigs, Free Soilers, Wilmot-Proviso and Anti-Nebraska Democrats, Silver Grays and old-time Liberty Leaguers, along with independents, from all of whom the slave states in general held aloof. This convention, by severing the Northern half of the Whigs and absorbing them into the Republican party, marked the official demise of the Whigs. The fatal illness had set in much earlier. The Compromises of 1850 were unsavory to the Northern Whigs and when the party failed to take a position on slavery they looked elsewhere. The dissolution of the Northern elements left Southern Whiggery stranded and with no place to find solid footing—with no acceptable national party to which it might attach itself. Still, in 1860, with Whiggery all but passed from the face of the earth, the North Carolina Whigs through their executive committee—obstinate perhaps, but commendably wholesome in their outlook—arranged a grand rally to demonstrate their solidarity and to proclaim to the world their faith in the old Federal government.

The noted men of the state and great crowds of the ordinary run of people converged on Salisbury. Among them was William A. Graham, perhaps the state's most distinguished citizen—former governor, senator, cabinet member and candidate for Vice President on the Winfield Scott ticket. Few Americans have had greater world influence. As Secretary of the Navy in the Millard Fillmore cabinet in 1852, Graham dispatched Commodore Matthew C. Perry with the American squadron which, on July 14, 1853, appeared in the Bay of Yedo and opened to world commerce the ancient secluded island kingdom of Japan. Graham after this Salisbury meeting was to become Zeb Vance's admirer and close friend.

Among the speakers to follow Graham was former Senator George E. Badger, whom nearly all observant historians of North Carolina place among the top few of the state's great men. He had served as Secretary of the Navy in the Harrison and Tyler cabinets, then after eleven years in the Senate had retired voluntarily. His greatness appeared to be ratified by the Senate itself when that body went through the unusual procedure on his retirement of passing a resolution unanimously expressing regret at his action in departing from them of his own choice.

But the fickleness of politics and the passions of the hour were never better illustrated than when this same Senate in 1853 failed to confirm him when he was nominated by President Fillmore just before leaving office to be an associate justice of the United States Supreme Court.[9]

Other orators of reputation in the state and nation were on the program for the giant rally—Representative William Nathan Harrell Smith, of Murfreesboro, graduate of Yale College and Yale Law School, who had just come within one vote of the Speakership of the House in the prolonged contest, and would long serve as chief justice of the North Carolina Supreme Court; former Congressman Nathaniel Boyden, a Whig of Massachusetts birth, transplanted to Salisbury, who would sit as associate justice on the state Supreme Court; former Congressman Kenneth Rayner, gifted speaker of Hertford County; the mellowing Alfred Dockery, Congressman during the Mexican War who had been the unsuccessful Whig candidate for governor in 1854; former Governor John M. Morehead, and others needed to pad out a program of two days.[10]

A special train was run over from Raleigh. Richard and Kemp Battle described the throng as "large to immense." Additions came all day. The formal program began in the morning and one by one the leading orators of North Carolina Whiggery held forth from a stand erected in the center of a square which was large enough to accommodate a vast crowd. Then came a noon dinner, called "copious," followed by more speaking, mostly extemporaneous, but "free and easy" and "full of animation, jocularities, and denunciations." The day wore on and the crowd wearied from standing so long, part of the time in a drizzle, but finally as the day waned Zeb Vance, who was little known to the leaders of North Carolina politics and not at all to the crowd that had assembled largely from the piedmont and eastern sections of the state, was called to the platform.[11] He was thirty years old and was a strong, rugged, handsome figure with his long black hair flowing to his shoulders. Any sentiment for secession which might have prevailed in the large gathering was at once swept aside by the powerful oratory which poured from this young man's lips. Richard Battle gave perhaps the best picture of what took place:

"His youthful face, his ruddy countenance, his twinkling eye, and his familiar greeting at once arrested the crowd. As they listened to his clear statement of existing conditions, his apt illustrations, his amusing stories and his impassioned appeal, or held up to their gaze dark pictures of the horrors to follow secession and disunion, all became subject to his magnetism. Their weariness and hoarseness were forgotten, and when he closed the streets of the town and the hills around long reverberated with their enthusiastic shouts."

What happened then was that some huskies among the enraptured crowd seized Zeb, hoisted him to their shoulders and paraded with him through the Salisbury streets. Barrels of tar had been hauled in and as darkness came on they were lighted. Pine knots and tallow torches were on hand and a torchlight procession moved back and forth through the streets. When the illumination was at its height Zeb was again sought by the crowd. He was taken from street corner to street corner and, in the words of his future secretary Battle, was "almost forced to speak, again and again, to admiring hearers of both sexes and all ages." How many acres of humanity Zeb addressed could only be conjectured, but combined, they would have made a good-sized farm.

Back in his office at Fayetteville, Edward Jones Hale, editor of the *Observer,* was getting the report of the convention and was amazed that Zeb Vance, the young Congressman from the hills, should "be represented as shining among the stars . . . of such magnitude as Badger, Graham, Morehead, W. N. H. Smith and Alfred Dockery." Then he quoted the story from his reporter son as it came into his office:

"At night those who remained in town assembled at the public square to see the fireworks. From the commencement of the display cries were continually made for 'Vance', and 'Let's hear the Mountain Boy.' After considerable exhibition of the fireworks and an hour's calling for him, Mr. Vance came forward and mounted on a pile of boxes." He began with a number of witticisms, then got the crowd silent and "held them steadily around him for over an hour. You can form some idea of the crowd when I tell you," continued the report, "that one of those wide streets of Salisbury was packed for three hundred feet of length—sidewalks and all—almost as close as it is possible for human beings to stand. In the midst of this vast assembly was Mr. Vance. Cheer after cheer followed nearly every sentence he uttered. And as he left his platform the enthusiastic crowd threw wreaths over his head and receiving him on their shoulders, bore him around the vast assembly amid deafening shouts."[12]

The greatest compliment paid to Vance on the day's work came from the distinguished former Senator and Cabinet member George E. Badger, who, when he was being complimented for his own address, directed the honors immediately toward Zeb. "But you ought to have heard young Vance," he said, as if the one who complimented him had missed the high note of the affair. "He is the greatest stump speaker that ever was! the greatest that ever was!"[13]

Locke Craig, a later governor of North Carolina and a kindred soul of Vance because (though born in the eastern section) he too came from Buncombe County and lived near the slope of the Black Mountains, took delight in describing this introduction of Vance to the masses east of the Blue Ridge and to the old-line Whig leaders who had until then played commanding roles in the nation's affairs.

"Reports about the young Congressman from the mountains had spread down into the state," said Craig. "When he spoke to the convention it was realized that the man for the times of approaching storm had appeared. Men heard him with wild delight, and the multitude bore him on their shoulders . . . Nothing like him had been seen. He was young, splendid in courage and in humor, in logic and eloquence. They acclaimed him then the born leader . . ."[14]

Vance went far to make himself governor of North Carolina in this Salisbury speech, though the election did not come until two years later, after his ideas about disunion had suffered abrupt change and after the nation had been pitched suddenly into civil war.

Vance had another opportunity a little later to put in some good words for the Union. Congress recessed for the holidays in late 1860 and he passed through Raleigh on his way home. South Carolina already had called a convention for the clear purpose of seceding. Zeb arrived in Raleigh when secession was in the air. The Columbia, South Carolina, convention was to meet on December 17 and, after adjourning to Charleston, to adopt its ordinance of secession unanimously on December 20. Meantime two South Carolina representatives, William W. Boyce of Winnsboro, who was serving his fourth term in Congress, and Lawrence M. Keitt of Orangeburg, both ardent secessionists, stopped in Raleigh en route home from Washington. Keitt had stood by protectively as though to hold off interference when his South Carolina associate, Representative Preston S. Brooks, had rained blows with his gutta-percha cane on the head and shoulders of the Massachusetts senator, Charles Sumner. He had dropped out for a term because the House passed a resolution censuring his action, but had been re-elected in 1856. Later he would serve in the Confederate Congress and throw his life into the Confederate cause at Cold Harbor.

The North Carolina legislature was in session when Boyce and Keitt reached the Yarborough Hotel near the capitol on Fayetteville Street, where they were waited on and invited to speak by a group of Democratic legislators who favored secession. They addressed a crowd which assembled in front of the hotel and were driving home their case for secession when Sion Hart Rogers, a native of Raleigh and an attorney who had served earlier as a Whig Congressman, feared violence. The capital city at that moment strongly opposed secession.

Anger over the speeches of the South Carolinians began to be expressed along the streets. When Rogers heard the mutterings he rushed to the courthouse and had it lighted, then told the caretakers to ring the bell, the customary signal for an assembly of importance. The crowds began to assemble and Rogers announced that a meeting for the Union was about to be held inside. A mild wave of excitement ran through the tense gathering when he announced that the speaker would be western North Carolina Congressman Zeb Vance. The crowd that followed them into the court room was sizable.

Vance recognized that he could not deal with the inflammatory situation too severely else an outbreak was likely to occur between hostile groups, possibly leading to bloodshed. So he began a speech that was "semi-jocose and semi-serious." Little of the text remains except a few cursory press reports and Richard Battle's comments, but he dealt with his "South Carolina friends" gently, saying they would have to be excused because they were "crazy fanatics" on whom it would be a waste of time to vent true indignation. The crowd became so wrapped in his stories—one was about a kitten whose sex a woman could not determine and mistakenly called Julia—that it forgot the South Carolina Congressmen and shouted "Hurrah for Vance!" Vance thought the visiting dignitaries were as mistaken about North Carolina as the lady had been about the sex of the cat. After the danger of a collision had passed and Vance had held forth for two hours, he judged that his hearers were in good humor for the rest of the evening. The meeting was adjourned and the Raleigh citizens went back to their homes.[15]

It is significant that in all of his talks during this period Vance never opposed the legality, but only the expediency, of secession.

Vance at this time began to be noticed as a speaker of some national standing. He was sought after. In the spring of 1860 he joined with other Whigs and American party adherents in the formation of the new Constitutional Union party, which was an effort to drive a wedge between the abolitionist Republicans and secessionist Democrats and create a vehicle for the preservation of the Union. Zeb's first appearance for this new group was in Carroll Hall in Baltimore April 12, 1860, at something of an organizational meeting, and that night he joined with others—chiefly Southern members of the American party—a designation now employed more frequently than Whig—in addressing an open-air rally at Monument Square. When the convention of the party was held in Baltimore May 9, Zeb attended as a delegate.

His brother Robert was writing him from Asheville a warning against parties, and adding the news that his recent adversary Coleman was pretty well out of the political picture. "I think I would have as little to do with parties as I could," wrote Robert on April 16, "as parties are so torn about now no one can scarcely see his own standing place . . . Dave Coleman never can make half a run for Congress. The whole Western delegation to the Convention here, Bill Thomas [a Democrat of Union sentiments] in particular fell out with him." Coleman's offense was that he had defeated Thomas as a delegate to the Charleston convention of the Democratic party. Robert confided that Old Bill Welch, whoever that might have been, had cursed Coleman all over town. Neither Robert nor Zeb could know that the last thing in which they would be interested was another campaign for Congress from the mountain district.[16]

The Baltimore Convention nominated John Bell of Tennessee for President on the Constitutional Union ticket and Edward Everett of Massachusetts for Vice President. Thus two old-line Whigs were offered as conservative candidates devoted to the Union. That the ticket appeared at the moment to please the South was indicated, as a sample attitude, by Zeb's close friend William John Brown. He wrote May 17, "I see the Balt. Conv. have made a good ticket & as I think in the proper manner, both as to time, place & platform, & if its *Providence's will*, hope we shall be able to elect it, & thereby calm down the troubled waters & drive all factionists & commorants out of place & power & give a quietus to the disorganizer of all sections."

Knowing how the Washington atmosphere was surcharged, Brown added some homely remedies for Zeb's comfort: "Abstain from heating stimulants on account of the irritation of your bowles, use good olive oil frequently in broken doses with occasionally divers powder & Blue pill. At night, to stimulate the free action of the liver, avoid preparation with *aloes*. Knowing your predisposition to piles I recently got an almost infallible cure." This came from a Charleston doctor who visited Asheville frequently and who invariably used the cure "with great success." Brown did not prescribe it but offered to send it if needed.[17]

Mrs. Vance was ill during parts of the session. Robert wrote to Zeb that she suffered from *weed*, a fever which affected chiefly nursing mothers. Their third son, Zebulon Baird, Jr., was born March 22, 1860. Mrs. Vance had written Zeb about two weeks before he was born, telling mainly of the difficulty of keeping the home establishment running during his absence. ". . . I am willing to make any sacrifice that we may get out of debt," she told Zeb on March 6, "having almost abandoned the idea of going to Washington at all. I guess you will be willing. I couldn't I suppose go before the first of May and if Congress adjourns as early as you hope for now it will hardly be worth while to go. . . ."[18] Making the trip to Morganton, the nearest railroad, by stage would have been difficult with a baby who by May 1 would be only about five weeks old.

In those days of early January, 1861, reports filtered through to the mountains that a cabal of Southern Congressmen had been formed to act as a shield in Washington for the new government which would be set up in Montgomery, Alabama, the following month. From all such discussion of secession and the formation of a new republic, Vance held aloof. Some of the news stories gave a fairly accurate view of what was soon to transpire, though the plan as then outlined in the press reaching the mountain area was to make Senator Robert M. T. Hunter of Virginia, who had been prominently discussed for President of the United States in 1860, and had been offered the post of Secretary of State by both Pierce and Buchanan, provisional president of the new Southern government. "Mr. Hunter possesses in a more eminent degree the philosophical characteristics of Jefferson than any other statesman now living," said the dispatch. Colonel Jefferson Davis, "distinguished for gallantry at Buena Vista," former Secretary of War, and "not second to Gen. Scott in military science or courage," was to be commander-in-chief of the Southern army.[19]

From the strictly Southern viewpoint Vance's voting record in the House was spotty. He opposed the resolution introduced by Representative Roger A. Pryor of Virginia condemning the doctrine of coercion, a vote which the opposition Asheville *News* duly recorded for the western Carolinians with the observation that it was "utterly indefensible on any grounds." Yet Zeb stood with the solid Southern membership in opposing a resolution endorsing the conduct of Major Robert Anderson in holding Fort Sumter after South Carolina seceded. "This," exclaimed the *News*, "was a good vote."[20]

Zeb's attitude during these frenzied months could be seen from his letter to his friend William W. Dickson of Caldwell County, on December 11, 1860, which he wrote after a conference with Senator John J. Crittenden of Kentucky, leader of the compromise efforts in Washington. He thought the only chance of saving the Union was to gain time.

"This is the general opinion of our friends here," he said. "The whole southern mind is inflamed to the highest pitch and the leaders in the disunion move are scorning every suggestion of compromise and rushing everything with ruinous and indecent haste that would seem to imply that they are absolute fools." They were precipitating the people into a revolution "without giving them time to think." Zeb thought they feared a resort to the public mind, hence their haste in South Carolina and elsewhere to call conventions, but give a very brief time for the election of delegates. Vance showed that he had about the clearest picture of anyone of the dire consequences of secession.

"But the people *must* think," he continued, "and when they do begin to think and hear the matter properly discussed they will consider long and soberly before they tear down this noble fabric and invite anarchy and confusion, carnage, civil war, and financial ruin with the breathless hurry of men flying from a pestilence. If we can gain time we can get the advantage of this sober second thought." Vance had confidence a compromise could be worked out if the South would but wait. He had no dread of the Railsplitter.

"Fear of Lincoln when he comes into office is perfect humbuggery, and those who urge it know it to be so," he declared. "If we go out now we can't take the army and navy with us, and Lincoln could as easily employ them to force us *back* as he could to prevent our going out; and the Yankees would as readily fight to whip us back as they would to keep us in! Its all stuff. I tell you this great rashness that burns the public mind *must and will burn out,* and cooler councils rule the day; but it must have time . . . We have everything to gain and nothing on earth to lose by delay, but by too hasty action we may take a fatal step that we never can retrace—may lose a heritage that we can never recover . . ."[21]

Vance named a number of others to whom the letter should be

showed—Merrimon, Calvin J. Cowles, a unionist storekeeper of Wilkes County; and Augustus H. Martin who like Merrimon was a member of the state legislature. Vance approved the idea that North Carolina should call a deliberative convention and thought "our friends" should lead in the movement in order to control it; but mainly he wanted to confide the question to the people, who, after they heard what the North had to offer, could make the decision.

"If *they* choose to undo the work of their wise and heroic ancestors, if *they* choose to invite carnage to saturate their soil and desolation to waste their fields, they can not say their public servants *precipitated* them into it! The people must and should rule, but we must see to it that we do our duty in warning, instructing, and advising them . . ."[22]

Vance thought also that a convention in North Carolina, a key state, would hasten the North into action for a settlement. He looked on it as different from the hasty secessionist conventions. "For when North Carolina gives way, they in the North must almost look upon the sheet-anchor of conservatism as gone."

## Chapter Seven

## Zeb and His State Are Crowded Out

Traditionally the state took pride in her associations in the Union. North Carolina had been a heavy provisioner of Washington's army in the Revolutionary War, though the overland haul was long and arduous. One of the inspiring events in Washington's army in 1777 occurred at Middlebrook, New Jersey, with the arrival of the North Carolina brigade of six regiments under General Francis Nash, which had marched to his relief after Sir Henry Clinton had been repulsed in Charleston, South Carolina, harbor in 1776. Though powder was never plentiful, Washington was so pleased at the arrival of the brigade that he fired a salute of thirteen guns.[1]

Nash soon after was fatally wounded at Germantown. Seven North Carolina officers were killed in that battle. One of the distinguished services of the war went to Colonel Thomas Polk, whose North Carolina regiment Washington selected to convoy the treasures of American independence—the Declaration of Independence, the Liberty Bell, and documents of state—to security in Allentown, Pennsylvania, when he was forced to evacuate Philadelphia. North Carolina troops were at Valley Forge, and there Washington's army, severed from the Northern states, received most of its food and provisions by wagon train from Virginia and North Carolina, while Governor Richard Caswell, much as Vance was to do in a later war, kept his state at work making shoes, uniforms and blankets, and raising pork and bacon for the patriot troops.

North Carolina took pride also in the participation of her frontiersmen at King's Mountain, and, in the campaign of Greene's army, heavy with North Carolina units, against Cornwallis, ending at Guilford Court House, the prelude to Yorktown. Her soil had given the nation two Presidents, Jackson and Polk,[2] and numerous leaders in Congress, the cabinet and the courts. The majority of her people were Union-minded. Nothing but the most severe wrench, some action which would be interpreted as an affront, or the threat of invasion by hostile troops would be likely to break the old association, however much secession might be agitated by militant groups.

Two weeks after his letter yearning for time, Vance wrote from Washington to Walter Waightstill Lenoir, a grandson of Waightstill Avery and of General William Lenoir, and a planter of Happy Valley in Caldwell County. Lenoir had led his class at the University of North Carolina and had become a man of influence and large affairs. Vance in writing to him, during the short session and after South Carolina had seceded, disclosed his full contempt for President Buchanan, and was immoderate in his remarks.

"The crisis here is rapidly approaching its denouement," he said. "The Administration is literally dropping to 'smash.' The timidity, vascilation and corruption of the President; the recent discovery of enormous frauds and defalcations [the Secretary of War Floyd scandal concerning which the House was just initiating an investigation][3] and the known and acknowledged complicity of the Executive with all the plans and schemes of disunion, make every honest man damn the day that placed Buchanan in office. So there is no help but constant harm from that quarter."[4]

North Carolina was different in many respects from the other Southern states. She was a state not so much of great plantations, though some were maintained within her borders, as of small, independent farmers who possessed few slaves or none at all. Collectively the state had a goodly number of slaves, but they were concentrated in the plantation areas, chiefly of the eastern and north-central counties, where in some the Negro slave population exceeded the white.[5] The farmers, with small-town merchants, white laborers, professional men and others, held many meetings across the state during the period of ferment in the interests of peace and against disunion. Secessionist meetings were held also, but not in such abundance. Truly the state seemed less explosive than some of her Southern neighbors, either at home or judged by the expressions of her Congressmen in the legislative halls. The ablest men of the state were unionists, their position being tempered by the belief that the state could reach a satisfactory accommodation with the North. They might be better described as wary unionists. The strong unionist quality of North Carolina statesmanship had been established much earlier by the able Democratic Senator Bedford Brown, aptly called North Carolina's "State Rights Unionist," who served in the Senate from 1829 to 1842, but remained a strong factor in public opinion until the Civil War.[6]

In his own mountain district Vance had the resolute support of the dean of the western North Carolina bar, Nicholas W. Woodfin, brother of John W. Woodfin, under whom Zeb and Merrimon read law. Merrimon called Nicholas Woodfin one of the best lawyers, if not the best, of the western circuit, and with this most would agree. He worked so hard he weakened his constitution but defied expectations and survived to the stage of senior and dean. He missed the United States Senate by an eyelash when the state legislature voted, but was unsoured. Abraham Lincoln could have obtained from him—and may have—the seed of his famous phrase "of the people, by the people and for the people," though both Woodfin and Lincoln may have recalled a similar expression from the antislavery speech of Theodore Parker of May, 1850, in Boston. Woodfin had come to Asheville a barefoot country boy on a mule, and by energy had won not only wealth but also the distinction of being, along with Clingman, one of the two most conspicuous men of the western part of the state.[7]

Woodfin analyzed the theory of secession and found it untenable. "Sir," he said, "as well tell me of a conditional marriage or of a reserve right to secede from it at will after its consummation." He questioned how the new states carved out of former national territories would be bound by the Federal laws on one day and the next would have a right to disassociate themselves. He put his finger on the danger of fragmentation inherent in secession: If one state had a right to secede, then California might secede and sever the country from the west coast, or Louisiana might secede and bottle up the Mississippi, even though the central government had paid France $15,000,000 for the province of Louisiana and the port of New Orleans.[8]

Zeb Vance at the moment of crisis was concerned with forwarding this line of thought. His feeling was that the North would offer no terms of convenience to the South, but still he saw no reason for North Carolina to part company. "The Union is dissolved, of course," he continued. "S.C. is already gone and I make not a doubt but every Gulf State will be with her by the 4th March. Must N.C. and the border states go with them is our question? We are not compelled to do so."[9]

Vance here advanced the novel suggestion, not as his own proposal but as one being booted about the capital city with which he was somewhat sympathetic, of a buffer country between North and South. Many felt the best course "is to form a great middle confederacy, composed of the border slave and border free states. In this way we preserve this Capitol, the public lands, the form and prestige of the old government, secure greater homogeniousness, and finally reorganize and reconstruct the whole Union around this grand and over-shadowing neuclus!"[10]

Vance was still thinking about as clearly as anyone in Washington. As was evidenced by his letter to Walter Waightstill Lenoir, December 26, 1860, he could foresee that secession meant war and war meant drenching the South in blood. Governor Henry A. Wise of Virginia was holding that the South, not the North, was the section of the country adhering to the Constitution and that the North instead of the South should be the one to secede. It was the section overriding the Republic as established by the ratification of the Constitution. Vance's was not a far departure from this thinking. He wanted no part of a Confederacy embodying the "peculiar dogmas" of the cotton states. He suspected the intent was to keep out the border states until they could establish a government and adopt a constitution providing a reopening of the African slave trade, and direct taxation and free trade. "The voice of the great border states is against this of course; hence their hasty action. The confederacy once formed, we go into it acceding to their policy or we stay out and be their border guard against abolitionism.—*They don't care which!*"[11]

He thought the controversy was between New England and the Deep South and that most of the country was being ground between the upper and nether millstones. He believed at this late hour, after South Carolina had departed, that the key to the situation was Georgia, where Alexander H. Stephens, Benjamin H. Hill and Herschel V. Johnson had been conducting a stubborn rear-guard action against secession. The Central Confederation, once formed, could dictate a compromise between the sections which Georgia, he believed, would be compelled to accept, and if Georgia resigned it would "break the back bone of the whole seceding Kingdom." The next step would be to get rid of an irksome sore. "As for New England," he said, in an explosion of angry inconsistency, "we would *kick* it out if it refused to secede, and would never let it back unless as the single state of New England with only two Sumners in the Senate to play the blackguard."[12]

Vance asked an opinion about conditions from his friend and adviser Lenoir. He explained that though "great excitement pervades all ranks and classes," little would be done until after the holidays. "Then I think ten days will bring things to a head." He was fairly accurate in his time schedule. Mississippi joined South Carolina and seceded on January 9, 1861, to be followed by Florida and Alabama within the next two days; then, after eight days, Georgia capitulated, and soon Louisiana and Texas joined the rest of the Deep South.

Meantime Lenoir wrote on January 7, 1861, heartily endorsing Vance's plan for a central buffer government which might ease the departing states back into the fold, a plan which he had already forwarded by having resolutions embodying it passed at a meeting in the town of Lenoir. Numerous other North Carolina communities during this period were continuing to hold Union rallies which indicated that the temper of North Carolina was not to follow the lead of the Gulf States, but to abide for the time at least with the Union. Lenoir thought the states to the south were making a grave error. His letter, ably written, contained much pertinent thought which he summed up with an endorsement of Vance's suggestion.

"Our resolutions show that I stand out as stoutly as any southern man ought for full justice from the north as an indispensable condition to union with the north, or any part of it. But if we are to have an entire separation from the north, I am opposed to joining our state with the schemes and policies of the cotton states, and prefer a union with Virginia, Kentucky and Tennessee, with Maryland, Delaware and Missouri if they would join; or even our separate independence."[13]

Lenoir's letter to Vance is fairly indicative of the thinking in North Carolina on other aspects of the impending conflict: "I am utterly opposed to reopening the slave trade, have no faith in the new political dogmas which I believe they will engraft in their constitution, and have no desire to engage in the silly project of trying in vain to carry slavery into Mexico and Central America [the Golden Circle scheme], two old long inhabited countries, which have rejected slavery once, and wont receive it again, even if the north remains quiet. Nor do I wish to take part in a civil war between North and South, . . . which will be sure to come about unless we have a central government to keep the peace." However much Lenoir may have disliked the idea of a civil war, he would be wearing a gray uniform before the summer winds blew.

Vance clarified in a letter to George N. Folk of Watauga County, written January 9, 1861, his advocacy of a convention in North Carolina —a convention which secessionists were advocating also in order to take North Carolina out of the Union. His letter reflects how the country was being uprooted and swept almost helplessly as by a hurricane: "We are swallowed up and hurried along the rushing tides of time, and, having reached a point where we can no longer steer it, it now becomes us to prepare, if possible, for our safety and honor, by steering with, and not against the rushing volume. Unable to do as we wish, we must do as we can."[14]

As to the concrete proposal of the hour, he continued: "I do not regard the call of a Convention as a disunion movement; I regard it rather as the conducting steel to the lightning freighted cloud. Firm, temperate and decided action may save our rights and the Union, too, non-action will precipitate us into disunion. We want a Convention for other purposes than secession alone, though others, I know, desire it for no other object. We want it for the purpose of demanding terms of the Northern people."

If the North declined to give terms, then North Carolina should make its voice heard along with the Southern states. As it was, these states were rapidly inoculating the people with the dogmas with which North Carolina sentiment did not then concur. Vance emphasized that he wanted an open and uninstructed convention as the best method of promoting peace.

The demands of his correspondents were varied. One showed in this early December period of turmoil that he had other thoughts than peace. "Please buy and send to me by The Express a Pistol . . . Reflection Satisfies me that rebellion ought to be arrested by force . . ." The letter came from Knoxville, Tennessee, and was indicative of the unionist sentiment there.[15] Another wanted him to have the *National Intelligencer* republish an address by Daniel Webster—brilliant and picturesque—delivered at Capon Springs, Virginia, in 1851 against disunion, but denouncing also the code of the "higher law," a favorite resort of abolitionists who wished to transcend the Constitution.[16]

Throughout the season of storm and trial, Vance's fellow mountaineer, Clingman, was for secession. But he was the last of the Southern senators to resign his seat. One of Vance's Wilkes County devotees wrote that the North Carolina legislature ought to oust Clingman, whose policy was fashioned by personal ambition. "I recon he thinks That if he can succeede in getting a Southern Confederacy that he will Mount the presidents Chair."[17]

Just how wild the rumors flying about North Carolina were might be seen by a letter to Vance from J. C. L. Gudger of Hominy Creek, southwest of Asheville. The community had "learned" that fat and combative Senator Robert Toombs of Georgia and the pompous General Winfield Scott, puffy and seventy-fivish, had fought a duel. The first report was that Scott had been killed, the second that Toombs had fallen. Who had won this first clash of the approaching conflict? Gudger had received no newspapers for eight or ten days but "I find contradictory reports in them also."[18]

He told of a slander being circulated that "Zeb Vance is a dead dog, he's gone in for coercion." The trouble was that half of the people didn't know what "coercion" was and apparently were judging it something frightful. Another advised him that in the mountain counties secession has "split Whig & Democracy all to hell."

An interesting contention of those who insisted, contrary to Woodfin's view, that North Carolina more than other Southern states was the custodian of her own destiny, dealt with her early meditation before approving the Constitution. She was not a part of the United States when the Federal government was organized under Washington in April, 1789, but remained until November 21 of that year, according to this reasoning, an independent republic. Only Rhode Island had been more deliberate in ratifying the Constitution.

The claim that the two states were free and separate governments entitled to go their own ways may not be as specious as it appears. Congress acknowledged that they were outside the Federal jurisdiction. The customs duties imposed by Congress applied to North Carolina as they did to European or other powers. This was probably not so much to force North Carolina's hand as to prevent the European countries from making all their shipments through North Carolina and Rhode Island ports and avoiding the duties altogether.

An analysis of this relationship made in later years from a study of five acts of Congress led to the conclusion that "the United States did in 1789 formally and officially acknowledge the absolute independence and sovereignty in that year of North Carolina and Rhode Island, and of the latter state in 1790 also; and that these two states . . . were countries as much foreign to the United States as France or Spain."[19] Thus the notion that Texas and Vermont were the only independent republics to affiliate voluntarily with the United States would yield to the addition of North Carolina and Rhode Island to the list. The argument was that an independent state which joined of its own will could depart at its own choosing, and that North Carolina had a freer right to secede than any other Southern state. North Carolina delayed her ratification of the Constitution in order to influence enactment of the Bill of Rights amendment, a circumstance which was persuasive with Vance when he became governor, influencing him to keep the safeguards to personal liberty always operative during the stress of war.

The action which broke the back of North Carolina unionism was not the firing on Fort Sumter or the defense of the fort by the Federal garrison. Possibly Jefferson Davis had sanctioned the firing to force decision by the border slave states. It was Lincoln's call for volunteers and his decree of the blockade. Most particularly it was the assessment in the call of a quota of troops from North Carolina to fight against her sister commonwealths of the South. Lincoln asked North Carolina to supply two regiments. Governor John W. Ellis replied with spirit that he would not send a man. Vance was a part of the transformation which swept across the state.

"The argument having ceased," he said, "and the sword being drawn, all classes in the South united as if by magic, as only a common danger could unite them."[20]

Nicholas Woodfin, like other North Carolina unionists, had held to the central government only unless some "stronger cause" for secession might appear, and that is what did happen when President Lincoln, even before the state seceded, imprudently perhaps, declared on April 27 the ports of North Carolina under blockade. Eight days earlier the coasts of the cotton states which had already seceded were blockaded—a paper blockade at first, having no valid standing in international law, but later more effective. Lincoln may have concluded that North Carolina was not likely to remain in the Union after Virginia seceded on April 17, 1861, but since there were no vessels available with which to blockade the North Carolina coast, an exception in the case of North Carolina would have moderated secession sentiment or at least prevented further inflaming it. Conceivably with more consideration from Washington and a withholding of the blockade from North Carolina ports, the state might have been held in the Union for a time, and delay might have reopened avenues of conciliation. North Carolina did not pass its ordinance of secession until May 20, more than a month after Virginia, and was the last to join the Confederate States government. Slow to join the Federal Union, she was slow to leave it.

Someone in Washington might well have called Vance into consultation. The Lincoln administration was skating on thin ice. Had Kentucky followed her border state neighbors North Carolina, Tennessee, Virginia and Arkansas out of the Union, it would scarcely have been reasonable to hope for a conquest of the South. As Lincoln himself put it, the jig would have been up had Kentucky seceded. Losing North Carolina at a time when there was such a strong sentiment in the state to keep her old ties was one of the big factors that made the war so long and so deadly. North Carolina could not have been expected to fight her sister Southern states, but with a little better play of statesmanship in Washington at the beginning, and some attention to Vance's urging, her efforts might have been neutralized, as were those of Kentucky. The unionists needed help, and it was not forthcoming.[21]

Kemp Battle gave as clear an analysis as anyone of the situation in North Carolina after the firing on Fort Sumter. He, like Vance, had been "a violent Union man" before Lincoln's call for troops. He felt Lincoln's election was a misfortune, theoretically at least, but other elections would come and with them perhaps fair legislation for the South. He did think the Lincoln administration was wanting in a conciliatory attitude and "should not have declared war against the seceding states, which the call for 75,000 troops amounted to." He recalled that President Jackson had refused to use troops to enforce a Supreme Court decision, and the wisdom of his moderation had later been established. When Lincoln issued his call for volunteers, the North Carolina unionists, who had hoped for a cordial hand from the Washington administration, felt ignored and snubbed. With Northern troops coming down, they had to stand with their own people. Battle explained it thus: "It is better to go out together, even if we are whipped back together. If we do not go with the South we shall certainly have civil war at home. That will be much worse than fighting the North."[22]

However they may have reached the decision, the old unionists quickly became secessionists. The legislature called a convention unanimously and the convention passed the ordinance May 20, 1861. Certainly as far as North Carolina was concerned, it was a war which could have been avoided. Vance had seen clearly that the thing required was time. If, as Winston Churchill said, "war is little more than a catalogue of mistakes and misfortunes," this was an instance where, as much as any other in modern history, the haste of both sides assured the rupture. Battle compared his own attitude to Vance's. Vance made a Union speech one day and was scheduled to make another the next. Meantime he received news of Lincoln's call for troops. "Fellow citizens," he said, as he opened his second address, "I died last night a Union man. I am resurrected today a Secession man."[23]

Zeb's own version varied from Battle's. He was making a speech when he received news that Lincoln had called for troops and had included North Carolina in the levy. He had his arm raised in a gesture for the Union. But let him tell it: "When Fort Sumter was fired upon, immediately followed by Mr. Lincoln's call for 'volunteers to suppress the insurrection,' the whole situation changed instantly.

"The Union men had every prop knocked out from under them, and . . . were plunged into the secession movement.

"For myself, I will say that I was canvassing for the Union with all my strength; I was addressing a large and excited crowd, large numbers of whom were armed, and literally had my hand extended upward in pleading for peace and the Union of our Fathers, when the telegraphic news was announced of the firing on Sumter and the President's call for 75,000 volunteers.

"When my hand came down from that impassioned gesticulation, it fell slowly and sadly by the side of a Secessionist. I immediately, with altered voice and manner, called upon the assembled multitude to volunteer not to fight against but for South Carolina. I said, if war must come, I preferred to be with my own people. If we had to shed blood I preferred to shed Northern rather than Southern blood. If we had to slay I had rather slay strangers than my own kindred and neighbors; and that it was better, whether right or wrong, that communities and states should get together and face the horrors of war in a body—

sharing a common fate, rather than endure the unspeakable calamities of internecine strife."[24]

Vance had left Washington when the Thirty-sixth Congress died with the inauguration of President Lincoln, March 4, 1861. Long before the Thirty-seventh Congress met in extraordinary session, July 4, 1861, he was in the Confederate Army. His last speeches for the Union were delivered in Marshall, the old Lapland of his boyhood days, and in Asheville. In Marshall he spoke with unusual fervor and it was noticed that he did not insert a single anecdote into his remarks. It was no time for jest or punning. According to his brother Robert, "sorrow and gloom were depicted on the faces of the people." That night when he returned to speak at Asheville, he found the city in a frenzy of excitement. The news of President Lincoln's call for troops came while he was speaking to the people of his own town.

In the sequence of events, Lincoln had not only called for volunteers, but had placed North Carolina under blockade even before the meeting of the state legislature which was to provide for the selection of delegates to the state convention. This convention would then decide whether or not the state should secede. The national government had not left it much room for choice, even had it been disposed to defer secession.

As Robert summed up his brother Zeb's position, "He had taken ground in Congress against secession, which he strongly opposed, but at the same time he declared his belief in the right of revolution. He earnestly warned the country of the danger of attempting to coerce the states of the South by force of arms. He had in the closing hours of Congress, with all the warmth of his heart and the power of his eloquence, exerted himself for the preservation of the Union, and that this should be done peacefully."[25]

Now the day of debate had passed. In Zeb's own words, "It is a fight to the end. All you can expect is War! War! War!!"[26]

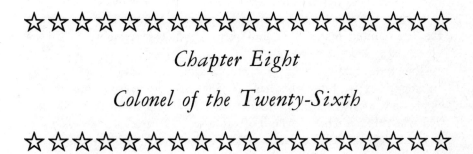

# Chapter Eight

## Colonel of the Twenty-Sixth

Zeb Vance could either bemoan the wreckage of his efforts for the Union and retire from public sight, or join in the wave of exultation over secession which swept across the Old North State, and he preferred the second course.

Now that the tensions and uncertainties had abated, the state abandoned itself to wild rejoicing. Indifferent to the need that would soon be felt for gunpowder, cannon were fired in the towns. Bells were rung, orators expounded, farmboys came down from the hills carrying old muskets and paraded as recruits through the streets.

Such editors as had stood for the Union quickly shifted their position after Lincoln's call for volunteers. All of the state's newspapers, thirteen in number, shouted ardently for secession and the Southern republic.

Exhortations flew about and filled the columns: "A thimble would contain all the conservatism in the North. . . . If we get justice, and right, and peace . . . the sword and bayonet, the ball and grape and canister must get it. . . . The South cannot be conquered if she will do her duty. . . . North Carolina must meet [the test] if it takes every dollar and every drop of patriotic blood. . . . Organize and arm! . . . Stir them up. Blow the fife, beat the drum!"[1]

The Raleigh *State Journal* carried the paean of delight that burst forth when the state reasserted her independence:

"Amid the ringing of bells and booming of cannon, mingled with the deafening shouts of thousands of loyal voices issuing from the stentorian lungs of many true freemen, we have the pleasure to announce that at 5½ o'clock Monday evening, the Good Old North State, God bless her and her sons, passed the Ordinance of Secession unanimously by declaring her eternal separation from the government of the late United States . . . and resuming her sovereignty in all its elements and departments.

"No tongue can describe the enthusiasm that prevails. It can only be conceived by him who has studied the patient suffering of the oppressed Jews while in the land of bondage, and the joys which they felt when they reached the land of promise. The persecuted secessionists —and all are secessionists now—have had glory enough for one day."[2]

None of course could look ahead and see that there was scarcely a family in the state but that would be touched by death during the next four years.

The militia units were mustered and the state legislature provided for calling 50,000 additional volunteers to serve for one year. Camps were established, companies assembled, officers were elected, regiments formed.

Despite the outward show of unanimity, there were pockets of dissent. Toe River Valley, mountain-rimmed along the Tennessee border, divided. The northern, unionist portion withdrew from Yancey County and formed a new county named after the mountain explorer Dr. Elisha Mitchell, and the schism was permanent.[3] Always there was dissension in the mountains, but Asheville became at once a citadel of loyal Confederate sentiment. Perhaps its former Whiggery and unionism led to a reaction and contributed to its new-found ardor for the Southern cause. Said a later press appraisal: "It was one of the most bitter towns in the state in its hatred of all things northern. The Federals called it 'That Damned Secession Hole.' "[4] The leading men, whether former Democrats or Whigs, promptly espoused the Southern cause. David Coleman, Vance's old political opponent, and his four brothers entered the Confederate Army and all became officers. Merrimon enlisted, and soon found himself for a time under the command of his early adversary Vance.[5] Nicholas Woodfin had turned secessionist before the firing on Sumter, but was still looked on with enough doubt that he was defeated for the Confederate Congress.[6]

Recruiting was begun quickly for two Asheville companies. The first was the Buncombe Riflemen, which had been formed when John Brown raided Harpers Ferry, and had begun drill in December, 1859, under the leadership of Captain W. W. McDowell. McDowell, cashier of an Asheville bank, was the grandson of Major Joseph McDowell who had fought at King's Mountain and joined his battalion of North Carolina riflemen to Daniel Morgan's sharpshooters just before the battle of Cowpens. Captain McDowell's company, being well organized, was filled up quickly. It left Asheville April 18, 1861, for Raleigh, well ahead of secession. It became Company E of the 1st North Carolina regiment and fought at Bethel, the first formal engagement of the war. Woodfin, the old unionist, was the speaker who sent the company off from the great gathering at the Asheville square.[7]

The next company was the Rough and Ready Guards, in which Vance enlisted as a private. When the election of officers was held, the company readily saw that he possessed the required leadership traits and elected him captain. Colonel James M. Ray of Asheville, who commanded the 60th North Carolina at Chickamauga, knew all the western North Carolina officers and judged Captain Vance "a remarkable man in never being at a loss as to what to do or say." He had, as had been seen at Chapel Hill and in Congress, mastered the art of being perfectly natural. The name of the company, a tribute to the Mexican War general and Whig President, Zachary Taylor, was soon transferred to the captain. Zeb's friends began to call him "Rough and Ready," which seemed to fit him, though when the company called on him for a speech with the name as an introduction, he responded that he was "most awfully rough but scarcely ever ready."[8]

The term "Tar Heels," cherished by many North Carolinians and possibly of Revolutionary War or earlier origin, is sometimes attributed to Zeb's first company, and since none knows the exact origin, though extensive research has been done by the state's journalists and historians to discover it, this is probably as good a version as any as to how it was confirmed in state pride. Zeb was leading the company past some Virginia soldiers lying along the roadside when one of them, familiar with the pine tar industry of North Carolina, shouted, "Oh, you Tar Heels!" "Yes," Vance shot back, "if you fellows had some tar on your heels you would have stuck yesterday in that fight, instead of running."[9]

The company when Vance took command numbered 151 enlisted men, of whom 119 were from Buncombe County and most of the others from the neighborhood. Though it passed to the command of other officers, the Roughs were always Zeb's boys. Brother Robert went to the square to see them off and found the streets crowded with families from over the county. This company could not know it was destined to share in great achievements—to hold the "Bloody Lane" at Sharpsburg; march with Stonewall Jackson and strike the enemy in the thickets at Chancellorsville; to turn the Federal flank again at Gettysburg; to march with Jubal Early on Washington; and to serve long under one of the most intrepid young officers ever to wear the gray uniform, Major General Dodson Ramseur, scarcely older than the men he commanded when he fell mortally wounded at Cedar Creek.

Sending off companies to the war appeared to have become common-place already in Asheville between the departure of the Buncombe Riflemen on April 18 and the Roughs on May 3. The Riflemen had been honored with a flag, sewed by Asheville women and presented to the company by Miss Ann Woodfin, the lawyer's charming daughter, who offered the colors with a neat little speech at the ceremonies where her father delivered the more formal address of farewell. This flag had a history, for it was adopted as the regimental colors of the 1st North Carolina and was carried at Bethel; it might therefore be regarded as the first flag of the Confederate Army baptized with blood. The color-bearer was Zeb's first cousin Alfred H. Baird of Asheville.[10] The flag now hangs in the North Carolina Hall of History at Raleigh.

Apparently the Roughs got no special flag from the Asheville women, for there was no reference to it in the description of the company's leave-taking. Robert Vance did give one surprising bit of intelligence. The fifes and drums played "Dixe" on the Asheville square. If his memory was correct this must have been coincidental, because "Dixie," a Broadway minstrel tune, had not yet been enthroned as the war song of the South. The air had been played a short time before, in February, 1861, at the swearing in of Jefferson Davis as the Confederate presi-dent, but this song of Ohio origin did not have its impact on the Confederate Army until carried to Virginia by the Washington Artillery of New Orleans.[11]

Zeb marched his company down South Main Street past Newton

Academy on the hill, down the Hendersonville Road to the Swannanoa River, where he turned left and marched up the right bank of the River, then turned on to the main highway toward Morganton. The company camped that night in a cove north of the road known as West's Old Field, where the side road leading to Bull Mountain and the Great Craggies moves up the Haw Creek valley. This was near enough to Asheville to allow Vance, a mounted officer, to ride back home that night, then the next morning to ride over Beaucatcher gap to rejoin his command.

His fondness for Asheville, the locale of his political triumphs, was deep and abiding. He more than most could anticipate the deadly struggles that would mark the oncoming war as one of the most sanguinary of history. Asheville, a town of about a thousand, even then was the "Queen City of the Mountains." Possibly Zeb was viewing it for the last time. As he passed over Beaucatcher Mountain—the gap was little more than a name for the mounting roadway—he stopped to look down on the houses nestled between the Black and Craggy Mountains to the north and east, and the mighty form of Pisgah to the west. Far in the distance might be seen the tender outline of the first fold of the Great Smokies. Beneath him flowed the French Broad, at times placid, here and there tossing and stormy as it cleaved through a mountain barrier. Did Robert accompany him to the height? The elder brother knew enough of the scene to compare it with Boabdil looking back for the last time on Granada and the Alhambra, in the "last sigh of the Moor."[12] Still Vance was to enjoy many later triumphs in Asheville, and there would find his final resting place; for Boabdil the scene was closed forever.

Vance's command became Company F of the 14th North Carolina Infantry, a regiment commanded at the outset by Colonel (later General) Junius Daniel, a West Point graduate of Halifax, North Carolina, and an officer of superb fighting qualities. Later it passed to the command of Colonel Risden T. Bennett when Daniel was promoted to head a brigade.[13] The first lieutenant was Philetus W. Roberts, but one of the second lieutenants, James M. Gudger, was to become captain and lead the company during the stubborn battles. He was fearfully wounded but emerged from the war about as sound as anyone could hope. One bullet was stopped by the Testament in his breast pocket.[14] Gudger wrote a letter on May 8, 1863, after the battle of Chancellorsville, where the regiment fought in Ramseur's Brigade, saying, "On the

3rd day of May, 1861, the Roughs, one hundred strong, left our beautiful little village to meet the enemy, and on the day of our second anniversary we were drawn up in line numbering twenty-four war-tired men." But that was not all: "I am proud of being at the head of such a company. I think a more gallant regiment than the 14th never fired a gun, and a more gallant company is not in it than the Roughs. We have driven 'Fighting Joe' back and sent him over the river whence he came."[15]

While camped near Smithfield, Virginia, when Daniel commanded the regiment, Zeb had as his tentmate and messmate the Reverend Richard N. Price, who preferred to sleep off the ground. He set up his bedstead on poles held in place by forks, while Zeb threw himself on a straw tick on the ground. Once Price was awakened by a thrashing about and found it was pouring rain. "I'm floating," groaned Captain Zeb, as he put his pallet on higher ground. Vance was usually writing letters at night, chewing tobacco while he scribbled and sometimes spitting recklessly. The minister before going to sleep cautioned him, "See here, Zeb, I'm afraid you'll spit on me!" "No, Brother Dick," he replied. "I'll spit in the water bucket." Reassured that he was joking, Price went to sleep.[16]

The Reverend Mr. Price was Vance's brother-in-law, who in later life was to have a marked religious influence over the South as minister, founder and editor for the three decades of the Holston *Methodist*, and long a contributor to the Nashville, Tennessee, *Christian Advocate*. At times during his editing he was professor of mathematics at Emory and Henry College and president of the Holston Conference Female College. He had been a circuit-riding preacher when he enlisted in the Roughs as a private, but he quickly was made the company chaplain, and as such he followed Vance into the 26th North Carolina, of which he became regimental chaplain. In no regiment could he have had to minister at more funerals and battle deaths. His devotion to the military service could be seen from his later enrollment as chaplain of the 4th Tennessee Volunteers during the Spanish-American War. His wife was Ann E. Vance, Zeb's sister.[17]

Vance seemed to touch the units he commanded with the inspiration of his own unyielding spirit. That was the case with his first company, the Roughs, and with the regiment he commanded later, the 26th North Carolina Infantry, one of the most celebrated military units in the state's history. General Ramseur told General Rodes that in perfection of drill and marching the company of Roughs was the equal of West Point cadets.[18] In the course of the war, every member of this company who marched out from Asheville with Vance was either killed or wounded, except one. Their fellow townsman, Colonel Ray, who gave this figure, did not identify this fortunate man, but the company was a participant and heavy loser in most of the sanguinary battles of the Army of Northern Virginia.[19] Colonel Bennett said that of the 1,400 officers and men on the regiment's rolls in the war, "scarcely fifty" came out unscratched.

The equipment carried by these first two Asheville companies was mostly obsolete. The canteen was the little cedar keg made at the arsenal at Fayetteville, which the state took over from the Federal government. They were of the same type as the canteens carried by Wellington's army, but they were standard equipment for Confederate troops. They were one reason why Northern canteens were so prized when captured on the battlefield, another reason being that the Confederate metal canteens later introduced were scarcely more satisfactory than the cedar kegs.

The small arms were a distinct improvement over those used in the wars of the Revolution and 1812, though many of the soldiers from the mountain regions carried their old squirrel rifles or shotguns. Instead of pouring the powder from a horn, old style, and then putting in the bullet, the soldier merely had to bite off the end of a paper package, drop the powder into the barrel, put in the lead ball, more wadding, and then ram down the charge with his ramrod. Colonel Ray considered it "an immense improvement over the old style." These paper cartridges, which were used by armies over the world and were of the type that had ignited the Sepoy Rebellion of 1854, had an abiding influence on the American Army. They required that a soldier have teeth strong enough to bite through the heavy, tough paper. Thereafter an army requirement was that a recruit have good teeth. Wars are no longer fought hand to hand and teeth are really no aid in combat, but the old requirement endured through two world wars. Colonel Ray repeated a story of a backwoodsman who came down to enlist during the Spanish-American war. The enrolling officer noticed he had several teeth missing and rejected him. "But I don't want to eat the Spaniards," the old man said. "I just want to fight them."[20]

Soon after his enlistment Zeb began to detect, or at least to suspect, that the old-time unionists were not being given favorable consideration at Raleigh, but preference instead went to those who had espoused

secession heartily before the attack and defense of Fort Sumter. Two
weeks after he left Asheville he wrote to his wife from camp near
Statesville, saying he was rather low-spirited "at the way things are
managed at Raleigh." He saw strict partisanship in the conduct of
affairs: "none but Locos [the Locofocos were a radical Democratic off-
shoot of the Jackson era] and Secessionists will be appointed to the
Offices: the old Union Men will be made to take back seats and do most
of the hard work and make bricks without straw." But he was prepared to serve his country "in spite of the small men who control
its destinies." He took pride in his command: "Many persons pronounce us the finest company in the state."[21]

Vance's letter to his wife is significant as indicating the formation
of views which controlled him throughout the war; that the South was
in the control of small minds; that the leaders were disposed to be
punitive and that they took about as much delight in suppressing former
unionists as they did in combating the forces of the Union itself. While
in the beginning this feeling was directed against Governor Ellis of
North Carolina, it came to vent itself in time against the Confederate
President, Jefferson Davis.

"I am sitting in my tent now listening to the whip-poor-wills," he
wrote. ". . . I think so much of you and all the dear pleasures & sweets
of home—our children, our garden, our flowers . . . It is so late I must
go to my straw."[22]

For a time Zeb's letters were from Suffolk, where his company was
on guard and garrison duty, but before the Roughs got into action, he
was notified on August 26, 1861, that he had been elected colonel of
the 26th North Carolina regiment of infantry.

When he was reflecting after he became colonel, Vance wrote on
September 18, 1861, a letter to a constituent, N. G. Allman of Franklin,
North Carolina, which showed his thinking about the Union and secession quite as well as Robert reflected it for him. Allman had written
asking him to become a candidate for the Confederate Congress but he
promptly rejected the thought.

"Ardently devoted to the old Union," he said, "and the forms which
the Federal fathers had established, I clung to it as long as I thought
there was a shadow of hope for preserving, purifying or reconstructing
it." He recalled that in his last official address to his constituents he
pledged that if his efforts for peace and justice at the hands of the
North should fail, then "their cause was mine, their destiny was my

destiny, and that all that I had and was should be spent in their service."
When peace failed, "civil war was thrust upon the country, and the
strong arm of Northern despotism was stretched out to crush and subdue
the Southern people." Now, "after having acquired sufficient knowledge
of military affairs to begin to be useful to my country," he had no
intention of escaping the army by seeking or even accepting a civil
appointment.

Then he spoke an appreciation he felt of the friendship of the people,
an attitude which accounted for the warm sympathy always existing
between him and them:

"Certainly if there lives a man in North Carolina who ought to do all
and suffer all for his country, I am that man. Since the time of my
entering upon man's estate the people have heaped promotion and
honors, all undeserved, on my head." He could never repay them but
he was determined to show that he was "not altogether unworthy
of their regard." He recommended that his cousin, Allen Turner Davidson, be retained as representative to the provisional Confederate government.[23] He could not avoid in a letter to his wife an expression of regret
that his friends had not tendered him the offer of this distinction as
Congressman to Richmond, but the reason clearly was that he was in
no position to accept it.[24]

A sad event for Vance and all Asheville in this early period of the
war was the death of Lieutenant William Henry Hardy, youngest son
of the beloved old pioneer doctor who had set Zeb's leg after he fell
from the apple tree. Dr. Hardy, a close friend of Zeb's father, had lost
his first son, James Patton Hardy, at the storming of Pueblo in the
war with Mexico. The three remaining sons entered the Confederate
Army, one, Dr. John Geddings Hardy, being the regimental surgeon of
the 60th North Carolina Infantry in the Army of Tennessee. Another
son, Washington M. Hardy, entered the 60th and eventually became
colonel. The youngest, William, was in South Carolina when the war
broke and enlisted at once in the 2nd South Carolina Infantry. He
became aide on the staff of Colonel Joseph B. Kershaw and was shot
through the head at First Manassas, the first Buncombe County soldier
to fall in battle. Before the battle he had written a note which was
found in his pocket. "Dear Mother: We are about to go into an engagement. I want you to know that if I should be killed, all is well.
Willie."[25]

Zeb loved Hardy's family and suffered with it. Of twelve doctors practicing in and around the Asheville community before the war, the elderly father was the only one who did not enlist in the Confederate service. His was one of the heaviest tasks of the war, the single doctor for a mountain population that had supported twelve, and into which refugees from Virginia and Tennessee were soon crowding.

Writing from Camp Burgwyn, named after the youthful lieutenant colonel of the 26th regiment, near Morehead City, Vance told his wife on September 15 that "we are still on the sand banks, and see the Yankee vessels every day," and that the enemy evidently was preparing for a grand demonstration. Zeb's regiment was guarding Fort Macon, which protected Beaufort, one of the few accessible North Carolina harbors. An earlier fort dated back to colonial times. A later fort, being ungarrisoned in 1861, had been seized by a small North Carolina band acting on its own responsibility just after the fall of Fort Sumter. Fort Macon was renovated and strengthened and on June 28, 1861, was transferred to the Confederate government. Vance's regiment guarded it for three months before going into winter quarters, experiencing little more excitement than epidemics of measles. A hospital was established on the mainland and at one time a severe fever overcame many soldiers, caused possibly by the fact that they had to wade out a distance in the shallow water to fetch in the supplies carried by vessels from the mainland. They established their winter camp midway between Morehead City and Carolina City,[26] a large Confederate encampment a square mile in area.

Vance's hope all through this period was to go to Richmond and have his old company, the Roughs, transferred to the 26th regiment, but he was never able to make the trip, though he did procure an assent from the governor to a reassignment of the company. The company was always dear to him.

The 26th regiment was mobilized at Camp Crab Tree, three miles north of Raleigh, in July and August, 1861. Its numerals in North Carolina history came to be synonymous with gallantry and blood. Some of the company names showed their county origins—the Chatham Boys, Moore Independents, Caldwell Guards, Pee Dee Wildcats, Wilkes Volunteers, the Jeff Davis Mountaineers of Ashe County in the far northwestern corner of the state. Most of the counties which supplied the men were in the central and western sections and in nearly every instance were counties which opposed secession prior to Fort Sumter.[27]

After the officers had elected Vance colonel they went on to elect the camp drillmaster, Harry King Burgwyn, a lad from Northampton County, lieutenant colonel. Mistaken as regiments were at times in their elections of officers, never was one more discerning than the 26th when it picked Burgwyn. Though he had not yet reached the age of twenty-one, he was a soldier of distinguished bearing, a graduate with the highest honors of the University of North Carolina, and a graduate of Virginia Military Institute, who had commanded the attention and compliments of the austere professor of artillery tactics, Thomas Jonathan Jackson. Peculiar as was the companionship of the mountain politician Vance and the martinet young drillmaster Burgwyn, it was for a period the closest of Zeb's life and the memory of it never left him.

Burgwyn, born to plantation affluence, had received his preliminary education from private tutors, then, before going to Chapel Hill or Lexington, Virginia, had taken courses at the military academy at Burlington, New Jersey, and at West Point, where he was instructed by John G. Foster, who was to become a general in the Federal Army against whom he fought at New Bern.

Corporal John R. Lane, later in the war the colonel of the regiment, described Burgwyn as "a youth of authority, beautiful and handsome; the flash of his eye and the quickness of his movements betokened his bravery. At first sight I both feared and admired him."[28]

Vance was well liked by the regiment, and by experience and diligent study he acquired an understanding of military practices and battle tactics, but he left the drill work and camp routine and management largely to Burgwyn. This diligent young man was so exacting that he gradually won the disfavor of the men. The regiment had been enlisted for one year's service and at the end of that time, after a stirring address by Vance, it re-enlisted in a body. Meantime the battle of New Bern had been fought.

Vance and Burgwyn were re-elected colonel and lieutenant colonel respectively, but it was the talk of the regiment that, had the election been held before the battle, Burgwyn would not have had a chance. Some disliked his martinet methods so heartily that threats were made he would not survive the first brush with the Yankees, and would not fall from enemy fire. After the battle, during which the men witnessed his combat ability, efficiency and courage, and learned that they owed their safety to his conduct, he was the pride and darling of the regiment, all the way from New Bern until the few survivors buried him with grief in a gun case beneath a great walnut tree on the battlefield of Gettysburg.[29]

Another pride of the regiment was its band, which came to be regarded as "the finest in the Army of Northern Virginia."[30] It was a factor in the splendid drill performances which made the 26th a model among Lee's regiments. This band, which has been called also "the pride of Tarheelia" and the "Johnny Reb Band from Salem,"[31] was before the war the brass band of the Moravians, the religious sect who had settled Salem in 1766, in the remote wilderness. Most of the story of this band remains because of the diary kept by one of its members, Julius Augustus Leinbach, a talented musician and diligent recorder. The band was given new life a century later by Professor Frederick Fennell of the Eastman School of Music of Rochester University, New York, an enthusiast and buff of Civil War tunes and military marches. His interest was aroused when he visited Gettysburg and read how this band, during a bombardment on the second day of the battle, had enlivened the battlefield with a medley of waltzes and polkas. Thereafter he haunted the small North Carolina towns and finally at Winston-Salem, into which Salem had merged, found the band's original books and music stored safely in the archives of the Moravian Music Foundation and the Wachovia Museum.[32]

The band had a warm spot in the heart of Zeb Vance not only because of his association with it in the regiment, but also because it played at his inauguration as governor of North Carolina. The band performed sentimentally for Vance on the day of his leave-taking of the regiment. He followed it and the regiment's activities closely throughout the war. So striking and inspiring were its performances that it was sent on home-front as well as army tours.

Samuel T. Mickey, organizer and captain of the band, told of meeting Vance ambling through the lobby of the Gaston House at New Bern at the time he was seeking to affiliate his band with the 26th regiment. "A man wearing a colonel's uniform came in with a loaf of bread under each arm. This was Zeb Vance. I spoke to him and told him my errand. 'You are the very man I am looking for,' said Zeb. 'You represent the Salem Band. Come to my regiment at Wood's brick yard four miles below New Bern.' "[33]

On the next morning Mickey was there and the historic association of the band with the famous 26th regiment began. Mickey was still conducting the band in Salem forty years after the war, and while he was described as a "prosperous mechanic," he was always a bandmaster at heart. Often during the war his musicians serenaded General Lee and other officers. At Bunker Hill, Virginia, on the retreat from Gettysburg, where Lee was cheered by their music, Colonel Walter Taylor, his adjutant general, followed the band to its quarters, thanked the members and commented that their music was "different from that of the other bands of the army." Again, when Lee visited the regiment just before the Wilderness campaign and talked over his plans with Colonel Lane, while outside the tent the band played, the commanding general remarked, "I don't believe we can have an army without music."[34]

Vance made an arrangement to pay the band with subscriptions obtained privately from the officers of the regiment, which showed the value he and they placed on its music. One of its early duties was to accompany him on tours of the different regiments. Most of them had been recruited for service of one year and it was essential to procure their re-enlistments. Vance, being the best stump speaker in the army, was customarily called on to address the regiments before the expiration dates and he reinforced his appeals with the stirring martial refrains which the Moravian musicians seemed best able to produce.[35]

Dr. Thomas J. Boykin, regimental surgeon of the 26th North Carolina and in later years a Baltimore physician, gave the most vivid picture of Vance's appeal to that regiment to re-enlist for the duration of the war. According to the doctor, it was "the best and most eloquent, effective and practical speech I ever heard any one deliver."[36] That was generous praise, but the talk was manifestly practical, because when the drum roll sounded the end of the address and the call was made for re-enlistments, *"every man* in the regiment marched up and re-enlisted for the war." A good many gray-haired fathers had come to the camp to escort their sons back home at the expiration period. Many of these older men wept and a good number, the doctor reported, came forward and wanted to enlist also. The men had been paid and given a new suit of clothes. Vance formed them in a hollow square and took his place on a box in the middle and made his appeal, in the doctor's words, "in the most impressive and burning language I ever listened to in all my life." The theme was the duty of these young men to remain in the ranks and defend their homes and families from ruthless invasion.

Who could have judged that this inspired orator for Southern rights was the same man who only little more than a year before had been one of the foremost champions of the Union?

Major Charles M. Stedman of Chatham County, a member of the 1st North Carolina and later the 44th, who served with Lee from beginning to end and was the last Civil War veteran in Congress, liked to relate the story of Zeb's appeal to this regiment "whose name will gild with splendor the pages of history as long as the world loves enduring courage and patriotic heroism." He told how the enlistments had expired, and

"The men were packing their knapsacks and preparing for their journey home. They were singing gay songs of happiness in anticipation of meeting again those so near to their hearts . . .

"Vance ordered the drum to be sounded and calling the men together addressed them. He urged them to re-enlist, to protect the honor and glory of North Carolina. The sweet and happy memories of their homes faded from their vision as he appealed to their supreme sense of duty in an effort, pronounced by those who heard it, to be unequaled and unrivaled. Every man in the regiment re-enlisted as they cheered for Vance, and then sang in full chorus 'The Old North State Forever.' "[37]

This song had been written by William Gaston, judge of the North Carolina Supreme Court, an office he long held by election of the general assembly and the common consent of the people, though the antiquated constitution of the state prohibited, prior to 1835, Roman Catholics from holding office. He was living in Raleigh at the home of a widow whose daughter attended a concert of Swiss musicians. They won marked applause with a tune that struck the young lady's fancy. She hummed the tune for the judge and asked if he could write words for it. The next day he brought in the words, famous during the war and still treasured in North Carolina.[38] The only line Kemp Battle did not seem to fancy was that saying "scorners may sneer at and witlings defame us," which seemed to him an uncalled for admission, but the soldiers were not disturbed by it.

## Chapter Nine

## New Bern — The Test of Combat

The battle of New Bern was the first trial of the 26th regiment under fire. The Federal General Ambrose E. Burnside descended on New Bern, situated up the Neuse River from Pamlico Sound, on March 12, 1862, with a combined land and naval force. His infantry, formed into three brigades, aggregated 11,000 bayonets; the squadron consisted of fourteen naval vessels.

Co-operating with the army, this squadron already had reduced the main defenses of Albemarle Sound to the north. In his operations Burnside had captured Elizabeth City, destroyed the eight little vessels which composed the Confederate "mosquito fleet," seized Roanoke Island, occupied Edenton, the early capital of the state, and raided Winton up the Chowan River from Edenton. Now he had arrived at New Bern, the second largest city of North Carolina, which on the river was defended by a number of hurriedly constructed forts and a brigade of troops commanded by Brigadier General Lawrence O'Bryan Branch.

The battle which ensued was of high significance in the career of Zeb Vance because it was the first test of his command abilities in an engagement of consequence; it emphasized to him that North Carolina was standing virtually alone in defending her own coastline; and it contributed to his election as governor five months later.

Branch, a resident of Raleigh, a Princeton graduate and North Carolina Congressman before the war, was commonly regarded as a man of ability and leadership in civil life. He had been tendered two posts in President Buchanan's cabinet, the Treasury and Post Office departments, but had preferred his legislative role. When the state seceded he became quartermaster general of North Carolina, then went into the line when elected colonel of the 33rd North Carolina Infantry, and rose to command a brigade ably until he was killed at Sharpsburg.

The loss of New Bern, another early capital, was a severe blow to North Carolina, but one Branch could not have expected to prevent except with heavy reinforcements supplied by the Confederate government and these were not forthcoming.

Branch's defending force consisted of six North Carolina regiments and two companies of North Carolina cavalry, in all about 4,000 men. Mostly they were green troops. That was not true of the attacking force, which had engaged enemy forces at several points in earlier fighting in Virginia or on the sound. Branch occupied some weak works that had been thrown up before his arrival, but while he was awaiting Burnside he strengthened them as much as he could, being handicapped by a lack of entrenching tools, with which the state, having relied on Northern and European manufacture of nearly all implements, was never well supplied. He circulated handbills over the territory calling for the plantation owners to loan slaves to help erect defenses, but he got just one Negro. The spirit of the state had not yet been stirred, as it was to be a little later by Vance. His troops constructed additional forts along the Neuse River, but when the action opened the odds were soon seen to rest with the heavy Federal naval flotilla.[1]

Burnside effected a landing on March 13 on the west bank of the Neuse and the mouth of Slocum's Creek well below the town and began a march up the right bank of the river. His army, composed of the brigades of Generals John G. Foster, Jesse L. Reno, and John G. Parke, bivouacked that night in a rainstorm that held from darkness till dawn. The Federal soldiers pulled out of the mud the next morning and came up to the Confederate defensive line five miles below New Bern, where Branch's Brigade waited. The Federal naval vessels moved up the river along with the infantry advance, shelling and disabling the forts until they were abreast Fort Thompson on the river at the left of the Confederate line. The Confederate front was protected by felled trees while Fort Thompson with thirteen guns secured the left flank, ten of the guns bearing on the river approach and three on the land.

Branch's line extended from the Neuse River and Fort Thompson on his left to the swampy land along Bryce's Creek on his right, a distance of two and a half miles, or a long front for a single brigade, even one of six regiments. The New Bern-Beaufort highway and railroad up which Burnside was moving his three brigades bisected the Confederate position. The railroad ran on a causeway through the swampy ground and this causeway proved to be the most important feature in the terrain of the battlefield. The strongly entrenched Confederate left covered the mile and a quarter between the river and the railroad. At the railroad the right was recessed 150 yards so as to take advantage of Bullen's Creek, which flowed parallel with the Confederate line and emptied into Bryce's Creek, which in turn flowed into the Trent River above New Bern.

The weak point in the Confederate line was consequently the gap of 150 yards in the center. Here, close to the railroad, was a brick kiln, which, as a protection covering the ingress up the railroad tracks, Branch had loopholed for infantry fire. As a further protection he ordered up two guns to play down the railroad, but their arrival was delayed. The main mistake apparently was that at this weakest point in his line he chanced to station his weakest troops, a militia battalion commanded by Colonel H. B. J. Clark. The battle turned largely on the circumstance that in laying out their line, the Confederates did not dig their entrenchments through the railroad right of way, but left the causeway intact, judging, apparently, that it was sufficiently defended by the troops inside the brick kiln and by the two guns that were supposed to sweep the railroad approach.

Branch remained in the center and gave command of his right wing to Colonel R. P. Campbell of the 7th North Carolina and his left wing to Colonel Charles C. Lee of the 37th North Carolina, but as the battle was joined, Vance, who had the only full regiment on the right of the railroad, aided by one detached infantry and two cavalry companies, directed the fighting in that quarter and assigned to Burgwyn the command of the regiment.

The Federals attacked with Foster's brigade on their right, nearest the river, and Reno on their left, confronting Vance, who was protected on his right front by Bullen's Creek. Parke was in support in the rear of the Federal center. Foster assailed the Confederate left with much spirit while Reno carried the brick kiln without much difficulty, then

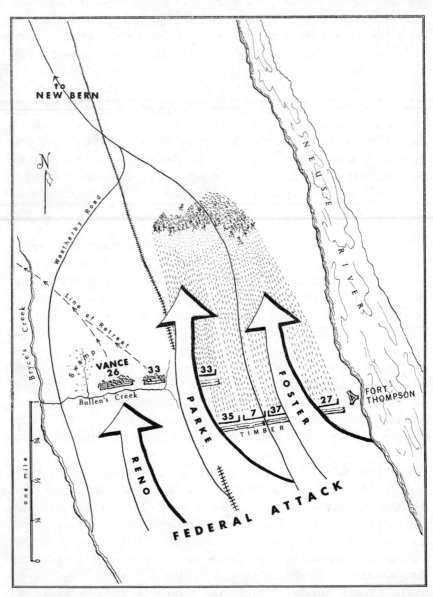

*Battle of New Bern, March 14, 1862. The arrow showing Parke's attack covers the brick kiln on the railroad, the key to the center of the Confederate position.*

turned on the militia defenders of the center and watched them flee
ingloriously from the battlefield. The next regiment, the 35th North
Carolina, taken in flank, retired precipitously. The 7th North Carolina
by a spirited counterattack stayed the Federal advance.[2]

At this juncture Parke moved his reserve brigade up the railroad,
and Colonel Isaac P. Rodman of the 4th Rhode Island noticed the
passage up the causeway through the Confederate center. He told Parke
he could carry the Confederate line, and the brigade commander supported him with the 5th Rhode Island and 8th Connecticut. This heavy
column drove through the center of the Confederate position, turned
to the right and carried the entire line of a mile and a quarter, moving
along the flank from the railroad to the river. Despite all of Branch's
efforts to rally his men, the main part of his army collapsed and rushed
back into New Bern. The Federal gunboats shelled the woods, which
added to the rout.

On the right, where Vance was fighting Reno, the story was altogether
different. At the time when the brick kiln had been carried, Branch had
sent the 33rd North Carolina to support Vance's left, which was severed
from the rest of the line and exposed. This regiment, commanded by
Colonel Clark M. Avery, had as its lieutenant colonel an officer of
unusual excellence, Robert F. Hoke, and the regiment held its position
with tenacity, as did Vance's 26th, though there were wide gaps in
the extended line and Reno attacked repeatedly with vigor. After the
left had collapsed, Branch sent several messengers with orders for
Avery and Vance to retire, but they did not get through the waves of
Federals and the battle on the right was maintained by Vance, Avery,
and Hoke for more than an hour. The Federals moved through the gap
and at length appeared some distance in the rear of the two North
Carolina regiments before these were forced to cease firing and retire.
Colonel Avery was captured. Major Abner B. Carmichael who commanded the hot corner of the left of the 26th was killed, a heavy loss
to Vance.

He was shot through the head while, as Vance stated it, "gallantly
holding his post on the left, under a most galling fire. A braver, nobler
soldier never fell on field of battle. Generous and open hearted, he was
endeared to the whole regiment."[3] Before being elected major he
had been the captain commanding the Wilkes County Volunteers.

Vance and Hoke led their commands across Bryce's Creek and did
not follow the routed forces into New Bern. The best compliment for

the 26th and 33rd regiments came from Lieutenant Colonel William S. Clark of the 21st Massachusetts: "These two regiments were the best armed, and fought the most gallantly of any of the enemy's forces. They kept up an incessant fire for three hours, until their ammunition was exhausted, and the remainder of the rebel forces had retreated."[4]

Vance gave a full report of the combat, in which he explained that his regiment had been posted in a series of redans by Burgwyn, on the right of the railroad and in the rear of Bullen's Creek. The battle opened at 7:30 A.M. and at 9 A.M. Hoke came to his relief with two companies of the 33rd regiment. They fought until twelve noon, when Vance's adjutant, Captain J. J. Young, after a hazardous passage across the field, reached him with intelligence that the enemy had turned his left by way of the railroad track, had reached and pillaged his camp in the rear, and were several hundred yards down the railroad between him and New Bern. Young reported that all the Southern troops on the field were in full retreat except his own. Vance ordered an immediate retreat.

Burgwyn's discipline now manifested itself and no doubt saved the regiment from disaster, as the private soldiers readily admitted. The men retired from the trenches and rallied and reformed in the woods without panic or confusion. Burgwyn was on the right and when Vance's command to retreat reached him he withdrew in good order, and the regiment, accompanied by Hoke and a portion of the 33rd, moved to Bryce's Creek, which was in fact a river seventy-five yards wide and too deep to be forded. On the bank only one small boat could be discovered. Branch's line of retreat had been supposed to be into New Bern and no provisions had been made for a hurried crossing of the formidable stream on the little army's right flank.

Some who could swim plunged into the water immediately and reached the other shore. Vance wanted to hunt more boats on the other shore. He got across but was nearly drowned in the effort. He rode into the stream, but his horse refused to swim; he was thrown off and was weighed down by his clothing and heavy accouterments. The men along the bank saw him sink into the dark water, and some of them rushed down to pull him out. According to his own story of the incident, he then swam across with his sword, pistols and cartridge box on. Somehow he got his horse across, rode quickly to the Trent River, and procured three boats from a riverman. He and his men carried the boats on their shoulders to the point where the regiment was crossing.

Burgwyn, coming up, had seen that some of the men were drowning. He drew his sword and had his close Chapel Hill friend, Lieutenant William A. Graham,[5] who had come up from one of the cavalry regiments, draw his and stand with him at the crossing. There they held back the men to prevent panic and the mass drowning that would have been likely had all plunged into the stream. They saw that the boats were loaded without confusion or crowding. Four hours were required to get the regiment on the opposite bank. When the last man was over, the intrepid Lieutenant Colonel Burgwyn, who had recognized that the Federals might at any minute discover the crossing point and pounce on the divided regiment, but who had maintained discipline and remained calm, stepped into the boat and was the last man across.

Lieutenant Graham told how he had got into a boat—one of those brought up by Vance would hold eighteen men—but was called back by Burgwyn, who told him he must help prevent the men from overloading and swamping the boat. "I stood facing Colonel Burgwyn, and each time we counted eighteen we halted the column. When we had all across except Colonel Burgwyn and myself, I entered the boat and, leading the horse into the water, swam him over along its side. The boat returned and Colonel Burgwyn came over in like style."

The 26th never forgot Burgwyn's management of the regiment in the battle and at the crossing. He was not yet twenty-one years old. When Vance was elected governor and the regiment was in Robert Ransom's Brigade, Ransom opposed the elevation of Burgwyn to the command and declared he "wanted no boy colonel in his brigade."[6] The men promptly bristled and declared they would have no other colonel than Burgwyn and stood so firm and rallied such support that to accommodate them he was promoted and the regiment was transferred to the brigade of J. Johnston Pettigrew.[7] A little later, by the time of Gettysburg, he was being looked on as one of the model colonels of an army rich with unusually able regimental commanders.

When a check was made it was found that three of the 26th were drowned in the crossing of Bryce's Creek. The total casualties were eighty-seven killed, wounded, and missing. The losses in the 33rd regiment were higher.

Lieutenant Colonel Hoke with part of the 33rd regiment joined Vance after crossing his men over the creek in a boat found downstream, and the little command, the unworsted portion of the army that had defended New Bern, retreated to Trenton where stragglers were collected, and thence to Kinston, which it reached at noon March 16. It had marched fifty miles in thirty-six hours.

Parts of the army already were in Kinston. One cavalryman reported he covered forty-eight miles from New Bern in eight hours. Anxiety was being felt over Vance's 26th, about which nothing had been heard since the left wing of the Confederates had left the field. Trains ran into Kinston during the day after the battle, bringing infantry units which had been loaded at Tuscarora,[8] on the line of retreat, ten miles out of New Bern. On the second day after the battle the defeated army was delighted to see Vance come marching in, his regiment in good order, the famed Moravian Band from Salem moving in advance of the column, playing the stirring notes of "Dixie."[9]

The 26th reached Kinston nearly threadbare, its camp having fallen into enemy hands after the left wing of the army had given way. Clothing had been lost at the crossing of the river. Colonel Hoke told how a boy sixteen years old threw away his clothes in order to save his gun when swimming the creek.[10] Vance wrote a letter to the editor of the Raleigh *Standard* the next day: "Will you please announce to the good people of the State, that my regiment is here in a most destitute condition. Any persons that will send a coarse cotton shirt, drawers, or socks, will be doing us a great kindness, as it will be weeks before the State can supply us."[11] The Fayetteville *Observer* and other newspapers reprinted the appeal and the returns were in some instances generous. One of the most heartfelt and sympathetic must have been Kemp P. Battle's contribution of $114, which was the emolument he drew as a member of the last session of the convention.

Zeb, on March 20, wrote for his wife a description of the action, highly commending his regiment. He must have felt the exhilaration of battle: "For five hours the roar of the small arms was uninterrupted, fierce and deafening. Thirty odd pieces of artillery (field) were in constant play, whilst the great guns of our batteries and the enemys ships made the earth tremble. I was surprised at my feelings, excitement and pleasure removed every other feeling and I could not resist cheering with might and main. . . . We feel quite proud of the good name we have obtained and are determined to maintain it."[12]

Vance's achievement of retiring in good order and saving his regiment from panic can be judged by the pandemonium set loose when the left wing of the Confederate force retired into New Bern. Some of the militia which had been stationed in the center had not stopped running until they reached the town. Vance's adjutant, Captain Young, tried to rally them, telling them the newspapers would be filled with accounts of their cowardice. One shouted, "I'd rather fill twenty newspapers than one grave."[13] One of the men ran himself to death, like the militiaman before the British redcoats at the battle of Bladensburg on the outskirts of Washington in the War of 1812. This Confederate militiaman died just after reaching the safety of a train, crossing the river into New Bern, after he had raced five miles from the battlefield.

But the flight did not end at New Bern. There many civilians and other soldiers besides militia joined it. A description of the exodus was provided by Dr. Edward Warren, a volunteer doctor with the army, who later under Vance was to become surgeon general of North Carolina; he offered a diagnosis of the flight which followed the shelling of New Bern by the advancing Federal flotilla. The panic was set off when someone yelled, "The Yankee cavalry is coming."

"A panic must be witnessed and participated in to be appreciated," the doctor wrote, "and even then it cannot be described. The men who were thus flying in terror from an imaginary danger—for the enemy possessed no cavalry, and never dared to leave the town—proved eventually the bravest soldiers the world ever saw. From the Valley to Appomattox they left a record of their heroism which the nations have regarded with admiration and their own people will treasure as the most precious of heirlooms.

"Panics are nothing more or less than a species of emotional insanity temporarily affecting masses, under the influence of which manhood succumbs, reason is silenced, and the fear of death predominates to the exclusion of every other sentiment and consideration. I can only express the hope that it may never be my misfortune to witness another, and certainly not to be called to participate in one, for I have had sufficient experience in that line to last for a lifetime."[14]

W. A. Curtis of Murphy, one of the cavalrymen under Vance's command, said that when his troop passed the camp where they had left their extra clothing and equipment, it was in flames. They had on hand there a large supply of blankets, quilts and clothing which friends had sent from their homes to keep them comfortable during the winter. All they had carried into battle except guns and ammunition were a few rations. "Among the articles which I lost, I mostly regretted the loss of a Bible, a present from my mother. . . ."[15]

Curtis passed within view of New Bern, which he saw was already occupied by the Federal forces. The town was on fire in several localities "and the dense, black smoke arising from the lurid flames darkened the elements over us." The Federal soldiers were trying to extinguish the fires "they had so wantonly kindled themselves." The Federals contended that the fires were set by retreating Confederates. Scattered along the roadway out of the town he saw "trunks, boxes and household plunder, of all kinds, together with army equipment. . . . It was a sad spectacle to see ladies, both young and old, many of whom appeared to be unaccustomed to hardships and toil, trudging along the road in mud and water, on foot, carrying immense loads of their household articles."[16]

The loss of New Bern, defended by a small force of North Carolina troops, to a formidable Federal amphibious army was the first evidence of the indifference—which endured throughout the war—of the Davis administration to the North Carolina waterfront. It was an unconcern which General Lee, though always pressed for more troops himself, happily did not share when he later became commander of the Confederate Army in Virginia. But the victory was of top significance to the Northern Army because the Confederates never recaptured the city. The Federal force which remained there was a dagger always poised at the heart of the Confederacy. The railroad which was the main life line of Lee's army, connecting Richmond with Wilmington, North Carolina, and thence with Augusta, Atlanta, and the South, was but sixty-one miles from New Bern, and only twenty-four miles from weakly defended Kinston. It was continually menaced and Lee could undertake no aggressive movement, such as the invasion of Pennsylvania, without first weighing the danger of a deeper penetration into North Carolina and the loss of this vital railroad.[17] His strategic movements were always rendered hazardous. Clearly the attitude of Richmond was ground for Vance's complaints after he became governor that North Carolina was holding the front line in Virginia but was being dealt with casually in the vital coastal areas at home, which were raided and plundered by the enemy at will.

The New Bern campaign of March 12-14, 1862, was conducted by Burnside at a time when the main Confederate Army was lying idle at Centerville, Virginia. It is easy to see in aftersight that the cars which carried provisions forward to Joseph E. Johnston might have transferred one or two good brigades of soldiers on the return, via Richmond,

Petersburg, and Goldsboro, to repel the Burnside expedition. The danger had been signaled well in advance, first by the Butler descent on Hatteras the preceding August, and his capture of the fort and Hatteras Inlet. Burnside had concentrated his forces in the North Carolina coastal waters of Pamlico Sound as early as February 4, 1862. Roanoke Island fell February 8, at a time when heavy Confederate forces in Virginia were unemployed, the officers often whiling away the time at cards.[18]

McClellan did not land his Peninsular army at Fortress Monroe until early April. Johnston did not begin the transfer of his army from the Centerville, Gordonsville, and Fredericksburg areas until after the McClellan movement was defined. The first of his divisions joined General Magruder's command defending the Peninsula on April 9.[19] Thus there was abundant time—weeks of it—to have detached a brigade or better still a tested division to save New Bern, after which it would have been easier for this force to reach the Peninsula by rail from Kinston and rejoin Johnston than by marching overland from Centerville. The use of interior lines, perhaps the greatest advantage possessed by the Confederacy, does not appear to have occurred to President Davis and his advisers in this instance, though it could readily have saved New Bern and prevented the festering of an irritating sore on the vitals of the Confederacy for the balance of the war. Vance as governor was continually irked by it, but could not remove it.

On the plus side for the Confederacy, the victory so magnified the military stature of General Burnside as to lead to his promotion to the command of McClellan's left wing at Sharpsburg, where his slowness was an important element in saving Lee's army, and later to his command of the Army of the Potomac and the ill-advised slaughter of his brigades in front of the stone wall at Fredericksburg.

George C. Underwood, the assistant surgeon of the 26th, summed up the popular reaction after the battle: "The press of the state heaped eulogies upon the officers and men of the 26th regiment and recruits flocked to its standard."[20]

Because of this Vance decided to organize a legion, a Civil War name for a unit of lesser numbers than a brigade, but ordinarily having its own cavalry and artillery detachments. Hampton's Legion from South Carolina had been a noteworthy augmentation to the army in Virginia at the beginning of the war. Thomas R. Cobb, Howell's brother, had recruited a Georgia Legion, which he led gallantly on the Peninsula.

He won promotion and was killed defending the sunken road at Fredericksburg.

The Asheville *News,* quoting the Raleigh *Standard,* reported the movement on April 26: "We learn there is much anxiety felt in different quarters to raise a Legion in this State to serve during the war to be called the 'Vance Legion,' to be commanded by the gallant Z. B. Vance. The idea is a popular one & we have no doubt it could be raised in 30 days. Let the ball be put in motion."[21]

Vance had, in fact, meditated about the legion before the battle of New Bern. On March 4, while stationed in that town before the battle, he wrote to his cousin Allen Turner Davidson, Confederate Congress in Richmond, asking him to explore the situation. Zeb was enthusiastic. "In thirty days, I could raise another regiment for the war, two companies of cavalry and one of artillery . . . Do you suppose the President would give me authority to raise it? Can you feel out the authorities for me? Try it & write me. If you think it probable I would run up to Richmond. . . ."[22]

What Davidson may have done is not clear, but Zeb followed this with a letter addressed directly to Secretary of War Randolph, dated April 3, 1862, requesting authority to raise the legion and guaranteeing to have the requisite number of men in thirty days. The secretary gave the authorization and on April 18 Vance announced for an additional regiment of infantry, two companies of cavalry and one artillery company, which would give him command of a demibrigade or legion. He offered a bounty of $100 for each soldier on enlistment. Cavalrymen were required to furnish their own horses. "The best arms and equipments to be had in the Confederacy will be furnished. Recruits will be received singly or by companies. Turn out, and let's make short work with Abe." He asked the Fayetteville *Observer,* Greensboro *Patriot,* Charlotte *Bulletin,* Salem *Press* and Asheville *News* each to copy the appeal four times.[23]

After Zeb's project had been well launched, it met a chilling response from the North Carolina governor, Henry T. Clark, an Edgecombe County Democrat and an original secessionist, devoted to routine, who was not likely to go out of his way to advance the fortunes of a recent unionist and Whig, whose name was being linked with the governorship by some of the newspapers. Vance wrote to Adjutant General James G. Martin, who replied on April 23 that the governor declined to clear the way for the legion because the law did not recognize any such organization. Another letter from Martin on April 26 showed the governor throwing up obstacles. North Carolina already had filled its quota. ". . . he is not inclined to encourage formation of new Companies . . ." Martin, friendly, congratulated Zeb on his unanimous re-election as colonel of the 26th. They were to have a close and mostly a compatible relationship but at the moment Martin could not or did not help.[24] Vance also wanted a leave to go into several towns and raise his force but this General Theophilus H. Holmes, who commanded the department of North Carolina, declined to grant.[25]

There appeared to be no doubt in Vance's old regiment that he was being given a runaround about the legion. One of his officers wrote a letter to the Raleigh *Standard* July 23, 1862, declaring that as soon as Vance's name began to be mentioned for governor "every impediment was put in the way of the Legion." When a quartermaster of one of the new companies applied for cooking utensils in Raleigh, they were refused. The legion recruits had to borrow pots and pans from families in the neighborhood in order to prepare their food. One of the captains was paid the regular $50 state bounty for his men on their enlistment but within an hour he was recalled and the money was taken back from him. The paying officer explained that he "knew nothing of Vance's legion."[26]

Vance did get to Richmond in early May, where he was squeezed for time because Randolph told him the muster rolls of his new organizations would have to be submitted by May 17. "I hurried home and attempted to get them prepared," he wrote. "But inasmuch as they were scattered over different portions of the State, in counties remote from the Telegraph & daily mails I have found it impossible to get them." He did have the rolls of five companies, but he thought the plan for the legion would be a failure unless he should be allowed more time. A week later he was still optimistic. "My Legion is thriving and will be a success, I think."[27]

This last letter, written May 25, shows how Vance, while occupied with refitting his troops at Kinston, was being carried on the buoyant wave that was sweeping over the South, even though McClellan had a great army inching up toward Richmond: ". . . McClellan is almost certain of being whipt if he attacks Richmond by land and without his boats. In the West, the whole country relies with implicit confidence in the glorious Beauregard who has 100,000 of the bravest men on the continent under his command." No doubt Beauregard would have been elated if he had had half that number of effectives. "He is gathering strength every day, & the impression begins to prevail that he will annihilate Hallecks whole army. General Banks has retired across the Blue Ridge to Fredericksburg, leaving the open road for old Stonewall Jackson into Maryland & Penna. He is going certain, & it is said he will be joined by 30,000 Marylanders with arms in their hands. God grant it."[28]

Truly the accounts of numbers reaching down into the Confederacy were as untrustworthy as those being fed to McClellan by his secret agents and scouts. But Zeb was entitled to a moment of optimism and elation about the war. He was usually a stark realist whose judgment did not go far astray. His plans for the legion gradually petered out. One of his recruiting agents, A. M. Erwin, reported on June 4 that Adjutant General Martin "says you never *consulted he* or the *Gov* about your Legion & he would not do anything for you." One company was being raised by Captain Thomas J. Dula (not the same Tom Dula whom Zeb defended in the celebrated murder trial after the war). Dula eventually took his company into the 58th North Carolina and did well in the Army of Tennessee until wounded at Chickamauga. On June 15 Vance was writing a protest to Secretary Randolph against the plan of General Holmes and state authorities to disband the companies he had already recruited, again on the ground that the state had filled its quota. "I find it impossible to raise and organize troops with both State and Confederate authorities against me, and have therefore quit trying to get my companies together." He wanted to know what to do with those he already had in his camp.[29]

The recruit-hungry Confederate government, which could have used good troops in any theater, was indeed treating Vance cavalierly. Randolph wrote a rather ambiguous endorsement on Vance's final letter, directing his clerk to "inform him that" Governor Clark had sent no advice, he was uninformed about any obstacle raised by General Holmes "but considering the attempt as abandoned order already received," whatever such a clause may have implied. Then he directed that Holmes be ordered to "disband such companies as could not be made efficient by discharging all not liable to conscription and by transferring the conscripts to the old regiments." He added that any promising companies could be attached to the regiments needing companies. Thomas Jefferson would have frowned on the foggy language of such an endorsement written by his grandson, but the general purport seemed to be that Vance's legion was finished and buried in a heap of red tape, and the troops he had been gathering diligently were either to be sent home or gobbled up by other regiments, as was the case with Dula's men.

Quite obviously neither Richmond nor Raleigh wanted to recognize the clear-speaking Zeb Vance as a factor, else they would have given him the promotion he deserved after the way he conducted himself and his regiment at New Bern. Someone was even kindling a series of back-fires against him in the newspapers. This hostile propaganda campaign mounted to open flame and involved some character searing when, about this time, mention began to be made in some of the newspapers that Vance would make a good candidate and a capable governor. He was disgusted over the political maze being created around the legion. He attributed his failure to "the opposition to the scheme on the part of the State and Confederate authorities."[30]

His Asheville friends were disappointed. The Asheville *News* on May 15 already had told of his promotion: "We learn that Col. Z. B. Vance has been appointed Brig. Gen. by Pres. Davis. This will be grati-fying news to the people of this section with whom the gallant Zeb is a great favorite. He will wear his new honors most worthily." But one could not always rely on the reports that found their way up the moun-tains. A little later under the heading of "Good News, If True" the newspaper told that Andy Johnson had been killed by the former chief of police of Nashville, George Brown. The same report had "Picayune" Butler being killed in New Orleans, but the public was cautioned, "we are a little afraid this is too good to be true." Still, $10,000 had been offered to any man who would slay "Picayune." "If George Brown killed A. J. we will open a subscription to raise a monument on Black Mountain." A few days later the *News* was forced to concede that the Andrew Johnson report was false.[31]

Zeb suffered for some weeks after the battle of New Bern with an injured hand (hurt when he fell on the logs of one of the breastworks) which interfered with his writing, but on March 23 he was able to report improvement.[32]

In camp at Kinston he had an unusual experience in recruiting. Among those coming to join the regiment because of its fame after New Bern were two young persons who enrolled as L. M. and Samuel Blalock. They were brought into Company F, the Caldwell Guards, by a private, James D. Moore. The first, known as Keith Blalock, confided to Moore that Sam was his bride and said he would not enlist unless Sam could go with him. Moore agreed but Vance had no suspicion of the deal.

Sam was taken to be a boy of sixteen, dark haired, five feet four, 130 pounds, while Keith, supposedly Sam's brother, was about six feet. Sam drilled well, became an expert in the manual of arms, did the regular company chores, and none in the company suspected her until her husband developed sumac poisoning and hernia. Then Sam divulged to the company commander that she was a female and the captain told Vance, who promptly discharged her. Both of them—Keith and Malinda—became bushwhackers in the western counties later in the war.[33] The instance was one of several female enlistments which occurred in both armies. Zeb would have done better for the cause had he slapped them in prison for misrepresentation, but he could not anticipate their future careers.

At the end of a year, with the regiment at Kinston, Vance had fallen naturally into the responsibilities of command. While the steadfastness of his regiment in holding the right wing at New Bern probably had not given it the celebrity attained by the 1st North Carolina in the much smaller clash at Bethel, nor the 6th North Carolina which had charged and captured the Federal guns at Manassas, it had won applause aplenty and the distinction made Vance's name better known over the state in military than it had been in political affairs before the war.

How did the soldier regard Vance? One of his men thought his strength was in his warm sympathy for the ordinary private and his concern over the men's wants. He never neglected the matters of shelter, food, clothing, equipment. Those virtues were indeed the mark of a good commanding officer.

"I well remember the first time I ever saw him," said this member of the 26th. "He had no appearance in the world as a soldier; his hair was long and flowing over his shoulders, and he was wearing a little seal skin coat, from which I judged him to be a chaplain. He had not long been absent from the hustings of Western North Carolina, and had but little experience in war as captain of the 14th Regiment. When he came to camp he soon began to display the same qualities which made him so popular all over our State.

"In the first place he had the keenest sympathy with his men. They soon came to feel that Colonel Vance loved them, and made their troubles his own. In the next place, Colonel Vance was able to inspire his men with the belief that he had confidence in them. These two essentials to a good commanding officer were, perhaps never possessed by any man to a greater degree than by Colonel Vance."[34]

As to drill and discipline, he was at first deficient, but he was the one to recognize it. Instead of allowing the regiment to deteriorate, he employed the superior drill experience of Lieutenant Colonel Burgwyn. The result was that the regiment "became almost a perfect instrument of war." It was devoted to its commander and, as was seen after New Bern, to Burgwyn as well. As to Vance's conduct, "In battle I always marked him as cool and courageous . . ." As governor he was to benefit much from having been a colonel. "He had a sympathetic knowledge of the needs of the Confederate soldier . . . he knew how with all his kindness to deal firmly with men and affairs."

But Zeb was about to enter into one of the most trying ordeals of combat ever experienced by an American army, a massed frontal attack against an enemy position of unusual strength, which was to impose a severe test not only of his own courage, but of his regiment's stamina and responsiveness.

On June 20, 1862, Ransom's Brigade, which included Vance and his 26th regiment, was ordered to report to Major General Benjamin Huger on the Williamsburg Road on the Virginia Peninsula below Richmond.

☆☆☆☆☆☆☆☆☆☆☆☆☆☆☆☆☆

## Chapter Ten

## Malvern Hill

☆☆☆☆☆☆☆☆☆☆☆☆☆☆☆☆☆

Malvern Hill, along with the third day at Gettysburg, was one of Lee's tragedies. By collecting available forces in Virginia and North Carolina he had amassed an army of approximately 90,000 men, the largest he ever commanded.

Stonewall Jackson, the whipping boy for most of the Peninsular failures, commanded his left wing, which was farthest from the James River. Extending toward the river were the commands of Huger and Magruder, with Longstreet and A. P. Hill forming the reserve on the right.

The day was steaming hot—it was July 1 in tidewater Virginia—and the Federal Army, which had been changing base from the York to the James River, was drawn up in a carefully prepared position on an elevated plateau rising about sixty feet above the woods and farmland of the neighborhood, a height known as Malvern Hill.

This was not a supply point which the Federals could use on the James, and consequently it might have been calculated that they would have to retreat farther, to Harrison's Landing, six miles down the river, or beyond. But Lee decided to attack them in force. The maps were inadequate. Major General D. H. Hill knew of the terrain along the river, his information having been obtained from a chaplain who had lived nearby. He described the land and told Lee, "If General McClellan is there in force, we had better leave him alone."[1]

After Lee ordered the attack, much difficulty was experienced in forming in the woods and the lines were not ready until afternoon. Even then, never was there co-ordination between the different units. The Federal guns had been skillfully placed and their locations had been inspected on the previous evening by McClellan personally, a careful engineer, assisted by perhaps the best engineering officer in the Northern Army, Brigadier General A. A. Humphreys.

McClellan described his line as "very strong"[2] along the whole front of the open plateau, though it weakened on his right, where it extended to the lower land. But the road from Richmond and White Oak Swamp, on which Lee's men were following the Federals, threw his army more to the Federal left along the river. It was there Mc-Clellan anticipated attack and massed his infantry and it was there the heavy blow fell, instead of on his weaker right flank, which Stonewall Jackson's Corps faced. The plateau, being about a mile and a half long, with a width of half that distance, was cleared of timber and had a number of easily defended ravines in front of it. To the north and east were clear sweeps for the Federal artillery, while on the northwest the plateau fell off abruptly, as McClellan viewed it, into a ravine reaching to the James River. Expecting the attack on his left near the river, here McClellan concentrated his artillery fire.

Lee's failure has been attributed to the slowness or mistaken direction of some of the divisions, Huger's and Magruder's especially; to a breakdown of staff work; to the alleged lethargy of Stonewall Jackson, who was supposed to assail the weak part of the Federal line, where it trailed off from the plateau into the low farmlands; and to the fact that green brigadier generals had to form the lines at the base of the hill. Longstreet thought the inability to get the batteries into position was to blame. But perhaps the better diagnosis of the battle is that it never should have been fought at all, because McClellan was retreating, and of all the places to bag him, this was probably the worst of any along the James River. "We were repulsed at all points with fearful slaughter," said Longstreet, "losing six thousand men and accomplishing nothing."[3]

Vance's 26th regiment was among those to feel the full impact of the disaster of charging into the sheet of flame blazing from the Federal works.

The carnage was frightful on the slope and plateau. Some of the

Confederates, unable to withstand the fire, hit the ground and lay in the depressions, being unable to go forward and unwilling to retreat. Other waves went through them.

"We passed over four lines of men," said one officer. "Our men trampled them into the dirt like logs, and moved on." These were not of Vance's regiment, but nearby. These attackers, too, were hurled back. One panic-stricken soldier, rushing past a Georgia officer, shoved him aside at the exact instance a cannon ball tore off the fleeing man's head, and splattered his blood and brains over the officer's face.[4]

Robert Ransom's Brigade, consisting of five North Carolina regiments, among them Vance's 26th, made one of the last formidable assaults, at 7 P.M., but with Magruder's rather than Huger's Division. The regiment had been on picket duty for several dark nights in front of Kearny's Federal Division on the Williamsburg Road. When the battle was joined on July 1, Magruder called on the brigade commander three times for help, even if he could send only one regiment. Ransom sent the 24th North Carolina first, then followed it with the balance of the brigade, all moving on the run.

As the three leading regiments reached the combat line they were thrown into the action one by one. The last two, commanded by Ramseur and Vance, were halted so they could regain their breath, then were pushed forward, as Ransom described it, "under as fearful a fire as the mind can conceive." They pressed ahead up the slope as best they could until within two hundred yards of the fortified line, where the Federal guns blasted them with canister and grape, and the infantry, protected behind their works, blazed at them with successive volleys. Still, the two regiments moved ahead. By this time it was twilight, but the entire brigade kept its forward motion until the Federal guns were now only one hundred yards away.

Masses of Federal troops could be seen moving back and forth, strengthening the weak points. Couch's Federal Division was reinforced by the arrival of the Irish Brigade under Meagher and the Excelsior Brigade under Sickles. Vance's 26th, along with the other North Carolina regiments, now let loose the Rebel Yell and dashed up to within twenty yards of the guns, where they met what Ransom described as "a perfect sheet of fire from muskets and the batteries." The onrush was stopped, the brigade line wavered, then the survivors fell back in front of a fire "the intensity of which is beyond description." Ransom bespoke the brigade's regrets: "It was a bitter disappointment to be compelled to yield when their guns seemed almost in our hands."[5]

General D. H. Hill witnessed Magruder's assault, which included Ransom's Brigade with the 26th, and said: "I never saw anything more grandly heroic than this advance after sunset of the nine brigades. . . . Unfortunately they did not move together, and were beaten in detail.

"As each brigade emerged from the woods from fifty to one hundred guns opened upon it, tearing great gaps in its ranks; but the heroes reeled on and were shot down by the reserves at the guns which a few squads reached."[6]

Viewed from the Federal side, the Confederate attack was poorly organized and capricious. Lee's army began feeling out the position near the river between nine and ten in the morning, and while in the early afternoon the Federals could observe marching columns in the distance, nothing happened until 3 P.M., when a sharp attack was hurled against the center of the Federal line, which held its fire, then delivered a deadly volley. Then a lull came over the battlefield about four, but at six the Confederate artillery fire was resumed and Lee delivered a more earnest attack. As McClellan described it: "Brigade after brigade, formed under cover of the woods, started at a run to cross the open space and charge our batteries." Heavy artillery fire and the infantry volleys sent them reeling back and covered the ground with gray-clad bodies.

Again at seven and until darkness around eight thirty the Confederates threw their brigades against these same or nearby heavily defended works. About nine the artillery fire ceased and the battle was ended.[7]

The Confederates had difficulty in getting their batteries into position, and those placed effectively were dismounted by the fire of the better placed Federal guns. "The enemy," said Longstreet, "concentrated the fire of fifty or sixty guns upon our isolated batteries, and tore them into fragments in a few minutes after they opened, piling horses upon each other and guns upon horses."[8]

But the heart of the story was that Lee attacked brigade by brigade, in sequence, not in concert, and was defeated in detail.

There were some lightening incidents. Even while waiting amid the havoc of the artillery fire, Vance injected one or two gaieties. As the regiment began to move, a rabbit darted ahead in front of the line. "Go it, cottontail!" Vance shouted. "If I had no more reputation to lose than you have, I'd run, too!" That did not sound like some such normal cry as "Forward, men, with might and main!" But it was breezy, designed to ease his tense troops, and it showed Zeb retained his familiar coolness.[9] Again, while the men were lying down awaiting the order to charge, while the Federal guns were bombarding furiously, Zeb noticed a soldier nodding his head and bowing each time a shell whizzed past. "Why are you so polite in the presence of the enemy?" Zeb asked smilingly.

Another incident was the loss of the pay of Company G. Captain John R. Lane, later the regiment's colonel, had it in his blouse, wrapped in a newspaper. In the excitement of the charge the money not only disappeared, but was not missed by the captain until the battle was over. Then he realized it must have slipped out somewhere on the battlefield. None knew until the next morning that McClellan was retreating, but Lane went out alone, early, chancing capture, and hunted back and forth over the ground littered with bodies and equipment, where the company had waited and over which it had charged. Finally, to the surprise of everyone whom he told of it, he found the package lying among some bodies. It had never been opened.[10] Amid the carnage of such a fearful attack, money was the last thing anyone was thinking of. Lane had another peculiar experience. The night of the attack the enemy fire continued and bombs exploding in the air looked like a gala Fourth of July celebration. Lane lay down on the field to sleep between two other soldiers. When he awoke the next morning, both were dead. The roar of the battle had not disturbed him in his exhausted condition, but they had been hit, and, as the regimental scribe suggested, his reveille was in this, theirs in another, world.

In the nearby 30th North Carolina of General George B. Anderson's Brigade, Company A, the color company, was in the center, charging with bayonets fixed. Corporal Pipkin's eyes moved back and forth from the point of his bayonet to the enemy line close ahead, but not attentively enough to shut out sight of a brand-new pair of cavalry boots, tied together, lying on the ground. As he passed he held his gun and bayonet in his left arm, and with his right hand reached down and scooped up the prized boots. He was described by his colonel as "a most excellent soldier" and, again, a "gallant fellow." He did not break the alignment as he stooped nor even take his eye off the point of the bayonet as he threw the boots over his shoulder. But he did not get to wear them. Next day they found his body on the slope, the boots missing.[11]

About the only loot the 26th obtained was a fine brass horn which some Federal bandsman had dropped. The unidentified soldier who found it turned it over to Captain Mickey's band from Salem and the musician who received it used it during the rest of the war. Deduction has established that it was probably a large bass horn known as a bombardon, and since it had a better tone than a like or similar instrument the band had brought with it from Salem, it was played regularly. At the end of the war it was given away because it was "too heavy to carry home." The only other stroke of fortune for the band after Malvern Hill was a furlough just after payday. The bandsmen were so elated that when they reached High Point, North Carolina, in the middle of the night, they "worked off exuberant spirits" by waking up the town with a serenade.[12]

One of the inexplicable events of the war was that after he had gained so crushing a victory, McClellan should order a retreat that same night. Some Federal officers demurred, some wept, some refused at first to obey. Phil Kearney could sense the condition of affairs. "We ought, instead of retreating, follow up the enemy and take Richmond." He declared before a group of officers that the retreat order "can only be prompted by cowardice or treason."[13] By the night of July 3 the last Federal train had reached Harrison's Landing and the Peninsular campaign was ended—ended on a note of despair for the North, in a bath of blood for the Confederate Army.

As much of a test as the battle for Vance and the 26th was the chaos of the defeat, which seemed to overpower the army despite the failure of the Federals to counterattack. Vance's close friend Dr. Edward Warren, of Edenton, his surgeon general throughout most of the war, who was caring for his wounded in the field hospitals, left one of the best accounts of behind-the-lines conditions. As he observed it, "the repulse was complete and overwhelming." The confusion and demoralization were so supreme that "for several hours after the engagement the Confederate army had absolutely no organic existence—was nothing more or less than a heterogeneous mass of stragglers extending from Malvern Hill to Richmond."

His observations give support to the claim of Federal General Kearny that the Federal Army had Richmond within its grasp. That was the doctor's contention: "McClellan could, in fact, have marched during that night or on the succeeding morning into the Confederate capital with as much ease and as little opposition as he actually traversed the space which separated him from the river."[14]

What Vance's 26th and other regiments had experienced, Warren vividly described. Early the next morning he rode over the field and found it "literally gray with Southern jackets—completely paved with the bodies of dead and wounded Confederates." He went into an old icehouse inside the Federal lines and found twelve bodies there. A shell had come through the roof and killed all the occupants. This doctor went on to other battles and, in Africa, to other wars, but when he wrote he told of Malvern Hill: "In all my experience I have never seen anything comparable with the slaughter upon those fatal hillsides." Nothing he ever saw equaled the "desperation of the assault and the obstinacy of the resistance at Malvern Hill."[15]

Another Southern officer going over the field the next morning found it covered with dead and dying. "Men mangled in every conceivable manner, to the number of ten thousand, were strewn out before me."[16]

The appalling nature of the Confederate defeat does not appear to have been emphasized in accounts of the Peninsular Campaign or Seven Days Battles, and at times Malvern Hill is treated as a "drawn battle," because McClellan did retreat and left possession of the battlefield to a Confederate Army which had degenerated in large portion into a disorganized mass.

Malvern Hill rates with both Gettysburg and the battle of Franklin, Tennessee, among the severe repulses suffered by Confederate armies in frontal assaults. The story of the carnage grew at times as the years passed. It came to be told about Franklin that one of the five Confederate generals killed on that field did not fall—that he was shot in such a fierce storm of bullets that the piles of dead around him held him up and he was found standing in military erectness, though stone dead.[17] At Malvern Hill the slopes were covered heavily with the bodies of the attackers, but not heavily enough that any were standing!

## Chapter Eleven

## Governor by a Landslide

Not often has a man thirty-two years old been elected governor of a great state without lifting his hand for it, but that is what happened to Zebulon Baird Vance in the summer of 1862, while his regiment was guarding the Confederate rear at Petersburg, while McClellan was dragging his weary army back from the Peninsula, and Stonewall Jackson was beginning another of his swift movements that, supported by Lee in late August, were to develop into the spectacular campaign of Groveton and Second Manassas.

The situation over the governorship had been complicated in North Carolina because the regularly elected governor, John W. Ellis, had died three months after the coming of war, and the presiding officer of the state senate, a planter from Edgecombe County, Henry T. Clark, had, in the absence of any lieutenant governor, succeeded. The convention, a superbody that had taken the state out of the Union and met on occasions thereafter, judged that the governorship would be open at the expiration of Clark's term as state senator. It set as the election date the first Thursday of August, which fell on August 6, but provided that the soldiers might vote in their camps a week earlier, on July 31. A new legislature was to be elected at the same time and the inauguration would be on the second Monday in September, which that year fell on September 8.

Long before the election a groundswell developed for Vance. The old-time Whigs had not forgotten his performance at Salisbury and the old-time Democrats and their sons observed with satisfaction his solicitude for his own 26th and other regiments, his ardent efforts to raise a legion, and his determined stand at the battle of New Bern. The first opinion around the state was that, instead of putting a young man into the governor's chair, the people in such a trying hour should turn to a veteran, which meant the state's most distinguished citizen of the era before the secession discord, the former senator, former governor, and former cabinet member William A. Graham. He was fifty-eight years old and now, after Fort Sumter, secessionist. But Graham would not entertain a call and attention began to turn gradually but definitely toward Vance. His old friend and antagonist Augustus S. Merrimon, who was becoming one of the strong men of the state, was a leading factor in lining up newspaper sentiment behind him.[1]

One of the fears was that Zeb would reject the governorship as promptly as he had the suggestion that he run for Confederate Congress from his home district. That apprehension was reflected in the letter from Henry W. Miller, of Raleigh, a leader of public opinion in the shifting political faiths of the day, who had been nominated to run against Lawrence O'Bryan Branch for Congress just before Fort Sumter, but withdrew when the guns sounded there. His main distinction seems to be the statement that he "never wanted office, never had office, and never was fed from the Federal crib."[2]

Miller could discern the trend and his words to Vance were sharp: "It will never do in the world for you to withhold your name from the People as a Candidate for Governor. You can do more for the Cause, and for the State, in the Executive Office than you can in the field. Your election is certain. There is great enthusiasm for you."[3]

He added that the secessionists—which meant the originals before Fort Sumter—were creating the impression that Vance would not serve. That should be put to rest. The only thing Zeb's friend wanted him to say, according to Miller, was that he did not seek the office, was honored by his rank in the army, but "if the people of the Old North State elect me their Governor, I cannot refuse to serve them." That is substantially the course Vance was following, and Miller's letter, dated June 18, must have crossed his own announcement that was then being sent to the press.

Edward Joseph Hale, editor of the Fayetteville *Observer*, of which his father, Edward Jones Hale, was proprietor, recorded the incidents of Merrimon's visit in Fayetteville in support of Vance and obviously did not regard Editor Holden enough of a factor in the Vance movement to mention his name. The senior Hale was looked on as the leading Whig editor of the state, though the independent William W. Holden with his *Standard* undoubtedly issued in Raleigh the most complete and intellectually lively paper published in North Carolina. The junior Hale, who had left his editor's desk for the army, was home on leave and escorted Merrimon around the town. He said Merrimon had conferred with "a few friends" and at this meeting it was determined to bring out Vance for governor. Hale's support was essential and Merrimon had come to get it. He and the elder Hale agreed that if Zeb would run, he should address a letter to the editors of the Fayetteville *Observer* giving a sort of platform. Vance wrote the letter but gave it to Holden's *Standard* first, perhaps with the thought that it had a larger spread over the state.[4]

The Raleigh *Register* had come up with a farfetched notion of putting over a candidate without a contest and to do so had begun a movement which turned up one of the least likely men in the state, an obscure Charlotte railroad official named William Johnston. He is not to be identified as the son and aide of Albert Sidney Johnston of the same name, who was serving on the staff of President Jefferson Davis after his father's death at Shiloh. Confusion might have occurred because the candidate bore during the campaign the half-complimentary title of "Colonel," gained from a few months as commissary general.[5]

When they encountered opposition, the backers of Johnston turned to a campaign of verbal eye gouging and groin kicking which the press, hostile to Vance all the way from Richmond to Philadelphia and the North, chorused. The effort might have been more effective had they not made one of their main issues Vance's conduct on the field of New Bern, where all his regiment knew his steadfastness was as firm as that of anyone in the army, and much better than most. The patriotic urge to increase enlistments with the legion venture was named shabby political manipulation. Vance had observed strictly not only the military regulations, but the amenities and niceties of the service, and if he had grumbled that the former unionists were being rebuffed in favor of the original secessionists, it was mainly in the confidence of letters to his wife and not in front of his troops or in the public press.

The chief issue that could be advanced favorable to Vance's opponent,

Johnston, was that he had seen the secession light a little earlier than had Vance, and had come closer to being an original advocate of the parting. The time element was the test of rectitude imposed by a segment of the press. Johnston, like Vance, had been a Whig, but one much less influential and therefore the affiliation was the more readily forgotten. He ran as a "Confederate," but without the qualities that catch the ear and the heart, and had Vance been free to take the stump, Johnston's defeat, disastrous as it was, would likely have been overwhelming. But the colonel of the 26th, after his original announcement, made not one political statement and not one partisan address. He was, in fact, more deeply immersed than normal in his military tasks because his efficient young lieutenant colonel, Burgwyn, was sick on leave during the pre-election period; his experienced major, Carmichael, had been killed at New Bern; and his newly appointed major, James S. Kendall, had become ill with yellow fever (from which he soon died) and had resigned.[6]

One canard was that Vance had not been at the battle of New Bern at all! In those days of slow communication and lack of general education, political orators did not always have to be on guard against speedy refutation. But the Charlotte *Western Democrat* did make a correction of its statement that "Colonel Vance was not in the fight at New Bern" by undertaking to explain that this meant he was never under fire.[7] The Raleigh *Register* showed equal ignorance of the battle when it averred that Vance's regiment was not in the actual fighting but only technically engaged. When a more truthful account was published elsewhere defending Vance, the opposition press insisted that the story was "concocted for party purposes." One of the difficulties in this and other situations was the lag of time between a battle and the publication of the official reports. These reports in both armies were often no more reliable, and at times not so much so, as the press accounts filed by war correspondents on the scene. While they were ordinarily slanted in favor of the regiment or larger unit making the report, they usually were not deliberate fabrications.

When the newspapers supporting Vance got around to it, they were able to give a fair account of the battle, and as the Fayetteville *Observer* said, "The truth is, he fought the enemy for one hour and a half after General Branch had left the field."[8]

One of Vance's militant advocates was Holden, the forty-four-year-old printer and typesetter seasoned to become publisher and editor of the North Carolina *Standard,* of Raleigh, perhaps the leading Democratic organ of the state. He studied law at night school and became an assertive man of positive views. Holden is at times mistakenly credited with making Vance governor in 1862. A reading of the record and developing news stories suggests he was in truth more an expedient hanger-on than a political entrepreneur—that while he gave Vance powerful support, he was a sympathetic cackler and not the hen that laid the egg. Courageous, industrious, domineering, sharp of word and mind, Holden was enough of a factor to threaten and at times exercise control over one or another of the political parties of the state, but he never seemed to harvest the affections of the people, possibly because of his shiftiness and a sort of determination, the curse of many politicians, to either rule or ruin. When he finally reached the governor's chair with the aid of Northern bayonets during the reconstruction years, it was only to be impeached, on reasonable and not political grounds, but he was long a close part of the Vance story and, in 1862, a combative partisan and in his own opinion the explorer, discoverer and commanding general in Vance's cause.

Zeb's announcement, made in a letter to the *Standard* dated June 15 and published June 16, and printed in the Asheville *News* June 26, mentioned that his name had been put forward by a number of meetings and a respectable proportion of the state's newspapers. He recalled that he took the field at an early date with the intention of remaining there until independence was achieved, but he recognized that "a true man should, however, be willing to serve wherever the public voice may assign him." If his fellow citizens believed he could contribute more as governor than in his military assignment, he would not feel at liberty to decline. "I should consider it the crowning glory of my life to be placed in a position where I could most advance the interests and honor of North Carolina." He went on to deprecate the growth of party strife and prayed for "unity of sentiment and fraternity of feeling" in the prosecution of the war.

One of the minor campaign developments was the disclosure that while candidate Johnston lived in Charlotte, he was president of a South Carolina railroad and actually had his office in Columbia, South Carolina. His business concerns were with the southern state. The reaction of the Iredell *Express* of Statesville to this revelation was to undertake to show that Vance had no claim on the state, either: "We have no doubt," said the *Express,* "that the *Standard's* candidate Col. Vance, desires to serve his State as best he can but what has he ever done for her? The *Standard* can not point to a single monument except his speeches, which are well enough in sound." Then the newspaper almost belied its own words: "Col. Vance is a gallant soldier, and for that we honor him as well as many other good qualities of head and heart. We deeply regret that he affiliates with a journal so corrupt as the *Standard*."

The Asheville *News* took some delight in recalling that as recently as 1859 the *Standard* had been attacking Vance among the Black Republicans and Southern Know-Nothings, but now he was being styled "the glorious Vance." "How can Col. Vance's friends have any confidence in the present professions of the political gambler of the *Standard?*"[9]

While the newspapers bickered, Vance remained with his command at Petersburg, Virginia. As his political document, he stood on his letter of June 15. His group was known as the "Conservatives," and the opposition was the "Confederate" party. The principles of the Confederate party were stated succinctly on an electioneering card: "An unremitting prosecution of the war; the war to the last extremity; complete independence; eternal separation from the North; no abridgement of Southern territory; no alteration of Southern boundaries; no compromise with enemies, traitors, or tories. Jeff. Davis, Our Army and the South."[10] Vance issued no platform. The newspapers of the state split about evenly on the two men and the issues, such as could be developed. Aside from Holden, but perhaps of greater influence, Vance had the stanch support of Edward J. Hale and his Fayetteville *Observer*.

The selection of Vance as a candidate was something of a reaction against the effort of the few oldtime Democratic newspapers to reach an agreement on a candidate and avoid a campaign. The South after secession was, in fact, substantially without political parties, and certainly without national parties. One reason was the nearly universal acceptance of secession, over which parties had battled before the war. Another was the constitutional provision, regarded as wise by many Southerners, that the President of the Confederate States, who held a six-year term, could not succeed himself. The President was consequently aloof from politics. Partisan interest slackened, candidates usually ran for the Confederate Congress as individuals more than as party representatives, and a one-party system, or more accurately a no-party system, was, in general, enthroned.

But North Carolina, as in the matter of secession, differed in the field of politics, where partisanship was not subdued but aggravated. Holden was one who condemned the no-contest idea, saying in the *Standard* that "Honest men do not fear a public discussion, but only the venal and corrupt." That was a little beside the point because none was trying to corrupt the office, but Holden, who had become a master of vigorous prose, was undoubtedly correct in his demand that an accounting be made to the public in wartime just as in peace.

As early as March 8, before the battle of New Bern, the *Standard* was inveighing: "We might give our bodies to be burned as a sacrifice to Southern liberty; and still after all this, there are secession partyans in this State who would insult our ashes and say we were too slow. . . . If we did not believe the people in August next would put their feet on the partyans referred to, we would despair of free government itself." A little later, on March 28, the *Standard* was analyzing the battle of New Bern on the basis of authentic information about how the right wing of the army had withdrawn in orderly manner: "This retreat by Col. Vance and Lieut. Col. Hoke evinces fine judgment and military skill and merits the applause of the country." Here was accurate intelligence set against the preposterous charges that Vance had not fought in the battle at all!

The Asheville *News,* Vance's old competitor, which had not been unfriendly to him as a soldier, hit at the candidate by striking at Holden: "The Raleigh *Standard* by insidious appeals to the late Union party, has succeeded in sewing the seeds of dissension." The *Standard* had "traduced Graham" but had found him "too old to be caught in a trap," then was trying to take up Vance because he was popular. "The editor of the *Standard* is determined there shall be strife." The *News* did see that "for several years he [Holden] has itched distressingly for the position himself," which seems to have been at the heart of Holden's intransigence now and on later occasions, but the *News* avowed, in a hand-washing gesture, that "if a curse of a divided and distracted people is to be visited upon us we do not intend to be responsible for it in any way."

Then this home town newspaper moderated its attitude: "Col. Vance has acted as a true man and patriot in the struggle for independence. We honor him for it, and had his name been presented under the same circumstances as Mr. Johnston's was, would have urged the propriety of casting for him an undivided vote." This editorial of June 19 bore the signature of Thomas W. Aiken, editor. When Vance's official announcement of his candidacy came to the mountains a week later, the

*News* showed impartiality: "We advise the freemen of the State to look dispassionately and without prejudice at the facts as they stand before them, spurning all attempt at dictation, vote as the interests of their country demand."[11] The *News* had announced for Johnston on June 5, and held to him until the election.

Not Johnston's contacts with South Carolina, but North Carolina's relationship with Virginia proved an underlying, scarcely mentioned, but ever-present factor in the campaign. Something of the feeling generated in colonial times, that Virginia looked patronizingly on North Carolina as a cast-off province, became again a subconscious element in the North State attitude. Vance's rejoinder that the Virginians who taunted his men needed tar on their heels was not out of keeping with the common lack of cordiality. Researchers still have been unable to unearth any solid cause for the latent hostility between the two states one and two centuries ago. The best reason advanced is that North Carolina's coast and outer banks, especially along her northern waterfront, rendered impossible the development of adequate harbor facilities, with the result that this area and much of the piedmont depended on Norfolk, Virginia, and the Carolina planters felt dissatisfied with the treatment accorded them by Virginia shipmasters and exporters and tradesmen.

Even before Vance's election (after which the relationship flared into an open controversy), North Carolinians were becoming restless because their soldiers were too frequently commanded by Virginia officers. J. G. de Roulhac Hamilton, an able historian of the state in an earlier generation, rated this antipathy against Virginia as one of the influential side elements which entered the campaign in Vance's behalf; the *Standard* did not miss the opportunity to comment freely on the unwonted Virginia hostility. Nothing could have reacted more to Vance's advantage than that the Richmond *Enquirer* should choose this time for launching a series of attacks on North Carolina, apparently for no more than whimsical reasons, because none could complain justifiably about the manner in which the state was meeting its war obligations.[12]

Though there was substantial public interest in the approaching election, the attention of the press and people was focused more on the current glories of Stonewall Jackson, one of Vance's idols. The Asheville *News* took delight in telling that "Stonewall's face is said to be as sour as a half gallon of crab apple vinegar in a black jug," but it could be lighted. "Two things on earth relieve his acidity. When a park of ten pieces of artillery opens on him at point blank range his deep set eyes gleam merrily like a tallow candle in an excavated pumpkin. When he sees a four-horse wagon captured from the Yankees, he grins horribly a ghastly smile like a hyena over the corpse of a defunct Affaganistan."[13] Clearly, had Stonewall been a candidate in North Carolina— and he might have claimed the state as his home because his wife was living there[14]—Vance would have had little better chance with the electorate than Johnston.

Even Stonewall's horse came in for praise during interludes from political news. The horse was as peculiar as Stonewall himself. "He is a young horse with a very old head" and he had "very odd manners." Stories told how the devout Jackson would go to sleep in church. As to the horse: "When his master dismounts to go to bed under a tree the horse lies down also, stretches out his forefeet, puts his head between them and begins to snore like a Christian."[15]

After the Federal Army had obtained a lodgment on the North Carolina coast, President Lincoln, under his plan of setting up state governments loyal to Washington in Southern areas as they were conquered, appointed Edward Stanly as military governor of North Carolina. Stanly was a native of New Bern and a former Whig Congressman. On May 26, 1862, President Lincoln made him a brigadier general and sent him back to the scenes of his boyhood, ostensibly to rule North Carolina from the new state capital, by Federal designation, of New Bern. About his only services were to act as a medium of communication with individuals in the North and forward letters suggesting that North Carolina abandon the struggle.

One letter chanced to help Vance's prospects. Ex-Senator George E. Badger, the former Whig unionist, wrote to a New Yorker and transmitted the message through Stanly, and it came to have bearing on the campaign. Badger made the letter public, showing it to be a defense of the former unionists and a reassurance that they were deeply loyal to the Confederacy, and fully opposed to reunion with the Washington government. Northern newspapers, misunderstanding the situation in North Carolina, were looking toward the election of Vance for a signal that North Carolina was sickening of secession. Badger's letter was their answer.[16]

Some of Vance's opponents were proclaiming that his success would interfere with the Confederate war effort, though how they could attribute lukewarmness to one who had just stormed up the slopes of

Malvern Hill remained a question which only the politicians could answer. Clearly the public was not impressed. Most certainly neither were his troops, many of whom had beseeched him in advance of the battle, knowing that he was a candidate and sensing that he would be elected, not to risk the welfare of the state by exposing himself to an enemy fire that manifestly would be destructive. He brushed aside the suggestion and, like any good colonel, led his men.

A few could not yet recognize that Zeb was serious and responsible, in the midst of a desperate war. Said the North Carolina *Whig,* "If the state is to be governed by fun and jokes, Vance is the man."[17] This paper had forecast only a few days earlier that three months after Vance's election North Carolina would be invaded by a Yankee army of 50,000 men. "People of North Carolina," rang its call, "your liberties are worth a world of Vances and Holdens."[18] While Holden was in some respects helpful, he was also the heaviest load Vance had to carry.

Many did vote for Vance in the belief that he would be inclined toward peace more than Johnston, and would not press the new conscript law, but he could be more accurately described as the war candidate than the peace candidate. When his own regiment voted, of approximately seven hundred ballots only seven were marked against him. The total army vote was 15,374. Probably the majority of the North Carolina soldiers in 1862 were not of voting age. Vance received 11,683 soldier ballots, his opponent 3,691. Johnston had difficulty in establishing himself as the war candidate when he was occupying a safe railroad berth in Charlotte. Nor could he make of Vance a peace candidate when Zeb was at the head of a rugged combat regiment.

Vance won a landslide victory with the civilian as well as the army vote. His total was 54,423 to Johnston's 20,448, a majority for Vance of 33,975. Of the eighty counties in the state at that time, Johnston triumphed in but twelve.[19]

Even before the returns were available Zeb was elated and shared his enthusiasm in a letter to his wife: "I have every assurance that I will be governor by a large majority, but it is not certain. From 38 regiments in the army I have recd more than two to one."[20]

When the results were clear, Zeb took his farewell from the regiment which was never to lose the flavor of his association with it, though perhaps a majority of the lads he commanded would fall in later battles. The regiment, together with onlookers who swelled the crowd to about two thousand men, gathered on the night of August 15 in the Petersburg camp to tell their old commander farewell, hear his parting words, and present him with a testimonial sword, handed to him from the regimental officers by Sergeant Major L. L. Polk, legislator and editor in later years and founder of the *Progressive Farmer*. Captain Mickey's regimental band had returned that day from its leave in Salem and participated. Vance's talk dwelt not on the pleasant promises familiar to politicians but on the rigors the men could expect in a battle to the finish with the Northern invaders. He left camp the following morning never again to don in active service the uniform he had come to love.

Said a member of the 26th: "Though rejoicing that he had been chosen Governor of the State by such a complimentary majority, with a pang of regret we saw Colonel, now Governor-elect Z. B. Vance, exchange the sword for the helm of State. He received almost the unanimous support of the regiment . . . which well attests his popularity among the troops."[21]

Passing through Raleigh, Vance made a unifying address which the press received favorably and which, like that to his troops, promised vigorous prosecution of the war. He talked in serious vein and as if to signal a new phase in his conduct, which involved a less outward revelation of his inner joy of living, he told a heckler who called for a story that the well of his jocundity had dried up. The speech was delivered in front of the Yarborough Hotel, where a good Saturday night crowd assembled and shouted for the governor-elect. In his call for unity he conceded that "some hard things had been said in the campaign" and statements had been made that he had not fought at New Bern and Malvern Hill. He said he might be willing to admit he had never seen either of those fights, "but I keep remembering bullets whistling by my ears."

He called for an adjournment of partisanship. "Now the first, great absorbing purpose should be to beat back our invaders and establish the independence of this glorious Confederation of States . . . Gentlemen, our people are properly and terribly in earnest . . . I want you and I want all the people of the State to aid me with *all* their energies, all their means, and all their confidence in this mighty struggle until the Confederate States shall stand proudly among the nations, free and independent."[22]

The election returns came to the mountains slowly and although Vance was the apparent winner, judged from the first trickle of reports, not until August 21 was the Asheville *News* able to announce—graciously, for a paper that had opposed him—the popular verdict: "The returns . . . are not all in, but enough has been received to show that

Col Vance is elected by a large majority. . . . Col Vance is the youngest man ever elected to this responsible position, being only 32 years of age. That his position will be no bed of roses needs no argument to demonstrate. . . . Firmness, energy and financial skill are requisite. . . . Taken up, and without an effort on his part, elected to the highest office in the gift of the State, he has but to follow the dictates of his heart, and guard with jealous care the important interests committed to his care—discarding from his confidence the bitter and ultra men . . . he can make for himself a name as enduring as time."[23] Before the end of the year this newspaper, once strong in its opposition, was saying "In the election of Gov Vance the right man was certainly put in the right place."

Someone from Virginia, who left no better footprints than the pseudonym "Virginius," wrote a letter to the Norfolk, Virginia, *Landmark*, January 15, 1885, saying he happened to be in Asheville in the late summer of 1862, recovering from a wound, when the newly elected governor came home from the army for a brief visit before assuming his duties at Raleigh. Vance was admired by the mountain people but many of them had no interest in or sympathy for the war. Some were hostile to the Confederate cause. When the word spread across the hills and valleys that Vance was in Asheville, crowds of country and mountain folk came to town to shake hands with him. Then they called on him for remarks and he spoke from the courthouse steps. His uncompromising stand on fundamental principles was at once disclosed.

"I heard the address," wrote Virginius. "The youthful looking orator began by telling the people that he had heard many of them were complaining about the burdens of the war, when, happily for themselves, they knew nothing of war.

" 'You should go into our sister state of Virginia!' Vance declared, 'to see her bloody fields, blackened homesteads, and fleeing families to learn what war is.' "

Virginius continued: "Then he told them he had heard many of them had voted for him because they thought he would not enforce the conscript law. That law, he said, he considered a wise and proper measure. . . . Concluding he said, and I think I give the very words: 'All I have to say is, that if there is any in North Carolina who ought to be in the army, and who is not there, I will make the state too hot to hold him.' I had never seen Governor Vance before, but there was a ring of truth and honor about him which every act of his subsequent career has confirmed as being the very soul of the man."[24]

Vance made another address while in Asheville and it was of the same purport. Four volunteer companies passed through town and the governor-elect was again called on. Again he pledged himself to enforce the conscript law, which had become the number one irritant in the mountains, and he reiterated that he would make the state too hot to hold the recreants. The law was necessary and should receive the cordial support of every patriot. His other pledge, and it proved to be no idle one, was to do all in his power to provide for the comfort of the army.[25]

The inauguration in Raleigh on September 8 smacked a little of the gala days before the deadly pall was cast over the state by the seriousness of war and by the casualty returns. The Johnny Reb Band of Salem, from Vance's own 26th regiment, persuaded Colonel Burgwyn that their presence was urgently needed to give Zeb a good induction, and gained added time so they might tour several eastern North Carolina towns and inspire the citizenry with concerts. Diarist Leinbach told the story of it. The band polished their instruments "nice and bright" and on the Saturday (September 6, 1862) before inauguration Monday (September 8) left Petersburg, and arrived in Raleigh that evening. The committee of arrangements met them at the station, and put them in a big bus, in which they rode around the city that night playing some of their choice army airs. They had good rooms at the Yarborough, the leading hotel, and "received excellent treatment."

On inauguration day the band marched from the hotel to the west front of the capitol and played a concert while the crowd was gathering. Perhaps the most important offering was a new "Governor Vance's Inauguration March" composed by Edward Leinbach, brother of the diarist Julius A. Leinbach, which was here played publicly for the first time. The diarist gave a reaction to Zeb's remarks: "The Governor's address was short, but good, and seemed to please his hearers. After he was done speaking, we again played to dismiss the crowd."[26]

Vance in his inaugural address promised again full enforcement of the conscript act and did much else to allay the heat generated by the spirited newspaper election campaign. Of secession: "It was not a whim or sudden freak, but the deliberate judgment of our people. Any other course would have involved the deepest degradation, the vilest dishonor, and the direst calamity. . . ."

Foreshadowing how he would marshal civilian sentiment and put the state to work, he called for unity and industry. Success would depend quite as much on the people at home as on the army. "One of the most vital elements of our success is harmony. On this great issue of existence itself let there, I pray you, be no dissenting voice. . . ." Newspapers of both factions and citizens of all beliefs and faiths applauded the address.

The lately opposing North Carolina *Whig* chimed in, but harshly: "Well the election is over, Col Vance seems to be the new Governor, of course we succumb to the majority we done what we could for Mr. Johnston as was our duty no doubt he would have made a good governor but it was otherwise ordained, never mind Mr. Johnston, we will give you another chance if nothing happens."[27] The editor was as stingy with punctuation as with felicitations, the paragraph having just four commas and nothing more. Was it pulling Vance's leg with hillbilly jargon? Or was the editor on leave?

When the *Whig* reported Vance's inaugural it was in better rhetorical form and more hospitable disposition. It referred to the "perspicacity of ideas which it embraces, classical purity of its language, elegance of its style, force of thought—political matter never surpassed." Then it told the instance of the editor who in opposing Henry Clay remarked that his mouth was "large and unseemly," to which a more friendly editor replied that "Mr. Clay has a mouth that generally speaks for itself." The *Whig* enjoined: "Read Gov Vance's Inaugural; it speaks for itself."[28]

One of the first to write him, on August 15, was his old professor, David L. Swain, who had been elected governor of North Carolina just thirty years before. He had some good advice. He saw that Zeb owed nothing for his election.

"Your election by the people," he said, ". . . will afford you an opportunity to discard party and the selfish tools of party. Beware of hasty committals to applicants for office. Gov. Clark has taken sides with high soldiers. Will not one able and trusty friend suffice?"[29]

He made the practical suggestion of a private secretary possessing "learning, talent and integrity," and supplied two names. One of these individuals, Richard H. Battle, friend of Zeb's Chapel Hill days and son of his old mathematics professor, became his confidential secretary and one of the reasons why he was a great governor.

On September 6, 1862, two days before taking office as governor, Zeb became the father of a fourth son, named Thomas Malvern Vance. The charge up the Virginia hillside had not been forgotten.

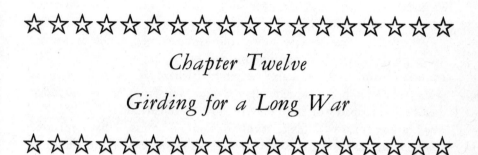

## Chapter Twelve

## *Girding for a Long War*

Vance at this period was tall, straight, "handsome of form and feature," too heavy surely, carrying 230 pounds, but the weight in the middle years he was now entering was mainly in his big shoulders and full chest and not yet at the waist. A good many pounds were stored in the muscles of his large, thick neck.

Possibly from the latent power that seemed to go with him, or from a sort of magnetism which individuals sometimes possess from a source which is not clear, he caught the full attention of everyone the moment he came into a room or appeared on a platform, and as one of his closest acquaintances said, "his listeners gazed at him with tireless and ever increasing admiration."

Such comments sounded excessive but had a foundation. Something accounted for the fact that this young man who issued no platform, made no promises, conducted no campaign, and was running with a party hurriedly thrown together, loosely named the "Conservatives," that had never been entered in a campaign before—something, indeed caused him to triumph in the balloting by a count of better than two to one. The phenomenon is the more impressive when it is considered that he had the hostility of much of the Southern and the apparent backing of the Northern press, and that he ran against an original secessionist who, however weak he seemed to be in the final tally, was at least carefully selected and judged by his backers to be a likely winner.

When Locke Craig came to examine the reasons for Vance's political triumphs he struck on this same quality. "His personal appearance was unique," said the latter-day governor. "He did not look like other men. No man who saw him ever forgot him. His magnetism charmed with a peculiar and indescribable power."[1]

With Vance installed in office, things developed about as former Governor Swain had suggested. Instead of having many advisers, he confided mainly with his able secretary Richard Battle, who was six years his junior but who remembered him well from having attended as a lad the debates of the Dialectic Society at Chapel Hill when Zeb was holding forth with his classical allusions and puns. What impressed young Battle even in those days was Zeb's command of the Bible, of Shakespeare and the other peaks of English literature, and of the romances of Sir Walter Scott, whose works he read and reread avidly both before and after college.

Few families were more closely associated with Vance than the Battles—Judge William Horn Battle, Zeb's professor of mathematics and law, and the two sons, Kemp and Richard. As he observed Vance during three years of war, Richard saw him develop his administrative powers, which the younger man thought were "phenomenal." The relationship became close. Richard took note not only of the governor's work methods, but also of his family and social conduct. Richard expressed the surprise of a man from the piedmont or lowlands. Zeb's manner contained "nothing of the roughness or want of refinement, which one would naturally expect in a successful politician from our mountain district." He was "kind, attentive and indulgent" to his wife and children, and regardful of the feelings of the domestic servants. Richard could observe readily, because he was frequently a visitor and worker at the governor's home at the southern end of Fayetteville Street, known ostentatiously in those days as the "Governor's Palace."[2]

Battle was the only person who helped Vance on his messages and state documents, and respecting them he made no pretense of being a "ghost writer." Vance did his own composing. Battle helped mostly with the "copying and arranging," as he put it. Because of the demands of callers, the governor could not undertake serious composition in his office in the capitol. When under pressure he had to work at the "palace," with Battle often sitting alongside, and the orders were that they were not to be interrupted. Immersed as he might be in some message to the legislature, the governor would toss it aside the minute they entered the dining room for the midday meal. He would become "easy, natural and sparkling" with his four boys and his "little red-haired wife."[3]

Hattie Vance, whose hair was more auburn than red, took no part in his official work, having her hands full with her active and at times boisterous boys, and with the supervision of the servants. Hattie was strict in her discipline and Zeb would sometimes intercede as an advocate for the children. The servants were devoted to him—Alex Moore, who helped at the office, and William, who waited table, gardened and blacked boots at the "palace."[4]

Zeb liked to break the routine by dropping into his secretary's office to report some experience. He made it a rule to see all callers, which his rugged constitution allowed him to do at a time he was carrying a heavy schedule of official duties and conducting a voluminous correspondence, the important part of which, such as letters to advisers and officials of the Confederate government, was in his own hand. The callers served to keep him in touch with the people, even if they did involve hearing numerous petty problems. He had an executive staff of four persons: his secretary, Battle; two aides, Colonels George Little and David A. Barnes; and an executive clerk, A. M. McPheeters, and with these and with long working hours he carried on the state's business.

The opposition Raleigh *Register* assailed Vance for building up such a large staff, modest as it may seem by modern standards, but the *Standard* promptly came to his defense, though with a note of concern on the score of his availability:

"The Executive office is open to all. It is almost constantly thronged with persons—with officers, soldiers, citizens—who call to see the Governor on business, or to obtain information. Every one is civilly received and respectfully listened to. As the official head of the people, and at the same time their servant, the Governor labors to hear and do justice to all. The labor is, in itself, very heavy; and from what we have seen of it, we fear that the health of the Governor, aided as he is by the two gentlemen referred to [Little and Barnes] will ultimately give way under it."

Then the article, which must have been one of Holden's choice personal compositions at the season when he was feeling his greatest cordiality and deference toward Vance, went into a rhapsody over the manner in which the newcomer had taken the reins of state control. "There is no man in the State to whom so many look, and on whom so many hopes rest, as Governor Vance. We say this in no spirit of flattery, but as the simple truth. He estimates justly, we believe, the responsibilities which are upon him, and he has too much of human nature, though yet a young man, and has too much sound common sense, to be injuriously affected by the position which he fills in the public eye. He is the same plain, honest, straightforward, laborious man, that he was in former days; and though naturally kind-hearted, he can be severely just upon those under his control who are either faithless or negligent in duty."[5]

A story about Vance's callers, which Battle remembered as typical, related to a back-country woman who had an assignment. "Governor," she said, "I want you to search the records and see when I was married. They want to conscript my son John and I say he is not old enough."

"Well, suppose I find out when you were married," said Zeb, "how can I tell when John was born?"

"Oh, Governor," exclaimed the woman, "there's no trouble about that! John was born just three months before we were married."[6]

How General Lee came to appreciate Vance's drollery was illustrated by his treatment of "Aunt Abby" House of Franklin, who became such a privileged character she could go into the governor's office almost at will. She was deeply sympathetic with the Confederates, nursed the wounded, but thought her nephew Jack could stand a furlough because, she claimed, he had bad health. She urged Vance to write a diplomatic sort of letter to General Lee which she would carry personally to Virginia. Zeb wrote the letter, telling Lee that according to the information he could get from the bearer, the soldier's aunt, the odor of a combination of nitrate of potash, sulphur, and carbon (which added up to gunpowder) was the best tonic to soothe Jack's jangled nerves. Aunt Abby took the letter happily and went off to Virginia. In two weeks she was back in such jubilant spirits that Zeb was curious.

"Aunt Abby," he said, "did you give my letter to General Lee?"

"Of course I did," she replied, "and I got Jack a furlough, too."

"What did General Lee say when he read the letter?"

"He laughed and said that Vance was a mighty smart feller."[7]

His secretary Battle noticed that amid the trials of war the governor found time to continue his reading habit.

Probably the key to Vance's indefatigable efforts in the Confederate cause, his readiness to undergo any personal sacrifice, his composition over long hours, and his rugged adherence to the principles of personal liberty and individual freedom for the people of his state in wartime, was to be found in the character of his reading. One of the works which won his absorbed interest during this period was John Lothrop Motley's *The Rise of the Dutch Republic*, which the Harvardite historian had published (at his own expense because commercial publishers would not accept the risk) in 1856, after having lived for many years with the archives in Holland, Belgium, and some of the German principalities.

This monumental history, which Motley had undertaken because he saw similarity between the Prince of Orange and George Washington, appealed strongly to Vance and he talked of it much.[8] He found an analogy different from Motley's. He likened the heroic struggle of the Dutch against Philip II to that being made by his own Southern people for independence, and the resolution of Orange steeled him in his own perseverance. As Motley, Zeb's Yankee idol, had labored ten hours a day "like a brute beast" to get his history completed, Zeb worked even longer hours with equal faithfulness toward the ideal of independence it espoused. Motley had written that "if ten people . . . hate despotism a little more and love civil and religious liberty a little better in consequence of what I have written, I shall be satisfied."[9] Probably he never knew the influence his book had on the conduct of the Confederate war in North Carolina, but Zeb Vance surely could have been counted a leader among any ten Motley might hope to inspire.

Battle noticed that, from this and other reading, Vance's writing style improved. He gained vigor and terseness, and a sort of patriotic fervor entered into his eloquence.

Zeb's reading was of great help to his understanding of military affairs, an essential requirement for a wartime governor. When he had become colonel of the 26th, Lieutenant Colonel Harry King Burgwyn, fresh from the Virginia Military Institute, had taught him the rudiments of drill. The difference between the two men was suggested by a commonly told story of how Vance, drilling a company, had just taken it from "present arms" to "order arms." Burgwyn came rushing over and told Zeb one could not take a company from "present" to "order." The customary method was to go through "port arms." "But I have just done it," replied Zeb simply.[10]

Burgwyn was no help to Vance in a larger understanding of military affairs. Only the best students and readers of military history in the army, such as Stonewall Jackson, could have informed him. As an acquaintance said, "He was fond of taking Cyrus, Alexander, Caesar, Hannibal, and getting the gist of their campaigns, comparing them with similar campaigns of modern times." The observer said he even found time to make detours into astronomy and geology, but history seems to have been his jealous mistress during the war years.[11]

Zeb's task was well near Herculean because the preceding governors, Ellis and Clark, served only partial terms and neither had sufficient opportunity—even had they possessed the capability—to come to grips with the stupendous task of organizing and conducting a populous and independent-minded state through the most bitter and devastating of American wars.

Most of the constructive war measures of North Carolina consequently are attributable to Vance, in either their inception or their effective implementation. That is true as much with the industrial gearing of the state to a surprisingly high rate of production, as with the impetus given to agriculture, which was subjected during the war years to a veritable revolution. Beyond this was the governor's day-by-day attention to the splendid regiments which were continually being recruited and augmented and kept as near to regulation strength as circumstances allowed, and clothed and equipped with the best materials obtainable in the South or overseas.

When Vance took the reins, North Carolina was still almost wholly an agricultural state. Cotton, a lucrative prewar crop, was coming up from the south, and tobacco was coming from the north, chiefly from Virginia, Maryland, and Pennsylvania. The raising of foodstuffs, urgently needed in wartime, had been losing ground. Vance himself provided an excellent summary of the prewar economic situation. Only in relatively small industries such as "naval stores," which meant products of the pine forests, and in fisheries did North Carolina stand ahead of the other Confederate states.

North Carolina had been called the "Rip Van Winkle state" and the "Ireland of America" as late as the 1830s,[12] and was looked on at times as the poorhouse of the South, but by 1861 the state had attained a good level of employment and substantial material welfare. The people were conservative and industrious, and were forging ahead. As Vance said, "Average wealth was considerable, and prosperity and comfort abounded." The public credit was excellent. Along numerous lines the state was far from self-sufficient and had to depend on Northern or European manufacture for even the hand implements of agriculture and home comfort.

Vance used some striking examples: "Like most Southern people, we were slavish tributaries to Northern and British manufacturers; the simplest article in common use bore their impress, from a broom or an axe-handle to a water bucket."[13]

Though the South grew all the cotton it needed, it manufactured few textiles, but shipped its product in bales to the New England and British mills. North Carolina was ninth among the eleven seceding states in cotton production but third in general manufacturing. Still, all the cotton manufacturing plants in the state would not aggregate a capital investment of over a million and a half dollars, and the wool manufactories not over $300,000. "Of cotton goods," said Vance, "not half a supply, even of the coarser sorts, were made for our own consumption; of woolen goods, scarcely a tenth."[14]

North Carolina had been passing out of the "poorhouse" stage for three decades and there was nothing stagnant or decadent about the society over which Vance was called on to preside; rather it was dynamic and high spirited, with fewer class distinctions among the white population than prevailed in some of the other states where cotton had been longer enthroned. Then as now, North Carolina agriculture was conducted by numerous small farmers instead of great plantation owners. Already the state was promising to develop a number of thriving cities of moderate size, enterprising and forward-looking, with none large enough to dominate the culture or economy of the general population. North Carolina was lacking in homogeneousness, there being little social or economic kinship between the plantation dwellers along the rim of the Dismal Swamp of the northeast and the small farm residents of faraway Cherokee County in the rolling countryside and fertile valleys of the southwest corner. The state stretched 503 miles from the Atlantic coast to the Tennessee border at the crest of the Great Smokies. Vast areas had no railroad connections.

The slave population was centered largely in the east-central portion, roughly around the Raleigh neighborhood and extending northward toward Virginia, a tobacco-growing area. In three counties, Edgecombe, with Tarboro the county seat; Halifax, with a town of the same name; and Warren, on the Virginia border, slaves outnumbered white residents. Other large slave counties were Wake, the county of Raleigh, where domestic slaves were numerous, and Granville, another Virginia-border tobacco-producing county. The whole white population was 631,489; the slave population, 331,081; and the state had 30,097 free Negroes.[15] Little slavery existed in the mountains and that mostly of a household character in the towns, or, in the case of the farms, individual workers.

In total population North Carolina was fifth among the eleven seceding states, but in white population she was third, with only Virginia and Tennessee having larger white populations. Vance rated the state seventh in wealth among the eleven, fourth in the value of all agricultural products. Her rank was third in the production of wheat, rye, and oats; fourth in horses and cattle; and though third in manufacturing, that did not imply any manufacturing or heavy industries of consequence. The state, like the rest of the South, lagged far behind the North in substantially all types of industrial output.

About the only way such a far-flung state with diversity of geography, enterprise and political interest could be welded into a unit for the prosecution of a relentless war was through inspirational leadership supplied by some commanding figure who could rally the people irrespective of their economic or partisan outlook, and fire them emotionally with an absorbing devotion to the task of supporting the armies and repelling the enemy. That is what Vance with his unsparing industry, commanding oratorical powers, and zealous personal leadership set out to accomplish.

As has been said of the South, an agricultural people without the appliances to put an army into the field "were converted into soldiers, as with a magical wand. There were no looms to weave the cloth; no furnaces to mould the cannon; no plants to make the muskets; no outputs of lead for shot; no manufactories for powder in all this fair Southland."[16]

The transformation of the state was evidenced by the busy communities mainly in the piedmont, and by the increasing production figures. Of such requirements as cotton, wool, and iron products, and shoes and leather, the state under Vance's stimulus soon was not only filling its own needs and supplying large quantities of goods to the army, but also selling heavily to other Confederate states.

Vance may be looked on as the guardian and patron saint of the North Carolina textile industry almost from the beginning. When he was in the state legislature and North Carolina textiles consisted of a few minor plants, he had sought to stimulate home manufacture. He introduced an amendment to the revenue bill of 1855 providing that all persons trafficking in ready-made clothing not manufactured in North Carolina would be required to pay a tax of one per cent on each hundred dollars of invested capital. The bill was obviously unconstitutional by old standards and was defeated, but it disclosed Vance's interest in this feeble industry which he was able to nourish during the war years.[17]

Vance from the beginning crossed swords with Confederate Quartermaster General Abraham C. Myers, a graduate of West Point in 1833 (the period just after Jefferson Davis and Lee), who had continued in the regular army, mainly in the supply services, until his state of South Carolina seceded. Colonel Myers, while diligent, adamant, and quarrelsome, like many good quartermasters, did not appear to recognize that war had become big business, with whole societies involved, but thought in terms of the armies that had gone against the Seminoles and Mexico. Vance's first clash with him came in October, 1862, over leather which the quartermaster's agents were procuring in North Carolina.

Leather was exceedingly scarce, partly because none had thought to conserve it properly in the early stages of the war. In civilian circles the army was charged with the principal waste. No effort was made in the first year or more of the war to save the hides of beef slaughtered for army rations.[10] Perhaps it was simply another manifestation of the impression that the war would be of brief duration.

By the winter of 1862-63 the shortage had become acute and most of those who had leather demanded excessive prices. Speculation was rampant. A tanner in Henderson County in the western section wrote to the Raleigh *Standard* inquiring if hides could be purchased in the capital city, and the reply was of course in the negative. He reported that persons who described themselves as government agents were in the western counties buying up all the leather and shoes they could obtain and taking them out of the state. This was probably a part of the legitimate Confederate effort under the ordnance and quartermaster departments.[19]

Uncertain, the Raleigh newspaper sounded a warning: "Persons who sell to such individuals should always beware that they are *bona fide* government agents. No encouragement whatever should be given to speculators in leather or any other article of prime necessity."[20]

Vance's complaint was that two thirds of the state's leather was being made into harnesses when the crying need was for shoes. Always aware of the improvisations of mountain life, he wondered why harness strong enough for all normal purposes could not be made of heavy cotton goods, such as was being found satisfactory in North Carolina. Vance suggested in a letter to President Davis that the Confederate government terminate all its leather contracts in the state and allow the full output of the North Carolina tanneries to go into the manufacture of shoes.[21]

Davis replied to Vance a week later with a hair-splitting letter which pointed out that the Quartermaster Department had "very inconsiderable" contracts in North Carolina and those Vance spoke of must be of the Ordnance Bureau.[22] A difficulty in the Confederate organization for war—which Davis might have corrected at this moment—was that shoes were indeed under the quartermaster while harness was under the ordnance branch and, instead of leather being allocated in keeping with the greatest needs, competitive buying prevailed between the departments and between the states and the central government as well. Davis thought the suggestion of utilizing the leather supplied for shoes was commendable but said Myers thought cotton harness, while perhaps satisfactory for plantation use, was unfit for the wear and tear to which army harness was subjected. Davis sent Vance's letter to the Secretary of War with instructions that "as far as possible" the leather of the South should be used for shoes. What Vance needed was an experimental laboratory for the development of heavy cotton harness, which was not impractical, given a little time for research and testing.[23]

Less than two weeks after assuming office, Vance found Quartermaster Myers beginning a bombardment to have the state turn over its clothing contracts to the central government. This became the issue in a long argument in which Vance never yielded. The merits in the case are not easily determined. Undoubtedly in theory the contracts for army clothing should have have been held by the central government, but there was no reason why it should not have gone out and made contracts of its own, instead of calling on Vance to surrender those he held. Vance was busily engaged in setting up new textile plants, in trying to prevent profiteering, and in putting women and children to work spinning and weaving and sewing clothing in the homes, and he held no monopoly over such enterprise. But the more important consideration is that Vance did produce the uniforms, and in a volume that was not likely to be attained by the quartermaster general. Myers probably could have achieved better results for the cause by co-operating with Vance and winning him over than by opposing him.[24]

The conflict of methods arose because the Confederacy, being cast into war before it had opportunity to prepare for it or even organize a departmental government, called on the states at the outset to clothe and equip their regiments. Originally the soldier had to clothe himself, with the Confederacy making reimbursement. Then, as a second step, the soldier was allowed money for the purchase of uniforms and shoes. The North Carolina legislature passed a law under which the state assumed the duty of supplying uniforms, shoes, and blankets in return for which the state would receive from the Confederacy the aggregate of the commutations due the soldier for his equipment, which was $50 a year. The Confederate War Department assented to this arrangement.

In October, 1862, the Confederate government discontinued the commutation and assumed the responsibility of providing for the soldiers directly. Even before the Confederacy abolished the commutation system, but in anticipation of the action, Myers again wrote to Vance saying he found the manufacture of clothing still carried on by state agents, and: "I think it is very desirable, with a view to systematizing and extending this branch of the service, that there should be a complete transfer to the Confederate Authorities of all contracts and facilities held by North Carolina for the manufacture of Army clothing." He asked Vance to sanction the transfer and allow the same staff to supervise the work.

Vance replied through his aide David A. Barnes, saying he was unwilling to make such a transfer without consulting the general assembly which would meet soon. All through the bombardment, lasting two years, which continued after General Alexander R. Lawton of South Carolina and Georgia became quartermaster general in the autumn of 1863, Vance was adamant in his refusal, although he readily turned over his surpluses of uniforms to out-of-state commands. The point often lost sight of is that at the beginning of the war North Carolina's cotton manufactories were so limited that the state was a heavy importer of clothing, fabrics and textiles. It shot ahead under the stimulus provided by Vance until a substantial, thriving industry had been established and Fayetteville had become the leading cotton manufacturing center in the South. Since the state was third from the bottom in the Confederacy in the production of cotton, there was no economic reason why it should take top place as a manufacturer of cotton goods. Vance stated that the capital invested in cotton manufactories in North Carolina at the beginning of the war was less than $1,500,000.[25] Recent research by Dr.

Richard W. Griffin, editor of the *Textile History Review*, has placed the capitalization of North Carolina's thirty-nine mills operating in 1860 at $1,272,750.[26] It is difficult to estimate the wartime growth. Such factors entered as the loss of the state's records, inflation, and the fact that Sherman's army and other forces in the final invasion flattened the industry and leveled or burned the mills. Despite this severe setback, in 1869 the forty-six mills listed had a property valuation of $2,272,-000.[27] These figures are indeed puny compared with the state's present textile industry. They fail to show the sharpness of the spur applied by Vance's contracts, under which he bought the full output of all the textile mills in the state.

A good reason for Vance's desire to retain the contracts and supply North Carolina troops could be seen in a letter from Lieutenant Thomas J. Jarvis, of the 8th North Carolina, who told on November 3, 1862, that he had only thirty blankets for his entire company, which was suffering from the cold, with not half enough to go around, and said, "I have made requisition on the Q.M. time and again but cannot get them."[28] This company could not send home for blankets or carpeting because their county, Currituck, was inside the enemy lines.

Direct pleas like this made Vance want to look first after his North Carolina regiments. Quartermaster General Myers informed him on December 8, 1862, that the Confederate government would no longer reimburse the state for clothing and equipment, and reiterated his request that the state turn over its contracts, but it was again a vain entreaty.[29]

Other factors entered into the governor's firmness. Before he became governor and took over the responsibility of supplying clothing, the press was complaining that North Carolina troops were shabbily uniformed. "The regiments from other States are well clothed," said the Raleigh *Standard*, "because the other States have no war establishments and ours has, and their troops are turned over as fast as raised to the Confederate government." The paper charged that North Carolina had on hand an immense quantity of "slop shop clothing which no captain will purchase if he can possibly avoid it," but which the Raleigh authorities were forcing on the soldiers at $4 a shirt and $4 a pair of drawers. North Carolina troops in the summer of 1862 were declared to be the worst clad of any around Richmond, the fault being not with the legislature but with Governor Clark's administration. Meantime the

Confederate government, relying on the state as the provider, was turning its back on North Carolina units. A captain in Virginia "picked out an excellent uniform for his men in Richmond, but the Richmond government refused to give it to him though his regiment was in rags."[30]

Clearly the state's determination to equip and clothe its own troops worked a hardship on the men early in the war, before Vance's inauguration. Soon they were the best uniformed and best equipped of the army. Holden's *Standard* had wanted the duty turned over to the Confederate government "where it properly belongs," but Vance held the contrary view. Even after Vance took over, Holden was calling the state clothing and adjutant general's departments "cesspools of corruption." Vance and the Conservative party were sometimes denounced as traitors.[31] Instead of abolishing the system, Vance made it the most productive of any source of supply in the Confederacy.

How extensively he made distributions of clothing to army units from other states cannot be determined with any accuracy, but his disposition appears to have been generous even before his wholesale allotment of uniforms to Longstreet's Corps, which did not include a single North Carolina company. Uniforms of North Carolina origin had a manner of working their way into the other commands, where they were not sufficiently prized to satisfy Vance, who was constantly aware of the effort that went into their procurement. Though the governor might supply the clothing, he had no control over it after it reached the army.

Finally, late in 1863, he felt impelled to write to General Lee directly and ask gently, "Would it be within your power to suppress the practice among soldiers of selling clothing?" He declared he had recently "been much outraged" to see English shoes, jackets and flannel shirts, "which I had imported at so much risk," being worn by civilians and slaves. The difficulty, as he reported it to Lee, was that regimental quartermasters would come with requisitions for from 800 to 1,000 men when there were not half that many in their regiments. They procured a double supply, with the result that when Vance encountered a temporary shortage in his imports or manufactures, other soldiers got nothing. Zeb had the temerity to give General Lee some hints about soldiering: "The extra amount taken to the field is an encumbrance lost on the first hasty retreat and constitutes a dangerous temptation to the honesty of the parties in charge. In every respect it is desirable that their requisition should come in approved only according to their actual present and not prospective wants." He expressed confidence that Lee would recognize the difficulties "under which the Home Department labors in procuring supplies"—difficulties which were increasing constantly because of the diminishing resources of the South.[32]

One of Vance's major problems was common to the South—the curbing of speculators and extortionists. His most effective weapon was arousing public sentiment. In a letter written ten days after his inauguration he inveighed against the high prices prevailing and declared it appeared to be impossible to clothe and shoe the troops.

"The Cotton & Woolen factories have advanced their prices to an unheard of extent," he declared, "and refuse to make contracts which would prevent them from raising next week, if they saw proper. The price of common shirting, for example, is fifty cents per yard." To provide every North Carolina soldier with two shirts and two pairs of drawers would require a million yards. "This," he continued, "amounts to 500,000 dollars, simply for underclothing. When you take in the shoes and clothing (coats and pants) which have advanced in the same ratio, the sum will be almost incredible." He had obtained calculations indicating that twenty-five cents per yard for cotton cloth would "actually pay the mill owners 300 per cent."[33]

Applications were being made that the convention reassemble to rectify some omissions in the Constitution, and Vance threw his support behind the movement, not to curb the liberties of the individual in wartime, but to protect the average citizen from exploitation at the hands of the unscrupulous element among the millowners. That was the burden of his letter:

"The cry of distress comes up from the poor wives and children of our soldiers also, from all parts of the State. If these prices bear so hard upon the government, what will become of them, when in addition we consider the enormous rates at which provisions are selling? It is a subject that distresses me beyond measure, the more so as I feel powerless to remedy any of the evils." He went on to denounce the "inhuman spirit of averice which is rampant in the land."[34]

He had trouble with food speculators as well, who were as active in North Carolina as in Richmond, where they continually drew the ire which the Rebel War Clerk John B. Jones spat into his diary. Complaint against the price gougers—some of whom no doubt could have made out a good case for themselves in view of the erratic but generally downward trend in the value of Confederate money and uncertainty about the acceptance of North Carolina script—was widespread, and the people were reduced to extreme want.

A typical plea was that of R. L. Abernethy, a teacher and Methodist minister of Marion, who entreated: "If it is Constitutional, and if your position as Governor of N. Carolina gives you the power to do so, in the name of *God*, of suffering humanity, of the cries of widows and orphans, *do* put down the Speculation and extortion in this part of the State.

"Here in Marion, beef is being sold to poor wives of soldiers who get $11 per month in the field, at the enormous price of 11 and 12 cents per pound! Leather at $4 per pound! Bacon at 40 & 50 cents per pound! And every thing in proportion.

"If this thing is not put down, our Country is *ruined* forever. Many children of the soldiers in the Camps are nearly barefoot and naked without the possibility of getting clothes or shoes."[35]

Vance early issued a proclamation appealing to the citizens to make voluntary contributions to the Quartermaster Department of shoes, socks, blankets, drawers, shirts, and pants. "If every farmer," he besought, "who has hides tanning would agree to spare one pair of shoes, and if every mother in North Carolina would knit one strong pair of thick cotton or woolen socks for the army, they would be abundantly supplied. A great lot of blankets also might yet be spared from private use and thousands could be made from carpets upon our parlor floors. With good warm houses and cotton bed clothing we can certainly get through the winter better than the soldiers can."[36]

The use of carpeting became widespread in the army for blankets and ponchos. The ponchos gave a varihued appearance to some units of Lee's army as they marched in the rain.

Vance appointed agents to collect the clothing and offered to pay if the owner felt unable to donate it. Then he issued another denunciation of the price gougers: "And now my country men and women, if you have anything to spare for the soldier, in his name I appeal to you for it. Do not let the speculators have it; spurn him from your door and say to him, that our brave defenders have need for it and shall have it without passing through his greedy fingers. Do not place yourself among the extortionists—they are the vilest and most cowardly of your country's enemys and when this war is ended and people come to view the matter in its proper light, you will find that the most detested tories are more respected than they."

Zeb must have been recalling some of his own campaigning experiences when he added a clincher to his appeal: "Remember, when you sit down by the bright and glowing fire, that the soldier is sitting on the cold earth; that in the wind, which is whistling so fearfully over your roof, only making you feel the more comfortable because it harms you not, he is shivering in darkness on the dangerous outpost, or shuddering through the dreary hours of his watch. Remember that when you come forth in the morning, well fed and warmly clad, leading your families toward the spot where the blessed music of the Sabbath-bells tells of the peaceful worship of the God of Peace, the soldier is going forth at the same moment perhaps half fed, after a night of shivering and suffering, to where the roar of artillery and shout of battle announce that he is to die, that your peace and safety may be preserved. Oh remember these things generous and patriotic people of North Carolina, and give freely of your perishable goods to those who are giving all that mortal man can give for your safety and your rights."[37]

The response was instant and generous, as scattered items in the press attest: a collection of $91 at the Henderson Calvary Church; the receipt of blankets, carpeting for blankets, shirts, drawers, and 276 yards of cloth to the Soldiers Aid Society of Asheville; contributions elsewhere throughout the state. The spirits of North Carolina were buoyed as it entered the second winter of the war by confidence in Confederate triumph. From the New York *Times* came the acknowledgment, reprinted in North Carolina: "Another year may see anarchy and civil war extended through the Free States and the Southern Confederacy triumphant and unassailable."[38]

In November Vance put through the legislature a drastic law prohibiting the distillation of liquor from "any kind of grain including rice, also potatoes, sugar cane seed, syrup, molasses, peas, peanuts, and dried fruit of every description." Observed the Raleigh *Progress*: "We learn that Gov Vance said recently that he had determined that not another Still should run in the State during his term. He thinks as all other honest people do that bread is better than whiskey."[39]

Companion to this measure was Vance's decree against the planting of cotton and tobacco, a decree proscribing everything, in fact, except food. Cotton was already piling up in the bales and could not be eaten; tobacco, while prized, had not yet become an army essential. The Raleigh *Standard* fell in behind the governor's address to the farmers: "The man who plants cotton and tobacco now, while the demand for breadstuffs is so urgent, is doing his country more harm than the open and avowed Lincolnists can do. Give the Confederacy a plenty of bread and meat, and the Yankee nation with all its foreign backers, can never conquer us."[40] The Salisbury *Watchman* gave support: "We do hope for the honor of our country, that no man in Rowan County will plant any more cotton or tobacco than will be necessary for his *own* use. Our large planters should vie with each other in the production of corn this season, as upon it depends the very *salvation* of our country."[41] Similar support came from the Wilmington *Journal* and Iredell *Express*.

Probably nothing during the war amused Zeb more, at least in afterthought, than the reaction to his sharp enforcement of the law against distilling liquor. In the hill country, distilling had been looked on as almost a prerogative of citizenship. The state tax on liquor was thirty cents a gallon and one dollar on any brought from outside the state. The hill people who lived on the edge of poverty could not be expected by an intelligent officialdom to pay tax on liquor they made for home consumption, and liquor was regarded as almost a necessity during the sharp winters in the mountains. Zeb said the liquor restriction was viewed by many as "a peculiar hardship," and no doubt in many instances it was.

" 'Old Rye,' " said Vance with a chuckle, "grew to be worth its weight in silver, and 'Mountain Dew' became as the nectar of the gods. Even 'New Dip' [a snuff] became precious, and was rolled as a sweet morsel under our rebel tongues. Yet, true to their character as the most law abiding people on the continent, all respected the act of Assembly."[42] Probably most did, but surely not "all."

Zeb's enforcement of the antidistilling law disclosed as much as any other measure his hold on the people of the state. He had such a serious regard for the restriction that when President Jefferson Davis wanted to have liquor distilled in North Carolina in substantial quantities for medicinal use, Zeb put his foot down and held the state law to be superior to the President's wish. Davis never did get his liquor, nor did the North Carolina farmers who sent appeals to the governor for exemptions in their particularly grievous cases.

"Many thirsting souls," said Vance later, "fancied that I was invested with that illegal power, the exercise of which lost James II his crown, of dispensing with laws, and petitioned me accordingly for a dispensation."[43]

When Jefferson Davis and the Confederate government were denied such a dispensation, the focus was on the question of jurisdiction. The central government, it developed, did not abate its efforts. Still, there was curiosity in both North Carolina and Virginia over the Confederate government's gargantuan demands for whisky. The Lexington, Virginia, *Gazette* inquired: "What does the Confederate Government do with its whiskey?" It then explained that Rockingham County was manufacturing it for the government at the rate of 200,000 gallons a year and Augusta County at the rate of 300,000 gallons. This would mean 500,-000 gallons for two Virginia counties. Suppose, the *Gazette* continued, that they made one tenth of all the government procured in the state, which was regarded as a low estimate, then Virginia would be contributing 5,000,000 gallons a year "to this line of supplies. Now if the other states together furnish as much more, we have no less than 10,000,000 gallons. This is enough to deluge all the hospitals of the Confederacy with all the patients they contain."[44]

Vance late in the next year, 1863, had to thwart again Confederate efforts to get North Carolina whisky. He wrote to Secretary Seddon saying he had learned large distilleries were operating in Charlotte and Salisbury making spirits of the grain due to the Confederate government under the tithe tax, or tax paid in kind. They were distilling, he was informed, under orders of the War Department and 30,000 bushels of grain had been diverted into the distilleries. He very firmly stated two propositions to the Secretary of War: that the grain was needed for bread for the poor, and that the laws of the state positively forbade distilling. He said he was "sure you will agree that no person under the authority of the Confederate Government can violate State laws with impunity."[45]

Vance clearly was reasoning that he could not restrain his own people who were urgently requesting the privilege to make whisky for their own use, and at the same time remain indifferent to a clear violation of the state law by the Confederate government. His attitude was by no means illogical. As it developed during the war, he was quite willing to have the courts determine the areas in which state and Confederate laws prevailed, but in the absence of any high Confederate tribunal as a court of last resort, he was compelled to adhere to the supremacy of state law and state courts within the borders of North Carolina. Certainly none could expect him to submit matters to final adjudication by a Virginia court, or a Georgia court, or any other state court.

Manifestly much government liquor was finding its way into other than hospital channels. In a country which for three or more years lived on the edge of starvation, Zeb's restrictions against distilling and insistence that grain be used for food did not seem unreasonable.

Among his home people who requested dispensations, the excuses given were ingenious. "One had much sickness in his family, and would I permit him to make a small 'run' for medicine? Another wanted to make just enough 'to go in camphor'; and still another gave it as his solemn opinion that it was going to be a terrible bad season for snakes, and they must have a little on hand in case of bites!"

His sense of humor at times dictated his replies. One man who wanted to distill only ten gallons thought he might appeal through the governor's appetite or cupidity, and said that if Zeb would give permission for the run, he would send the governor a quart. "A quart!" thought Zeb. "I replied in all seriousness, that I could not think of violating my official oath for less than a gallon. That broke the trade."[46]

Vance let loose his wrath upon a firm which he said had declined to provide the state with cotton goods at a 75 per cent profit over the cost of production, the limitation imposed by the law exempting their employees from military service. The merits of the case cannot be determined at this late date because of the inflationary conditions, the question of whether the manufacturer's costs for raw materials were pegged likewise and a great many other factors, but Vance saw only his side.

"It is melancholy in every sense," he stormed. "If the standard of patriotism was no higher in the great mass of people, we might treat with the enemy tomorrow and consent to be slaves once and forever. Poor men, with large and often helpless families, go forth to bleed and suffer at $11 per month, supporting their wives and children God knows how, with flour at $20, shoes and cotton goods at fabulous prices and yet men who stay at home in protected ease to reap a harvest of wealth, which might be truly called a harvest of blood, from the necessities of the country, cannot afford to take 75 per cent above the cost for the garments in which their protectors stand guard and do battle for their liberties!"

He grew warmer as he pursued the subject: "What per cent, gentlemen, do you suppose the soldier is reaping, with a half starving family, a shattered constitution, ragged and bare-footed, sleeping on the bare earth, and languishing with gaping wounds or raging fever in loathsome hospitals? If he can incur personal and pecuniary ruin for his country's sake, can't you afford to eat good food, sleep in a warm bed every night on 75 per cent profit for the country's good also? Alas, Alas, that such a state of things should exist in North Carolina."[47]

By such denunciatory letters Vance was able to keep clothing manufacturers in better line, though manifestly most of them were as patriotic as members of any other group, as their good relations with the state government attested. The extent of profiteering is difficult to gauge. John Christopher Schwab, professor of political economy at Yale, in his investigation of this question as applied to the entire South but with reliance on the contentions of the Virginia editor and author, E. A. Pollard, found instances of excessive profits, such as that of a woolen mill declaring dividends of $530,000 on a capital of $200,000, and a paper mill declaring dividends of 575 per cent for the years 1861 and 1862. Another profit, with the industry unnamed, was placed at 645 per cent. The Virginia tax assessments in 1863 showed 120 concerns taxed on profits upwards of $3,000,000.[48] In all these instances the effect of inflation does not appear to have been measured, for if a manufacturer bought raw materials when money was firm, as after Lee's Second Manassas campaign, and sold the finished products after Gettysburg, the profit undoubtedly would seem fantastic in terms of Confederate dollars. But as money continued down, the raw materials probably could not be procured at what the manufactured articles sold for a brief time before. Nevertheless, fortunes undoubtedly were made in North Carolina textiles during the war. Richard W. Griffin in his study concluded that despite its loss of plants and material, the North Carolina textile industry came out of the war better than most neighboring industries: "They had not been as loyal as many of their critics felt they should have been. . . ." But this comment applied also to the industry all the way from the Potomac to the Rio Grande. Throughout the war the cotton manufacturers were under continuous public attack.[49]

By his own drive, his zeal for the Confederate cause, and his ability to lead and persuade, Zeb put the state to work. His regulations, even the most stringent, were, he felt, "cheerfully sustained by a patriotic public voice and generally obeyed." With the young men gone from the farms, the old men and women took to the plows in the furrows while children followed with their hoes, grubbing the weeds in the corn rows.[50]

Saltpeter was in acute demand and mines long idle through neglect or low yield were reopened and worked diligently. The churches offered up their bells to be made into cannon. Patriotic citizens took lead window weights from their homes, along with pipes and all other leaden articles, for use in making bullets. The whisky stills, no longer being needed on farms of devoted Confederates, and turpentine stills as well, were turned in so that the copper might be used for percussion caps.[51]

All of the credit for the North Carolina war measures cannot be assigned to Vance personally, but he was the main impetus, or, to use a word of later origin, the *dynamo* that supplied the prime power. When the Norfolk Navy Yard, situated in nearby Gosport, was lost to the Federals in early 1862, such machinery and equipment as could be salvaged and transported was set up in Charlotte, North Carolina, where for three years a navy yard flourished and did highly valuable naval construction work, especially in marine engines, propellers, forgings, armaments, warship projectiles, and much else, though more than two hundred miles from tidewater. The Charlotte Navy Yard was one of the anomalies of the war.[52] Vance gave it every aid and encouragement; undoubtedly much of its splendid record under adverse circumstances during the war resulted from his orderly conduct of the state and the protection of essential workmen in war industries from the ravenous appetites of the conscription officers.

Another naval contribution was the ram *Albemarle*, which was built in a cornfield shipyard on the Roanoke River at Edward's Ferry, out of timbers cut nearby, the keel being of large oak stumps. The tools were provided by a blacksmith shop. After early spectacular service, the ram eventually was sunk, but she was a symbol of North Carolina enterprise and, as has been said, "no vessel was ever constructed under more adverse circumstances."[53]

North Carolina was virtually without heavy industries. Of the supply of iron required in the state, she did not produce at the beginning of the war one twentieth, and as Vance mentioned, "there was not a manufactury of arms worth mentioning in the state."

By the autumn of 1862, within a few weeks after Vance took office, superior army rifles were being manufactured in his home town of Asheville. Iron was produced from the Cranberry mines of nearby Avery County. The Napoleons set up to command the western approaches to the munition works gave to this Asheville eminence the name it still retains of "Battery Park." Another battery was erected on Beaucatcher Mountain to command the eastern approaches. When the Confederate government had to enlarge the facilities, the plant was removed to Columbia, South Carolina, and was blown up when Sherman's army approached that town, but it was credited with making some of the best Enfield-type rifles used by Confederate soldiers.[54]

The Cranberry mine, two and a half miles from the Tennessee line, on a branch of the Nolichucky River, was believed in that day to have as rich a vein "as any yet discovered in any part of the world." The state geologist, Dr. Ebenezer Emmons, analyzed the ore and pronounced it to contain 99 per cent pure oxide of iron. Two veins of outcrop were worked, each four feet wide, and a belief was expressed that the veins would widen and the lode might be inexhaustible.[55]

Under the spur of necessity and the threat of an iron famine, Robert R. Bridges, a member of the Confederate Congress, and his brother John L. Bridges, both University of North Carolina graduates, purchased, renovated, and enlarged the High Shoals Iron Works and soon had furnaces, forges, rolling mills, foundries, and nail factories lighting the night skies in three counties of the piedmont—Lincoln, Gaston, and Cleveland. These busy plants handled large orders not only for the Confederacy, but for North and South Carolina as well, and composed the second largest iron works in the Confederacy, yielding only to the Tredegar Iron Works in Richmond, which had been engaged in heavy manufacturing since 1840.[56]

Vance had been governor only two and a half months when the North Carolina *Whig,* which could criticize him unhesitatingly, recognized his worth by republishing from the *Mountain Eagle:* "Gov. Vance—our soldier Governor—is earning for himself the esteem of every man, woman and child in his State by his exertions in behalf of our suffering State. He is not only exercising his official power to clothe and feed our troops, but we find him nobly sharing the post of danger with our gallant soldiers. He is the right man in the right place and long will North Carolina bless the day he was made her Chief Magistrate."

The phrase "right man in the right place" intrigued the editors so much it recurred in the comments.[57]

Wharton J. Green, an officer on General Junius Daniel's staff until he was wounded at Gettysburg, later a Congressman and long a devoted friend of Vance's, observed the manner in which Zeb launched and conducted his administration: "His ambition seemed to be from the start that North Carolina should not only have the fullest rosters at 'roll call,' but the fattest graveyards on hard fought fields, if needs be, of any of her sister States."[58] Those of Daniel's Brigade would know the truth of this. Though it is mentioned but scantily in the accounts of Gettysburg, it suffered the second highest casualties there; more than any of Pickett's brigades, and surpassed only by Pettigrew's, another all-North Carolina brigade.[59]

As to Zeb's provisioning of his troops, Green told how an old veteran in a regiment that was being relieved by a North Carolina unit blurted out in tears: "If we were only as well shoed and cared for as them damned Tar Heels, we'd know how to stick and die as well as they do."

To provide an understanding of Vance's administration it is possible to give only a broad outline of his major undertakings and develop those which had bearing on the morale of the armies and the home public. Almost all he did contributed to maintenance of the war by the Confederacy against the much greater resources of the North. Except for his personal exertions the Confederacy undoubtedly would have collapsed much earlier.

When Vance in the decade after the war undertook to compile the record, he did so in the belief that both postwar public opinion and the spate of histories being written gave the impression that the Old North State had lagged in her war duties. He felt that the histories prior to 1875, when he made his own compilation of facts, had so far "either designedly fed this unjust impression by a studied silence on the subject, or else have been too much trammelled by the necessity of local panegyric to give ample motive to the *whole South*." Conceding that other states produced the great leaders of the war (North Carolina had no Lee, Stonewall Jackson, Nathan Bedford Forrest, Jefferson Davis, or Joseph E. Johnston), he made his celebrated pronouncement which has echoed through later North Carolina accounts:

"In the number of soldiers furnished, in the discipline, courage, and loyalty and difficult service of those soldiers, in amount of material and supplies contributed, in the good faith and moral support of her people at large, and in all the qualities that mark self-sacrifice, patriotism, and devotion to duty, North Carolina is entitled to stand where her troops stood in battle, behind no State, but in the front rank of the Confederation, aligned and abreast with the best, the foremost and the bravest."[60]

Vance was handicapped after the war in compiling statistics about his state because the principal records were taken to Washington in 1865 and closed to the scrutiny of Southern writers and historians for thirteen years after the conflict, but he used his money and had the former adjutant general of the state, Martin, check some of the figures, and judged that he reported with "approximate exactitude." As to the state's military duties, Vance held: "So far as I have been able to learn, North Carolina furnished more soldiers in proportion to white population, and more supplies and material in proportion to her means, for the support of the war, than any State of the Confederacy."[61]

He was concerned also after the war that the histories being written dealt with the leaders, not the followers, much as, in the words of Macaulay, the history of Great Britain dealt with the kings and not the British people. This has been substantially corrected by some publications since Vance's day, but to him, the story of the war was that of the sufferings, sacrifices and labors of the ordinary people, the sustenance and material they furnished to the men in the ranks, "their feelings, hopes, patriotism, and their despair."

When Vance described the type of history he desired, he revealed his deep respect for the Southern people based on his firsthand knowledge of what happened in his own state.

"The broad, catholic, cosmopolitan history of this most remarkable struggle has yet to be written," he said, "wherein the story of the people shall be told; wherein, when it is said how a great general won a victory, it will also be mentioned what troops and where from fought it for him; how the artisan in the shop, the ploughman in the field, the little girls in the factories, the mothers at the old hand looms, the herdsmen on the mountain side, the miner in the earth's bowels, the drivers and brakesmen on the railroad engines, how *all these* felt, and strove, and suffered equally with the soldier, and yet without his stimulus of personal glory."[62]

But Vance did not make the essential point or draw the major lesson from the state's performance. When he told of the resources and determination which a people may exhibit under the pressure of circumstances, and how the state "sprang forward with astonishing activity," he did not stress that the vast measure of this response grew out of volunteer co-operation and was continued while his state, and his alone among those which fought the Civil War, maintained, unshaken and against continual coercion and odds, the marks and guideposts of individual liberty—the supremacy of the civilian over the military courts in handling offenses; the right of the *habeas corpus,* which collapsed elsewhere to satisfy military demand. It may be repeated that the performance of this state, in which civil rights were so jealously guarded, is a contradiction of the proposition advanced after the war, and reiterated by writers since, that the South fell from an excess of democracy. Vance's story supports an opposing belief that war is prosecuted most vigorously in an advanced country when democratic institutions are preserved—that people familiar with freedom respond more eagerly when capable leadership fires their fervor than when they are coerced by severity, regimented drastically, and watched by diligent informers.[63]

Enlightened public opinion, the great moral power in peace, can be made, as Vance demonstrated, the great driving force in war.[64]

## Chapter Thirteen

## The Crises Come in Clusters

When the harvest of 1862 was being gathered and stored, Vance had
to strip the foodstuffs clean from the eastern counties open to Federal
raids from the coastal towns.

Federal concentrations of manpower threatening North Carolina
remained heavy, even after Burnside had withdrawn his 9th corps in
July to unite it with McClellan's army. They were reported by the Confederate commander in North Carolina, Major General Samuel G.
French, in late October, 1862, to be 25,000 at Suffolk, Virginia; 12,000
at New Bern; and 2,000 at Washington, North Carolina. Federal gunboats commanded the waters. Opposing them French had a meager army
of varying size since North Carolina had been drawn on heavily for
troops for Lee's campaigns.

The state was exposed on its flank either to hostile raids for fresh
provisions, or to a deeper invasion in force, which might cut the arteries
of the Confederacy reaching from the capital at Richmond down into
the South. Some of the richest farmlands along the coast were in enemy
hands and other productive counties were in constant danger of having
their stock and stores of grain carried off by raiding parties.

Vance and most of North Carolina were never able to understand why the Richmond government did not give greater attention to the ejection of the Union armies which remained as garrisons of the seaboard towns. The governor's correspondence and the autumn newspapers of 1862 were heavy with complaints against the Confederacy and entreaties for more adequate protection. Community leaders wrote, mass meetings were held. The local attitude was represented in a letter to Vance on September 18, 1862, from John Pool, speaking for the leading farmers and citizens of Bertie County. This county was washed by Albemarle Sound and the Chowan and Roanoke rivers and the smaller Cashie and Salmon creeks, all navigable.

"Along the streams," Pool wrote, "lie the main body of the excellent farming lands of the county, and several thousand slaves are upon these lands. The gun boats of the enemy are traversing these waters almost daily. Occasionally the enemy lands a few troops at unexpected points, but so far, has committed very little depredation. . . . There is not a Confederate soldier here, and not the least show of protection extended to the citizens." The people, he told the governor, were completely at the mercy of the enemy and nothing but Federal clemency prevented their total ruin. They for the most part were loyal to the Confederacy and "have acted with surprising prudence and faithfulness." How long is it wise, he asked, to allow them to depend entirely on the enemy for safety and feel that they were abandoned by the Confederate government?[1]

The people held a mass meeting in Windsor on September 15 and asked Vance to use his influence with Confederate authorities to have three measures adopted, and any others they deemed prudent. The three were: quarter two companies of cavalry in Bertie County; exempt the county from the conscript law; and relieve the county of any military orders requiring slaves to work on fortifications. How the last tied into the protection was not explained, except for the assumption that if the slaves were worked on fortifications they might flee to the Northern armies.

Vance, anxious to obtain the cavalry protection, was compelled ten days later to write General Gustavus W. Smith, the department commander, in protest. He had learned that cavalry in the eastern sections was to be brigaded, but that "the very first order calls all of them to Garysburg." This was in Northampton County up the Roanoke River, well removed from the coast. Thus the whole area would be exposed. "Without the protection of the cavalry," he stormed, "the finest provision region of the State can be desolated by the enemy in a few days. It is not to be thought of for a moment and I earnestly protest against it." He delivered one of the pregnant remarks which more and more were to characterize his wartime correspondence: "If it is not the intention of the President to protect us, we must protect ourselves."[2]

Vance got a reply dated October 6 from the assistant adjutant general, Captain Graham Davis, reassuring him that the number of companies on vedette or outpost duty was as great as at any time, and listing the companies. Nine captains were on duty, four in Onslow and adjacent counties and five near Kinston. How many men each captain led was not disclosed.[3]

The Raleigh *Standard* inserted its comments in the October 15 issue: "The President doubtless is not unmindful of North Carolina. He surely must feel the claim which our noble State has upon the Confederacy. Her blood has been freely spilled, her treasury has been open to the common cause; and shall our whole East be neglected? One-seventh of her wealth is now in the hands of the enemy—delay may soon place one-third of it beyond hope."

The editor made felicitous and exonerative remarks about the governor: "We are sure no one feels more deeply the importance of this matter than Gov. Vance." But Holden's best suggestion was weak indeed, and amounted to no more than recommending that the legislature be called. This "might . . . lead to action which could not easily be accomplished otherwise."[4] The situation was one which required soldiers, not laws.

Resolutions which Vance sent to President Davis from Onslow County (in which Camp Lejeune, the Marine Corps training ground at New River, is now located) caused the executive in mid-October to report fully and gently to the governor: "I have not been unmindful of the condition of the Eastern portion of your State and can make allowance for the anxiety felt by those who reside there. Efforts are industriously made to organize and instruct the new levies of mounted troops, that force being most relied on to protect your exposed districts; and you may be assured that the government will do everything in its power to defend the citizens of Onslow against the depredations of the enemy." He told Vance that Major General French had been ordered to send a force to prevent marauding expeditions and protect private property. The Federal concentration at Suffolk threatening the Virginia-

North Carolina communications required the Confederacy to answer with a concentration there, he explained. This would be understood, he believed, by the intelligent citizens of the county and state.

Davis, who was not then and never would be companionable toward Vance, took this opportunity to extend a deserved compliment which might assuage the governor's ruffled feelings: "I gratefully acknowledge the earnest and patriotic manner in which since your assumption of the Executive Authority in North Carolina you have labored to fill her battle-thinned regiments and recruit her armies in the field. I am happy in the confidence that you will continue to afford this government your valuable cooperation, and beg to assure you of the deep interest I feel in all that relates to the security and welfare of your State." They were no more than words, but Davis, too, had his problems.[5]

"Wheat! Wheat!" shouted the Raleigh *Standard* in early October. "The high prices of wheat and flour should admonish our planters throughout the State to sow largely of wheat for the next spring crop —Let every effort be made to sow a full crop."

Planters in 1862 were testing a rustproof wheat, which appeared to provide such a good yield that the *Standard* suggested it be called "Vance Wheat" because it was reliable.[6]

A week later came encouraging forecasts about the 1862 harvest. Lenoir, a small county along the Neuse River, was producing 125,000 barrels of corn and would have also a large amount of pork and beef. An "intelligent planter" reported that the estimate, while large, was "below the truth."[7]

With this a key to the eastern section, the estimate was made that the area east of the Wilmington and Weldon Railroad not under Northern control would produce 1,500,000 barrels of corn, "besides an amount of bacon and beef cattle beyond our ability to speculate." The same amount of corn had been produced in earlier years in the counties held by Northern troops, but the yield would be lower there in 1862 because so many slaves had departed—"been run off," according to the Raleigh *Standard's* version—and because of the shortage of animals.[8]

Similarly the North Carolina sweet potato crop was excellent, though there were complaints that the planters were keeping the prices high. Possibly to curtail the demand and help toward more reasonable prices, the Raleigh *Standard* downgraded their food value, saying that a bushel of Irish potatoes would go twice as far in a family while "a bushel of meal will go farther than two of Irish potatoes, or four bushels of sweet potatoes."[9]

Through the whole eastern section, mules, oxen, and wagons had been impressed by the Confederate government after the loss of New Bern and the owners had not yet received a penny for them. The paper felt that in simple justice the owners should be compensated and that the remaining counties should be defended "to the last extremity."[10]

The governor reported to Davis his compliance with a suggestion made by the Confederate commissary general, Colonel Lucius B. Northrop. Northrop asked Vance on November 2 to find a reliable businessman who could clear the hogs, beef, peas, beans, and potatoes from the part of the state accessible to the enemy. The regular commissary agents were not getting satisfactory results.

Vance answered through his aide Barnes, saying he would cheerfully undertake the task of clearing of produce the counties subject to invasion. He considered all of the counties west of Raleigh safe. In the piedmont and west the only danger of losing the pork was in the salt shortage, to which he was giving his most earnest attention. Crises never came singly, but in batches. Vance did designate a purchasing agent, but found that "speculators were ready to dog his steps."

"Two of the richest counties in the State," he wrote to Davis, "are Gates and Hertford, and I am extremely anxious to strip them first." But he wanted the protection of troops and reiterated his demand for them. He asked Davis to order General French to send to Winton on the Chowan River a regiment which had been raised in that district, and a section of artillery. By holding Winton with artillery, supplies from Gates County on the eastern side of the river might be brought across safely and the two counties could be stripped effectively behind the screen of soldiers.[11]

By his own diligence and acting through state agents when he found the Confederate government too occupied in other theaters, Vance succeeded in gathering in the harvest from some of the best agricultural areas and making it available for the armies, when inactivity probably would have allowed a substantial portion of it to fall into Federal hands. But his trouble with the enemy in the eastern counties was merely beginning, and would plague him until the end of the war.

In early November, 1862, Raleigh was filled with excitement over reports that the Federals were on the move again thrusting toward the Weldon Railroad; that Federal steamboats were passing up the Tar

River, and that six enemy regiments had crossed Swift Creek north of the Neuse River. The operation, measured by the reports, appeared major. Farther north, Colonel Burgwyn was reported to have advanced with a portion of Zeb's old 26th regiment and fought an engagement near Hamilton.

Vance immediately left Raleigh with Adjutant General Martin and reached Tarboro on November 3, at a time when the Raleigh *Standard* was recalling how it had warned everyone against the impending danger. "If the government would not be cut off from North Carolina, and practically from all the Southern Atlantic States, and indeed entirely cut off from them, with the exception of the means of transportation furnished by the Danville Road and the East Tennessee Road, it must rouse itself to the dangers which threaten it, and make the necessary efforts to drive back the enemy to his gunboats." The main hope, the newspaper seemed to think, was that the government at Richmond would find itself actually isolated from the rest of the South. "In other words, the *necessities* of the government, which has so long neglected our State, will, we trust, lead to such measures as will relieve Eastern Carolina of the presence of the enemy."[12]

The governor found the reports of a Northern push inland to be based on little more than a shifting of troops and returned to Raleigh.

An early and always an emergency problem was salt. As powder and lead were prerequisites for the firing line, salt was almost the prime necessity of the home front; in a country which possessed little or no refrigeration, it was the sole means of preserving meat and making bacon and ham available to Lee's army and the home public.

Mindful that salt had been a major problem during the Revolutionary War, the North Carolina State Convention early provided for a salt commissioner, who began works in Morehead City and on Currituck Sound, only to have them destroyed when Federal troops took over the northern and central coastal sections. John Milton Worth, salt commissioner, who because of the emergency was required to make a monthly report, did not get his work well under way until Vance became governor. At Currituck Sound he had merely bargained for supplies, but at Morehead City was producing one hundred bushels of salt a day when New Bern fell and he lost his saltworks, along with all the pans used in boiling down the sea water. He moved to Wilmington, where private saltmakers were already busy, attracted by the high prices.

Well before Vance became governor, the Raleigh *Standard* had been sounding the alarm without offering any practical solution. "Salt! Salt!" it cried, then foretold dire consequences: there was not enough salt in the state to last six months; cut off as they were likely to be from the ocean, salt would have to be obtained from mines or springs. "Without salt man and beast will become diseased and die." Asiatic cholera had been attributed to lack of salt. Let the authorities look into this matter at once.[13]

Vance encouraged and stimulated the state's activity, though because of the great demand for pans Worth had to make heavy outlays for them and all materials. His report ten days after Vance took office showed that he was making two hundred bushels of salt a day at Wilmington but was beset with numerous difficulties. He had to pay from $1 to $1.50 a cord for wood on the stump two miles distant from his works and hire teams at unreasonable rates. He was selling salt at cost price to the counties for public distribution at from $3 to $4 a bushel, compared with the price of from $8 to $13 obtained by private saltmakers. He, too, regarded it as fortunate that salt went so high, because the combined output of his own and the private works was about eighteen hundred bushels per day in mid-September and he hoped that by October 15 he would reach a daily output of twenty-five hundred bushels. With two thousand additional bushels expected daily from the North Carolina saltworks maintained in Virginia, the supply, if all went well, would be adequate.[14]

With the pork season coming on, Vance applied every spur. He wrote to Worth on October 1, 1862, that "in the present emergency it is desirable to have salt without regard to expense. The vast amount of meat that will be lost without salt renders the price of it a small consideration." He wanted the number of kettles increased so that production could be stepped up at once. "I can furnish conscript labor, any amount of it," he promised. "I suppose the yellow fever will hardly trouble you on the coast. Let me beg you, my dear sir, to push forward this matter with the greatest possible rapidity."[15]

Vance's reference to yellow fever may have been intuitive, because the production difficulties Worth already had encountered were trivial compared with the devastating yellow fever plague which suddenly struck Wilmington that autumn. Worth reported on October 7 that the works were virtually suspended. One of the early victims was the commissioner's son, seventeen years old. Unable to procure nurses, Worth cared for the boy, who died in his arms. Worth took the body back to his

Asheboro home for burial, leaving the works under the direction of a brother, Thomas C. Worth, who had conducted the river steamboat line from Wilmington to Fayetteville.[16] Before the month of October was out, he, too, would succumb to the disease. While yellow fever raged in Wilmington, smallpox broke out in several Southern cities and seemed to follow the railroads, adding to Vance's difficulties in getting salt.[17]

Each week the Raleigh press carried the health report from Wilmington; one week in late October showed 431 new cases and 102 deaths; another, 267 new cases and 82 deaths. The mortality was believed larger because obscure cases were not reported. Entire families were wiped out. Forty years had passed since Wilmington had experienced a single case of yellow fever. Opinion in the city was that it was brought from Nassau by the blockade-runner *Kate*. Authorities groped about for an explanation, though of course they could find no true one. The Raleigh *Standard* quoted a "medical gentleman": "It is positively asserted that the healthiness of the place, previous to the arrival of the *Kate,* traces the first case to her; but be that as it may, I am sure that the condition of the town is now, and for some time has been, so far as I can judge by the appearances I see, most neglected and filthy. There is apparently no provision for scavengering, and the cellars are filled with water, but a gentleman informs me that is always so."[18]

Vance wanted the salt despite the yellow fever and smallpox. He wrote through his aide David Barnes that he deeply regretted the epidemic, but deplored the stoppage of production: "This suspense if long continued will result in great public injury." Meantime he urged the official in charge to provide himself with such additional kettles and articles "as will enable you to produce salt in a much larger quantity." He wanted money spent prudently, "but salt must be had at any cost."[19]

Finally, to provide further incentive, Vance went to Wilmington on December 12 and addressed an assembly of the private saltmakers held in Commissioners Hall, his object being to get the most salt at the lowest possible price. He exhorted the producers and promised that if they would stabilize their prices he woud in turn procure laborers for them, provide transportation and guarantee to take their salt. The trip appears to have been beneficial because production was maintained for a time, in the face of constant irritations. The production cost was based mainly on the distance of the kettles from timber, the main cost factor being the hauling of firewood. One thousand pounds of sea water would boil down to twenty-seven pounds of salt. That was an easier process than scraping the floors of farm smokehouses for the accumulated drippings of the years, to which the farmers resorted.[20]

In order to conserve North Carolina salt and restrain speculators from other states, Vance renewed an export restriction which General W. H. C. Whiting at Wilmington enforced. He lifted it on occasion, as when Governor Joseph E. Brown of Georgia interceded in behalf of an Augusta resident who had bought Wilmington salt earlier, only to have it held up, first by the yellow fever and then by Vance. Vance explained that his order did not relate to salt purchased prior to its date or to persons from other states making bona fide purchases for their individual use, nor did it hamper communities which wished to make charitable distributions. The only purpose was to prevent extortion and speculation.[21]

While in Wilmington, Vance inspected the fortifications being strengthened by General Whiting, then visited encampments of North Carolina troops at Kinston and Goldsboro.[22] Fort Fisher, which guarded Wilmington, was under continual threat, and Whiting, commanding officer at Wilmington, and Colonel William Lamb, who commanded the fort, were naturally more solicitous about saving the fort and city than making salt. "Should the place fall," Whiting said, "the salt works will be lost." Vance's journey was partly in apprehension over a letter from Whiting December 6, 1862, saying he had few troops and the port was likely to be attacked, and recommending speedy action to secure the quantities of salt on hand there. He wanted the independent owners to ship it promptly by any of the four routes—three railroads and the Cape Fear River.[23]

In January, 1863, Salt Commissioner Worth complained to Vance that Whiting had impressed the steamboat and barges which brought the sea water to the saltworks. Then he impressed all teams and hands in the area to build breastworks and bridges. The result was that the state's saltworks and nearly all private producers had to suspend operations again. Applications accumulated and prices advanced daily. Vance immediately wrote to Major General Gustavus W. Smith, commanding the Department of North Carolina at Goldsboro, and complained that stoppage of the state's works at a time when production was at 350 bushels per day was a major calamity, coming in the midst of the pork-packing season.

"I can scarcely conceive of any such emergency as would justify it," Vance wrote. "A little trouble on the part of General Whiting's Quarter Master would have enabled him to press teams in adjacent counties, and a requisition upon me for labor would have furnished as much as he wanted." Vance demanded that the teams and workmen be restored to saltmaking. "It is almost as important to the State as the safety of the City, as our people cannot live without salt."[24]

Eventually the production was resumed and was carried on with occasional stoppages until the loss of Wilmington in 1865, but Whiting in the emergency of late 1864 halted the operation once more by drafting the employees, who had been exempted by state ordinance. Another stoppage occurred when Federal troops raided and held the works for a few hours in 1864, but during that year the state produced 66,100 bushels of salt from sea water at Wilmington and sold them at an average of $7.75 per bushel, or at less than half the market price of $19 for salt made by private works at Wilmington that year.[25] Vance based his price on costs and by the end of 1864, with inflation in swing, the price went to $13 for state salt and $25 for private, and before the war ended salt was selling at $70 a bushel in Raleigh. All through the war the saltworks were self supporting and paid back their investment. Vance gave them his continual, at times almost daily, attention. Without him it is not likely they would have performed and without them North Carolina would have had no cured meat and no bacon and many persons undoubtedly would have starved. Probably most of the privately made salt was taken out of the state after the lifting of the temporary export restriction, but so active was the market that these producers made about two thousand five hundred bushels per day during the latter part of the war.

Vance was equally attentive to the state's interests in salt production at Saltville, near Marion, Virginia. This was the leading salt-producing center of the South, with a daily output of above seven thousand bushels in late 1862. Though Virginia controlled the supply and obtained the largest portion for her own use and for distribution through the counties at a below-market price, North Carolina entered into the production at its own works and at the end of 1862 had on hand at Saltville what Vance described as a "vast amount of salt."

At the season when the need for salt was most acute, his problem was transportation. He called on Quartermaster General Myers of the Confederate government for help. Nearly all the locomotive power south of the Tennessee railroad was controlled by the government. He was prevented, he told Myers, from sending engines and cars from North Carolina railroads because the gauge of the railroads differed—a common plague to the South—and requested that Myers either provide engines or make exchanges for North Carolina engines.

He emphasized the urgency in his letter of December 26, 1862: "The season is now far advanced and the condition of every class of our people will be truly deplorable unless Salt is brought to them. Independent of that, the supply for the Army will be seriously diminished. A large amount of pork is now awaiting for salt, to be packed, and unless it is received very soon, an immense loss will ensue."[26]

What help Vance got from Myers is not clear, but the state did bolster its salt supplies from the Virginia source, as did other states, but usually with much friction with Virginia.[27] The press seemed as excited about a rich salt strike in Louisiana as it might have been over the discovery of gold, but the mines there were of scant help to the East and of none after the loss of Vicksburg. Governor Brown of Georgia was in a constant struggle for salt and, like Vance, maintained works at Saltville, Virginia, until Federal troops crowded into that section in late 1864.[28] North Carolina maintained an agent, Nicholas W. Woodfin, at Saltville, who sold to county agents at cost.[29]

Governor Vance had not only to get salt produced, but also to obtain equitable and timely distribution in the counties. The problem is best seen from a specific instance. A group of citizens of Burke County signed and sent to him an appeal for an act by the legislature—their confidence in laws seemed naïve—"for a prompt and cheap Supply of Salt." The innkeeper and salt agent for the county, Thomas G. Walton, had told the people to come for salt December 4. ". . . the people had their hogs fat redy to kill and Corn Scarce" but Walton allowed them only three pounds per family. They suspected that "Sharks" who had salt hidden were waiting to buy up the pork at distress prices. "Here Stood Women thinly Clad wives of our Suffering Soilgers in the mud in front of Thomas G. Waltons Salt House from early in the morning till near night eighteen miles from home waiting till Thomas G. Walton could weigh out Salt for a hole County." They claimed that salt which cost $1.50 a bushel at Saltville, Virginia, was sold for five dollars by Walton at Morgantown.[30] Vance did his best to satisfy all complaints, but few if any wartime problems were as ever-present as this.

Zeb's appeals for more considerate prices of food commodities drew the response of many patriotic citizens. The Raleigh *Standard* co-operated by publishing a feature at intervals entitled "The Roll of Honor." This was not for deeds of valor on the battlefield, but of quiet sacrifice and generosity in the remote neighborhoods on the home front: ". . . John Swicegood, near Abbotts Creek, is selling flour at only $6 per hundred, and still lower to soldiers families . . . Burwell Cashion, living near Davidson College, [is] another patriotic man who sells corn to soldiers families at $1 per bushel." Morrison Parker at Round Hill sold corn to destitute neighbors at below market and sole leather at 75¢ per pound.[31] A citizen from abroad had sent two cases of cotton cards for distribution among the soldiers' families of Edgecombe County. Editor Holden disclosed in this and other ways that he could stimulate the war effort as well as criticize those at the top of it in Richmond.

Meat was always in scant supply. North Carolina editors took delight in copying an advertisement which the publisher of the Cleveland, Tennessee, *Banner* inserted in his own paper when he found his revenues would no longer garnish his table: "Wanted. We want to buy a coon and 'possum dog, to hunt our meat with during the coming year. It is foolish for a man to think about buying hog meat who is printing a paper at $2 a year. A dog that will hunt coon, 'possum, and kill a sheep occasionally, will command a good price in these 'headquarters.' "[32]

Under Vance the powder mill of Waterhouse and Bowes near Raleigh became operative and began to supply powder directly to the Confederate government, which, in turn, under an earlier agreement, began to provide a working supply of four thousand pounds of niter per week. In this instance Vance quite naturally had no interest in injecting the state into what was clearly a matter for the Confederate departments.

Among Vance's early and essential achievements was the organization of a state Medical Department, under the direction of one of the most striking and charming characters to appear in the North Carolina of the war years, Dr. Edward Warren, who had returned from Baltimore to his home state at the outbreak of the war. He has been met with in these pages caring for the wounded during the Confederate rout at New Bern and the repulse at Malvern Hill.

Warren was born in Tyrrell County and reared in New Bern by his doctor father; then, after attending the University of Virginia, he was graduated from the Jefferson Medical College in Philadelphia. Following study in Paris and practice in Edenton, he had become an able and popular lecturer at the University of Maryland—a chair which, incidentally, was closed to him after the war and his faithful service to North Carolina. His failure to recover it, even after instituting court action, was perhaps fortunate for posterity, for he went on to other work and eventually became the chief surgeon for the Khedive of Egypt and subsequently a prominent practicing physician in Paris. These adventures and the rich reminiscences they stored enabled him to write in later life his fascinating and rewarding book, *A Doctor's Experiences in Three Continents,* which gives intimate pictures, among many other things, of his association with Zeb Vance.

Vance's close friend Dr. T. J. Boykin, surgeon of the old 26th regiment, who idolized the governor, recommended Warren, and Vance appointed him surgeon general of North Carolina. How Vance made solid friendships was seen in Warren's remarks about Boykin—"a more loyal and pure hearted man never lived"—then, "his love for Vance was like that of Damon for Pythias—a sentiment incorporating itself into his entire life."[33] Warren, too, came under Vance's spell and remained his devoted friend for the rest of his wandering life. Vance awakened in him a desire to serve North Carolina, "from which I can say with truth, and without vanity, incalculable benefit accrued alike to her soldiers and her people." The doctor assuredly was not boasting, for his value to the state was incalculable.[34]

On Vance's recommendation the legislature appropriated $100,000 annually (a figure later raised to $300,000) for the surgeon general's office, with which Warren established a number of conveniently located wayside hospitals scattered over the state and a Soldiers' Home in Richmond, a stopping place for North Carolina soldiers en route to and from Lee's army in Virginia. Here Warren or members of his staff "fed, warmed, sheltered and clothed thousands of weary soldiers as they journeyed homeward or campward."[35] From Europe he purchased a large quantity of medicines, surgical instruments and hospital supplies, which he distributed (and here he was following Vance's policy of first looking after his own) to North Carolina troops "with a liberal hand," at a time when the Confederate government had exhausted its supply of such stores.

Dr. Warren systematized the collection of clothing and supplies offered by the charitable home people. He established collection centers on the railroads and one at his Raleigh office, then gathered up each month everything useful the public sent or deposited and shipped it off to the fighting front. He organized a corps of capable surgeons. Of two he spoke most highly: one was Dr. Eugene Grissom, a graduate of the University of Pennsylvania School of Medicine, who had begun the war as a line captain in the 30th North Carolina regiment. After he had been wounded at Seven Pines, someone, apparently Warren, saw he was needed more in his profession and brought him into the Medical Department, though he had been elected to the assembly in the election when Vance won the governorship.[36] The other was Dr. David Taylor, who, like Grissom, was sent wherever there was an accumulation of wounded or sick soldiers or other kind of need.

When the smallpox epidemic struck the state shortly after Vance became governor, Warren by his energetic measures—supplying good serum and appointing a vaccinator in each county, and then checking on their work—stamped it out. In this drive, 70,000 persons, according to the records of his office, were vaccinated. When the militia and home guard regiments were formed, Warren organized a medical staff to serve them, gave each regiment the required surgical instruments and provided each with an abundant supply of hospital stores.

Vance showed his appreciation by promoting Dr. Warren from colonel to brigadier general in the state military service, with an increase in pay and emoluments. Not on account of this, but because of the admiration stirred in him as he watched Vance's performance, Warren's fondness for the governor grew, and perhaps there was no more discerning man than the doctor who came into frequent contact with Zeb during the war. None expressed deeper attachment:

"In my judgment no nobler man than Zebulon Baird Vance was ever created—with an inherent kindness of heart which tempers and softens his entire nature; a respect for justice and right which asserts itself under all possible circumstances; a sense of the ridiculous from which wells out a stream of humor at once copious, sparkling and exhaustless, and an intellect which like some great oak of the forest is at once a 'tower of strength' and a 'thing of beauty forever,' now braving the hurricane's breath and the lightning's flash, and then adorning the landscape by its grandeur, its symmetry and its verdure.

"I have analyzed his heart from core to covering, and I know that in its very cell and fiber it is of the purest gold, without the trace of alloy or a taint of counterfeit."[37]

Warren's association brought to light Vance's sharp attention to everything going on around him. Clearly he possessed a good volunteer intelligence service, though its meddlesome diligence irked him. The surgeon general told of being out with a crowd on a drinking bout in a nearby city where he had been on duty. The crowd was composed of Vance's friends and although Warren drank nothing he was companionable. When he returned to Raleigh and reported, the governor remarked seriously:

"I heard all about your big spree, Warren."

"My big spree!" exclaimed the doctor. "Governor, what in the world are you talking about?"

"Now don't crawfish," Vance continued. "I know the whole thing. How you and Tom —— made the place howl while I thought you were devoting yourself to public affairs."

Warren, growing impatient, told the governor he must explain himself, whereupon the governor handed him a letter marked "confidential" and said, "Well, read this." The letter was an account of how the doctor had neglected his business while he was making merry in the big party. Warren, now fully angered, asked if the governor believed the letter. But Vance, a twinkle showing at length in his eye, said he had not waited to answer the letter by mail, but had sent a telegram to his informer. Then he handed over a copy of the telegram, which said:

"Tell Warren sorry not to join him there."[38]

Reading in these few words Vance's contempt for the informer, the doctor seized his hand and avowed: "The man who could be anything else than true to such a friend as you are, does not deserve to live."

Warren told another enlightening story of an effort he made later in Vance's term, when relations between the governor and Editor Holden were growing strained. Warren, hoping to prevent an open rupture between the two, went to see Holden one night, then called on the governor the next morning. Before he could tell about it Vance opened the conversation:

"And so you paid Holden a visit last night?"

"Yes, but how in the world did you know about it?"

"Well," said Vance, "you have some enemies who would prejudice me against you if they could, and you had hardly entered Holden's office before three persons came running to my house, each so out of breath that he could scarcely articulate, to inform me that my 'dearest friend' was closeted with my 'most malignant enemy.' "[39]

When Warren asked what the governor said to them, Vance continued: "Oh, I thanked them very much for their interest in my affairs and said that's all right, I suppose the visit is on my account, for I knew that *they* were instigated entirely by malice and that whatever *you* might do, it would be prompted by a desire to serve me."

With New Bern in Federal hands, President Lincoln began an effort at the piecemeal reconstruction of North Carolina by appointing the Union military governor, Edward Stanly. He had practiced law in North Carolina, gone to Congress, and served as Speaker of the house of commons in the legislature and as state attorney general, then had moved to California and taken leadership in the West in the development of the Republican party, a ready transition because he had been a steadfast North Carolina Whig. He appears to have been a personable and intelligent man, who had suffered the stings of political defeat both in North Carolina, where he had lost the seat he held in Congress, and in California, where he had sought the governorship in 1857.

High hope existed in Washington that North Carolina would crumble and re-establish an allegiance with the old government, an impression which was part of the persistent thought in the North that the state had not been sincere with herself in seceding and that large elements of the people, perhaps the preponderance, were at heart unionists. That confidence was sufficient to convince Stanly that he could hold a governorship by appointment where he could not win one by ballots, so he appeared at New Bern with a shield of Federal gunboats and carrying an official scroll from Washington which presumably made him governor of the state. Thus Vance, when elected, found he was not the only claimant to the title.

Stanly ordered a Congressional election held from the partially conquered district and took many other measures, one of which was to request in a letter from New Bern dated October 21, 1862, an interview with Vance, whom he addressed as "His Excellency," but not as "Governor." He said he had returned to North Carolina because of the "strong affection which I have inherited and cherish for the people of my native state." He told Vance that nations, like individuals, sometimes quarrel through misunderstanding. Such, he felt, was the situation between the Federal government and North Carolina. He expressed confidence that he was in a position to "confer blessings" on the people if those in high station would give their assistance. He suggested that if Vance declined, one or more "good citizens" might be authorized by him to confer. The letter was delinquent in one respect, that it gave no hint of any plan or program Stanly wanted to discuss.[40]

Vance was in an abrupt mood in his reply, which he addressed on October 29 to "Hon. Edward Stanly." No governorship was mentioned here, either. He said to grant an interview would be incompatible with his duty. If the subject Stanly wanted to discuss related to peace between the United States and the Confederacy, then he had no authority, since the power to make war and peace rested with the Confederate President and Senate. If he wanted to discuss a separate peace between North Carolina and the United States, then the conference was still more inadmissible because the state had entered into a solemn compact to adhere to the new government of the Confederate States. He unloaded some stronger language.

"Your proposition is based on the supposition that there is baseness in North Carolina sufficient to induce her people to abandon their confederates and leave them to suffer alone all the horrors of this un-natural war, for the sake of securing terms for themselves, a mistake which I could scarcely have supposed anyone so well acquainted with the character of our people as yourself could have committed.

"North Carolina having committed the question of War and Peace to the authorities of the Confederate Government has now no cause to distrust their ability or their patriotism, or to withhold that generous support to their measures which has thus far characterized her."[41]

Stanly shot back a reply claiming Vance had made unbecoming remarks and Vance grew more heated in his second letter, which told Stanly how his name was execrated and cursed and that "damnable atrocities" were committed daily almost under his eye. His mission was a failure.

"Coming to the people who have often honored you, in the wake of destroying armies; assuming to be governor of a State by the Suffrages of abolition bayonetts red with the blood of your kindred and friends, how could you expect it to be otherwise?"

Vance's final paragraph was a bit prophetic. North Carolina might be subjugated, he said. Stanly might reach her capital: "But I assure you upon the honor of a Son, who will follow as he has followed and main-tained her, *whether right or wrong*, who has every means of Knowing the sentiments of her people, that you can only do so over the dead bodies of the men who once respected you, through the smoking ashes of the homes which once greeted you with hospitable welcome, and through fields desolated, which once gladdened your eye, rich with the glorious harvest of peace."[42] Stanly was not there to witness it, but that was substantially the manner in which North Carolina fell.

Stanly, it developed, had retained his proslavery sympathies, though he had been a Free Soiler in the West. President Lincoln issued his Emancipation Proclamation effective January 1, 1863, and Stanly resigned fifteen days later. He thought the proclamation altered the purpose of the war and destroyed any chance he might have in North Carolina.[43] The exchange with Vance had left no doubt as to who was the real governor. He returned to California and indicated his disgust by breaking with the Republican party there. The unionist elected to Congress was denied a seat in the House in Washington and Stanly's departure ended the fiction of a Federally controlled state government.

Thereafter, of the numerous military campaigns in the eastern part of the state, the most distinguished was the recovery of Plymouth. Lee in the spring of 1864 detached one of his best divisions, under General Robert Hoke, who conducted a brilliant surprise movement, captured Plymouth on April 24 and went on to the capture of Washington. But before he could undertake the capture of New Bern, Lee's urgent need for troops required him to recall Hoke, who arrived in time to participate in the costly check administered to Grant at Cold Harbor. Hoke was back in eastern North Carolina again in the late stages of the war.[44]

In a country strained to the limit in a war effort, there were continually problems about railroads. Apart from the roads being needed for transportation, any surplus iron they might possess in little-used sidings or spurs was sought eagerly by ordnance officers.

An early request came for iron for plating gunboats with armor. Secretary Mallory wanted a railroad. His first quest in North Carolina was unfruitful. On November 4, 1862, he wrote to Vance: "If you will let the Department have the rails and facilitate its transportation to Richmond, they will be immediately rolled into plates for the vessels in question and for such other defenses as may be built in the waters of your State."[45]

Vance replied through his aide David A. Barnes saying he assumed the secretary referred to the iron in the Atlantic and North Carolina Railroad. The state, said Barnes, was only a stockholder in the road, the large portion of which belonged to private individuals. A meeting of the directors was called to consider the question. Vance finally gave all the iron on the railroad from Kinston to New Bern "if they will only come and get it." The offer applied to fifteen miles of the track which remained inside the Confederate lines. Vance wrote to Mallory that the iron should be secured from the torn-up portion of the railroad nearest the enemy.[46]

Then he told something about the condition of Southern railroads. The iron taken from the Atlantic road which was nearly new should be used to replace worn-out iron on other roads, and the damaged rails from the main lines would serve just as well for rolling. He also gave Mallory the bolt iron on the damaged bridges across the Neuse River.

This situation set the stage for one of Vance's stubborn controversies with the Confederate government. Secretary Seddon wanted to complete the gap of forty miles between Danville, Virginia, and Greensboro, North Carolina. Linking these two cities would give Richmond a reserve railroad in case the Confederacy lost the line through Weldon and Kinston to Wilmington and on to Charleston, South Carolina, which was always exposed as long as the enemy occupied New Bern. But Vance took the view inferentially that the reserve road would make the Confederacy less resolute about holding the route through eastern North Carolina. At least he was not highly interested in completing the link. He wanted to recover the eastern counties, not lose more of them. He assented to the new road, but did not put his shoulder behind the construction work.[47]

He seemed to be on reasonable ground when he questioned the wisdom of putting iron into a new railroad at the time the existing roads were going down hill toward ruin for lack of rails and rolling stock.

Vance was first requested by Secretary Randolph to assist in building the new road. He replied through his aide that he would give whatever help he could "but at the same time hopes it will not be improper to remark that the government should at all hazards and at all times defend our present Railroad connections at Weldon. That section of the country is of the utmost importance to the Government, abounding in abundant supplies for the Army."[48]

Richmond had still a third railroad extending through Lynchburg and Bristol, Virginia, to Knoxville, Chattanooga, and the deep South. But the Confederate government decided to build the link, appropriated money and went ahead with the work, though there was much opposition to it in Richmond among legislators from South Carolina and Georgia. The next step was to call on Vance again for help, which Secretary Seddon did when he found North Carolina slaveowners indisposed to hire the slave labor needed for the project.

Vance answered saying he favored the road but would not impress slave labor to help it, because for many months the eastern part of the state had been furnishing labor on all public works from Wilmington to Petersburg and few slaves were owned in the region through which the new railroad would run. Then he stated what seemed his main objection that "this railroad is viewed with almost universal disfavor in the State, as entirely ruinous to many east of it," and that the charter to build it never could have been obtained except as a pressing war necessity. He said there was "strong feeling that upon completion of the Danville connection the eastern lines of our roads would be abandoned to the enemy."[49]

At the very time, Vance was receiving a letter from S. D. Wallace, president of the Wilmington and Weldon Railroad—the main line connecting Richmond with the southern seaboard—saying he needed from three to four hundred tons of new rails due to the heavy war duties being imposed on the road. Nor did he want the rails of the side lines taken from North Carolina for the renewal of roads outside the state, as had been suggested. The line proposed to be stripped was the Wilmington, Charlotte and Rutherford Railroad and he would regret any contingency which would cause the destruction or abandonment of that improvement.

Eventually, after two years, the Danville-Greensboro link was completed, when it might have been built in a fourth that time. It did serve the Confederacy during the last eleven months of the war when it was in operation.[50] Vance did not retard it but it stands as an example of how things moved slowly when he did not get behind them and push. In any event, his attitude clearly was that of the majority sentiment in his state, and while the majority did not dictate to his conscience, it had a right to be heard.

In the rush of events, Zeb had no time for anything but forthrightness—even if he had had an inclination toward the devious, which he did not. Nevertheless, it was the nature of politics that motives be interpreted cynically and Vance's wartime governorship has often been described as infested with politics to the very core. In truth, he was never in all his career a politician in the accepted sense of carrying water on both shoulders, or, in a latter-day meaning, avoiding sharp issues and conforming to popular trends, which, again in a later sense, would involve basing policy and principle on the polls and straw votes. More accurately, Vance took a position and the polls, the straw votes, and the people gravitated to it. Neither during the war nor later did he maintain a political organization. He governed for no group. He sounded off the cadence and the state kept time.

The skepticism with which his early years were marked—much as were Lincoln's, but which in Vance's case was more an indifference to religion than any deep-seated doubt—had given way, before he reached the governorship, to a faith, if not yet to any religious discipline. Perhaps Vance's most frequently quoted remark was about his brother's religion and his own. "Bob is a Methodist," he said, "and believes in falling from grace but never falls. I am a Presbyterian and don't believe in falling from grace but am always falling."[51]

At the time of the war he had not yet joined the Presbyterian Church, which he did during his postwar residence in Charlotte after the affliction, suffering, and death of his wife Hattie. The opinion of his chaplain and brother-in-law, the Reverend R. N. Price, was that through most of his life he was a "worldian" who was upright, honorable, paid his debts, was quick to forgive, but had made no avowal of religion. That would have been his spiritual situation during the war. The avowal came later. He had reasoned with himself and obviously had concluded that a faith which gave his wife such comfort during a long illness was one he should espouse and share with her in memory.

## Chapter Fourteen

## Sharpsburg Wounded

In that late summer of 1862, when the Carolina wheat was threshed and stored, the sweet potatoes turned with the plow, persimmons waiting for the frost and pumpkins golden on the withering vine, when the apples reddened, and grapes hung in white and purple clusters in nearly every farmyard, Lee led his triumphant army, with its thirty-one regiments and three batteries of North Carolina troops, across the Potomac into Maryland.

Vance had been governor but nine days when the Northern and Southern forces lunged at each other in front of the village of Sharpsburg, along Antietam Creek, September 17, in such a desperate combat that the day probably remains, after other and more far-flung wars with vastly greater armies and grander weapons of destruction, the most sanguinary of American history, and certainly the bloodiest of the Western world.

Vance's old troops were there, his company of Roughs in the 14th North Carolina, commanded by Colonel Risden T. Bennett, that had carried the flag at the first battle at Bethel and now was in the center of the most deadly battle yet fought, at Sharpsburg; but Zeb's heart went out not alone to these, but to all the Southern troops engaged in this clash of stubborn armies, neither of which knew, for at least a day after the battle, which had won. Then Lee's retreat acknowledged not only his defeat, but the rebuff which had been given to the Southern cause by the apathy of their sister slave state Maryland.

Maryland's indifference seemed to sting the North Carolina home public as much as the repulse of Lee's army, and unkind references to the state began to appear in the North State press.

North Carolina troops might well, and did, claim credit for saving Lee's army on two of the critical turns of the battle. First, when the weight of Federal numbers threatened to crush Lee's center and left, the two North Carolina brigades of Walker and Ransom were shifted from their position on the extreme right to the Dunkard church in the left center just in time to stay the Federal breakthrough. Again, in the late afternoon, when Burnside had finally crossed Antietam Creek and was about to roll up Lee's exposed right flank, the brigades of Pender and Branch composed an important part of A. P. Hill's Division, three brigades of which arrived from Harpers Ferry just in time to strike Burnside in flank and roll him back. It was one of the instances where it might be truly said that with a delay of ten minutes they would have been too late. Moreover, North Carolina troops of George B. Anderson's Brigade held the historic "Bloody Lane" in the army's center until, by North Carolina accounts, "thrice their number of Federals lay dead in their front in musket range."[1]

A striking feature of this battle, one of the most stubbornly fought of modern history, was that the Confederate Army, though on the defensive, did not on any part of the field resort to breastworks. That undoubtedly contributed to the heavy Confederate and North Carolina casualty lists. The terrain favored their lines at times, such as along the sunken road, but most of the fighting was in the open fields. North Carolina troops, according to the finding of the official North Carolina commission, composed more than one fourth of the men in Lee's line of battle.

The governor's principal relation with the battle was in the aftermath. Expectations had been high when Lee, after his series of brilliant victories over the Federal General Pope, and the withdrawal of McClellan from the Peninsula, sought to annex Maryland to the Southern republic. Since North Carolina had no newspaper correspondents with Lee's army, the press had to rely on reprints from other papers, mainly from Virginia, which were the first to reach the North Carolina towns. The nature of the fighting in Maryland was at first not clear. Jackson's capture of Harpers Ferry was hailed with huzzahs. But when it was known that Lee had retreated across the Potomac the outcome of the Maryland campaign was no longer uncertain.

As soon as Vance learned of the magnitude of the battle and the desperate fighting into which the North Carolina troops had been plunged all along the line, he summoned Surgeon General Warren, collected the available surgical and medical supplies, and hurried off to Virginia to be on hand when the great numbers of North Carolina soldiers began to come back from the battlefield.

Perhaps there was more to this trip than merely carrying up medical supplies and encouraging the North Carolina troops. A young, virile man like Vance, who had just experienced the excitement of front line duty, was not to be confined to his desk in Raleigh if he could find justification for leaving it and getting nearer the scene of active campaigning at a time of high drama in the Southern cause.

In Richmond the governor and surgeon general called at the hospitals. Vance, with his abundant store of good spirits and ready remarks, gave all the cheer he could to the wounded. Then, seeing that most of the wounded were not yet being brought to Richmond, he sent Dr. Warren to the rear of the army as it was moving down into Virginia. Warren on leaving Richmond went first to Charlottesville, where he cared for about fifty who were in "a condition of great destitution."[2] Undoubtedly the army was lower on uniforms at the time of Sharpsburg than at any other period except the last phases of the war, because Vance's efforts to provide them to North Carolina troops and subsequently to others were just getting under way. Clothes were scarce for the men in Charlottesville. Warren always made known to the wounded that he had been sent to them by the governor personally. Those who have misunderstood Vance during the war years and sought a political implication in nearly every action he took would regard the doctor a good cog in the Vance political machine, but anyone who observed Vance closely would have been impressed that politics was his last consideration in the anguish and stress which followed a great battle. Warren's messages from the governor to the wounded men were manifestly a part of his therapy and at the same time no more than a genuine expression of the governor's deep affection for these soldiers—an affection which, as has been noted, extended for several decades to all the common run of people in the state.

"Their delight at seeing me and learning that you had sent me to look after their wants," the doctor reported, "cannot be expressed in words. Many of them cried like children, and declared that they would never forget you." Most of them, in fact, never did. Dr. Warren answered all their pressing wants, then went on to Staunton, where he was met by an aide with more surgical and hospital stores. The army surgeon in charge at Staunton gave him free access to the hospitals, which he found crowded with three thousand wounded soldiers, one fourth of whom were from North Carolina.

"I had supposed the condition of the sick and wounded at Charlottes-ville bad enough," he wrote to Vance, October 11, "but it is infinitely better than that of the poor creatures in these Hospitals. Dirty, naked, without shoes, hats or socks, wounded in every possible manner, utterly dispirited and entirely indifferent to everything, they present a picture of wretchedness and misery which no tongue or pen can describe."[3]

Wounded were reaching Staunton at a rate of one thousand a day in trains running from the army at Winchester, Virginia, and a week was required to make the comparatively short journey up the Shenandoah Valley, during which hunger was added to their other woes. Dr. Warren was thoroughly familiar with scenes behind the lines after a battle. Few surgeons had had more battle service. His work at New Bern and Malvern Hill has been noted in these pages. He helped care for the wounded after First Manassas and for one thousand two hundred typho-malaria cases in the Charlottesville hospital early in the war. He was at Mechanicsville and Gaines's Mill, and was back and forth during the early stages of the war in service in Virginia and North Carolina. But the aftermath of Antietam seemed almost to overcome him.

Ordinarily as restrained in his statements as in attending his patients, he nevertheless let loose a torrent of complaint. "Taking all things together," he wrote in pencil to Vance, "the condition of these poor unfortunates is enough to wring tears from hearts of stone, and to stamp the authorities of the Confederacy with a brand of unutterable disgrace. Thank God, I have been able to do something at least for the poor fellows from North Carolina." He visited every ward of every hospital, took the hand of every North Carolina soldier, and told them Governor Vance had resolved they should not be neglected. He distrib-uted all the supplies brought from Richmond and expended $300 in the purchase of more, "mostly clothes to cover their nakedness." He cheered Vance to the extent of saying, ". . . you have the prayers and blessings of hundreds who have been made comparatively comfortable by your kindness."[4]

The wounded were being transferred from Staunton to Lynchburg and Richmond. Warren returned to Richmond via Lynchburg and installed a surgeon in charge of North Carolina's wounded in the Confederate capital. One of the severe shocks to North Carolina was the death of Brigadier General George B. Anderson, which resulted from what appeared at first to be a trivial wound. He was hit in the foot by a ball. He was sent back through Staunton and, when the foot became infected, to Raleigh, where amputation failed to save him. "He bid fair to be one of the most useful and able of our North Carolina officers," said the Raleigh *Standard*.[5] The distinguished brigade commander and former Congressman General Lawrence O'Bryan Branch, who had commanded Vance at New Bern, was killed by a sharpshooter shortly after his arrival on the field, but he played his part in saving Lee's right wing from disaster.

His brigade, which had been worsted at New Bern, had already won since that unhappy affair the tribute of Stonewall Jackson. On the death of Branch, the command passed to Brigadier General Stephen Dodson Ramseur, under whom it became further distinguished and known as "the Ironsides of the Army."

The Raleigh *Standard* gave North Carolina an account of Vance's trip to Richmond after the battle, obviously grapevined because the surgeon who wrote it as a volunteer contributor gained little information about the governor's official conversations, but did observe him at the hospitals. "Our Executive is as remarkable for his discreet reserve on State subjects, as he is for his cordial and agreeable *abandon* in the private circle," said the account. Otherwise, the sick and wounded from the North State were "cheered and delighted by a visit of our beloved and popular Governor," who made the rounds of the hospitals in company with Surgeon General Warren.[6]

No doubt Zeb's cordiality and homespun jokes did brighten the day for the convalescents, but this was more than a trip of good cheer, because he and Warren "minutely inspected the hospitals," as the correspondent surgeon affirmed, and adopted some new measures that would greatly relieve those who were suffering most severely. Precisely what the measures were was not specified, but: "A visit to Richmond will convince anyone of the valuable service which may be rendered by an energetic and intelligent Surgeon General for our State." Dr.

Warren arranged suitable conveyances for the wounded, and it was promised that "those who could be safely removed will soon be sent home to North Carolina."

Gradually news of the sturdy participation of the North Carolina regiments at Sharpsburg began to filter back in soldiers' letters. One from a member of the Oak City Guards, raised in Raleigh, told how Colonel Risden T. Bennett's 14th regiment, to which he belonged, resolutely held the line along the Bloody Lane in Lee's center. This was of more than average interest to Vance, because the 14th contained his old company, the Rough and Ready guards of Asheville.

After such a fight the private might be excused for regimental pride: The regiment "fought all day, and while other regiments and men were running, the 14th stood 'like a Stonewall' and repulsed three heavy columns of the enemy." The fourth assault found them with ammunition gone and they were forced to give ground. "The next day I carried rations to the regiment and found 27, men and officers. Noble fellows, they were glad to see me. The next day we had collected 52 men of the immortal 14th, who had come out unhurt."[7]

Confidence in the superiority of Southern arms had before the battle fired the people to extraordinary sacrifice. Why should not the average citizen accept it as self-evident, after the collapse of McClellan's Peninsular campaign and Lee's brilliant victory at Second Manassas? Typical of the news stories was a Raleigh reprint from the St. Louis *Republic* quoting a Northern colonel who, with his arm in a sling, was holding forth in a Washington hotel surrounded by a group of eager listeners: "There is a dash about these Southerners absolutely terrific; we can't stop the devils when they charge, without killing them all—and sometimes we do that—but if we don't, they are bound to take our batteries."[8]

This was the glory, but the grim side came in the close-set columns of casualties among North Carolina troops, which day by day followed the bloody affair along Antietam Creek.

So depressing was news coming from the hospitals that soon it had to be lightened, the Raleigh *Standard* seemed to think, so it printed a vintage story of a colloquy:

Lady (at bedside of sick solider)—How dy'e do. Is there anything you want?

Soldier—No, I believe not.

Lady—Isn't there *something* I can do for you?

Soldier—No, I think not.

Lady—Oh, I do want to do something for you. Can't I wash your hands and face?

Soldier—Well, if you want to right bad, I reckon you can; but if you do, you will be the fourteenth lady who has done so this morning.[9]

In North Carolina a note of disgust over the campaign was directed partly against the performance of Maryland, whose song had been the top hit of the soldiers in the early days of the war. Now, after Sharpsburg, the Salisbury *Watchman* commented: " 'Maryland, My Maryland,' whistled and sung by almost every body capable of these performances, sounds a little flat since the return of Gen. Lee from that unfriendly territory. The population of Frederick City gave him a cautious reception as if fearful of the consequences; but when Abe Lincoln subsequently visited them, they became enthusiastic in their demonstrations of joy. 'Maryland, My Maryland' is about sung out, we would think, after these signs of submission to the tyrant. Their intimate relations with the money worshippers of New York and Philadelphia, have, we fear, so far corrupted their patriotism as to render the State hopelessly mercenary. Our Government has petted her people no little, since the beginning of the war, by crowding them into offices, and, so far, without any important good results."[10]

Holden in his Raleigh *Standard* was blunt in his criticism of the campaign: He reported that Lee's army was concentrated around Winchester. "This ends the boasted invasion of the North, an idea which we never entertained as either possible with our means, desirable or wise."[11]

Soon after the retirement across the Potomac, Brigadier General W. Dorsey Pender wrote to Vance from Bunker Hill, Virginia, urging stringent enforcement of the conscript law in the state as a means of restoring some of his missing men to his brigade. The practice of Confederates going home for a spell after the battles was beginning to be seen after the campaigns on the Peninsula and against Pope. Pender stated that some of his officers who left after the battles around Richmond to get conscripts had not yet been heard from. "I have not only needed the conscripts," wrote Pender, "but also the officers sent after them. I had to fight in several battles with less than 300 men in my Brigade and without an officer in some of the companies. Two of my regiments have frequently been with only one & two Captains."

Pender asked that the civil officers of the state arrest and hold any officer or soldier home without leave. "There are at least 500 men &

officers & too large a portion of the latter absent without any excuse
or reason from my Brigade alone."[12]

Pender's was by no means the only skeleton brigade in the battle of
Sharpsburg. Lee's army was so grievously weakened by straggling and
absenteeism that he fought the battle with somewhere between 35,000
and 45,000 men. He reported his strength as "less than 40,000 men."
In writing to Davis September 21, just after regaining the Virginia
shore, Lee gave the startling figures that in the battle Evans's Brigade had
present only 100 men, Garnett's 120 men, and Lawton and Armistead
together, 600 men.[13]

McClellan gave his strength as 87,000, with 60,000 bearing the
brunt of the fighting.[14]

Lee's army had been threadbare—so different observers described it
—when it entered Maryland. The hard marching of the Maryland campaign wore out such clothing and shoes as had been serviceable. Vance
had not yet set up his import channels or extended textile manufacturing
and was hard pressed to supply the North Carolina regiments. Said
a volunteer correspondent who wrote to the Raleigh *Standard* from
Martinsville, Virginia, about the 48th North Carolina, another regiment
which had gone through the sanguinary fighting in the army's center:
"Our boys have only one suit of clothing (well worn) and very little
bed clothing, having left them behind in our retreat, and not a blanket
for every half dozen men, and many of them barefooted. They are half
starved, half clothed, hard marched, hard fought, and still are cheerful
and make little complaint. Something must be done for them, in the
way of bed clothing in particular, and that quickly."[15]

The broader picture was contained in a dispatch to the Savannah,
Georgia, *Republican*, written nine days after the battle: It told of the
suffering, straggling and difficulties attending such a trying campaign:
"I can recall of no parallel instance in history, except Napoleon's
disastrous retreat from Moscow, where an army has ever done more
marching and fighting, under such great disadvantages, than General
Lee's has done since it left the James River."[16]

Another of Vance's army problems was pay. While Lee was in
Frederick, Maryland, Lieutenant Colonel Thomas Ruffin, Jr., son of
Chief Justice Thomas Ruffin, of the 13th North Carolina, wrote to the
governor saying the regiment had received no pay for six months and
that the men were in great want. Nor had the state bounty, due the
soldiers on their enlistment, been paid. Ruffin excused the Confederate

government for not paying the regular monthly amounts because "it has been our misfortune not to be able to make our Muster-rolls for a long time, we being Either on the march or engaged in fighting on every muster day." The state had no excuse because the proper muster rolls for the bounty were made out and $10 had been paid on them. "Our men are without clothing & shoes," Ruffin continued, "as the government cannot furnish them their only Chance to get them is to buy them: Our other regiments are provided with money, While ours is destitute. Even this does not make them murmur. . . ."[17]

Vance had been governor only a day when the letter was written. Neglect of the soldiers he would not tolerate. As soon as he received it he hurried off a reply.

"I will send the paymaster to your regiment as soon as possible. He has gone to Cumberland Gap to pay off our troops there and will return in a fortnight. I will telegraph him, and if he has money sufficient to pay off your regiment, to call by on his return, and if he has not, I will send him on . . ." The regiment was entitled to considerate treatment. Its performance would be outstanding at Gettysburg and on other fields.[18]

One of the best descriptions of the North Carolina regiments at this time was provided by Murdock J. McSween, a controversial lawyer, journalist and soldier from Richmond County, North Carolina, who later became a thorn in Vance's side, but in November, 1862, when he wrote to the governor, was a stanch friend. He was something of a wanderer between regiments without anyone seeming to be certain of his precise affiliation. In the autumn of 1862 he made a circuit of several North Carolina commands, and the conditions he reported were such as to impel the governor to redouble his supply efforts.

McSween observed that units stationed around Petersburg and Richmond were well equipped and clothed. The soldiers of the Army of the Potomac (Lee's army had this name both in the North Carolina press and in private correspondence, the later official name of the Army of Northern Virginia not yet being employed) were in woeful need of shoes, blankets, and clothes. Sharpsburg had been an eroding battle. McSween found that the North Carolina companies with Lee, after the casualties in Maryland, averaged thirty effectives. "About one third are barefooted or the same as barefooted—I saw many men marching in the snow entirely without shoes or any substitute. There are perhaps ten men in a company well shod." The scarcity of blankets was distressing, for it was moving into late November, a season in which the Virginia weather is subject often to severe cold spells.

Another difficulty, and it was a true hardship, was that the troops had not changed clothes for several weeks and possessed nothing fresh, having lost or stored their baggage during the hard campaigning in Virginia before entering Maryland. The baggage left behind in Virginia had been "damaged, stolen or misplaced," during their absence, according to McSween.

"They are of course ragged and dirty," he reported to Vance, "and itch vermin and disease are very prevalent." All he said confirmed the distressing report from Dr. Warren. He listed as the articles of greatest need shoes, blankets, pants, and coats, and "any sort of a hat or cap will do." The men were making their own gloves and socks from the rags of the old clothing. "It matters but little what is the color of the clothing —so it is not blue."[19]

McSween's letter, direct from the army after one of its most grueling campaigns, was of course influential with Vance and affected him deeply. One could not but be moved by such lines, coming after Dr. Warren's report that "many a sick soldier lies for weeks in rags & filth and actually rots away with disease. The proper vegetables & nourishment for the sick are much needed especially in Richmond, Gordonville & Culpepper & there is no way to get them." McSween made some pertinent recommendations and an observation which certainly must have interested Vance, in view of his thinking along the same lines. One recommendation was that the state should assist in the manufacture and purchase of medicine. Clearly, from his description, the wounded and sick still needed more medical supplies, even after Dr. Warren's energetic efforts. Another: "It would be to the interest of North Carolina & her soldiers if the state should retain control over her manufactures & resources till her own troops are supplied." The Confederate quartermasters were endeavoring to get supplies and Quartermaster General Myers could not promise much until later. McSween must have talked with Myers, for he quoted that officer as saying he would be seriously embarrassed if he could not gain control of the resources and manufactures of North Carolina. McSween's warning against this was based on the dire need of the whole army, and the fact that he noticed troops from some of the other states were even worse off than the North Carolinians. The Myers plan would mean that North Carolina supplies "might be exhausted on others while her own sons were suffering." Still another sensible suggestion was that the hospitals acquire and retain stores of underclothing which the soldiers might use when recovering. The change and cleanliness would speed the recovery, he felt.

The observation, which must have interested Vance particularly, indicated that General Lee was fully aware of the hazards of overloading the soldiers with clothing—the matter about which Vance was to caution him at a later date. "Gen. Lee says he does not wish the troops to have two or more supplies and hopes that economy and system can be practiced—He regards an over abundant supply as a useless waste of our scanty resources & a serious impediment to his movements & plans."

Overcoats, according to McSween's observations, were not "strictly necessary." They were certain to be lost if the army had to march or fight much. "A good common suit with plenty of under clothing and a good large blanket is amply sufficient and as much as the soldiers can possibly carry & save." It is to be remembered that Southern soldiers at times scoffed at their Northern enemies saying the reason they could not fight as well was that they carried on their backs too much extra clothing. McSween put his finger on a serious difficulty—that too many Southern soldiers were wearing Yankee uniforms. He thought the captured blue coats ought to be dyed another color, though how they could have been dyed from dark blue to gray was not explained.

Northern plenty was in the Carolina news. The debacle of McClellan's campaign against Richmond was being described to the home public. After the blue and gray armies had moved away from the James River, civilians explored McClellan's old campsite along the river. They found thousands of torn and rotting tents; rusty axes, spades, shovels and tools aplenty; beef and fish barrels and liquor cases and much else strewn over the countryside. The abandoned riches were being gathered by residents along the river and sold to later comers. "Leaden balls are worth 25¢ per pound and thousands of pounds can be gathered up with little trouble. The cloth of the abandoned tents is worth 7¢ per yard and any quantity of this can be obtained from there."[20]

Apparently Vance could have outfitted a good-sized Carolina brigade with what McClellan in his haste had left behind.

## Chapter Fifteen

## Doughty Runners of the Blockade

After the loss of the towns and forts commanding Albemarle and Pamlico sounds, North Carolina was reduced to the single port city of Wilmington, twenty-eight miles upstream from the mouth of the Cape Fear River. Under Vance and two able Confederate officers, Major General Whiting and Colonel William Lamb, Wilmington became the rendezvous of blockade-runners and for the better part of three years perhaps the most important city of the Confederacy.

Richmond might be lost without heralding the collapse of the cause, but neither Lee's army nor the home public could survive long without the commerce which plied into this busy port, bringing food, medicines, shoes, clothing, machinery, and munitions of different types, all the prime needs of the army, ranging from cargoes of powder for muskets and cannon to heavy Whitworth rifled guns.

Vance's main part in this vast import and export operation was to procure a North Carolina squadron, headed by one of the fleetest and sturdiest of the blockade-runners, the *Ad-Vance*, and to set up an organization abroad and in his state by which he could exchange cotton or cotton credits for the most urgently required supplies, which he passed on to North Carolina troops, to the Confederate government, Lee's army, and the home public.

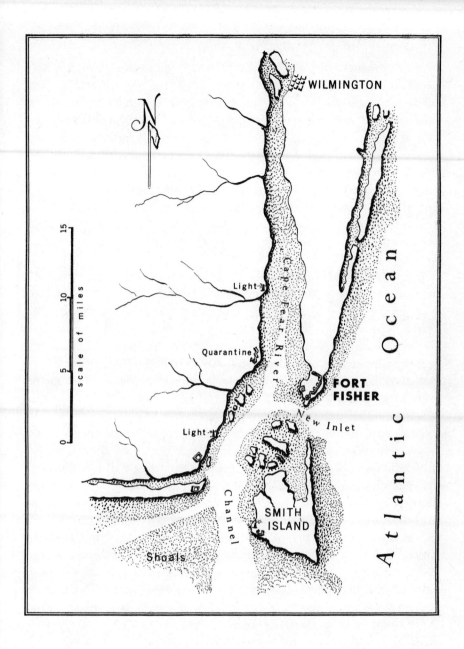

*Fort Fisher, captured by Federal sea and land forces January 15, 1865.
The map shows the channels at the mouth of the Cape Fear River and
the city of Wilmington upstream.*

Many privately owned blockade-runners took advantage of the port of Wilmington and to a lesser extent Charleston, South Carolina, and made enormous profits out of the war, but Vance conducted his state's business on a cost basis, for the benefit of the troops and the people, and of all his enterprises, this was among the highly successful, though he seemed to be impeded at nearly every turn by the Richmond authorities. Confederate officialdom, as in the instance of his manufacture of clothing, wanted to crowd in on his activities instead of initiating government-owned blockade-running on a large scale on their own account. He was finally forced in a note of disgust to inform his state legislature that Wilmington was "blockaded more effectively from within than without."[1]

One or two enterprising Confederate officials did see the advantage of blockade-running by the government and entered the trade in a limited way, among them Josiah Gorgas, chief of ordnance for the Confederate States, who without co-operation from the War Department bought five vessels which made successful voyages through the blockade, bringing in badly needed ordnance stores. An alert Navy Department representative, James D. Bulloch, likewise brought in munitions, but on the whole the central government appeared to be more dilatory along this line of essential endeavor than almost any other.

Blockade-running was no especial prerogative of North Carolina. All of the seceding states had coastlines except Tennessee and Arkansas, while the shore line of Florida was greater than that of all the Northern states combined, but Wilmington did have the advantage in that it was fairly close to Lee's army and had a direct railroad connection through Kinston, Weldon, and Petersburg with Richmond.

The gulf ports, many of them less tenaciously held by the Confederacy than Wilmington, were in turn closer to the armies in the western theater of the war. They were more remote from European provisioners, but some were closer to the exchange port of Nassau.

Something of a fort had been evolving below Wilmington after April, 1861, on the tongue of land on the left bank of the Cape Fear River at its mouth, an area known as Federal Point but renamed Confederate Point when North Carolina seceded. Here the batteries protected the New Inlet, the most favored but not the only channel into the river. The Federal blockading squadron which ordinarily numbered upwards of twenty-five ships, and often many more, patrolled a considerable section of the coast, a difficult task because of its broken nature and a number of shoals and islands, one of which, Smith's, was ten miles long and lay directly in the mouth of the river. This island separated the Old from the New Inlet.

Renamed several times, the works at the end of Confederate Point were in 1862 called Fort Fisher in honor of Colonel Charles F. Fisher of Salisbury, North Carolina, who fell at First Manassas while commanding the celebrated 6th North Carolina regiment, one of the state's famous combat units. Fisher was killed just after the regiment and the 33rd Virginia of Stonewall Jackson's Brigade charged and captured the Federal batteries of Ricketts and Griffin at the critical moment of the battle.[2]

Lamb strengthened and extended the fort continually almost until the hour it fell in the final phase of the war, and gave it undoubtedly the strongest sand and earthen ramparts in the South, and a model for a harbor defense which was studied long after the war. The fort ran across the point where it was half a mile wide, then down the beach a mile, and so powerful did the Federal Navy think it to be that it was approached gingerly and did not come under any all-out attack until near the end of the conflict. Meantime, this life line of the Confederacy, a haven for ocean-going ships, was preserved, though in the post mortems following the war there was considerable amazement about it. Said a *Harper's Magazine* article in 1866, "It is singular to us that the United States should so long neglect to close the only port, almost, of the Confederacy, into which every 'dark of the moon' there ran half a dozen or so swift blockade runners, freighted with cannon, muskets and every munition of war, medicine, cloth, shoes, bacon, etc."[3]

Of similar purport was the comment of one of the romantic blockade-runners familiarly known in Wilmington as "Captain Roberts," who proved to be the son of the Earl of Buckinghamshire, commander of Queen Victoria's yacht. Captain Roberts, who later as Hobart Pasha commanded the Turkish grand fleet, seemed surprised: "We were much struck with the weakness of Fort Fisher, which, with a garrison of twelve hundred men, and only half finished, could have been easily taken at any time since the war began by a resolute body of five thousand men making a night attack. . . . I fancy the bold front shown so long by its occupants had much to do with the fact that . . . an attack was not attempted till just before the close of the war."

Vance entered blockade-running on behalf of his state at the suggestion of Adjutant General James G. Martin, who had proposed it to

Governor Henry T. Clark shortly before Vance took office. If Vance hesitated momentarily when he became governor, the reason was that strong opposition existed to the project, notably from the able Raleigh lawyer and former attorney general of the state Bartholomew Figures Moore. His assertion that it would be unconstitutional was not to be taken lightly, coming from one who had helped to draft the revised code of the state and was a senior authority well versed in constitutional principles. Another respected opponent, who made wariness essential, was Vance's erstwhile supporter, Editor Holden of the *Standard*, who was likely to be against anything not of his authorship. That Vance soon adopted the plan wholeheartedly and made it successful showed his courage to risk sharp criticism if he believed a course to be correct.[4]

In truth, the opportunities were so inviting he could not ignore them. After perfecting his plans he went to the legislature in closed sessions and by his able presentation prevailed on that body to make an appropriation of $2,000,000 for the inauguration of his venture, which broadly was for the state to purchase the cotton grown by its own citizens, sell what it could in the export trade and hold the balance in storage, and issue against it certificates or warrants which could be sold for the purchase of supplies abroad.

The first step was of course the purchase of a blockade-runner. Vance designated for this purpose and to act also as his European agent a Warrenton merchant of Scottish birth, successful John White, forty-eight years old, a native of Kirkcaldy, Fifeshire, who had reached North Carolina when he was fourteen years old.[5] His dry goods business in 1862 was probably the largest in the state, and to house it he had built during the 1850s three handsome brick buildings, which when the war came he was operating with his son-in-law as partner under the name of Arrington, White & Company. Vance never made a better appointment because White proved to be an agent of high intelligence and strict integrity, but apparently the governor was not acquainted with him before making the designation and relied on the recommendations of Colonel John Devereux, quartermaster general of North Carolina, and Major Thomas D. Hogg, chief ordnance officer of the state.

White sailed from Charleston November 15, 1862. With rare discernment and the assistance of Thomas M. Crossan, a fellow townsman, of Warrenton—"Glorious Tom Crossan"[6] he came to be called—who had fought with Vance at New Bern and had a record of service in both the old United States Navy and the Confederate Navy, he bought for

$190,000 the *Lord Clyde*, a fast steamer built for the Dublin-Glasgow trade. Captain Crossan took command, rechristened the ship the *Ad-Vance* in the governor's honor, and procured the services of a hardy and experienced Scotch sailing master, Wylie. He signed a crew and made ready for the first voyage, which was begun from Cardiff, May 30, 1863.

White's difficulties in disposing of his cotton certificates were multitudinous and were not eased by the Confederate emissary in Great Britain, James M. Mason, who induced him to suspend his efforts while the Confederacy was undertaking, through Mason, to negotiate a British loan. Eventually White made a financial arrangement which proved favorable to both parties with the London banking house of Alexander Collie & Co., and began the purchase of supplies for shipment to Bermuda, whence they would be transported to Wilmington by the newly acquired *Ad-Vance*. Thereafter she carried cotton from Wilmington mainly to Bermuda and at Bermuda loaded for the return voyage with the treasured items Vance felt were most urgently needed by the state's troops.

Back in North Carolina Vance began to have troubles almost at once, though they were minor at first. After White had been selected and was about to depart, the Confederate War Department declined for a time to release his son-in-law, S. P. Arrington, from line duty to other work, in order that Vance might assign him to conduct White's business in Warrenton. Secretary George W. Randolph refused to make the transfer when Vance wrote to him on November 1, but soon Seddon succeeded Randolph as Secretary of War and nineteen days later, after White had sailed, Vance had his aide David Barnes renew the request. He explained that White had extensive mercantile interests in Warrenton but had accepted the duty of acting as the state's agent to purchase supplies. It was necessary for him to leave someone in charge, and the knowledge of the business was possessed only by his partner and son-in-law Arrington. The evidence that the request was at length granted is that Vance did not continue to write about it.[7]

Vance commissioned William H. Oliver of New Bern to purchase cotton for blockade-running purposes. The instruction Oliver received through the state's quartermaster general, Devereux, was to buy every bale of cotton he could put his hands on and to pay a stipulated price of twenty cents a pound. That was substantially higher than cotton was commanding in some areas at the time, but it meant ready sales. He went first to the areas near the Federal lines, to clear out all cotton within reach of Federal raiding parties. In a brief period he purchased 7,000 bales for which he paid $700,000, but the tedious aspect of the job was to get the cotton moved, because of the scarcity of railroad engines and cars. Vance borrowed a steamboat, the *Cotton Plant,* for transporting part of this cotton on the Roanoke River. A large part of the purchases were taken to Graham, North Carolina, a safe repository between Greensboro and Chapel Hill, and against it Vance issued his North Carolina cotton warrants with which he purchased the cargoes for the *Lord Clyde,* or *Ad-Vance.* Heavy consignments of cotton had been shipped when Agent John White sailed from Charleston on the steamer *Leopard* in November.[8]

Large quantities of the cotton purchased by the state were delivered by Oliver, under Vance's order, to the manufacturing firm of John Newland & Sons, at Saxapahaw, where it was manufactured into cloth, which in turn was delivered to Quartermaster General Devereux for use in making uniforms. This plant also made yarn which Vance exchanged in Virginia for much needed leather, which was quickly fashioned into shoes. These were by-products of his blockade-running operation. When machinery for making cards, which were required for the manufacture of cloth, began to arrive on the *Ad-Vance* it was set up in the factory of William H. Willard, and Oliver was thereby enabled to distribute a large number of pairs of cards over the state.[9]

The story of the *Ad-Vance* was told in some detail by James Maglenn, chief engineer, who joined the ship as an engine room assistant when she arrived in Wilmington on her first voyage and remained with her until she was captured in September, 1864, after a highly successful career. Her name had a double application, he explained: first an honor to the governor, meaning "To Vance," and the second signifying that she was the state's pioneer ship. Though the second significance seems remote, some have preferred it and have called the vessel the *Advance,* but that name was not employed by Vance, nor by the crew, nor by the editor of North Carolina's best-known war accounts. Since Vance, representing the state, owned the vessel, he may be looked to as giving the official name.

Maglenn described some of the trips as "exciting and hazardous." Though some might appear to have been fairly routine runs between Bermuda and Wilmington, taking cotton one way and returning through the blockade with the urgently needed uniform cloth, shoes, medicines, and military stores, all were loaded with tension and excitement. One trip was a return to Liverpool for repairs. Buffeted by gales, chased by formidable Federal squadrons, filled with water to within six inches of the grate bars of her furnace, she was often in dire peril, while her crew at times almost abandoned hope, stranded as she once was on the shoals within enemy range. She was attacked often by Federal gunboats, but she made eleven full voyages into Wilmington through the presumably tight blockade.[10]

Laden as she was on incoming voyages, she nevertheless had room for the Reverend Moses D. Hoge of Richmond to bring in a large consignment of Bibles and religious tracts for soldiers. On that particular voyage she had a narrow and fortuitous escape from the Federal blockaders and the nature of the cargo may have helped her to get in, though she was aided also by a direct hit by one of the Fort Fisher Columbiads on the nearest pursuing Federal gunboat. "It was a scene of intense excitement," wrote the Reverend Mr. Hoge in his account.[11]

James Sprunt, purser of the companion blockade-runner *Lilian*, left another account of the *Ad-Vance,* in which he credited Vance with both inaugurating the venture and supplying the energy behind all the state-operated blockade-running. The *Ad-Vance*, as he understood it, was named "in compliment to the distinguished war governor."[12]

The first arrival of the *Ad-Vance* in Wilmington on Sunday, June 26, 1863, was not only the signal for rejoicing in the port and a little later throughout North Carolina, but also the occasion of one of Vance's severe ruptures with the Confederacy because, as on other occasions, it had sent a Virginia officer to a North Carolina command, and in this instance one who had the temerity to affront the strong-minded North Carolina governor personally.

When the *Ad-Vance* reached the protection of Fort Fisher down the Cape Fear River, Vance hurried down to Wilmington. With a group of friends and officials, he boarded a river steamer, the *Flora*—having obtained permission from both the harbor and military authorities for the trip—to greet the *Ad-Vance* officially. The meeting was supposed to be at the quarantine station fifteen miles below the town. Zeb, in his enthusiasm over the initial success of his venture, boarded and visited around the ship, examining the cargo and talking with the officers, while the *Ad-Vance* meantime pushed up the river and made fast at the Wilmington Custom House wharf.

At this juncture Lieutenant Colonel Charles E. Thorburn, who had held a variety of assignments under the Confederacy in Virginia but was now commander of the city and river defenses of Wilmington, acting under General Whiting, the district commander, who was absent, came to the wharf in full uniform and pompous manner. In "a loud and commanding tone," as Sprunt described it, he ordered that the *Advance* be turned about and steered back to quarantine. There she would be compelled to languish for a period of fifteen days, even though no communicable diseases happened to be reported among her crew. Vance, who had obtained clearance for the vessel, was standing near the gangway when the pretentious lieutenant colonel delivered his ultimatum. As Sprunt gave it, the governor "heard the rude speech of the military satrap and noticed his offensive manner." Vance, whose passions could flare, bristled immediately, but with outward calm, inquired firmly:

"Do you dare to say, sir, that the Governor of the State shall not leave the deck of his own ship?"

Colonel Thorburn replied curtly—and the words were well remembered and noted down—that he would not let anyone pass off the ship "if he was Governor Vance or Governor Jesus Christ."

For a moment there was danger of an eruption. As was said "the Governor was young then and his blood was hot." But some of his party stepped in front of him. Meantime the colonel gave orders to his soldiers to shoot down anyone who tried to leave the ship. This was not exactly a cordial reception to accord the most important blockade-runner ever to reach the Confederate shore, and one bursting to her load limit with supplies urgently needed for the prosecution of the war and the comfort of the army—supplies upon which the outcome of a battle might depend. By the arbitrary orders of a lieutenant colonel they were to be held in quarantine for fifteen days. Whether or not the officer was correct, his manner was highly offensive. Had he been discreet, Vance's authority would have been sufficient to relieve him of any responsibility or blame he might have incurred for passing the vessel.

Someone had sent for the Chairman of the Board of Commissioners of Navigation, P. W. Fanning, who had charge of clearing vessels in the harbor. He arrived hurriedly and quickly issued a permit allowing entry for the ship and authorizing any passengers on board to land when they desired. Governor Vance was the first down the gangplank. He saluted Fanning with respect and proclaimed in his stentorian voice for the crowd which had gathered, "No man is more prompt to obey the civil authorities than myself, but I will not be ridden over by epaulettes or bayonets." The crowd, clearly siding with the young governor, gave him three hearty cheers as he left to make arrangements to load the cargo of the *Ad-Vance* on a special train waiting to transport it to Raleigh. Then the crowd had time to cheer the ship, which was flying from her masts and yards numerous flags, flapping in the morning breeze.[13]

Probably it was the circumstance that Colonel Thorburn was an out-of-state officer in charge of a North Carolina post which rankled most with Vance, but he was not one to forget a discourteous challenge to his authority by anyone. As quickly as he could he wrote directly to President Davis about the incident, dated July 8, 1863, explaining that he had obtained the consent of General Whiting for the trip down the river and had displayed the permit to Lieutenant Colonel Thorburn before that officer employed his rude language. Vance quoted his words and told Davis the officer had posted a guard on the wharf and given it orders to shoot anyone attempting to leave the vessel. Vance's schedule had been seriously upset by the functionary because the delay while awaiting the arrival of the commissioner of navigation caused him to miss his train for Raleigh.[14]

Then in vigorous terms he stated to Davis his complaint against Thorburn: "Having thus deliberately, wilfully and without excuse inflicted a gross insult upon the people of North Carolina through her Chief Magistrate, in their name I now demand his removal from the State, and that he be no more placed in command of her troops. If it be indispensable that North Carolina soldiers be commanded by Virginians, I should regret to see the Old Dominion retain all her gentlemen for her own use and furnish us only her blackguards."[15]

The governor's ire created one of those taut situations which the observant Rebel War Clerk J. B. Jones liked to dwell on in his diary and he gave full treatment to the incident. When Davis received the letter he endorsed it for Secretary Seddon saying it required his attention "if the case be as stated."[16]

Meantime, General Whiting had relieved Thorburn of his command and had written apologetically to Vance, July 1, 1863, explaining that the governor was in no manner at fault and that the *Ad-Vance* had in fact already been cleared when he boarded her. Technically the lieutenant colonel was within his orders to carry out the ordinances of the Wilmington commissioners of navigation, but he admitted to Whiting that he had used disrespectful language. Whiting explained that the *Ad-Vance* had not been held up at quarantine, as supposed, but had grounded on the Rips before inspection. "On ascertaining that she was from Bermuda," he wrote, "and with a clean bill of health and knowing also that she belonged to the State, I at once sent to her my steamer to lighten her. This had been going on for several days and accordingly I gave readily the Steamer *Flora* and permission to your party to visit the *Advance*. To quarantine the *Advance* after so much previous communication and the breaking out of her cargo was in my opinion useless." Whiting regretted he had not been in Wilmington at the time, for he could have prevented the disturbing incident.[17]

Lieutenant Colonel Thorburn submitted his resignation from the Confederate Army from Petersburg, Virginia, August 5, 1863, and it was accepted to take effect October 1, 1863.[18]

Purser Sprunt described the *Ad-Vance* as "a first-class ship in every respect." Her engines had great power and were "very highly finished," and with a pressure of twenty pounds per square inch she averaged seventeen knots; at thirty pounds "she reeled off twenty knots without difficulty." That explains why she could outstrip pursuers. Her only shortcoming was her heavy draught which made it difficult to take her across shoals that were plentiful in the Cape Fear River. As a precaution she was never sent out or brought in fully loaded. Sprunt said "the regularity of her trips was remarkable and could be calculated upon almost to the very day; indeed, it was common to hear upon the streets the almost stereotyped remark, 'Tomorrow the *Ad-Vance* will be in.' And when the morrow came she could generally be seen gliding up to her dock with the rich freight of goods and wares which were so greatly needed by our people."[19]

Sometimes she was incorrectly referred to as the *A. D. Vance* and as such she appears in the United States Navy Records.[20]

Governor Vance managed to get some peculiar officers and sailors aboard the ship. One was James Fauntleroy Taylor II, son of the solicitor general of North Carolina, whose manner of speaking and pronunciation was close to absurd, yet he insisted on having others conform to it. When General George Washington Haywood, an eminent Raleigh lawyer, broke down mentally during the war—plagued by the notion that because he had not favored secession he was being spied on by government agents—Fauntleroy Taylor II became his escort. Taylor took him to his brother in Alabama and it was the tale that those they encountered en route were unable to determine which was the crazy man and which the caretaker.

Taylor was known as the Bard of Ram-cat, a section of Wake County he called Rham-kart. Having one blind eye, he still obtained a berth as a petty officer on the *Ad-Vance,* and managed to serve without spending his time in irons below decks. Kemp Battle told how he demanded from others such pronunciations as go-at for goat, to-ad for toad, and ah-li-gah-tor for alligator. When the captain of the vessel was giving him orders, he would stop him in the middle of a sentence and correct his pronunciation, to make it conform to his own strange standards. He had a rule for safety in blockade-running or battle: "A bullet, gentle-men, has a path called its line of trajectory. All you have to do to ensure safety is to stand to the right or the left of this line."[21]

But even with the Fauntleroy Taylor IIs, who showed how hard pressed Vance was for nonmilitary personnel, he got the cargoes through.

Colonel William Lamb, who from the ramparts of Fort Fisher had the closest view of the blockade-runners and as much as anyone was respon-sible for the success because he made a sort of Gibraltar of his fort—a Malakoff was the word employed in that day because the Crimean War had just been fought—took command of the Confederate Point de-fenses, including Zeke's Island, on July 4, 1862, at a time when serious blockade-running there was just beginning. The defensive works were meager then and could have been carried by even a puny Federal expedi-tion. Fort Fisher had but three heavy guns and only fourteen others, while Zeke's Island had two 32-pounders. A Federal squadron might have steamed past with impunity, but that was not the case after Lamb had been at work for a time erecting sand ramparts and parapets, which many, including some of the enemy, said he could not do, and if he could, that they would not be effective.

Vance, Lamb, and Whiting are the three names which dominated the on-shore phase of blockade-running, and they began their association with it at about the same time: Whiting a few months after Malvern Hill, Lamb three days after the date of that battle, and Vance about two months later. The first blockade-runners entering Wilmington that summer were nondescript steamers and old sailing vessels—anything of light draft. Quickly steamers designed for the trade were built in Great Britain. They were low, long, narrow, and sleek, about nine times as long as wide, having side wheels or double screws, and being dull gray in color for low visibility. They ranged, as Lamb described those which passed him, from 400 to 700 tons. Their stacks might be lowered close to the deck, lessening the distance at which they might be sighted; they never showed lights and they used coal that made the thinnest, whitest smoke.[22]

Nassau, on its sandy island of New Providence, suddenly became one of the world's busiest ports and most cosmopolitan cities, and none could have been more ideally suited for the stealthy trade, because the Bahamas had banks, coral reefs, shoals, and difficult passages, and the blockade-runners always had on board a Bahaman pilot who knew the channels as he knew the palm of his hand. The heavy Federal vessels, which remained at sea off Alaco Light and occasionally sent in a small boat to the American consul, were not equipped to deal with the runners, who came and went almost at will. Nassau was 550 miles from Wilmington. Sprunt, who was there often, described the conditions: "The wharves of Nassau were piled high with cotton during the war, and huge warehouses were stored full of supplies for the Confederacy. At times the harbor was crowded with lead-colored, short masted, rakish-looking steamers; the streets alive with the bustle and activity of the day, swarmed with drunken revellers at night. Almost every nationality on earth was represented there. . . ."[23]

These blockade-runners came to be the life line that sustained Lee's army and allowed it to fight during its last years, when the area of the Confederacy was gradually being pushed in. The success of such operations, considering the size of the Federal blockading squadrons, must be looked on as one of the astonishing phases of the war. Sprunt gave the number of vessels engaged in the Wilmington trade as eighty-three while Lamb placed it at one hundred; Sprunt numbered the losses at thirty-seven captured by the enemy, twelve destroyed or sunk, eleven lost but with their cargoes partially saved, and one foundered, a total loss of sixty-one. Lamb put the losses at sixty-five captured or destroyed. Few were taken before they had made several trips; one, the *Robert E. Lee,* made twenty-one trips, and three others made eighteen, the *Fanny,* the *Margaret,* and the *Jessie.*

But they made 363 voyages to Nassau and 65 to other ports, such as Bermuda and Halifax, and they brought in freight of enormous value, ranging from $300 to $1,000 per ton. The success cannot be measured so much by the number of ships lost during the whole war as by the frequency of the successful voyages. It seems almost incredible that with a large hostile fleet lying off the mouth of the Cape Fear River watchful as a cat at a mousehole, a vessel arrived with a rich cargo every day in August, 1863, and that an average of an arrival each day was almost attained from January to October of that year. Vance was often at Wilmington and maintained the closest harmony with Whiting and Lamb. The fort had a meager guard, consisting mainly of the 36th North Carolina regiment, designated also as the Second Artillery, with Lamb the commander.

But the hazards and romance were with the runners and not the defenders. The ships were commanded by Confederate and British naval officers, the British using assumed names and being on leave from Her Majesty's service. They were manned by skillful sailors, many of them British. The pay made the risks worth taking. The sailors received monthly wages of $100 in gold and a bounty of $50 at the end of the voyage, while the captains and pilots received up to $5,000 for a single run. Sprunt, one of the articulate participants in the trade, paid a high tribute to those who took the heavily loaded vessels past the watching Federal patrols: "The Cape Fear pilots have long maintained a standard of excellence. . . . The story of their wonderful skill and bravery in the time of the Federal blockade has never been written. . . . Amidst impenetrable darkness, without lightship or beacon, the narrow and closely watched inlet was felt for with a deep-sea lead as a blind man feels his way along a familiar path, and even when the enemy's fire was raking the wheel-house, the faithful pilot, with steady hand, and iron nerve, safely steered the little fugitive of the sea to her desired haven."[24]

Vance was as closely in control of the state's blockade-running as any competent businessman would be in the efficient operation of his factory or store. One of his heavy tasks was his correspondence with White and his later temporary agents, Duncan K. McRae and George N. Sanders. He directed the sale of the North Carolina cotton and rosin bonds and he placed the orders for the merchandise required. He worried about the "corruption" that entered into the buying, which was not a reflection on his agents but related to price gouging on the London market. He rationed his cargo space as a planter would allot his acreage to the most essential crops.

Vance would send such staccato orders as: Need no more cloth; shoes and blankets wanted. Shoes mostly too narrow. Blankets too heavy and large.[25] He took pride in what he called his "long legged steamer" and listed as the important supplies she brought in especially grain scythes (the reaper and binder had not yet made headway in the South), card clothing for the factories, handcards for the old-fashioned looms, medicines, and "large quantities of shoes, blankets and army clothes." He seemed to delight in the fact that she often entered the port "in broad daylight, in the face of the blockading fleet."[26]

Thirty years after the height of the blockade-running Colonel Lamb wrote: "There was scarcely a dark night that I was not called upon the ramparts to admit a friendly vessel . . . The running through the [enemy] squadron and safely over the bar in daylight of the powder-laden *Cornubia,* in 1862, and the *A.D. Vance* . . . in 1864 (the latter steamer rescued by a timely shot from a ten-inch Columbiad in the fort) were incidents never to be forgotten."[27] This was the instance when the Reverend Moses D. Hoge's consignment of Bibles was saved —an event which seemed to have had considerable impact in the South. The Confederacy had a feeble printing industry, and even with starvation always looking in at the door, a devout people appeared to be happy to sacrifice cargo space in order that copies of the Scriptures might be placed in the hands of the soldiers.

Arrival of the vessels came to be quite commonplace, as when the Raleigh *Standard* announced in a mere item May 27, 1863, that Wilmington had eight blockade-runners in the port with a good assortment of stores.[28]

Not to be ignored in Lamb's armament at Fort Fisher were four rifled Whitworth guns which he had salvaged from the wrecked *Modern Greece* and posted to range five miles. When they announced their presence with a salvo, they suggested that the blockading Federals should move farther out to sea. But the guns were so good they were coveted and three were transferred, while the fourth eventually was lost when sent to the relief of a wrecked blockade-runner along the shore.[29] It was the gun that had saved the *Ad-Vance* and the Bibles and, according to General Whiting, "dozens of vessels and millions of money." His need for long-range guns was so great that he eventually got six other Whitworths from the blockade-runners. Vance of course could not know that the Reverend Mr. Hoge who brought in the Bibles would deliver his funeral address in the United States Senate chamber thirty years later.

Judge Walter Clark, a boy veteran of the war and later chief justice of the North Carolina Supreme Court as well as the state's most diligent contemporary war historian and editor of regimental accounts, was frank in his praise of Vance, sharp in his criticism of President Davis on the score of blockade-running. Vance, he said, "organized a basis of supplies beyond the ocean and sent the steamer *Advance* back and forth like a weaver's shuttle, through beleaguering and hostile fleets, bringing needed supplies alike for army and people. Had the President of the Confederacy possessed equal foresight and enterprise the catastrophe [of losing the war] might possibly have been avoided. The ability and patriotism then displayed by their chosen chief impressed his memory indelibly upon the affections of the people of North Carolina. To his latest hour they never forgot him or took away his lineaments from their heart of hearts." Judge Clark added a comment which seemed to epitomize Vance's public career: "As for money, there was not enough to buy him."[30]

Wharton J. Green, of West Point and the University of Virginia Law School, Confederate officer, and later Congressman, told how some in North Carolina felt Vance was stretching the powers of his office by operating his ships, and could fancy he heard "the stereotyped big oath of North Carolina's biggest son: 'By the eternal! these glorious fellows shall not come to want through any neglect or omission of mine.' " Green said that while Vance drafted a general outline of the freightage desired "on these momentous trips of the little craft," the list was augmented by his efficient coadjutor, "Honest John Scotch White." What appealed to Green was that Vance, Captain Crossan and Agent White maintained their strict integrity—"what a splendid opportunity for nest feathering was lost by these three thoughtless men"— during transactions in which "almost every pound of cargo was worth its equivalent in silver, and sometimes even in gold."[31]

At about the time Vance was beginning his cotton operations, Vice President Alexander Stephens was voicing regret, in an address at Crawfordville, Georgia, in November, 1862, that cotton was not being purchased by the Confederacy and used to stabilize the currency. He wanted the government to secure all cotton that growers would exchange for 8 per cent Confederate bonds at a price of ten cents a pound. That was half of what Vance was paying and he could well afford the higher price, considering he could sell it in Liverpool for up to eighty cents a pound. Stephens believed there was power in cotton, which there might have been had the central government purchased and employed it as Vance was doing, in exchange for commodities so urgently needed from overseas.

But even with Vance's operations, uniforms of good material were by no means cheap on the open North Carolina market. Lieutenant Colonel James M. Ray of Asheville, who commanded the 30th North Carolina at Chickamauga, bought material for a uniform, a bolt of best Crenchaw cadet-gray waterproof cloth that had been shipped from England on the *Ad-Vance*. He said the material ought to be good because it cost him $1,500—in Confederate money, of course. But in defense of the expenditure he told of the man who rode a fine horse into camp, where an eager soldier offered to buy him. The owner said he was not for sale. "But I'll give you three thousand dollars," said the soldier. "Huh!" said the officer. "I just paid a thousand dollars to have him curried."[32]

Colonel Ray was not wholly pleased with his uniform because his wife made it and had an impression that he was larger than he actually was, so the fine imported cloth was rarely seen in front of the regiment.

None will ever know just what was brought into the Confederacy or from where, because no records existed from which a computation might be made. Vance's figures were patently estimates, made by him in different addresses, as to the Maryland Line in Baltimore in 1885, but they are usually accepted for the share of goods his North Carolina vessels carried into Wilmington. What the privately owned blockade-runners brought into the state none could guess. There is an element of mystery about it because Vance's list does not appear large for four ships averaging numerous voyages, yet he had on hand large quantities of imported material at the end of the war. This was held in the supposition that the war might be of much longer duration and that North Carolina troops would have to be supplied from the stores when other sources failed. He did well to keep the North Carolina troops reasonably well clothed and equipped for nearly three years and still have sizable surpluses on hand at the end. Hampered as he was in his commerce by the Richmond government, it is understandable that he did not turn over to it his surpluses as the war advanced, but held them for his own disposal.

Vance, before any others, could see that blockade-running would have a term. The Federal fleet was constantly being augmented and Fort Fisher, strong as Colonel Lamb had made it, was always vulnerable to a combined land and naval attack in force, and this was certain to be made as the Federal government tightened its cordon about the Confederacy. More than others, Vance awaited the signal that would be flashed by Lee's invasion of Pennsylvania. Elated before the invasion, he seems to have misread the signs, for he wrote to John White on July 10, 1863, at a time when the outcome of Gettysburg was still uncertain in the state, saying "the war is evidently nearing its close." His next sentence left no doubt that he believed the Confederacy would triumph: "The resources of our State and the Confederacy have developed in such a degree that we have every assurance of being able to clothe our troops with our own goods, and our vast amount of captures has given us an abundance of arms."

But he took a practical view when it was clear that the invasion had proved a costly failure. Still he was not one to weaken his efforts under stress and in the end the handicaps imposed by the Richmond administration more than the repulse of Pickett and Pettigrew on Cemetery Ridge were what caused him to curtail his blockade-running as a state enterprise.

He wrote on September 3, 1863, to White in Manchester that blockade-running was becoming more and more perilous and that purchases should be suspended. He expressed hope that White had already bought plenty of cotton and wool cards, which he emphasized as "very important!" His report to White on the course of the war was enigmatic. "I must refer you to the papers for the news. Since my last, reverses have befallen us, as was to have been expected: and we look for still others. But rest assured it will all come right—and don't believe one half the Federals say about our condition." That was not a message of despair, but still not one of high confidence.[33]

His letter of July 10, telling White to suspend purchases, caught that agent overloaded with goods already bought, so it proved impossible for Vance to cut blockade-running short, even had he desired to upon serious reflection and the further revelations that the war was not ending, either in victory or defeat. He was, in fact, just about to enter into blockade-running more extensively, through the purchase of part ownership by the state in three additional vessels—the *Don,* the fleet little ship that had been commanded by the scion of the Earl of Buckinghamshire but which the Federal blockaders captured soon after North Carolina became interested in her; the *Hansa* and the *Annie.* Vance used cotton certificates to cover the cost of one-fourth interest in the ships.

Majority control—and the cargo space was to be allotted in proportion to the ownership—rested with the London and Manchester house with which White had maintained favorable relationships, Alexander Collie & Company. At about the same time Vance sold half interest in the *Ad-Vance* to a Wilmington firm, Power, Lowe & Co., for $350,000, an excellent bargain, which pleased the governor because she had cost $190,000. He affirmed in February, 1864, that he had built up a credit for the state in the Bank of England of $400,000; had sent about $6,000 to North Carolinians in Northern prisons for the purchase of heavy clothing for the winter; had given 10,000 uniforms to the commands of Generals Longstreet and Johnston (these gifts were continued until Longstreet's Corps had received 14,000 uniforms), and had on hand 10,000 complete suits; 14,000 pairs of English shoes; 24,000 English blankets, and about 50,000 suits of ready-made clothing. He was elated also that North Carolina warrants in England were commanding a premium.[34]

Two months later he was quoted in the Raleigh press as having remarked in Wilkesboro that North Carolina troops had such good clothes he understood they sometimes traded them for liquor! This and much else confirm that Lee's army was by no means ragged—that a great many soldiers, and especially the North Carolinians, were well clothed during the 1863-1864 winter and spring seasons. Shoes were never plentiful and uniforms would wear out in hard campaigning, and the picture of destitution and want usually associated with the army was no doubt correct in the early and later stages, but the mid-war period, if not of plenty, was one of moderate comfort. This was at about the time when Vance was writing to General Lee asking if measures could not be taken to prevent the men from selling clothing to nonmilitary personnel.

But the security of abundance which Vance seemed to enjoy was not shared by the Confederate government, which coveted more of the cargo space of the blockade-runners. The private runners brought in, of course, what they could sell at the best profit and this was not necessarily army goods. Often it was coffee, laces, silks—the most prized articles of public consumption.[35] In late 1863 the Confederate government commandeered one third of the cargo space of all blockade-runners entering Confederate ports, then Wilmington, Charleston, and to a lesser degree Mobile, Alabama, and Galveston, Texas, but exempting state-owned vessels. Vance seemed to feel that vessels partially owned by the state would be exempted also and under that impression his agent negotiated the deals for the *Don, Hansa* and *Annie.* But they were rudely disillusioned when the first runner, the *Don,* sailed. A little later, instead of giving relief, the Confederacy increased its requisition and required the rental of one half of the cargo space to the central government. Thus, after failing to enter into blockade-running on its own account, and to follow Vance's plan of exchanging cotton and cotton credits for goods, the central authority moved to expropriate the property of a state that had been more enterprising.

Vance vigorously protested the commandeering of space on the *Don* and thought it "remarkable" that his efforts at blockade-running, instead of being encouraged, should meet with "little else than down-right opposition," especially when they had been so beneficial to the Confederate cause. He threatened to cancel the scheduled sailing of two of the other ships. Secretary Seddon relented in this instance and allowed the *Don* to depart, leaving the issue of sharing the cargo to later adjustment in conference with Vance. When the regulations became effective under which the Confederacy commandeered one half instead of one third of the cargo space, Vance was thrown into a rage. Since he owned but one fourth of the space in three of the vessels, the regulations would mean that he would be allowed only one eighth, for all his efforts in operating the ships, paying the crews, and setting up the organizations by which North Carolina cotton was converted into essential articles and supplies.

Vance unloaded his wrath on overburdened Secretary Seddon: "Is it possible that such an unblushing outrage is intended by the Government? I have no comment to make on such a proceeding further than that I will fire the ship before I will agree to it." Similarly he told President Davis that the terms were so severe the ships owned by North Carolina could not conform to them; that "money would be lost by each trip, and of course the State cannot incur losses for the benefit of the whole which are not to be shared by the whole." Vance's complaint, in order that it not seem petty, must be viewed in its relation to the whole pattern of what he regarded as impositions on his state by the central government on many other scores. This requirement, which would strip the state of the benefits it had been gaining through its own diligence and good management, was but a section of the montage he thought he saw of concentrated authority and oppression of the sovereign states. But President Davis, rarely in a mood to compromise, was not so disposed in this instance and contended he did not possess the power to suspend the regulations in Vance's behalf. After long negotiation, the *Ad-Vance* was to some extent excepted but her course was about run.

Vance exhausted almost every recourse to have the other ships freed from what he termed "inquitous and absurb regulations"; he appealed to Senator William A. Graham for legislative succor and attended a meeting with Governors Brown of Georgia, Watts of Alabama, and Clark of Mississippi, at which a memorial of protest was addressed to President Davis. This memorial espoused Vance's plan of the states providing for their own troops. He appealed to the North Carolina legislature, which twice passed resolutions asking North Carolina Congressmen in Richmond to get the shipping restrictions repealed. Davis vetoed a bill by the Confederate Congress which would have given him relief. In the end, he was compelled virtually to withdraw the vessels from blockade-running, after losses incurred by detentions, the surrender of cargo space and other causes had mounted to $200,000 in gold. John White well before this had come home from his noble service in Great Britain. In the closing days of the war Vance won a hollow victory in the Confederate legislature, which in March, 1865, voided the regulations he had fought against so bitterly, but by that time blockade-running was history and all the Southern ports were closed.[36]

Vance's letters to Richmond during his controversy over the blockade-runners suggest either an inability or lack of responsibility on the part of Confederate authorities to meet their financial responsibilities or take advantage of inviting opportunities. As early as November 13, 1862, he was writing to Secretary Christopher G. Memminger, saying he had applied two weeks earlier for $250,000 in Confederate bonds which he would send abroad for the purchase of shoes. He continued: "I thought I could certainly get them inasmuch as the Confederate government owes this State near five or six million dollars. I have sent two special agents for them, but have been put off for the reason that the papers were not in form, etc."[37] It is clear why Rebel War Clerk Jones inveighed so bitterly in his diary against "red tape," his bugbear that seemed to account for most Confederate failures.

"As the vessel was about to sail," Vance continued, "in which my Agent was going, I instructed my Agent to ask for the bonds anyhow and to say that any papers would be signed afterwards that might be required by the forms of the Department. This was refused also and my Agent has probably lost the vessel. I am compelled Sir to complain of such treatment; it displays either an incompetency on the part of your subordinates or an unwillingness to accommodate me with the bonds which I would not have and do not want after my Agent is gone."

Few governors have used such forthrightness and vigor in addressing the department heads of their central government, whether Federal or Confederate, but it is clear that none in the conduct of the Confederate civil affairs, from Jefferson Davis down, possessed the driving energy and dominating ability of Vance, who, had he been in control at Richmond instead of at Raleigh, would have given the Southern states a different picture of how to conduct a war.

Another complaint was that the coal he procured and had delivered to Wilmington for his blockade-runners was confiscated by the Confederate government for its own ships, in this instance the *Cornubia*. Later, coal for the *Ad-Vance* was confiscated, with fatal results.

Vance also experienced difficulty in getting cotton returned which he had loaned to the Richmond authorities. On December 23, 1863, he was compelled to write to Secretary Seddon complaining that it had been eight months since he had loaned the Confederate government 1,800 bales of cotton, which he needed urgently to pay a debt for commodities abroad. Again on January 7, 1864, he entreated Seddon to give him his cotton; he had eight or ten cargoes of supplies backed up at Bermuda and urgently required his 1,800 bales to cover what he owed for this rich store.[38]

Hard-pressed Seddon, lean and cadaverous, must have found his mouth watering when he read Vance's list of the goods in the Bermuda warehouses: 40,000 blankets, 40,000 pairs of shoes, large quantities of army cloth, leather, 112,000 pairs of cotton cards, dyestuffs, lubricating oils, large quantities of bacon, machinery and parts to refit twenty-six of the state's principal cotton and woolen factories. The list shows how Vance kept abreast of the state's requirements when he sent in his requisitions, which he filled out personally, to Agent White. He tried to explain to Seddon that what he was doing was for the good of the cause and that he was meeting little except hostility from the Confederate government.

Though it is apparent that the Davis administration looked with disfavor on Vance's blockade-running, for reasons that were never altogether clear, these were among his highly successful ventures until they were impeded and eventually brought to an end largely by the

Richmond government's hostility. Still, few other wartime transactions so lifted the morale of the North Carolina home public or added to the fighting ability of the state's front-line troops.

Meantime, ill fortune had overcome the *Ad-Vance*. Sailing Master Wylie, now her captain, had taken her out of Wilmington on September 9, 1864, loaded with cotton for Halifax. That day she remained anchored in the New Inlet, within easy view of the Federal blockading squadron of twenty-five to thirty vessels, who knew that the insolent craft would make a run for it that night.[39] Even in this last fatal event in the stormy story of the *Ad-Vance*, involving the greatest disaster in the history of Confederate blockade-running, the culprit was the Confederate government, which commandeered all the good coal in Wilmington for one of its own cruisers, the *Tallahassee*, leaving nothing but low-grade fuel called "Egypt coal," described by the head engineer as "nothing but slate or the croppings from the mine."[40] One version was that part of the coal the *Ad-Vance* had already loaded was transferred to the *Tallahassee*.

That night the Federal fleet threw numerous rockets to light the New Inlet. The *Ad-Vance* had enough good coal to take her over the bar; despite the vigilance of the Federals, she made her way out, and when dawn came not an enemy craft was in sight. But there remained the telltale trail of black smoke from the slate coal and this the tenacious Federals continued to follow.

About 8 A.M. a pursuing vessel was sighted and as the day wore on she gradually gained on the *Ad-Vance*, which grew sluggish under the poor fuel. Every effort was made to speed her so the pursuer might be shaken off after darkness, but before sunset the Federal warship, the *Santiago de Cuba*, was in range and throwing shot over the *Ad-Vance*, which had no other course than to surrender. She was taken into Norfolk and her career as a blockade-runner was ended. She reappeared off Wilmington bearing what had been an honored name in the British navy of the 1812 period, the *Frolic*, and was a part of the Federal fleet in the final bombardment and which lay off Fort Fisher after the end of the war.[41]

☆ ☆ ☆ ☆ ☆ ☆ ☆ ☆ ☆ ☆ ☆ ☆ ☆ ☆ ☆ ☆ ☆ ☆

# Chapter Sixteen

## Recruitment and Promotion Controversies

☆ ☆ ☆ ☆ ☆ ☆ ☆ ☆ ☆ ☆ ☆ ☆ ☆ ☆ ☆ ☆ ☆ ☆

Most of North Carolina's soldiers were volunteers—well over 100,000 by the old count—and conscription, the recruitment policy adopted by  the central government, aimed partly to bring in new men and more pointedly to stimulate re-enlistments among the short-term volunteers, was never popular anywhere in the Confederacy and especially not in the North Carolina mountains.

Vance wrestled with no more difficult problem. He called the enforcement methods ruthless and unrelenting. His trials arose likewise from the reluctance of lukewarm young men to bear arms, many of whom had no interest in either side of the conflict. But he was eminently successful, for he enrolled far more conscripts than were secured from any other Southern state.

Though North Carolina was often charged with indifference to the cause and rebelliousness toward the Davis administration, Vance demonstrated that not only with its volunteers but also with its conscripts he could make his state the most responsive section of the Confederacy. Of all the conscripts inducted by the Confederate armies, Vance brought in one fourth. The number was 21,348. This was about one third, or roughly 7,000 ahead of that of any other state. Vance himself modestly placed the number at 18,585,[1] but the final official figure was the larger.[2]

Perhaps the greatest influence toward this record was Vance's talent for genial persuasiveness. When he put his resolute endeavors behind the conscription act, they drew a response which delighted him and seemed above his expectations. The day-by-day problems attending enforcement of the act continued to the end of the war. The governor's controversies were not mainly with the conscripts or their families or with the refractory areas, but with the Richmond authorities, who often did not appear to recognize the vast personal contributions he was making to the cause. Probably conscription would have fared even better in the state had the Richmond government worked entirely through Vance and not so often at cross-purposes with him.

At the beginning enlistment was by volunteering, stimulated a little later by the offer of state bounties and a Confederate bounty of $50, the bounty method being a heritage from the Revolutionary War. Conscription was adopted April 16, 1862, by the Confederate Congress. It extended to all white males between the ages of sixteen and thirty-five, while the volunteers were arbitrarily given a term of service of three years from the date of their enlistments. On September 27, 1862, after the failure of the Sharpsburg campaign and Maryland's rebuff to the South, the age limit was raised to forty-five, but Davis did not call up the older men until July 15, 1863, after Lee had been defeated in Pennsylvania.[3] Again, in February, 1864, after Bragg had been worsted in the battles around Chattanooga, the age limits were fixed at from seventeen to fifty, but the seventeen-year-olds and those above forty-five were enrolled in home defense groups which became known as the Junior Reserves and Senior Reserves.

The states and their courts went along with the conscription acts with some reluctance but regarded them essential to waging war and winning freedom. For a time the hiring of substitutes was allowed. The price had risen to $5,000, when in August, 1863, after substitution had become common and it was estimated that 60,000 substitutes were in the service, the privilege was discontinued by law in order to still a cry by Vance and others that it was "a rich man's war but a poor man's fight." The new act and War Department regulations provided that those who had previously hired substitutes were no longer exempt, which threw into the courts the question of the sanctity of the old contracts and created for Vance one of the knottiest situations he had to untangle—or endeavor to untangle—during the war.

What he accomplished in sending men into the Confederate armies—

volunteers and conscripts alike—was one of his major achievements. He did, as was often charged, exempt more men, but he was conducting much more active state industrial operations and was less disposed than some governors would have been to give the Confederacy *carte blanche* in these affairs.

He was stimulating extensive manufacturing and he exempted all who were making supplies for state troops. The Confederate law made numerous exemptions, with some of which, such as the so-called "Twenty-nigger law," Vance disagreed. This law exempted one white overseer for every twenty plantation slaves, a provision intended to promote food production and retain some white males in the country districts, but it came to be denounced as class favoritism and was dropped.

Vance's policy respecting conscription was summarized in his statement that he was not among the politicians "who made the 'night (and day) hideous' with cries of States' rights and was rather accused of consolidationism," but was not willing "to see the state of North Carolina in effect blotted from the map and her government abolished . . ." and, "God forbid that the rights, honor, and the existence itself of the States should rest upon the grace and mercy of a bureau of conscription."[4]

Since conscription was the law, Vance threw his full energies behind it and, true to the assertions in his Asheville speech en route to the governorship, he tried to make the state "too hot to hold" draft dodgers and skulkers. Almost his first state paper was a ringing proclamation, issued September 18, 1862, denouncing opposition to the law and avowing it his sacred duty to repress opposition to its enforcement.

"Whilst thousands upon thousands of our best and bravest," he declared, "have cheerfully obeyed the law and by their patriotic valor have driven the enemy back to the Potomac, it would be an intolerable outrage upon them, to permit others to shirk or evade the law, or worse still, to resist it by open violence. Let no one then be deceived, the law will be enforced. . . ."[5]

Even before this Vance gave instructions to the militia officers of the state to assist Colonel Peter Mallett, commander of the state's camp of instruction for recruits near Raleigh, in rounding up and bringing in reluctant conscripts for induction and training. This would expedite enrollments and also spare regular soldiers from the disagreeable and unsightly spectacle of rounding up conscripts on the streets. The governor found much confusion existing because Confederate officers and agents were enlisting soldiers in the state in a most haphazard manner. He wrote at once to Secretary of War Randolph asking that he refrain from conferring authority on persons to enlist men in North Carolina without securing the endorsement of the state, and requesting that he revoke any authority he might have given anyone not a citizen of North Carolina. If enlistments were being made in North Carolina beyond the Blue Ridge by General E. Kirby Smith, who commanded in eastern Tennessee, as they were at the time, Vance wanted this authority revoked also.

His reasons: "Much confusion has been produced. Many soldiers have been enlisted in the Confederate service without this State's being credited with the same in her quota of troops." The operation of the conscription was being hampered by the manner of enforcement and it would be difficult if not impossible for the state to fill its thinned regiments already in service.[6]

Much of the complexity and controversy with conscription resulted from the insistence by the conscription officers that they should determine the validity of an individual's claim to exemption, while Vance held this to be a function of the state and its courts. The antics of the Confederate agents were often high-handed and at times brutal, and this more than any other factor led to Vance's long, spirited, and in the end fruitless correspondence with Davis which pulled the two apart and left their relationship formal and strained.

But Vance first came up against the ravenous appetite for recruits which existed with the department commander at Petersburg, Major General Samuel G. French.

Back on the night of February 23, 1847, Lieutenant Samuel Gibbs French of Gloucester County, New Jersey, a graduate of West Point in the class of 1843, was assisted into an ambulance after being severely wounded that day in the battle of Buena Vista.

The incident was memorable to him on several counts, the first being that he was helped into the ambulance by two of the most distinguished officers of the American army, General Zachary Taylor, its commander, and Lieutenant Colonel Charles May, head of the hard-riding dragoons, who fought ably and won his colonelcy on that field.

Inside the ambulance French found two other wounded officers who were to be transported with him from the hacienda of Buena Vista to the hospital at Saltillo. One was Colonel Jefferson Davis, whose Mississippi Rifles had formed a V with the 3rd Indiana—the famous "V of Buena Vista"—and had caught the charging Mexicans with a cross fire and turned a likely defeat into a resounding American victory. No doubt Davis's wound explained General Taylor's presence at the ambulance that night, for the Mississippi colonel not only shared the glories of the field, but also had married the commanding general's daughter. The other wounded officer was a young lieutenant described by French as being from Illinois, George E. Pickett, fresh from the recent class at West Point, where he had achieved the most difficult role at the Academy, that of skating on the thin ice well enough to avoid sinking, but not so well as to be more than last in the class.[7]

French resigned from the army in 1856 to supervise his wife's Mississippi plantation, and, when war came, he espoused the cause of his adopted, rather than his native, state, a decision he dealt with engagingly in his autobiography, *Two Wars*. He became chief of ordnance for Mississippi but seemed favored by the falling stars of promotion. By August 31, 1862, though he had participated in no engagements of note, he had advanced to the grade of major general. Likely he was not the only one who remembered fondly the acquaintance made on that night ambulance ride from Buena Vista. He remained throughout life eloquent in his praise of Jefferson Davis. Thirty years after his promotion he was saying the assaults on the character of the Confederate President were more bitter than those of the English people against Napoleon, but that Davis "has left a notable instance of a man, while living, obtaining a victory over error and silencing the tongue of slander."[8]

French was dispatched to New Bern to supersede Branch. Before he could arrive Branch had been defeated and the Burnside expedition had captured the town. Then for the next year, except for the brief period of Gustavus W. Smith's service, French was in North Carolina or commanded the department embracing it from Petersburg, the headquarters for the region south of the James River. He was consequently the Confederate officer in the field with whom Vance had closest contact, until French was ordered back to Mississippi in May, 1863. His attitude toward Vance was friendly, though he pointed out in his letter of October 22 that the requirements of General Lee for his campaign into Maryland in the early autumn of 1862 had stripped North

Carolina of troops and prevented him from striking the blows he had hoped to make at points where the Federals had small forces along the North Carolina coast.

Vance's sharpest controversy involving French was over the right of North Carolina recruits to select their own regiments. In respect to all recruiting the governor had begun his relations with the Confederate government buoyantly and zestfully and with a spirit of full co-operation with both the army and the civilian authorities. In making a résumé report to Secretary of War Randolph a month after he took office, he said that on assuming his duties he found conditions at low ebb, with few recruits coming in, but after he issued his proclamation and directed Adjutant General Martin to publish an order promising all comers the privilege of choosing their own regiments as long as those they selected were not filled, the situation changed sharply. "The good effect of this was instantly manifest," he told Randolph. "The number coming in was trebled and a cheerful spirit of alacrity prevailed everywhere." He recalled that he had mentioned this improvement to President Davis when in Richmond, and in Randolph's presence, and understood that both approved the recruit's right of selection. Yet when he returned home he found that Major Mallett, who commanded the induction camp near Raleigh, had received orders to send all recruits to specified brigades irrespective of the wishes of the inductees or the promises made to them by General Martin. They were being sent to General French at Petersburg to be incorporated in two brigades—Pettigrew's and Daniel's—which were being augmented there.

"This has produced the greatest disaffection and rightly too," Vance declared. "What the particular exigencies of the service may be I do not know; they must be great indeed to justify bad faith toward the soldiers on the part of the government. If such is to be the policy, as I do not wish to become a party to such transactions, I shall countermand the orders issued to my militia officers and leave him [Mallett] to hunt up the conscripts as best he can."

Then he gave Secretary Randolph some free advice, saying he regarded it a serious error for the War Department to decline to receive the counsel of anyone except the general who commanded the department. While not a military man himself, he did claim he ought to be heard. He felt he might safely assert that with regard to political movements which would mean popular support in the execution of the conscript law, "I know more than all the West Pointers in the service."

Still, as far as he was aware, "no one suggestion of mine . . . has received the approval of the Department."[9]

On the same day Captain James C. McRae, adjutant, was writing from Petersburg that the Secretary of War deemed it of vital importance to strengthen the commands near Petersburg and the two brigades mentioned were being filled. The fact that both Pettigrew and Daniel commanded all-North Carolina brigades was not a mitigating circumstance because the recruits had been promised the right of selection if they would come in and the promise was being violated. Many preferred regiments where they had kin or friends, or those which had won distinction. Most of the old regiments were depleted and urgently needed fresh personnel.[10]

Vance cut across channels and wrote to Major Mallett directly, saying the violation of General Martin's promise was creating the greatest dissatisfaction. He regarded the guarantee as so important, he said, that he had mentioned it to President Davis when in Richmond and had gained his approval of it. He hoped Mallett thereafter would conform and send the recruits to the regiments they chose. "The men come up," he said, "relying on the published order of Gen. Martin, and it is an outrage to deceive them in this way. I desire to sustain the Confederate Government with all my power, but certainly don't intend to assist it in duping the soldiers in defiance of its own published orders."[11]

Vance undoubtedly understood that no deliberate deception was intended on the part of the President or Secretary of War. In the disorganized state of the new government often one hand might not know what the other was doing. Nevertheless, in his role of protector of the North Carolina common people, Vance was justified, by the facts as he received them, in employing vigorous language. Late in the month he was reproving Davis because Randolph had not favored him with the courtesy of a reply to his letter of October 10. Meantime, a more grievous circumstance had developed. About one hundred enlistees from a region Vance described as "lukewarm" had come in cheerfully under the promise that they could select their regiments. General Martin confirmed this to them and wrote to French soliciting his consent. "He refused of course," Vance told Davis, "and according to a note received from him, the men were stopped at Petersburg and distributed equally to certain regiments as quarter Masters' stores or any other chattel property alleging that by not coming in sooner they had forfeited all claims to consideration.

"Of the shortsightedness and inhumanity of this harsh course towards our people, I shall offer no comment. I wish not only to ask that a more liberal policy may be adopted but to make it the occasion for informing you also of a few things of a political nature which you ought to know."

Vance, confident, fresh, and thirty-two years old, then began, much as a schoolteacher would in instructing a class, to deliver a lesson in the historical concepts and public-opinion trends in the Old North State which Vance felt distinguished it from the other states of the Confederacy, to the President of the Confederacy, a veteran in politics and learned in the precedents of state, but an aloof man surely not as understanding of human nature and the emotions that sway an aroused people as was the younger governor. Vance explained that the people were "eminently conservative and jealous of their political rights." The transition to revolution and war had been sudden and extraordinary. Prior to Lincoln's proclamation the people exhibited a popular majority of upwards of thirty thousand against secession on the ground of any of the causes that then existed. The last election, after sixteen months of war, in which the Conservatives triumphed heavily, disclosed that the original secessionists did not hold the ear of the people. Without the "warm & ardent support of the old Union men," North Carolina could not "so promptly and generously have been brought to the support of the seceding States," and without the same influence being unremittingly brought to bear "the present status could not be maintained forty eight hours." Then he emphasized his remarks by underscoring the words, "*These are facts.*" He said he alluded to them not to remind the President of any earlier political differences "which I earnestly hope are buried in the graves of our gallant countrymen" but simply to give him information.

His points were again that the old unionist leaders should be listened to, that the conscription law could not be executed by one of other political antecedents than his own without incurring outbreaks among the people, and that enforcement even by himself would be difficult unless he received the co-operation of the central government. "If on the contrary," he asserted, "West Point Generals who know less of human nature than I do of military service, are to ride rough shod over the people, drag them from their homes and assign them or rather *consign* them to strange regiments and strange commanders without regard to their wishes or feelings, I must be compelled to decline under-taking a task which will certainly fail."

He wanted to know what the other states were doing about the con-script law and said "a very general impression prevails that this State is doing vastly more than her share." That was, as it later developed, precisely the case.[12]

Davis was wary of any commitment to give his ear to the old union-ists. He answered on November 1, expressing regret at the disappoint-ment suffered by some of the recruits but explaining that certain restric-tions existed on the right of selection. Still, his purpose was, as far as possible, to associate men together who would best harmonize with each other. He said the emergency on the North Carolina coast had led to the exertions to fill up French's regiments. He hoped there would be no future grounds for dissatisfaction. He concurred in the wish that party distinctions which once existed would be buried in the graves of those who had fallen. He was still writing in a generous and pacific tone, but with some inclination, it appeared, to sweep Vance's com-plaints under the rug.[13]

Vance crossed swords with Secretary Seddon about the appointment of officers as replacements in the first group of North Carolina regi-ments. In the beginning the right of appointment with state troops remained with the governor, and Vance never recognized any other arrangement with these regiments. But when in early 1863 Secretary Seddon issued a commission, Colonel Isaac E. Avery of the 6th North Carolina protested to Vance and Vance put in an immediate protest to Seddon, saying the right of the governor to fill vacancies was recog-nized by Seddon's predecessor. He hoped the secretary would allow no more such commissions in these regiments to be issued by the Con-federate government.

Vance conducted a long but bootless battle on this proposition and eventually desisted without surrender late in the war before an adverse ruling by the Confederate Attorney General George Davis, a North Carolinian. Seddon acknowledged his first letter and asked him for more particulars, saying no distinction was made among the North Carolina regiments by the Adjutant General's office. Vance in reply submitted a list of regiments in which he as governor claimed the right to make appointments. This list included all of the state's original regiments enlisted for the duration of the war, regarding which the state law under which they were recruited required that the governor make the appointments and fill vacancies. The others, known as "conscript regiments," were originally enlisted for twelve months and the right of appointment of the officers was accorded the President of the Confederacy. Vance contended that the distinction having been recognized by the War Department, dissatisfaction and confusion would result from change.[11]

Despite his rights under the state law, Vance was not on firm ground in demanding the right to appoint regimental officers. The best test was their conduct in the field and of that the recommendation of the commanding general to the President naturally would have the greatest weight. Adjutant General Cooper gave no heed to Vance's claims, despite the governor's assertion that the law was on his side. When the Attorney General ruled that the President was the final authority on appointments, Vance no longer pressed his fight.[15]

He was on more solid footing in insisting that the state be dealt with fairly in the promotion of general officers. While he did gain concessions, the record at the end of the war shows that he never won major recognition along this line. Though the Confederacy was lavish in the bestowal of high military rank, the state which supplied the largest number of privates was grievously scant in generals. Of the 480 Confederate brigadier generals appointed during the war, twenty-five were from North Carolina.[16] In some instances the troops themselves were responsible for their out-of-state brigadier generals, as in the case of Brigadier General James H. Lane, a Virginian, graduate of Virginia Military Institute and the University of Virginia. Still, he could be looked on as almost a North Carolinian because he went to that state just before the war to instruct at the North Carolina Military Institute in Charlotte, then was elected major in the famous "Bethel Regiment." After Branch fell at Sharpsburg, Lane commanded an all-North Carolina brigade known as the "flower of the Cape Fear section" and was loved and respected by his troops from Bethel to Appomattox. Brigadier Archibald C. Godwin was another Virginian to command competently an all-North Carolina brigade, the old brigade of Hoke and Avery, from the time of Avery's death at Gettysburg until Godwin was killed at Winchester in 1864. He, too, had come up with North Carolina troops, having recruited and commanded the 57th North Carolina while he had charge of the military prison at Salisbury. Nor was there opposition, but to the contrary pleasure, among the North Carolina soldiers who served for a period under Brigadier General Raleigh E. Colston, of French birth but Virginia reared and educated.

Vance injected himself into Confederate military affairs at any instant when he thought the state was being slighted. General Gustavus W. Smith, after his wound at Seven Pines and brief ad interim service as Secretary of War, was assigned to the North Carolina Department. Then, just after he had informed himself about the state's defenses he was relieved and French was appointed, which brought from Vance a protest that much time would be lost while a new commander was acquainting himself with North Carolina conditions.

Vance was again angered in late January, 1863, when a Virginian, Colonel T. P. August, was appointed, to the general amazement, commandant of conscripts in North Carolina, succeeding Colonel Peter Mallett, who had been wounded in December, 1862, commanding some conscripts in an engagement at Kinston. War Clerk Jones, who commented to his diary on Vance's latest flare-up, pointed out that the commander of all conscripts in the Confederacy was General Gabriel J. Rains, a North Carolinian, who was Colonel August's superior. "But the War Department has erred," Jones conceded, "in putting so many strangers in command of localities, where natives might have been selected." He observed that Richmond had never been under the command of a general from the deeper South.[17]

Vance was not so restrained. His letter to Secretary Sedden recapitulated his grievances: "Merely alluding to the obvious impropriety and bad policy, of wounding the sensibilities of our people by the appointment of a citizen of another state to execute a law, both harsh and odious, I wish to say, Sir, in all candor that it smacks of discourtesy to our people to say the least of it. Having furnished as many (if not more) troops for the service of the Confederacy as any other State, and being, as I was assured by the President, far ahead of all others in the number raised under the conscript law, the people of this state have justly felt mortified in seeing those troops commanded by citizens of other States, to the exclusion of claims of their own." The feeling was heightened into general indignation when it was announced that "North Carolina has no man in her borders fit to command her own conscripts, though scores of her noblest sons and best officers are now at home with mutilated limbs and shattered constitutions."

He officially protested the appointment as unjust and impolitic, then gave Seddon a final load of his wrath: "Having submitted in silence to the many, very many acts of Administration, heretofore, so calculated to wound that pride, which North Carolina is so pardonable for entertaining, it is my duty to inform you that if persisted in, the appointment of strangers to all the positions in this state over her troops, will cause a feeling throughout her whole borders, which it is my very great desire to avoid."[18]

Vance was heard in this instance because General Rains relieved Colonel August, and Mallett on his recovery was restored to his old post. But the August case was followed by an even more presumptuous appointment by the Richmond authorities, of Colonel Edmund Bradford of Virginia to be the Confederate tax collector in North Carolina. The appointment came at the time of Lee's invasion of Pennsylvania and overshadowed the battle of Gettysburg in the North Carolina press, which was quickly filled with editorial protests and accounts of indignant mass meetings of citizens. When it was discovered that the tax collector was actually a Northerner—a native of Pennsylvania who had settled in Virginia after graduating from West Point and serving in the army—the storm grew more intense. Many seemed to think it was a studied insult to the state.

The tithe tax, which Bradford was to collect, was unpopular, being an unfamiliar type of levy in kind, effective in 1863, under which farmers would be required to give the central government one tenth of their produce. After allowing the farmer certain small exemptions of some produce for his own use, the tax fell on a specified list of agriculture commodities—wheat, corn, rice, sugar, molasses, hay, tobacco, peas, potatoes, and several others. The required amounts would have to be delivered to the army depots. The idea of the tax was that the army could be supplied without resort to money and that less money would therefore have to be printed.

Such a tax was difficult to collect and fell mainly on the easily accessible districts; it irked the poor landowners who had never paid any sort of taxes. The tax collectors, whatever their origin, came to be detested.[19] When it developed that the collector in North Carolina was a Virginian and former Yankee, he was roundly and publicly denounced. Said a writer to the Raleigh *Standard*, Colonel Bradford was "a warm Southern man before the enemy appeared at Norfolk; after they did come he betook himself to the back woods of North Carolina."[20]

Vance wrote on July 6, 1863, directly to President Davis again emphasizing that much dissatisfaction had resulted from appointment of citizens of other states to offices "that should of right be filled by our own people.

"The last appointment of the Quartermaster General of a Colonel Bradford of Norfolk to the Chief Collectorship of the tax in kind for this State has given almost universal offense." The letter continued in more respectful terms than Vance ordinarily employed with Secretary Seddon. Vance felt that this was such a purely local office that the state had a right to demand it for one of her own citizens.

Here Davis was for once tractable, even apologetic. He wrote on July 18 saying some competent person was needed and that while Bradford was from Virginia, he had spent much time in North Carolina. But he would correct the matter and watch in future instances. "I am aware," he wrote, "of the embarrassments you may have in carrying out your patriotic efforts, to aid the Confederate Government in this struggle . . . and would be very far from willingly allowing any additional obstruction to be thrown your way."[21] Davis in a later letter asked for a recommendation and Vance said he would be in Richmond and offer a list. The appointment of John Devereux of Raleigh followed. The Raleigh *Standard* closed the exciting case with: "Mr. Devereux is a native of this state—a gentleman of intelligence and business habits."[22]

Though these matters were settled, the sorest wound remained. This was the appointment of out-of-state officers, principally Virginians, to command North Carolina regiments and brigades, and Vance inveighed against it frequently. The instance of Garland's Brigade was one on which attention came to be focused. When Garland was killed in the Maryland campaign, Colonel Duncan K. McRae of the 5th North Carolina took command and led the brigade at South Mountain and Sharpsburg, but when Colonel Iverson was promoted ahead of him on November 1, after the army was back in Virginia, McRae, an able officer, resigned in a storm of indignation. Alfred Iverson, Jr., son of the Georgia senator who had been one of Jefferson Davis's close friends in the prewar Senate, had been colonel of the 20th North Carolina. McRae was not only Iverson's senior, but an officer of superior attainments as Iverson's costly fiasco at Gettysburg soon demonstrated. The McRae-Iverson case came to involve Vance sharply and brought out so forcibly the governor's issue of out-of-state command of North Carolina troops that this, a glaring instance, should be examined.

Colonel Duncan McRae was of a prominent Fayetteville family, a graduate of the University of North Carolina, whose brother later became dean of the law school there and justice of the North Carolina Supreme Court. Duncan, a Raleigh and Wilmington lawyer active in politics, had served in the legislature, been United States consul at Paris, then had run for governor unsuccessfully against John W. Ellis in 1858. Active in advocating secession, he had been elected colonel of the 5th North Carolina, one of the first ten regiments raised after Fort Sumter, and had led it through the hard fighting of the Peninsula. An unusual opportunity came to McRae and the 5th at Williamsburg and in it he and the regiment acquitted themselves nobly. When the Federal brigade commander Winfield S. Hancock turned the left of the Confederate line and threatened its rear, Jubal Early's Confederate Brigade was recalled by D. H. Hill, with General Joseph E. Johnston's assent, to confront Hancock and try to sever him from the balance of McClellan's army. The battle which ensued between Hancock and Early was that in which Hancock won his title of "the Superb" and the 5th North Carolina and 24th Virginia equally lasting glory.

Early ordered his brigade to charge. Of his four regiments, the 5th North Carolina was on his right, the 24th Virginia on his left. These two regiments responded with alacrity. The two center regiments lagged and were satisfied with long-range firing. McRae, advancing on the far right, saw that the 24th Virginia on the far left was unsupported. Risking the flank fire of both the enemy and the two center Confederate regiments, he moved the 5th North Carolina across his brigade front until he could form a line of assault with the 24th Virginia regiment. These two regiments attacked Hancock with such vigor that the charge remained one of the most intrepid of the war after many other charges and many larger battles. Hancock, who met it, said that night, "Immortality ought to be inscribed on the banners of the 24th Virginia and the 5th North Carolina for their great bravery," while the regimental historian recorded, "The charge of the 5th North Carolina on this occasion has rarely been surpassed in the history of war for its heroism and gallantry."[23] Early was wounded and McRae took command of the brigade. His fellow colonel, Hamilton C. Jones, referred to him as "the Gallant, high-toned Chivalrous McRae."[24]

Still, after Seven Pines when the army was organized as nearly as possible into brigades of troops from the same state, and the West Point North Carolinians, William Dorsey Pender and George Burgwyn

Anderson, were given commands of North Carolina brigades, McRae was passed over and the North Carolina brigade into which his regiment fell was placed under the Virginia Military Institute graduate Samuel Garland, Jr., a Lynchburg lawyer. McRae talked of resigning then but the army was still heavily engaged with McClellan and he yielded to the urgency of both Garland and General D. H. Hill and remained with his regiment. When Garland was fatally wounded at South Mountain McRae took command and conducted against heavy odds what D. H. Hill called one of the best fought engagements of the war.

Then, six weeks after the Maryland campaign, when McRae was again passed over and Iverson, a Georgian, whom he had commanded at South Mountain and Sharpsburg, was jumped above him, he resigned. One of his first acts was to write Vance a lengthy letter of explanation and justification. "I could not consent that a junior officer of my own command should be promoted to command me, when no allegation is made of my unfitness or unworthiness. But severe as is the trespass upon the individual pride of No. Carolina officers who have lately been obliged to submit to the promotion in several instances of citizens of other States to the command of Brigades exclusively North Carolinians, the slur upon the state is broader and demands the resentment of her sons in the only mode they can manifest it. In the spirit of an earnest protest against this injustice, individual and to my state I resign my commission."[26]

McRae asked Vance to make use of his services "*in any capacity* however subordinate" that would not subject him to a "renewal of the wrong" imposed on him.

The Fayetteville *Observer*, an opponent to the appointment of McRae to the command of the 5th North Carolina at the beginning of the war, and of Branch also, both being lawyers and politicians, now acknowledged that in both instances "we have lived to see our mistake." Both had been faithful and capable, but received different treatment: "Gen. Branch was on the favored side in politics—he was a Breckinridge man and secessionist. Col. McRae, though also a secessionist, had committed the unpardonable sin of being a Douglas man. Here lies the secret of the different treatment of the two officers—Branch promoted before he ever smelt gunpowder—McRae always *after* the fight recommended for promotion by the great Generals who commanded him and knew his worth and his services, and always rejected." The newspaper felt it was but another exhibition of that "great defect in the President's character," which had marked his course since the war began—that in respect to old political differences, "like the Bourbons, he forgets nothing and learns nothing."[27]

McRae was getting precisely the treatment accorded Vance before he was elected governor, about which he had complained in his letter to his wife.

Vance appointed McRae an agent in the purchase of European supplies and he went to Europe with George N. Sanders in 1863. One of the excellent junior officers was thus lost to the army because of the practice of appointing junior officers from other states to command North Carolina units. And he was lost after he had been recommended for promotion by Generals Longstreet, D. H. Hill, Early, and Rodes. D. H. Hill endorsed his resignation, saying, "I have at times recommended Colonel McRae for promotion. North Carolina has furnished more troops and has fewer general officers than any other State. I approve Colonel McRae's resignation believing that his self respect requires it."[28]

Another grievous case thrown into Vance's lap was that of Thomas Miles Garrett, the young diarist of Chapel Hill who wrote about the high jinks of the university students of Vance's era there, and who went into the 5th North Carolina, Duncan McRae's regiment. The instance allowed Vance to establish beyond reasonable doubt the strength of one of his old tenets, which was that the former Whigs and unionists were indeed discriminated against in President Davis's selections of officers.

Captain Garrett had been wounded and captured in the regiment's celebrated charge at Williamsburg. When restored to duty by exchange, he was touted by the other officers to succeed Colonel McRae, who was considering resigning after the appointment of Garland to command the brigade. Garrett already had been passed over when recommended for major and there seemed to be such a pattern of rejection that he wrote Vance, the incoming governor, on September 1, 1862, complaining that prejudice existed against him because he was a former Whig.[29] Soon after leaving Chapel Hill he had served in the state senate as a Whig member.

When the colonelcy of the regiment became vacant after the lieutenant colonel was killed in action and McRae had finally resigned, a sharp contest developed between Garrett and Captain Peter J. Sinclair, a Scot whose father, a Presbyterian preacher, had immigrated to

Pennsylvania, where Peter became a lawyer. The young man moved to Fayetteville, North Carolina, shortly before the war, edited a newspaper, became a secessionist and raised a Cumberland County company which went into the 5th regiment. Sinclair had won the major's commission over Garrett, but the officers clearly favored Garrett for regimental command. Lieutenant Colonel Hamilton C. Jones of the 57th North Carolina, who had served as a captain in the 5th, wrote to Vance on December 19, 1862, that his old regiment was being torn apart by internal feuding. The question was whether the regiment would continue to be "one of the best in the service, or whether it is to become an unmanageable mob." He told Vance that Garrett alone could restore the regiment because he commanded the esteem of all, had fine talent and unflinching courage, whereas Sinclair he believed to be "morally and mentally incapable of commanding the regiment" with credit.[30] Vance, who was exercising the right of appointment of the early regiments, named Garrett, upon which Sinclair resigned from the army.

Garrett made an excellent regimental commander, was wounded at Sharpsburg and again at Chancellorsville, and won commendation and citations for bravery especially from Rodes, who was understood to have recommended him for promotion to brigadier general. Vance acted on this information and made Garrett one of his principal exhibits in thundering against Davis because of the mistreatment of former Whigs. When Iverson was relieved after his mismanagement of the brigade at Gettysburg, Garrett was passed over and Colonel Robert D. Johnston of the 23rd North Carolina regiment was made brigadier general. Garrett, who continued to serve ably, declared on the eve of Spotsylvania that he would "come out of the fight a brigadier-general or a dead colonel," and was buried a colonel.[31]

Other instances were brought to Vance's attention by protests and were grouped with Garrett's case. Colonel William J. Clarke, of the 24th North Carolina, an enterprising lawyer and businessman who had dropped his extensive affairs to become a soldier, wrote to the governor November 13, 1862, objecting to the elevation over him of Iverson, a Georgian, and calling attention to the fact that Colonel John Rogers Cooke, though a Virginian, commanded an all-North Carolina brigade. Cooke, J. E. B. Stuart's brother-in-law, Missouri born, proved to be one of the finest brigade commanders in the service and no complaint against him could be made by anyone on the score of merit. But Clarke wanted Vance to write to President Davis about these and other cases, believing only North Carolina officers should command North Carolina brigades.[32]

The matter built up so that on March 9, 1864, Vance unloaded on Davis a highly spirited and telling letter about the treatment of the antisecessionists and Whigs. He said he could not prove, of course, that other than military considerations influenced Davis in his selections, but "out of some twenty-five or thirty generals appointed from North Carolina" only three antisecessionists were among them. Two of these, Richard C. Gatlin and Laurence S. Baker, were West Point graduates and old regular army officers. The third was the governor's brother Robert B. Vance.

"Now it does seem strange," the governor continued, "when it is remembered that two-thirds of the people of this state were opposed to secession until Lincoln's proclamation, that God should have endowed the remaining one-third with all the military talents; that 'military considerations' should divest two-thirds of our citizens, however brave, patriotic and intelligent, of the capacity to serve their country except in the ranks or as subordinate officers? Branch, Clingman, Scales, Ransom, and Gordon—all politicians—are promoted at once. What representative of the old Unionists was thought fit to receive similar favors? Col. McRae, of the Fifth North Carolina Regiment was the senior colonel of his brigade. On the first vacancy a junior officer from another state was put over him. He was a Douglas Democrat. Colonel Garrett, his successor, was an old Union Whig previous to the war; had fought for three years and was covered with wounds. On the next vacancy in the brigadiership Lieutenant Colonel Johnston, a secessionist, was put over him."

The other instance cited to Davis by Vance was that of Colonel John S. McElroy of the 16th North Carolina, who "had fought his glorious regiment from 1,200 down to 150 men, and was himself disfigured with wounds." Vance said he had learned that McElroy had been recommended for promotion by General Pender, but had been superseded by Colonel Alfred M. Scales, a secessionist. He made no complaint against the men selected, "but only wonder at the passing strangeness of this singular freak of nature in so partially and arbitrarily distributing the military capacity of the country."[33]

McElroy had entered the 16th regiment as captain of the company raised in his home county of Yancey, distinguished himself on the Peninsula, rose to regimental command and was severely wounded leading his men at Chancellorsville. Said Lieutenant Benjamin H. Cathey, regimental historian, "No braver soldier or more chivalric gentleman graced the 16th with command than Colonel McElroy."[34] He does not appear ever to have solicited Vance's influence, but was satisfied to serve and win the citations of his superiors. Davis denied that any recommendation for his promotion to be brigadier general was on file in the War Department but contended that Pender, "that noble soldier, whose name is a glorious legacy to his mother state," had twice recommended Scales. On the first occasion there was no vacancy; on the second, Scales, the senior colonel of the brigade, was approved by A. P. Hill and Lee, by his regiment and, according to Davis, by the North Carolina delegations in both houses of Congress. Vance was correct in not underrating Scales, but it did seem that McElroy's capabilities entitled him also to promotion.[35]

Vance might have cited other cases, among them that of his old political antagonist, Colonel David Coleman, who had led the 39th North Carolina ably at Chickamauga, then had commanded the brigade when Brigadier General Evander McNair was wounded. With it he had been a leading factor in Bushrod Johnson's penetration of the Federal center, which won the battle for the Confederacy. His claim to promotion might be seen from the fact that North Carolina had eight regiments in the western army—enough for two brigades—but had no brigadier general after Robert B. Vance was captured.[36] Still, Coleman had been a Democrat and a secessionist and Vance was making a case that the former unionists were the ones being snubbed. He was on firmer ground when he was contending that the state as a whole never received its proportionate share of brigade commanders.

Nothing was clearer evidence of the slowness of promotions for North Carolina Whigs, against which Vance was protesting, than the case of Rufus Barringer, who recruited his cavalry at the outbreak of the war and was still a captain at Gettysburg, though he had served with high merit in virtually all of the army's engagements. He did not complain to Vance on that score, but did write a stinging attack on his colonel after the Maryland campaign, saying he had "relapsed into a former habit of hard drinking" and that the regiment was fast going to ruin. Vance could do nothing more than forward the letter to Secretary Seddon saying no indulgence was due one of the habits described, but the colonel, Lawrence S. Baker, a West Point graduate, either must have reformed or been steadier than Barringer thought, for he gave gallant service and was wounded often in Wade Hampton's cavalry brigade and was promoted to brigadier general after Gettysburg.[37]

Barringer married one of the Reverend R. H. Morrison's six daughters and therefore was the brother-in-law of both Stonewall Jackson and D. H. Hill, but he would have had many marks against him if President Davis did indeed keep a political blackball book. He had studied law under Chief Justice Richmond M. Pearson of the North Carolina Supreme Court, whose name was anathematized in Richmond. He had served as a Whig in both branches of the state legislature and had been a presidential elector on the Bell ticket in 1860, which Vance had supported. Vance's complaints to Davis must have helped him because after Gettysburg he jumped from captain to brigadier general in less than a year and commanded a brigade in W. H. F. Lee's cavalry division.[38]

Vance did complain that the prejudice against old unionists extended to civil offices and cited the case of Robert P. Dick, former Federal district attorney, who was dropped for reappointment because Davis had said, as Vance quoted him, "he was slow to leave the old Government."

"A majority of 40,000 were quite as laggard as Mr. Dick," declared Vance, "and among them the writer is not ashamed to class himself."

Davis in his reply did not recall making the statement about Dick but said that if he did, it "was simply the mildest form of indicating distrust."[39]

Davis pleaded ignorance of any recommendation for Garrett, saying none ever reached the War Department. This Judah P. Benjamin, Secretary of War at the time, confirmed by making a certificate, which Davis sent to Vance. The President claimed not to know the previous political affiliations of the officers referred to, but said Lieutenant Colonel Johnston's elevation was recommended by Rodes and concurred in by Ewell, the corps commander, and General Lee. The disparity in the figures cited by Vance tend to support his, rather than the President's, claim, for the fact was that an officer who was a North Carolina unionist prior to Lincoln's call for volunteers had about as much chance of becoming a brigadier general in the Confederate service as in the army of Siam. If President Davis did not know the political antecedents of the newly elevated brigadier generals, apparently somebody else in the government was keeping a close check on them.

Vance was far from standing alone in his castigations of the Confederate procedure with promotions. Editor Holden declared in the Raleigh *Standard:* "North Carolina is badly treated. She is ignored. She has no voice in the cabinet. [The attorney general was not regarded in early times as a cabinet officer.] She is raked for conscripts as with a fine tooth comb. Her troops are always placed in the forefront of the hottest battles. . . . A large portion of her people are suspected of being disloyal. The people of North Carolina are long suffering; but Mr. Davis would do well to bear in mind that it is the last straw that breaks the camel's back." He went on to declare that if the state did not receive equal treatment in the Confederacy she would leave it, a threat which Vance was not prepared to make.[40]

Long before this, the proadministration Wilmington *Journal* had complained about the dearth of North Carolina brigadier generals though they were "as plenty as hops from other states." This was when the aging Theophilus H. Holmes was the only North Carolinian with a star, and that because he was one of the few field officers of the old army to discard the blue and put on the gray uniform. Braxton Bragg, North Carolina born but long a resident of Louisiana, and other emigrant generals were not looked on as part of the North Carolina list.

Vance carried his fight to the state legislature, to which he said: "It is mortifying to find entire brigades of North Carolina soldiers in the field commanded by strangers, and in many cases our own brave and war-torn colonels are made to give place to colonels from distant states, who are promoted to the command of North Carolina troops over their heads to vacant brigadierships."[41]

Vance finally felt compelled to deliver to Davis a more spirited protest against an accumulation of acts and impositions by the agents and troops sent into the state to round up conscripts. He began by recalling his letter of October, 1862, in which he had tried to picture North Carolina conditions, and mentioned his two visits to Richmond for meetings with the President, being anxious, he explained, to give him "a true insight into conditions. . . ." Though professing respect and expressing a fear that he might be considered importunate and discourteous, he nevertheless may have seemed to talk down to the President and treat him as one who did not have his grip on the throttle of the war.

Davis had wondered why in previous complaints about military outrages against civilians, the governor had kept the elucidating papers in the files at Raleigh instead of forwarding them to Richmond for study and action. He had also stated that no complaint had been made to him without redress being made when that was possible. Vance now took the word "redress" as his theme. He seemed irked a little that Davis would think he held the files in Raleigh and declared he had sent many complaints of wrong and outrage to the War Department, "and to my knowledge, no case whatever has ever been redressed." Others had been forwarded to the departmental commander or officer in the field who, "after going through the circumlocution of military reference for several weeks, perhaps months," returned them to the governor "for his information." Such cases were closed by "acceptance of the story of the accused party as full exculpation."

Then Vance described for the President some concrete instances. Sometime in 1862 a cavalry company went into Tyrrell County, North Carolina, and "stole," as he put it (explaining that they had no authority to impress and made no attempt to do so under the law), numerous horses from owners who actually had them at the plow. "The poor farmers thus robbed" pooled their resources and employed a neighbor named Lewis to go to Richmond either to get their horses returned or to receive compensation for them. The kind of pay Lewis got was to be lodged in Castle Thunder prison on charges made by the very men who had stolen the horses.

Again, in the winter of 1862-63, a squad of cavalry sent from Atlanta into Cherokee County, at the far western tip of the state, seized, according to Vance, a number of old citizens above the age of conscription, "chained them together like galley slaves, and drove them before their horses 120 miles to Atlanta." One was a man upward of sixty years. In Atlanta they were thrown into prison and informed that they could either volunteer in the army or remain in prison for the remainder of the war. The action was heartless and served the Confederacy no whit.

"Upon my earnest remonstrance," Vance stated, "they were finally liberated. Was that wrong redressed? Was anybody punished for that outrage?"

As another case he cited the dispatch of the 56th North Carolina regiment from the army to Wilkes County, to arrest conscripts and deserters. As Vance explained, "some disorders existed and some disloyalty had been manifested" in the section. The soldiers pillaged indiscriminately the families of both deserters and patriotic citizens. Vance was so concerned when he heard of it that he went to the county for a firsthand inspection. He found the loyal citizens complaining about the "most outrageous conduct" of the troops. "Whole districts were represented to have been robbed and the inhabitants reduced to the verge of starvation. Cattle and horses were seized from the loyal men, carried into neighboring counties, sold, and the money divided."

Vance then took up the question of redress. The robberies had rendered some respectable farmers destitute and unable to pay their taxes without selling their land. He applied to the Secretary of the Treasury, Memminger, to have these damages deducted by the tax collectors and credited against the amounts the farmers would have to pay. The secretary replied "he had nothing to do with it," and referred it to Secretary Seddon, whose reply had come in while Vance was writing his letter to Davis. Seddon said he could do nothing except withhold the amount of the damages from the pay of the officers concerned if they could be convicted of permitting the pillage. Vance consequently regarded it impossible to get redress for this offense. "The women and little children, ruined by this conduct, must be fed by this state or starve to death. . . . I know these things in a greater or less degree are inseparable from a state of war . . . But they do add to the discontents in North Carolina . . . and prompt and kindly efforts to redress would cause these poor people to love their government and support its laws far more than the terrors of the suspension of the writ of *habeas corpus* and a display of force."[42]

In his reply Davis, growing petulant, reported a lack of knowledge of any of the three cases, the outrages in Tyrrell, Cherokee, and Wilkes counties. That he had never heard of them was indeed surprising, for they were notorious. He sought protection behind the statement that Vance had not forwarded the papers to him or stated what redress he deemed it within the power of the President to give.

"If I have no power to grant redress," he continued, "as seems to be intimated by some of your expressions, it is difficult to understand why such acrimonious complaints should have been addressed to me." Surely they were more properly addressed to him than they would have been to President Lincoln! Vance's letter, in fact, seemed free from acrimony. While it may have talked down, it exuded courtesy. But it contained frank statements of unpunished outrages, which tended to indicate that the Richmond authorities exercised no more than the loosest control over their agents and scattered forces in the field. True, war inevitably unleashed the basest passions in individuals, but it did not seem to be the occasion, on that account, for the President of the Confederacy to turn fretfully on his ablest governor because he had described unpleasant conditions the executive did not seem to know what to do about. His closing paragraph suggested he was more concerned with his personal dignity than with redress, compassion, or the good of the Confederate cause.

"There are other passages in your letter in which you have so far infringed the proprieties of official intercourse as to preclude the possibility of a reply. In order that I may not again be subjected to the necessity of making so unpleasant a remark, I must beg that a correspondence so unprofitable in its character, and which was not initiated by me, may here end, and that your future communications be restricted to such matters as may require official action."

Meantime the poor distressed farmers of three counties, about whom Vance in his human understanding and commiseration was genuinely concerned, were still without redress or prospect of obtaining any.[43]

One disadvantage to the Confederate authorities was that Vance, virile and vigorous, able to labor sixteen to twenty hours a day, was confronting in President Davis and Secretary Seddon men who were physically weak and easily exhausted, one of whom, Davis, blind in one eye, did not come to his office until eleven in the morning, and during his recurring illnesses came not at all. Sometimes he did not visit his office for stretches of ten days, but worked at home privately, without permitting callers access. War Clerk Jones said of the President: "I think he has been ill every day for several years."

Secretary of War James A. Seddon, who had been a Congressman from Virginia well before Vance's service in the House, was said by the industrious, diary-keeping clerk in his department, Jones, to "resemble an exhumed corpse after a month's interment."[44] Kemp Battle, on a wartime trip to Richmond, found him stooping and coughing as though suffering from tuberculosis.[45] Vance, rugged and dynamic, could tilt with the two of them on even terms intellectually and far outstrip them in the splendid physique he brought to the job.

That Vance could cope with Davis and, as the correspondence clearly evidences, often get the better hand was a tribute to his powers of reasoning and his clear, eloquent expression, for Davis was a master of rhetorical deftness and none could surpass him in the meticulous examination of a point at issue. His letters to Vance show his artistry of expression, but they are not impressive as indicating any close grasp of the details of Confederate affairs, as did Vance's of transactions within the borders of his state. Too often Davis had to plead ignorance of something a President of the Confederacy might be expected to know. Vance at times might be misinformed but rarely, if ever, uninformed.

Among the groups exempted from conscription were state officials. Each governor was empowered to designate those essential to the conduct of his state's affairs. In most of the totals passed around at the time, and often recorded, none of which seemed authentic, Vance was credited with the largest number of exemptions of state employees. That would not have been surprising, considering that the state was highly active in promoting military work, making salt, running the blockade, and much else, and many employees were giving far more service to the cause as civilians than if they had been in the army. Still, the largest total of exemptions attributed to Vance for state officers was 14,675, which would seem small in consideration of the fact that the state in 1860 had 46,000 officeholders, a figure that must have been augmented during the war. An estimate of around 60,000 would seem reasonable in view of an increase to 94,000 in 1876. Among 60,000 state employees it was not out of line that 14,675 would fall in the conscription age group of from eighteen to forty-five years,[46] or a little later, seventeen to fifty.

Complaints were made against Vance that he exempted justices of the peace, which he must have been compelled to do at times. The dearth of law-enforcement officers remaining in the state during the war is suggested by the letter he wrote to Judge James J. Osborne at Charlotte, February 28, 1863:

"I am informed on undoubted authority that there are quite a number of distilleries in operation in Lincoln and adjoining counties in open defiance of the law. People expect me to do *everything* now-a-days and have therefore called on me to enforce this law, and as there is no Solicitor for that district, I am compelled to call on you. It requires a prompt remedy. Will you please issue bench warrants against the offenders, or take such other steps as to you may seem best to bring them sharp up and put a stop to these operations?"

War Clerk Jones inserted in his diary April 14, 1863: "Gov. Vance is furious at the idea of conscripting magistrates, constables, etc., in North Carolina. He says it would be an annihilation of State Rights." But Jones thought they were liable under the conscription act.[47]

The letter shows Vance's diligence against distilling in wartime, but also discloses there was no solicitor available for law enforcement in an important district, an office which surely would have been filled had the governor been trying to employ exemptions for political ends. The disputed figures showed Georgia second in exemptions, with 8,229, and on down to Florida with 109, but the North Carolina conscript officer thought those for his state were high and others regarded the figures as out of line. Another calculation reported in February, 1865, brought the North Carolina figure down to 5,589, which must have been too low, and left Georgia unchanged and therefore in the lead. The general impression gained from the figures, in spite of their unreliability, is that Vance produced the most conscripts and had the largest number of exemptions and was attentive to the fair demands of the service in both respects.[48]

Once Vance was set back on his heels by the lawyer and editor and governor of Virginia, John Letcher, an able executive who knew how to defend the good name of his state. Vance had written him pleasantly at times, once protesting against a Virginia recruiting officer crossing the state line and getting conscripts in Ashe County, in the far northwest corner of North Carolina. But Vance bombarded him once too often about the Virginia salt mines and made reference to the North Carolina units in front of Richmond. Vance's letter to Letcher of December 6, 1862, is missing from his letter book but its spirit can be judged by Letcher's aroused reply:

"You tell me," said Letcher in his summation, "that North Carolina is exerting her whole energies in the defense of the State of Virginia. A more just and at the same time more gracious mode of stating the services of your state would have been to say, that North Carolina was defending herself and her people upon the soil of Virginia, which has been selected as the safest battlefield by the Confederate authorities. This is not a war of Virginia; it is a war of all the states of our Confederacy, and the citizens of no one of the states south of us can say, that in fighting battles on their own soil they are defending themselves alone . . .

"If Maryland had gone with us her soil would have been drenched with much of the blood that has watered Virginia's and we should never in all probability, have heard of Manassas, Bull Run, Karnstown [Kernstown], Port Republic, Seven Pines, Chickahominy and other glorious fields, over which the Confederate banner has waved in triumph. Away then with the idea that the states south of us are fighting Virginia's battles. They are with Virginia fighting the battles of the Confederacy in the just and noble cause of Liberty, Equality and Independence and let the struggle between the states be, to see which can do the most, to achieve success."

This was a letter to which Vance does not seem to have undertaken a reply, but he did insert it in his Letter Book.[49]

## Chapter Seventeen

## Needed: A War Correspondent

Vance had a clear vision of what might happen and actually did happen with respect to much Confederate war history.

He could see that because the North Carolina newspapers of limited circulation and resources did not send correspondents to the front, the combat contributions of the North Carolina regiments were not being recorded publicly and probably would be largely lost.

The official reports might serve well enough for later governmental purposes, but they were often prepared and mulled over long after the battles and in virtually all instances after a lapse of days, and usually a public impression of an engagement had been established long before the reports were written. Probably more often than the report influenced the press, it itself was influenced by the newspaper phraseology.

The Richmond newspapers, being close to the scene of action, usually had correspondents with Lee's army, as did, at times, newspapers from Petersburg, Virginia; Savannah, Georgia; Charleston, South Carolina, and other cities. The North Carolina press depended a good deal on clippings from Richmond and even Northern newspapers, on random letters from officers and soldiers, and on chance volunteer correspondents. Vance could not know how long and bitterly the argument would ensue between North Carolina and Virginia writers over the

266

treatment accorded North Carolina units by Virginia journalists and historians, but he was by no means satisfied with the public record as it was being compiled.[1]

One grievous controversy related to the conduct of North Carolina troops in Longstreet's assault on July 3 at Gettysburg, where the column which attacked abreast Pickett's was commanded by Pettigrew. The supporting column was commanded by Major General Isaac R. Trimble. These troops, mostly North Carolinians, were inaccurately charged in the Richmond press with wavering and exposing Pickett. North Carolina units claimed, to the contrary, and presented much evidence in support of their contention, that they made the farthest advance into the Federal position.[2]

But the belief that press reports were deceptive arose prior to Gettysburg. Vance felt that while North Carolina troops played the major role in the victory at Chancellorsville, they received meager credit, if any at all, in the accounts. This prompted him to protest. He wrote to Secretary Seddon on July 3, 1863, the very day of the desperate Pickett-Pettigrew-Trimble attack on Cemetery Ridge, but well before he knew of it, calling to Seddon's attention the fact that North Carolina was not being mentioned in the battle news. This resulted in some measure from the fact, he explained, that there was no correspondent from North Carolina. He respectfully requested that M. J. McSween, of the 53rd North Carolina, be detailed "to attend the Army of Gen. Lee as an Army Correspondent."[3]

McSween, whose letter to Vance about the clothing of North Carolina troops after Sharpsburg has been noted, had chanced to meet Vance at Statesville when the newly elected governor was en route from Petersburg to visit in Asheville before his inauguration. When Vance wrote to Secretary Seddon, he called McSween "a gentleman of intelligence, a graduate of our University and in such feeble health that he cannot render any active service in the field."[4]

Vance selected him undoubtedly because he seemed presentable and the letter he wrote reflected deep solicitude about the condition of North Carolina troops.

Secretary Seddon in reply transmitted a communication from General Lee, to whom Seddon had referred Vance's letter. Lee expressed regret that any impression should prevail of injustice to any portion of his army and said he knew of no injustice nor had he heard of any. He said that if the official reports of officers commanding the troops could not be relied on he knew of no way of obtaining the truth. Clearly he wanted no half-scribe, half-soldier attached to his army. "The plan proposed by Governor Vance," he said, "will I think work great evil and produce embarrassment to the service. I cannot recommend that it be adopted. It must then be extended to all states and it can readily be seen what would be the result." He added that if the officers commanding the troops did not tell the truth they should be removed.[5]

Able general though he was, Lee did not seem to appreciate some public relations aspects of the North Carolina situation. Clearly he did not attach great importance to what the newspaper correspondents wrote. Propaganda in that day had not been developed very effectively to augment a campaign or foster desired attitudes among segments of the home public or behind the enemy lines. Certainly Lee was correct in his belief that officers should tell the truth in their reports, but these reports were usually brief, rarely critical of brother officers, and often became justifications of a course and were truth as seen from one viewpoint. Even had they been available, they were, in fact, as inadequate for newspaper purposes then as they are for historical purposes today.

Rebel War Clerk Jones, who handled this correspondence, entered in his diary on July 30, 1863, a digest of Vance's reply to Lee and Seddon: "An indignant letter was received from Gov. Vance today, in response to the refusal of the government and General Lee to permit him to send with the army a newspaper correspondent to see that justice was done the North Carolina troops. He withdraws the application and appeals to history for the justice which (he says) will never be done North Carolina troops in Virginia by their associates. He asserts also that General Lee refuses furloughs to the wounded North Carolinians at the battle of Chancellorsville (one half the dead and wounded being from North Carolina) for fear they would not return to their colors when fit for duty!"[6]

Vance's letter had other points which Jones did not cover. He explained he had no reference to the official reports as doing any injustice to North Carolina soldiers and he felt it "strange that Gen. Lee and yourself should so utterly misconstrue my meaning." The official reports, he pointed out, were rarely furnished to the newspapers and never except by consent of the War Department. Then he stated his object more succinctly: "I simply desired to correct as far as possible the daily neglect and frequent slander of a portion of the Richmond press, which has its corps of reporters in every department of the Army—by sending a similar corps to report for the press of this State."

He recognized that without Lee's assent no reporter could move with the army or have access to reliable information. The Richmond press, he said, alleged as an excuse for not speaking of North Carolina troops that there were no North Carolina correspondents to send the news, and this Vance was trying to remedy. He further explained that he merely wanted the North Carolina man to have the same access to information as was given others. "But as Gen. Lee objects to it and has seen proper to think that I object to official reports, which have never yet been published, I beg leave to withdraw the requests."[7]

Vance was, in fact, on solid ground, and some method might have been devised by which the North Carolina newspapers could have been supplied with accurate information, to the benefit both of the Confederate cause and of history. The last portion of his letter made a telling point: "The Richmond *Enquirer* in recent articles on the authority of its special correspondent charges our defeat at Gettysburg upon the cowardice and incapacity of the North Carolina troops composing Heth's Division.

"Such things are hard to bear, if true, and if untrue we are denied the right of having a correspondent in the Army to correct them, and must wait for the publication of official reports—which may or may not be published. How such things can contribute to the success of the cause I am unable to say."[8]

Vance's assiduous reading of history gave him understanding of how it was formed, and his apprehensions were well founded. The article to which he referred in the Richmond *Enquirer* has colored Civil War history with an inaccuracy persisting even to the present day. Long before the official reports of Gettysburg were published—Lee's not until after the war while Pickett's never yet has been discovered—a faulty historical verdict had been delivered. The Gettysburg reports of the Southern officers were bundled up by the Northern Army at the end of the war and sent to Washington and were not available to Southern writers until thirteen years after the conflict.

What the Richmond *Enquirer* correspondent wrote from Hagerstown, Maryland, dated July 8, five days after Longstreet's assault, and which Vance questioned so vigorously, became prime source material. It blamed the troops under Pettigrew for the repulse of Pickett's

Division. The North Carolinians were referred to as "the wavering line of raw troops." Said the correspondent, who signed himself "A," about Pettigrew's command: "I saw by the wavering of this line as they entered the conflict that they wanted the firmness of nerve and steadiness of tread which so characterized Pickett's command, and I felt that these men would not, could not, stand the tremendous ordeal to which they would soon be subjected."[9]

This was the division of Harry Heth, commanded by Pettigrew after Heth was wounded. It contained some of the most seasoned and tested units in the army, which on July 1 had won one of the most sanguinary battles of the war in ousting the Iron Brigade and other Federal units from McPherson's Woods and pushing Doubleday's line back to Seminary Ridge. Another difficulty with Lee's reliance on the official reports was that the press accounts of an action, which were the first things written, apparently did, as has been mentioned, give guidance to some officers, unconsciously perhaps, in the preparation of their accounts. Possibly they had read the news story before they wrote their reports. In any event, nothing could have been more absurd than calling Pettigrew's command "raw troops," yet accounts of the battle written nearly a hundred years later told how Pettigrew's supporting column failed Pickett because of its rawness.

Historians often have a gregarious tendency and many apparently never undertook to examine closely the units Pettigrew commanded. The florid Edward A. Pollard, who wrote one of the earliest accounts available to the South, accepted the story of correspondent "A" and wrote: "But where is Pettigrew's division? where are the supports? The raw troops had faltered . . . Pickett is left alone to contend with the masses of the enemy now pouring in on him from every side."[10] Nor did Pettigrew's Division fall back and expose Pickett, because it moved in echelon on Pickett's left and delivered its main attack, as numerous eyewitnesses attested and recorded in later North Carolina accounts, after Pickett's gallant brigades had been pressed back.

Pollard's history was published in 1866 and in that same year William Parker Snow, an English author, published his *Southern Generals,* which picked up the same Richmond *Enquirer* line about Pettigrew's performance: "These latter, however, being mostly raw soldiers, wavered; but Pickett's Virginians pressed forward under terrible fire of grape, shell and canister . . . Pettigrew's line has been broken and his men fly panic stricken to the rear."

The flank brigade on Pettigrew's far left did retire, but it had no North Carolina units, while the two supporting brigades on Pickett's right failed to come up and give protection, but neither of these had a North Carolina unit. Vance was indeed justified in being apprehensive about the kind of news that would be reported and which would color history unless someone was on the field guarding North Carolina's interests.

The Raleigh *Register* had enough confidence in North Carolina soldiers to challenge the Richmond *Enquirer* account at the time. Pettigrew's command included the 11th North Carolina, which was a reorganization of the old 1st North Carolina, the Bethel Regiment that had fought the first engagement of the war. The inspector general of the army had reported to General Lee that the 11th North Carolina was the best drilled and best equipped regiment in his service.[12] Pettigrew's Division contained Field's old brigade, which Stonewall Jackson had honored after Cedar Mountain by riding before it and dropping his cap on the ground, as an appreciation after it plugged the hole left by the retirement of his own Stonewall Brigade. It contained Archer's Alabama Brigade, long battle tested, which had been distinguished in the victory at Chancellorsville. But the Raleigh *Register* had no correspondent on the field to speak as an eyewitness.

Long after the battle the charge reflecting on North Carolina troops rankled with the state's publishers and historians, who never did see the truth catch up with the first error. Their only recourse was to add to the state's motto of "First at Bethel" the phrase, "Farthest at Gettysburg," to which they would attach with equal justice the final, "Last at Appomattox."

Testimony by both North Carolinians and others was overwhelming that, instead of faltering and fleeing, the North Carolina troops who marched with Pettigrew and Trimble attacked on the left of Pickett with a courage and tenacity fully equal to the Virginians'. There is persuasive evidence that the 55th North Carolina of Davis's Brigade made a farther advance into the Federal position than any of Pickett's, whose farthest brigade was led by one of the Old North State's gallant native sons, Lewis A. Armistead.

The casualty lists tell the story that both Pettigrew and Pickett made the assault with vigor and stanchness. The losses of Pickett's fifteen Virginia regiments aggregated 214 killed, 940 wounded, and 1,499 captured. The losses of the five North Carolina regiments in Pettigrew's front line aggregated 229 killed, 1,074 wounded, and none reported captured. Thus one third the number of North Carolina regiments had casualties in killed and wounded exceeding Pickett's. Of the fifteen North Carolina regiments in Pettigrew's and Trimble's full commands, the loss in the battle was 372 killed, 1,745 wounded, and 110 captured.[13]

North Carolina could scarcely be blamed for stating her full case after the war, having been put on the defensive by the Richmond newspaper account so influential with other writers after Gettysburg.

Lee wrote on the subject again on September 9, 1863, to Seddon, who forwarded the letter to Vance as an answer to his of July 26, withdrawing his request. Apparently Lee had in mind the Richmond *Enquirer* calumny against the North Carolina troops after Gettysburg. "I regret exceedingly," Lee wrote, "the jealousies, heartburnings and other evil consequences resulting from the crude misstatements of newspaper correspondents who have necessarily a very limited acquaintance with the fact about which they write and who magnify the deeds of troops from their own states at the expense of others. But I can see no remedy for this. Men seem to prefer sowing discord to inculcating harmony."[14]

He added that the reports would correct the situation, but that they could not be released at present because they would give information to the enemy. But he seemed to think the important thing was what was done in a battle, and not what was said about it. He gave Vance, through Seddon, the reassurance that he had been making more appointments of North Carolina officers to command North Carolina troops as replacements occurred. He quite clearly had in mind the appointment of Robert D. Johnston of Lincoln County, North Carolina—the early secessionist who won the place over Colonel Garrett—as Iverson's successor, effective September 1, 1863. Johnston proved capable. His brigade was an important factor, perhaps the leading factor, in holding a temporary line until Lee could form a new one in the rear after Hancock's Federal Corps had broken through Edward Johnson's Division which manned the Confederate salient at Spotsylvania. Robert Johnston, wounded, went on to win other distinctions at Winchester and to give the brigade abler leadership than it had experienced under Iverson.

McSween's historical ventures never matured. Before Vance had mentioned him to Lee, he had begun collecting material for a history of North Carolina in the war. The Raleigh *Standard* on May 20, 1863, called on officers, chaplains, and others to supply him with items, descriptions of battles, acts of individual merit, marches, and "a full, connected and impartial history of regiments, companies and detachments." Obviously he had sold his idea to the newspaper before he approached Vance.

"He designs especially," said the editorial comment, "as far as he can, to award to North Carolina her just deserts. Anything pertaining to a fair and faithful record of the part performed by North Carolina and her people in this great struggle will appropriately belong to this work." The editor agreed to forward any pertinent information if left in his care. "It will of course require much time and labor to prepare such a matter as this, but North Carolina will never get justice except at the hands of her own sons."[15]

An item which was influential in Vance's and the state's general attitude that the state was being neglected came from Richmond in late May and was published in an issue of the *Standard* with an additional two and a half columns of North Carolina casualties at Chancellorsville. It was an indignant tale from a North Carolina citizen who went to the Richmond depot when the train carrying wounded from Chancellorsville arrived. The incident showed how the discourtesy of a single person could help poison the attitude of an entire state. The North Carolinian asked if any from his state were aboard the train, and the head of a Virginia committee who was standing at the door was quoted as answering, "Oh, yes, these are all North Carolinians. They always manage to get off with trifling wounds." The writer of the account added that this "poor slanderer" represented a very large class in Virginia, "who never have done, nor never will do justice to our State." He said it had been twelve days since the battle was fought, yet none would know from a Virginia newspaper that there was a single private from North Carolina engaged. He charged a studied neglect by Virginia editors. "One of their regiments losing 40 or 50 men, will have a column or two devoted to their exploits but a North Carolina regiment like the 18th may lose 248 out of 410 men, or like the 7th, 199 out of 317, and yet there is great probability that not one line will ever be published."[16]

No doubt the Virginia editors were preoccupied with their local news, as good journalists would be, but North Carolinians saw discrimination and the impression had attached itself firmly to Vance. The writer to the *Standard* cited that a correspondent had made complimentary references to D. H. Hill's Division and had mentioned troops in it from three or four states, but had scrupulously avoided reference to North

Carolina, though perhaps three fourths of the division were from there. The deep-seated reason for the North Carolinian sensitivity is difficult to determine, but its existence was one of the most manifest factors in the state's war attitude.

This writer from Richmond concluded: "Now, Mr. Editor, these things have existed from the fight at Bethel. I fear that North Carolina need never expect anything from a vain-glorious Virginian but cold contempt and gross slander . . . It is to be apprehended that those Virginians who have essayed to write the history of these troublous times, may treat the Old North State with the same injustice that she has been subjected to by the springs of Virginia aristocracy." It was signed "A Thorough North Carolinian."[17]

The undercurrent of opinion which affected Vance and the leading Raleigh newspaper, that North Carolina had long suffered from a poor press, and that neither the state nor her sons had been accorded their proper position in the affairs of the nation, was not new in the Civil War period. A notable example of alleged slight was former senator and cabinet member George E. Badger, noted Whig orator, whom the Reverend R. H. Whitaker in his inimitable reminiscences of antebellum days in the state saluted as one who had never received credit:

"If he had hailed from some Northern state instead of North Carolina, where we have not learned to properly appreciate our own great men, a shaft would, long ago, have been reared to his memory, and our school books would have been filled with extracts from some of his great speeches."[18]

The result was that he passed from the memory of the children of a later day, when in truth some of his remarks were as worthy of preservation as were Daniel Webster's, which, it might have been pointed out, were in nearly every school reader of the nation.

Vance and Holden at this time were yearning for greater respect for North Carolina because the state was sweating under the attack of a fresh and vigorous Richmond editor, John Mitchell, newly come from Ireland to take command of the Richmond *Enquirer* and to establish himself as enough of a Southerner to challenge Congressman Foote of Tennessee to a duel, a presumption which found Foote unwilling to receive his messenger.[19] Mitchell published an article tending to create an impression that North Carolina conservatives were bent on destroying the existing Confederacy and conspiring to form a Middle Confederacy —the old prewar plan of some moderates. The Raleigh *Standard* was prompt and personally insulting in its response: "It is bad enough to have to endure the gross partyism of Mr. Davis' administration, but it is intolerable to be libeled by this seedy foreign adventurer. North Carolina is treated like a *province* in the appointments which are made, and on the back of this she is hunted and her reputation blackened in the eyes of those who do not know her by the miserable hounds of power. This writer [Mitchell] appeals to our soldiers in the field and tells them that those who have the management of the State affairs are not true to them or the Southern cause."[20]

The army units understood Vance and his intense loyalty to them, and John Mitchell's editorial comments, however widely they may have been read, were not influential against him. He seemed much more concerned at the moment with historical than current impressions.

Vance never lost his belief that the story of North Carolina's participation in the war had not been properly appreciated by general historians. The thought recurred through his speeches. When he was asked to go to Winchester, Virginia, to deliver the oration at the dedication of the Confederate Cemetery there, he found the reason was that the graves of North Carolina soldiers exceeded those of any other state. When he referred to it later he said it showed "that in all the glorious campaigns of Jackson, Ewell and Early, in that blood-drenched valley, North Carolina soldiers were either very numerous or else had an unusual share of the hard fighting; neither of which facts would be so much as suspected by reading the popular histories of those campaigns." When he looked over the mounds he epitomized it all in the statement: *"Dead men do tell tales."*

He went on to relate that almost the only commands of Lee's army remaining intact and serviceable at Appomattox were North Carolina brigades, and that it was uncontradicted that North Carolina surrendered there twice as many as did any other state. At the same time, Hoke's Division of three brigades of North Carolina troops at Greensboro, "in splendid condition and efficiency," constituted one third or more of Johnston's entire army.

Then he summed up: "I mention these facts, not by way of ill-tempered or untasteful boasting, but by way of proper self-assertion, a quality in which the people of my State are charged, and justly charged, with being deficient; and also because they testify to the state of things which in the hands of a just and discriminating historian must greatly redound to the credit and honor of North Carolina."[21]

Nearly forty years were to pass before an authoritative compilation of information about North Carolina in the war was made under the auspices of able Chief Justice Walter Clark. The articles about the regiments were more the memories of a surviving officer in each regiment than a fresh and living account. Some were complete, some woefully inadequate, and the gap left by McSween's failure to carry on the projected work was never quite filled. Clark's five volumes, a monumental achievement of assembly and editing, are the main source record of North Carolina's part in the war, but they have influenced only latter-day history and some of that to a minor degree.

Likely it was fortunate that Lee did not accept McSween as an army correspondent, valid as Vance's request had been. McSween seemed prone to misadventure, became involved in controversy with Colonel Matt W. Ransom, served a military prison sentence, and eventually turned against Vance, only to regret it and seek reconciliation. As a writer he was able and probably suffered from impulsiveness and a hot temper, which were not qualities that made a good war correspondent. After the war he edited a newspaper in Fayetteville.[22]

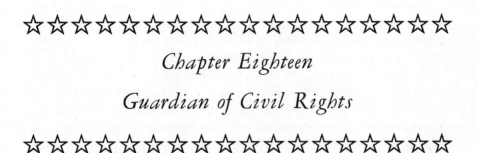

## Chapter Eighteen

## Guardian of Civil Rights

One of Vance's tasks was educational work with the Richmond authorities, who, like most governments in wartime, were disposed to be arbitrary and, unless checked, to run roughshod, especially by measures adopted by junior representatives in the field, over the very principles for which the Southern states felt they were fighting.

The war was mainly for state rights, and if the states were to have no rights the conflict seemed of hollow purpose.

Throughout much of the history written since the war there has remained an underlying theme that because the states, some more than others, demanded the reservation of certain basic rights from Richmond, the South lost the war, when something approaching a despotism would have won it. This view is relished by those who find confirmation out of the circumstance that sometimes despotisms have won wars. But they might, if they chose, chalk up for absolutism an equal or longer list of failures. They tend to forget the South faced stupendous odds and conducted against them one of the most gallant struggles of history, and approached at times a draw which would have been tantamount to victory.

A case equally attractive might be made of the thesis that both the Southern home public and soldiers in the front lines began to question the worthiness of their cause when the Richmond administration showed more despotic tendencies. Men went home or into hiding in the mountains when the war became conventionalized and lost its ecstatic and volunteer quality. Alexander H. Stephens could not have been the only one to detest it when Richmond began to bypass the states and deprive citizens of civil rights.

Desertions, it might be pointed out, became more general after the central government began to press down, at times with galling severity, on the home public. Certainly it is clear that increasing harshness of the central government did not bring the South nearer to victory.

Manifestly the reason the South lost the war was that her population, strained to the limit, yielded an army of not more than 700,000 men, a figure in excess of most calculations, while the North mustered 2,213,000, at a bottom figure. Not the excess of freedom but the scarcity of naval vessels to break the blockade was a major contributing factor.[1]

Vance dealt effectively with this question in his own summation. He absolved Jefferson Davis of any personal aura of despotism and said the Confederate President never abused the extraordinary powers granted to him by Congress; on the other hand, "so great was his reverence, and that of the Southern mind at large, for all the old-time muniments of personal liberty, that nearly every claim of the States in behalf of their citizens was conceded." Vance was speaking here after the mellowing processes of more than twenty years, for neither he nor Davis withheld the rapier when they were parrying over the civil rights issue in the war years.

Vance in this résumé went on to say that "the proudest boast" he could make about his war governorship was that the old legal maxim *inter arma silent leges* was expunged, and that in its place was written *inter arma leges audiebantur.* "The laws were heard amidst the roar of cannon. No man within the jurisdiction of the State of North Carolina was denied the privilege of the writ of *habeas corpus,* the right of trial by jury, or the equal protection of the laws, as provided by our constitution and the bill of rights."[2]

Thus his insistent struggle was to demonstrate that personal liberty could be preserved during war. The framers of the original Federal Constitution, whom Vance had come to know intimately under the stimulating tutelage of richly endowed President Swain, and the devisers of the Confederate constitution as well, understood this when they refrained from awarding broad extraordinary war powers to the Executive. Vance apparently would have preserved at all times the writ of *habeas corpus,* which the Constitution allowed to be suspended in cases of rebellion or invasion as the public safety might require. Certainly the South was being invaded and Vance did not cotton to having the writ set aside.

A glaring case of abuse of power which Vance had to correct was that of the Reverend Robert J. Graves, who was snatched from his home by Confederate authorities, covertly transported to Richmond, and lodged in the notorious Castle Thunder prison without the semblance of legal proceedings. Vance looked on the action, taken under the orders of Brigadier General John H. Winder, provost marshal of Richmond and chief of the Confederate prisons, an officer odious to the North and disliked by many in the South, as nothing other than an invasion. While as an individual Graves was not significant or apparently entitled to much veneration, his captivity shook the Confederacy because it aroused Vance to a full measure of indignation.

Graves was a rolling-stone lawyer and minister, British born, who immigrated to Massachusetts, moved to Albany, New York, to practice law, and journeyed south to William and Mary College and the Union Theological Seminary, both in Virginia. He was graduated by both schools and engaged in teaching, then became pastor of the Bethlehem Presbyterian Church in Orange County, North Carolina, the county of Chapel Hill, Hillsboro, and the station that became Durham.[3]

Graves in late 1862 decided to go North—his version was that he wanted a New York surgeon to operate on his throat—but when he applied to Winder for a passport he represented himself as a New Yorker who wanted to repatriate himself. But he returned to North Carolina after his trip, resumed his pulpit, and at the suggestion of one of his congregation wrote a letter about his impressions gained on his visit and sent it to the Richmond *Enquirer.* The parishioner who suggested the letter, William J. Bingham, a distinguished educator, merely thought it would be helpful for the people to know of the serious war efforts being made in the North, to counteract any impression that the North was apathetic. The Richmond authorities read the letter in type and it seemed to them to give comfort to the enemy and stir discontent at home.

When the letter was published, Captain T. E. Upshaw of the Confederate Army wrote a letter to the *Enquirer* and the editor took it to

General Winder. It said that one of Upshaw's soldiers had been returned as a prisoner and was present when Pastor Graves came to Harrison's Landing under a flag of truce from the North, and that while they waited he had heard Graves give much information—"everything he knew" as the soldier put it—about the affairs and conditions in Richmond and in particular about the gunboat *Richmond* which was building there. The exchange became so intensive, the soldier reported, that the Federals brought out drawings and plans of the *Monitor* and showed them to the pastor, presumably to get points of comparison or elucidation of a highly detailed nature.[4]

Vance knew nothing of this and other later disclosures, but when Winder had the private's story he sent a detective to the clergyman's church at The Oaks in North Carolina. The detective, Captain McCubbin of the Richmond police force, on service under Winder, sat in a pew one Sunday morning while the pastor preached, then arrested him after the sermon, and, before anyone in Raleigh was aware of it, carried him off to Richmond. As soon as Vance heard of it he had the cars searched in Raleigh in an effort to intercept the pair. When he found he was too late he rushed a request to the Mayor of Richmond asking him to stop the preacher and his guard, but that, too, was belated and the next heard of Graves was that he was lodged in the notorious Richmond prison.[5] About this prison one letter writer said, "they donte have mutch mircy on a man" there.[6] The question was not whether Graves might have given all the secrets contained in the War Department files to the Northern officers—there was little likelihood he had learned much about the gunboat in Orange County—but the sovereignty of North Carolina had been affronted by his unannounced seizure. The legal forms were ignored and the arrest was made by an unauthorized agent from outside the state. Vance, who always looked at the center of the issue, saw that before anything else was done respecting his innocence or guilt, the Reverend Mr. Graves must be restored to North Carolina. In this he had the immediate and ardent support of some of the state's leading newspapers, which did not know whether or not Graves was guilty of an offense, but knew that his personal rights had been trampled underfoot because he had been arrested without a warrant or a specific charge. The General Assembly passed unanimously a joint resolution demanding his return for examination and the state became thoroughly inflamed.

The resolution had the prestige of having been introduced by the former senator and cabinet member William A. Graham, who was representing Orange County in the legislature before going a little later to the Confederate Senate in Richmond. Vance dispatched it together with his own demand on December 24, 1862, to President Davis, who happened to be visiting the armies in the west. He received a full letter of explanation from Secretary Seddon dated December 27, telling that he had inquired of General Winder, who said Graves was being held as a spy. He described the pastor's letter to the *Enquirer,* saying that without judging the real intent "it seemed to many well calculated to cause mistrust and discouragement among our people." He told of the incident at Harrison's Landing and of the statement of a Richmond clergyman, the Reverend Mr. Norwood, who said Graves had told him that he had found it difficult to gain permission from the Federals to travel North. He claimed he was held a prisoner at McClellan's headquarters for two weeks for declining to take the oath of allegiance. Finally, he obtained his permit from the Northern Army by affecting to give information about the gunboat which would in no manner help the enemy. Of this Seddon commented: "This attitude confessed by a minister of the Gospel for an end of private advantage affecting to act the spy is certainly not calculated to diminish the suspiciousness of his conduct. . . ." It also, Seddon felt, tended to confirm the soldier's statement.[7]

The *Enquirer* had received another letter, this from George P. Miles, who called himself a "zealous citizen of North Carolina fully acquainted with the antecedents of Rev. Graves." He described the preacher as "a Yankee undeserving of trust and of more than doubtful loyalty."[8] All these matters were apart from the fact that he had been snatched out of North Carolina without being charged and was to be tried by a military court although he was a civilian. To that Vance would not assent. Winder claimed he did not know Graves was a North Carolinian when he had him arrested, but regarded him an alien enemy and as such subject to arrest as a spy. Seddon conceded that Winder "acted with over zeal" in not satisfying himself first that the man was a citizen of North Carolina. As such, Seddon agreed, "he could with no propriety or legality be removed from the state," but should have been handed over to the proper authorities to be dealt with according to law.

What President Davis would have done in the instance is doubtful, for he loved to examine close points. Seddon held that any doubt about the man's citizenship had been cleared by the action of the state legislature and "there can be neither prudence nor justification for not promptly admitting the error of his removal and rectifying it by his immediate return and delivery under your Executive's demand."[9]

So the Reverend Mr. Graves was sent back to Raleigh and Vance was so highly gratified that it appeared a fresh rapport had been established between Raleigh and Richmond. "Nothing tends more strongly to preserve harmony and cordial feelings," he wrote to Seddon, "than for a State, naturally and properly jealous of its rights, to perceive such a courteous disposition to respect and defend them, on the part of the General Government." He explained his own position by saying "the greatest motive actuating me in this matter is my earnest desire to see all the forms of law and liberty observed."[10]

Vance wrote on December 30 to Justice Matthias E. Manly of the North Carolina Supreme Court saying he had "the body of R. J. Graves" and hardly knew what to do with him, but was sending him to his own county to be bailed and to answer any charges that might be lodged against him. He wrote also to George V. Strong, the Confederate district attorney at Goldsboro, saying Graves, "who was arrested and sent to Richmond, as a spy or something of that kind," had been returned and bound over for examination before Justice Manly. The Secretary of War had been notified to send such evidence as he had against him.[11] The Reverend Mr. Graves's offense, if anything more than using bad judgment, was venial, it appeared, for the grand jury never indicted him and he was never brought to trial, though he might have been hanged if tried by court-martial in Richmond.

Brigadier General Winder never snatched any more citizens from North Carolina for transport to Richmond, but numerous other civil rights cases demanded the governor's continual vigilance.

Vance used the Graves case as a precedent when later in the war an enterprising colonel arrested and sent beyond the state lines a former surgeon of a North Carolina regiment, Henry P. Retter. In another instance of more touching character the governor declined to let the law stand in the way of a humanitarian service, and assumed the responsibility for the technical infraction. A magistrate's order prohibited the Wake County committee charged with distributing provisions to the needy families of soldiers from including the families of deserters. Commissioner Isaac Rogers declined to make the distribution to a Mrs. Thompson, a deserter's wife, but told her to see the governor. When Vance heard her dire need, he could not refuse the woman food, but gave her a letter to Rogers ordering the distribution. Later when he saw

Rogers he said he had no legal authority for the letter, but the desertion of the woman's husband did not alter the laws of humanity; that the wife and children should not be visited with the sins of the father, and that if objection were made, to refer the complaints to him.[12]

One of the most flagrant cases of indifference to personal rights occurred when General French moved into eastern North Carolina in late 1862, and officers under his command arrested forty citizens on the suspicion that they were disloyal. Apparently not knowing what to do with them, French sent them to the military prison at Salisbury for safe-keeping. As soon as he heard of the mass arrest, Vance wrote to President Davis November 11, 1862, stating that as governor it was his duty to see that they were protected "in whatever rights pertain to them."

"First among them," he continued, "is undeniably the right of a trial of their alleged offenses." He added that a number of other citizens had been taken to Salisbury under similar circumstances—in all, fifty to sixty civilian prisoners. As this was in the early stage of his administration and grievances had not mounted, his attitude toward Davis was cordial. He said he would be glad to know what disposition was to be made of these cases or if there was any grave public reason why they should not be investigated.[13]

Davis referred the letter to General French, who told Vance he had instructed officers not to molest citizens unless they had positive proof of an offense against the government. Otherwise, if nothing could be proved against them, they would go home more embittered. In addition, the practice would open the way for the enemy to retaliate by arresting loyal Confederates inside their lines. He regretted that the arresting officer had taken the forty men beyond Tarboro. He would instruct that charges be made against those where necessary and issue orders that the others be sent back via Goldsboro to Greenville, from where they could be returned to their homes.[14]

Vance was probably more emphatic verbally to French or others than he was in his rather mild letter to President Davis. Fourteen years later, when in a heated political campaign, he referred to the incident and said there was quibbling in Richmond about what should be done with these citizen prisoners. He told the authorities, he said, that if the prisoners were not either tried or released "he would issue a proclamation recalling the North Carolina soldiers from Virginia, and call out the state militia to protect the liberties of the citizens." The prisoners, he declared, were speedily released.[15] He undoubtedly did make that threat. In all likelihood had he not gained an accommodation he would have begun to execute it, but it did not appear in his correspondence over this case.

President Davis had been given temporary authority to suspend the writ of *habeas corpus* well before Vance became governor, the first instance being the law of Congress February 27, 1862, after the South's first great tragedy, the loss of the army defending Fort Donelson. The President was authorized to declare martial law and he did declare it in March in the Richmond area in apprehension over McClellan's advance up the Peninsula. He declared it also around Memphis when the Federals approached.[16]

These declarations were what provoked the outburst of Vice President Stephens, who thought Congress had no more right to authorize martial law than Davis had to proclaim it. Congress now and then extended the authority and even more frequently debated it. The doctrine of suspension of the writ of *habeas corpus* was compared to the policy of the Duke of Alva, "one of the bloodiest tyrants of ancient or modern times," and no reason was found why citizens should be deprived of their liberty without proof "for reasons of state!" Such choice reflections on the Davis policy were given to the North Carolina public by the *Standard*.[17]

Opposition against suspending the writ and substituting military for civil jurisdiction built up over the months despite Davis's discreet use of his powers. John Christopher Schwab, the Yale political economist and student of these subjects of more than half a century ago, found that the Confederate authorities in suspending normal civil processes "did not employ this extreme war measure with the stringency characteristic of the policy adopted by the Federal government." Martial law in the North was "much more effectively and harshly used as a means of cowing the opposition and restraining the disloyal."[18] The *Standard* made this same comparison when the writ was first suspended, and at the time rebuked the Richmond *Enquirer* for its barbs at North Carolina. It did not seem enough, said the Raleigh newspaper, for the former Union men to go into the army or send their sons or give financial support, but they were expected to ignore all their principles and give sanction to all acts by the Confederate government and "submit without a murmur to the violation of the military upon the civil power.

"This is the cup presented to us, and if we do not drain it to the dregs, we are pronounced untrue to our native land. . . . We have urged separation of the South and desperate prosecution of the war because of the assumption by Mr. Lincoln of despotic power, his overthrow of the liberty of speech and of the press, and of the writ of *habeas corpus,* his arrest of women and children and imprisoning them without a hearing because they claimed the great American right of thinking and speaking for themselves, and his disregard of the States, and the right of property in the Southern States. Opposition to all such acts of tyranny is inborn with the people of North Carolina. . . . We have opposed tyranny without, but we have labored to maintain liberty within."[19]

Vance's outburst against suspension had the background of widespread public agitation and newspaper comment, but was founded more securely on his personal aversion to autocratic government and a profound confidence in the civil institutions of long test and wise development. His fresh correspondence with Davis came at the time when Congress with increasing reluctance prepared to extend the period of suspension of the writ.

When he learned that a new act authorizing the President of the Confederacy to suspend the writ was pending in early 1864, and would pass, Vance, though he had found little fruit in his correspondence with the President, boldly plunged into a dissertation of human and civil rights, which elicited from Davis, ever ready to dwell on imponderables, an even more lengthy reply.

This correspondence, which is the very heart of the prolonged and at times wrathful misunderstanding between the two men—though impatience seemed the quality more of Davis than of Vance—was provoked because Vance believed the suspension was to be aimed especially at North Carolina and not the entire South, due to the circumstance that the state, while it did produce more conscripts than any other, was the scene of widespread mass meetings and public denunciation of the conscription act.

Vance took a more unquestioning view in the early days of Davis's drift toward autocratic powers. But in 1864, presiding over a state most jealous of its personal freedom and civil and local prerogatives, and more articulate in its defense of them than it had ever been in opposition to the old government, he would have been driven into the role of champion of personal liberty in the South, even had he not found it congenial.

While the bill suspending the *habeas corpus* was pending, Vance, not having seen it, could express no final opinion about it, but he warned

Davis that if it should be judged unconstitutional and "revolutionary in itself," it would be resisted. He urged Davis that, should it become law, he should "be chary with exercising the powers with which it will invest you. Be certain to try at least for a while, the moral effect of holding this power over the heads of the discontented men before shocking all worshippers of the Common law throughout the world by hurling freemen into sheriffless dungeons for opinion sake."[20]

The mere suggestion that the President might resort to such arbitrary acts could not but have disturbed the sensibilities of one of Mr. Davis's personal confidence and high attainments, but it was only the beginning of the innuendoes Vance packed into his letter. When he undertook to fathom Davis's purpose, he seemed wanting in deference: "I do not speak this factiously, or by way of a flourish, nor do I believe that as an enlightened lawyer, and a Christian statesman you could feel any pleasure in the performance of such an ungracious task. I am on the contrary convinced that you believe it to be the only way to secure North Carolina in the performance of her obligations to her confederates. The misfortune of this belief is yours."

He asserted that if the people were left "untouched by the arm of military violence" their reason and patriotism would be expressed at the ballot box. At that time threats of reassembling the convention were being heard around the state, the inference being that the superlegislative body which took North Carolina out of the Union might consider as well taking her out of the Confederacy, but Vance with ardent patriotism opposed convening such a group. His eyes were always on the stanch loyalty being displayed by the state's superb fighting units in Lee's and other armies. He told Davis:

"Hundreds of good and true men, now acting with and possessing the confidence of the party called Conservatives [his own party] are at work against the dangerous movements for a convention, and whilst civil law remains intact will work zealously and with heart." He said he expected to take "the field," meaning to begin a stumping campaign, as soon as his duties would allow him to get away, and expressed confidence in his ability to restrain revolutionary tendencies. "Never yet Sir," he declared, "have the people of North Carolina refused to listen to their public men if they show right and reason on their side. I do not fear to trust the issue now to these potent weapons in the hands of such men as will wield them next summer: I do fear to trust bayonets and dungeons."

Vance then went back to his earlier efforts to make the President aware of conditions in North Carolina and recalled the two visits he had paid Richmond to clarify his views; then he reiterated that the people of North Carolina had been suspected by the Confederate government because of the reluctance with which they severed ties with the old Union. This consciousness of being suspected "has been greatly strengthened by what seemed to be a studied exclusion of the anti-secessionists from all the more important offices of the government, even from those promotions in the army, which many of them had won with their blood."

Vance posed for Davis the most telling question: "Discussion it is true has been unlimited and bitter and unrelenting criticism upon your administration has been indulged in, but where and when have our people failed you in battle, or withheld their blood or their vast resources?"

He built up his case by emphasizing the looseness of control held over the agents of the central government sent into the state. He asked to be shown any exactions upon their patriotism to which the people had not submitted, and: "Conscription, ruthless and unrelenting has been only exceeded in the severity of its execution by the impressment of property, frequently intrusted to men unprincipled, dishonest and filled to overflowing with all the petty meanness of small minds dressed in a little brief authority. The files of my office are filled with the unavailing complaints of outraged citizens to whom redress is impossible. Yet they have submitted and so far performed with honor their duty to their country though the voice of these very natural murmurs is set down to disloyalty."

Vance's personal reference to Davis was ordinarily respectful but could not be looked on as complimentary: "I do not hold you responsible for all the petty annoyances, 'the insolence of office' under which our people lose heart and patience; even if I did I cannot forget that it is *my country* that I am serving, not the rulers of that country." He made it clear that he did not threaten. "I desire only with singleness of purpose and sincerity of heart to speak those words of soberness and truth which may with the blessing of God best subserve the cause of my suffering country. Those words I now believe to be the advice herein given to refrain from exercising the extraordinary powers about to be given you by Congress, at least until the last hope of moral influence being sufficient, is extinct."

Though the North was mustering its vast resources of men and materiel, and preparing to press the Confederacy with great armies simultaneously on all fronts, Vance had by no means despaired of success. He had seen the fighting qualities of his own people when fired with patriotic and dynamic leadership, in contrast with the lethargy which springs from being harassed and badgered. He summed it up for Davis in two sentences: "Our success depends not on the numbers engaged to support our cause, but upon their zeal and affection. Hence I have every hope in persuading, not one in forcing the sympathies of an unwilling people."[21]

Quite obviously the reading of Motley was fresh in his mind. Those who have charged Vance with being controlled during this period by no more than political considerations patently have not given attention to the deep human sentiments and the devotion to fundamental Anglo-Saxon institutions which motivated him above all other aims. Certainly one having no more than political advancement in mind—the desire to win re-election at any cost—would not have repeatedly alienated the Confederate government. Davis was not without influence and could do damage if he chose.

Davis had many enemies; still the intemperate campaign being waged against him by Vice President Alexander Stephens in Georgia was driving moderates toward him, and ratifying an affection between him and some of the generals which could not be accounted for on any other score than sympathy for an upright man laboring to his full but limited capacity. As had been said of Millard Fillmore for his approval of the Compromise of 1850: "Every piece of artillery which belonged to the camp of his adversaries was brought into action against him . . . every arrow aimed against him had poison on its point";[22] so it might be said of many of the public attacks on Davis from his own people. Much of it issued from the opposite viewpoint to Vance's complaints—it was because of a softness, because "he was a constitutional ruler, not a revolutionary chief." A few no doubt would have preferred a military dictator, and their number increased.

Vance did not make Davis's trials easier, nor did another indefatigable letter writer who was less co-operative than Vance, the embattled Governor Brown of Georgia. Senator John J. Ingalls of Kansas, "a man as noted for his hatred of the Southern people as for his brilliant talents," often Vance's adversary in later years in the United States Senate, said from his seat there that he could understand the South's reverence for

Davis, and that he "honored them for their constancy to that heroic man." He added what Vance knew from his studies of the Dutch Republic and of Wallace and Robert Bruce in Scotland, that "Ideas can never be annihilated" and "no man was ever converted by being overpowered." Davis, according to Ingalls, remained to the end "the immovable type." He was the exponent and representative of "those ideas for which he had staked all and lost all."[23]

The President was receiving more severe handling close at home than was being given him by the fairly restrained language of Vance. After the death of William Lowndes Yancey in Alabama, July 23, 1863, the Richmond *Enquirer,* of which E. A. Pollard, the most irritating thorn in Davis's side, was editor, used praise of the deceased legislator as the occasion for a fresh assault on the executive. As it was boiled down, Davis was "unfortunately and hastily *inflicted* on the Confederacy at Montgomery, and when fixed in position, banished from his presence the heart and brain of the South—denying all participation in the affairs of government to the great men who were the authors of secession."[24]

The charge that the President was ingrowing had some merit, though he was now accused of ignoring the original secessionists, while Vance charged he ignored those who last left the Union fold. The fact was that Davis needed, or responded to, little advice from anyone, and Vance could have spared himself many unhappy hours had he curtailed his fruitless correspondence with Richmond.

Davis waited sixteen days before replying to Vance's letter, explaining that the close of Congress imposed on him engrossing duties. As before, he immediately detected a personal affront in Vance's direct remarks, claiming that the governor made "unjust reflections upon my official conduct" and assertions "which you would in vain attempt to sustain by proof."[25] These were not the main burden of the letter if they characterized it at all, and Davis's belief must be attributed to the delicacy of his antenna in searching for criticism. He declared unjust the statement that North Carolina had been slighted in civil appointments and army promotions and although this was old and well-covered ground he insisted on a specification. He declared there was not an instance of promotion recommended because of political opinion or party affiliation. He denied that the people of North Carolina had been "suspected" because of their reluctance to secede. Categorically he denied most other assertions in the governor's epistle. His letter ran upwards of one thousand six hundred words of closely reasoned composition. Whether the fault was Vance's in drawing him out, or the President's in not compressing his reply into two hundred words or so, considering that he was faced with hand composition and inevitably some editing before his scribe made a final copy, the correspondence was patently a drain on the time of the busy executive, who in February, 1864, was in some of the most critical hours of his republic's existence.

He regretted as much as Vance did the excesses of subordinates in enforcing conscription, but again contended that lack of redress could not be complained about as long as Vance kept the papers in his files. Davis asserted that no complaint had come that had not received respectful consideration and redress, as far as was in his power to do justice.

Not until the last hundred words or so did he reach the main subject of Vance's letter, which was a caution to go slow in exercising the extraordinary powers he was about to be granted. About this: "I can only say that they will be used, if at all, with a due regard to the rights of the citizen, as well as the public safety. Arbitrary measures are not more congenial to my nature, than to the spirit of our institutions. But should the occasion unhappily arise when the public safety demands their employment, I would be derelict in duty, if I hesitated to use them to the extent required by the exigency."

Vance did not read this letter with pleasure, and said so in his reply. But the barren correspondence was developing into a wrangle with a deal of explaining on both sides as to what they did and what they did not mean. "I trust," said the governor, "I am incapable of needlessly and wantonly insulting the Chief Magistrate of the Confederate States, and have ever endeavored in making unpleasant statements to you to avoid discourtesy, while expressing myself with candor."[26] The correspondence tends to bear out Zeb in that respect. The main issue remained whether or not the Confederate administration had been guilty of a studied exclusion of the old antisecessionists from appointments and promotions and on that no possibility of agreement existed. Vance conceded, as before, that though he considered it apparent, he could not prove that other than military considerations had governed the President's army appointments.

However Davis may have intended it, he never had a chance to suspend the writ of *habeas corpus* in North Carolina. The story of that failure is tied to the steadfastness, or perhaps stubbornness, of Zeb Vance and to the undeniable stubbornness, mixed with some judicial acumen and devotion to human rights, on the part of controversial Chief

Justice William Mumford Pearson of the North Carolina Supreme Court.

He was from Rowan County, North Carolina, the county of Daniel Boone, Hinton R. Helper of *Impending Crisis* fame, and in the era between them, of the tall, redheaded, taciturn schoolteacher Peter Stewart Ney, whom many believed to be the French Marshal mysteriously escaped from the Bourbon firing squad after Waterloo. Though Pearson was coming up at that time and reading law in the county, there is no evidence that he was influenced by the stately, brooding, wistful French teacher. He was the son of a Revolutionary War lieutenant who had fought, barehanded, a famous battle with a Tory colonel in Davie County.

Pearson led his class at the University of North Carolina twenty years ahead of Vance's studentship there. He studied law under Supreme Court Justice Leonard Henderson at Mocksville, became a practicing lawyer, then ten years later a superior court judge and in 1848, at the age of forty-three, an associate justice of the Supreme Court.[27]

He gained his chief justiceship by seizure. Chief Justice Thomas Ruffin had resigned from the three-member Supreme Court in 1852. Six years later, on the death of Chief Justice Nash, when there was a legislative deadlock on all others, the General Assembly again elected Ruffin a justice. The court picked its own chief justice, usually giving precedence to seniority. The question of Ruffin's seniority was open, due to the break in his tenure. Of the other two, Pearson ranked William Horn Battle. When the three met, Pearson at once said, "According to precedent I am to preside. I call the court to order." Neither of the others objected and much Civil War and Zeb Vance history was bound up in the assertion.[28]

Justice Pearson was plunged into the conscription issue when the case of John W. Irvin came before him in March, 1863, on a request for a writ of *habeas corpus* which he granted on examination of the facts. Irvin was drafted under the first conscription act and hired a substitute, as the law allowed. The substitute was above thirty-five years of age. When the second conscription act was passed after the Sharpsburg campaign and the age limit was extended to forty-five, those who had hired substitutes between the ages of thirty-five and forty-five were thrown back into the pool of eligibles. Irvin was in consequence again drafted. The conscript officers held, under War Department regulations interpreting the laws, that he was no longer protected by a substitute who was himself eligible for conscription. Pearson held to the contrary, supporting the sanctity of the original, lawful contract between Irvin and his substitute.[29]

Colonel Mallett, head of the conscription camp, by order of the War Department rearrested Irvin, and the state and central authorities were brought into immediate confrontation. Secretary Seddon declared that the department was within its powers and offered the dictum that the opinion of Chief Justice Pearson was not regarded as a sound exposition of the Act of Congress. Mallett was directed to ignore it. Vance in opposition requested Mallett not to send Irvin outside the state and rushed off a protest to Seddon, and the exchanges grew protracted. Vance held that the War Department might not be bound by the decisions of the North Carolina courts but the governor surely was, then absolved the state from blame with this assertion:

"It is certainly no fault of this Government that there exists no competent tribunal to decide these issues and it is certainly not unreasonable for the State of North Carolina to object when a decision of its Chief Justice is ordered to be disregarded by a Department of the Confederate Government invested with no judicial powers whatever."[30]

He stated his regret over the clash, but made it clear that according to his concept of duty his powers as an executive officer were "absolutely bound by the decisions of the State Courts" and that it was not competent for him to review them—that they "must of necessity be to me the supreme law of the land." In this he was obviously sincere, not merely bellicose. "Having thus stated," he continued, "the plain path of duty, which I am bound to pursue, I desire nevertheless to assure you of the great concern which I feel in the issue, and of my earnest wish to assist the War Department in maintaining the efficiency of our Armies and avoiding conflict with the local authorities."

Though he declined to recognize a decision by an administrative bureau, he promised to get a decision from the full Supreme Court of North Carolina, which was then sitting. Meantime, he asked Seddon for any suggestions about how such difficulties might be avoided.

Seddon was in one of his unyielding moods, feeling that he had made enough concessions to Vance already. The nub of his conclusion was: "When a Confederate officer, in performance of a legal duty, under the constitution and laws of the Confederacy, is in possession of one charged as an offender against those laws, it does not belong to the power of a State officer to take that person from his custody." Seddon employed the phrase, "under the constitution and laws of the Confederacy." He was not one privileged to interpret the constitution, which was the province of existing tribunals. The matter of the constitutionality of a statute and War Department regulations was involved and, since the Confederacy possessed no Supreme Court, for better or worse Vance had to choose between the ruling of a bureau in Richmond and his own highest tribunal. He chose the tribunal. When he had Seddon's final, unyielding word, he abruptly issued a general proclamation May 11, 1863, and published it in the newspapers, directing his militia officers not to arrest any man as a conscript or a deserter who had been discharged under a writ of *habeas corpus* issued by a Supreme or Superior Court judge of the state; and further, "to resist any such arrest upon the part of any person, not authorized by the legal order or process of a Court or Judge having jurisdiction of such cases."[31] He sent a squad of militia soldiers and the man was released.

The full court to which Vance had the issue submitted sustained Justice Pearson in a companion case, the justice having the privilege of delivering the decision in which he held that Congress had committed an error. Having given to conscripts the right to hire substitutes who were not liable to military duty, none could have anticipated that these substitutes could have been conscripted by another act or by War Department regulations which attempted to cover a gap Congress had left open. The court seemed to look on it more as a loophole in the law than a case involving the sanctity of contracts. But as in such matters where no court had jurisdiction over both parties in a controversy, the one defeated ordinarily would be contemptuous, and Secretary Seddon remained just that. Adamantly he had his conscript officers enroll during the Gettysburg period the men who had hired substitutes under the original act, and they in turn sought and obtained legal relief through the embittered jargon of Justice Pearson and personal security behind the strong protective arms and even more powerful invectives of Zeb Vance.

Vance was reasonable in arguing that if the Confederacy wanted a high tribunal to pass on constitutional questions or conflicts between the states and central government or among the states, it should have created one. Some in analyzing Confederate institutions have found worth in two provisions not contained in the old Federal procedures, judged meritorious alterations. One, previously referred to, was the provision that the President, who served a six-year term, could not succeed himself. The other was not constitutional, but a legislative choice through stalemate—the lack of a supreme court and therefore the absence of any agency which might set aside the acts of Congress. The result was that Congress itself had to judge the constitutional soundness of its enactments and therefore would be more attentive to its measures on that score.

Vance, from his references, appeared to feel that the country would be better than worse served by a Confederate tribunal of highest jurisdiction. Whether or not its competency extended to the laws of Congress, it could adjudicate issues involving the rights of citizens in conflict with the officials of the central power. Great justices seem to have appeared less frequently in American history than great executives, and the tendency of courts has been the human drive toward the acquisition of power, or to participate more in the game than to umpire the plays of others. But if a true function of the judiciary is to safeguard the weak individual in all his inherent rights from the excesses of strong government, which in emergencies will always have overzealous administrators and agents, then Pearson came close to greatness in the firmness of his stand during this long controversy over a few recruits. He came even closer to impeachment later during the stresses of reconstruction. Vance, too, had no other course than to uphold the state's highest judge, and though he did seem restive at times under the decisions, and contrary to an historical impression was as eager as anyone in the state to keep the army ranks filled and more active than any in trying to bring this about, he worked as an agent of the law. In all these matters of conflict Vance, as an attentive executive should, kept the General Assembly closely informed, through messages to it, or by personal appearances, either to address it or to confer with its members in closed sessions.

The legislature had some of the state's top figures, but also, with most of the spirited talent in the army, some crudities. Some of the legislators must have reminded Vance of the story told about a state senator in Maine, who was described as so much of an ass that he could not distinguish the Capitol from the Federal Arsenal. He went to the Arsenal instead of the Capitol to take his seat, and when he had signed all the papers presented to him, discovered that he was regularly enlisted in the United States Army for seven years.[32]

But the governor, having risen from being a rather crude state legislator from the mountain district himself, and a backwoods Congressman in Washington, was deferential to all legislators and his administration was characterized by harmony between the two branches. What he asked he nearly always received. His respect for the General Assembly was in keeping with his respect for the state courts.

Vance was a good constitutional student, though not the peer of Webster of an earlier, or Borah of a later, day. His policies recognized, as Secretary Seddon's might have, the change in the wording of the preamble of the Confederate Constitution. Where the Federal Constitution read, "We, the people of the United States in order to form a more perfect Union, . . ." the Confederate Constitution substituted, "We the people of the Confederate States, each State acting in its sovereignty and independent character. . . ." A great many reasonable restrictions were placed on Congress. The state was recognized to be sovereign and independent and the confederation was therefore loose. The whole idea was that of a voluntary union. The judicial power, as under the old constitution, was to be in a supreme court and such inferior courts as Congress might establish. There was no general welfare clause to give courts open running fields. In the Confederate Congress itself, there always appeared enough members who cherished states' rights and the principles which seemed to have been embodied in Confederate institutions to forestall the creation of a powerful court, such as had interposed itself between the other institutions and God in the old government. At the ardent solicitation of delegate Thomas R. R. Cobb of Georgia, who as a Confederate general was to die defending the stone wall at Fredericksburg, the preamble of the Confederate Constitution made reference to "Almighty God," thus rectifying the omission in the Federal Constitution. Good minds worked on the drafting of the instrument, some features of which marked a distinct advance in Anglo-Saxon jurisprudence which were regrettably lost with the collapse of the military power supporting it.[33]

One reason that Vance was never able to address an inquiry to a Confederate supreme court was Congressional antipathy to the able and shrewd Judah P. Benjamin, who more than any other person in the cabinet held the President's confidence. As Henry S. Foote, the Mississippi senator in Washington turned Tennessee representative in Richmond—an implacable Davis hater—stormed: "There is no necessity of a court in war times. A court with jurisdiction over the State would only create discord. I shall never consent as long as Judah P. Benjamin shall continue to pollute the ears of His Majesty with his insidious counsels; . . . as long as he shall continue to occupy his official position which he now disgraces, no supreme judge will ever be elected, except in accordance with his advice. . . ."[34]

An equally telling objection was Wigfall's, who held that the old United States court did more to disrupt the Union than anything else; that "had Chief Justice Marshall been a man of bad character, the Union would now be in existence, but he was so unimpeachable in character that he fastened his principles of nationalism on our institutions." Marshall had turned the "beautiful republic" into the "monstrous despoilism" from which the South had been compelled to detach itself. The old Supreme Court, he held, drew its opinion of its rank out of the circumstance that the Book of Judges preceded the Book of Kings.[35]

Vance was on the ground, had his militia in hand and possessed the courage to use it, and the decisions of Justice Pearson's court prevailed. Powerful influence had been asserted throughout the South among those who cherished local institutions and individual freedom by the resounding letter written by Vice President Alexander H. Stephens against martial law and republished in the Raleigh *Standard* October 15, 1862, after Davis had instituted martial law in the Richmond and Memphis areas. The *Standard* commented it was a misfortune that the Vice President was not at least an advisory member of President Davis's cabinet. "His brilliant intellect, deep penetration and thorough statesmanship, and his calm, conservative views, would doubtless have suggested plans of vast moment to the interests of the South."

The Stephens letter, copied from a Georgia newspaper, filled a close-set column. It was dated September 8, 1862, and addressed to James M. Calhoun, whom General Bragg had appointed "civil governor" of Atlanta, Georgia, and who had inquired of Stephens what his powers were. Stephens was not surprised at the inquiry because he could not himself find anything in any written code that would enlighten him. "The truth is," he said, "your office is unknown to law. General Bragg had no more authority for appointing you civil governor of Atlanta than I had; and I had, or have no more authority than any street walker in your city. Under his appointment, therefore, you can exercise no more power than if the appointment had been made by a street walker."

He expressed easily understood views that seemed precisely in accord with Vance's: "We live under a constitution. That constitution was made for war as well as peace. Under the constitution we have civil laws and military laws; laws for the civil authorities and laws for the military. The first are to be found in the Statutes at Large, and the latter in the Rules and Articles of War. But in this country there is no such thing as Martial Law, and cannot be until the Constitution is set aside, if such an evil day shall ever come upon us."

He went on to say that all lawmaking power was in the constitution and that martial law is nothing but an abrogation of all laws. The government could suspend the writ of *habeas corpus*, but that would not interfere with the right of one arrested to a speedy and fair trial by a jury.

That the letter was printed by the *Standard* and prominently displayed in column one of the back page, in itself showed the editor's idea of the temper of the state in its insistence on the preservation of constitutional guarantees. Vance was altogether in line with that sentiment, though he was gradually drawing apart from Holden in certain aspects of the editor's superhostility to Richmond.

Largely because of the popular agitation by Vance in North Carolina, Stephens and Brown in Georgia, and executives of other states, and because of the leadership of Vance and resolutions from the North Carolina General Assembly, authority to set aside the writ expired on August 1, 1864, and Congress declined to renew it. The Mississippi governor and the Virginia state senate opposed it. Georgia had enacted unanimously a law providing that any justice who declined to grant a writ of *habeas corpus* should forfeit $2,500 to the applicant he denied. Vice President Stephens renewed his attack in his address to the Georgia legislature and Georgia declared the suspension void. Opposition to suspension had become a fetish among numerous highly articulate Southerners. The law giving Davis the unusual power in this respect fell before the weight of public opinion.[36]

Like Vance's state, Georgia could not be accused of any lukewarm support of the war, however loudly her statesmen denounced Davis. She had drained her manpower long before hostile armies ever reached her soil. Casualty figures are difficult to arrive at but Georgia's war losses at the time of this discussion, or in mid-1863, appear to have been second only to North Carolina's, and by one calculation, at the very top.[37] Demanding free institutions at home was not inconsistent with devoted service against a common enemy in 1863, any more than it was when the Greek states fought the Persians or the thirteen colonies battled for independence.

Both North Carolina and Georgia had larger populations than South Carolina or the Gulf States and naturally would have larger casualty lists, but they exceeded on a proportionate basis as well, and both were unstinting and unflinching in their sacrifices to push back the invaders.

Confederate authorities undertook to retaliate against Vance by not allowing a sheriff to pass through the military lines bearing a writ of *habeas corpus.* It appeared for a moment that Seddon had triumphed. But the state became inflamed, the state legislature remonstrated, and Seddon, perceiving that the widespread agitation was laden with more dangers to the Confederacy than allowing one or two conscripts to have access to a state judge, gradually came to relent on any interference with state officials or state powers.

When Assistant Secretary of War John A. Campbell, recently an associate justice of the United States Supreme Court, wrote Vance in reply to one of his letters to the War Department, he intimated that the judicial department of North Carolina "lent itself" to the protection of deserters. Vance replied with high indignation, asserting the charge was untrue and declaring the North Carolina judges would have his protection. North Carolina, said Vance, had been wronged by calumnious imputations which had caused many in the army and elsewhere to believe she was not putting forth her full energies. He countered this by saying the state had "furnished" more than half the killed and wounded at the two great battles on the Rappahannock, Fredericksburg and Chancellorsville.[38]

Ten years later, when he was addressing the graduation exercises at Wake Forest College, June 26, 1872, Vance spoke in a manner that throws light on his thinking during the war years. He stated his concepts of "the principles of Anglo-Saxon liberty—trial by jury, liberty of speech, freedom of the press, the privileges of parliament, the right to petition and bear arms, three branches of government each equal and independent, subordination of military to civil authority, the franchise of municipalities, prohibiton of *ex post facto* laws." These he said were the bulwarks of our freedom. "They are all the children of oppression and born of the stern exigencies of the hour."

He told how Roman liberty gained life "among the shepherds of the Latin hills" and how it "perished miserably in the palaces of the Caesars." He summarized his understanding and ideal of the American government, which would have been applicable either under the Confederate or the Federal Constitution: "If, in short, the meanest citizen in all the land cannot instantly command for his protection in the commonest, simplest personal right, the entire physical and moral weight of the Republic, then, indeed, is its glory but the false gilding and glamour which dazzles and deludes, and is no more entitled to your reverence and attachment than is the autocratic splendor of the Czar or the idle magnificence of the Grand Turk."[39]

Vance's view, as it appears to have been during the war crises, was that government was unreasonable when it enforced rules which were handed down and not passed up, and which were neither sanctioned by nor regarded tolerable by local public opinion. The country was organized into states and these might be regarded as the local entities. Why should North Carolina leave one government considered by many a near despotism merely to encounter a despotism in another? What was the purpose of the Southern revolution except to gain freedom from remote government judged to be headstrong and unfair? Is freedom impossible of attainment because always there will be some distant government heedless of local rights? The Federal constitution was set up to avert the very trend toward centralization that had meant the downfall of Rome and many others. Certain provinces of rule were allotted to the central and local governments and there was no danger of fragmentation as long as each was content with its restrictions. His reasoning was sound for any period, and might well be studied more often and adverted to by succeeding generations. Perhaps Davis grew to dislike Vance because he was so everlastingly right.

Vance's apprehensions about civil liberties were more than academic. Southern administrators might be induced, if the opportunity allowed, to follow the pattern being established in the North, where the War Department pursued ruthless and patently unconstitutional methods to stamp out what it and some of the state authorities looked on as simple treason.

The military commission which tried the Lincoln conspirators for what was clearly a civil crime had its precedents in earlier military courts. These tribunals administered severe penalties from which there was no easy appeal. How many citizens were imprisoned and held incommunicado without formal charges being filed against them will perhaps never be known. They had no Zeb Vance to safeguard their constitutional privileges as he did in the case of the Reverend Robert J. Graves. An estimate has been made that in Washington alone hundreds were confined under a suspension of the writ of *habeas corpus* and under a policy of assuming guilt when there was no positive proof of innocence. The notorious instance of General Charles P. Stone, though he was an army officer, had points in common with civil rights cases, in that he was arrested without any charge and incarcerated for six months obviously without any guilt, presumably because of administration displeasure over the manner in which he had conducted the Ball's Bluff campaign.

Military courts were not restrained from administering quick and harsh sentences to civilians until after the war, when the Supreme Court ruled in the Lambdin P. Milligan case, which was argued by one of Vance's idols, Jeremiah S. Black. The decision held that, where the civil courts are open, a civilian may not be tried by a military court even when the writ of *habeas corpus* has been suspended. The ruling coincided with Vance's position, and that of Alexander H. Stephens also, where it held that the Constitution is the law equally in war and in peace. The opinion by Associate Justice David Davis sounded much like the language Vance would have employed: "No doctrine involving more pernicious consequences was ever invented by the wit of man than that any of its [the Constitution's] provisions can be suspended during any of the great exigencies of Government."

Undoubtedly the danger Vance sought to guard against has been present in all wars. Disaffection is rarely attractive and few want to seem to champion it. But when established institutions are cast aside the risk is to the loyal as well as the disaffected. That was the case as late as World War II, an instance being the unhappy internment of numerous loyal citizens of Japanese ancestry during a war when many of their sons were giving faithful service to the country in front-line combat. Not all wartime executives have had the broad understanding of constitutional principles which Vance possessed, or the resolution to uphold them against challenge from any quarter. The easy course has been to agree with the dictum that in war, personal liberty is first to fall.

At about this time came the first discussion of Vance as the possible successor of Jefferson Davis if the Confederate States won their independence. The use of his name seems to have grown out of the meeting in Richmond, to which Vance went to discuss civil rights and other topics of common concern with the view of advancing public support of the war. The first published report, as far as North Carolina knew of it, was in the New York *Herald*, whose correspondent in New Bern talked with "a prominent citizen" recently arrived from Richmond, who said that at a meeting of governors in the Confederate capital, Vance was offered the succession to the Presidency "provided he would wheel the Old North State into line and keep her in the traces." The *Herald* said Vance had returned to Raleigh "a fierce war man, and would hereafter do his utmost to prevent the state from returning to the Union."[40] The governor never had any other thought than fighting the war to the finish, though the belief was widespread in the North that the state would like a chance to drop out of the Confederacy. Substantial pockets of opinion favoring that action did exist, as was to be evidenced when the political campaign developed the next year, but Vance was the last man to consider such a course.

To project the *Herald* story further, there was little doubt that Vance would have made a strong candidate had the South been success-ful. John C. Breckinridge, who would naturally have been thought of for the office, would not seem to be eligible because he was a resident of Kentucky, which was not a part of the Confederacy. He also seemed to be developing a liquor problem which might have raised a question as it had with Toombs. General Lee made it emphatically clear that he had not the slightest interest in political office and his statement was so emphatic that none could misunderstand him.[41] Vance would have been the best campaigner in the South and would have been a logical meeting point between the army and the Alexander Stephens-Georgian school of thinking. The report was so intriguing that the *Standard* republished it and added some speculation of its own. It thought the statement that the governors had made an offer would be news to Vance.

"We have no idea," said the editorial comment, "the succession to Mr. Davis was even mentioned to Governor Vance while in Richmond, much less that a bargain was made he be the next President of the Confederacy. Governor Vance went to Richmond as strong a war man as he was when he returned. He visited that place at the request of the President, to confer with him on the best means of promoting the Confederate cause, especially as to the proper policy to be pursued by the administration at Richmond toward the people of North Carolina, who had just been insulted by the appointment of a resident of another state to be chief Tithingman. Governor Vance did us the honor to confer with us before he made the visit to Richmond, and we can bear witness he returned with the same sentiments and feelings with which he went there."[42]

Holden obviously had talked with Vance on his return also, for he wrote authoritatively. He emphasized that there was no necessity of "wheeling the Old North State into line" because "she was there already, with more troops in proportion to her population than any other State; and she will remain there as long as there is any hope for achieving the independence of the Confederate States."

Then the editorial reflected Vance's position: "Governor Vance is not a candidate for the succession to Mr. Davis. His thoughts are turned mainly to the best means of defending his state, and extricating his country from its present condition. But if, in the future, Governor Vance should aspire to the Presidency, or if his friends should desire it for him, his chances will be as good to obtain it as those of any man, provided he should adhere unflinchingly to the Conservative principles on which he was elected Governor of the State. . . . Those principles we are satisfied are destined to prevail, and to shape the character of the Confederacy." Just what principles Holden had in mind he did not enumerate. Vance had been elected on no platform whatever. What the last part of the editorial seemed to mean was that if Vance was going higher, Holden wanted to ride along with him and fill as much as possible the role of presidentmaker, as he had felt he had as governormaker.

Holden apparently countenanced a report a little earlier that others were trying to steal Vance from him. He published a letter from Roxboro signed "Sketo," which saw a plan to change the administration and separate Vance from the party which had elected him. "Just look for a moment," said Sketo, "at the course of events. The men and papers that used to abuse Vance and the party which elected him, are beginning to praise him. Even the President, who never yields to men or reason, it is said, yields to the representations of Governor Vance." This last remark was based on Davis's removal of Tithingman Bradford at the governor's urging. Sketo concluded: "How the base curs that barked and howled at his heels, now wag their tails and fawn upon him."[43]

Vance's trip to Richmond was made in early August and he returned August 8, 1863. An unidentified acquaintance who reported to the *Standard* said he "was treated with much attention and courtesy by the authorities in Richmond." While there he was the guest of surgeon Otis F. Manson, who though a Virginian had begun practice in Granville County, North Carolina, where he attained great distinction through his medical publications, his study of malaria and smallpox and his pioneering in the use of quinine. During the war he served as the chief medical officer for North Carolina in Richmond, won Vance's deep affection and, according to the governor, "endeared himself not only to me but to every man, woman and child in North Carolina."[44]

# Chapter Nineteen

## Massacre in the Mountains

Early in January, 1863, one of the bloodiest little side wars, or more accurately brutal slaughters, occurred near Zeb's early home town of Marshall, and although hostilities in that region had long been forming, the clash leading to the bloodshed developed over what had become the most sought after article in the mountains, salt.

Few matters disturbed Vance more than this fratricidal outbreak among his home people.

So scarce was salt that winter, when transportation into the French Broad country was difficult over primitive roads often impassable after the rains, that the price ranged from $75 to $100 a sack. Madison County, named after the peacefully disposed President, as the town of Marshall was after the great Chief Justice who favored the code over the shotgun, was divided in its sentiments, and the animosities between Union men, called "Tories" after the odious designation of Revolutionary War days, and "Loyalists," a reversal of the old-time term, which in 1863 meant people of Southern viewpoint, were sharper than those between Lee's and Burnside's armies as they faced each other across the Rappahannock, along the hills, often frozen, sometimes muddy, that winter.

Hordes of newcomers had poured into the mountain area, some

homeless waifs cast up by the war, some refugees of quality who came to live in Asheville and the towns, among them Mrs. Leonidas Polk, wife of the bishop-general. At times Asheville, with its cool air and clear summer skies, was enlivened by groups of Jeb Stuart's rollicking cavalry officers on leave, attended by their guitar players and banjoists.[1] But the arrivals were mainly conscript dodgers and deserters from both Federal and Confederate armies who avoided the towns and crowded into the back areas, where they banded into mounted gangs riding stolen horses and terrorizing farm abodes, pilfering hams and bacon (they rarely looked for money because little remained in the mountains and it was of doubtful value compared with goods) and at times torturing citizens or shooting them down in cold blood.

As Copperheads and Knights of the Golden Circle dwelt in large areas of the North, so deserters, escaped prisoners and conscript dodgers overran the North Carolina mountains and "Buffaloes" (another name for Southerners sympathetic to the Union) served as guides to Federal army units. Often in some sections, as in Southern Ohio, Indiana, and Illinois, it was neighbor against neighbor, friend against friend, families divided—truly a fratricidal war.

Perhaps the prevailing sentiment outside of the towns was unionist, though none ever made a tally, but Confederate units which tried to patrol the area were fired on often from ambush, and Northern soldiers escaping from the prison at Salisbury always found havens farther west of the Yadkin River. Some pushed on to the Federal armies in Tennessee; others took squatter rights to a back mountain cove and lived off the distressfully poor countryside. Bandit's Roost in Wilkes County got its name from the bands which roamed Wilkes, Watauga, Alexander, and Caldwell counties, killing those who resisted.[2]

Vance kept an eye on the mountains as much as he could because he knew the character of the people and understood their deep passions and resentments and the poverty to which they had been reduced by a war that was not of their choosing. Being a tolerant man, he was not vindictive against those who wanted no part of the conflict, though in his intense desire to see the South win he was not disposed to temporize with them for any hostile acts committed against Confederate soldiers. Perhaps the most distressing feature of mountain life from an economic standpoint was that, unlike the piedmont or coastal plantations, the farms had no slaves. Most of the young men went into the armies or into hiding, leaving the plowing and harvesting to the

old men, boys, and women. These looked with resentment on the
"Twenty-nigger law" which eased life in the rural areas of the older
sections, but gave mountain people no comfort.

Two singular Confederate units composed the mountain patrol during
this winter. One was the Thomas Legion, composed mainly of Cherokee
and headed by their white chief, William Holland Thomas, of Welsh
ancestry, born in a log cabin on Racoon Creek on the site of what is
now Waynesville. Just before he was born his father was drowned in
one of the frequent flash floods of the Big Pigeon River.[3] Six years
later the Indian patriot Tecumseh came into this fastness in an effort
to align the Cherokee with his new tribal confederation. Junaluska and
Yonaguska, great Cherokee chiefs, lived nearby, and Thomas, who
became a storekeeper, was reared with closer companionships among
the Indians than the whites. His legion, which seemed rarely to consist
of more than a skeleton regiment, had wide fame as a mountain guard,
but never possessed the strength or discipline to patrol effectively the
vast, wild country of western North Carolina and eastern Tennessee, a
wilderness empire as large as many states. They were a picturesque but
not a strictly military aggregation as they went about the hills. Said the
Franklin *Western Carolinian,* after a glimpse of Thomas and 104
Cherokee warriors: "As they passed through the town they made the
welkin ring with the terrible Indian war whoop."[4]

The other Confederate unit was the 64th North Carolina regiment,
raised by Colonel Lawrence M. Allen and having as lieutenant colonel
James A. Keith, both of Marshall. The unique feature of the 64th
among North Carolina regiments was that although well equipped and
beautifully drilled, it never fought a battle. Of the ten companies, six
were raised in Madison County, one in Henderson, one in Polk and two
across the line in Tennessee. Those who knew the regiment described it
as composed of strong, sturdy men numbering 1,110, most of whom
were destined to spend the better part of the war amid the rigors of
prison life at Johnson's Island in Lake Erie.

Allen was known to be fearless; many who did not admire him had
confidence in his leadership if they reached the battlefield, though it
was said he could put away a goodly amount of liquor. "Colonel Allen
was not an attractive man,—rather otherwise," said Captain B. T.
Morris of Company A, who left an account of the regiment. Keith was
described as intrepid and one who had bitter enemies among the Tories;
it was conceded: "He did severely punish some of the enemies of his

country—some far too severely." Major W. N. Garrett of near Warm Springs appears to have been a good officer. His father had been murdered at his own door by bushwhackers, presumably unionists, and had fallen back into the arms of his wife and daughters. This, taken with the harassment a part of the regiment suffered along the trails and roadways, embittered it against the wandering marauders and unionist residents alike.[5]

Lieutenant Colonel Keith commanded the 200 men left in the Madison County area, while the balance of the regiment drilled in Knoxville.

Near the edge of Madison County close along the Tennessee line, on upper Laurel Creek, a little settlement grew of unionists and Tennesseeans who had crossed the line to avoid one army or another; it became known as Shelton Laurel. It suffered severely from lack of provisions and claimed the Confederate authorities in Madison, when they rationed the salt, denied any to Shelton Laurel on the grounds they were Tories and not entitled to the Confederate distribution. Fifty or sixty men from the Shelton Laurel district thereupon organized, marched on Marshall, captured the town, seized the salt—the Union viewpoint was that they simply took their share which had been withheld from them—then broke into stores and did some plundering, and pillaged especially the home of hard-bitten Colonel Allen, commander of the 64th regiment.

The raid caused a sensation through the state and in East Tennessee, where Brigadier General Harry Heth, who later commanded one of Lee's divisions and brought on the battle of Gettysburg, commanded with headquarters at Knoxville. Vance called on him for protection and he immediately ordered Brigadier General W. G. M. Davis, a Floridian who commanded from Greeneville, Tennessee, to Warm Springs, North Carolina, to go with his brigade and a part of Thomas's "battalion," as Heth termed the Cherokee Legion, into Madison County to quell the disturbance, and drive back any enemy force in the region.

Vance, knowing the passions of the mountains, warned Heth and the officers he could communicate with to be "cool and just" and entreated Heth against permitting "our excited people" to deal too harshly with "these misguided men." He ordered that those captured be delivered to the proper authorities for trial.[6] But he told Heth not to relax until the Tories were crushed. From Vance's position in Raleigh it was impossible to discern the extent of the uprising or to know how grave a threat it imposed to law and order in the western part of the state. General Davis's plan was to round up all the unionists and transport them to Kentucky, a recourse which Vance said might be applied to all who wanted to go. He cautioned that he did not want to exile women, children, or old men if they preferred to stay in North Carolina, even though Davis thought it would be a service to the state to "get rid of such a population as that inhabiting the Laurel section."[7]

None was prepared for the horrible aftermath of the Marshall raid. Lieutenant Colonel Keith reached the area first, but the perpetrators of the raid had gone into hiding and few were apprehended. Instead, Keith went about the Laurel area and arrested thirteen men and boys, mainly those who had had nothing to do with the raid. They had not resisted him on his approach though a few had sought cover in the bushes. The list that reached the Memphis *Bulletin,* which published a long account of the episode with all its details, indicated that two of the thirteen were sixty years old, one was fifty, one was forty-five, one was thirty-five, and then boys of ten, twelve, fourteen, fifteen, seventeen and nineteen. Augustus S. Merrimon's list, which he prepared for Vance, indicated that some were "desperate men," the eldest being fifty-six, but he too listed several boys.[8]

Colonel Allen was not in command—according to the Memphis account he had been suspended for six months for drunkenness—but he appeared and told the prisoners they would be taken to Tennessee for trial. They were marched out of town a few miles, and five of them were ordered to kneel in front of a file of soldiers, whereupon Keith gave the command to fire. The soldiers were so horrified that when they brought up their muskets not a trigger was pulled, while the kneeling men, praying to be spared, reminded their captors that Colonel Allen had promised them a trial. They were informed, according to the Memphis story, that Allen was not in command. Keith meantime commanded the hesitant soldiers to fire or he would make them change places with the kneeling prisoners.

"Old man Wood and Shelton were shot in the head, and their brains scattered upon the ground, and they died, without a struggle. The other three lived only a few minutes." Then the others were killed, first five and then three, including the lads, regarding one of whom, named Billy, twelve years old, a pitiful account was published. He had asked not to be shot in the face, as his father had been. He was hit in both arms in the first fire, then he rushed up to an officer, clutched as best he could the man's legs, and pled with his captors: "You have killed my old father and my three brothers; you have shot me in both arms. I can forgive you all this. I can get well. Let me go home to my mother and sisters." But he was dragged back and eight balls were sent through his body.[9] The Memphis story told also of how a soldier from an out-of-state company attached to the North Carolina regiment jumped on the bodies and asked some men to clap their hands for him "while I dance the damned scoundrels down through hell." When the wives of the men heard of the massacre and came out the next day they found the common grave had been covered so lightly that hogs had rooted up one body and eaten off the head.[10]

Keith took his men back to Shelton Laurel, flogged some women severely and tied ropes about their necks, and made surely the saddest spectacle of a Confederate officer encountered during the war. Vance, shocked when he heard the horrible account, asked Augustus S. Merrimon, state attorney and an original secessionist, to investigate. Merrimon reported that probably eight of the thirteen were not in the company making the raid on Marshall. He supposed they were "shot on suspicion." He could not learn the names of the soldiers who shot them, but said "some of them shrank from the barbarous and brutal transaction at first, but were compelled to act." He told how after the massacre the women had been whipped and haltered, and summarized, "One thing is certain, thirteen prisoners were shot without trial or hearing whatever and in the most cruel manner."[11]

Wilma Dykeman, one of the best known present-day authorities on the history of the North Carolina mountains, said of the slaughter: "Much has been written of the large battles and decisive deaths of the War Between the States, but nowhere is there a microcosm more chill and revealing than this episode of war at its heart and core."[12]

Heth relayed General Davis's report to Vance and it tended to minimize the matter, saying "Colonel Allen's 64th North Carolina regiment and his men are said to be hostile to the Laurel men and they to the former, a kind of a feud existing between them." That was already clear to all the world. Of the men killed, he said all but two were deserters from Colonel Allen's regiment. He could scarcely have meant by this to include the boys. "They formed part of the expedition against Marshall and no doubt plundered Allen's house."[13] The whole force that raided Marshall did not exceed fifty men, he said.

"The attack on Marshall," he reported, "has given rise to wild rumors of organizations of armed tories throughout the mountains, bent on sacking towns and the plunder of loyal men. The reports, greatly magnified as they went to Raleigh, have no doubt led the Governor of North Carolina to call on the Confederate Government for a protecting force. I think you can safely assure him that the militia are not needed."

The 64th regiment, most of which had no part in the massacre and was worthy of a better reputation than that left to it by the slaughter of unarmed men and boys, went on to join the command of Brigadier General John W. Frazer that summer at Cumberland Gap. Frazer, a West Point graduate of high repute, was told by President Davis to evacuate the gap, called the "Gibraltar of America," on the approach of Burnside with a Federal army into East Tennessee, but Frazer declared he could hold it. When the gap was invested he surrendered ingloriously and the 64th was sent off to Johnson's Island with never a chance at a pitched battle.

Vance was not disposed to drop or whitewash the Laurel massacre. He declared he would follow Keith to the gates of hell to see him punished. As soon as he had Merrimon's report he sent copies to General Davis at Knoxville and to Secretary Seddon. He wanted Davis to investigate and proceed against those guilty. "I cannot reconcile it to my sense of duty," he wrote, "to pass by in silence such cruel and barbarous conduct as is alleged to have characterized a portion of them, and more especially as the officers mentioned are citizens of this State."[14]

In his report to Seddon he said he had ordered out the militia as soon as he heard of the raid but that General Davis had suppressed the outbreak before the militia arrived. "But in doing so a degree of cruelty and barbarity was displayed, shocking and outrageous in the extreme, on the part of Lieut. Col. J. A. Keith, Sixty-fourth North Carolina troops, who seems to have been in command, and to have acted in this respect without orders from his superiors, so far as I can learn." He asked Seddon to read Merrimon's report, "which you will see discloses a scene of horror disgraceful to civilization. I desire you to have proceedings instituted at once against this officer, who, if half be true, is a disgrace to the service and to North Carolina."[15]

Seddon referred the letter to General Daniel S. Donelson, who by that time commanded at Knoxville, and asked him to investigate. In the end Keith was allowed to resign. His defense was that Heth had told him not to take prisoners, which Heth heatedly denied.[16] Such an order was not likely from one of the most courteous and honorable West Point officers in the Confederate service, as he had been in the old regular army before the war.

After the war Keith was arrested and jailed in Asheville, but before he could be brought before the Federal Circuit Court, President Johnson issued a general amnesty which relieved him of trial for his offense.

The governor issued a proclamation intended to heal as much as words could the ever-deepening rancor existing between the hostile factions in the mountains and to bring deserters back into the army. Some of the community names in this area show the earthy quality of life there—Upper Pig Pen, Lower Pig Pen, Hard Scrabble, Shake Rag, Possom Trot, Loafer's Glory, and the like. Some of the primitive terms have given way to more sophisticated designations, but then and later, life was a matter of much scratching for a living. Yet there were fertile valleys, coves, and folding hills which the inhabitants dearly loved, perhaps more than they honored the distant capitals in Richmond or Washington. For Zeb Vance it was home country and never was it threatened by a Federal force coming from East Tennessee—an area which after the fall of Cumberland Gap was in Federal hands—but that it aroused his immediate concern and brought him into prompt action.

That was the case in the autumn of 1863, when information reached Raleigh that the enemy was moving on Asheville. Colonel George W. Kirk, later notorious in North Carolina reconstruction history because of his part in the Kirk-Holden War, was a Union Tennesseean who commanded a mounted Federal regiment raised in western North Carolina. He raided the countryside and became more dreaded perhaps than any other commander operating in the area. In late October a Federal force captured Warm Springs, thirty-eight miles over the mountains from Asheville, the town where Zeb had sold flowers as a child. The news which came back from the minor engagement there was that John W. Woodfin, the genial and capable lawyer under whom both Vance and Merrimon had read law, and who had managed to become both wealthy and beloved, a hard feat in a region where most persons had little, had led a force of mounted Confederate home guards and had been one of the few to fall in the little battle.

In Raleigh, more than 250 miles away and without telegraph connection, the extent of the invasion was unknown. Brigadier General Robert B. Vance, the governor's brother, commanded in Asheville, and the first report of the affair added that he had left for the scene of action. The mountains had such scant protection that Kirk was able to raid the next year as far east as Morganton, but in late October, 1863, the Federals had to be content with the dash on Warm Springs. Kirk, it developed, was not in the action, which was conducted mainly by an Indiana regiment. But Governor Vance, not knowing the minor extent of the operation, left Raleigh as soon as he heard of it, to be on the scene if fighting occurred. "His presence," said the Raleigh *Standard,* "will be valuable in embodying the Home Guard and adding to the regular forces under General Vance."[17] The newspaper was confident the enemy could be driven back. Vance got as far as Marshall, eighteen miles from Warm Springs, from where he sent back word that the enemy force, of about eight hundred men, had retired to Tennessee. In a letter to Raleigh the governor expressed his relief, and also his belief that the mountain passes to the west should be fortified at once.

## Chapter Twenty

## Vance's Plagues: Deserters and Cavalrymen

Not from invasion, but from sporadic plundering by deserters and irresponsible Confederate army units, did Vance suffer with his state from the greatest depredations during the middle period of the war, when Lee was fighting his grueling battles in Virginia and Pennsylvania, and Bragg was gradually being forced back into Georgia.

The deserters went to the hills first, then the cavalry went after them, or at times the horsemen were sent to a quiet sector so both they and their mounts might recover from hard service. Often it meant a dual plague descending on the countryside, the deserters and their pursuers, and it was difficult to tell which stripped the farms down most.

As to the deserters, the postwar statistics tended to show that the crippling absenteeism was no more prevalent among North Carolina than other units—that North Carolina held pretty close to the average for the armies as a whole, North and South. But General Lee seemed to feel at times that North Carolina was a particular offender, though he did complain to Secretary Seddon about desertions among the Virginia troops as well.[1]

Likely a great deal of the blame against North Carolina units during the war and in later accounts was that the mountainous areas of the state offered the best nearby haven for deserters from all parts of the

South, and while the roving bands might be looked on as North Carolinians they were in fact a conglomeration from many states.

Among the North Carolinians, perhaps the greatest cause of desertion was hardships at home. Understanding this, Vance spared no effort to relieve such suffering, much of it coming from acute want of food. When the cavalry sent to round up the deserters ate the provisions and further reduced the people to want, they were in fact tending to stimulate rather than reduce the emotional plague of desertion which infested Lee's army, especially during the quiet periods. Many a deserter intended to return to his comrades in time for the next battle but could not make it, and often a deserter would write a letter of explanation about his family conditions that would touch any heart; still, the war had to be won and Vance aligned himself sharply on the side—in some sections of his state the unpopular side—of coercing the men back into the ranks. To that end he employed the state militia to arrest deserters and set watches at the fords and strategic points along the highways, and reported to Secretary Seddon his measures to refill the depleted ranks.

Here Vance was brought into conflict with his alert Chief Justice Pearson, who could see no legal process by which the governor, whose duty was to enforce state law, could in turn enforce Confederate law, which came under the jurisdiction of the conscription officers working out of Richmond. True to his concepts of the supremacy of the law and the courts, Vance bowed to the writs of *habeas corpus* which Justice Pearson issued freeing deserters the militia captured, but he did go to the legislature, where he requested vainly for a time, but at length successfully, a law which would empower him to round up the straggling fringes of Lee's army that infested the Carolina hills. Even after the legislature grew more tractable, a great deal of friction ensued between the executive and judicial branches of the North Carolina government before Vance finally gained full authority to use the militia to arrest deserters and turn them back to the army for service or punishment, as their cases might warrant.

Vance became disturbed over Pearson's involved legalistic reasoning when what he wanted was a clear-cut decision about his right to employ Home Guards to take deserters. He had won from the legislature the right to employ the militia, but the Home Guards were merely the old militia under a different name. Still, the name Home Guards did not appear in the authorizing legislation. He told Pearson that all should remember the almost insurmountable difficulties of his position.

"I know," he wrote, "that it is almost impossible to bend every energy of the state to the support of the military power which is struggling for national independence, and to maintain intact all the rights and majesty of the civil law without offending both. Yet I told the people of North Carolina this when they unsolicited called me to this position and I intend to keep this promise or perish in the attempt."[2]

Chief Justice Pearson indirectly tended to stimulate desertion by the overzealous hairsplitting of his decisions, which were misconstrued at times in the army into an impression that he had outlawed the conscription act altogether, as far as it affected North Carolina troops. Some actually left the army under that impression. More influential as a check to desertion than his militia was Vance's personal influence and his continued use of proclamations, which were published widely and, of more importance, read by those to whom they were directed. The Raleigh *Standard* of February 18, 1863, reported on his appeal for the return to their commands of all absent soldiers: "We learn that his first proclamation has had a fine effect in inducing our soldiers who were absent to hasten back, and many more are on their way. In issuing these proclamations the Governor has at heart the good of the service and the honor of the soldiers. He can be actuated by no other feeling." The newspaper went on to stress how unjustly the soldier in deserting acted toward his comrades.

In his proclamation of January 26, 1863, Vance gave deserters until February 10 to get back to their commands if they wished to escape trial. "The state," he said, "is trying to provide food for your families and each company is making a similar provision, and as your Chief Magistrate I promise you that the wife and child of the [soldier who is] in the army doing his duty, shall share the last bushel of meal and pound of meat in the state." The date was later extended to March 5 because of the time required to get the word into the remote sections.[3]

That Vance had come to hold something of the father-image to North Carolina troops could be seen in the moving letter addressed to him June 16, 1863, from Cottage Home in Lincoln County:

> It is with sorrow I communicate to you, this morning, the contents of this letter, but I see no other alternative; it is the only way for me ever to gain the affection of my friends. Sir, I have brought on myself disgrace and the contempt of my friends as long as I live by absenting myself from my company without leave. I got home the 12th of this

month. My old grayheaded father met me at the gate with joy—happy to see me. After passing the usual compliments, he asked me if I was on furlough. I told him I was not. The old man broke into tears, and told me I could not stay with him, that I must go and join my regiment. I replied to him, I intended to do so; I did not come home to stay. He then told me if I would go back he wouldn't have me arrested, but if not he certainly would. I told him I wanted some clothes and a pair of shoes. He gave me a pair of shoes, and told me he intended to send me such things as I needed, and asked me why I didn't stay and wait for a furlough? I replied that I hadn't been home in so long, I wanted to see them all once more. He replied, "I had much rather never to have seen you, than for you to come home in that way." He asked me if I hadn't seen the Governor's proclamation? I told him I had not. He then got the paper.—"See here—read this, my son; this teaches you what fruits desertion brings on. Now," says he "you are ruined—undone forever. This sort of conduct will never do; you must return, and that immediately." I promised him I would. "Go," says he, "and stand by your colors until you fall, or until your country is free." Governor, this is a lesson taught me I never can forget. I am actually sorry I done so. I will promise you I never will do so any more. I beg your pardon. I want to return to my regiment, if you please. Give me a pass or something of the kind to show, in order that I can get back without being arrested. . . .

Vance's sympathy and tolerance and respect for a noble father were shown in his reply, June 22:

Your letter asking for a pardon and a pass to return to your regiment, has been received. Enclosed I send you a pass, and will give you when you report to me in this City, a letter to Gen. Pender, which I have no doubt will secure you exemption from punishment. I am sure there is nothing that a brave officer would not grant to the son of such a father. I desire you to present him my regards and to say to him that I would feel honored to shake his hand. I feel refreshed in the contemplation of such unalloyed patriotism and such Roman virtue; and I thank God that such men can be found in North Carolina. And while they are, I feel it impossible to despair of our ultimate success. Would to God that every father in the land would receive his erring son in like manner. How many noble soldiers, who have been induced by hardships and disappointments to take this fatal step, would be redeemed from unavailing regret and sorrow and disgrace which the remembrance of all their glorious fights cannot extinguish. How gladdened would be the hearts of our Generals, and how despairing those of our foes, could it be known that even the ties of nature were as nothing, and the strong bonds of filial affection but as dust in the balance, to a people who have dedicated their sons to slaughter and their homes to desolation for their country's independence.

Take your father's advice. You could not follow the counsels of one more glorious and patriotic, and return to your brave comrades, as gallant a regiment as ever stepped upon a field of battle, and show by your good conduct that you desire your error to be forgotten, and that you are worthy of your lineage.[4]

Vance's proclamation, his second, which had been issued February 10, 1863, had not only returned the Lincoln County lad to the colors but in all 2,000 men in a single month, according to his estimate.[5] His aide David A. Barnes advised General Lee that "the reasonable expectation of its effect was fully realized and hundreds were induced to return to their colors."[6] Major General D. H. Hill, who had taken command of the North Carolina department, was so delighted with the wording of Vance's proclamation of May 11 that he requested a hundred extra copies to have read and circulated through his regiments. The proclamation promised dire vengeance to those who "hide your guilty faces by day and prowl like outlaws by night, robbing the wives and mothers of your noble defenders." But he promised that no man would be shot if he would return to the army voluntarily.

On September 7, 1863, Vance issued a highly emotional and eloquent plea urging the people to persevere amid the fiery trials of war. "A great and glorious nation is struggling to be born," he said, "and wondering kingdoms and distant empires are stilled with listening hope and admiration, watching this greatest of human events. Let them not, I pray you, be shocked with the spectacle of domestic strife and petty malignant feuds.

"Let us show that the God of Liberty is in His Holy Temple—the hearts of freemen—and bid all the petty bickerings of earth keep silence before Him."

While upholding the inalienable right of the people to assemble and exercise freedom of speech—rights which "shall never find a disturber in me"—he cautioned that the same instruments which guaranteed the fundamental freedoms also limited the exercise of them within the bounds of law and imposed a solemn duty of watching that the bounds were not transgressed.[7]

Desertion was induced at times by want and the severe living conditions in both eastern and western armies during the winter of 1863-64. Accounts from East Tennessee, where elements of Longstreet's command were wintering near the North Carolina border, at Morristown and Strawberry Plains, were that soldiers would take hides from the butcher's pen and bind them around their feet for shoes, and that blood, left by the lacerated feet of unshod men, could be seen on the frozen ground.[8] A Tennessee lad virtually barefooted on the frosty night at Chickamauga decided to dig holes and bury his feet for warmth. As was observed, it was a good idea, for "he was there to stay anyhow."[9]

When Bushrod Johnson's Division, which had cut through the Federal Army at Chickamauga, was transferred to Virginia in the spring of 1864, it marched through Richmond. "Never before," said a member, "was seen such a ragged set of soldiers, many of them without shoes and with their feet tied up in rags or in green cowhides. These were the men who held Butler's army at bay until an army could be gathered together."[10] These ragged veterans from the west were indeed the saviors of Richmond.

Vance had his own explanation of desertions. He told Seddon in a letter May 13, 1863, that the promise in the law of conscription that the recruits would have furloughs had never been honored. He said the men invariably gave that as an excuse when arrested.

"Another great cause," he continued, harping back to an old quarrel with the War Department, "is that they were refused permission to enter the regiments of their choice with their neighbors and relations. Large numbers actually threaten to desert before they leave camp, and generally make good their threats." Explaining that he had mentioned this matter before, he went on: "I am now fully convinced that the service loses in attempting to fill up certain regiments first, without regard to the wishes of the conscripts. The remedy is plain here, and we should no longer neglect it."[11]

Due to hardships, lack of food and clothing, ill-kept promises, and many other reasons, desertions became commonplace and more readily understood by the loyal soldiers who remained faithfully in the ranks. As General Pettigrew remarked before setting out for Gettysburg, "the great majority of my brigade would shoot a deserter as quick as they would a snake," but the story was changing even late that year. The pitiful letters reaching Vance were numerous and distressing.

Richard Bardolph of the University of North Carolina at Greensboro, in his excellent study of desertions, observed that it was impossible to measure the number of desertions among North Carolina troops, but there appeared to be "an irregularly increasing flow." Acceleration occurred after military defeats or hard campaigning, when rations were short over a substantial period, after the receipt of depressing news from home, after "peace" meetings, crop failures, the exactions of tax collectors, or depredations by skulkers. Desertion was more frequent in summer, when there were more battles and a better chance of living off the country en route home or into hiding.[12]

Vance in writing to Seddon January 5, 1863, disclosed the frightful conditions existing in some sections due to the ganging up of deserters. He said he could make arrests through the local militia in the eastern and central parts of the state. "But in the mountains of the west the case is different. The enforcement of the conscript law in East Tennessee has filled the mountains with disaffected desperadoes of the worst character, who joining the deserters from our Army, form very formidable bands of outlaws who hide in the fastnesses, waylay the passes, rob, steal and destroy at pleasure. The evil has become so great that travel has almost been suspended through the mountains. The militia has become too feeble to resist them, as that section has turned out its proportion for the war with the greatest patriotism and unanimity."

Vance was charitable to his home area in his use of the word unanimity, but he offered a plan: "I propose to organize about 200 men, put them under the command of experienced officers, arm and equip them at State expense, if the President will accept them into the Confederate service, and pay them only when actually engaged."[13]

He hoped the War Department would accede because the example of the marauding deserters was operating almost ruinously on the efficiency of the army while injuring citizens and damaging property in the western section. He said he was maturing a vigilant system of general police for the whole state for the prompt arrest of deserters and conscripts. At every turn he was trying to keep the ranks of the army filled. His suggestions were numerous, but in the end the most effective results appear to have come from his personal leadership and appeals to the loyalty and common sense of the people.

In early February, 1863, Vance wrote to Seddon suggesting that the 16th North Carolina be sent home to gather deserters and recruit conscripts, but when the question was referred to General Lee, he had already established a plan of sending details of different North Carolina regiments home on furlough to bring back recruits and absentees and could not spare another full regiment.[14] Pettigrew before the march north to Gettysburg, from which he would not return, wrote to Vance enclosing letters from homefolks who induced desertion, then added some remarks about the home-front attitude.

"We have watched closely, for some months, the course of certain newspapers, and of a majority of the Legislature. I regret to say I have not seen from either a single word calculated to aid us in our efforts to save the country from subjugation to the worst of all tyrannies. They utter nothing but declamations calculated and intended to make us dissatisfied, not only with the Confederate cause but to impress us with the hopelessness of the struggle and thus to unnerve us preparatory to submission. . . .

"I sympathize with every party in its effort to arrest the first steps of our Government toward despotic power, and even abuse of the Government I consider a matter of relative indifference, though it had as well be left out, but I have no manner of sympathy with those who overlook their country in their opposition to a government or a party. I would rather see the whole State desolated as Virginia is, than dishonored by an effort to look back on its escape from the Yankee Sodom."[15]

The letter appeared very much in line with Vance's attitude, though he had to give practical recognition to the existence of newspaper reproaches against the Davis administration and widespread public apathy, extending to clear-cut opposition to the war, in several areas of the state. If he were to lead them he could not break with them openly. Moreover much of the press agitation against the administration was well founded. Vance went along with it, but always he kept his aim on the winning of the war. His appeals and complaints to Richmond were to give strength to the war effort and to rally support, not to create dissatisfaction at home or in the ranks.

Vance's correspondence in mid-1863 contained various suggestions for meeting the deserter problem in the western counties. He wrote to Seddon July 25 saying the number "in the mountains and inaccessible wilds of the West" was 1,200. They were plundering and robbing and he had found it impossible to get them, but through their friends they had made propositions that they would come out and enlist for the defense of the state alone. He thought the effect on the army might be injurious but it seemed the only way of gaining service from these men. He said he could get at least 1,000 and asked Seddon's opinion.[16]

That was a bargain into which no respectable government could enter, and Seddon of course did not accept it. On August 26 Vance wrote him again about the accumulation of deserters who set the local militia at defiance. His Home Guards were "poorly armed and inefficient and rendered timid by fear of a secret vengeance from the deserters." He thought that if General Lee could send a depleted brigade or a strong regiment to North Carolina with orders to report to the governor good results might follow. "I could make it increase its ranks far more than the temporary loss of his brigade in a very short time."[17] The governor never lost confidence in his personal appeals to the western people, but recognized the value of strong-arm work in some contingencies.

Lee early the next month responded by sending two regiments and a cavalry unit of Hoke's Brigade to North Carolina, and Vance requested that it take out warrants before a civil magistrate against any persons found harboring, feeding, or abetting deserters and commit them to jail. The situation was bettered but desertion was by no means cured. Many deserters did come in voluntarily, others were arrested, but most went farther back into the woods.[18]

Vance told Davis he did not believe one deserter in a hundred was actuated by disloyalty, but rather by homesickness, fatigue, poor food in the army, plus the matter of unredeemed furloughs and refusal to make good the promise that they could select their own regiments.[19]

Late in January, 1863, Vance received a letter from Brigadier General A. G. Jenkins, with whom he had served in Congress before the war and who was now commander of a Confederate cavalry brigade. He said that Virginia was overcrowded with horses sent out by the army at Fredericksburg to be foraged until spring, and that it was imperative to forage some of them in North Carolina. He encountered an indisposition by the people to sell produce for Confederate money and wanted Vance's authority to make impressments. He said the authority could be circumscribed so there would be no injustices. He recalled the pleasure of his personal acquaintance with the governor when they were members of the old Federal Congress.

In denying the request, Vance gave a picture of conditions and of the unruly conduct of the cavalry. "The horses," he said, "are unfortunately in the midst of a section which was almost ruined by drouth last

summer." This, with the diminished amount of labor in the northwestern region of the state, had produced such a scarcity of corn as to render
suffering imminent among women and children unless relief was afforded them promptly. He had gone to the legislature, gained approval,
and was removing corn from the eastern counties to relieve the near-
famine conditions in the region under question. He said he had written
the Secretary of War requesting the removal of the horses as a matter of
humanity, but suggesting that they be transferred to the eastern section
where corn was abundant and likely to be destroyed by the enemy. He
hoped Jenkins's good opinion of him would in no wise be changed "by
my great anxiety to protect the wives and children of our soldiers from
suffering for want of bread."

Then Vance informed the cavalry general of what was occurring:
"Allow me to say that I am sure you are not aware of the conduct of the
men in charge of these horses. I am informed by citizens that they are
under no sort of control. They feed their horses on the ground, wasting
more than half in the mud. At night they ride them all over the country,
frequently breaking open granaries, drinking and insulting citizens and
making themselves a terror to the whole population. I trust you will
inquire into these reports, and have the evil corrected if true."[20]

War Clerk Jones a few months earlier had a good suggestion for the
use of these and other surplus horses, which were to give Vance concern later in the year. Jones said the South had as many horses as the
North "and twice as many good riders," but in infantry the North
could put three men in the field to the South's one. Yet 10,000 mounted
men on the enemy's border would be equal to 30,000 infantry—not in
combat, but to employ that number in watching and guarding against
cavalry strikes. He thought this was the only way of equalizing the war.
None seemed to pay any attention to his suggestion, perhaps because
it was confined to his diary, or else because it was made just after Second
Manassas, when Southern riders were in sight of the Federal Capitol
and with good glasses could see the roof of the White House. About
President Lincoln and his cabinet Jones wrote: "It is said they sleep in
their boots; and that some of them leave the city every night for fear
of being captured before morning."[21] This was not a season to dread the
enemy's infantry, but the plan had merit.

In his letter to Seddon, Vance apologized for the frequency of his
complaints, but, judging from the contents, this one seemed equally
justified. He said a large number of horses belonging, he believed, to

Jenkins's command were quartered in Wilkes, Ashe, Surry, and Yadkin counties and the officers were impressing corn and forage at less than half the current rates. He referred to the drouth and the difficulty of feeding the wives and children of absent soldiers. He suggested to Seddon as he had to Jenkins that the horses should be sent to a region where there was plenty, but where the abundance might fall into enemy hands.[22]

Seddon paid no attention to Vance's letter, but the governor would not let the matter drop. He wrote again February 25, 1863, mentioning that three weeks or a month had passed without a reply and all the while the horses were devouring the substance of a people threatened with famine.

"With every possible disposition to aid in the support of the army," he told Seddon, "I have the strongest reasons conceivable—the existence of my own people—for declining to permit those horses to remain in that section of the state. When the question of starvation is narrowed down to women and children on the one side and some worthless cavalry horses on the other I can have no difficulty in making a choice. Unless they are removed soon I shall be under the painful necessity of calling out the militia of adjoining counties and driving them from the State."[23]

Two months later, the picture had changed sharply. The effects of Vance's regulation of agriculture, giving precedence to food, were becoming evident. The wheat harvest promised to be bountiful, and a little later the promise was fulfilled, the harvest being heavy and the wheat in general free from rust.[24] Vance wrote to Seddon on April 27, 1863, what must have been a heartening letter. He said passage of the impressment act and the approach of a harvest of promised abundance had brought to light many hoards of food which the fear of famine had kept off the market. Provisions were going to the quartermasters: "The call for aid to the army has met with a liberal response from our generous people, and I trust all fears may be dismissed."[25]

In addition to purchases and requisitions and taxes in kind going directly to the Confederacy, Vance had made purchases on behalf of the state with which to feed the suffering families of soldiers and by that means keep down disquiet and desertion. The demand for these stores had been less than expected and he would consequently be in a position soon to turn over 250,000 pounds of bacon and some corn to the central government. He said the purchases of Confederate agents also could be increased.

Though the coming of spring grazing and an ample harvest relieved the stress for a time, they did not solve the problem of the broken-down horses, which was with him again the following winter. He eventually became so exasperated over the illegal seizures of property and depredations of bands of cavalry that on December 21, 1863, he demanded that the War Department stop the "stealing, pilfering, burning and sometimes murderous conduct" inflicted on a loyal country by these detached bands.

"If God Almighty," he wrote to Seddon, "had yet in store another plague—worse than all the others which he intended to have let loose on the Egyptians in case Pharaoh still hardened his heart, I am sure it must have been a regiment or so of half armed, half disciplined Confederate cavalry! Had they been turned loose upon Pharaoh's subjects with or without an impressment law, he would have become so sensible to the anger of God that he never would have followed the children of Israel to the Red Sea. No Sir, not an inch!!"

This time he delivered a direct threat. Unless Seddon did something, he would be compelled to call out his militia "and levy actual war against them."[26]

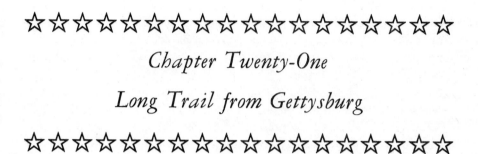

## Chapter Twenty-One

## Long Trail from Gettysburg

Gettysburg was a dividing point, almost imperceptible at first, marking an end to elation and high confidence; not of lessening of effort, but the beginning of wonder, doubt, and reappraisal.

Vance's first emotion was that of deep grief over the fate of his old 26th regiment, which not only fought one of the most gallant, unyielding actions of the battle, but also suffered the highest casualties there, or the highest of any regiment of any battle of the war. The intrepid young colonel, Harry King Burgwyn, who had helped make Vance a soldier and had received in return, as had the balance of the regiment, some of the firmness and ardor radiated by the governor's fervent spirit and personal leadership, had been killed at the front of his regiment, leading its attack.

Burgwyn had been buried in a gun case on the battlefield that night after his and Vance's old regiment had been almost annihilated, while it, too, was nearly extinguishing its enemy, the 24th Michigan, and parts of two other Federal regiments. But enough of the 26th remained to participate on the third day in the costly, sanguinary assault delivered by the divisions of Pickett, Pettigrew, and Trimble against the enemy center on Cemetery Hill.

In all, the regiment which had held the line with Vance at New Bern and marched with him up the slope of Malvern Hill lost above 83 per cent of its strength at Gettysburg. Well might Pettigrew write to the governor after the battle of his pride in the regiment's performance.

First to cross the Potomac in Lee's invasion was Jenkins's cavalry that had caused grief to Vance and the northwest counties. It was now well rested after its North Carolina grazing. On the invasion, in the rich enemy country of Maryland and southern Pennsylvania, it could command fresh horses and corn and fodder in plentiful supply, though most of the horses proved to be Percherons or other such big draft breeds as to be little suited for cavalry or artillery use. First of the infantry to ford the Potomac River was Vance's old Asheville company, the remnants of the Rough and Ready Guards, along with the 14th North Carolina regiment under Colonel Risden T. Bennett, to which it belonged. Vance was truly present in the Pennsylvania campaign in the spirit of soldiers he had recruited, trained, loved, and led.

Before he learned of the step-off for Gettysburg, Vance had to bear up under the long casualty lists from Chancellorsville, which perhaps more than any other was North Carolina's battle. The names from Lane's Brigade alone required two and a half closely set columns, with the names run into the paragraphs, and not listed separately, a new paragraph to each. Mrs. T. J. Jackson had left Charlotte to be with her wounded husband after the battle and some of his dying words to her saddened and inspired readers of the May 20 newspaper: "If I had not been wounded," Jackson had said, "or had had an hour more of daylight, I would have cut off the enemy from the road to United States Ford, and we would have had them surrounded, and they would have been obliged to surrender or cut their way out—they had no other alternative. My troops may sometimes fail in driving the enemy from a position but the enemy always fail in driving my men from a position."[1] The words were those Longstreet quoted to Lee on the field at Gettysburg.

The account of Chancellorsville came from the Richmond *Sentinel,* but the Raleigh *Standard* commented regarding Jackson's death: "The loss which the cause has suffered by his removal from the world cannot be overstated. From the beginning of the war he has been a light, always flaming onward to victory."

The Gettysburg campaign was ushered in with a blast from the Raleigh *Standard* because Harry Heth had been given command of the newly created division in Lee's army, instead of young but able Dodson

Ramseur. What had Heth done to be a major general, the paper inquired. "General Heth is one of the pets, and we believe, a relation of the President." Davis's motives were usually suspect in Holden's back sanctum. Heth was not a kinsman of Davis but a cousin of two other Confederate generals, George E. Pickett and Basil Duke. The flare-up shows Vance had been no more than responding to the sentiments in the state when he continually demanded a better share of generals for North Carolina. The *Standard* stormed:

"Gen. Ramseur, of this State, with his brigade, executed a movement at Chancellorsville which even the famous Stonewall Brigade had failed to perform. He charged through them and routed the enemy, turning the tide of battle; and Generals Hoke and Pender of this State, also aided materially with their brigades in achieving the victory. But they are overlooked, and Harry Heth is promoted. Why, there are North Carolina captains and Colonels, and even privates, who deserve this honor more than Heth does. Yet he received it, just as Pemberton was placed in supreme command in an important department, because he was a pet of the President. Almost every honor or office which is bestowed at Richmond, is the result of favoritism or partyism."[2]

Outside of a few greats such as Lee, Jackson, and Joseph E. Johnston, Davis was, in truth, no more adept than Lincoln, or President Madison in an earlier time, in picking his generals; and there was just enough merit to Holden's charge that he chose pets to give it color. His military education and familiarity with the army as Secretary of War caused a presumption that he knew the merits of the officers well. These were, it appeared, handicaps to the freedom of his judgment. Lincoln picked many failures but dropped most of them speedily when they did not prove themselves, while Davis adhered tenaciously to some of his faltering choices in the face of widespread criticism, as if stubbornly determined to demonstrate that he had made the appointments on meritorious and not personal grounds. Neither Holden nor Vance had been unjust in inveighing against the lack of recognition to their state. Still, Heth was a good officer, and Pender, whose promotion had been notoriously delayed before the Gettysburg campaign, was given his major generalship shortly before the step-off and not long before his death.

Vance and the North Carolina newspapers, which again brought the subject of promotions into focus just before Gettysburg, seemed at the time to have occasion for their reproaches. Davis might have wiped the slate clean at the beginning of the war and promoted Confederate officers strictly on the basis of merit, instead of adhering rigidly to the system of seniority obtaining in the old regular army. And had some of the young North Carolinians and the meritorious fighters from other states been pushed ahead from colonelcies as rapidly as A. P. Hill, Ewell, and others had been, the army undoubtedly would have had abler commanders of the 2nd and 3rd corps at Gettysburg and in the later phases of the struggle.

General Lee was recommending and acceding to promotions from among those in the top seniority brackets—major generals to be corps commanders and the like—but the top brackets were composed of those who had won the earliest appointments from colonels to brigadiers before there was much fighting, and in the period when the North Carolinians, having yet no Vance to press their cause, were largely overlooked.

The *Standard* had not delivered its full load. It held that wherever North Carolina troops were engaged, the enemy was defeated and "it so happened that where the South was defeated she had no troops." The state, it was reiterated, had no voice in the cabinet, was raked for conscripts as with a fine-tooth comb, her men were in the forefront of the hottest battles, and then the claims of men like Heth, Pemberton, and Winder were honored, while the North Carolina brigadier generals and colonels "who storm the breastworks and win battles are passed by unnoticed." Then came a bold threat that "North Carolina will never hew wood and draw water for those who slight or underrate her."[3]

Soon the march up to Pennsylvania was in the army news and the home public awaited the outcome of what obviously was the great gamble of the war.

Gettysburg was a fearful ordeal for North Carolina troops, who were heavily involved in the opening of the battle by Heth's Division and in the other divisions which participated in the engagement of the first day—Rodes's, Early's and Pender's. The only North Carolina major general on the field, W. Dorsey Pender, fell on the afternoon of the second day, while Pettigrew was mortally wounded during the retirement to Virginia and later died at Bunker Hill, Virginia. Much North Carolina writing has been centered on the point that Pickett, who nobly commanded three brigades of Virginia troops, exercised no control over the eight other brigades, which were composed mainly of North Carolina troops but included regiments or battalions from five states. Pickett commanded fifteen of the forty-eight regiments and two battalions in the assault on the third day.

Vance had every right to feel that at Gettysburg North Carolina had done her duty. One of the last letters Pettigrew wrote, dated July 9, 1863 (he received his death wound July 14 at Falling Waters), was to give Vance a report on the conduct of his beloved 26th.

"Knowing that you would be anxious to hear from your old regiment, I embrace an opportunity to write you a hasty note. It covered itself with glory. This is no passing elogium I pay them. My Brigade and that of Colonel Brockenbrough were held in reserve on the evening of the 1st of July. It fell to the lot of the 26th to charge one of the strongest positions possible. They drove, certainly three and we have every reason to believe five regiments out of the works with a gallantry unsurpassed. Their loss has been heavy, very heavy—but the missing are on the battle-field and in the hospital. Both on the 1st and 3rd your old comrades did honor to your association with them and to the State they represent."[4]

From Sergeant Joseph J. Young of the 26th came a story of the regiment's frightful loss of officers. The letter to Vance was dated July 4, from "near Gettysburg." It explained that the army would fall back about five miles to draw the enemy from his impregnable position. Then came the summary of the battle: "It was a second Fredericksburg affair, only the wrong way."[5]

Perhaps the most touching and painful letter came from Major Samuel McDowell Tate, of the famous 6th North Carolina which had been a leading factor in the capture of Rickett's and Griffin's batteries at First Manassas and had shown its mettle on later fields. Hoke, who commanded the brigade of which the 6th was a unit, had been wounded in the Chancellorsville campaign and was absent from Gettysburg. The commander of the 6th, Colonel Isaac E. Avery, of the distinguished and patriotic Morganton family, had taken charge of the brigade, only to fall at the outset of its assault on Cemetery Hill on the evening of July 2. Major Tate assumed command of the 6th regiment and Colonel Archibald C. Godwin, the Virginian commanding the 57th North Carolina, succeeded Avery as brigade commander.

The North Carolina regiments of Hoke's Brigade, Tate with the 6th at the front, and the Louisiana "Tigers" of Hays's Brigade, broke through the Federal lines on the summit of the hill and threatened to gain a lodgment in the center of the Union position. Being unsupported at the critical moment by Early, they were compelled to fall back. As it was, two isolated, unaided brigades captured the stone wall on East Cemetery Hill, captured the Federal batteries, and, had alert commanders been present in the places of Early and Ewell—had Stonewall Jackson survived to lead his old corps—very likely would have given Lee the advantage he had been seeking in his assaults all along the line from Round Top to Culp's Hill.

Tate wrote to Vance July 8 from near Hagerstown, in the belief that because his state had no high-ranking officers present, and Early was not disposed to be charitable, the story of his regiment's heroic assault would be lost. He wrote with a pencil, saying moments were precious. He assumed he might fall like so many of his companion officers, because another battle was momentarily expected. He felt that while yet spared he should perform a sacred duty for his gallant men. Apparently the thing that puzzled him was how he had stayed alive so long.

"The great reason for this," he said, "is the fact that it was North Carolinians only who succeeded in entering the enemy's works at Gettysburg—that our Brigade Commander was slain and we have no friends who will tell of our success on the night of the 2nd of July, *because all but the 6th Regt. failed.*" He said he had made a promise to the regiment to acquaint the governor with the story, "that history may hereafter speak truly of them." He said he wished nothing for himself, "but I do want the glorious band of veterans in this regiment to be appreciated and honored. They are rapidly passing away but North Carolina will have reason to point with pride to their valorous deeds."

He related the story of the advance on the enemy, posted behind the stone walls on the summit of the hill. The regiment charged the fortified heights, carried the wall, captured the battery playing on them, and lost more men than did all the rest of the brigade. "This battery will be credited to Early's division—see if it don't," he told Vance. After a struggle on the heights, which he held to be without parallel in the war, seventy-five members of the 6th North Carolina and twelve Louisianians of Hays's Brigade scaled the wall and planted the colors of the 6th North Carolina and the 9th Louisiana regiments on the guns. Tate continued: "It was now fully dark. The enemy stood with a tenacity never before displayed by them and with bayonet, clubbed musket, sword and pistol, *and rocks from the wall we cleared the heights and silenced the guns.* In vain did I send to the rear for support. It was manifest I could not hold the place without aid, for the enemy massed in all the ravines and adjoining heights and we were fully half a mile from our lines."

The enemy advanced and Tate with the 6th battled on the heights, then took a second position until the Federals began to reach toward his rear. In the retreat the regiment lost not a man, but was forced to surrender the ground and what the men had accomplished in some of the most desperate fighting of the battle.

"On arriving at our lines I demanded to know why we had not been supported and was cooly told it was not known we were in the works.

"I have no doubt the Major General will report the attack of the Works by Hokes and Hays brigades *which could not be taken.*

"Such monstrous injustice and depreciation of our efforts is calculated to be serious injury, and then always to divide the honors due us among all our division is a liberality which is only shown in certain cases.

"Of course the reports are not written out—but I know the disposition so well that I look for no special mention of our Regiment while it is the only one in the A. N. V. which did go in and silence the guns on the heights, and what is more, if a support of a brigade had been sent up to us, the slaughter of A. P. Hill's corps would have been saved on the following day."

By the last he meant mainly Pettigrew's Division, which took part in the Longstreet assault directed at the little clump of trees. Tate showed very clearly that he placed no confidence in any report which Jubal Early might offer of the engagement. When he wrote he forecast another battle at Hagerstown or near the Potomac, then concluded: "This regiment has had a reputation, you know, and I fear no harm can come to it while any are left, but it is due to the noble dead as well as to the living that these men be noticed in some way. Such a fight as was made in front of the fortifications has never been equaled. Inside the works the enemy were left lying in great heaps and most all with bayonet wounds, and many with skulls broken with the breeches of our guns. We left not a living man on the hill of our enemy. . . . All we ask is don't let old North Carolina be derided, while her sons do all the fighting."[6]

Tate's letter gave a view of what Vance was talking about when he told Seddon and Lee that North Carolina needed a news correspondent with the army. The presence of a North State scribe would have given greater confidence in instances like this heroic attack of Avery's Brigade and especially the famous 6th regiment.

An interesting postscript was affixed to Tate's letter. It told of the many vacancies left among the officers in the 6th. "How are they to be filled?" he asked Vance. "By election? or by appointment?" Although the war was well into its third year, not enough system had been introduced into the method of promotions that the commanding officer of a regiment knew what it was. He had to write back and ask his governor.

President Davis likewise took pride in the achievements of the battle. He wrote to Vance about the heroism of a single Asheville soldier, who happened to be, though Davis was not aware of it, one of Zeb's first recruits.

"In the action of the 1st of July near Gettysburg," said the President, "the Sharpshooters of Brig. Gen. Ramseur's brigade under command of Lt. F. M. Harney, 14th North Carolina volunteers, dispersed the 150th Pennsylvania Regiment. That gallant officer with his own hands wrested the standard from the color bearer of the Pennsylvania Regiment and soon after fell mortally wounded.

"General Ramseur on communicating the above particulars informed me it was Harney's last request that the flag should be presented in his name to the president.

"The wish of the dying hero has been complied with. The flag is in my possession and will be treasured by me as an honorable memento of the valor and patriotic devotion which the soldiers of North Carolina have displayed on many hard fought fields."

Davis thought it due the lamented officer to communicate the circumstances not only to the chief magistrate of the soldier's state, but through him to the man's family and comrades, along with the President's sincere sympathy "for the loss of one so worthy of their admiration and esteem."[7]

Vance took pride in the letter. Lieutenant Harney had been born in Kentucky, had gone to Central America with the filibusterer William Walker, and had become a carpenter in Asheville. There he joined the company of Roughs Zeb Vance had raised. Zeb made him an orderly sergeant. The governor told Davis that by good conduct and hard fighting Harney had risen to be a first lieutenant. He had no kinsmen in the state, but Vance said North Carolina "will be proud to see his name placed on the long list of heroic dead, and all will welcome his memory among their bravest sons, and mourn him as a noble brother slain for her defense. . . ."[8]

Vance and all North Carolina had difficulty in following the Gettysburg campaign or determining its outcome. As late as July 8 the confused reports from Pennsylvania and Maryland seemed to portray have been served by having correspondents in the field with General another grand success for Confederate arms, and here the state would Lee, to satisfy the hunger of the home public for news of the great invasion.

On July 15 the Raleigh *Standard* knew General Lee had fallen back from the heights near Gettysburg, and observed: "If General Lee is retreating toward Hagerstown the inference is that the tide is against him." On July 22 it was clear that the gray wave had receded from Gettysburg. The long, ghastly casualty lists began to appear in North Carolina newspapers, which were also clipping and reprinting some of the battle accounts sent by correspondents to the Richmond press.

Then on July 29 came the funeral of brilliant, much beloved General Pettigrew, with Governor Vance marching in the funeral procession from the capitol, where the body had lain in state. The cortege included a military escort from nearby Camp Holmes, headed by the commander, Colonel Mallett. Two of the fallen general's brothers, William S. and Charles Pettigrew, marched with Vance to the muffled roll of the drums.

"Thus has passed away in the prime of manhood, one of the noblest and brightest ornaments of our State."[9] Vance could scarcely have sustained personal losses more severe than those of the admired young colonel of his old regiment, Burgwyn, and the rising young generals he had come to know well, Pender and Pettigrew.

Such was the beginning of the long trail back from Gettysburg, toward the Wilderness and Appomattox.

Davis in autumn that year made a swing through the South, partly to allay the controversies that were continually arising in Bragg's army and partly to rally the people to a cause which had met its most severe reverses in early July at Gettysburg and Vicksburg. Returning home he spoke at Wilmington, North Carolina, largely in defense of his actions but paying a tribute to the state for its war contributions. Editor Holden could not omit the opportunity to call attention to the fact that he had formed two cabinets—an overstatement because Benjamin had remained a fixture from the beginning—all of original secessionists; that all the ministers he had sent abroad had been original secessionists; and that of some 200 brigadier generals appointed, nearly all were from the original secessionist party; and of the numerous appointments he had made in North Carolina nearly all were secessionists. Holden by his reiterations seemed to be dropping into mere quarreling, but that did not deprive his case of merit even if it was becoming tiresome.

North Carolina tightened its belt after Gettysburg. Whatever had been done before by an industrious population was done with renewed vigor. Vance himself was not the less but the more determined to win after the shocking losses, many of them closely personal, which the state had received in the last two battles, Chancellorsville and Gettysburg. In both the fighting seemed to fall heaviest on North Carolina regiments.

How the people, according to an old Southern saying, "learned how to do without," and met privation at times joyfully, might be seen from the item in the home section of the Raleigh *Standard* headed: "A Few Words About Chicory." It told how *chicorium intybus,* a perennial plant indigenous to Europe and naturalized in this country, answered all the purposes of coffee. The root, cut into thin slices, roasted and ground, was an admirable substitute for coffee "and when combined with the latter in the proportion of two to one improves the flavor of coffee very much."[10] In time of blockade when only the very wealthy could afford coffee, chicory would serve very well itself. The custom was formed and chicory has been used in much Southern coffee since.

Vance in one of his jocular moods after the war gave his unflattering opinion about Confederate beverages: "When the last grain of coffee had been used, and the last pound of sugar which could be obtained from captured Louisiana had gone with it, then, and not till then, did we realize that the crisis of our fate had come, and blank despair had settled down upon the Southern cause. Without the flavor or the shadow of a pretense of the flavor of coffee, we were reduced to the honest truth in the shape of a drink made of parched rye sweetened with sorghum molasses! With a cheerful melancholy this was spoken of as coffee, in deference to the customs of antiquity. It might with propriety be described as the fluid form of secession—and as the last and a most faithful support of the Confederacy."

He wondered if any to whom he spoke had ever tasted it, then: "I am firmly persuaded that if you . . . had lived upon it for one week, as we did for three years, you would rise as one man from your seats and extending both hands toward me, would exclaim: 'We forgive the war, O Rebel; we pardon secession; friends and brothers you have suffered enough!' To say, as was the custom, that the hopes of the Confederacy depended upon the brave hearts of its defenders was in effect to take an unpardonable liberty with science; these hopes rested chiefly on the strong stomachs of their defenders! Patriotism had become a question of dyspepsia and nightmare."[11]

Vance tried to place provisions where they were most needed. The schools had difficulty. He gave a special permit to Sheriff Augustus Fogle of Forsyth County and to the principal of the Salem Female Academy, Professor de Schweinitz, to pass through the Confederate lines on their quests for food. Not only did the academy take care of its girl students, but large numbers of refugees from the war-torn sections of the South crowded in and had to be fed. When sugar was exhausted Vance would send them a couple of barrels from the scanty state supply. The sheriff and principal would harness the horse to a wagon and scour the surrounding country looking for vegetables, meat—whatever would keep the wolf of hunger from the academy door.[12]

Vance was a trustee of the University at Chapel Hill and visited it at the commencement exercises for the small classes in 1863 and 1864. In the early summer of 1863 he met there four ex-governors, Swain, Morehead, Graham, and Manly. The last was a justice of the Supreme Court, who attended with another justice, Battle, leaving the third, Pearson, to labor over his learned and controversial decisions. The military touch in the 1864 commencement was supplied by the presence of the 43rd regimental band, but the ten seniors being graduated listened, along with the governor and other trustees, to addresses far removed from the deadly conflict raging around them. Albert M. Boozer of Lexington delivered an oration on "The Omnipotence of God," while J. Burton Williams, Jr., of Warren County spoke on "The Career of Hannibal."[13]

Vance himself, in later years, gave what was perhaps the best summary of conditions during this intense period of the war, when the North was toughening and tightening its pressure and the new nation, with hopes for recognition by other powers all but gone, fought on doggedly with a yearning and at times with the confidence and inner trust that the hand of the Almighty must at length intercede, or that the invading enemy would grow weary of the tremendous task of subjugation, and allow the South to go the way of its choosing.

The situation, said Vance, called into active play all the mechanical talents of the people. The village or crossroad blacksmith enlarged his shop and made tools and agricultural implements for his neighbors; shoemakers, coopers, wheelwrights, tanners, all came into sudden demand. "Even the druggist compounded from the wondrous flora of the country substitutes for nearly all the drugs of commerce, which if not so efficacious were at least more harmless than the genuine article." He thought that of all the ingenuity displayed, the greatest contriving was from "our woman-folks." No longer could they get "store clothes," the silks, merinos, and alpacas. The old ones of such materials were carefully put aside for use at weddings and occasions of high state. The women wore calico prints from the state's cotton mills, or dresses of cloth woven on the hand looms of the old homesteads and plantations. Bonnets were the favorite headgear of women of that generation and as Vance said, there were three million bonnet wearers in the South and not a bonnet factory inside the Confederacy. Let him tell of the improvisers:

"The situation was indeed most appalling; but my fair country-women were equal to it, as they had been to all other emergencies. . . . As in the War of the Roses, the women were greater partizans than the men, and with them the memories of the struggle were longer in dying out. . . ." So it proved with the South, where the cheerful patience of the women amid hardships "shamed the boasted courage of the men." The women showed the noble qualities that were beneath the thin veneer of personal vanity. "They took the bright straw of the wheat, oats and rye, and the husk of the corn ears, rich in the beauteous color-ing of silver and old gold, and with deft fingers wove for themselves all manner of head-gear, as charming as any which ever came from the shops of France or Italy."

He found a sharp effect produced. On gazing at the Southern girls "thus arrayed from top to toe in home-made striped cottons, which we called Alamance plaids, set off by corn-shuck bonnets, the work of their own hands, I have felt all the usual symptoms of violent attack. . . . I became sadly aware of the fact that it did not matter how they dressed, they had the same power to find the soft spot in our hearts every time." Then he added that, in the language of St. Paul, "Brethren, I speak as a man."[14]

Men frequently wore hats of the same rustic material and nearly all men's clothing was home woven, of cotton or wool or a mixture.

Closely as he was concerned with the home population, Vance's thoughts always were directed more to the young men in the ranks. He had visited often the units, usually companies or battalions, stationed at different points in eastern and central North Carolina, and at times the larger units at Kinston and Goldsboro. He longed to see the brigades and regiments which had grown famous in Lee's army, and all through the winter of 1863-64 when the army was in quarters south of the Wilderness, he was projecting a visit there.

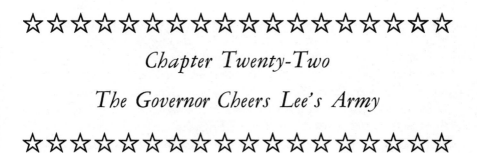

## Chapter Twenty-Two

## The Governor Cheers Lee's Army

Vance's governorship reached its high point with his visit to Lee's army, which was resting in winter quarters south of the Rapidan River centered around Orange Court House. He arrived there March 26, 1864, for a speaking tour of ten days with North Carolina troops.

He had decided to seek a second term as governor and the trip was by some interpreted as of strictly political motive, but as one of his staff analyzed it, his true purpose "was to rekindle the fires of patriotism in the hearts of the North Carolina troops; and to cheer and stimulate the entire army."[1]

He did exactly that. "I had supposed that I knew him thoroughly and appreciated him fully," his aide continued, "but I had no conception of his gifts as an orator and of the potency of his personal magnetism until this memorable occasion."[2] Whatever his motive may have been, the result far transcended any partisan significance, for Lee himself testified to its great value to his army, and virtually all the high-ranking officers, Jeb Stuart in particular, were enraptured as thoroughly as the men in the ranks.

Surgeon General Warren, who accompanied him, said he transcended himself and "produced an impression on the army—from its great captain to its humblest private—which displayed itself in the wildest enthusiasm."[3] Big, handsome, vibrant, he made an impressive figure before the troops, who were so seasoned that they could sense leadership qualities instinctively.

In Lee's army at this period were thirteen North Carolina brigades, comprising sixty-five regiments, which was more than half of the army. Longstreet's Corps, which had no North Carolina troops, was absent, wintering in East Tennessee, and the corps of Ewell and A.P. Hill, both heavy with North Carolina units, were stretched at intervals along the bank and back country of the Rapidan, with Ramseur's North Carolina Brigade on the extreme right and Lane's North Carolinians on the extreme left. Vance began his tour on the army's right and found on his arrival at Ramseur's headquarters that Generals Lee, Stuart, and other of the army's notables were on hand to welcome him. For several days he progressed down the line of brigades, arousing all the fervor that might be expected from a religious revivalist of extraordinary power. After the first one or two speeches the entire army was aware of what was transpiring and of the high quality of the young governor's eloquence. Eager soldiers from Virginia, South Carolina, and Georgia brigades, and regiments from other states, along with large crowds of civilians, including the belles from the surrounding country, were crowding into the North Carolina area to be caught up in the wave of patriotic ardor.

Colonel Joseph C. Webb of the 27th North Carolina, Davis's Brigade, returned from a leave to find the army "ablaze with excitement."[4] This was the only occasion of its kind during the war and it was the most rousing event of the dull, rainy winter which preceded the opening of Grant's Wilderness campaign with its sanguinary battles and relentless pressure.

Vance had made the journey to the Rapidan because the North Carolina units had become restive about the peace meetings being held in the state. Distaste had grown to bitterness over Holden's editorials and now his apparent candidacy for the governorship. Nothing could have given the troops greater assurance of the steadfastness of the people back home than Vance's ringing orations, with their fervid outbursts of eloquence, humor, pathos, and the sparkling admixture of droll anecdotes with which his memory and fertile imagination abounded.

The tour of the brigades, which lasted more than a week in the Orange Court House area, was followed by a review of the troops, the only one accorded a civilian by General Lee and the Army of Northern Virginia.

The story of the review is best told by one who was there, Dr. Warren, whose description is a trifle flamboyant but perhaps the best for details of any written by an observer.

"Upon an immense plain," he said, "in the immediate neighborhood of Orange Court House, there were the troops which composed the then unconquered Army of Northern Virginia. They were clad in rags but wreathed in victory; their flags were soiled and tattered, but upon them were inscribed the immortal names of Coal [sic] Harbor, Manassas and South Mountain; their arms were battered and blackened, but their fire had startled the nations and reverberated around the world; their bands were decimated and out of tune, but they still discoursed the inspiring strains of 'Dixie,' 'The Bonny Blue Flag' and 'The Girl I Left Behind Me,' and though many a gallant leader was absent because 'off duty' forever . . . Stuart, Early, Ewell, Hill, Rhodes [sic], Gordon . . . Hampton and Fitzhugh Lee were there to do honor to Carolina's illustrious son.

"Arrayed in two confronting lines and with their bronze faces beaming with pleasure and expectancy, the noble veterans awaited the coming of the old chieftain whom they had followed in triumph so long, and of the youthful governor, whose devotion to the cause and tender care of his own troops had already made him the idol of them all. Finally the cannons boomed, and General Lee and Governor Vance appeared, and, amid a storm of enthusiastic cheers and an avalanche of friendly greetings, rode slowly along the excited lines. It was a stirring scene, and as I rode with this distinguished company, and gazed into the battered but radiant faces around me, and listened to the grand 'Confederate yell' with which they hailed their great commander and his honored guest, I felt that it was indeed an occasion to be remembered, and realized that I stood in the presence of heroes and conquerors—of the men who had made history, and had earned even from their enemies the reputation of being 'the bravest soldiers who ever marched to the music of battle.' "[5]

An elevated platform had been prepared for the speaker in the center of the vast field and around it now crowded the great mass of the Southern army, men from all the brigades irrespective of states. No transcript remains of what Vance said here or in any of his talks to the brigades elsewhere, but scattered summations were noted down in letters or were recalled later, and it was clear that this was not only Vance's greatest test, but the most glorious acquittal of any he ever faced.

His staff member, Dr. Warren, was beside himself with ecstasy. "A more appropriate, effective and eloquent address was never uttered by human lips," he declared. "Under the influence of his rich and varied imagery, his happy and graphic illustrations, his masterly grasp and inner meaning, his trenchant thrusts and touching allusions . . . and, in a word, his magnificent and resistless eloquence, the audience was stirred, enraptured, enthused and carried away as if by the spell of a magician. Not a man who heard that impassioned outburst of patriotic inspiration would have hesitated to die for his country. . . ." Warren added that if any lukewarmness or despondence had been "produced by the machinations of a selfish faction at home" they vanished "as the morning mist before the rising sun under the spell of this good man's matchless eloquence."[6]

Warren was the source of the tribute ascribed to the commanding general: "I heard General Lee remark that Governor Vance's visit to the army has been equivalent to its reinforcement by fifty thousand men."[7]

On this occasion, as in his earlier retort to the Virginia troops when he was commanding his company of Roughs, Vance is credited in some accounts as having originated the term "Tar Heels." Probably what he did was to give it elevation. Long used contemptuously, the name became an honor when Vance addressed his auditors as "Fellow Tar Heels." Ever after, it implied the sticking quality of North Carolina troops. The term has not been noticed by this writer in North Carolina newspapers of the Civil War era, and only infrequently in contemporary writing of any sort, but there are instances of its use prior to Vance, who is often credited with originating it, when clearly he did not.

For many, "Tarheel" has remained a name of top endearment. Dr. Warren commented that for Vance, it was synonymous with tenacious courage. Afterwards, "during the war and up to the present moment, the most subtle compliment which can be paid to a North Carolinian who followed the banner of the Confederacy . . . is to call him by that homely but blood-baptised appellation of 'Tarheel.' "[8]

When Vance finished, the excited soldiers cheered for General Lee as though they wanted him to speak, but he was not one to believe that military ability implied talents along other lines, and though pleased with the demonstration of affection, he mounted and rode away. Still, the soldiers wanted more and they obtained a few responses. Good-natured, boyishly exuberant Jeb Stuart, who was bubbling over with the fervency kindled by Vance's remarks, came to the platform easily and gracefully. He lifted his hat with its long plume, bowed, waited until the shouts had quieted, bowed again in recognition of them, and made a military officer's speech. "Fellow-soldiers, I am a cavalryman, and, consequently, not an orator. But I would be untrue to myself if I failed to command words enough to thank you for your kind reception, and to say that I have commanded many soldiers, but never braver and more trusty than those from the Old North State. God bless her!"[9]

Warren, who heard him, said the simple remarks from the great cavalry leader aroused the audience, and especially the North Carolina part of it, more than would the eloquence of Demosthenes. The men shouted so loud and long that the officers began to fear the Federals on the other side of the river and hills would grow concerned and be aroused to the sudden opening of a new campaign.

Jubal Early, a lawyer and facile speaker, addressed the men engagingly and forcibly and fell into the spirit of the day by warmly applauding the heroism of the North Carolina troops. Vance had unloosened a veritable tide of oratory. Rodes, who had been a professor for a time after his graduation from Virginia Military Institute, seemed nevertheless nonplused when the troops got him to the stand. He recalled an incident of the Gettysburg campaign:

"I never attempted but one speech before this in my life," he said, "and that was at Carlisle when we raised a Confederate flag over its arsenal last year. I did not finish that speech because an attack was made upon us while I was in the midst of it; but with God's help I intend to finish my speech at Carlisle."

That remark aroused the men to as high a pitch of excitement as Vance, who stood near by, had done in his oratorical flights. It was a plain statement that Rodes wanted to launch another Pennsylvania campaign. Suddenly thousands took up the cry, "At Carlisle! At Carlisle!" The army was ready to begin the march, if Rodes truly meant it. But by that time the day had worn on, and the drums beat and bugles sounded assembly, and with a precision that surprised the onlookers, the ranks were formed and what had been a mass of men suddenly became orderly formations moving off, not to Pennsylvania, but back to the humdrum of winter hibernation.[10]

Dr. Warren thought Vance had given North Carolina the standing the state's soldiers deserved, for "from the Roanoke to the Susquehanna their bones are scattered upon every field which General Lee lost or won," and though late to enter the Confederacy, she "ensanguinated and impoverished herself in maintaining it."[11]

Edward Joseph Hale, the young Fayetteville editor who had sent back the enthusiastic report of Vance's Salisbury address just before the war, was a staff officer with Lane's Brigade, which at Liberty Mills was on the extreme left of Lee's army, where it would be the last brigade to entertain Vance and hear him. So a day ahead, Lane and Hale rode together to Scales's Brigade, the next North Carolina brigade to their right, to hear him and escort him back to their own camp. Hale described the series of army appearances as "the most picturesque episode of Vance's life," then told of his talk to Scales's men.

"It was pitched in a lofty key. General Lee, General Stuart and other big wigs of the army, arrived just at the close, owing to a misunderstanding of the time set for the speech, but we learned from them that they had been following Vance up from brigade to brigade."

Hale described the scene as inspiring: "There lay the unconquered Army of Northern Virginia, like a lion at bay, along the foothills of the Blue Ridge. Or, we might say that the Great Commander was holding his dogs of war in leash for what soon proved their long death grapple, when they were let loose on the flank of Grant's marching army five weeks later. Traitors at home were sowing discord among the people, with the expectation that the infection would spread to their brethren in the army.

"At this crisis, the young Governor of the State which supplied such a great portion of that army, appeared upon the scene. What a setting the picture had! The Great Commander and his brilliant escort, many hundreds of fair women of Virginia on horseback and in carriages, and the grim veterans and their tattered battle flags! And what a theme . . . this was a last appeal to the men at the front to stand to their colors, even though that required turning their deaf ear to the wails of those dependent upon them. His fiery eloquence bewitched the great Virginian and his companions, while it wrought our North Carolina soldiers up to the highest pitch of patriotic fervor. No wonder they made their imperishable record in the unprecedented campaigns that followed."

Hale said that twenty-one years later he sat on the platform with Gladstone in Manchester and heard his memorable speech there opening the Home Rule campaign. "Having in consideration the fact that each speaker's object was to sway great bodies of men in behalf of a people's freedom, I believe that Vance's was the greater effort."[12]

Brigadier General James H. Lane, who was perhaps the only general officer present in the eastern army from Bethel to Appomattox, and was "dearly beloved by his entire brigade," told of the large civilian gathering which came to hear Vance. The governor was due at his brigade the day following his visit with Scales but the weather was so bad—snow followed by rain—that the address had to be deferred a day, greatly to the disappointment of many who had come from a distance, including, Lane said, a number of fair damsels. It appeared bad the next morning, but at 2 P.M. the rain stopped and, despite the dampness and a high wind, Vance spoke for an hour and a half, then left the next morning, Sunday, for Johnston's Brigade stationed at Hanover Junction nearer Richmond.[13]

In Gordonsville, on the morning of April 3, when Lane wrote, Governor Zeb was called on for a speech but refused because it was Sunday, believing apparently that some of his humor and episodes would not fit well on the Sabbath, though there was apparently no vulgarity in any of his army talks, else the choice stories would have been passed around. Then, too, Lee was often present.

Lane gave a description in a letter: "It is the first time that I have had the pleasure of meeting him. He is a large, fine-looking man and one of marked intelligence. In him is happily blended true eloquence and sound reasoning, with an inexhaustible fund of anecdotes. His speech at Scales's Brigade was a much finer intellectual effort than the one delivered to ours. His appeal to the soldiers to stand by the Colors, his enumeration of the qualities of heroes out of whose blood spring nations and empires, and his showing that all things earthly as well as heavenly that are truly worth having must be purchased at the sacrifice of blood, were really grand, and brought tears to the eyes of many of the old battle-scarred veterans. It is an interesting sight to see these old heroes wipe away tears, and a few moments later be convulsed with laughter. J. E. B. Stuart followed him around and seemed to be completely carried away with his speeches, and I understand General Lee on one or two occasions forgot his usual dignity and laughed heartily at his anecdotes. I am sure the visit of such a fine speaker to the army has had a beneficial effect upon the soldiers. The governor must be heard to be properly appreciated."[14]

Colonel Webb of the 27th North Carolina of Davis's Brigade, Heth's Division, told of his glimpse of Vance in a letter he wrote April 4, 1864, to his aunt Robina Mickle of "Happy Valley" in Caldwell County, along the upper Yadkin River. Rain delayed the governor's appearance before the brigades of Davis and Kirkland, but he spoke before 6,000 soldiers on April 6, though the field where the men stood was still a quagmire. The colonel found that many from other states vied with the North Carolinians in admiration of the spirited governor.

"General Stewart [Stuart] has been with him nearly all the time since he came, and a number of other generals have been to hear him every time he spoke. Gen'l Lee has heard him twice, and I understand that old Gen'l Ewell has nearly shaken his wooden leg to pieces laughing at his jokes. I don't think I ever saw a more attentive or enthusiastic audience than he had here, nothwithstanding the men had to stand in mud and water all the time he was speaking."[15]

One of the appreciative accounts of Zeb's visit was left by the Reverend George Patterson, who referred to himself as "a cross between a Boston Yankee and a Greek," and was, in fact, one of the remarkable characters of Lee's army. His story gave fresh sidelights on Lee's reverence and Vance's oratorical powers.

The Reverend Mr. Patterson was the son of Petro Papathakes and Louisa Miles, the father a member of the Greek Orthodox Church and the mother a Unitarian and descendant of a colonial Massachusetts family. When George, born in 1828, was baptized and christened in the Episcopal Church, his father's name was translated into what was regarded as an English equivalent and became Patterson. The quality noted about him was his deep learning, which he seems to have acquired more in remote and primitive Wisconsin than scholarly Cambridge, for he trained for the ministry at Nashotah House in the northwestern state, then for reasons that are not apparent, but possibly because of his deep regard for the welfare of the slaves, he applied to the Episcopal Bishop of North Carolina in 1850 for an assignment. He became a candidate for orders in the North State, was ordained deacon in 1852 and priest in 1856, and took over the pastorate of Somerset Place on Lake Scuppernong, near the eastern shore. There he devoted himself to the welfare of the slaves, though he defended the right of slavery on Biblical grounds.

When war broke he became chaplain of the 3rd North Carolina regiment, and, as a student of his career stated, his work was "magnificent."

The men were attracted by his personality quite as much as by his learning and eagerness to serve them—"he shared every hardship with them, and was in the thick of every fight, and ministered to them in camp and hospital and in the midst . . . of shot and shell." His preaching was forceful, frank and direct, and everyone came to trust him. Later he was made chaplain of the Chimborazo Hospital in Richmond, but in the winter of 1863-64 he was active at the front and the great event of his army life was Vance's visit.[16]

Patterson estimated like others that the North Carolinians composed half of Lee's army at that time, but thousands of soldiers from other states crowded to the North Carolina brigades to hear the governor, famed as an orator of repartee, ornate forensic outbursts and ready wit, while officers of all ranks were there. Patterson mentioned Ewell, "Maryland" Steuart, and Rodes as among the governor's auditors, while Jeb Stuart followed him from brigade to brigade, "fascinated, and heard every speech."

When announcement was made of the review, the North Carolina regiments polished their muskets, patched and sewed their uniforms, and made ready to put on their best appearance. Someone asked the chaplain what he intended to wear. "My uniform, of course," he said, by which he meant his cassock instead of his gray battle suit, though the priestly garb was faded and torn. In it he lined up with the staff in front of the regiment.

Lee rode in front of his staff, with Vance at his side. When the commanding general reached the regiment and saw Patterson, he took off his hat, bowed low on Traveler's neck, and in a clear voice, easily heard along the line, said, "I salute the minister of the church of God." Patterson's heart beat with pride that Lee would recognize through him the devotion to God which governed his military conduct quite as much as it had his life in the days of peace. The address which followed this review was described by Patterson as outstanding among those the governor delivered.[17]

Major Charles M. Stedman of Kirkland's Brigade gave his account of the visit and said Lee and others were captivated by Vance's eloquence. He confirmed that Lee, like Stuart, accompanied the governor from one brigade to another. "The enthusiasm of the soldiers knew no bounds. It was the prelude to the campaign which soon thereafter commenced, in which they won imperishable renown. His last speech was made at a general review of Lee's army near Orange Court House. It was ordered by that great commander as a special compliment to Vance, an honor bestowed upon none other in all its history."

Stedman grew more enthusiastic as he recounted the incidents of the visit. "No orator in all the annals of time ever had an audience whose presence was more calculated to inspire heroic sentiment and high resolve," he said. "It was the remnant of the Army of Northern Virginia. Upon its banners were names which will long live during the ages to come—Manassas, Chancellorsvile, Sharpsburg, Fredericksburg, Gettysburg. The greatest commander of the English-speaking race was beside him. Stonewall Jackson had gone to his final rest. Pettigrew had joined him in immortality."

He mentioned some who survived and were present—A. P. Hill, Ewell, Early, Gordon. "They forgot the fields of their glory as they listened to him. J. E. B. Stuart was there and never so happy, unless at the head of a cavalry charge. Hoke of North Carolina, who had established his reputation forever as one of the foremost of all the great soldiers of the Civil War, gazed upon him with mingled pride and affection. He knew him and loved him."

Matt Ransom shared Hoke's exultation. The unrivaled artillery officers, Pegram of Virginia and Haskell of South Carolina "leaned forward to catch his every utterance. History has no more splendid scene to record."[18]

After General Lee's, perhaps the greatest tribute that went to the young governor was delivered by the even younger commander of Lee's cavalry, Jeb Stuart, who said of Vance's address following the review: "If the test of eloquence is its effect, this speech was the most eloquent ever delivered"[19]

When Vance visited Ramseur's Brigade, the honor of entertaining him at dinner fell to the 14th North Carolina, which contained his old company, the Rough and Ready Guards of Buncombe County.

Something of a minor crisis was created when the governor accepted the invitation of Colonel Risden T. Bennett, because the regiment, though possessing good quarters for a repast, built of slabs from the nearby forests, was short on pots, pans, and all manner of equipment needed for the preparation of a worthy feast.

Before the 14th had gone into winter quarters it had been employed for a number of weeks cutting timber for the construction of plank roads needed during the muddy season. The regimental chaplain, W. C. Power, with the volunteer help of the men, set up a chapel at the lumber camp, built of upright slabs covered with horizontal planking, but within two weeks after the sturdy building was consecrated the 14th was ordered back to its old front-line position.

Neither Chaplain Power nor the soldiers were to be defeated and by patient labor they took down the chapel in the woods and reassembled it close behind their lines. There all that winter they held their divine services. They had to abandon it when, as Colonel Bennett said, "the fierce blast of spring fighting broke upon the peaceful face of nature." Meantime during the winter the men did routine duties—"on picket, prayed, snow-balled, polished our weapons and prepared our revenge." The failure at Gettysburg was not forgotten and the army hoped to retaliate with a resounding victory. Desertions were a serious problem in some commands, but the 14th was virtually free of the contagion and because of its steadfastness Lee sent it back to Bowling Green, Virginia, as a rear-guard patrol to catch deserters heading south.

When the governor came there was rivalry among the regiments of the brigade, all being from North Carolina, over which should have him for dinner, and the 14th was selected. Chaplain Power, who had a reputation of being a good provider and possessed also one of the jewels of the regiment, a good cook, brought the cook, his provisions and his impressive but still pitiful supply of kettles and pans to augment the limited number at regimental headquarters.

Instead of the regiment showing the governor that it had to live on lean fare, it pooled its resources to give him the most sumptuous dinner possible under the conditions of in-the-woods campaigning. Still, there were not dishes or room at the table for all the officers of the regiment, or even the ranking members and the full headquarters staff, along with the governor and his small retinue, so some had to await a second table. Unhappily neither the colonel nor other officers left an account of the conversation, but all must have eaten heartily, for the second table detail saw the food dwindle down to the fried tarts, which proved a delicacy of which there was an ample quantity.

Good Colonel Bennett, who with the regiment had held the center of the "Bloody Lane" line at Sharpsburg and stormed down from Oak Hill to break the enemy on the first day at Gettysburg, modestly declined the first table and waited on the governor and his party.

In his later comment he noted the change in Vance's attitude: "He was an advanced Confederate, having learned rapidly as events were accomplished in his view and under his intelligent observation." Apparently the colonel, deeply imbued with the cause from the start, harkened back to Vance's fight against secession, or else had heard the spurious reports that neither he nor the folks back home any longer had their hearts in the cause.[20]

Nothing in the visit gave Vance more pleasure than this dinner and visit with his old comrades, many of whom were the lads he had recruited in the first days of the war.

The estimate that half of Lee's army was from North Carolina was not excessive, in view of Longstreet's absence and that of Pickett's all-Virginia division. The states which contributed the heaviest numbers to General Lee were North Carolina and Virginia, and to the Virginia soldiers Vance was cordial and deferential. However he may have complained to President Davis about the excess of Virginia officers commanding North Carolina troops, Vance had nothing but deep respect for the conduct of Virginia soldiers in the field and in battle. He praised them so highly in one speech that it seemed the Virginians were doing most of the cheering. Just when the North Carolinians were feeling neglected, Zeb turned the whole matter into a joke, saying the Virginians were born leaders and the Carolinians were always glad to follow, and "it was well we did follow you and keep close up to you, too, for if we hadn't, those heavy battles around Richmond would have been mere skirmishes." That brought a delighted yell from the North Carolina elements and his good humor was such that both states were pleased.[21]

At the time Vance was with the army in Virginia getting a testimonial of warm affection from the shouts of the soldiers, he was receiving an equally sincere and more touching tribute from North Carolina prisoners on Johnson's Island, off Sandusky, Ohio. The letter they wrote, dated March 30, 1864, was signed by a number of committee members, of whom Wharton J. Green of Warren, later Congressman, was chairman. On the committee also were Thomas S. Kenan, the intrepid colonel of Daniel's Brigade who commanded the 43rd North Carolina at Gettysburg, and Joseph J. Davis of Franklin County, a captain of the 47th North Carolina, who came to be termed "one of the state's best known, best loved and most distinguished sons."[22] A member of Pettigrew's Brigade, Davis was one of the group who went farthest into the Federal lines on the third day at Gettysburg, and was wounded and captured inside the stone wall, 150 yards beyond the spot where General Armistead fell. In later years he served on the

Supreme Court of North Carolina and in Congress. The letter bore the signatures also of 224 North Carolina prisoners on Johnson's Island. It disclosed not only their affection for Vance, but the resolute spirit of the state's soldiers even while undergoing an onerous captivity:

> Sir—At a meeting of the officers from North Carolina confined in this prison, on yesterday, we, the undersigned, were appointed a committee to express to you the intense satisfaction with which we have watched the distinguished ability and lofty patriotism which have characterized your administration. It has been with peculiar pride, during this, our long and tedious imprisonment, that in every wind that has brought to our ears a whisper from the land of our birth and of our unchangeable love, we have heard the utterances of our own sentiments, the echo of our own prayers, of our highest hopes and purest aspirations, in the manly and patriotic language of the Governor of our State. Exiles from our home and country, captives in the land of those who hate and would destroy us, we watch with anxious concern the progress of events and the course of the war, and note with unmingled pleasure the manifestation of ardent patriotism and unyielding firmness among the masses of the people of our State. But, sir, it is with peculiar pleasure that we advert to your late noble effort at Wilkesboro—so genuine in its eloquence, so exalted in its patriotism, so forcible in its arguments and withall so hopeful and confident of success, that every son of the Old State felt a glow of pride in the reflection that these grand utterances emanated from his own honored Chief Magistrate.
>
> Sir, your exposition of the policy of the Federal government, your startling portraiture of the miseries that would be endured by our unhappy country and the oppressions and indignities that would be heaped upon her, in case of submission, are so forcibly verified by the actions of the dominant party in this country, that no reasoning man, enjoying, as we do, an unlimited access to the leading journals of all political parties here, can fail to realize the fact that even the most appalling apprehensions of misery that have presented themselves to the minds of our most sagacious statesmen, even the most hideous pictures of ruin that have been painted by our most eloquent countrymen, would fall far short of the realities of the doom that would await us, should we be so demented as to lay down those arms and disband those armies that have hitherto protected us from the fury of our enemies. . . .
>
> War may cover the land with sorrow and mourning, but peace on the terms of submission would cover it with the blackness of the shadow of death. War has still the blessing of hope, but in such a peace there is only the darkness of despair. In such a state of existence the order of

nature would be reversed. Life would be the king of terrors and death its only solace. In final, eternal separation lies our only hope, our only safety. Other terms were dishonorable, were dangerous. As soldiers of North Carolina, as citizens of our young Confederacy, we can be content with no peace that does not recognize us as a free and independent people.

So long, sir, as you tread the path of duty with the same manly unfaltering step as heretofore, so long will our hearts go with you in gratitude; so long will we hail you as among the great deliverers of the State we reverence, from a tyranny more revolting than the visage of death.[23]

Vance had written a little earlier, January 20, 1864, to Governor Horatio Seymour of New York, saying he was informed of the suffering of North Carolina troops confined in New York for want of winter clothing. He transmitted three sterling bills of exchange drawn on a London house for £1,200, about $9,000 at current rates, which he wished the governor to expend for clothing for North Carolina prisoners in whatever prison confined. "In venturing to ask you to take so much trouble upon your hands," Vance wrote, "I feel sure that the suggestion of humanity and the common courtesy existing between honest enemies will be sufficient apology." He asked the opportunity of reciprocating if it became possible to do so. The lot of the prisoners was thereby made a little easier, and Vance did reciprocate by his attention to the welfare of Northern prisoners at Salisbury.[24]

★☆★☆★☆★☆★☆★☆★☆★☆★☆★☆

## Chapter Twenty-Three

## *Vance and Holden as Adversaries*

★☆★☆★☆★☆★☆★☆★☆★☆★☆★☆

Longstreet's absence from Lee's army at the time Vance visited it in Virginia was due to the detachment of his corps in September, 1863, to reinforce Bragg after the Federals under Rosecrans captured Chattanooga and threatened Georgia.

The transfer of two divisions and the corps artillery by railroad, the first extensive operation of its kind in the history of warfare, indirectly came to involve Vance in another flare-up with Richmond, and this on behalf of his old but parting friend, Holden.

The clamorous editor, whose self-assertion often extended to arrogance, was rapidly becoming a politically ambitious enemy intent on unseating the governor and taking over the office, much as young Carson had unseated his erstwhile friend Dr. Robert B. Vance, Zeb's uncle, leading to the bitter reproaches and the doctor's death in a duel.

Zeb was fashioned from a much larger mold than his irascible little uncle and had no intention of being succeeded by one of Holden's principles, largely expedient, but which, out of a common but mistaken appraisal of the temper of the state, were being covertly directed toward a withdrawal of North Carolina from the war. Such was the governor's devotion to legal processes that despite his awareness of the editor's probable intentions, he was the first to complain when Holden and his newspapers were subjected to mob violence. Holden was exercising freedom of the press to its full tensile strength and was going beyond the snapping point in the opinion of large numbers of spirited soldiers from North Carolina and other states.

When Longstreet's Corps headed south toward Chattanooga it had to take an eastern route because of the threat to Knoxville, Tennessee, by Burnside's invading army. The city fell September 6, 1863, thus cutting the railroad which ran southwest from Richmond through Bristol and Knoxville. The eastern route took the soldiers through Raleigh and Wilmington or Charlotte, Augusta, and Atlanta.[1]

One of Longstreet's several stellar brigades was Benning's, composed entirely of Georgians, in the command of which Henry Lewis Benning, a man of large capacities and distinguished public service before the war, had won the sobriquet of "Old Rock." He is appropriately remembered by having the largest present-day military installation in the United States, situated near his home town of Columbus, Georgia, named for him.

Benning's Brigade, riding flatcars and boxcars, was unloaded at the Raleigh depot on the evening of September 9 and Benning's car arrived between nine and ten. He busied himself about the transportation of his men out of the city, then lay down near the railroad, used a crosstie for a pillow, and went to sleep until 11 P.M., at which time the cars arrived from Goldsboro, the troops boarded them, and the brigade was carried southward.[2]

While Benning slept some of his soldiers, apparently abetted by a detail of North Carolina troops, went to Holden's home, their purpose unexplained but it clearly was an intent on Holden's person. Not finding him there—he had heard their approach and fled to Vance's protection—they went to the *Standard* office, tore its doors down, sacked it and broke it apart, scattered the type on the floor and in the street, pied all the type that had been set, upturned the make-up stones, then decorated the place mournfully from the kegs of printers' ink. The presses in a back part of the building seemed to be too formidable or else escaped notice, and were unhurt, but the newspaper was so badly damaged that it had to suspend operation for a time.

Retaliatory silence was inflicted with equal severity the next morning on its rival newspaper, the *State Journal*, organ of the stanch secessionists. After Benning and his soldiers had left, and word had spread around town of their punitive action against Holden, that editor's partisans gathered. About half a hundred, led by pro-unionist Mark Williams, went to the *State Journal* office and did a more effective job of destruction than the soldiers had inflicted on the *Standard,* and left the presses an irreparable wreck.[3]

Vance was not intimidated by either mob but he arrived too late in both instances. When he heard the mob was at Holden's he rushed to the plant and exhorted the soldiers, and by his personal appeal and bold front probably saved the office and building from total ruin. He identified some of the men as Georgia soldiers, though he knew the name only of a Major Shepherd, and sent a police officer to find Benning at the depot. But the troops there crowded up closely and would not let the policeman enter, and claimed that the general was asleep and could not be disturbed. After the mob was dispersed, Vance rushed off a telegram of protest to President Davis and requested that other troops passing south not be allowed to enter the city else "the most frightful consequences may ensue."[4]

On the next day, September 11, he wrote a full letter to Davis placing the principal blame on the brigade commander Benning and saying that he saw several officers in the crowd at the newspaper plant. "I have also reason for believing it was done with the knowledge and consent of General Benning, as he remarked to a gentleman an hour or two previous, that his men had threatened it." Vance said he intended to enforce the law rigidly against the Raleigh citizens who participated in the second mob and he demanded that punishment be inflicted on the Georgia officers who assisted or countenanced the first mob. If the army gave no punishment he would feel compelled to request the state of Georgia to deliver the officers to him to answer the demands of justice. That would have been a most unlikely concession from Governor Brown of Georgia, and Vance must have inserted the suggestion to bring added pressure on Davis and not in any expectation that the officers would be handed over to him. But he did include in his letter to the Confederate President a ringing paragraph that must have had an effect:

"I feel very sad in the contemplation of these outrages. The distance is quite short to either anarchy or despotism, when armed soldiers, led by their officers, can with impunity outrage the laws of a State. A few more such exhibitions will bring the North Carolina troops home to the defense of their own State and her institutions. I pray you to see that it does not occur again. Should any newspaper in the State commit *treason,* I would have its editor arrested, and tried by the laws which many of us yet respect."[5]

He thanked Davis for complying speedily with his request that the passing troops not be allowed inside the city.

Benning was assailed by the Raleigh *Progress,* the only newspaper left unscathed, and by the *Standard* in the middle of October, after Holden had returned from hiding in the country and unconcernedly resumed publication without apology or restraint. But the Georgia general and the Georgia press gave an entirely different picture of the occurrence and no doubt the truth was in that elusive midland between the two accounts. The Atlanta *Intelligencer* denounced the charge of the Raleigh *Progress,* which linked Benning with the sacking, as a "base falsehood."[6] Nobody in Georgia seemed to believe Benning was accountable and he and his officers were allowed to go on to play a forward role in the crushing of Rosecrans's right wing at the battle of Chickamauga. Governor Brown had no thought of punishing them or extraditing them to North Carolina to "answer the demands of justice."

Benning declared the charges against him were entirely false and countered by saying he had met a party of North Carolinians in Weldon under a lieutenant looking for deserters, who requested and obtained permission to ride on the top of his cars to Raleigh and on to Charlotte. He said after they had left Raleigh some of the North Carolinians bragged that they had been the leaders of the attack on Holden's paper. Likewise there was a rumor in Raleigh that North Carolina troops were the leaders. The fact was that Lieutenant Colonel William S. Shepherd (whom Vance identified as Major Shepherd), who commanded the 2nd Georgia, the principal regiment charged with the infractions, had helped Vance stop the disorder and saw no other Georgia officers present. Also the fact that the Georgia troops left in a body after Vance had remonstrated with them indicated that the affair was not wholly riotous or wholly Georgian. Probably the higher officers were not privy to it until, as Benning contended, it was too late for them to take preventive measures.[7] Vance did not think the soldiers withdrew so tamely. He declared to Davis that they threatened his life if he interfered. "This thing is becoming intolerable. For sixty hours I have traveled up and down, making speeches alternately to citizens and soldiers, without rest or sleep almost, engaged in the humiliating task of trying to defend the laws and peace of the State against our own bayonets."[8]

Benning wrote his letter to Vance from his headquarters near Chattanooga, September 28, after Lieutenant Colonel Shepherd had been wounded at the head of his regiment at Chickamauga and much water had gone over the dam, but the comment in the *Standard* of October 28 was that Benning's letter was "not satisfactory" because it did not account for his prophetic remark that he would not be surprised if he read his men tore down the *Standard* office. The Fayetteville *Observer* injected a new element when it reported in palliation of the offense that some of Holden's friends had gone to the depot and got into an altercation with the Georgia soldiers, which led to their descent on the newspaper.[9] This the *Standard* denied by saying no rumor of the sort had been heard in Raleigh and manifestly the *Observer* had fabricated it.

The significance of the episode lies in the fact that, although Vance extended his protection to Holden, who came cowed to his office while the mob was on the streets, it brought into focus the divergent paths the two men had been following. Vance later wrote to his friend Hale in Fayetteville: "Holden is in continual terror and alarm, sleeps I am told away from home every night. Alas, alas!"[10] The governor was not one to be tied to a peace movement whose leader had to slink through the streets of his own city to avoid a mob any more than he was one to condone the action of the mob in taking the law into its hands. No doubt the break was overdue. There never had been a warm, personal affection between them. It was not that Vance severed himself from Holden's peace party; he had never joined it. His peace aims were under the terms laid down in his letter to President Davis. He was, in fact, standing out more and more as the leader of the loyalists, despite his tiffs with Davis. Holden on the other hand had become the rallying point of the old peace factions gradually growing more vocal, or of new ones emerging as the grim war showed no signs of abatement. Vance was still as ardent as ever in support of the constitution and free institutions; but the sacking of the *Standard,* while the occasion for fresh protests to Richmond, seemed to draw him a step nearer to the Confederate government, on the general theory that there was more danger of anarchy and chaos in the peace movement as it was being conducted than there was of despotism from Richmond, from which he was able to shield his state with some degree of effectiveness.

Peace meetings became much more common throughout North Carolina after Gettysburg and Vicksburg. Most of them appeared to be a genuine yearning for a negotiated cease-fire with the Union instead of treasonable design against the Confederacy. Still, the basic cause, the heart of the disaffection, could be found in the measures regarded as oppressive taken by the central government, especially the conscription of manpower and the impressment of foodstuffs.

Different shades of opinion went into the peace movement. Abetting it were a number of organizations, largely secret, formed in different parts of the South, of which the Heroes of America was not only the most virulent and effective in North Carolina, but also the least appropriately named. The Heroes had the objects of fostering desertions, carrying on espionage, aiding escaped Federal prisoners and, in general, accomplishing the overthrow of the Confederacy. But mainly the people who attended the peace rallies were no other than the common run on whom the burden of war fell hardest and who could expect to reap from it little, even in intangible benefits. They would rather have peace, as most persons always would prefer peace, if it could be achieved on anything approaching a reasonable understanding.

Back in 1862 Holden had been adverting to the catastrophe of the war. From a review of his files between October, 1862, and June, 1863, it is understandable how Pettigrew obtained the impression the *Standard* was giving comfort to the enemy. Gradually that impression had been established in the army, as resolutions passed by North Carolina troops in Virginia began to attest. After stating in October, 1862, that the debt incurred by Lincoln and the war party in the North could not be less than two billion dollars, and that through the North "wrecklessness of moral principle" and "stark mad infidelity" were almost universal, he continued:

"Upon the South the ruin is incalculable. One hundred thousand brave men have either died, or their constitutions broken down, or they are maimed. . . . The loss in property cannot now be estimated. And when is the ruin to end? From the North there is nothing to hope— from Europe we can look for no sympathy. Nothing, perhaps could gratify English statesmen more than the utter ruin of both North and South." No course was suggested, but the tone was not reassuring. By June of the next year Holden was threatening openly that North Carolina must have better treatment from the Confederacy or she would leave it.[11] So far had the discontent advanced that by May, 1864, a peace meeting was being held in Raleigh itself.[12]

The nature of the peace propaganda could be seen by an unsigned letter from Buncombe County to the editor, published May 20, 1863, approving the course of the *Standard* since 1860, and asserting that three fourths of the people held the same opinion. The writer thought opposition to secession was on the increase, that many were deceived who voted for secessionists before the war; that they would never vote again for an original secessionist for office, and that the Conservative party would grow stronger the longer the war lasted. Holden published a long extract from this unsigned letter, rabidly antiadministration, which would tend to indicate his own leaning. The letter said the people recognized the necessity of accomplishing independence, that they had burnt their ships behind them, but held that the old Union might have been preserved with a little more effort. It concluded:

"The people, therefore, hold the original secessionists responsible for the war and all the consequences that have flowed from it—the bloodshed, all the attendant horrors, the privations and sufferings of the people, and the immense taxation of our people, even after peace shall have been restored, to the fortieth generation. Look at that picture before the war, and now look at this since the war!—Imagine the thing on canvas. We were for preserving the old picture—the secessionists were for destroying the old and painting a new one. They have succeeded."

One diagnosis of Vance, that he was controlled utterly by politics, attributed to him the ability to discern what the people needed and wanted ahead of their knowledge of it—a rare gift indeed, and one which is often called not politics but leadership. More accurately, he could foresee needs and prepare in advance to safeguard or satisfy them, which is sometimes termed statesmanship.

Possibly Vance was a little naïve for a time in absolving Holden from harmful intent or a desire to break away from the Confederacy. His disposition after his election in 1862 was to be agreeable, for Holden had been a factor in his success. At his instance the editor was given the lush bit of patronage of being elected by the legislature in November, 1862, as public printer. But the parting came as the peace meetings grew more numerous. In two summer months of 1863, a hundred peace meetings were held in the state by the notorious Heroes of America, with Holden always seeming to supply the impelling force. His paper made mention of such gatherings, but he disavowed any connection with the secret order. Still, there is little wonder that thirty-odd North Carolina regiments denounced Holden and the peace campaign in resolutions. So apprehensive were the troops that they held a convention on August 12, 1863, at Orange Court House protesting the peace movement and urging steadfastness by the people in the Confederate cause. Their voice, it happened, was heard louder than Holden's.[13]

Vance's proclamation of September 7, 1863, cautioning the people not to try to solve the problems of one revolution by plunging the country into another, showed his open hostility to the kind of peace campaign Holden was fostering. His peace letter to President Davis, written out of a sincere conviction that a negotiated peace with the North, if obtainable, would be the prudent course, has been misunderstood at times as bringing him into line with the Holden agitation, or as keeping the gate open if he found it expedient to join in the peace crusade. The clearest understanding of his intent is gained from the letter itself. He did indeed have the difficult role of holding the discordant factions together and preventing open outbreaks. He wrote December 30, 1863, saying that because of the discontent in the state, he had concluded it was "perhaps impossible to remove it except by making some effort at negotiation with the enemy."

Many seemed at the time to detect evidences in the North that people there wearied of the war. The suggestion was altogether seemly that the South put out another feeler.

"I am promised by all men who advocate this course," he told Davis, "that if fair terms are rejected it will tend greatly to strengthen them and intensify the war feeling and will rally all classes to a more cordial support of the government. And although our position is well known as demanding only to be let alone, yet it seems to me that for the sake of humanity, without having any weak or improper motives attributed to us, we might with propriety constantly tender negotiations. In doing so we would keep conspicuously before the world a disclaimer of our responsibility for the great slaughter of our race and convince the humblest of our citizens who sometimes forget the actual situation— that the government is tender of their lives and happiness and would not prolong their sufferings unnecessarily one moment. Though Statesmen might regard this as useless, the people will not, and I think our cause will be strengthened thereby."[14]

Vance's purposes were clear and twofold—earnestly to open the way for peace on reasonable terms, and to strengthen the war spirit if the proposal should be rejected. Peace movements at this time and a little later were virulent and widespread in the North. Vallandigham was preparing to run for governor of Ohio *in absentia*. That there was a much deeper peace movement in Ohio than in North Carolina would be evidenced by the fact that he gained 185,000 civilian votes against his adversary Brough's 247,000. Lincoln's defeat in the 1864 election was accepted by many as a virtual certainty. Peace meetings such as the giant rally in New York City under the auspices of Horatio Seymour and Fernando Wood, attended by 30,000, in the early summer of 1863 were far from unusual in the North, though perhaps not again of that size. Lee had held in advance of the Pennsylvania campaign that peace should be made to appear inviting and that the Northern peace party should be encouraged, not spurned by the South.[15]

Certainly Vance's letter was not out of step, though the reaction in Richmond appears to have been that the ceiling had fallen down. Mary Boykin Chesnut entered in her diary January 4, 1864, how her husband had nearly annihilated her with the latest news: "North Carolina wants to offer terms of peace. We only needed a break of this kind to finish us. I shivered as one does when the first handful of earth comes rattling down on the coffin in the grave of one we cared for more than all."[16]

President Davis answered in good spirit and with apparent understanding that Vance sought a general and not a separate peace for his state. But he was not encouraging. He had already done what Vance had in mind—he had thrice undertaken to communicate with Washington authorities only to be rebuffed, the last time being only a few months before, when the enemy refused even to allow his peace representative, Vice President Stephens, to pass through their lines for the purpose of a conference. Davis did not subscribe to Vance's notion that peace overtures, if rejected, would consolidate home-front opinion in favor of pursuing the war. He thought that by an "over earnest desire to reclaim by conciliation men whom you believe to be sound at heart, but whose loyalty is more than suspected elsewhere, you will permit them to gather such strength as to require more violent measures than are now needed."[17]

The two men remained widely apart in their approach. Where Vance would try to win recalcitrants and doubters back into the war effort by demonstrating the folly of their beliefs, Davis thought in terms of coercion.

On the same day he wrote to President Davis, Vance wrote to his friend Edward Jones Hale, publisher of the Fayetteville *Observer*, a letter which stated the principles on which he would seek re-election: He wanted to "make a record showing every desire for peace except at the expense of my country's ruin and dishonor; and I want the question narrowed down to *Lincoln or no Lincoln*, and I don't intend to fritter away my strength on any minor issue. I advise you therefore to make no fight on the substitute questions—the country will settle that— on taxation, schools, or anything of that kind."[18] His phrase "Lincoln or no Lincoln," with the words underlined, is puzzling. The words could have meant that he expected peace only if Lincoln was defeated in the election that year; or the implication could have been exactly the opposite, that the question was peace with honor, taking Lincoln if necessary. Probably he had in mind that peace could not involve accept- ance of Lincoln's wartime policies.

Holden never went quite as far as pledging he would take North Carolina out of the Confederacy and sue for peace separately, but that was the implication of the North Carolina peace movement. His two principal supporters, Jonathan Worth and John Pool, were old-time Whigs and unionists.[19] Worth, later governor, was a brother of Salt Commissioner John M. Worth. The two had opposed secession and then had sided with the South when the state seceded, but Jonathan never lost his ardent peace views, while John labored as effectively as anyone could to produce salt and in the later stages took the colonelcy of a regiment of Senior Reserves. John Pool had been defeated for gov- ernor by Ellis in 1860, then sat on the side lines of the war until he shifted counties and returned to the state senate in 1864 to introduce peace resolutions.

As the issue narrowed it became one of Holden and the peace party against Vance, who would fight the war to the finish but strive for honorable terms. Vance wrote to William A. Graham about his old Conservative party—that he would see it "blown into a thousand atoms and Holden and his understrappers in hell" before he would ever consent to a course which he thought would dishonor the state and the Confederacy.[20] Holden and his followers in turn demanded a state convention and notified the governor that if he did not call one he would have opposition for re-election. That was the signal for the final break. Holden wrote for his own newspaper an announcement of his candidacy for governor. He published it in a special issue on March 3, 1864, since he had again suspended regular publication in late

February, not to resume until May. Vance launched his campaign in what was looked upon as the heartland of disaffection, the hard core of the peace movement, Wilkesboro, on Washington's birthday.

Holden's party was for the best peace terms obtainable, as contrasted with what was called Vance's "last man and last dollar" stand. For Holden it was said: "If the people of North Carolina are for perpetual conscription, impressments, and seizures to keep up a perpetual, devastating, and exhausting war, let them vote for Governor Vance, for he is for 'fighting it out now'; but if they believe, from the bitter experience of the last three years, that the sword can never end it, and are now in favor of steps being taken by the States to urge negotiations by the general government for an honorable and speedy peace, they must vote for Mr. Holden."[21]

Holden actually insinuated much greater indifference to the Confederacy's welfare than this. In his January 19, 1864, issue of the *Standard* he declared North Carolina had a right to hold a convention "without being responsible for so doing to any power on earth," which would seem to flout President Davis and the Confederacy. He concluded: "North Carolina is true, and will be true to the Confederate government as it was formed, in its integrity and purity; but she would not be bound by a government which had lost its original character and had been perverted to despotic purposes against her own rights and liberties of her citizens." In his published announcement he disavowed that he had desired to seek the governorship, though anyone would have been warranted in judging that it had been his controlling impulse for a long time, and declared that Vance had left the Conservatives and gone over to President Davis. He said his own views were well known and would not be altered. "If elected I will do everything in my power to promote the interests, the honor, and glory of North Carolina, and to secure an honorable peace."

As in most campaigns, the issues were muddied by the overlapping areas of the two candidates and their platforms, but, as matters developed, Holden came to be looked on as the peace-now candidate and Vance the fight-it-out candidate. That was how the voter simplified it when he went to the polls.

Vance's platform was altogether sensible, and as brief as a forthright platform ought to be. He stood for:

"The supremacy of the civil over military law.

"A speedy repeal of the act suspending the writ of *habeas corpus.*

"A quiet submission to all laws, good or bad, while they remain on the statute books.

"No reconstruction or submission, but perpetual independence.

"An unbroken front to the common enemy; but timely and *repeated* negotiations for peace by the proper authorities.

"No separate State action through a convention, no counter revolution, no combined resistance to the government.

"Opposition to despotism in every form and the preservation of our republican institutions in all their purity."[22]

Vance himself was able to say long after the canvass, when he rose in the Senate to defend Jefferson Davis against a calumny, and to refuse what was offered as a compliment by General Sherman to the effect that he had been disaffected and anxious to separate his state from the Confederacy, that the one thing those who had gone down with the sinking Confederacy had retained was the knowledge that they had served their country faithfully, honestly and devotedly as they had understood it, a satisfaction which General Sherman was trying to take from him.

"It is well known," he said, "that I was drawn into secession unwillingly; it was also well known that in regard to many of the details of administration I was at variance with the authorities of the Confederate government; but it is equally well known, I hope, that, after my own honor was engaged and the honor of my native State, there never was an hour during all that unhappy time in which I did not give every energy of my body, mind, and soul to the success of the cause to which I had pledged my allegiance."[23]

Certainly the record of his administration attests to the truth of that statement. His policy has been aptly described as one of "fight the Yankees and fuss with the Confederacy."[24]

The 26th regiment "Johnny Reb" Band from Salem had been granted a leave and reached Raleigh to change cars on the late afternoon of February 1. Vance chanced to be in the crowd at the depot when someone pointed and said, "There is the band of the 26th." The governor was at once excited. "Where? Where?" he queried, then dashed off so impetuously it was feared he would run over the crowd. What he wanted was to make a date for the band to meet him in Wilkesboro for the launching of his campaign February 22. The bandsmen readily agreed, then went on to High Point to greet their families and friends who had conveyances that would take them to Salem, where they would relish nearly three weeks from army routine and sowbelly bacon.[25]

Vance selected Wilkes County for his campaign opening not because it had been one of his main supports in earlier elections, but more because Holden's pacific overtures could be met there head on. He could demonstrate that he did not fear to deal with the main issue of the campaign squarely. Meantime, on February 20, the eleven members of the 26th regiment band loaded themselves into two wagons at Salem to keep their appointment with their old commander. Some Salem residents who wanted to hear Zeb filled the vacant spaces and gaily over the country roads went the tooting musicians, to reach Yadkinville the first night, then journey on to Wilkesboro and arrive on the afternoon of February 21, after covering in the two days a distance of about fifty miles. Vance was already in town, with headquarters at Trainor's Hotel, where the musicians, delighted with the reunion, the first with the former colonel of the 26th since they had played at his inauguration, had supper, and as the crowd gathered that evening, gave a short concert and quickly won the toe-tapping accord of the taciturn people.[26]

On the following morning the band began at eleven o'clock its prelude to the momentous political occasion. The crowd that assembled during the next hour was estimated variously at between twelve hundred and two thousand persons, which was quite complimentary to Vance, considering that the county seat town was then small and remote. Their reaction was not all he had hoped. His two main points were that he had not despaired over the outcome of the war, and that if a convention took North Carolina out of the Confederacy her condition would be rendered infinitely more difficult instead of being improved. Band diarist Leinbach made an entry that day which pictures the meeting well:

"Of course the Governor's talk was strongly in advocacy of the war but it was evident that the feeling of his audience was not entirely in sympathy with him and it was an open question whether he had accomplished much good.

"The people of Wilkes county were somewhat independent in their ideas and did not take kindly to anything that interfered with their freedom of thought and action. They had no Negroes to fight for and did not believe in being shot at for the sake of somebody else.

"We saw something new under the sun, for us, in Wilkesboro, to-wit, viz.: women going into the grog shop to drink whiskey with the men."[27]

That night the band gave a concert in the courthouse at an admission fee of $2, and considered the affair highly successful, with a take of nearly $350. Vance wrote them an official pass extending their leave until February 27, but they did not make it back to camp in Virginia until March 6. Something of the carefree nature of the army in winter quarters was seen by the fact that nobody bothered about their over-staying their leave. Their stage had overturned en route from Salem to High Point and they missed their train. Vance took advantage of the mishap and had them give a concert in Raleigh, from which they netted $480. As they were badly in need of clothing, the governor gave them an order allowing them to buy new uniform material from the state quartermaster, but one of the boxes was lost or, they felt, more likely stolen, on the way through Weldon to Richmond.[28] Vance followed them to the army for his speaking tour of the North Carolina brigades later in the month.

Judged by the Wilkesboro test, Vance's campaign prospects did not seem auspicious. He is to be credited with taking a courageous stand for what did not appear at the outset to be the popular side of the issue. But he put on a bold front when he wrote to Editor Hale in Fayetteville, after talks at Salisbury and Statesville, saying he had a fine acceptance.

Doubt has been expressed that anyone not having Vance's superb stumping ability could have defeated Holden. The editor held up the seductive temptations of peace where Vance offered the onerous hard-ships of war. Battles had a treacherous allurement in 1861 but had become fields of blood, death, and horror in 1864. Offhand it would seem that Vance had only a slight chance of victory and the pollsters and prophets of his day were sanguine during the summer months over Holden's prospects.[29]

But the electorate was made of strong timber. Perhaps Vance's political sense was so delicately tuned that he understood the people better than others, for he concluded after two or three speeches that the convention idea was not catching on for Holden. On the other hand, reaction to his speeches was excessively enthusiastic in the Con-federate press. That could be the only interpretation placed on the Richmond *Dispatch's* comparison of him with Virginia's own Patrick Henry, and its statement that some of his passages "thrill the heart and make the blood burn like the notes of a clarion."[30] The Wilkesboro speech stirred so much interest in Virginia that the Richmond *Enquirer* sent a special correspondent to North Carolina to get further samplings of Vance's oratory.[31]

William M. Robbins of Trinity in Randolph County, a member of the 4th Alabama regiment throughout the war, having gone to Eufaula in that state to practice law, was at his old home in North Carolina, after taking a wound in the Wilderness, when Vance came to nearby High Point for a campaign speech in the summer of 1864. Robbins, a veteran of Law's Brigade and the desperate assault on Little Round Top at Gettysburg, was in later years a Congressman and long the Southern Commissioner on the Gettysburg Battle Field Commission. He had never seen Vance but on that day at High Point he gained a lasting impression.

"His speech . . . won my admiration not only for its sparkling wit and rare humor, but still more by the zeal and vigor with which he advocated the strenuous support of the cause of the South in the great sectional conflict. This impressed and pleased me the more when I learned, as I did that day, that he had not originally favored the policy of secession, but when North Carolina cast her lot with her sister Southern States, he had gone with her, heart and soul. . . . His course in that matter was an index to his character and career. . . . Above all things, he was a North Carolinian, devoted to the welfare and glory of the State, and proud of her, as he was her pride."[32]

Vance told in later years about some of the distillations made, during the war, not from restricted grain, but from potatoes, turnips, sorghum cane, or a host of other nutritive ingredients, some of it called "new dip" and some which on the shortest notice "could furnish its victims with the panoramic view of a full menagerie." Then he spoke of a brandy made from native persimmons and said that during the campaign he made a speech under the refreshment of this fluid, which had some good traits, "one of which was that it partook of the highly astringent qualities of the fruit." His friends pronounced this the best speech of his life because the astringent drink had "tended to shut me up—and I said less than usual!" He won laughter and applause as he recalled the incident by saying, "Congress could not do wiser than to purchase a quantity of that beverage for its own use."[33]

Most of his campaign speeches ran an hour and a half to two hours. That was not lengthy for the era, when people who came to the rallies had time to listen all afternoon. The only requirement was that the speaker be entertaining.

Vance went into the stumping campaign with his usual enthusiasm. Even under the pall cast by the war and the constant inpouring of the casualty lists, he charmed his audiences with his anecdotes and good humor. Crowds followed him at times from one town to another. For an organ he had to bring about the establishment of his own newspaper in Raleigh, the *Conservative*, which showed he had not surrendered his party's name. Could Vance have been hurt deeply by Holden's defection? He wrote to Editor Hale that "the man who has been deepest in my confidence and whom my friends have persisted in apologizing for, has at length showed his purpose." But that seemed more a sigh of relief than a cry of anguish. Some feared the governor was too sanguine—"he is exuberant in confidence of his own strength" —and Holden appeared pleased with his own progress, for in June he was writing that his intelligence was cheering and, amazing as it might sound, "I feel sure of a decided majority in the army."[34]

Vance was offering a telling argument, to this effect: "Secession from the Confederacy will involve us in a new war, a bloodier conflict than that which we now deplore. So soon as you announce to the world that you are a sovereign and independent nation, as a matter of course the Confederate government has a right to declare war against you, and President Davis will make the whole State a field of battle and blood. Old Abe would send his troops here also, because we would no longer be neutral, and so, if you will pardon the expression, we would catch the devil on all sides."[35]

And the sober reaction of the public seemed contained in a letter signed "Junius," touching the same point: "For North Carolina to secede from the Confederacy, would be to erect a foreign state in the very heart of the Confederacy—and *imperium* in *imperio*. No argument is necessary to show how we would be crushed between the upper and nether millstone. To suppose that North Carolina could maintain her sovereignty under the circumstances is supremely preposterous, and it is equally so to suppose that she could in any way do anything toward effecting an honorable peace. There is such a thing as jumping out of the frying pan into the fire."[36]

The voters reached that conclusion. When the army vote came in from the polling in the regiments, held two weeks prior to the general election, Holden was due for a rude surprise. Vance received 13,209 to Holden's 1,824. The civilian vote was equally devastating. Vance received 44,856 to Holden's 12,647. Holden carried only two counties, Johnston and Randolph. Vance, with a total vote of 58,065 to Holden's 14,471, won by better than four to one. The peace movement had been strong in type in the newspaper columns, but frail in voting strength at the polls.

About all Vance said was, "My competitor, a bold and popular demagogue, made the issue distinctly of peace on terms less than independence and I have beaten him worse than any man was ever beaten in North Carolina." And Charles Manly, Whig governor of North Carolina from 1848 to 1850, wrote to President Swain at the university, agreeing that "Vance is a character." He thought the executive from Buncombe equaled the county's lofty peaks.[37]

Armed with a resounding popular mandate, Vance threw himself intensively into the war effort, first along lines that had no historical precedent in the United States. He conceived that because of the composition of the Confederacy, being a grouping of sovereign states cast abruptly into war before there had been any accumulation of precedents or stabilization of institutions, impetus could be given to the war effort by joint action of the governors. To open the way for it he proposed a meeting of all the governors of the Confederate States east of the Mississippi.

Had the Confederacy possessed a virile and inspirational chief executive who could have aroused the people emotionally and spiritually and commanded the warm attachment of state officials all the way down the line, Vance likely never would have thought of summoning the governors into conclave. He looked on the meeting not as an evidence of fragmentation in the Confederacy, but more as a process of consolidation, and as such it was accepted by those who approved it. Nevertheless, he recognized he was moving into an area where his purposes might become suspect, and was willing to risk censure or encounter misrepresentation provided he could accomplish benefits for the Southern cause.

Vance's purpose is best understood from the letters he wrote on September 23, 1864, to the governors of Virginia, South Carolina, Georgia, Florida, Alabama, Mississippi, and Tennessee. The letter to Governor Milledge Luke Bonham of South Carolina—the others being of the same tenor—pointed out that the legislatures of states would soon be assembling and that such steps should be taken by them "as the perillous and straightened condition of the country demands." His main object was to have the states pursue joint action to get more soldiers into the ranks.

"The great evil of desertion must be broken up, if possible," he wrote; "provisions must be made to feed the poor and the feeble and desponding must be encouraged and inspired with hope; and beyond all else, *men must be sent to the armies of Gens. Lee and Hood. To* find where and how to get these men is the great object of inquiry."

Vance thought that no doubt large numbers of eligible men were in the various civilian departments of the Confederate government, but to put them into military service and fill their places with noncombatants would be the responsibility of the central authorities. He felt that many engaged in the civil departments of the states might be spared. He appeared to believe that recruits were being withheld for emotional or jurisdictional reasons. That was suggested by his statement:

"And there is yet a large class of state officers in all the states withheld from service, not only on account of the necessity for them in administering the governments, but also because the principle of state sovereignty rendered it improper to allow the Confederate Government to conscript them. This latter class I suppose to be quite numerous in all the States; and could there be a way prescribed to put, at least, a portion of them into service, without injuring the efficiency of the State Governments, and without infringing on the rights of the States and their dignity as sovereigns, they could constitute quite a material reinforcement to our hard pressed armies."

Then the North Carolina executive clinched his point by adding: "It seems desirable . . . that action on this and all kindred matters should be uniform, or as nearly so as possible. It would avoid much discontent for every man to know that he was required to do only that which everyone else has to do, and that the burthens of the war are fairly distributed.

"In order to obtain this uniformity as well as to consult on any other matter of public concern which might present itself, I beg leave respectfully to suggest a meeting of all Southern Executives this side of the Mississippi at some point such as Augusta, Georgia, during the coming month of October, when and where some general plan of action might be agreed upon for the relief of the country, and recommended to our several legislatures."[38]

Vance was here stepping naturally into a role of leadership, though he was the youngest of the Southern governors. Was he, in effect, bypassing President Davis and the Confederate Congress in Richmond and arranging direct action between the state executives and their legislatures for the adoption of common practices and laws? There is no doubt that he was, but there was some justification in the fact that he was moving into an area that was being neglected and where understanding and uniform measures were badly needed. Perhaps a more dominant and robust President of the Confederacy than Mr. Davis would have summoned the governors of the states to meet with him in Richmond from time to time, to counsel with him, tell him of their problems, gain his views, and arrive at some pattern for legislative action in the states. What Vance was striving for was a common approach, a regularity and equality of methods which had been lacking under the auspices of the central government.

The response was gratifying. Governor William "Extra Billy" Smith of Virginia said that while such a meeting "may give rise to much misrepresentation, I can see no solid objection to it, but can well see, that great good may result from it." He suggested Columbia, South Carolina, instead of Augusta, and favored an early date because he would convene the Virginia legislature on the first Monday in November, if not earlier. Bonham in his reply understood the purpose as one of "filling the ranks of our army," and gave the meeting his entire approval, with Augusta being a suitable place. Governor Brown of Georgia, while agreeing wholeheartedly, took exception to Vance's remarks about state officers, saying they were not applicable to Georgia "where every officer civil and military who can possibly be spared and keep the state government in existence, is and for months past has been in military service. . . ." He suggested a meeting date of October 17.[39]

Vance had written a letter to Robert L. Caruthers, who had been elected governor of Tennessee but had never been able to take office in Nashville because of the Federal occupation. The letter was sent in care of Brown, who sent it in turn to the care of Brigadier General Marcus J. Wright, commanding the District of Atlanta with headquarters at Macon, but Caruthers apparently did not receive his letter and did not attend.

The fact that the governors met was of more significance perhaps than the accomplishments of the session. This was the first occasion under the American system of an effort at joint state action by the governors meeting in person, and to Vance goes the credit for having initiated it. The governors passed resolutions which Bonham, who seemed to have been the recorder of the proceedings, forwarded to Secretary of the Treasury Trenholm in Richmond, who in turn placed them before President Davis. The main one—and it is sometimes mistakenly believed that the conference was called merely to deal with blockade-running—respected the Confederate government's claim to a heavy share of the cargo space on state-chartered blockade-runners. As

Bonham explained it, the governors who assembled believed they could help the government in procuring needed articles if they were allowed the cargoes in chartered vessels, as well as in those owned by a state outright, the latter class being exempt by law. He tried to get across the point that the governors felt the states in their importations would be auxiliaries of the central government and did not see that the common object would be impeded, but instead, that it would be promoted by chartering.

The governors adopted resolutions strongly supporting the Confederacy in its war efforts. "The effect," observed Trenholm, in accepting them, "will be [to] . . . convince the enemy that the struggle can be terminated only by the recognition of our independence." The meeting at least served the purpose of showing that the states presented a common front.[40]

Trenholm did nothing about amending the regulations covering blockade-running but merely sent a copy of those proclaimed by the President and already in effect. Vance did his share by trying to cut down exemptions, as the meeting suggested, but his and the other states were all but stripped bare. Had the meeting come earlier in the war it might have been more fruitful and have led to other meetings of more consequence. Occurring at a time when Lee was besieged in Petersburg, Mobile had fallen, and Hood, after losing Atlanta, was concentrating in Alabama while Sherman prepared for his march through Georgia, little could be expected toward saving the Confederacy. Vance was merely doing what he could to keep the sinking ship afloat. It did influence the messages to the legislatures, but at this late date these appeals were of little moment.

Apart from the fact that this was the first meeting of a group of governors to deal with problems of mutual concern, it was significant because of a bit of phraseology to come out of it in the form of one of Zeb Vance's quick remarks. Wade Hampton liked to tell the story in later years of how Vance, who during the lean times after the war supported himself and family by making lectures over the country, was traveling in the West, when he met a man "of convivial habits." After talking of various things, the stranger turned to Vance and said, "As the Governor of North Carolina said to the Governor of South Carolina . . ."

He did not know he was addressing the author of the famous saying of old soldier Vance to old soldier Bonham, "It's a long time between drinks."[41]

☆☆☆☆☆☆☆☆☆☆☆☆☆☆☆☆☆☆

## Chapter Twenty-Four

## Grinding Up the Seed Corn

☆☆☆☆☆☆☆☆☆☆☆☆☆☆☆☆☆☆

War in late 1864 and early 1865 narrowed to its ultimate stages for North Carolina, to become a battle fought by the stalwarts—men who would rather die than submit, many of them veterans returned to the ranks after wounds on other fields—and by the boys.

The boys were mostly members of the Junior Reserves, one of the most gallant bands in the history of the state, who at the battles of Averasboro and Bentonville formed the largest brigade in the skeleton armies with which Generals William H. Hardee and Joseph E. Johnston made the last stand of the war in the east, and every member in the ranks was *under eighteen years old*.

Nearly every line officer was under eighteen. They were termed by Vance, President Davis, and others "the seed corn of the Confederacy," and in the desperation of the closing months of the grueling struggle this seed for future generations was tossed recklessly and despairingly over the parched, unproductive battlefields of North Carolina and Virginia.

Vance recruited and organized the Junior Reserves, whose story has never been adequately written, though it compares favorably with that of the gallant and justly heralded service of the Virginia Military Institute cadets at New Market. At Bentonville the Reserves had ten times the strength of the cadets at New Market. Under the law, the

Junior Reserves were restricted to service within their own state, but North Carolina's went to Virginia and fought where Robert Hoke could find good fighting.[1]

Who were Zeb Vance's Junior Reserves? William Franklin Elkins, of Cabarrus County, after the war a resident of Plainview, Texas, told how as a lad he had seen the Cabarrus Guards march off Sunday morning, April 21, 1861, wearing their handsome, dark blue dress coats and light blue pants, with white belt and trimmings and caps topped with red, white, and blue plumes. The resplendent uniform was the most attractive he had ever seen. Then Cabarrus had sent her company of "Black Boys," the name a heritage from pre-Revolutionary War days. When the royal governor, Lord Tryon, ran short of powder and sent to Charleston for a supply, some young patriots blackened their faces to disguise themselves as Negro slaves and so avoid suspicion. They put fuses to the powder wagons and blew them up. The descendants of these young patriots preserved the name when the company was revived after the Revolution and when war began among the states the "Black Boys" were well armed and drilled according to Hardee's tactics. Elkins knew soldiering by observation.

"When our beloved Governor, Zeb B. Vance, saw fit," he said, "he called us boys, seventeen years old, to report to our respective county sites and then to Raleigh, the capital, where the Governor ordered us to Camp Holmes, and assigned us to quarters." As Elkins continued the story, Vance put them under drillmasters, who taught the school of the soldier. Soon "guns were issued to fit our size." They apparently were sawed-off rifles such as Colonel Henry Kyd Douglas had made especially for squat little Wesley Culp of the Stonewall Brigade, which he was carrying when he fell while fighting for the South on his father's farm and his own birthplace on Culp's Hill near Gettysburg. Zeb Vance's juniors drilled morning and evening, then went off to the war, where the seed corn would become fuel in the battle's blast.[2]

Who were Zeb's Junior Reserves? Charles Dickerson Dowd, a boy of sixteen, volunteered, became captain of Company B, 6th battalion, 70th regiment of the seed corn, and fought at Bentonville. He had distinguished forebears. He was a grandson of Cornelius Dowd of the Constitutional Committee which admitted North Carolina into the Union, and a great-grandson of Brigadier General Richard Montgomery who fell in the attack on Quebec. A bit of Americana might be seen in one of his obituary notices fifty-five years later. "Not only in the Confederate army did Captain Dowd serve his country with honor, but during the twelve years of infamous reconstruction days, as a Klansman, he served his country and section with no less fidelity."[3]

Walter Clark, who became chief justice of the state, enlisted as a Junior Reservist. He recalled that when the defeated army passed through Raleigh after Bentonville, three days after Lee had surrendered at Appomattox, they knew that the end must be near but were determined to stay in the ranks until the finish. Most of his companions had been thirteen years old when the war began at Fort Sumter. "They were now four years older and they were veterans. They had driven back the gunboats at Fort Branch on Christmas Day, 1864. They had gone to Belfield, Virginia, to check Warren's corps in its advance on Weldon. Attached to Hoke's division, the heroes of so many battlefields, they had crossed South West creek below Kinston under fire and aided in the capture of 2,500 Federal prisoners."[4]

Zeb Vance's spirit was one of the sparks that fired these lads with the ardor that withstood the long marches, scant rations, and ordeal of the nearly hopeless battlefield. Other states had young soldiers. In Arkansas, when the war broke, the boys from St. John's College at Little Rock, ranging from fourteen to nineteen years, enlisted almost in a body in the celebrated 1st Arkansas, and the professors became the officers. Chance placed them under Stonewall Jackson at First Manassas. When Lee retired from Gettysburg, another group of lads, Parker's Boy Battery, made up of boys from Georgia and Maryland schools, covered the retreat and lingered long on the field after the infantry had departed. Boys were scattered heavily through the ranks of both armies; many were seasoned veterans while still in their teens.[5]

But probably of all the boy brigades, the one raised by Zeb Vance was the most formidable. Virtually all the senior officers had been wounded earlier. Colonel Charles W. Broadfoot of Fayetteville later became a leader of the bar and trustee of the state university, and with Vance labored to revive the school when it lapsed in the days of poverty and indolent government of the reconstruction. John W. Hinsdale, another colonel, distinguished as a sophomore for declaiming, went to war in 1862 without his diploma, but he got it nearly half a century later, in 1911, when the scrolls were awarded to all surviving members of the classes from 1862 to 1868 who had missed them in the war. He too became one of the state's leading lawyers.[6]

Any excess of democracy which may have existed in North Carolina because of Vance's preservation of the writ of *habeas corpus* and his careful scrutiny of all Confederate enactments did not prevent the sixteen-year-old boys from rushing to the colors when he issued the call, and perhaps they would not have responded with such eagerness to a despotism.

The denouement of the Confederacy came rapidly. North Carolina, which had been spared invasion except in the eastern and western counties, found her defenses failing and great armies moving in from the south and east and cavalry raiders from the west. The great tragedy for the state and the Confederacy was the loss of Fort Fisher, long inevitable but no less a shock when it came. The greatest military engagement on North Carolina soil was at the battle of Bentonville, a futile last-stand affair. The loss of that field opened Raleigh to capture by General Sherman.

Vance considered it apparent to every intelligent observer as 1865 dawned that the Confederacy was doomed. Lee was holding Richmond with what he described as "a mere skirmish line." In twenty miles of trenches, Grant faced him with 180,000 men. Savannah had fallen and while the South still held Wilmington and Charleston, their loss was inevitable. Sherman had marched through Georgia to Savannah. "It had been demonstrated not only that the Confederate military forces in the Southwest were unable to stay him," said Vance, "but that no hostility was to be expected from the despairing people whose homes he ravaged."

Sherman with 75,000 troops was preparing for the "home-stretch toward Richmond," driving the scattered Confederate detachments— amounting to not more than 22,000—before him. Enemy cavalry overran the interior of the Confederacy. "Nowhere," Vance continued, "was there a gleam of hope; nowhere had there come to us any inspiriting success. Everything spoke of misfortune and failure." The motive of the more intelligent people was that energetic action would secure better terms than a premature and abject surrender and such feeling he found predominant in North Carolina as Sherman's army began its northward movement on February 1.[7]

Vance had expected Sherman to enter North Carolina by the old route used by Lord Cornwallis and take Charlotte. Vance judged that the winter mud in the hill country, plus the fact that "he did not care to trust himself to such combinations of Confederates as might cross his path so far in the interior," caused Sherman to leave the Cornwallis route at Winnsboro, South Carolina, turn to the right, cross the Catawba and Great Pee Dee and march in two divisions, for Fayetteville. Vance was most critical of the conduct of Sherman's army and the "stragglers and desperadoes following in its wake." He was severe in his castigation of the Federal commander:

"When a general organizes a corps of thieves and plunderers as a part of his invading army, and licenses beforehand their outrages, he and all who countenance, aid or abet, invite the execration of mankind. This peculiar arm of the military service, it is charged and believed, was instituted by General Sherman in his invasion of the Southern States. Certain it is that the operations of his 'Bummer Corps' were as regular and unrebuked, if not as much commended for efficiency, as any other division of his army, and their atrocities were often justified or excused on the ground that 'such is war.' "[8]

Vance in his denunciation of Sherman was not able to look ahead to wars in which supposedly enlightened nations would make civilians their main target, devastate entire cities to break down morale and the will to resist, and degenerate warfare to a barbarity that would have appalled the horde of Genghis Khan.

Vance cited Sherman's report in verification of his charge and could not resist the temptation, nor could his friend Cornelia Phillips Spencer, who wrote under his auspices, of contrasting the gentler invasion of Cornwallis in 1781 with that of the Federal commander in 1865. Mrs. Spencer, daughter of Vance's old professor, distinguished for her authorship and called by the governor "the greatest woman North Carolina ever produced," cited Cornwallis's order from Beattie's Ford, January 28, 1781: "It is needless to point out to the officers the necessity of preserving the strictest discipline, and of preventing the oppressed people from suffering violence at the hands from whom they are taught to look for protection," and to his later order condemning as an outrage and "disgrace to the army" the firing of several houses.[9]

Vance, continuing his comparisons and distinctions, recalled how some Pennsylvania German farmers had come to Longstreet during the Gettysburg campaign to complain "of the outrage which some of his ferocious rebels had committed upon them, *by milking their cows.*"[10]

In contrast, he told how four citizens of Fayetteville were hung up by their necks until nearly dead to force them to reveal where they had hidden valuables and one of them was shot dead. Vance gave a blow-by-blow description of Sherman's property destruction in Fayetteville. A touch of sadness for him was the burning of the Fayetteville *Observer* office, the newspaper always cordial to him. The Hale family which had supported him loyally thus passed out of the Fayetteville publishing field.

Let Vance sum up his opinion about the two leading invaders of North Carolina history, Cornwallis and Sherman: "The whole policy and conduct of the British commander was such as to indicate unmistakably that he did not consider the burning of private houses, the stealing of private property, and the outraging of helpless, private citizens as *War,* but as robbery and arson. I venture to say that up to the period when that great march [Sherman's] taught us the contrary, no humane general or civilized people in Christendom believed that 'such was war.' Has civilization gone backward since Lord Cornwallis' day? Have arson and vulgar theft been ennobled into heroic virtues? If so, when and by whom? Has the art of discovering a poor man's hidden treasure by fraud or torture been elevated into strategy which wins a campaign? If so, when and by whom?

"No, sir, it will not do to slur over these things by a vague reference to the inevitable cruelties of war. . . . Truth like charity never faileth." He went on to contrast Sherman's march through the Carolinas and Georgia with Lee's invasion of Pennsylvania and the striking forbearance of Lee's order commanding the respect of private property. He cited witnesses of the good conduct of Lee's army, down to the instance reported by a correspondent of the London *Times* of how he saw with his own eyes General Lee and one of his surgeons stopping to repair damage to a farmer's fence.[11]

Vance's ideas of warfare were obtained from his earlier reading of Chancellor Kent, one of the idols of his erudite Professor Swain at Chapel Hill. In dealing with Sherman and Lee, he cited Kent's commentary on plunder and depredations on private property. Kent said such conduct had been condemned by the wise and virtuous in all ages and usually was severely punished by "commanders of disciplined troops who had studied war as a science, and are animated by a sense of duty or love of fame." Kent said, as Vance cited him, that when a commander went beyond these limits wantonly, and seized private property or destroyed dwellings or public buildings for civil use, when it was not clearly indispensable for the purposes of war, he was sure "to be held up to the general scorn and detestation of the world." Vance mentioned also that Kent was studied by Sherman at West Point. He cited Major General Henry W. Halleck in similar vein on the usage respecting private property, and brought out much other evidence, like a lawyer presenting his case, capping it with similar or more severe quotations from the code prepared by the government to control the armies of the United States.

Many cases have been made out in condemnation and defense of Sherman, but it is not likely there was ever a more telling and annotated arraignment than Vance's, supported as it was by references to eminent writers on public law—Woolsey, Vattel, Grotiers, Puffendorf, Polson, Jomini, and back to the humane injuctions of Caliph Abubekr, one of the "cruel and bloodthirsty" followers of Mahomet, and to the ancient Xenophon's comments about the forbearance of his hero Cyrus.[12]

The propriety of Sherman's military methods will always be debated, as will be, perhaps, the question of their efficacy in the broad picture of war. They kept alive pockets of bitterness in three states for more than a century. If they hastened the end of active war, they delayed the return of true cordiality. The British Field Marshal Montgomery of World War II appeared to doubt their military value when he compared Sherman's activities to Sir Redvers Henry Buller's, commander of the British forces in South Africa, in burning the homes of the Boers, for which the Boer women, left homeless, never forgave the British.[13] Sherman probably could have won his campaigns as easily by fighting the weakened Confederate armies without wanton devastation of the country or, as Vance charged, the slaughter of animals unneeded for food, and without making his name perhaps permanently abhorred, especially by the women in a large area of the country, as Buller's was with the Boers. The case made out that Sherman's methods were necessary to the winning of the war was not impressive as Vance viewed it.

Each student of the war is entitled to his own view about Sherman, but in a study of Zeb Vance it is necessary to report that in Vance's opinion he was a despoiler where there was no need to despoil and one who came very close to being a monster. Sherman took the role of conqueror and scourge and not a deliverer, and students of military methods will no doubt note that he triumphed where Cornwallis failed, but whether Sherman's war on civilians was a justifiable military recourse (and it has been ratified by later commanders where Lee's concept of war confined to hostile armies has fallen by the wayside) will be argued as long as the Civil War is analyzed and discussed.

Despite the ardor of the young and the steadfastness of the stalwarts,

Vance could clearly discern in late 1864 an ebbing of public enthusiasm for the war. This ardor, he said, gave the Southern cause at the outset a "delusive victory, sustained it at the flood-tide, and strove fiercely to maintain it against the ebb." He spoke fondly in later recollections of "the noble exaltation of the heroic spirit which strives to overcome fate itself, and smiles defiance at misfortune," but he pictured "the final dying away of hope and the incoming of despair; the demoralization of even good and brave men; the humiliation of heart-broken women; the reckless disregard which follows when all law, civil and military is withdrawn."

Bursting into one of his oratorical flights as he described the coming of the end, he continued: "In kaleidoscopic array each phase swept across the stage, as storm-clouds are driven across the sky, culminating in that moral darkness of men ungoverned by law or motive, and women acting without hope. All these things, and more, I witnessed among my own people in those unhappy times; from the day when the first company of volunteers went forth amid the plaudits of the people, as to a festival, down to that dark hour when I saw the last regiment of beardless boys, the 'seed corn' of our hopes, pass through the unprotected capital of our State."[14]

A disturbing event, dwarfed by larger crises, was the capture of his brother, Brigadier General Robert B. Vance. The general made a foray into Tennessee in the winter of 1863-64 but was unsuccessful, even negligent, in his retirement. The feat of crossing the Great Smoky Mountains in late December and January was little short of sensational considering that General Vance used a "so-called wagon road" which was a difficult trail Colonel Thomas and his Indian legion had made across what is now called Collins Gap. The achievement was in the fact that Vance took a section of artillery with him; he had to dismount the guns and could not even use skids, but dragged them naked over the stones. Thomas's Legion later came into ill-favor in Richmond and Secretary Seddon wrote to Governor Vance that it was a refuge for deserters, that Thomas was disobedient, and that he always kept out of the way when the enemy advanced. But at the turn of the year he was co-operating with General Vance, who sent him to Gatlinburg while Vance was going on to Seviersville and to the capture of a train of eighty Federal wagons.

En route toward Newport, Vance halted at Crosby Creek Meeting House for dinner, but failed to put out pickets. As he was eating, a troop of Northern cavalry suddenly swooped down and took him and a number of others prisoners. He did not get back to western North Carolina until after the war, but he did not seem to encounter blame except triflingly in western North Carolina history. Such control as the Confederacy had exerted in the mountains lessened, and except for some of the towns, the region was at the mercy of wandering bands. After Longstreet returned from East Tennessee to Lee's army the area was exposed to Federal invasion, but apparently was not regarded as of sufficient military value for a major effort until the Federal cavalry broke in during the last stages of the war.[15]

Governor Vance, always disturbed about it, wrote to Secretary Seddon in mid-July 1864, saying that the western border of the state greatly needed protection but he had no arms for the militia. He had loaned all his guns to the Confederate government and requested urgently that one or two thousand stands be returned.[16] By late October the situation had become even more aggravated. He wrote to General John C. Breckinridge, commanding the Department of Southwest Virginia, October 29: "The murder of prisoners and non combatants in cold blood has I learn become quite common and in fact almost every other horror incident to brutal and unrestrained soldiery." Blaming Tories and renegades, he suggested that Breckinridge communicate with the Federal commander of East Tennessee "to ascertain if a check cannot be given to the passions of men whose thirst for murder and robbery disgraces the name of soldiers."[17]

In the summer of 1864, when General Jubal Early was defeated in the Shenandoah Valley by Sheridan, Vance seemed almost to despair of the Confederacy's fate, to his old and intimate friend President Swain at Chapel Hill.

Early had returned from his summer raid on Washington laden with spoils, in high confidence, but the Federals had collected a formidable army that pushed him out of Winchester and defeated him at Fisher's Hill, then pressed him farther to the fatal battlefield of Cedar Creek. He had fairly won there, but failed to keep his army in hand, and lost disastrously to Sheridan's counterattack.

At Winchester on September 19, 1864, the South suffered an irreparable loss when Major General Robert E. Rodes was mortally wounded. His division was composed largely of North Carolina troops. Ramseur, now a major general, whose division, like that of Rodes, included two North Carolina brigades, was deeply affected by the death of his companion under whom he had served long as a brigade commander, and whenever he spoke of him tears came into his eyes. Soon Ramseur, whom Vance admired and in whose first promotion he had played a conspicuous part, fell at Cedar Creek. James M. Garnett, division ordnance officer, made an entry in his diary—"In the evening I rode over to division Headquarters and witnessed dress parade, the band playing a dirge to Major Generals Rodes and Ramseur."[18] As after the death of Jackson, the Southern army would never be itself again after the loss of Ramseur and Rodes.

Vance and all North Carolina mourned the loss of Ramseur. One of the tributes came from Lieutenant, later Judge, Thomas R. Roulhac, the historian of Ramseur's old 49th North Carolina regiment, which always bore the imprint of its brilliant young leader: "North Carolina, whose soil has been made sacred by the ashes of so many great and strong men, her jurists, her statesmen, her magistrates, her teachers, her ministers and priests, her soldiers and her patriots, holds within her bosom the dust of no nobler or more perfect man than that of Stephen Dodson Ramseur."[19]

Nothing that had happened during the war seemed to distress Vance more than this Shenandoah Valley campaign, as it did Fitzhugh Lee, who wrote after Sheridan had passed through: "The beautiful Valley of Virginia was a barren waste, and from the mountain's breast was reflected the light of two thousand burning barns, seventy mills filled with wheat and farming utensils, while in front of the victorious army were driven thousands of head of stock."[20]

Sheridan had a remark better remembered than Lee's, that "A crow flying across the Valley now would need to carry its rations."[21]

After the loss of Winchester and General Rodes, but well before the death of Ramseur, Vance, who was unusually discerning about the military campaigns and their significance, was writing: "I never before have been so gloomy about the condition of affairs. Early's defeat in the valley I consider as the turning point of this campaign; and, confidentially, I fear it seals the fate of Richmond, though not immediately. It will require our utmost exertions to retain our footing in Virginia till '65 comes in." Even before it happened on November 8, 1864, he could see that Lincoln was defeating McClellan for the presidency. As he stated it: "McClellan's defeat is placed among the facts, and abolition is rampant for four years more." He thought the Confederate Army in Georgia was utterly demoralized, and: "By the time President Davis, who has gone there, displays again his obstinacy in defying public sentiment, and his ignorance of men in the change of commanders, its ruin will be complete."[22]

His words were prophetic, because Hood, who replaced Johnston, did complete the ruin of the army around Atlanta and at Nashville.

Vance disclosed in this letter his penetrating ability to examine a question, the fruit of his courtroom experience. Perhaps there has never been a clearer or more detached view of the reasons for the decline of the South, and, if one would carry the thinking a bit further, of how the Southern revolution differed in an important aspect from that of the colonies against the mother country in 1776.

"The signs which discourage me," Governor Vance wrote, "more than aught else are the utter demoralization of the people. With a base of communication five hundred miles in Sherman's rear, through our own country, not a bridge has been burned, not a car thrown from its track, nor a man shot by the people whose country he has desolated. They seem everywhere to submit when our armies are withdrawn. What does this show, my dear sir? It shows what I have always believed, that *the great popular heart* is not now, and never has been in this war. It was a revolution of the *Politicians,* not the *People;* and was fought at first by the natural enthusiasm of our young men, and has been kept going by State and sectional pride, assisted by that bitterness of feeling produced by the cruelties and brutalities of the enemy.

"Still, I am not out of heart, for, as you know, I am of a buoyant and hopeful temperament. Things may come round yet. General Lee is *a great man,* and has the remnant of the best army on earth, bleeding, torn, and overpowered though it be. Saturday night may yet come to all our troubles, and be followed by the blessed hours of rest. God grant it!"[23]

He groped for ways to help the cause which looked to him for assistance and declared he would "fain be doing." Then he ended with a note of personal vindication: "Duty calls me now to stand by the new union, 'to the last gasp with truth and loyalty.' This is my consolation. The beginning was bad: I had no hand in it. Should the end be bad, I shall, with God's help, be equally blameless."

As the year 1864 passed, Fort Fisher was subjected to two attacks in less than a month, after the first of which, abortive, Vance was on hand. The second, larger and more determined, was successful, and the guardian of the Cape Fear River and Wilmington, and of Southern commerce with the rest of the world, fell, and as it went down its defender, General Whiting, was mortally wounded.

Except for occasional and superficial tiffs, Whiting and Vance had been compatible during the years of their close association, and each, being learned above most of their contemporaries, enjoyed the intellectual play of the other. One of Whiting's admirers, writing in 1896, speculated that even then his record at West Point had not been matched, while the view was held by others that President Davis had sent him to a post remote from the fighting through failure to appreciate his high qualities, much as he had failed to appreciate Forrest's. When assigned temporarily under Beauregard, Whiting scrupulously avoided his enemy, liquor, which was present with him as the blockade-runners came in, and he honored his promise to Beauregard in that respect, but he was returned to Fort Fisher to defend it and die for it. He earned the tribute: "Few men have been born into the world with such astonishing endowments of body and mind. His personal masculine beauty was a splendid shrine for one of the most brilliant, comprehensive, and versatile intellects."

The story was told that he excelled at everything at West Point and elsewhere, even down to playing marbles.[24]

Fort Fisher, at the mouth of the Cape Fear, the last port the Confederacy possessed, came under attack at the Christmas season, 1864. A naval force commanded by Rear Admiral David Porter and an army under Major General Benjamin Butler began a joint operation to complete the Federal encirclement of the South.

Month after month the fort's garrison had lived in expectancy of attack, and on December 23 a fleet of fifty warships appeared. The bombardment was severe and kept the garrison of about a thousand men—half of whom were a battalion of boys of the Junior Reserves—behind the ramparts or in the bombproofs; but the gun crews replied and Private Kit Bland of the 36th North Carolina regiment made himself one of the heroes of the war when the Confederate flag was shot away, and dangled from its high staff above the fort. Amid the fearful bombardment from the ships, Bland, like Sergeant Jasper of the Revolutionary War, climbed the staff and refastened the flag, only to see it struck by another shot. Again he shinned his way up the pole and with his necktie fastened the flag so securely that it remained aloft through the intense bombardment of the next two days.

Butler's main hope rested in a powder ship with which he thought he could breach or level the sand ramparts and open the fort to assault. He loaded the ship *Louisiana* with 250 tons of powder—an immense charge for that day—and sent her under cover of darkness to within two hundred yards of the bulwarks. As the matches were touched at midnight the main Federal fleet moved offshore. The sky was lighted and the waters seemed to shake, but the scheme was a failure and about the only result was, as a droll Confederate soldier expressed it, "It pretty nigh waked up everybody in the fort."[25]

When the Federal fleet came back the next morning the fort looked unscathed. Another mighty bombardment was unloosened and though it appeared that nothing could withstand such a storm of shot and shell, the sand ramparts suffered little damage. On Christmas Day Butler landed most of his army and an assault column under Major General Godfrey Weitzel approached, but the fort looked too formidable and after consultation he and Butler decided against an infantry attack. They re-embarked the troops that day, and the next morning the transports steamed back to Hampton Roads and the warships to Beaufort to prepare for a larger expedition. Some of the junior officers were humiliated, believing the fort was ripe for picking.[26]

When Vance heard from General Braxton Bragg, who now commanded at Wilmington, that the fort was under attack, he issued an appeal for recruits, then hastened to Wilmington, accompanied by Surgeon General Warren. They learned of the powder ship explosion, being told it sounded in Wilmington like the "report from a pack of firecrackers." Accompanied down the river by courageous members of the Ladies Relief Society, they reached the fort on the day the last of the enemy troops departed. The fort defenders needed few ministrations, and about all Vance could do was to congratulate General Whiting and Colonel Lamb and "hurrah with the victorious garrison."[27]

When the Federals returned January 12, 1865, the fleet was larger and still under Porter, but the army, also augmented, was commanded by a better combat general, Alfred H. Terry, and three days later the fort was in Federal hands. Bragg's little army moved down from Wilmington, but Terry had thrown his forces across the peninsula between the Cape Fear River and the ocean and entrenched. Bragg and General Hoke, after reconnoitering, found that an assault against the vastly superior Federal force would be futile. Still, they had not expected the fort to fall so quickly. Easily holding off Bragg and Hoke from his heavily manned entrenched line, Terry assaulted the fort in different places. He effected an ingress on the river side and fought a bloody combat from one traverse to another until Whiting was mortally wounded, Colonel Lamb severely wounded, and the leaderless garrison captured. Bragg, a convenient scapegoat, was blamed by many for not getting to the rescue, but exonerated by others as being helpless to aid, as Joseph E. Johnston was at Jackson while Pemberton was besieged in Vicksburg. Perhaps he should have made more of an effort.[28]

Thus Zeb Vance lost his and the Confederacy's seaport, which he more than any other had employed in the desperate struggle for independence. Happily he was not present in Wilmington to see many of the commodities accumulated in the warehouses at great hazard go up in flames a little later. General Hoke, having no adequate transportation, was compelled to set fire to the large stores that would have fallen into enemy hands, then fire the two privately owned Wilmington shipyards. On the morning of January 21, 1865, he evacuated the city, which had been a symbol that the South was a nation. Terry moved his Federal army up the peninsula and into Wilmington. The Confederate coast from Texas to Virginia was sealed.

Colonel William Lamb, garrison commander under Whiting, who did much of the construction of the fort and a great deal of the fighting in its defense, later made a statement cherished by its defenders and others in the state: "When I recall this magnificent struggle, unsurpassed in ancient and modern warfare, and remember the devoted patriotism and heroic courage of my garrison, I feel proud to know that I have North Carolina blood coursing through my veins, and I confidently believe that the time will come in the Old North State, when her people will regard the defense of Fort Fisher as the grandest event in her heroic past."[29]

Some of Vance's Junior Reserves were among the prisoners captured in Fort Fisher; others were with Hoke and remained to contest the advance of Sherman's army. Sherman had crashed into North Carolina on March 11, leaving South Carolina half in ruins behind him. After giving the old Federal arsenal town of Fayetteville its first experience with "total war," he began his advance toward Goldsboro and Raleigh. Joseph E. Johnston collected the best sort of an army he could find. Finding that Sherman was advancing loosely with his two wings widely separated, Johnston decided to strike the one farthest inland and see if he could not destroy it. Sherman was not seeking battle, desiring first to unite with other Union forces, Terry's coming across from Wilmington and Major General John M. Schofield's, which had come up from New Bern. The juncture would give Sherman about 90,000, opposed to Johnston's poorly armed and equipped array of 30,000.

On March 19, 1865, Johnston struck Sherman's left wing, commanded by Major General Henry W. Slocum, at Bentonville, after Hardee had delayed him momentarily at Averasboro, thirty miles north of Fayetteville. Bentonville has been called the "battle of the generals" because so many high-ranking Confederates were on the field. Three full generals were present—Johnston, Beauregard, and Bragg; five lieutenant generals, Wheeler, Hampton, Hardee, Stephen D. Lee, and Alexander P. Stewart, and a host of major generals and brigadier generals. But the striking feature of the battle was not with the generals, but in the fact that so many ardent veterans and Junior Reserves were willing to throw themselves as a forlorn hope into a fray against Sherman's tough veterans when it was clear to all that the cause was well near lost. They went in with a battle cry, "We'll whip them yet!"[30] Johnston was successful at first, drove Slocum's leading division, alarmed Sherman, who was marching with his other column, and caused the Federals hurriedly to concentrate their full strength. The battle in its different phases lasted three days, the first the Confederate attack, the second a lull, and the third a counterattack and a Confederate withdrawal. Sherman did not undertake to follow the Confederates, but preferred to go into Goldsboro for his juncture with the other Federal armies from the North Carolina coast.

Johnston retired to Raleigh, and with him went "the unripe wheat" of Hoke's Division, the Junior Reserves who had carried a heavy load at Bentonville and fought like true soldiers. Some of the veterans who left that field had been in the little group of the 1st North Carolina which fought in the first battle at Bethel. One was Colonel Hector McKethan of the 51st North Carolina. One of his lieutenants commented: "Many, as was the case of our colonel and a number of others, saw the sun of the South rise in glory at Bethel, and set in its blood-red sheen at Bentonville."[31]

Captain B. L. Ridley, member of the staff of Lieutenant General Alexander P. Stewart, who at Bentonville commanded the remnants of the Army of Tennessee, which eighteen months before had won the stubborn battle at Chickamauga, went to Raleigh March 28 to get an overcoat, "and soldier-like, I called upon Governor Vance." Before meeting the governor he spent the night at the Yarborough Hotel, "miserably kept," and paid $55 for a day's board. He walked around the capitol, which he found to be made of "imported granite," excelling any capitol of the South except his own state's, Tennessee. He made his approach to the governor by explaining that North Carolina had been his father's birthplace, and "Old Vance" was so taken with his cheek, as Ridley gave it, that he got an order from the quartermaster for "smuggled" gray material for a suit and overcoat. The quartermaster was exceedingly kind. When he returned to camp he was scolded by two of the colonels for not remembering them when he asked for the cloth.

Ridley's journal—much gossip, much fact, and giving incidents of his stay around Raleigh—is affecting because it pictures a dying army, once magnificent and devastating as a thunderbolt in the hills of North Georgia, but now like a worn, desperate, thirsty wanderer, staggering across the desert, whose toiling steps foretell the approaching end. General Stewart, "Old Straight," had news of the death of his son in Auburn, Alabama, and took it hard. "Notwithstanding his stern, military character he is a tender hearted man." Selma had fallen, and almost the same breeze brought news that Lee had lost virtually all his artillery.

Still, on April 4, 1865, in the midst of countless misfortunes, with the night of the Confederacy coming on, defeated and forced back from the field of Bentonville, the Army of Tennessee, not yet worsted spiritually, held at Raleigh what would once have been termed a grand review. Governor Vance was on hand, with crowds and many Raleigh ladies, and "everything went off well," but the touching story is best told by the April fourth entry in Ridley's diary:

"I witnessed today the saddest spectacle of my life, the review of the skeleton Army of Tennessee, that but one year ago was replete with men, and now filled with the tattered garments, worn out shoes, barefooted, and ranks so depleted that each color was supported by only thirty or forty men. Desertion, sickness, deaths, hardships, perils and vicissitudes demonstrated themselves too plainly upon that old Army. . . .

"Oh, what a contrast between the Dalton review and this one! The march of the remnant was so slow—colors tattered and torn with bullets—it looked like a funeral procession. The countenance of every spectator . . . was depressed and dejected, and the solemn, stern look of the soldiers was so impressive—Oh! it is beginning to look dark in the east, gloomy in the west, and like almost a lost hope when we reflect upon that review today!"[32]

After the remnant of the Army of Tennessee had marched by the reviewing stand, Hardee's Corps, formed out of scattered units but including Hoke's Division, passed, and Ridley noticed that the cheers of the Raleigh ladies went to the young, intrepid General Hoke's Division. Was it for the veterans—or the boys of the Junior Reserves? On the next day came word that Lee had evacuated Richmond—"a city that has been protected for four years now to succumb to the world's minions," as Ridley put it—and that Jefferson Davis had issued a proclamation asking the South to stand by him in the reverses and, again as Ridley summarized it, "not to be discouraged, for he'll steer us safely through." A resolute but truly an impractical man! Could any have truly believed there was still hope?

Kemp Plummer Battle attended one of Davis's receptions in Richmond in the days when the Confederacy was in the yellow leaf and engaged in the "half sentences." The affair seemed in some respects to have been much like latter-day Washington cocktail parties, with only banalities offered. The conversation did not appear to Battle to come from the heart as the long stream of handshakers passed by the President. Amid such trivialities do republics die.[33]

Here and there had been brighter and historical interludes dropped into the sorrowful story of defeat. Vance received a letter from Petersburg, Virginia, dated July 20, 1864, which showed how heavily the anguish of war bore on both sides. Captain John S. Dancy of the 17th North Carolina wrote of Grant's ill-conceived assault on the Confederate lines:

"I forward to you a Yankee Flag captured at Cold Harbor, Virginia, on the 3rd of June 1864 by the 17th N. C. Regt. Col. W. F. Martin. It belonged to the 164th N. Y. Volunteers, who charged boldly up to within seventy-five yards of the line of the 17th Regiment and were literally cut to pieces. A few prisoners captured by us stated that themselves and three others who reached their lines safely were the only ones left of the Regt. All the field and company officers were killed in the immediate front of the 17th and the Yankee bodies were literally piled upon one another.

"I forward the flag to you as the Executive of the State, with the hope that it may be taken care of or measures taken to remember it as the capture of the 17th N. C. Regt."[34]

Another request which, like this, the governor acknowledged tenderly was from Colonel John R. Winston of the 45th North Carolina, whose flag seemed to tell the story of the regiment's glory and decline.

"I send you the flag of the 45th N. C. Troops," Winston wrote, "which the members of the Regt. desire your Excellency to have placed among the archives of our dear old State which we love the more the longer this inhuman and unnatural war continues. We have endeavored to take care of our flag, but it is much tattered and torn—a fair representative of the service this Regt. has seen. The staff has been shot nearly off three or four times. At Gettysburg two Color bearers were killed and all the Color Guard killed or wounded. Our losses around these colors since that battle have been fearful."[35]

The 45th was in Daniel's Brigade, which suffered some of the heaviest losses at McPherson's Farm and on Culp's Hill at Gettysburg. Vance said the colors would be placed among the sacred relics of the state.[36]

One of the high spots in North Carolina's participation in the war in Virginia came at Reams's Station below Petersburg, where North Carolina troops under Generals A. P. Hill and Harry Heth broke the famous 2nd corps of the Union Army commanded by Major General Winfield Scott Hancock. The Federal commander was so chagrined by defeat, with which his corps had not often been familiar, that he exclaimed to one of his officers, "I do not care to die, but I pray God I may never leave this field."[37]

Vance was writing to Lee about desertions and dropped in the line, "The information of our great victory at Reams's Station has caused general rejoicing. It is peculiarly gratifying to our State pride, as it seems to have been achieved in great part by North Carolina troops."[38]

Lee wrote to Vance a few days later about the Fort Fisher defenses and referred to the battle. "I have frequently been called upon," he said, "to mention the services of North Car. soldiers in this army, but their gallantry and conduct was never more deserving of admiration than in the engagement at Reams's Station on the 25th inst. The brigades of Generals Cook, McRae and Lane, the last under the temporary command of Genl. Conner, advanced through a thick abattis of fallen trees under a heavy five of musketry and artillery and carried the enemy's works with a sturdy courage that elicited the warm commendation of their Corps and Division commanders and the admiration of the army.

"On the same occasion the brigade of Genl. Barringer bore a conspicuous part in the operations of the cavalry which win no less distinction for boldness and efficiency than those of the infantry.

"If the men who remain in North Carolina show the spirit of those they have sent to the field, as I doubt not they do, her defense may be securely intrusted to their hands."[39]

Vance was able to write Lee in a few days, on September 5, 1864, that several hundred deserters had been apprehended or had surrendered and "I trust to be able to get most of them without again asking for regular soldiers."

These were not the last of General Lee's expressions of confidence in North Carolina. During the last campaign, at Sayler's Creek, where the Confederates were being driven, Lee sent a staff officer to rally the men. The officer had just departed when suddenly a gray column appeared in good marching order, as if it had been dropped by heaven for the emergency. Lee's countenance lighted with pleasure.

"What troops are those?" he called out to their leader.

"Cox's North Carolina Brigade," came back the answer.

Lee took off his hat and bowed his head. "God bless gallant old North Carolina," he said fervently.[40]

## Chapter Twenty-Five

## Sunset Hours of a Lost Cause

William A. Graham, former governor, senator, and cabinet member and again senator under the Confederacy, returned to his Hillsboro, North Carolina, home just prior to the evacuation of Richmond by the Confederate government and its flight to Danville, Virginia, and on to Greensboro, North Carolina.

Graham, one of the capable men of North Carolina history and, in 1865, perhaps its most respected elder citizen, son of the Revolutionary War officer Joseph Graham, who as a major had sharply contested the approach of Cornwallis and helped win for Charlotte the name, applied by the British general, of "Hornet's Nest," had held virtually all the honors at the state's command.

William A. Graham's younger sister had married the Reverend Robert Hall Morrison and become the mother of a set of charming daughters, four of whom married men destined to become distinguished Confederate officers—Lieutenant Generals Stonewall Jackson and D. H. Hill, Brigadier General Rufus Barringer, whose cavalry brigade was substantially extinguished while covering the retreat of Lee's army from Petersburg, and Alphonso Calhoun Avery, grandson of the Revolutionary War leader and brother of Isaac E. Avery who fell leading a brigade at Gettysburg.

Former Governor Graham, whose advice Vance often sought, stopped in Hillsboro only long enough to get some sleep after riding all night from Richmond, then hurried on to Raleigh to acquaint Vance with the chaotic governmental affairs and the worsening military situation in Virginia.[1] He had left Richmond persuaded that it was beyond hope that the South could achieve independence, that peace could not be looked for through President Davis as long as that unbending man had a platoon of soldiers left to fire rifles, and that the state governments should make overtures to the Federal government for ending the fighting. Many were inclined to bypass Davis and get peace.

That is the opinion he gave to Vance, in recommending that the governor convene the North Carolina legislature immediately. He said Richmond was about to be captured and that its fall would be followed by the rout or dispersion of Lee's army, if for no other reason than want of sustenance. He thought that while the Confederate government knew the distressful hour was at hand, it had formulated no plan or policy for what might follow a military collapse. He felt General Lee was anxious for an accommodation and that Johnston could not gather an army adequate to contest the further advance of Sherman. He told Vance he had talked with Davis before leaving Richmond and had found the Confederate President anxious about the turn of events, but unwilling to do what he called "commit suicide" by negotiating the Confederacy out of existence, nor would he seek to arrange the best terms possible for the states in case they desired to readopt on their own initiative the old Constitution of the United States.

Nevertheless, the wisest men with whom he had talked were solicitous for a settlement, he told the governor, but they were trammeled by commitments or had such a false sense of pride that they could do nothing except wish the initiative might be taken by another.[2]

Vance's first reaction was that those who wanted peace should seek it and not come to him. Those who were licked should be the ones to say so. According to the report of the conversation which Graham made to former Governor Swain, Vance was surprised, even incredulous of Graham's report. This attitude must have applied to Davis's failure to develop any sort of program, because it did not require prescience to know that the end might be near. But Vance was not in a frame of mind to initiate a surrender of the state to the Federal government, which was about what the Graham proposal involved. The best he would do was to agree to consider the situation further and call a meeting of his advisory board, the Council of State, in a week's time.

Graham, earnest in his desire to avert more useless bloodshed, returned to Raleigh after a week at home and encountered Vance on the train returning from Statesville, where he had moved his family for greater security as Sherman threatened Raleigh. Arriving in Raleigh, they had dinner together. Vance reported the council was equally divided on the question of calling the legislature and consequently he had not summoned it. He had talked with John A. Gilmer, with whom he had served in the Federal Congress and who more recently had been in the Confederate Congress. Vance had possessed enough respect for him to vote for him ten times in the long speakership fight before the war. Gilmer told him he ought to seek a conference with General Sherman and while Vance agreed that this ought to be done for the protection of property, he was reluctant to call the general assembly, and had no intention to treat for a separate peace for the state. Instead, he went to see the review of Johnston's depleted army, inviting Graham to accompany him. "I declined," said Graham, "not seeing any good to be accomplished there."[3]

Vance was proving almost as unwilling as President Davis to abandon the conflict and acknowledge the end of the Confederacy, though anyone could observe clearly that the death throes were at hand. He was under heavy pressure to act. Graham, reporting to Swain on his conferences, urged the university president to go to Raleigh and accompany Vance if he intended to contrive a meeting with Sherman.

"I do not think it necessary," Graham wrote, "perhaps not advisable myself, to visit him again on these topics. My conversations with him were very full and earnest. I told him I should attend the session of the General Assembly, and if desired would address them in secret session; that I had had confidential conversations with a committee of the Virginia Legislature, which had taken a recess for ten days, and that it was important to act in concert with that body; that my colleagues in the House . . . were ready to call a session of the assembly together by advertisement; but all this had no effect in procuring a recommendation to the council in favor of a call."[4]

All the while during these discussions Sherman was reorganizing his forces at Goldsboro after the juncture with the armies of Schofield and Terry, getting supply trains running from the coastal towns, and poising for the step-off toward Raleigh, fifty miles distant.

The chief reason for Vance's indisposition to initiate peace measures was that he had made, less than a year before, a determined campaign across the state against that very action. While he might follow others in the quest for peace, he could not with good faith become the spearhead of the movement. As long as the central government pursued the struggle he was under commitment to follow along with it. Moreover, that obviously was his personal choice at the hour, for he knew enough about history to understand that a cause is never lost until everything is over; that even in modern times Frederick the Great had triumphed after he was all but crushed; that the cause of the colonies appeared to be finished when Washington retreated across New Jersey; that Europe was prostrate before Napoleon after Austerlitz.

But he wanted to do what he could to safeguard state property and records. The burning of the South Carolina capital was uppermost in his mind, and Fayetteville seemed to have suffered from considerable incendiarism. He had some of the archives bundled and sent to Company Shops, a railroad point in Alamance County now embraced in the city of Burlington. He stripped Raleigh of surplus supplies and had them distributed at points along the railroad where they might be used by Confederate forces in their retreat. Property removed from Raleigh included 40,000 blankets, quantities of overcoats, English cloth sufficient for 100,000 uniforms; shoes and leather aggregating 10,000 pairs; cotton cards; great quantities of cotton yarns and cloth; 150,000 pounds of bacon; a large stock of medical supplies; 6,000 scythe blades, and many other articles of value. Vance and the state officers worked through the nights to get the supplies loaded and by noon April 12, with Sherman due the next morning, the shipments cleared the town.[5]

On April 10, 1865, Sherman, his army refitted and now, according to Vance's estimate, 110,000 men strong, began his movement toward Raleigh, and Johnston began his retreat. Vance's question was whether to remain in the capital city and accept capture and try to continue the operation of a government under Federal occupation and hope to prevent disorder and chaos throughout the state, or to flee before Sherman's advance and set up a capital elsewhere. The question was whether state control was in the city or in the governor's person and Vance determined to abandon Raleigh and carry the government, even if no more than in pretense, with him.

Meantime Graham had prevailed on Swain to go to Raleigh, and the elderly university president, the senior surviving governor of the state and as devoted to its interests as any man within its borders, took the train on April 10 for Raleigh from Hillsboro, where he had talked with Graham. That day Sherman began to roll northward again. Graham had drawn up an outline of what he thought Vance should do. The main points were the convening of the legislature, the passing of a resolution by that body requesting an opening of negotiations to stop the effusion of blood, and the election of commissioners to treat with the United States. The result of these negotiations should be reported to a convention which would have sovereign power. A final point was that if Sherman advanced on Raleigh, Vance should send a commission to treat for a suspension of hostilities until the state could act on the plan to terminate the war.

Arriving in Raleigh, Swain dined with Vance, and after a prolonged discussion—Vance not being much in favor of dealing directly with Sherman—prevailed on the governor to request that Sherman meet commissioners of the state. Vance put in the condition that he obtain the assent of General Johnston. He mounted at once and rode to Johnston's camp.[6]

Reports were reaching Raleigh—"painful rumors," Vance called them—on April 10 and 11 that General Lee had surrendered. The governor later gave an account of his talk with General Johnston. "Animated by these reports," he said, "and also by the fact that the Confederate forces were passing through and rapidly uncovering the capital of the State, and that all further operations were really intended to secure such terms as were possible, I consulted General Johnston as to what it was best for me to do. With the frankness of a soldier and a man of common sense, he advised me to make the best terms I could for the protection of my capital and people."

Vance questioned him about the propriety of sending an embassy through his lines to meet General Sherman, but did not report his reply.[7]

Johnston at that time was summoned by President Davis, who had reached Greensboro, and departed, leaving Hardee in command, and Vance had his further transactions with that general. He asked Swain to telegraph for Graham, who came at once. His train, due at 11 P.M., did not arrive until three the next morning. They found Vance at early dawn writing letters and dispatches by candlelight, then after an early breakfast they went to the capitol in company with Colonel James G. Burr, one of the State Guard officers serving on Vance's staff. There the two former governors wrote a letter to Sherman, the purport of which was to save the capital and remaining state papers from destruction. Vance signed it but did not have time to enter the text in his letter books and it does not appear to have been preserved, though what purports to be a version appears in the Official Reports. Hardee gave the ex-governors authority to pass through the Confederate lines. Vance gave them authority to act as commissioners. Accompanied by Surgeon General Edward Warren, Quartermaster General John Devereux and Colonel Burr, and with their special train flying a flag of truce, they set out from Raleigh in search of Sherman somewhere between the capital and Goldsboro. Warren had begged Vance's permission to accompany the party at the last minute, and the governor consented laughingly, saying, "Warren, I believe you would volunteer to go to the devil if an expedition were started to the domains of his Satanic Majesty."[8]

There appears to be no doubt that Johnston assented to the dispatch of the commissioners. Mrs. Spencer, whose account was published with Vance's blessing the next year, said that "the mission was not entered upon without the deliberate assent and advice of General Johnston, after a full conference with Governor Vance, and also with General Hardee's entire concurrence, and a safe-conduct from him in General Johnston's absence." The fact that Hardee supplied the locomotive was evidence of the military's concurrence. That Johnston approved was the impression of Sherman's leading biographer when he investigated the circumstances of the mission.[9]

Virtually everyone, it seemed, had descended on Vance with a recommendation or an insistence that he send the deputation to meet Sherman. Thomas Bragg, former governor and senator, who had been Attorney General of the Confederacy, and Kenneth Rayner, distinguished former Congressman and a dean of the North Carolina bar, were consulted and gave approval. But through it all, Vance held to an aim to save the city from a conflagration such as had devastated Columbia, and not to negotiate with Sherman a separate peace. Clear as was his object, it came to be grievously misunderstood by President Davis and some of the army officers.

The journey of the commissioners was filled with vicissitudes; they cleared Hardee's Corps and were passing through General Wade Hampton's cavalry—though Hampton seemed to honor Hardee's order reluctantly—when they were suddenly hauled up by an order from General Johnston, delivered to them by couriers who chased them for two miles and demonstrated that the speed of horses exceeded that of the broken-down Confederate railroads of 1865. The order directed that the train return to Raleigh.

The holdup occurred because Colonel Archer Anderson, who had served gallantly at Chickamauga as D. H. Hill's chief of staff, informed President Davis in Greensboro that the commissioners were being sent, and Davis, ever suspicious that Vance might be undertaking to negotiate a separate peace, did not intend that they should reach their destination. Vance had made no secret of the dispatch of the commissioners and had himself notified Davis of it. But Anderson's message got through to Davis first and the President at once passed down orders through Johnston to Hampton, directing Hampton to stop the commissioners. To deliver these orders Hampton's couriers outsped the train.[91]

The engine was turned about and the train was being pulled slowly back to Raleigh when they were overtaken by horsemen, these unhappily being a Federal cavalry detachment commanded by Brigadier General Smith D. Atkins.

When Swain looked out at the youthful General Atkins from Freeport, Illinois, tall and handsome, who had formerly commanded the 92nd Illinois regiment of Wilder's famous "Lightning Brigade," Army of the Cumberland, and had been first of Rosecrans's army to enter Chattanooga, he could not know that in less than five months this blue-uniformed officer would be the husband of his beautiful daughter Eleanor.

Atkins told them he would take them to the Federal cavalry chief, General Judson Kilpatrick, and brought up a regimental band to entertain them while they awaited a carriage that would convey them to Kilpatrick's headquarters a mile distant. Kilpatrick proved abrupt and impatient. He debated with them about their status, claiming that despite their papers and safe conduct from Hardee, they were prisoners of war since they had come into his lines while a fight was in progress between him and Hampton. He read them a general order Sherman had issued congratulating the army on the surrender of General Lee, of which he had just been advised by telegraph. He lectured to them considerably about law and political science, concerning which probably no two persons in the United States were better informed, and after an hour or two had them taken back to the railroad for conduct to Sherman's headquarters. But instead of the train, they had to ride this time on a handcar. They made an incongruous, even ludicrous, picture in their long-tailed coats and tall beaver hats which Dr. Warren termed "*ante-bellum* relics," and which created amusement among the Federal cavalry soldiers who lined the roadways and at times offered artfully conceived insults. But they remained stately and silent and, according to Warren, possessed the dignity of Roman senators.[11]

Sherman was at the little town of Clayton, seventeen miles southwest of Raleigh. For some miles before they reached the town, the commissioners passed the marching infantry columns of Sherman's armies. The Federal infantry, seeing the white flags and knowing of Lee's surrender, and being better informed and more alert than the scoffing cavalry, assumed the mission was to tell of Johnston's surrender also and greeted the handcar with cheers. Sherman was at the Clayton depot, attended by his staff, where he met the commissioners pleasantly and escorted them to his headquarters tent, being gracious and polite in contrast with Kilpatrick's brusqueness. Graham gave him Vance's letter and found the general apparently disposed to deal compassionately with Raleigh. He wrote a letter acknowledging that of Vance and enclosing a safeguard for the governor and any of his state government who might wish to remain in Raleigh. Since the train had come out of Raleigh in good faith he would allow it to return. "I doubt," he concluded, "if hostilities can be suspended as between the army of the Confederate government and the one I command; but I will aid you in all my power to contribute to the end you aim to reach—the termination of the existing war."

Sherman hoped that the two commissioners and their escorts could depart before midnight, but circumstances prevented it and he arranged that they should sleep, have a cup of coffee with him at daybreak, then depart for Raleigh on their own train. After the business of exchanging the letters was finished, they talked for two hours, with Swain introducing the conversation by recalling that before the war he and Sherman were engaged in the same calling, he as president of the University of North Carolina and Sherman as superintendent of the Louisiana State Seminary and Military Academy. Sherman said he was quite aware of it and Swain continued: "Two or three of your boys were with me for a time."

"Yes," said Sherman, "and many more of yours have been with me during the war, who came, poor fellows, before they were men, and when they ought to have remained with you; and they too frequently helped to fill my hospitals. I think, however, when they return, they will do me the justice to tell you that I treated them kindly."[12]

Sherman was speaking of Swain's pupils who had become his prisoners. Perhaps he referred to some of Vance's Junior Reserves whom the Federal armies had captured at Fort Fisher and in battles in North Carolina. Then Swain inquired about one of his old pupils, Major General Francis P. Blair, Jr., the Kentucky-born son of Andrew Jackson's close friend and editor of the *Globe* in Washington. Francis, Jr., had studied at Chapel Hill in 1837 prior to being graduated at Princeton in 1841, then had moved to Missouri and had served in Congress with Vance in 1859. Sherman said that Blair, who commanded the 17th Army corps, was only two hours behind. Sherman had been reading the "terrible accounts" in a Raleigh newspaper about what he had done in Fayetteville and said, "I will turn Frank over to you to answer for it all in the morning." Swain had the boldness to mention the burning of Columbia, South Carolina, and Sherman, obviously irked by the accounts, spoke with much emphasis.

"I have been grossly misrepresented in regard to Columbia," he said. "I changed my headquarters eight times during that night, and with every general officer under my command, strained every nerve to stop the fire. I declared in the presence of my God that Hampton burned Columbia, and that he alone is responsible for it. He collected immense piles of cotton in the streets and set them on fire; the wind rose during the night, and dispersed the flakes of burning cotton among the shingle-roofs, and created a conflagration beyond human control."[13]

Sherman, a strangely inconsistent man, was the soul of courtesy during the visit. Voluble in his discourse, vicious in war, he was nevertheless of a warm and companionable nature in his personal relations and was disposed to give the South much gentler terms for a reunion with the old government than it attained from the legislators in Washington who had never been on the battlefield. Graham accepted his invitation to share his headquarters tent with him that night. Swain received an invitation that was as pleasant as it was surprising. One of Sherman's aides came up, said he would like to give the ex-governor comfortable quarters because Swain's name was one of the most familiar in his household. Swain did indeed know nearly everyone! The officer's mother had been one of his schoolmates, and of Vance's mother also, back in the early days in Buncombe County. He was Colonel Henry Hitchcock of Sherman's staff, a native of Alabama who entered the Union army from Missouri and won distinction in the Georgia and

Carolina campaigns.[14] He later founded and headed the law school of Washington University in St. Louis.

Vance waited in Raleigh for the return of the commissioners, whom he expected by four o'clock on the afternoon of their departure. Raleigh was uncovered and the question of whether or not he should remain depended on the nature of Sherman's reply. His own explanation of his movements was that Sherman, having heard that the orders sending the commissioners had been countermanded, thought there would be advantage in keeping the governor in suspense.

"No doubt, also," said Vance, "as I have been informed, he utilized my engine by making it ply all night between his camp and Goldsboro. Meantime it had been reported to me that the Commissioners and their engine had been captured, and I had ceased to expect their return. At precisely midnight, accompanied by two volunteer aids, I rode upon horseback out of the city of Raleigh, leaving it occupied by the rear guard of Hampton's Cavalry, and stopped eight miles from the city in the camp of General Hoke . . . The other State officers had previously retired to Greensboro."[15]

State Treasurer Jonathan Worth had recommended that Vance remain and surrender the city, but the urgency of army officers that he retire caused him finally to depart without information about Sherman's intentions. General Hoke stated later that he compelled Vance to depart, but it appears no more than a matter of persuasion, for Hoke had gone ahead of him. He was not disposed to turn himself over to Sherman unconditionally, being the symbol of the North Carolina government, so he wrote another letter to the Federal commander on the night of his departure, April 12, designating Mayor William B. Harrison as his agent authorized to surrender the city.

"I have the honor to request the extension of your favor to its defenseless citizens generally," he said, "and especially to ask your protection for the charitable institutions of the State located here, filled as they are with unfortunate inmates. . . . The capitol of the State, with its libraries, museum, and most of the public records, is left also in your power. I can but entertain the hope that they will escape mutilation or destruction, inasmuch as such evidences of learning and taste can advantage neither party in the prosecution of the war, whether destroyed or preserved."[16]

Thus he made it clear again that his purpose was to save the capital

city from the sort of destruction that had befallen her neighbor capital
to the south, Columbia, and not to make a separate peace with Sherman
on behalf of the state, unless that should be dictated by further developments.

On April 13, the morning following Vance's departure, the commissioners returned to Raleigh on their special train, which Sherman
released to them, to find that Johnston's army had fallen back to Hillsboro. Vance had departed and a ghostlike emptiness had settled over
the streets, except that the railroad depot was in flames. Confederate
stragglers lingering behind from Wheeler's cavalry had plundered and
fired it, making it impossible for the commissioners to pass their
train along the track. They left the train and walked along Hillsboro
and Fayetteville streets, only to find the curtains drawn and the doors
of stores and houses closed, the capitol and the governor's palace locked
and deserted.

Cornelia Phillips Spencer who talked with them wrote: "The very
air seemed shriveled. In the brief interval that elapsed from the retreat
of her protectors to the arrival of her foes, the beautiful city of Raleigh
stood under the outstretched arms of her noble oaks, embowered in
the luxuriant shrubbery of a thousand gardens, just touched with vernal
bloom and radiance—stood with folded hands and drooping head, in
all the mortal anguish of suspense, in a silence that spoke, awaiting her
fate."[17]

Few seemed to believe that Raleigh would be spared, after the way
the torch had been thrown around Columbia, whether deliberately or
inadvertently.

Finally the two commissioners found the servant who tended to
the executive office in the capitol, but before they could enter Swain
noticed some fag-end members of Wheeler's cavalry breaking into the
stores on Fayetteville Street. He went down to them and remonstrated
and told them Sherman had guaranteed to spare the town and that the
Confederates should also, and urged them to desist and follow the rest
of their command. All he could get was a response of "Damn Sherman
and the town, too." Just then the head of Kilpatrick's Federal cavalry
appeared down Fayetteville Street. All of the plunderers except one
lieutenant mounted hastily and rode off; the leader, a young Texan
named Walsh, of the 11th Texan cavalry, waited until Kilpatrick was
within a hundred yards, drew his revolver, shouted "God damn 'em,"

fired five shots at the Federal cavalry chief who headed his column, then put spurs to his horse and dashed up Morgan Street.

Kilpatrick sent a dozen horsemen in hot pursuit. They overtook the Texan after his horse had fallen turning a corner. Kilpatrick would not even give him five minutes to write a letter to his wife, but had him hanged summarily behind the capitol grounds, though he appears to have done no more than what other Confederates in the same kind of uniform had been doing for the last four years—shooting at the enemy. "His crime," as Mrs. Spencer saw it, "was more the rash act of a passionate and reckless boy, an aimless bravado from one wild and despairing man to a hundred and twenty thousand." He was buried beneath his gallows.[18]

Swain was designated to stand by and surrender the capitol, Graham to seek a conveyance that would carry them in quest of Vance and the Confederate Army. With Swain looking on, the national flag was raised over the capitol dome, and later that morning, when Sherman's long dusty columns were marching in, Swain turned over the keys to the capitol to the Federal commander. Sherman arrived before 8 A.M. April 13. He expressed regret that Governor Vance had departed the night before and wrote a letter inviting him to return. Perhaps he had heard favorable comments about the governor from his brother John Sherman, Vance's friend in the old House. His note said: "Grant safe-conduct to the bearer of this to any point twelve miles from Raleigh and back, to include the Governor of North Carolina and any member of the State or city government, on his way back to the capital of the State." [19]

Dr. Warren witnessed and in his florid style recorded the events of Sherman's occupation and the grand review of his great army as it passed up Fayetteville Street and around the capitol. The reviewing stand was at the gate of the capitol grounds, a historic spot in the state's affairs. There Henry Clay had stood and addressed acres of humanity, and near by he had tossed away the Presidency in 1844 by changing his position and espousing the annexation of Texas, to the anger of Northern supporters.[20] There North Carolina governors, many great men—Vance, Badger, Graham, Swain—had been inaugurated. There Sherman, mounted on a beautiful steed, surrounded by his burnished staff, watched the army pass with all the aspect of conquerors—the army which a year before had stepped off from Chattanooga for Atlanta, and now, after its spectacular march to the sea and up through the Carolinas, had crushed the Confederacy behind General Lee, while Lee's Army of Northern Virginia had held Grant at bay around Richmond. "The entire mass," wrote observer Warren, "seemed endowed with the intelligence and spontaneity of a vitalized organism." Doctorlike, he thought in anatomical terms.

"As I listened for hours to the tread of those countless legions, so complete in their equipment, thorough in their organization and admirable in their discipline . . . I could but feel a profound admiration for the genius which had perfected such a mighty instrument of destruction and conquest, and a supreme realization of the heroism and fortitude of the ragged, half starved and completely unorganized army which for four years of unequal conflict had defied its power, and had finally succumbed, not so much to its prowess as to the force of circumstances and the laws of nature. . . ."

Dr. Warren thought the march-by gave Sherman an opportunity "to give free indulgence to that love of display which constitutes so important a factor in his singular character."[21]

Armed with Sherman's safe-conduct and supplied by Sherman with a rockaway carriage, the commissioners left Raleigh to deliver their report to Vance, traveling by an old stage roadway known as the "Upper Durham Road," and skirting thereby the cavalry patrols of both Kilpatrick and Hampton, until they reached the Strayhorn residence nine miles from Hillsboro. Vance was still suspect by Confederate officers who either wanted to fight it out with Sherman's vast host on their own volition or were under the influence of President Davis's doubts. This was evidenced by the events at Strayhorn's, which Wade Hampton was using as his headquarters. W. J. Saunders of Hampton's staff was sitting on the porch with Hampton when he saw the two men in their high beaver hats driving up. "Yonder come the commissioners!" he exclaimed, and Hampton merely commanded, "Introduce me."[22]

They talked in the parlor, but Graham, the spokesman, was reticent and gave Hampton no hint of what had passed between them and Sherman. After an exchange of no more than formalities, the commissioners took their leave and drove away. Hampton, puzzled, turned to his aide. "What do you think of all this?" he asked. Saunders voiced surprise that Hampton had not asked them, then, pressed to say more, exclaimed, "Why, couldn't you see that Governor Graham had a letter in his pocket for Vance?"

That alerted Hampton immediately. "Go and get your horse, sir," he directed, as he went inside and hastily wrote two letters, one to Graham and one to General Johnston. Then he told Saunders to ride his best, overtake the commissioners, give Graham the letter and demand that he turn over to Saunders Sherman's letter to Vance. If he could not obtain the letter before it was delivered to Vance, he was to get an engine in Hillsboro, secure Graham, and take him on to Johnston at Haw River.

Saunders pushed his mount at top speed through the black night, but failed to overtake the rockaway bearing the commissioners. On reaching Hillsboro he went first to the depot and located an engine, then got a major of the cavalry corps to accompany him to Graham's house. When Graham read Hampton's letter he flushed angrily, stood up with his full dignity, and said he was ready to accompany the officers to General Johnston.

"Governor, had you better not hand me that letter?" Saunders queried him.

"I have already delivered it to Governor Vance, sir," the elder statesman replied serenely. Saunders remounted; not feeling justified in taking the locomotive, he rode through the night—"through rain, mud and the darkest night I ever saw"—the eighteen miles to Johnston at Haw River, arriving at dawn.

The ends being taken to prevent Vance from communicating with Sherman, even though the conqueror held his capital city, were becoming a bit farfetched. They stemmed, of course, from President Davis's visionary notion that he could continue the fight with Lee's army gone and Johnston's being hunted down by Sherman, and from his suspicion of Vance which had its basis more in his own dreams than in Vance's confrontation with facts. Certainly there could have been nothing reprehensible about Vance surrendering his helpless state any more than Lee surrendering his hopelessly outnumbered army, even had an independent surrender been the governor's intention, which it was not. He had been the one to stand against the heavy pressure to surrender and was entitled to the confidence of the army and the President

Graham on reaching his home had found Vance awaiting him in his parlor. Only then, on the night of April 14, did the governor have full confirmation that Lee had surrendered. Graham gave him Sherman's invitation to return to Raleigh and both Graham and Swain encouraged him to accept it, but he had just received a message from Davis urging him to come to Greensboro. Since he was still opposed to taking his state out of the war separately, grievous as the situation might be, he decided to respond to Davis instead of to Sherman.

When Vance reached Greensboro he found that Davis and his cabinet, who had been living for five rainy days in a leaky boxcar on a railroad siding, had departed for Charlotte. The governor followed them and met Davis in the presence of Reagan, Breckinridge, and others. He told Davis he had come to advise with him about what to do and to learn the President's intentions.

"The conversation was long and solemn," as Vance described it. "Mr. Davis appeared still full of hope, and discussed the situation exhaustively. He told me of the possibility, as he thought, of retreating beyond the Mississippi with large sections of the soldiers still faithful to the Confederate cause, and resuming operations with General Kirby Smith's forces as a nucleus in those distant regions; and intimated rather than expressed a desire that I should accompany him, with such of the North Carolina troops as I might be able to influence to that end."[23]

Vance was actually observing the last sigh of the Confederacy and his description of it involved interesting detail. It showed that despite their numerous tiffs, he was not without some admiration of his falling chief.

"He was very earnest, and displayed a remarkable knowledge of the opinions and resources of the people of the Confederacy, as well as a most dauntless spirit. After he had ceased there was a sad silence around his council board. Perhaps one or more opinions were expressed in support of Mr. Davis's views, and then General Breckenridge [sic] spoke. I shall never forget either the language or the manner of that splendid Kentuckian. With the utmost frankness, and with the courage of sincerity, he said he did not think they were dealing candidly with Governor Vance; that their hopes of accomplishing the results set forth by Mr. Davis were so remote and uncertain that he, for his part, could not advise me to forsake the great duties which devolved upon me in order to follow the further fortunes of the retreating Confederacy; that his advice would be that I should return to my position and its responsibilities, do the best I could for my people, and share their fate, whatever it might be. With a deep sigh Mr. Davis replied to General Breckenridge: 'Well, perhaps, General, you are right.'

"I remarked that General Breckenridge's views coincided with my own sense of duty, and after a little more conversation I arose and offered my hand to President Davis to bid him good-bye. He shook it long and warmly, saying: 'God bless you, sir, and the noble old State of North Carolina.' With feelings which I am not able to describe I thus bade farewell to the Southern Confederacy. . . ."[24]

Jefferson Davis went on to Georgia and capture, and Vance returned to Greensboro, intending to go to Raleigh and, if permitted, to resume his gubernatorial duties. Breckinridge and Reagan returned to Greensboro, and learning on the evening of April 17 that Johnston was negotiating with Sherman, the three rode in a boxcar to Hampton's headquarters east of Hillsboro, where a council of war on the surrender terms was being held. An atmosphere heavy with uncertainty prevailed, because news had just been received of President Lincoln's assassination, and none could weigh its import.

That night there was much sideplay and confusion in the remnants of the Confederate Army and among the high officers and officials scattered over the seventy miles between Raleigh and Greensboro. Hampton occupied the Dr. Dickson home three miles from Hillsboro, and announced that a council of war would be held in the parlor that midnight. A train from Haw River brought General Johnston. When Secretary of War Breckinridge, Postmaster General Reagan, the cavalry generals Hampton, Wheeler, and M. C. Butler, and others arrived— there was drifting in and out of the meeting—the final council on the surrender proceeded.

Vance came with his executive clerk, Leo D. Heartt. Saunders left a record of this council for no other purpose than to give what he called the historical facts, as contrasted with much fiction about Vance's part in the last days of the Confederacy, and to show "how injustice was done this gallant war executive." The object of the council was to discuss the terms, about which Johnston had been in communication with Sherman. But some of those present applied sharp words to Vance and deeply wounded and angered him. Precisely what they were was not stated.

Saunders and others rolled up in their blankets and slept under the trees outside while the conference deliberated. Great secrecy was maintained because of Lincoln's assassination and because it was feared that if the army heard a surrender was contemplated, though who could have doubted it, it would disperse. That sort of conference was not held without all in the ranks being aware of it. The news of the imminence of surrender began to circulate the next morning and large numbers departed. Vance, after sitting for a time in the meeting, came outside and got under the blanket with Saunders, "preferring," as that officer put it, "the open air and grass with a friend to the company of men who had treated him so cruelly at the council board, as I was afterwards to learn from his own lips."

Next morning when Saunders awoke he found that Zeb had taken all the blanket. The staff officer filled a pipe, covered the governor carefully, realized he had been under great strain, smoked, and watched over him and got him a tin basin of water when he awoke. The governor had no towel and wiped his face and hands with his handkerchief.

After a breakfast of sorts Vance suggested a walk and when they were beyond hearing of the house, where some of the generals and officials still slept, Vance burst out: "I came here to explain that Sherman letter, and they wouldn't hear me. Me in communication with the enemy, me making terms for my State unknown to the authorities! Of all men, sir, I am the last man they can accuse of that infamy!" According to the officer, Vance was so angry that tears came to his eyes. Then Saunders recorded his own impression: "For four long weary years we had fought and struggled and given our all for the cause that now was lost—but God forgive me, as I gazed on this strong man in his agony of the shame put upon him, I felt all the bitterness of resentment, and for the first and only time, I, a soldier of the Confederacy, was untrue and disloyal to its colors."[25]

Who cut Vance off at the council was never stated, and with so many present, any guess would be futile.

Vance, relieved by his outbreak, went into Hillsboro to see Graham again, then returned that night to Greensboro, where he learned of Johnston's surrender at the Bennett farmhouse near Durham—on terms which Washington disapproved. Other terms had to be drafted. Vance spoke of the two surrenders:

"The first provided not only for the surrender and security of the military arm of the Confederacy, but for the full and complete recognition of the existing autonomy of the States, merely requiring that the various State officers should attorn to the government of the United States, taking the usual oaths of office to support the constitution, etc. The latter provided only for the surrender of men and property of the Confederate Army."

Then Vance spoke along lines generous to Sherman: "Because I have been severe in my denunciations of the conduct of General Sherman and his army towards unarmed and helpless citizens, I have no disposition to refuse him justice when I think he really merits it. In my opinion one of the wisest and most farseeing measures connected with the war was this first convention offered by General Sherman. It was as generous as it was wise. It has perhaps never been rated at its true value by people either North or South."

Had it been ratified, Vance explained, the dominion of the Union would have been completed over the South forthwith, the states would not have been reduced to military districts in which civil law was overthrown by bayonet law, nor would there have been any reconstruction, nor "eleven blood-stained, war-ridden and desolated States plundered of two hundred and sixty millions by the last and infinitely worse invasion of the army of carpet-baggers. In short, when I say that the terms offered us by General Sherman would have saved the South the horrors of reconstruction, I have said all that human eloquence is capable of saying; and I feel much inclined to forgive General Sherman the horrors which he did inflict in consideration of his efforts to avert those which came afterwards."[26]

Mrs. Spencer also reflected his view when she said Sherman showed an eagerness to prevent further devastation.

"Perhaps a late remorse had touched him," she said, "but . . . in the civil policy he has always advocated toward the South, he has shown himself at once generous and politic." She added that had he pursued an equally far-sighted course as a soldier and held his army in restraint, there were few in the South who would not pronounce him the hero of the war on the Northern side.[27]

Vance never regretted his refusal to accept Sherman's invitation to return to Raleigh, as his friends had urged him to do. His situation would not have differed. With the repudiation of Sherman's first convention came a withdrawal of the invitation. General Schofield came by way of Greensboro under the second convention to receive the surrender of Johnston's remnants two miles west of Durham on the Hillsboro road. Vance went out to Schofield and offered his surrender also, but Schofield declined to accept it and told him he was at liberty to go home. Meantime the various stores possessed by the state, which had not been issued during the final days, were seized or plundered, mostly, Vance said to his regret, by Southern soldiers. They felt they were justified on the ground that whatever they did not take would fall into the hands of the Northern Army.

When the governor looked about to assemble his personal property he might take home with him, the fruits of four years of war, more than two and a half of it in the governor's chair, all he could gather up were his saddle horse and a pair of old mules. He shipped them by freight car to Statesville, the town he now regarded as home. He rode in the same car with a group of friends. They saw the highways filled with soldiers walking home from the armies of Lee and Johnston. At every station groups of soldiers would crowd into the train. The car was jammed and Zeb at length became irritated when another soldier began to climb into it where there was scarcely room, through a hole that had been knocked out of the side boards to admit air. The governor ordered him away, then drew his navy repeater and threatened to shoot him if he did not stay back.

"You don't look like you'd shoot," the placid old soldier said unconcernedly, and came on in. Everyone laughed, including the governor, and the man got a cramped ride with the rest. Thus Vance journeyed to Statesville and closed his service as wartime governor of North Carolina.[28]

North Carolina was prostrate; civil law which Vance had fought to uphold so diligently was at an end. The state that had known the relatively benign rule of Swain, Graham, Badger, and Vance was to live largely under the bayonets of military law during the eleven years of reconstruction, administered by the severe Schofield, the indifferent Daniel Sickles, and the handsome and decorous E. R. S. Canby.

Vance, now a former governor, the Northern military having taken over before his term expired, perceived that while war excites evil passions, because it is both excessive law and the absence of law, the barbaric propensity in men soon exhausts itself, and "the people waited anxiously for the return of civil authority, as benighted men watch for the dawn." From April until October, 1865, North Carolina, in Vance's opinion, was without law, either civil or military. "There was not a judge on the bench, not a magistrate or sheriff, constable of any kind or civil servant or conservator of the peace to be found in the State invested with legal authority. A complete social chaos reigned, yet profound and perfect peace existed throughout our borders. The instincts of order were sublimely present, and never did any portion of the great race to which we belong give stronger proof of its capacity for self-government and its innate desire for civilization."[29]

The supplies which Vance had husbanded so carefully were dissipated in the general breakup of the state organization and the surrender of the armies. What he had on hand at the end of the war, as he calculated it, was a good quantity of uniforms plus "great stores of blankets, leather, etc." The uniforms, both those already made and those still in cloth (the proportions not being specified), amounted to 92,000. As security for the warrants the state had issued in order to purchase this material, Vance held 11,000 bales of cotton and 100,000 barrels of rosin. Part of the cotton was destroyed before the war ended, but several thousand bales were "captured" after peace was declared. Some question has existed as to how much of the cotton found its way to the Federal treasury. Large quantities of the 92,000 uniforms were issued to soldiers and civilians at the end and gave some comfort to residents of the state in the hard days of peace.[30]

The very clear and simple reason why Vance had so many supplies on hand at the end of the war was that the denouement came much more rapidly than he had expected it. While his common prudence told him that the lifeblood of the Confederacy was gradually being drained away, he always appeared to have a secret hope that a great military triumph would relieve the pressure and perhaps open the way for negotiation. This is not inconsistent with his statements that the fortunes of the Southern nation were waning after Gettysburg and Vicksburg. Many of his sentiments of despair were expressed in retrospect.

His high spirit and determination to fight to the end were evidenced by the series of mass meetings he held in North Carolina as late as March, 1865, to rally public sentiment, and by his dispatch to Governor A. G. Magrath of South Carolina of an appeal saying enough soldiers were absent from their command who, if they returned, would "render the armies of the Confederacy irresistible and triumphant." He sought measures which might be taken for their return. With all the other duties that were pressing in on him, he still took the time to address personally some of the patriotic rallies he had arranged in the early part of the year, which discloses exactly an opposite feeling from one that the Confederacy was finished. He was continually sending supplies to Lee. That he was husbanding uniform material and equipment after the port of Wilmington was closed and when he thought the war might last possibly another two years is scarcely an occasion for censure, though it has often been made such. As it was, Vance had to withstand the charge by his opponent Judge Settle in the campaign of 1876 that he had continued the war two years longer than was necessary and was blamable for the destruction of two thirds of all the property in the state.[31]

Apparently there were plenty of army rations. "I was told by General Johnston," said Vance, "that when his army surrendered he had in the depots in North Carolina, gathered in the State, five months' supplies for sixty thousand men, and that for many, many months previous, General Lee's army had been almost entirely fed from North Carolina." This was confirmed by the quartermaster general of the state.[32]

Certainly Vance is not to blame if Johnston's army had plenty in its possession while Lee's was poorly fed and poorly clad. Transportation was a problem in getting supplies from Johnston to Lee. But Vance's own surpluses at the end of the war were an expression of hope that the Confederacy had not yet run its course.

In any event, those who have blamed Vance for having stocks of material in his warehouses or in process in his factories never produced a request for supplies which he refused to honor. Always the demand was that the Confederacy be permitted to take over his manufacturing. He was conducting the work superbly and clothing approximately half of the Confederate forces in Virginia, plus many units elsewhere. The fault would seem to be that of distribution and the workings of the Confederate quartermaster corps, and a failure of Vance to hold omnipotent forewarning of the dates of Appomattox and the Bennett farmhouse.

In the breakdown of transportation and the confusion of the closing weeks, not all North Carolina soldiers were well supplied. B. F. Sugg of Greenville, North Carolina, a member of the 40th North Carolina regiment, wrote that he lost his shoes at Fort Fisher on January 16, 1865, "and never had any on my feet until April 22." He marched more than 250 miles barefoot and surrendered with a part of Johnston's army at Bush Hill, near Trinity College.[33]

☆☆☆☆☆☆☆☆☆☆☆☆☆☆☆☆☆☆

*Chapter Twenty-Six*

*Jovial Prisoner at the Old Capitol*

☆☆☆☆☆☆☆☆☆☆☆☆☆☆☆☆☆☆

Vance was at home on the early morning of May 13, 1865, his thirty-fifth birthday, when his house on West Main Street, Statesville, was suddenly surrounded by a squadron of Federal cavalry commanded by Major John M. Porter of Huntingdon County, Pennsylvania, who was polite in the extreme but had imperative orders passed down all the way from President Johnson and Secretary Stanton through Generals Grant, Schofield, and Kilpatrick. Stanton's order to Grant was unnecessarily contemptuous because it said the President directed the arrest of Z. B. Vance, "who has been claiming to act as the Governor of North Carolina." The vote was based on the vote of the people of the state by better than a four-to-one margin and would seem as valid as any earthly power could make it.[1]

Stanton ordered that he be sent under close guard to Washington, which the arresting officer interpreted leniently. Vance was not fettered and was, in truth, given a day of grace in which he might take his departure from his family and wind up his affairs, which would not have been troublesome for one who possessed little more than a riding horse and team of mules.

Federal General George Stoneman, in his raid through North Carolina in the closing days of the war, had ripped up the railroads and

411

there were no trains from Statesville. The Federal squadron had no surplus animals except pack horses. Such privately owned horses and carriages as remained in the town were not likely to be sent off with a horse-hungry Federal cavalry command. Vance was too heavy to make a long, arduous ride on horseback or muleback.

At this juncture an incident occurred which gave him, with his long memory, an enduring affection for the Jewish people and led to a rapport which causes his memory to be revered by North Carolina Jews to the present day. Samuel Wittkowsky, a Jewish hat manufacturer of the town, whose Benjamin Franklin type of slogan of "Push, Pluck and Perseverance" was to make him wealthy and one of the leading citizens of Charlotte in later years, came forward with a horse and buggy and asked the pleasure of driving the governor to Salisbury.[2]

Federal General Kilpatrick, a cavalry leader never greatly admired in either army, who in a vain burst had sent the gallant Farnsworth to his death charging an infantry line at Gettysburg, began after the war to think he had performed an exploit of proportions in subduing the much talked-about Governor Vance. Kilpatrick had done no more than send Major Porter to arrest Vance, yet according to a press account, as Vance described it, "he tamed me by capturing me and riding me two hundred miles on a bareback mule." The story was altogether fictitious. Vance wrote a letter about it to the editor of the New York *World*, saying of Kilpatrick: "I will do him the justice to say that he knew that was a lie when he uttered it."[3]

Zeb told how he had been sent home by General Schofield, to whom he had offered to surrender, and had remained there until arrested on May 13 by the cavalry detachment under Major Porter, "from whom I received nothing but kindness and courtesy." He traveled by buggy to Salisbury, where they took the cars.

"I saw no mule on the trip," Vance concluded, "yet I thought I saw an ass at the general's headquarters; this impression has since been confirmed."

Wittkowsky, who drove him, was a Polish Jew, thirty years old, who had reached New York twelve years before with three dollars in his pocket. He had worked his way south, settled in Statesville, and set up the hatmaking firm of Wittkowsky and Saltzgiver. He had come to know Vance because the governor after reaching Statesville would go often to the general store of Isaac and David Wallace, two German Jewish immigrants, friends of Wittkowsky, who had peddled in the neighborhood of Bamberg, South Carolina, then had established the leading mercantile institute in Statesville in 1850, when the town had a population of six hundred. They began a small banking business as a side line, and, of much greater interest to the piedmont and western North Carolina country, encouraged farmers to gather herbs and roots, especially ginseng, which was valuable in trade and prized in the oriental markets because the Chinese believed it to be an aphrodisiac.[4] The story was told that the Federal cavalry raided the Wallaces' home at Passover in 1865, sailed and darted the unleavened bread through the air with the prankish remark that it was merely more hardtack.

Wittkowsky later told of his ride with Vance, which began about 9 A.M., May 14, with the buggy surrounded by troopers, a party in front and a similar party behind, and four troopers riding on either side. Vance seemed distressed even to the point of tears about two things: the fact that he had not been able to leave one cent of money with his wife on which she might feed the family; the second, the fate of the state. "Poor old North Carolina," he said to Wittkowsky. "God knows what indignities she may yet be subjected to."

On the question of money he made this remark: "Many a man in my position, having ships constantly running the blockade, would have feathered his nest by shipping cotton to Europe and placing the proceeds to his credit, and in fact, I was frequently urged to do so, but thank God, I did not do it. My hands are clean and I can face my people and say I have not made money out of my position."

As was customary with Vance, the sunny side of the situation eventually triumphed, even while they were riding to prison, and, for all he knew, to possible trial and execution for his part in the war. The assassination of Lincoln had engendered deep resentment in the North. The policy of the Federal government with respect to war prisoners had not yet been established and there was widespread belief that the top governmental figures, whose situation differed distinctly from that of the soldiers and officers covered by the amnesty terms of the surrender, would be tried for treason. After they had ridden twelve or fifteen miles Vance had revived his good humor and when they stopped at a spring and the Federal cavalrymen crowded around, he emitted a few witticisms and told an anecdote or so. Wittkowsky saw one of the Northern soldiers poke another and say, "Why, this rebel governor is quite a jolly fellow."

Stanton's orders called for "close guard," but Major Porter, a more reasonable man, relaxed the rigidity of his patrol and allowed Vance to ride horseback for six miles to break the monotony of the buggy ride and gain exercise. Then, to prevent attracting the attention of curious onlookers, he permitted Vance and his companions to ride in the buggy well in advance of the cavalry squadron. As they approached Salisbury, Vance had Wittkowsky stop the buggy and wait for the cavalry to come up.

"You are giving me a good opportunity to get away," he told Major Porter.

"Governor, I know my man," said the polite Pennsylvanian. Then the officer made another generous suggestion: "Governor, we are nearing Salisbury. If you will give me your word of honor to present yourself tomorrow at the depot in time to take the train, I will not subject you to the indignity of marching you through town under guard."

Vance thanked him and agreed, then went to the friendly house of Lieutenant Colonel Charles E. Shober, an early captain of the 45th North Carolina and later colonel of the 75th Senior Reserves, where acquaintances gathered and pooled $65 from their scant resources, which was the only money Vance had with which to begin a prison stretch in Washington, where the prisoners were required to buy their own food. Wittkowsky completed his participation in the journey and his account: "The next morning I went to the depot to bid him good bye and found him surrounded by quite a number of Federal officers, all as jolly as if the Governor and they had been old friends, starting on a pleasure trip." These officers took Vance to Raleigh and thence by train to Washington, where on May 20, 1865, he was incarcerated in the most famous of jails, the Old Capitol Prison.

Sam Wittkowsky's kindness and friendship bore abundant fruit. He moved to Charlotte in the aftermath of the war and prospered both in the retail trade and in textile manufacturing and a little later by the organization of a successful building and loan association, until, after the turn of the century, he came to be called by one newspaper the city's most useful citizen. Vance, for his part, during the lean postwar years when the lyceum was an accepted form of education and entertainment, wrote a number of lectures. None was delivered more frequently or widely than that entitled "The Scattered Nation," his tribute to the Jews, which had its inception in the kindness of hat manufacturer Sam Wittkowsky on the May morning ride from Statesville to Salisbury. Sometimes this was rated as the most famous of all the countless lectures delivered in the old lyceum-Chautauqua era before the coming of motion pictures, the motor car, and the radio-television age.

In Raleigh, en route to Washington, Vance and his captors had to change trains. During the wait they stopped by the law office of Kemp P. Battle, which was being occupied as headquarters by an Ohio colonel. Friends began to drop by. Battle, hearing that the governor was there, went over and had breakfast with him. The considerate captor, Major Porter, invited by Battle to accompany them, declined with the pleasant remark that he would merely hold Battle responsible for producing the prisoner at the proper time. After breakfast they walked to the Raleigh depot, Battle on one side of the governor and his friend W. H. H. Tucker on the other, with Vance chatting pleasantly and showing not a symptom of anxiety.[5]

Why Vance was arrested and imprisoned never was made clear. No charges were filed against him; he was merely arrested and taken to jail. Brigadier General William R. Cox, whose brigade had fired the last shots of Lee's army at Appomattox, thought he had so distinguished himself as "the War Governor of the South" that those controlling the national government decided "he should vicariously suffer for the transgressions of his people." Cox called on him briefly in Raleigh when he was on his way to the prison, and said of him: "Notwithstanding the opportunities to enrich himself, which one less scrupulous would have availed himself of, he was without a dollar, save amounts contributed by a few friends from their scanty stores."[6]

The Old Capitol Prison in which Vance was held stood directly opposite the east front of the Capitol, where the United States Supreme Court now is housed in one of the world's most splendid buildings. The Old Capitol Prison was splendid in its own day, too, because it was built originally for the United States Congress and few buildings have had greater bearing on the course of the government. When the British Army burned the Capitol on August 24, 1814, discussion became earnest that the capital city should be moved westward where it would not be so exposed. John Law, the wealthy Scot who had first made a fortune in India, then married the daughter of Martha Custis Washington, and dabbled in Washington real estate, hurriedly built a temporary Capitol for $30,000—"a large and commodious building," the *Niles Weekly Register* called it—so that accommodations would be available when Congress met.[7] In front of it James Monroe had been inaugurated President. There, after the burned Capitol was rebuilt, Mrs. Lindenberger and later Henry Hill had kept their famous boardinghouse; there John C. Calhoun lived and died; there Ann Royal published her gossip sheets, *The Huntress* and *Paul Pry*, and kept her well-known "Black Book" about the capital goings on; there the radiant, young and "most sensational of the Southern spies," Belle Boyd, the "Secesh Cleopatra," fair-haired, blue-eyed and twenty, honorary aide-de-camp to Stonewall Jackson, had languished. There Major Henri Wirz of Andersonville Prison was being held and in its yard would stand the gallows on which he would be hanged.[8]

General William R. Cox thought that, when Northern friends of the prewar Congress visited him, Vance brought his imprisonment into ridicule "by his good humor and his apt way of presenting, in a ludicrous way, the mistakes of others." His anecdotes, more than any record of his past good conduct, were what, in Cox's opinion, finally turned the key and opened the jail door.[9]

Possibly that was the case. None could doubt that the gayest period of the Old Capitol Prison was when Zeb Vance held forth with his yarns while his perplexed and tactless fellow North Carolinian, President Andrew Johnson, grappled erratically with the problems of state down Pennsylvania Avenue.

Much of Vance's jesting was quite obviously a pose, or protective cover-up. When Wittkowsky noticed on the ride from Statesville that the governor was first in tears, then turned to jesting, he may have detected that his joviality was a cloak for deep emotions to which he refused to surrender openly. Often when he might seem blithe, as when walking to the Raleigh depot for the trip to the prison in Washington, he was in truth concealing anguish and despondency. That is no doubt the explanation of his conduct at the Old Capitol Prison, which could not have been a pleasant experience even for one ordinarily disposed to see the silver lining.

How easy it was to get in jail in Washington during the frenzied period of violent emotions after the assassination of Lincoln, when the civil law had all but disappeared under Secretary Stanton's quasi dictatorship, might be seen from the case of Vance's companion prisoners, Thomas Green and his wife. They were Virginians but long residents of Washington who had bought the old John P. Van Ness mansion, where the early landowner and mayor of Washington had lived. After Lincoln's assassination, in a season of wild rumors, someone circulated the story that the old Van Ness wine vault was intended to be used as the hideaway for Lincoln in the kidnap plot, before he would be carried across the Potomac. The rumor made the gossip column and without more ado and "in those mad days when no magnate [magistrate] waited for proof," Green and his wife were arrested and confined in the Old Capitol Prison, where there was nothing more to lighten their harsh treatment than Vance's presence. More than a month was required for the government to decide that there was not a shred of evidence against them and to let them out. The instance must have struck Vance as the sort of arbitrary arrest and incarceration without charge he had protected his state against during wartime.[10]

When Vance's old Ohio friend Thomas Corwin, former senator, cabinet member, and diplomat, came to see him, he inquired, "Vance, what are you doing in prison?"

"Holden pledged the last man and the last dollar for the Confederacy," he replied, referring back to the early period when the editor was an all-out war man. "I stood his security and am imprisoned for the pledge."[11]

The reply must not have had the sparkle Corwin, a master of humor and the oratorical arts, expected.

"What was the matter with you fellows down South?" he continued. "I don't get the hang of it."

"I don't either," said Vance, fingering his neck, "but I'm about to."

Corwin, who still mustered influence around Washington, went to the White House and told President Johnson it was foolish to keep a man of Vance's standing and good humor in jail. That has sometimes been regarded as the reason for his eventual release.

The prison seems to have been about as public as Pennsylvania Avenue, with persons coming and going in sufficient numbers that a small crowd would gather around Vance's cell to pass comments with him. These Northern curiosity seekers must have annoyed him at times, which is the only explanation for the conundrum he expounded.

"No, boys," he said. "I am too sad to tell you funny tales. But I can give you a riddle. Why is the Southern Confederacy like the Biblical character Lazarus?"

"Because it is poor," someone answered.

"No, that's not the reason," said Zeb.

"We give up," said another. "You tell us why."

"Because," Vance said, looking them over, "it was licked by a set of dogs."

Among the early visitors was Representative Thaddeus Stevens of Pennsylvania, whom Richard H. Battle, Zeb's secretary, described as "the arch enemy of the South and its institutions." He had served with Vance in the House before the war but he apparently came for no other purpose than to gloat. He walked in front of the prison cell and gazed at Vance "as at a caged animal in a menagerie." That was the way Battle described it. Zeb stared back at him but detected no sign of friendly recognition, then "dismissed him from notice with a gesture of contempt." Stevens turned away and no words passed between the two, though "Old Thad" had gone all the way to the prison to take a look.[12]

Vance in later years discussed his prison term very little. During it he was charged with nothing, sentenced for nothing, brought before no tribunal, faced by no accuser. His cellmate (of all persons!) was Governor John Letcher of Lexington, Virginia, with whom he had had sharp epistolary exchanges when they were presiding over their respective states during the war years. Letcher sustained his spirits with his favorite stimulant, brandy; Vance had whisky rations.

Letcher's detention, together with the fact that Jefferson Davis was arrested and held prisoner, and that other Southern war governors were jailed, suggests that someone in Washington had in mind proceedings of one sort or another against them, and such was quite clearly the case respecting Davis for a time. Still, Stanton's domination never extended to the courts. The trials, which would have subjected to judicial review the controversial question of the right of states to secede, a matter that had been irrevocably decided on the battlefield (if the historical tenet that victory makes custom and custom makes right is acceptable), caused the Federal government to avoid prosecution, and the governors, and at length President Davis, were released.

Vance's case appeared to rest on somewhat different grounds from that of the other governors. Clement Dowd, later his law partner in Charlotte, made a diligent search of the Old Capitol Prison records for the period without bringing to light any charge, indictment, or other evidence bearing on the case. When he was engaged in this investigation in Washington the intimation was made to him that President Johnson probably had an old grudge against Vance. They had been in Congress together, though in different chambers, Johnson having gone from the House to the Senate before Vance became a representative, and had been governors of adjoining states, though espousing conflicting causes, Johnson governor by appointment, Vance by election.

"This suggestion," said Dowd, "is strengthened by, and may have been founded upon, the fact that the order of arrest came directly from President Johnson."[13] Another thought was that the arrest was an expression of Johnson's dislike for the old-time aristocracy of the South, though Vance could scarcely have qualified in that, being a commoner by instinct and birth, of the mountain pioneers and not the plantations. The more likely explanation, borne out by subsequent events, was that Vance was arrested and held on the ground of complicity in the conduct of the Salisbury Prison, about which Stanton had recently been receiving firsthand accounts. That was the opinion of Kemp Battle, who reported that an attempt was being made to hold Vance responsible for the hardships of the Salisbury prisoners, much as Major Henri Wirtz was being charged with mistreatment of the prisoners at Andersonville.[14]

One of the graphic descriptions of Salisbury from the prisoner's viewpoint was that of the New York *Tribune* correspondent, Junius Henri Browne, who, with fellow *Tribune* correspondent Albert D. Richardson and Richard T. Colburn of the New York *World,* was captured when their tug was sunk as they were trying to run the batteries at Vicksburg. The incident was one which caused Sherman, who disliked correspondents and believed all on the tug had drowned, to say: "That's good! We'll have dispatches now from hell before breakfast."[15]

This far-off Mississippi River event came to have direct bearing on the fortunes of Zeb Vance, because the correspondents, after experiences in Castle Thunder and Libby prisons, were transferred to Salisbury in February, 1864, a place known in Northern Army ranks to be a sieve, from which they made their escape. The correspondents worked their way through the western North Carolina underground to Federal forces in Knoxville, Tennessee, and eventually reached Washington in January, 1865, where Browne and Richardson sought out Secretary Stanton and reported on what they regarded as the unbelievably foul conditions—the "superlative squallor"—at Salisbury.

Browne wrote of them: "The quarters in which we were confined were very undesirable, being about ninety by forty feet, with barred windows, dirty floor, partially occupied by rude bunks, and two broken stoves that gave no heat, but a perpetual smoke of green pine-wood that made the atmosphere blue, and caused us to weep as though we had lost the dearest mistress of our soul.

"There, with rags and vermin, filth and odors, as little Sabean as possible, we passed the long, cold, desolate nights, shivering in our light blankets, and striving, for many a dreary hour, in vain to sleep. What a dismal den it was!"[16]

But he compared it favorably with Castle Thunder or Libby because the prisoners had the privilege of a yard and opportunity to use it each day. When they arrived in late 1864, Salisbury had between six and seven hundred captives, described as "Rebel convicts, Northern deserters, hostages, Southern Union men, and all persons that the enemy designed to hold for a long time." The numbers increased to where the prison, a former cotton factory, was jammed.

Others attested to the hardships of the Salisbury prisoners extending to the trigger-happiness of the boy guards, the miserable food, and the lack of adequate shelter, which caused the prisoners to burrow and live in caves.

The Southern contention was that Salisbury was loaded with prisoners solely because of the Grant-Stanton policy which, as a part of the war of attrition, put a stop to all exchanges such as had been the practice in the earlier part of the war.[17] The escape of correspondents Browne and Richardson, their report to Secretary Stanton, and their subsequent public statements went far to end the Federal no-exchange policy. Their exposure of the suffering, and the attention focused on the Grant-Stanton policy caused so much public agitation and clamor that Stanton was compelled to reverse himself and in February, 1865, resume the exchanges.

As Browne wrote: "After our departure from Washington, such a storm was raised about the Secretary's ears, such a tremendous outside feeling was created, that he was compelled to make an exchange."[18] The system adopted in February, 1865, was that prisoners captured prior to July 1, 1863, were the first exchanged; then those on the first five days in July, which included the Gettysburg and Vicksburg prisoners, then progressively for the later periods. But between October 1, 1864, and February 17, 1865, the time during which the prison had its heaviest use, 3,419 died there, of whom 2,504 were prisoners of war. Considering that the number of prisoners housed there was about

10,000, the death rate by any modern standards was shockingly high. So were all prison death statistics of this war. The death rate from disease in the armies of both sides was grievously high as well. When the exchange from Salisbury was resumed, the sick were put on trains and about 2,800 who felt able were marched to Greensboro and finally were sent to Wilmington for restoration to their own army. The prisoners who remained at Salisbury after the general delivery were transferred to Charlotte on the approach of the Stoneman cavalry raiders, who entered Salisbury April 12, 1865.[19]

Jefferson Davis contended that although the South held 60,000 more Federal prisoners than the North had Confederate prisoners, 6,000 more Confederates died in Northern prisons than Federals in Confederate prisons. Both he and General Lee did try repeatedly to have the exchange cartel restored, but were met with Grant's denial.[20]

The treatment of Northern prisoners in the South became closely involved in the Vance story.

S. A. Ashe, the soldier-historian who investigated the Salisbury prison record after the war, concurred with New York *Tribune* correspondent Browne that the deaths were partly attributable to those who denied the prisoners the hope of exchange. Writing of all prisons, he charged: "It is probably within bounds to say that, including both sides, more than 30,00, perhaps 40,000 of these deplorable deaths were due to the actions of the Federal authorities."[21]

Ashe's figures probably are high. The War Department reported that of the 188,000 Federal soldiers captured, half were paroled, half imprisoned, and that 36,000 died in captivity. Ashe cited Stanton's report that 26,246 Confederates died in Northern prisons, but said some placed the figure at 30,000, most of them occurring during the last twelve months when the exchanges were halted. He placed the death rate of Southerners in Northern prisons at about 33 per cent.[22]

In deaths of prisoners of war, Salisbury seems below the average, but nowhere was the picture anything but sordid.

Vance obtained his impressions of Salisbury from Surgeon General Warren, who stopped there while passing, to get a personal view. "I found it overcrowded, dirty and poorly provided in every way," he wrote later. He said the prisoners were "surly and insubordinate to the last degree even in the midst of their squalor, filth and wretchedness." When he attempted to talk kindly to them, he reported they answered mockingly and insultingly. On his return to Raleigh he told Vance of the forlorn state in which he found the prisoners, then quoted the governor as responding:

"Poor fellows. I pity them from the bottom of my heart. It is true that the Confederate authorities give them the same rations as their own soldiers, and that the United States government is mainly responsible for their condition by refusing an exchange when we have declared our inability to provide for prisoners, but I can't help feeling sorry for the unfortunate creatures themselves. There may be no law but that of humanity for it, but I shall devote some of the stores belonging to the State for their relief. You must send them from your depot such supplies as they require, and I will instruct my commissary general to do the same."[23]

Warren said he would be happy to carry out the governor's wishes. He got together at once what he regarded as a liberal supply of stimulants, medicines, hospital stores, blankets, and shoes and forwarded them without delay to the Salisbury prisoners. Vance followed this with a request to the legislature which authorized further distributions.

For a firsthand impression of the prison, Vance went to Salisbury at once and the word passed among the Northern soldiers that he was concerned with their welfare. Going from Raleigh by way of Greensboro, the train was stopped a few miles beyond Greensboro by a wreck in a deep cut. An engine had left the tracks, but another train had come up on the other side of the block to take on the passengers after they had walked around the obstruction.

The waiting train had a large consignment of Northern prisoners for Salisbury. The weather was rainy and Vance, big and heavy, had difficulty in clambering up the bank. Finally he halted and it did not appear he could negotiate the steep ascent. Quickly a Northern soldier, dirty and emaciated, as Vance described him, rushed to the bank, put down his hand and pulled the governor up. Vance thanked him, gave him everything that was left in his lunch basket, and turned over what remained of a bottle of apple brandy, which the governor called "that sole consoler of Southern hopes at that time."

Then it was disclosed that the prisoner did not know whom he was helping. "Half starved as he was," said Vance, "he gave a fair shout of joy and inquired my name, which I gave him. Of course, I never expected to hear from him again—but I did." In some manner the soldier got out of prison and was present when Vance's home town of

Asheville, where his mother still resided, was captured by a Northern cavalry detachment a bit indifferent to private property. This soldier found the house of the governor's mother, which was on the outskirts and exposed, and stood guard over it. Like a watchdog, he slept at night in front of the door. He certainly did not give the governor a bad reputation during the period of his Salisbury detention.[24]

Another element now entered into the governor's captivity. This was the disposition of his letter books, their secretion and discovery, and eventual perusal by Secretary of War Stanton in Washington.

The letter books measure eighteen by twelve inches and are two and a quarter inches thick, with the first two volumes containing 640 pages each and volume three, 787 pages. In the last volume only seventy-one pages are filled. The three books and index probably would weigh about twenty-five pounds. The paper is of excellent quality and even though the books have had considerable use by researchers and historians, they show little wear. They have been an important source in the research for this book.

When Sherman reached Raleigh the bulk of the records remained there, though Vance and Jonathan Worth had taken some to Company Shops and some to Greensboro by wagons assembled for that purpose. Later they were moved here and there about the state, depending on the threat of cavalry raiders, and some were looted, though what a soldier would do with old records remains a question. Eventually in May most of them were returned to Raleigh, but from the general mass Governor Vance withheld his three letter books and the index, plus the great seal of the state. The letter books, which have great historical value to the state, were placed for safekeeping in the Greensboro branch of the Cape Fear Bank. The diligent Federal officers found them there in mid-May, much to Vance's benefit, as it developed. The great seal of the state and two boxes of Confederate records were sent by train to Raleigh, but the boxes were broken open at the depot and the great seal was pilfered, never to be heard of again. Possibly it still reposes with the descendants of some Northern soldier who would rather not have it but do not know what to do about it without casting a reflection on their forebear; possibly it was thrown into the rubbish heap. But Vance's letter books, neatly and faithfully kept, were carried to Schofield's headquarters, from where they were sent to Washington, taken into the office of Secretary of War Stanton, and left on his desk for reading.

The story of what happened to other state records, including those of the University of North Carolina, is one that reached saga proportions, but bits of the record are still appearing. The story has been brought together by State Archivist Houston G. Jones. The state adjutant general's report was discovered during a renovation of an old Greensboro homestead. A batch of the state archives turned up in a pool hall in Morrisania, New York (now a part of the Bronx), where nobody seemed to be paying much attention to them and they could have been carried out by any patron. No one knows what did happen to them.

A long struggle ensued to get the Vance letter books returned to Raleigh, and it was pressed after Vance became senator, but the War Department coveted them, and sometimes the letters from North Carolina soliciting their return were not even answered. Finally in 1886 President Cleveland signed a resolution which Vance had managed to get through Congress providing that certified copies of the books should be given to the state, and after the laborious task of copying the letters had been completed, mostly in the neat penmanship of the era, the copies were sent to Raleigh March 13, 1888. Not until 1962, when a representative of the North Carolina government was checking the roster of North Carolina soldiers in the war, was the matter of returning the originals revived, and in that year, a century after Vance's election as governor, Christopher Crittenden, Director of the North Carolina Department of Archives and History, applied for and received the originals, an evidence that the rancors of the war had been forgotten at last.[25]

While the big letter books were lying on Secretary Stanton's desk one of the New York correspondents who had come to see Stanton glanced through them, and remarked as he read, seemingly talking to Stanton, that "among much evil they exhibited redeeming traits of character," and again, that the letters of Governor Vance to Secretary Seddon and General Bradley T. Johnson, "who had control of the prisoners at Salisbury, *urged* upon both of these functionaries the immediate relief of the suffering prisoners, as alike dictated by humanity and policy." The correspondent could not know of Vance's conversation with Warren or request to the legislature, but it was clear that if Vance had been arrested for any part of mistreatment of the Salisbury prisoners, it had been an instance of false arrest.[26]

Vance had written to Brigadier General Bradley T. Johnson, commander of the Salisbury prison, on January 26, 1865, saying the most distressful accounts had reached him of the suffering and destitution of

Northern prisoners under Johnson's charge. The letter was based on Dr. Warren's inspection. "If the half be true," said Vance, "it is disgraceful to our humanity and will provoke severe retaliation." He hoped conditions were not as bad as represented, "but lest it be so, I hereby tender you any aid in my power to afford to make their condition more tolerable." He said he knew of the great scarcity of food, "but shelter and warmth can certainly be provided and I can spare you some clothing if the Yankees will deliver as much to North Carolina troops in Northern prisons."[27]

Vance at the same time, as the news scribe must have noticed, was having difficulty in getting Major W. W. Peirce of the Confederate quartermaster's department stationed in Raleigh to give clothing to Confederates returning from prison after the exchange cartel was revived. He wrote to General Theophilus H. Holmes, who in the last stages commanded the reserve forces in his own state of North Carolina, complaining and saying, "As I cannot see these men suffer I have been giving them all supplies, though we may not receive any pay for them."

General Johnson was absent in Virginia because of illness when Vance's letter reached Salisbury. Captain G. W. Booth, his adjutant general, replied that the prison was established only for Confederate prisoners, and sufficient ground and building space had been obtained for that purpose, but about November 5, 1864, suddenly 8,000 Federal prisoners were sent there because the Confederate government had no other place. The grounds were enlarged and tents were issued and all were under shelter of some sort at the time he wrote, February 3. The number reached 10,000 and their condition was described as "extremely bad." Wood was being issued to them, the amount being governed to an extent by the weather. That they had enough was evidenced by their sales of wood to the sutler in exchange for tobacco. They regularly received one pound of good bread, one pint of soup, and small issues of meat and sorghum. Captain Booth sent a schedule of the rations issued in late January. "As to clothing their condition is truly deplorable—most of them having been prisoners some 6 or 9 months. The Confederate Govt. cannot issue clothing to them, and none has been received at this Post from the North." An effort was underway to secure clothing, and Vance's generous proposition no doubt would readily be agreed to by the Federal government. Even as he wrote he learned that supplies of shoes and blankets had been shipped from Richmond.[28]

General Bradley T. Johnson answered Vance on February 12, saying none could deplore more than he the condition of the prisoners. "It is disgraceful to our country." He confirmed Captain Booth's letter that they were well supplied with food and fuel but suffered for clothes and shelter. Thirty-five hundred blankets were expected on the next day, which, with the tents, would make their condition tolerable. He urgently recommended some immediate deliverance of the prisoners if a method could be arranged with General Grant.[29]

Vance's concern served to stir other action in behalf of the prisoners. Mrs. Spencer, who, it will be recalled, wrote at Vance's request, thought it unavoidable that they would have to live on half rations because everyone in the state was doing just that, and she felt that future investigation would have to determine how far the Federal government was "responsible and criminal in this matter" because of its refusal to exchange prisoners. Then she quoted an incident from a member of the last state legislature, who said:

"I called at Governor Vance's office, in the capitol, and found him sitting alone; and though his desk was covered with papers and documents, these did not seem to engage his attention. He rather seemed to be in profound thought." The legislator said a surgeon had just returned from Salisbury, and the governor was shocked at what he heard of conditions there. "He went on to detail what he had heard, and testified deep feeling during the recital." He wanted the state to take some action, to which the legislator agreed. A resolution was introduced at his instigation authorizing the governor to make an arrangement for distributing blankets and clothing to Federal prisoners in like quantity to those which would be distributed to North Carolina soldiers imprisoned in the North. The resolution passed the legislature on the very next day without a dissenting voice.[30]

Vance had written a letter to Secretary Seddon on behalf of the Salisbury prisoners of much the same purport as that to General Bradley T. Johnson, based also on Dr. Warren's findings there. This letter, dated February 1, 1865, was equally emphatic. "Accounts reach me," he said, "of the most distressing character in regard to their suffering and destitution. I earnestly request you to have the matter inquired into and if in our power to relieve them that it be done. If they are wilfully left to suffer and we can avoid it it would be not only a blot on our humanity, but would lay us open to severe retaliation." He said he knew the straitened situation in the country and blamed nobody until he had further information.[31]

Happily Vance's letters about the prisoners were relatively brief and Stanton, who was an incessant talker more given to output than intake, had the patience to read them. When he did his attitude was that of the New York journalist. Stanton has been described as one "whom some people thought was not mild; whom some thought was even savage."[32] But when Stanton saw how Vance had tried to ameliorate the condition of the Federal prisoners, he called the deposed governor to his office and said: "Upon your record you stand acquitted; you are at liberty to go where you will."[33]

A summation of Vance's conduct respecting the Salisbury prisoners was made by Major Charles M. Stedman, which, he said, "will attract the admiration of the brave and generous from every civilized land." Though the people of North Carolina were making a supreme effort to provide for their own soldiers, at Vance's request they gave ungrudgingly to the prisoners, "in many instances depriving themselves of needed comforts."

Stedman, a florid orator of the nineteenth-century style, declared descendants of both Union and Confederate soldiers would bless the name of Zebulon B. Vance for his prison work. "When the full truth of conditions existing in the prison at Salisbury . . . shall be known, as well as the unselfish conduct of the people of North Carolina, prompted in their labor of charity and humanity by the greatest of all her sons in that era of heroic names, additional luster will be given to the name of the State already illuminated by the achievements of her children on the battle field."[34]

The actual terms of the parole Vance received were not complete, nor did they seem to result entirely from the Salisbury letters, though that was the major factor. Nor was the parole issued forthwith. Paroles were not being granted except on recommendations from the new state authorities who were being set up in the South. One of the most deplorable situations ever to come to North Carolina was that Editor William W. Holden, who had turned about on any number of counts, should now be the one selected by President Johnson to determine who from North Carolina should be pardoned and who should stay in jail.

Latent but deep hostility to Vance existed among the old Holden crowd. Kemp Battle told how some of the editor's followers had decided to organize a torchlight parade celebrating the capture of Raleigh by Sherman's army. The menacing word was passed around that the houses not illuminated for the event would have stones flying through their windows. Since humiliation of Vance and his followers was the main aim, Battle, who had become acquainted with one of General Terry's staff officers, had asked him to get the intelligence to Terry that the instigators were seeking merely to rebuke and belittle the best citizens of the town and not to show genuine sympathy with the Union. He thought that if stones began to fly they would fly in both directions and a general fracas would ensue. Terry had the good judgment to cancel the parade plans.[35]

But Holden was back on his feet. When President Johnson determined to reconstruct North Carolina according to his own plan, between the time of Johnston's surrender and the meeting of Congress in December, whom should he appoint as provisional governor of North Carolina but Editor Holden! By proclamation May 22, 1865, he gave Holden the duty of prescribing the method for calling a convention of those loyal to the Union to amend the state constitution and pave the way for readmission. The military government, which possessed the true power, was organized in late April with Schofield in command, and with Generals Joseph R. Hawley and John M. Palmer controlling the eastern district, Terry the central, and Jacob D. Cox the western. Holden served as provisional governor until defeated in an election that fall by Jonathan Worth, but the plan of readmission President Johnson envisioned was discarded by Congress when it met that winter.[36]

Meantime, though he retained a cheerful front, Vance's imprisonment became one of the most distressing periods of his career, because Mrs. Vance grew seriously ill during the time when she had the whole care of four young, active boys. That was the reason he submitted to President Johnson a petition for pardon, which he wrote on June 3, 1865, two weeks after reaching the prison. This document of about twelve hundred words was a straightforward recital of his attitude before and during the war, the problems which confronted him when North Carolina faced the decision of joining or fighting her sister states of the South, and his determination to go with his own people.

He made it clear that he desired no pardon on any false pretense. He had labored in every honorable way to repel the invasion of his state but now, in view of the condition of affairs, intended no further resistance to the authority of the Federal government. Again, it was clear from his petition that he had come out of the war and the governorship almost penniless; he said in his petition that he had very little property (his house in Asheville probably being what he had in mind); that his wife and four children depended entirely on his work, and that during his absence they were living on the charity provided by personal friends.

The obstacle to his pardon was the ungenerous Holden, whose attitude might be seen from his statement recommending Brigadier General Robert B. Vance's pardon, that "He is a different man from Z. B. Vance. He is honest, has no political ambitions, and is very poor." That related to the pardon, but enough pressure was brought to bear on Holden to cause him to recommend, though grudgingly, as his later statement manifested, that Vance be paroled so he could get out of prison and return to his family.[37]

Whether from Holden's parole, Corwin's personal recommendation, or because of the letters about the Salisbury prisoners, Vance was released on July 6, 1865, after being under arrest since May 13 and in the Old Capitol Prison since May 20, altogether an arrest and detention of seven weeks and five days. He was required to remain at home subject to President Johnson's orders. As he described it in a letter from Statesville: "So I am here, a prisoner still. Mrs. Vance during my confinement was seized with hemorrhage of the lungs and came near dying. She is now, however, after much suffering, mental and bodily, restored to her usual health. We are living very poorly and quietly, as I can do no business until I am pardoned or released from my parole."[38]

Any respect which may have remained for Holden with Vance and his followers was lost by the editor's prolonged refusal to recommend a full pardon. Vance could not help but remember how Holden had come fleeing to him for protection on the night the mob of soldiers sacked the *Standard* office. He not only recalled this in a letter to Swain, but also mentioned that he had more than once shielded Holden from incarceration in Castle Thunder. Vance had, in fact, been his stanch protector against the Richmond authorities, who would gladly have responded to the army's urgency that he be jailed and muzzled.

The situation long continued where a vain editor, suddenly cast into power in his shifting about, and finally hitting the winning side, controlled the destinies of the most important and capable men of the state—Thomas Bragg, William A. Graham, former governor Henry T. Clark, former Confederate senator William T. Dortch, Vance, and many others—and he was not likely to release his hold. Still, his defeat for the governorship by Jonathan Worth, about which he protested loudly to President Johnson, did not immediately alter Vance's situation.

Vance's efforts to see President Johnson were rebuffed, though the privilege was extended to former governors Brown of Georgia and Letcher of Virginia. Vance attributed the President's coldness to the vengeance of his arch enemy Holden. He did not get a pardon until President Johnson finally got around to issuing an executive order to that effect March 11, 1867.

While Vance late in the war had been hastening about from Raleigh, Hillsboro, Greensboro, and Charlotte, then back to Greensboro and on to Statesville, Mrs. Vance and their four boys had set up housekeeping in Statesville, using some of their own furniture and some transportable articles they had taken from the Governor's Mansion for safekeeping. When Stoneman approached Statesville, Mrs. Vance packed a large trunk with her silver, her most valuable clothing, and $2,000 in gold which a Statesville bank had asked her to safeguard by sending it with the valuables. But the trunk was intercepted en route by soldiers of the command of Colonel William J. Palmer of the 15th Pennsylvania Cavalry, who headed one of Stoneman's brigades. The captors, being delighted with the property of the rebel governor, divided the spoil. Colonel Palmer learned of it an hour later, halted the men, and had every one of the articles and, what is truly surprising, every dollar of the gold collected and put back into the trunk, then had the trunk sent back under guard to Statesville and delivered to Mrs. Vance with the colonel's compliments! Moreover, there was no plundering in Statesville and Mrs. Vance was respected and unmolested.[39]

Vance before his arrest had enjoyed eleven days at this Statesville home after his arrival there on May 2, 1865. This was his first opportunity to give full attention to his family. Occasionally in Raleigh in the press of war business he would have to take time off to help care for a sick child, the town being short of doctors. In Statesville, stripped of his duties, he could live quietly but poorly, as he described it, being entirely out of money.

In later campaigns the charge was made from time to time that Vance had made money out of the war, but nothing was clearer after the conflict than that he was down to nothing and had to begin to build up slowly from the bottom. Even in that he was restrained at the outset because without a pardon he had no status as a lawyer. About all he had was his often ill but always patient wife, Hattie, and his four boys, Charles, David, Zebulon, Jr., known as Zebby, and Thomas. The two elder boys, Charles and David, entered school in Statesville and as the father mentioned, "are studying geography, etc." Why he should have stressed geography above other subjects is a matter of interest, but perhaps they liked it, and Vance himself, far from being a provincial, was always looking out at the world. They remained in good health after moving from Raleigh, and this, in consideration of the family's other problems and close circumstances, was the greatest of blessings.[40]

Though Mrs. Vance had received consideration when Sherman's raiders passed through Statesville and had had her property restored by Colonel Palmer, she had encountered altogether different treatment while Vance was a prisoner in Washington. A detachment of soldiers rode up one summer day under the command of an apologetic Federal officer, who did not appear to relish his orders, and moved every stick of furniture out of the house, leaving it as bare as an empty barn. The removal, the officer explained, had been instigated by North Carolinians in Raleigh who wanted the items restored which had been taken from the governor's palace. The incident remains something of a mystery because not only were these articles taken—and no inventory appears to exist of just what they were—but everything else in the house was removed, what the Vances owned privately as well. Vance's transfer of the palace items to Statesville had been legitimate, because he was still the elected governor then, and was setting up a new household only because he was about to be driven from the capital by invaders. But the mystery was that none of the furnishings, whether publicly or privately owned, ever got back to the executive mansion in Raleigh. Mrs. Spencer, who was curious about the incident, asked two questions: "First, who were the North Carolinians who instigated this insult to Mrs. Vance? And second, Whatever *did* become of the furniture? Everything in the way of furniture was carried off, and Mrs. Vance, who was then ill, and her children were left without even a bed." Her questions have never been answered.[41]

As soon as intelligence of the affair spread about Statesville, the citizens began to bring in articles, and in less than twelve hours the house was completely refurnished and had a good deal more in it than before the extraordinary raid occurred.

At this period of both mental and financial depression, on his return to Statesville on parole, Zeb Vance cast about in many directions and contemplated removal to Australia so earnestly that he wrote to his old Asheville friend, John Evans Brown, who was living there. Brown, a Pennsylvanian who had come down to survey and live an outdoor life because of his health, had an adventurous spirit in his rather frail body and in 1849 joined in the California gold rush. Then, after a short return visit in Asheville, he went to Australia to mine and become a sheep rancher. There he prospered, as he did later in New Zealand, a country he did much to advance as legislator and Minister of Education. He and his father, William John Brown, were among the Vance family's closest friends. John Evans Brown's brother, William Caleb Brown, had been Zeb's law partner in Asheville before the war.

Vance gave his distant friend a picture of economic conditions in North Carolina: "Our Currency, of course, is gone and with it went the Banks and bonds of the State, and with them went to ruin thousands of widows, orphans and helpless persons whose funds were invested therein. Their Railroads destroyed, towns and villages burned to ashes, fields and farms laid desolate, homes and homesteads, palaces and cabins only marked to the owners eye by the blackened chimneys looming out on the landscape, like the mile marks on the great highway of desolation as it swept over the blooming plains and happy valleys of our once prosperous land. The stock all driven off and destroyed, mills and agricultural implements specially ruined; many wealthy farmers making with their own hands a small and scanty crop with old artillery horses turned out by the troops to die. This is but a faint picture of the ruin of the country which years ago you left blooming like the garden of Eden, abounding in plenty and filled with a population whose condition was the praise and the envy of all the earth! Alas, alas!

"To travel from New Berne to Buncombe now would cause you many tears, John, unless your heart is harder than I think it is. But thank God, though witchcraft and poverty doth abound, yet charity and brotherly love doth much more abound. A feeling of common suffering has united the hearts of our people and they help one another. Our people do not uselessly repine over their ruined hopes. They have gone to work with amazing alacrity and spirit. Major Generals, Brigadiers, Congressmen and high functionaries hold the plough and sweat for their bread. A fair crop was the reward of last season's labor, and there will hardly be any suffering for next year except among the Negroes, who forsaking their old masters have mostly flocked into town in search of their freedom, where they are dying and will die by thousands. Trade begins feebly . . . and a beam of hope . . . again to reanimate our long tried and suffering people. **Our loss in men was very great. Seven-tenths** of the spirited, educated young men of N. C. fell in this struggle. Many old families are almost extinct in the male line."

How close Vance came to leaving his native state may be judged from his uncertainties about the future of the South, similar to those besetting the many former Confederate officers who were moving to Mexico or taking service in the army of the Khedive of Egypt.

"Many thoughts have I directed towards the distant Orient where you are," he wrote. "The idea is so possible at the least that I would be thankful to you for any information germain to the matter. Climate, soil, water courses, Government, population etc., are all eagerly enquired after here. What would it cost me and how would I go to get there? What could I do there? Either in Australia or New Zealand? As a lawyer, grazier, merchant or what not? What would I do when set down at the Wharf at Sidney with a wife, four children and perhaps 'nary red?' Tell me all about it. Should these things happen which we fear, my Brother Robert (who was a Brigadier in the Southern Army) and I will go some where. At present there seems to be no prospect in the stability of the Govt. in Mexico or vast numbers of our people would go there. Such a lot have gone anyhow. . . ."

Vance indicated that when "released from my bonds" and his citizenship was restored he would make a decision. "I think of going to Wilmington, N. C. to practise law if I don't leave the Country. The mountains were much torn and distracted by the war, being almost the only part of the State which was not thoroughly united. The State of Society there is not pleasant, and I don't think I shall ever return there to live. Murder and outrage are frequent and the absence of civil law encourages the wickedly inclined." He could not know that he had many happy and fruitful years ahead of him in the western North Carolina mountains.[42]

He thought the anxieties of the war had left their marks on him. "I am getting very gray," he wrote. He had worn his hair shorter during the war but now, after a common practice of Southern legislators and lawyers of the day, let it grow long again.

At the age of thirty-five, on the threshold of middle age, he was without money or position or the immediate prospects of gaining either, paroled but not charged, restricted in his movements to a single small town, and with the requirement of seeking permission even for a trip to Chapel Hill. But behind him was more than usually occurs in a man's lifetime. He had been mountain lawyer, state legislator, Congressman, captain of the "Rough and Ready Guards," and colonel of the glorious 26th North Carolina regiment. He had conducted his state ably and provided to the Confederacy much of the motive power through one of the most desperately fought wars of history. Above all, he had been a champion of human rights and personal liberty, a votary dedicated to preserving the institutions which safeguarded the individual man and woman, which he knew had been won agonizingly from despotic rulers over a long course of time. None had fought the war harder and none had preserved a clearer vision—that a war being fought for freedom could not recklessly abandon that principle at the start.

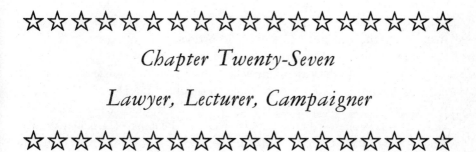

## Chapter Twenty-Seven

## Lawyer, Lecturer, Campaigner

Time, as Zeb Vance had thought from the beginning, would have showed ways for solving the intersectional discord. Time would have brought freedom to the slaves, which appeared to be the only benefit to come out of the Civil War.

Emancipation could have been achieved as quickly in peace as in war had the best thought of the government been focused in that direction, and in a manner much more orderly and beneficial to the Negro population. The former slaves were left stranded and virtually helpless for years. They received no mule and forty acres, but crowded into the Southern cities when the plantations were wiped out. Certainly emancipation could have been attained by purchase at vastly less cost in money and without the irreparable sacrifice in young lives and maimed bodies in both North and South. The best thought of both sections aspired toward emancipation, but government initiative lagged.

Vance, it proved, was one of the comparatively few legislators in Washington who from the beginning had had an unclouded vision of the catastrophe of war, and the understanding that both sides would lose by it. That is much clearer now, after the passing of a century, than then, when he stood with a relatively small group. He held no farfetched notion that the nation had to be fused by conflict—that a terrible blood

435

bath and the loss of the fairest young lives of North and South would serve as "a great unifying force." Had enough others possessed the statesmanship to see as Vance did the awful tragedy of war, surely more determined efforts would have been made at conciliation. But unlike him, the promoters of secession seemed to believe the parting would be cheap and safe, and thus the severance came, and the unwilling Northern leaders, who did not understand war either, would have none of it when the guns roared at Sumter. Again it had to be demonstrated to history that of all the methods of solving controversies, war, though often seemingly exciting and alluring, is indeed the least attractive.

To say that bloody war is unifying is merely to recognize that coercion, as in the days of ancient Rome, instead of a free choice by the people, has remained the accepted method of consolidating governments and attaining cohesion. Quite apart from the benefits of emancipation which were gained, many unfortunate consequences to the Federal government had their inception in the conflict, and have grown so much that the original purpose of the founders of a balance between Federal and state authority has been all but cast aside. If the South in 1861 was devoted too strongly to the rights of the states, the pendulum which in 1865 began to swing in the opposite direction reached another extreme.

But clear as was his vision, Vance also had a trait in common with Robert E. Lee, in that he was not one to look back. The decision had been made at Gettysburg, Fort Fisher, and Appomattox, and Vance was not disposed to ponder fruitlessly over what might have been had either the South or he personally decided a different way. As to events, he influenced them where he could, accepted them where he could not. He followed the Lee pattern of recognizing the Union as being re-established, and of resuming his journey with it in good faith. But he found that a deal of mirth could be gleaned out of the late conflict if handled delicately. When he began to be called on to lecture, first in North Carolina and then over the country, his repertoire of war stories became extensive and pleased the old soldiers of both armies, who were able after the passing of a few years to laugh at their hardships and deal more lightly with their old enemies and the causes for which they fought.

He would sometimes jibe at Massachusetts by telling how that state relieved herself of slavery. Massachusetts was like the old maid who was fond of garish jewelry but got religion and exhorted young pretty women against wearing gewgaws. "Oh, girls," she said, "I used to wear

ear rings and finger rings and laces and furbelows like you, but I found they were dragging my immortal soul down to hell and I stripped off every one of them."

"What did you do with them?" she was asked.

"Why," she said, "I sold them to my little sister."[1]

Vance went to Chapel Hill to deliver the commencement address in 1866, and while few if any more notable addresses have been delivered there, only three graduates heard it, though of course many visitors came from afar when it was known he would speak. Kemp Battle recorded that this class of 1866 did well, two becoming distinguished physicians and the other a lawyer and journalist. Zeb's address, entitled "The Duties of Defeat," placed him alongside Lee in advising the people to accept the decision of battle and work as loyal citizens of the governments, state and national, for the upbuilding of their society and the education of their children.[2]

Zeb seemed lightened by the fact that amid the carnage and ruin of war the University of North Carolina survived with "a goodly display of her ancient life and energy."[3] But though he had not yet had his full citizenship restored, he struck out boldly against the coming of carpetbag rule.

"With her homesteads burned to ashes," he said, "with fields desolated, with thousands of her noblest and bravest children sleeping in beds of slaughter; innumerable orphans, widows, and helpless persons reduced to beggary and deprived of their natural protectors; her corporations bankrupt and her own credit gone; her public charities overthrown, her educational fund utterly lost; her land filled from end to end with her maimed and mutilated soldiers; denied all representation in the public counsels; her heart-broken and wretched people are not only oppressed with the weight of their own indebtedness, but are crushed into the very dust by taxation for the mighty debt incurred as the cost of their own subjugation!"[4]

He said the country looked toward its young men to lead in preaching and practicing hope. Education was to become one of his great causes and none contributed more than he to its advancement for both races in the state, white and Negro. That year the faculty salaries went unpaid; the stock owned by the university was worthless.

Vance had attended the university, but was essentially self-educated. His single year at Chapel Hill, though he had diligently applied himself, had merely opened for him the great possibilities for advancement in the cultural arts and the law. No man of his generation understood better than he the need for general education, the maintenance of public schools, and the preservation of the institutions of higher learning. The University of North Carolina had all but dried up during the war. President Swain undertook in the early stages to prevent the draft of the whole of the able-bodied students, but as the emergency deepened they went into the ranks until at the time of Lee's surrender the student body numbered about twelve. Of eighty in the freshman class of 1860, only one, in frail health, stayed. President Swain held regular prayers and had the college bell rung each day, even when four thousand Federal cavalrymen were crowded into the village. Happily Swain did not survive to witness the closing of the college under the reconstruction government of the state. In August, 1868, while driving with one of his professors, he was thrown from the buggy and on August 27 he died. Of him Vance, who was later chosen to give a memorial oration at Chapel Hill, told how the word "great" is so variously applied and misapplied.

"It is often withheld when it is most richly deserved; not because of the injustice of contemporaries, for personal prejudice rarely outlives a generation, but because men rarely appreciate the full extent and character of the labors of a lifetime." Fame is more likely to come from sudden act than slow growth and long achievement. Thus a book may seem to make a professor great when it will not make him a great professor. Vance used the example of Spinoza, who was not recognized until the passing of a century. Of Swain he continued:

"In him there was a rounded fullness of the qualities, intellectual and moral, which constitute the excellence of manhood, in a degree never excelled by any citizen of North Carolina whom I have personally known, except by William A. Graham."[5]

When the college finally was forced to close, Vance became one of the most active members of the group that raised money to redeem the school's notes and put it back into operation. The amounts seem pitifully small today, but the canvassers were delighted that in six months they obtained $18,787. Zeb was on hand September 15, 1875, when the reopening of the university was observed in a great occasion of speeches, music and general celebration. The Salisbury Band played "Auld Lang Syne." Mrs. Spencer wrote a hymn for the occasion and headed a committee of women who hung pictures of the university's great. The trustees sat on the rostrum. Governor Curtis H. Brogden,

Goldsboro Republican who had succeeded on the death of Governor Tod R. Caldwell a few months before, spoke; and Vance, in what was described as "his usual felicitous style," introduced the main orator, William H. Battle of the class of 1820, ex-judge, ex-professor, but still current as one of the state's greats. As the Raleigh *News* said: "Judge Battle's was the tender task to awaken the echoes of memory, and bid us remember, resemble, and persevere." Thus with Vance one of the principal laborers and guides, the resuscitated university was ushered into its new era.[6]

Zeb held to his determination not to return to the mountains, but selected Charlotte, a thriving city of much promise, in preference to Wilmington, mainly because he believed Hattie Vance's health would fare better in the piedmont than the coastal lowlands. He set up a law partnership with Clement Dowd, who would later write and assemble a symposium biography of him, and Brigadier General Robert D. Johnson, who had commanded one of the North Carolina brigades in Lee's army at the age of twenty-four. Johnson withdrew soon to practice law on his his own in Charlotte and move to Birmingham, Alabama, where he became a bank president. Dowd and Vance continued as partners for six years. When Dowd left the firm in 1872, Zeb went in with Armistead Burwell for a time but withdrew upon his re-entry into politics in 1876.

Charlotte, named for Princess Charlotte of Mecklenburg-Schwerin, wife of the British monarch George III, was in the county of Mecklenburg, named for the birthplace of this princess and queen. There on May 20, 1775, the first declaration of independence from Great Britain was signed and read from the steps of the log courthouse—though Thomas Jefferson always disputed it. The town was already in the mid-1860s becoming a trading and manufacturing center that would make it known as the "Queen City of the South." Vance found himself much at home with the industrious descendants of the English, Scotch-Irish, and German who had come down from Pennsylvania and Virginia and the Swiss and Huguenots who had come up from Charleston, South Carolina, fusing into a city that had been incorporated in 1768 and had enjoyed continuous growth. He was gratified that the climate was generally pleasant, with four seasons, but with the winters ordinarily mild, the summers long but not ordinarily uncomfortable.[7]

This for ten of his middle years was to be Zeb's home. If he had any doubts about his popularity and drawing power they were quickly dispelled, because crowds came to hear him in court and callers dropped into his office, which was as open to visitors as his governor's office had been in Raleigh.

Zeb came to play an important role in the life of Charlotte and soon made friends of the community and business leaders. The British divine, the Reverend David Macrae of Edinburgh, who made an intensive tour of the United States in 1868 and in his book *The Americans at Home* wrote a fascinating volume of Americana, met Vance in the proprietor's office in the rear of a large Charlotte hardware store. The owner also was insurance agent, "medicinal practitioner," and other things, and his store was a gathering place. Zeb was sitting astride a chair as he would a cavalry horse, with his face to the back of the chair, on which he was carelessly carving with his jacknife. The minister gave a description of him:

"He is a tall, handsome man, with hard head and lurid-gleaming eyes of peculiar intensity. In manner he is exceedingly easy and frank, and his conversation is full of funny experiences and anecdotes."[8]

The visitor recorded one of them. When the 6th South Carolina regiment was guarding Sullivan's Island, a lieutenant posted a soldier, an Irishman, on sentry duty on the beach, but forgot to take into consideration the incoming tide. When the corporal of the guard came with a relief sentry, Patrick, the Irishman, could be seen in the moonlight struggling to walk his post with the water up to his waist. Pat challenged and was told his relief was at hand.

"Advance, thin," said the happy Irishman. "Advance and give the countersign."

"Advance!" exclaimed the corporal. "I'm not going in there to be drowned. Come out, and be relieved."

Pat declined vigorously. "The lieutenant told me I was not to stir from my post until relieved." Thereupon the corporal prepared to move on, saying, "I'll leave you there all night."

"Begorra you won't," declared Pat, bringing up his gun. "Halt! or I'll put a hole in ye. Them's my orders. No one is to pass without the countersign, and it's to be given in a whisper."

The poor corporal had no alternative. He had to shiver his way out through the cold water and whisper the word into the Irishman's ear.[9]

The conversation at the back end of the hardware store naturally dwelt on little except the war. Zeb told how his old regiment went into a campaign—apparently he was speaking of New Bern—with a wagon train a mile long and returned with only what they had on their backs, and some had not taken off their clothes for a month. They, officers and men alike, would resort to a "dry wash," which meant flapping their shirts against their saddles to loosen and shake off the vermin. When halted the men would take off their shirts, hold them up to the light, and look for the lice, which was called "reading linen."[10]

Macrae went to a Charlotte rally and noticed what others observed, that Vance had his audience in the palm of his hand from the moment he took the platform—that his hearers were with him, in anticipation, even before he was ready for them. He was not billed to speak on this occasion, but when the crowd saw him present and the announced speaker had concluded, they set up cries of "Vance! Vance!" and forced him to the platform. "His power over the audience was astonishing," the visiting Scot exclaimed. He regarded Zeb as little short of phenomenal. The ex-governor opened with half a dozen words and the audience roared. All he said was, "Fellow citizens, I once heard of an Irishman—" The crowd did not have the vaguest notion about the story or its point but broke out in an anticipatory roar of laughter.

"He kept the people laughing and cheering almost incessantly," said the Reverend Mr. Macrae. But then he sobered. Let Macrae give his account: "When he came to speak of the oppression of the South, he lashed himself into a state of great excitement, and strode up and down the platform gesticulating with such energy that the chairman had to back his seat more than once to get out of danger. . . . One picture he drew of a political opponent paddling out in mid-ocean on a single plank, and warning a majestic frigate to clear the way, elicited tumultuous applause, and caused great laughter at the expense of the person satirized."

Macrae studied the speech as Vance talked and found it to be a succession of what he termed "happy hits" instead of an orderly presentation of an argument. In the conversation after the meeting Vance conceded that the rough and tumble of stump speaking "spoiled" one for the logical presentation of a case in a deliberative assembly. It happened that in either circumstance he was superb.[11]

His courtroom speeches came to be the best entertainment in piedmont North Carolina, where the judges preserved decorum with difficulty, because laughter could scarcely be restrained. He was at heart a trial lawyer, one who could quickly establish an entente with a jury, charm it with the imagery of his language, stir it with the scorn of his benevolent satire, delight it with his wit and win its sympathy through his mastery of pathos. Most of the jurors of the day were scantily educated farmers, but they were sharp enough to understand his quick repartee and thoroughly at home with his broad humor.

One of Vance's celebrated cases and one of the few he lost before a jury was the murder trial of Tom Dula (pronounced "Dooley" and therefore mistakenly so spelled sometimes), which came about through a misunderstanding that served to show his abiding devotion to his old soldiers.

Tom Dula, a gay mountain blade who could strum a guitar, pick the banjo, scrape the fiddle, and sing a country ballad with the best of them, came back from the war to Happy Valley in Wilkes County. There he began to keep company with a chestnut-haired mountain lass, Laura Foster, who lived on German's Hill, and likewise to call on a married woman, beautiful Ann Melton, Laura's cousin. Thus the sort of love triangle almost as old as the Wilkes County hills was created. In January, 1866, Laura Foster mysteriously disappeared, after she had confided that she was going to meet Tom. She took a bundle of clothes, rode away on her brown mare, Belle, and the assumption was that she and Tom were to marry.

Days passed, Laura's mare strayed in and eventually a posse searched. One rider detected a stench in an ivy thicket and found a shallow grave, and the post-mortem showed that Laura had died from a deep knife thrust in the left breast. Tom Dula thereupon disappeared, as did several other young men who had kept company with Laura. But suspicion attached to Tom, and another posse headed by a local schoolteacher, Bob Cummings, who had often looked longingly toward Laura only to have his advances rejected, went to Tennessee after him. Without any such formality as an extradition—a writ was faked to serve the purpose—they brought Tom back. Ann Melton's sister talked. Ann conceded that Tom had been with her the day before Laura disappeared. Tom had borrowed a mattock, a link in the damaging chain of events that caused the grand jury at Wilkesboro to indict him as the principal and Ann Melton as an accessory before the fact in Laura's murder. The case had been so extensively discussed in Wilkesboro that everyone had an opinion. The trial was transferred to Statesville in adjoining Iredell County.

Zeb Vance came into it when some unidentified person rode up to his house and told him one of the musicians of his old 26th North Carolina regimental band—the band he had signed at New Bern and patronized fondly while colonel, and which had played at his inauguration and when he launched his campaign for a second term at Wilkesboro—was being charged with murder and did not have the money for a lawyer. Zeb, a direct actionist, went out, mounted his horse, and rode to the man's assistance.

Dula, it developed, was not a soldier of the famous 26th nor one of its bandsmen, which Zeb must have learned, though the point is not clear. But Tom had been in Company K, 42nd North Carolina, and had picked the banjo and fiddled ballads and battle hymns around the campfires, and, since he was a Confederate veteran without means and about to be tried for murder, Vance took the case without a fee and gave it his best efforts, as did two other prominent lawyers, R. F. Allison and R. F. Armstrong, who became associated with him. Tom had been with Hoke at Cold Harbor and in the Petersburg trenches and that was enough for Zeb.

Partly because of the love triangle involved, but more, perhaps, because Zeb Vance was going to perform, big crowds came to town and jammed the courtroom of Judge Ralph Burton, while newspaper scribes arrived from afar. The ever-enterprising James Gordon Bennett sent one of his top tear-jerkers to cover for the New York *Herald*.

Zeb was able to secure a jury composed mostly of Confederate veterans. He pitched his defense on the worth of a man's life who had been at Petersburg with Lee, compared with that of the mountain girl who had seduced this returning soldier. As the Greensboro *Daily News* correspondent, W. C. Burton, put it in a latter-day story: "The dashing Zeb Vance, founder and first colonel of the 26th, swashbuckled into the scene and tried desperately to save one of his boys from the gallows. He waved the fallen flag of the Confederacy. His defense was fiery and it seared poor Laura's name without mercy."

The question for Tom, as posed by Correspondent Burton, was: "Did he foully slay the pathetic young woman, Laura Foster? Or was it the vengeful work of the reputedly beautiful Ann Melton, the third person in that triangle of love, lust and homicide acted out so long ago in the hills of Western North Carolina?"

Zeb made a masterful speech in which, as reported by the Statesville *Landmark*, he declared, "The life of a Confederate soldier who has gone through the four-year war was worth a thousand wenches like Laura Foster."

Someone claimed to have overheard Tom Dula threaten he would "get even with the girl who was to blame for his coming down with a disease." But Tom resolutely maintained his innocence, though with his sense of chivalry he wrote a statement near the end completely absolving Ann Melton, who was freed. Throughout it all he kept his sparkle and jesting, and his sense of drama also, for when he and Zeb had lost before a stubborn jury, and had appealed and lost again, and been rejected through the Supreme Court, and Tom was finally en route to the gallows, he rode atop his coffin and scraped on his fiddle to amuse the trailing crowd.

Before the noose was placed he held up his hand and declared, "Gentlemen, do you see this hand? Does it tremble? I never hurt a hair on the girl's head."[12]

People still come to Tom Dula's grave on a ridge in the Wilkes County hills. Through the century since he returned to Happy Valley, many have thought he took the rap for beautiful Ann Melton and that the inscription on the stone raised up from the honeysuckle, with his name misspelled, "Tomas C. Dula Hanged For the Murder of Laura Foster," does not tell the full story of the crime. Ann never fared well in the community. She was killed finally when her oxcart upset, a retribution from Satan, some called it. Tom, the subject of an old mountain ballad, was a figure to be conjured with even on the gallows—handsome, dashing still, with his last grinning words to the hangman, "You have such a nice clean rope, I ought to have washed my neck."

About all Zeb could think was that nobody can win all of them, in courtroom trials any more than in sports. The most enduring thing to come from the case was the famous mountain ballad, "Tom Dula."

J. H. Whitaker told the story of Vance leaning back in his office one day when two woodcutters who had brought in loads to the market peered through the door and one said, "Ain't that old Zeb sittin' there?" Vance heard the remark and shouted, "Hello, old Stick-in-the-Mud and Turnip Tops! Come on in here and give me your paws! How are all at home, the wives and the babies?"

They talked for a while, but were still dazed when they went out, with the certainty that Vance was their old-time friend.

"Ain't old Zeb the best fellow you ever saw?" one asked. "He knows everybody, and even knows their names."[14]

The affection of the common people for him was understandable because he had time for them. An old man named Moore sold clay pipes with reed-root stems at the courthouse door, or would rig up a pipe with a new stem for a nickel. Vance was passing with the judge, also named Moore, after court adjourned.

"Hold on, Judge," he said. "I want to introduce you to my friend Mr. Moore, a name-sake of yours, by the way; a man who though not a judge of law, is a judge of a good pipe-stem, and can rig up a pipe in a jiffy, for a nickel, fit for any judge to smoke."

The judge said he was glad to get "an old-fashioned, reed-root pipe-stem and an honest old clay pipe" for a nickel. He paid it and went on with Vance, and the old pipe man never forgot the incident. "There ain't but one Zeb Vance in the world," he declared. "Stopped to introduce Judge Moore to his namesake, Mr. Moore. The Jedge's name-sake! Hurrah for old Zeb!"[15]

Vance liked to tell a story on himself, about the time he asked an old Negro what church he belonged to.

"Presbyterian church," the old man replied.

"Do you believe you have been elected?" prodded Zeb.

"Yes, sir."

"Do you think I'm elected?" Zeb continued.

"Well, boss," replied the old Negro, "I never heard that you were a candidate!"[16]

Once when Vance was going through the crowd that awaited his arrival to make a speech, a woman rushed up to the "Old Colonel" saying, "I've come ten miles this morning just to see Zeb Vance. Bless his soul, I love him enough to hug and kiss him!"

Zeb, undaunted, turned to her and said: "God bless you, madam, come to my arms." He liked to tell the story later of how he gave her a good hugging before the crowd. Her husband had been one of his soldiers who had liked to come to his tent and talk, and who had talked much about him at home also, to the point that Zeb claimed the wife wanted to kiss him "because her husband had told her what a good looking fellow I was." Someone asked him if she was good-looking.

"I don't know," said Zeb. "I never stand on looks in an engagement of that kind. The thing had to be did, and I did it in first class style."[17]

One of Zeb's common ejaculations was "By Gravy!" But as he got into his subject in conversation or on the stump he could grow more emphatic. Jonathan Worth, who was governor when Zeb renewed his law practice, a gentleman of Quaker background, never uttered an oath stronger than "Ding!" Zeb ran to the other extreme and such became his reputation. One day an old man came to his Charlotte office after a long journey, saying he had heard of Old Vance for years. "I'll die better satisfied," he said, "because I've seen you. I've heard a good deal about your brother Bob, too, and I've always heard he was the best character of the two."[18]

Few would have disputed the old man on that score. Bob had come home from his Northern prison in April, 1865, and as the Asheville *News* reported, "he looks rather worsted by his confinement, but . . . is full of life, cheerful and buoyant. The General is a great favorite of the people in his section." Bob devoted much time to the Methodist Sunday School and church and was a lifelong worker for temperance, being president at one time of the Friends of Temperance, a national organization he helped build and for which he worked unceasingly. With Zeb's earthy language and Bob's strict decorum, there was little doubt which one would judge from surface impressions the better character.

That would have been borne out when a delegation came to ask Zeb to declare himself publicly on the question of prohibition. He agreed, and made his statement: "My conscience is with you, but my stomach is on the other side." Though he did in fact become a serious student of the monetary system, when asked to make a statement about it he declared: "About the only financial principle with which I am entirely familiar is that it takes two names to float my notes."[19]

Vance never lost his ambition or drive, which revealed themselves in this postwar period, barren of political recognition, as fully as they did when he was gaining fame and directing an armed state in wartime. He had become one of the best informed citizens about the affairs of North Carolina. To bring his information into play and preserve it, he decided during the lean years to write it down. The result was a series of fact-crammed, attractively phrased articles entitled "Sketches of North Carolina." Dealing in large part with the state's history, he entered also into geography, industries, future prospects, and many other factors.

The articles were published in the Norfolk, Virginia, *Landmark*, of which James Barron Hope, admired throughout North Carolina, was the poet-editor. Hope was described by T. B. Kingsbury, in *Our Living and Our Dead*, the publication of the North Carolina branch of the Southern Historical Society, as "the only Virginia editor ever known to do North Carolina justice." He was a grandson of the commodore of the early American navy, James Barron, and a poet of sufficient merit to become known as the Poet Laureate of Virginia.[20] During the war, when the Federals captured Norfolk, he moved his family to North Carolina and never forgot the "generous kindness" with which he and they were treated. In return, he undertook to assist brother editors of North Carolina, as he put it, "by upholding the fame of their noble state."

Zeb accepted the opportunity eagerly and wrote the articles usually at night, after going home from the law office or court, or at hotels after court when he was on the circuit. He wrote with a lead pencil and the surprising element in the sketches is that he wrote them entirely from his retentive memory, without having access to histories, biographies, or statistical sources.

Of them publisher Hope said: "These sketches have done much to popularize the History of North Carolina. He ignored, on a sound theory, the more ponderous treatment and elaborate details of the analyst or historian. But in doing this he has still preserved the essential facts of Carolina's history: he has grouped these in a masterly manner, and through the whole performance, hasty as it was, he has shown an affluence of resources and a warmth of coloring which render his successive pictures worthy of an enduring place in our literature."

Hope spoke also of Vance's ambition to popularize the history of his state "in the robust and manly spirit which belongs to him."[21]

Vance did not prove one of the state's greater historians, but his sketches are easy reading, his conclusions clear, his facts in general accurate, and the result was a better understanding of North Carolina by a great many people. Unblushingly, he cut through the uncertainty which surrounds the place of Andrew Jackson's birth, and claimed him without qualification as a native North Carolinian.[22] Of the three North Carolina-born Presidents, only James K. Polk, a graduate of the University of North Carolina, was, Vance stated, an educated man. The third was the self-made Andrew Johnson. Vance thought not one of them would have made the journey to the White House "had they remained at home and partaken of our old-fashioned quiet." All three became President when residents of Tennessee. He thought the "fierce rivalries of a new land, swept by great rivers and alive with commercial activity, called forth their great qualities." In his opinion, the non-commercial features of North Carolina life did not operate so strongly on the genius of the people, who went forth to achieve elsewhere, like the Irish under English rule, who, he said, filled Europe with great men who had no field for their energies in the land of their birth.

North Carolina had a relatively greater place in the Union before 1800 than in the nineteenth century. North Carolina's slow growth had been improperly charged to a native inertness but was attributable to geography: "Our great navigable rivers speedily ran *out* of the State, our sea coast is cut up into shallow sounds and defiant sand banks, and our harbors are few and not first-rate. Therefore it is that we have little commerce; and having but little commerce we have no great accumulations of capital; having little accumulation of capital, we have no great cities; and having no great cities, we have no great home markets; and having no great home markets we have no highly stimulated and productive agriculture. . . . As trade and money-getting are the chief motive powers of this generation, it necessarily follows that we are somewhat behind in that kind of activity—all because of those sandbanks and the course of our rivers."[23]

He found plenty of vigor in the native North Carolina stock. Taking up the state after the Revolutionary War: "She began to be outstripped as soon as peace and settled governments allowed the development of those communities on the banks of great rivers and beside good harbors. That this was not owing to any sluggish inertness of her native population, may be easily shown by pointing to the thousands who under more favorable circumstances have attained the very highest honors in every department of life. North Carolina became, in fact, like Virginia, a parent hive from which poured forth annual swarms of honestly-reared, well-taught young men, who found vent for their native energy in distant and happier fields."

On the basis of one of his lectures a little later, the Wilmington *Morning Star* had observations about Vance's literary ability: "He writes well. His style is one of his very best points. He has cultivated the art of conveying his thoughts in limpid, direct, vigorous modern English. He writes with scholarly accuracy, and often with the felicity of the genuine man of letters."[24]

That was well enough of Vance the thoughtful writer, but in a rough-and-tumble, barbecue-pitched, political harangue there was striking contrast. Typical of the scores of political speeches he made during the 1866-1872 period in North Carolina, when he dropped the last traces of his early Whiggery and became an ardent Democrat, was that at the Ruffin Barbecue, reported by the Milton *Chronicle* September 18, 1868. While the texts of Vance's studied lectures show a finished side of his speaking career, perhaps the Milton *Chronicle's* extracts are as good an example as survives of his off-the-cuff, or what a later North Carolina governor, Charles B. Aycock, called "off-the-shoulder," remarks.

The Caswell County town of Milton, near which Vance spoke, had been having experience with the freaks of reconstruction. Sam Taylor, an illiterate, was made postmaster, though everyone knew he could not read the addresses on the envelopes. Still, he alone was eligible because everyone else in the town was a "Rebel" not qualified to hold office. But the government did hire an assistant for Sam Taylor—a former Confederate who did the reading and writing work.[25]

In Milton in 1856, "bright leaf tobacco" had been discovered, and an industry had been revolutionized, on the farm of the Slade brothers. The Slades had built a fire in a barn where the tobacco was drying. When the heat mounted they caught the brisk aroma and saw the leaves turn to golden yellow. They liked the taste and the smoke when they used the leaves, and told their friends, and thus the flue-curing of tobacco was born, an event which many believe was the greatest milestone in the popularity of the product.[26]

The Milton newspaper reported that "the rise of three thousand persons were present" to hear Vance, and among them five hundred ladies, to whom the reporter paid his respects: "The girls of old Rockingham and Guilford and Caswell [all counties in the Greensboro area of the state] were the rosette of rose-bud virginity and laughing beauty and by their lovely presence caused the hours to glide by softly like the patter of a lassie's foot as she trips o'er the grassy green of her springtime." First on the platform was "Duffy the Wisconsiner" who was "one of your round ruddy faced fellows, with a rocund [sic] form . . . short drab coat and tight pantaloons," who was much applauded. Then "Cowan of Wilmington," of deliberate elocution and graceful gesticulation, made three "capital points," about the familiar character then campaigning for governor on the Republican ticket. The points were, as reported:

"W. W. Holden—in the field—a coward.

"W. W. Holden—in his paper—a bully.

"W. W. Holden—in the courts—a liar."

In that setting the great Zeb Vance "unlimbered and lumbered," but the newspaper, which printed three columns of his remarks, regretted "we cannot give more than some of the headings of his great speech."[27] He began by saying he was thankful that amid much ruin "we are still left the freedom of speech; the freedom to denounce tyranny; and the freedom to meet together for a free exchange of our political opinions." Then he berated Thad Stevens, whom he termed the

"Fountain Head and Author of the Radical Party." Radical is a name which lingers in North Carolina, where Republicans are still often known as "Radicals." Stevens had freely declared, according to Vance, that the reconstruction acts were outside the Constitution.

Zeb warmed to his subject and rambled on: "I met up the other day with a fellow in Lincoln County. He got up and made a speech—said he abhorred radicalism and was opposed to its tenets—but he meant to vote for Grant and Colfax. He was one of your radical democrats—a heavenly hell of a fellow, who was entirely opposed to all the doing of hell, but mightily in favor of the devil himself. He didn't think the acts of Congress were *exactly* constitutional, but they were as near the constitution as any acts could be in such a case; that the Southern States were out of the Union and these measures had to be adopted in order to put them back. Right here, I shut my fly trap down on him.

" 'How did these States get out?' I asked.

" 'Why they got out by war,' he replied.

" 'How the devil is that, because they got whipped?'

" 'Well," he said, *'their relations got changed.* Like the fellow's pig—didn't exactly die, *it gin out.'*

"It reminds me, fellow citizens, of the limber johnnies your boys have seen in the shows—'now you see me—now you don't.' We are first *in*—then we are *out*. We are in—whenever they wish to oppress us; and whenever we claim their protection—we are out."

He made chiding references to his former fellow governor Joseph E. Brown of Georgia. He said all who would repent and favor the Chicago platform of the Grant party would have their sins washed white as snow, and: "Joe Brown of Georgia—who was he? An old original *he* secessionist. When the war first got to be talked about, he was so hungry for fighting that he took a snack before breakfast and seized Fort Pulaski. In 1860 and '61 if you had thrown him into a branch you might have heard him sizzle 3 miles. During the war he ate fire till he was as hot as a blacksmith's furnace—and since the war he has eat dirt till by virtue of it he has become a freeholder.

"Just go for Grant and—lo!—you are loyal. I could make a loyal man out of myself in a few seconds by simply telegraphing that I would support the Grant and Colfax ticket. My sins would be forgiven and they would tell me to 'depart in peace'—like a Buncombe magistrate of my town. The other day, a couple presented themselves before him to be married. He was a pompous sort of ignoramus and was smartly bothered 'how to do it'—as a crowd of town boys had collected to see the fun. After he had battle-whanged them through and tied them as man and wife—there was a kind of pause. The couple didn't know 'it was all over.' So straightening himself up, one arm akimbo—'my friends,' he said, 'depart in peace and sin no more.' "

His hearers, Zeb presumed, had had a dose of taxes, yet he declared the great mass of the Radicals did not pay taxes at all. He quoted "this carpetbagger Laflin from Pitt county" as proclaiming in the legislature, "I don't care a damn how much taxes are laid on the people of North Carolina, my constituents don't have them to pay." As to the Radicals' method of handling state affairs, he described some of the exorbitant increases in state expenditures, state salaries and the like. "I am very heavy on figures," he said, "like the little quack doctor who was called in to see a sick child. He looked at the child—felt its pulse—and shook his head. 'I don't exactly understand this child's case,' he said, 'but I tell you what I *can* do, I can give it some medicine that will throw it into fits—and I am hell on fits!' "

He said he had never had a chance to say whether he was in favor of Negro suffrage or not and launched boldly into the question of Southern disfranchisement. "My grandfather was at King's Mountain— and his old musket is now at home—I can just reach up and lay my hand on the muzzle—I am lineally descended from him—have been your Governor and worn the first honors, yet—*I can't vote.* But if I murmur a single word against the boy who blacked my boots last night and who is running for Governor of your State—as he has every right to do, HELL! BLOOD! FURY! THUNDER!—cry these radicals—'you are disloyal'—'you mean WAR!' Now fellow citizens, I, ZEBULON VANCE, tell you this truth:—I don't intend to live in a land where I am disfranchised—*and I don't intend to leave it.*"

Much water had gone over the dam since he had thought of the migration to Australia. He would stay and fight it out in North Carolina. He explained his political transition.

"My friends, old line whigs, I like you. I used to believe the old whigs were the salt of the earth, and I'm sorter of that notion yet. But the party is dead and buried and the tombstone placed over it, and I don't care to spend the balance of my days mourning at its grave." He thought if Henry Clay would rise from the dead he would not recognize the party headed by Billie Holden and a few "half whipped mangy looking fellows" at its head. He told a story of a Negro boy who caught a big catfish and stuck it in the bank and went fishing up the creek. Another boy came with a smaller catfish on his string and swapped cats. When the first boy, Jake, returned, he pulled up the fish. "Great Lord," he exclaimed, "is dis my cat? Here's where I stuck him, *but aint he swunk.*"[28] That was the condition in which Henry Clay would find the Whig party—"swunk."

Such was Vance's familiar method—always having at hand the anecdote. Some of the stories he must have concocted to fit the need, as Lincoln was suspected of doing. He told perhaps a dozen others in the course of that afternoon's talk at the Ruffin Barbecue. Yet as many others would pop up in another speech.

Vance had been a delegate to the Democratic National Convention in New York in 1868 which nominated Seymour and Blair, and had spoken for the ticket in Union Square. Two years later, after Holden had been elected governor of North Carolina in 1868, and just before he was impeached in 1870, Zeb was elected United States senator by the state legislature. Crowds serenaded him that night, November 29, at the Exchange Hotel in Raleigh. His old crowd, the conservatives, had recovered control of the state legislature in 1870. When Holden was at last impeached for his part in the Kirk-Holden war, Zeb made a well-remembered comment, "It was the longest hunt for the sorriest hide I ever saw."[29]

The Kirk-Holden war of the spring of 1870 illustrated the danger which Vance had guarded against scrupulously when the states collided —the abuse that would follow suspension of the writ of *habeas corpus.* The "war" centered in Caswell and Alamance counties. John W. Stephens had moved to Caswell from Rockingham County and become state senator of the carpetbag legislature. He was commonly called "Chicken" Stephens because of an accusation in his home county that he had been caught in a henhouse with nobody else there except the chickens. When complaints mounted against him in Caswell, he was "sentenced" by the Ku Klux Klan court, though never hauled before this extralegal body, after which a small band entered his office in the courthouse and garroted and stabbed him.

Another death occurred in a Negro lynching and Governor Holden sent the cavalryman and bushwhacker George W. Kirk and a little army, termed "mercenaries" by the Democrats, into the county. They seized the courthouse, burned and looted, arrested high and wide, and threw into jail eighty-two citizens of Alamance and nineteen of Caswell

County, then scoffed at the writ of *habeas corpus* which Justice Pearson issued.

Holden supported Kirk in ignoring the writ and a little dictatorship such as Vance had guarded against was established in the north central part of the state. It extended to Raleigh when the editor of the *Sentinel* was ordered held. The dictatorship collapsed when Grant in Washington declined to support it. The Democrats triumphed at the August election and Holden was impeached. Not until 1935, when the last of the "executioners" of "Chicken" Stephens died at the age of ninety-five, were their identities known, and then a sealed account was opened and placed in the state archives. Nine persons were named, but none attained the fame of the man they executed, "Chicken" Stephens,[30] and he mainly through a henhouse escapade.

The United States Senate would not seat Vance. The reflection was entirely on that august body, which has at times arrogated to itself the right to look foolish. It had but recently marshaled a commanding but insufficient majority to impeach President Johnson on a set of charges which today seem fanciful. The radicals were in the saddle and riding hard. The House passed a bill of amnesty for Vance, but he had been too stalwart a Confederate for the Senate's taste. Finally he resigned, though he had been properly elected, and the legislature sent Matt W. Ransom, another old soldier, who was seated. He soon had Vance restored to full citizenship, in possession of all his former voting and civil rights. In 1872, when Vance declined to run for governor again, his old Asheville friend Augustus S. Merrimon had been willing to make the race for governor but had lost. For this effort and sacrifice he was rewarded by election to the new Senate term. Vance would have liked it, but was forced to wait.

He was by this time a thoroughly indoctrinated Democrat. When the party in 1872 endorsed the old-time Republican editor Horace Greeley to run against Grant, he remarked, "If 'Old Grimes' is in the Democratic hymn-book, we'll sing him through if it kills us." Vance was about as puzzled as Sherman, who wrote from Paris to his brother about this campaign, "Grant, who never was a Republican, is your candidate; and Greeley, who never was a Democrat, but quite the reverse, is the Democratic candidate."[31] Still, Vance could understand such things better than Sherman. He could look back on his strange association with Holden and recognize that politics did indeed make strange bedfellows.

In many activities at Chapel Hill during those struggling years Zeb

Vance was a motivating force. With Kemp Battle, Cornelia Phillips Spencer, William A. Graham, and Dr. William Hooper he was an incorporator of the Historical Society of North Carolina. Graham was very properly chosen president of the society and guardian of its collection of letters from the greats—Washington, John Adams, Thomas Jefferson, Baron DeKalb, Nathanael Greene, James Madison, John Rutledge, Baron Steuben, Anthony Wayne, Count de Rochambeau, James K. Polk, Daniel Webster, and others. When Battle became president of the university, Vance supported his suggestion that October 12 be made a perpetual holiday commemorating the cornerstone laying of Old East Building on October 12, 1793. Rarely did Zeb Vance miss a commencement, but of greater bearing on the school's progress, he took part in the lecture series, speaking on "Practical Education and Its Importance to North Carolina," and other topics. During the same year he gave a number of lectures at the School of Education where North Carolina teachers were being trained.[32]

When he delivered in Chapel Hill in a later year his most famous lecture, "The Scattered Nation," a number of North Carolina Jews, in order to distinguish the occasion, presented him with a gold-headed cane. The cane was later stolen from a railroad car but a Jew in New York was able to locate it, purchase it, and return it to Vance.[33] The students were so aroused by the stirring tone of his great oration that during the night they wanted more. They came in an excited crowd to President Battle's residence and called for Vance. The university president produced him, then explained he had the right of first discovery. He told how he had accompanied his father, Judge Battle, to the mountains in 1848, and had met the young man filled with wit and familiar with the Scriptures, Shakespeare, and Sir Walter Scott, and had forecast then that the world would hear of him. Vance responded with what was called a speech of "unparalleled humor, wit, and eloquence."[34]

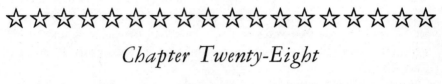

## Chapter Twenty-Eight

## Governor Again and Senator

After North Carolina had experienced twelve years of mixed military, carpetbag, and scalawag government which had gutted the treasury, grievously indebted the state with millions of dollars of bonds that had been sold as low as nine cents on the dollar, set up a barroom in the state capitol, exhausted the educational fund, and exhibited at almost every turn how woefully a government can be maladministered, the conservative elements turned in 1876 to Vance, much as they were looking at the same time in South Carolina to Wade Hampton as a liberator.

The Radicals, who had controlled the executive and judicial branches of the state government since 1868 and, at a critical time, the legislature as well, were indisposed to surrender their grip without a determined struggle. Forgetting the Holden type of expedient politician or his unimpressive successor, Tod R. Caldwell, they nominated Judge Thomas Settle, generally recognized as their ablest spokesman and strongest campaigner.[1]

Vance's party, a fusion of the conservative branch of the prewar Whigs with the Democrats, who had been brought together by the ordeal of the war and the more embittered years of reconstruction, took the name of the Conservative-Democratic party. The right of suffrage had been restored to the former Confederates and the large convention which met with the determination to nominate Vance for governor was described as an outpouring of "the best elements of the State" such as was never seen before. Delegation leaders had surveyed the possible candidates carefully and had decided that Vance, though he had acquired enemies by his strict enforcement of the conscript laws and his unrelenting arrests of deserters during the war, was the ideal of forthrightness, integrity, and stumping ability they wanted to follow. Other names were placed before the convention. Vance, the darling of the delegates, won by 962 of the 966 votes cast. He launched the party at once into what remains the most talked-about campaign in the history of North Carolina politics.

Settle, forty-five years old, a native of Rockingham County, had been the father of the Republican party in the state because he had introduced at the meeting of the Radicals in 1865 the resolution which identified them with the Republicans. He had served as president of the Republican National Convention in 1872. He had crossed swords with Vance as the prosecutor in the Tom Dula trial and had won, then had gone into the judiciary to serve as associate justice of the North Carolina Supreme Court from 1868 to 1876.

When Zeb went to the state legislature in 1854, Settle was there, a young and able member, a Democrat of strong Southern-rights leaning, a secessionist who was talking along lines that repeal or suppression of the Fugitive Slave Law would amount to a virtual dissolution of the Federal Union. Vance had voted against the hot resolutions he introduced then, and now, twenty-two years later, they were as sharply opposed in different political alignments, though it was scarcely the case to say that they both had reversed their positions. Except for the war years, when his reliance was on the constitution of the Confederacy, Vance had kept his foot on the base of the Federal Constitution and even now felt that the faults of the whimsical and shifting Federal reconstruction policies were to be found in the areas where they stepped outside of constitutional processes. Settle, who was acknowledged by the opposition in 1876 to be a "man of good family, good character, of a high order of ability," was also handsome and "an astute and powerful debater." But now the old secessionist wore another garb.[2]

Vance was in Raleigh when the convention met there and that night he spoke in front of the National Hotel, before the immense crowd that may have come expecting fun and frivolity but received what was referred to by listeners as a rare speech without an anecdote. What he did was tell "the story of the humiliation and suffering of the people during the era of reconstruction." He plunged boldly into denunciation of the Congress which authored the reconstruction legislation and inveighed especially against an act which empowered a military commander to order an election of members of a convention to frame a new constitution; to prescribe the qualification of voters; and in effect to disfranchise the most intelligent part of the population, consisting of all who had served in the Southern Army or held office under the Confederacy. Scores of thousands, he held, were voted illegally.

Undoubtedly the heaviest pain to Vance during the reconstruction era, in which he had borne no part in the government, was stated by his law associate Dowd, who summarized this address: "He told how he had struggled all through the dark period of the war to uphold the civil law and guard the sacred writ of *habeas corpus;* how he had succeeded by dint of persuasion, remonstrance, and at times by even threatening to call out the militia; and then how shameful and humiliating it was to know that after the last soldier had laid down his arms and peace had been proclaimed, that sacred writ was trodden under foot and reputable citizens cast into dungeon without cause or accusation, and . . . kept there without bail under Governor Holden's suspension of the writ. . . ."[3]

The campaign which ensued was termed "the battle of the giants,"[4] and few indeed have involved a keener play of wits, along with the exercise of strength, which the phrase implied. Vance displayed in his canvass the physical power his presence on the platform always seemed to suggest. He had a big, full chest, heavy neck and large head covered with thick, glossy hair, still mostly black, though he had commented on its grayness. A curled black mustache covered his upper lip. Perhaps his best speaking asset was his mellow, resonant voice, sometimes soft and flexible, always rich, thrilling, and melodious, and when raised, as stirring as an army drum.

But industry was as much a part of Vance as his natural talents, and during this and subsequent campaigns he amazed the state, which extends 503 miles from Manteo to Murphy, or from the Tennessee border tip to the northeastern Atlantic shore, by the manner in which he could cover it. "We told Governor Vance," said the Wilmington *Star,* "that he was a cast-iron man. He spoke at Burgaw in the afternoon for two and a half hours, and then taking an extra train for Wilmington, and with only a few hours intermission, he again, in the open air, with a slight rawness in it at that, spoke for two and a half hours. One hour thereafter he was on the river boat for his appointment at Point Caswell, where he spoke yesterday. A most wonderful man, physically, socially and intellectually."[5] In the three months he delivered sixty-nine addresses, most of them long, in sixty-five counties.[6]

Much after the fashion of the Lincoln-Douglas debates, Vance and Settle agreed on a joint stumping tour, beginning at Rutherfordton in late July, where Vance opened with a speech of an hour and a half. Settle followed with equal length, and each had half an hour for rebuttal. The opening debate was of note because Settle, who according to the Raleigh *Sentinel* "made a strong partisan appeal, and dodged the issues as best he could," read one of Vance's wartime letters, a copy of which he had procured from Washington. It was one of the many in which Vance had taken a stand against desertion. But Settle took some parts out of context, and Vance obtained the copy from him and read the parts that had been suppressed, then disclosed that though the Washington authorities had given Settle access to his letter books, they had refused to let him see his own letters, which Settle was able to garble to suit his fancy. The reaction favored Vance, and the crowd, as the Raleigh newspaper reported it, murmured "Shame on Settle" and "A villainous act!"[7]

At the Rutherfordton opening the campaign took its tone, and of it the Raleigh *Sentinel* said: "Vance arraigned Settle for sympathizing with the Kirk war, raising a company and resigning to run for office, and the Republicans for fraud and peculation, civil rights, hard times and heavy taxes. Vance's denunciation of the civil rights bill as one of the pet measures of the radical party was one of the best efforts of his life and must have a telling effect on the white Republicans of the mountain country if repeated in his future speeches. Settle made an appeal to the Negroes, went over the ku-klux raw-head and bloody-bones stories . . . and blamed Vance for faithlessness to the Confederacy. The Spartanburg band accompanied Vance. There was little demonstration for Settle. Both made powerful speeches. The mountains are afire for Vance."[8]

So it went for three months, mostly hot months of sweat and toil— Bakersville, Jonesboro, Carthage, Greensboro, Lexington, Wentworth, Kinston, and many other towns. Settle continued to read from Vance's letter books, which to Vance were still inaccessible. He declared Vance had betrayed the Union men who elected him, had "deserted" the Confederate Army as much as he had, and left it to run for office. He charged that Vance had "got to be such a war man that he wanted to fight till hell froze over and then fight on the ice."[9]

Vance said that if he owned a full-blooded Radical, "I would swap him off for a dog and kill the dog. [Laughter] All three of the coordinate branches of the government had agreed in declaring the States not out of the Union, yet Congress in 1867, had legislated them out for the purpose of perpetuating political power and to impose conditions on the people."

He referred to finances and said the cost of the state government for the ten years between 1865 and 1875 had been nearly twice as much as the entire cost for the seventy-two years before the war, and that of the $4,495,000 collected in internal revenue, $1,500,000 had been stolen. Officeholders had increased from 46,000 in 1860 to 94,000 in 1876.[10]

The pattern seemed to be that when Settle spoke first, the crowd could not see how Vance could possibly answer him, but when Vance rose he tore his opponent to shreds.[11] Still, that was not necessary, for as soon as he was on his feet there were cries of "Vance, Vance, Vance," and "Hurrah for Vance," which showed the bulk of the crowd was on his side. The stories handed down from this canvass have usually been weighted in Vance's favor, but discounting the partiality in the accounts, he did possess an added appeal springing from his down-to-earthness, which touched the crowds who came in homespun, arriving sometimes before sunrise, and who often followed the debaters from town to town, walking along the roadway where Vance and Settle would ride in a carriage. Vance won popular favor by jesting at the revenue officers, usually unpopular, who, he declared "could lie down and drink out of a branch and tell if there was a still five miles up it, and who could look at a man's track and tell whether he was toting a quart of whiskey or a two gallon jug." (Laughter)[12]

When the debate reached Charlotte, Settle, as was often the case, was heckled. He turned to Vance, awaiting his turn on the platform, and said: "Governor Vance, I'll be one of ten men to go with you and tie the first man that interrupts me again." The challenge aroused excitement, and a good deal of sympathy for the speaker. But Vance was on his feet quickly.

"Mr. Settle," he said, "I can't speak for your crowd, but the men I represent are the kind that can't be tied!" The only comment of the Charlotte *Observer* was, "Truly, this was a man."[13]

When the dust of the campaign settled and the ballots were counted, Vance had won a resounding victory, though his margin was nothing like those scored over Johnson in 1862 or Holden in 1864. He received 118,000 votes to Settle's 104,000. The significant feat was that he carried virtually the entire Democratic ticket into office with him. Tilden carried the state over Hayes. Every Democrat on the state and national tickets was elected save one Representative in Congress. With the withdrawal of Federal troops the next year, reconstruction, an era of bayonets, waste and sordidness, ended. Latter-day literature which has undertaken to brighten the reconstruction picture appears more to be history written to support a preconceived thesis than the revelation of new facts.

Vance's third term as governor was notable for many achievements, but mainly because of the impetus he gave to public education and railroad building, two of the state's acute needs. His return to Raleigh was a triumph. Little had changed about the physical aspects of the city. The rooster still stood atop the steeple of the Christ Episcopal Church at the southwest corner of Capitol Square, which had become a celebrity as the only chicken in North Carolina which escaped Sherman's army when it passed through. Not until the one-hundredth anniversary of the church in 1921 would he be taken down, for regilding. With his brilliant golden feathers restored, he was again elevated to his perch, where he still presides. "He is a great old bird," wrote a Raleigh resident after the regilding, "and has watched the wedding and burial of many a loyal son and daughter who gave all for the Stars and Bars."[14]

Vance was inaugurated January 1, 1877, in a blizzard which appeared more an omen blowing out the bitterness of the reconstruction than a harbinger of ill for Zeb Vance. The new governor was confident of the even sway of history when he said in his inaugural address: "For all the wrongs and inequalities of individual and national life there is a compensation, provided we do but patiently await its coming." He said his respects to the departing carpetbaggers, saying the state had been controlled by "unscrupulous and disreputable adventurers from the slums of Northern politics; a base and comorant tribe of reptiles which seems to spring like fungi from the rottenness and corruption of revolutionary times."[15]

Zeb went into the governorship with the same two assets he possessed on beginning his first term: the affection of the people and no complicating commitments to the politicians. He was as always his own master. That the education of the people was his first concern, both white and black on a common footing, was clear from his initial message to the General Assembly, delivered in January, 1877, in which he called on the members to make no discrimination in the matter of public education. Frenise A. Logan in his study of public education for Negroes in North Carolina between 1877 and 1894 found that for the first three years following the victory of Vance serious efforts were indeed made to equalize the schools of the two races.[16]

Zeb saw at once that the key to better education was the better training of teachers. He requested that the legislature establish two normal schools, one for each race, at which public school teachers might be trained. He declared a school for training Negro teachers was a deeper felt need than a school for the whites. The legislature responded and one result was the school at the University of North Carolina at Chapel Hill, where, as has been mentioned, Vance frequently lectured. The other was the Fayetteville Colored Normal School, the first institution in the South devoted to the training of Negro teachers. It was opened in 1877.[17] The state was appropriating money for this type of teacher-training under Vance before it was financially able to resume appropriations for the operation of the state university at Chapel Hill, which had to scrape along. The university received its first postwar $10,000 from the state in 1881, twenty years after the outbreak of the war.

Two years after taking office, Vance was able to make a report about the Fayetteville school, which was directed by a Negro of "excellent character and capacity," Robert Harris. "It has been managed with unexpected success. The first session opened with 58 pupils, about 40 of whom received certificates as teachers, some of a high grade. The second year began with 74 pupils and is now in progress." At the white normal school at Chapel Hill, 225 attended the first year and 400 the second. Vance appears to have been the first governor in the country to establish teacher-training in summer schools, and these were held at Chapel Hill.

Nothing could exceed Vance's candor when he appeared on invitation before Negro groups, the first occasion being the first public address of his new governorship, delivered in Raleigh the day after his inauguration. He informed the Negroes that their rights would be respected in common with those of the whites. He talked extemporaneously for an hour and won frequent bursts of applause. He admonished his hearers to vote as free individuals in accord with their own judgments and not in blocks as they were told.[18]

North Carolina began to experience its first Negro exodus after the

1876 election. The ousting of the carpetbag-scalawag government caused apprehension among Negro residents of the eastern counties, though Negroes were never predominant in the reconstruction legislature. Soon after Vance took office a group from Burke County in the piedmont wrote to him soliciting aid and influence in a colonization scheme, and stating their fears of oppression. He made it plain that the incoming party intended no harm. "I think your fears are idle," he declared. "So far as I am concerned, and the party with which I act, I know that there is no intention to oppose your people or deprive them of a single legal right."[19]

Still, the Negroes voted largely Republican, which led to some gerrymandering that remains one of the memorials to Vance. After he left the state house for the United States Senate, Granville and Franklin counties were closely contested by the two parties, with the outcome of both in doubt. But by taking a slice preponderantly Republican from each county and throwing them together into a new county, Franklin and Granville were placed more securely in the Democratic fold. This was effected in 1881 and the new county of 279 square miles, then heavily Negro in population, was named Vance County in Zeb's honor. It came to be known familiarly as "Zeb's Black Baby," and as such is sometimes referred to facetiously in the present day, though it has become a thriving industrial and agricultural center[20] which voted strongly Democratic in the 1964 election. Vance County produced Henry Plummer Cheatham, perhaps the most distinguished member of the Negro race sent by North Carolina to the national House of Representatives. He served two terms from 1889 to 1893.[21]

Vance's interest in education was genuine and manifest. Just before he made the race for governor he had been requested to head the University of North Carolina and shoulder the heavy but pleasant load that had been borne so nobly and long by President Swain. The tender was made to him informally when the school was revived in 1875 and his reply was characteristic.

"No, say to my friends," he responded, "that it would kill me in a few weeks to be obliged to behave as is required of a college president in order to furnish an example to the boys."

Vance stands with Governor Charles B. Aycock (1901-1905) as one of the two great educational governors in the state's history. No other has approached these two in constructive achievement. Vance saw clearly the need for practical training as well as education in the cultural arts and was the first governor of North Carolina to sponsor it.

On Sunday evening, November 3, 1878, Zeb's wife, Harriet Newell Espy Vance, died in Raleigh at the age of forty-six, after suffering ill health uncomplainingly and with deep faith over a long period. Zeb had just experienced the loss of his mother, Mira Margaret Baird Vance, who had died October 4 at the age of seventy-six. She had been the source of much of his early inspiration, as Hattie had been the companion of his turbulent years. The loss of both in a single month caused a grief from which he did not quickly recover. Funeral services for Hattie Vance were held in Asheville, where court was adjourned and all the stores were closed. The services were conducted by Mrs. Vance's Raleigh minister, the Reverend Dr. J. M. Atkinson, and burial was in the cemetery of the Asheville Presbyterian Church, where their first-born son was buried.

When Merrimon's term in the Senate expired, the legislature by acclamation elected Vance. He gratified his old ambition to return to Congress, and resigned the governorship on January 28, 1879, to be succeeded by his lieutenant governor, Thomas J. Jarvis, who had been permanently disabled in the right arm during Lee's 1864 campaign. He was elected to a full term in 1880 and after six years in the governor's chair and later diplomatic service, he would again succeed Vance, as senator.

Vance in 1880 remarried, the bride being the widow Florence Steele Martin, of Louisville, Kentucky, whom Zeb's friend Dowd described as a "lady of wealth, attractive presence and manners, and high intellectual and social qualities." She had one son by her first marriage, J. Harry Martin. She was a member of the Catholic faith. Before the wedding Vance wrote to his close friend Mrs. Spencer reflecting delight over the prospects of the union, except on the one point that "she is a Catholic."

"Think of it!" he exclaimed. "What *will* my Presbyterian friends say to me? This part of it gives me much concern, but I am . . . still enough of a boy to scorn policy in such a matter, and to listen somewhat to the suggestions of my heart." They retained their own faiths and the marriage proved happy.[22]

In the Senate Vance quickly won the reputation of top raconteur. He cared little about patronage and built no personal organization, as did his colleague, the senior senator from the state, Matt W. Ransom, who developed a political machine controlled for years after his death by his protégé Furnifold M. Simmons. When Vance was criticized on the score that he had fifteen relatives on the Federal payroll and opposed the Civil Service bill, he pleaded guilty to his brother, who had been elected Congressman from the western North Carolina district, and his son Charlie, who served him as secretary, but said all the other names listed by the New York newspaper were unknown to him. He seemed to know enough about them to say "they are all Republicans." He had been responsible for none of them.

Some of the senators, their wives and other ladies went on an outing in Chesapeake Bay. They had to climb the ladder to board the vessel. Zeb happened to glance up just as the lady ahead of him looked down and saw that he had a view beneath her skirts.

"Senator," she admonished, "I can see that you are no gentleman."

"I beg your pardon, madam," Zeb replied quickly, "but I can see that you are not, either."[23]

Much as he had complained against Virginia for holding the lion's share of high commissions during the war, he came in the Senate to have a genuine attachment for the Old Dominion. The Richmond *State* told of the new accord in its report of the Democratic National Convention of 1884: "One of the most striking incidents of the convention . . . carries with it the name of this distinguished son of North Carolina. The Virginia delegation, grateful for this able statesman's services in behalf of their people, called upon him in a body and expressed their heartfelt thanks. Since Virginia's two seats in the U. S. Senate have been occupied by a brace of renegades Senator Vance has been looked to as the representative of the Commonwealth. How well he has defended the honor of her people, the history of the last Congress has fully told. The Old Dominion and the Old North State now share alike a worthy pride in such a bold and earnest champion of the right. May his great fame and that of his native State continue to grow, is the wish of every true Virginian."[24]

Virginia at the time was served by Senator William Mahone, Lee's brilliant major general of the Petersburg trenches, who had fought from Seven Pines to Appomattox. He had won the disfavor of many old army associates by becoming a Republican and winning election to the Senate in 1880 on the thinly disguised "Readjuster" ticket. The other Virginia Senator was Harrison H. Riddleberger, a former Confederate soldier elected on the "Readjuster" ticket in 1881. Their records did not appear to entitle them to the severe reproaches of the Richmond *State,* but their novel party status did cause many Virginians to look to Vance to safeguard their interests. When Vance was elected to a second term in 1884, the Fayetteville *Observer* had this to say:

"The extraordinary demonstrations at Raleigh in the General Assembly which accompanied the reelection of the great Senator, last week, . . . were not only the exact expression of the will of all true men of North Carolina, but they prefigure, we verily believe, the sentiment of the American people at no distant day. The reputation of Governor Vance long since jumped the bounds of his State. Our neighbors across the border have already gratefully called him 'the Senator of North Carolina and Virginia.' And so rapidly has he grown since he entered the Senate, that the Union now claims him as one of its great statesmen."[25]

Senators came to know, what Senator George Gray of Delaware remarked, that no debate in which Vance engaged was dull and "no one cared to leave this chamber when Vance was on the floor." They recognized the verity of Zeb's remark that "Mirth does for the soul what sleep does for the body."[26] One of his early speeches, rich with anecdote, was delivered on the appropriation bill of 1880 for the legislative, executive, and judicial departments, in which he emphasized what those in government are frequently forgetting: the need of the people for breathing time. In jocularly partisan remarks he paid his respects to the opposition:

"If I thought the Republican party were standing upon the brink of a precipice, beneath which seethed those cold waters of oblivion, instead of warning them, I pledge you my word I would try to induce them to step over the edge; in fact, I might lend them a push. [Laughter] At least, I should feel as indifferent about it as the lodger at an inn did, who was awakened in the night when the meteors were falling, and told that the day of judgment had come. 'Well,' he said, testily, 'tell the landlord about it; I am only a boarder.' [Laughter]

"And now, Mr. President, if the breath was about to leave my body and I was permitted to say but one word as to what my country most needed, that word should be, *Rest.* Rest from strife, rest from sectional conflict, rest from sectional bitterness, rest from inflammatory appeals, rest from this constant, most unwise, and unprofitable agitation. Rest in all the lands and in all literature is used as the symbol of the most perfect state of felicity which mankind can attain in this world and the next. 'And the land had *rest*,' said the old Hebrew chroniclers in describing the reign of their good kings. . . . Cannot we give rest to our people? I know, Mr. President, that those from whom I come desire it above their chief joy. The excitement through which we have passed for the last twenty years, the suffering and the sorrow, the calamity, public and private, which they have undergone have filled their hearts with indescribable yearnings for national peace, for a complete moral as well as physical restoration of the Union."[27]

He told that across the Potomac one could scarce find the battlefields of "blood-watered Virginia," and dense forests of saplings spread over the hills that knew the tread of marching armies.

"Waving seas of wheat cover the open fields so lately plowed by the bursting shells while charging battalions met in deadly shock; and green grass has so covered the lines of intrenchment as to give them all the seeming of the cunning farmer's ditches. Restoration is nature's law; let us imitate her. God of all mercy and grace, may not these gaping wounds of civil war be permitted to heal, if they will?"[28]

Being a senator involved considerable humdrum and dullness for one of Vance's volatile humor and active nature. He was forced to listen to much dross in the sluggish dissertations on the floor. "I heard your speech," a colleague remarked tauntingly one day, "but it went in one ear and out the other."

"Nothing to stop it," was Vance's quick reply.

Some of the senators did not warm to his jokes. Dr. R. N. Price, professor of mathematics at the American Temperance University at Harriman, Tennessee, sent him a clipping from the Knoxville *Tribune,* saying that Congressman John Mills Allen of Mississippi, widely known as "Private" Allen and a famed raconteur of the House, would not transfer to the Senate wing of the Capitol: "Mr. Allen's jokes are well enough in the House, but if he should undertake to spring any in the Senate he would be frozen to death. Zeb Vance tried it once, and he still has to wear his overcoat when he enters the Senate chamber."[29]

But not all the senators were such prigs, and Vance gradually came to be recognized at his true worth. He maintained his deep reverence for the old institutions, and while he had become among the stanchest of Democrats, he remained a conservative at heart. He introduced Senator Thomas F. Bayard of Delaware, a leader of his era, as the speaker in Charlotte in 1882 at the anniversary celebration of the Mecklenburg Declaration of Independence:

"One hundred and seven years ago this day," said Vance, "the foundations of our liberties were laid broad and deep on this spot; and now that through the intervening years of war and peace, of rejoicing and sorrow, through good and through evil report, we have contended earnestly for the faith which was once delivered to us by the fathers, and held fast the form of sound words in which they are embedded, we have met once more to do them honor. We have met to worship once again at the shrine of American liberty, upon the very spot where it was born."

An account of a Senate visit was written by a special correspondent to the Goldsboro *Transcript-Messenger,* January 16, 1880, who had doubted that North Carolina was ably represented and went there to find out. Signing himself only "G. W. S.," he told how he had known Vance and Ransom since he was "a stripling soldier," but had misgivings as to whether Vance, "noble as are his talents, would be able to display the forensic ability and wield the power of Merrimon" or if Ransom had any capacity. The visit dispelled all doubts. "I found that Vance wielded a power second to no man in the Senate. . . ."

While in the cloakroom with the North Carolinians, "G. W. S." had an unusual experience. He was led to a settee where an undersized, compactly built, pleasant-faced man with a luxurious mustache was conversing earnestly with Senator Theodore F. Randolph of New Jersey. Ransom introduced him: "General McClellan, permit me to introduce you to a young man who fought square against you through the war."

McClellan rose to his feet, extended his hand. "Well, I feel none the less kindly toward him for that." Then the general continued: "The truth is, there is no earthly need of sectional bitterness and strife. If matters at issue had been left to the arbitrament of the private soldiers of both armies North and South, they would have been settled long ago, and Mason's and Dixon's line would long since have been blotted out. Or if these matters had been referred for decision to a few of our prominent generals on either side we could and would have met and after confabbing together would have so arranged everything so that today we would have a union in heart and mind—a union in *fact* as we have a union in *name.* The warfare at present going on between the sections is a warfare waged mainly by band-box warriors and bomb-proof statesmen."

What Vance thought of the remarks was not clear, but he and Ransom must have concurred with McClellan. Then "G. W. S." told Little Mac that the Southern soldiers had a profound regard for him and believed that had he "received the moral and material support in his operations which were afterwards accorded to him who is now the hero of the hour [Grant], he would have whipped us out and terminated matters long before they were terminated, and that, too, without such fearful loss of life, since skill would have been as much brought into requisition as brute force."

Stilted as was the correspondent's language, he got his idea across to McClellan, who bowed and expressed great pleasure at having the regard of Southern soldiers who were his countrymen. "I confronted him," said the visitor, "at every battle where he commanded—Mechanicsville, Gaines's Mill, Cold Harbor, Malvern Hill, Sharpsburg, Shepherdstown. One of the pleasant experiences of my life was to meet him as an earnest advocate of peace."[30]

A flurry of opposition arose against Vance before his re-election to the Senate in 1890—his fourth election to that body but the beginning of his third term. It was centered in a farm group headed by Leonidas LaFayette Polk, who looked on Vance as an "Old Stager" and was impatient for quick action. The tolerant Vance advised him to seek gradual reform and added epigrammatically, "The danger is that oppressed freemen become impatient, and impatient men are often unwise."[31] One of Vance's supporters and workers before this election was Charles B. Aycock, who eleven years later would be governor and leader of another campaign, similar to Vance's, for the improvement of public school education in North Carolina.

An interesting bit of North Caroliniana was the comparison by Robert Watson Winston of Vance and Aycock, the two North Carolina representatives in Statuary Hall in the national Capitol. Winston spoke at Chapel Hill on University Day, October 12, 1941, in accepting a tablet jointly memorializing Vance and Aycock. He dwelt on the companion purpose of the two governors: "The cornerstone of Governor Vance's philosophy was universal education. Aycock took up Vance's work and became our great educational governor. Vance early conceived the idea that a good teacher was an essential and soon became the acknowledged founder of normal and summer schools and of the modern teacher-training college. Aycock made the public education-minded."

Winston was a schoolmate of Aycock at Chapel Hill. Of Vance: "One day in early June, 1876, when he was nominated for Governor, I, a callow youth of sixteen, a sophisticated rising sophomore in the University, was present, an interested spectator of the scene." He heard

Vance speak often and, like Aycock, became one of his lieutenants. He compared the methods of the two, who would rank in any top group of orators.

"On the stump Aycock was sometimes fierce and impetuous and his speech turbulent, sweeping away all opposition. Vance was more deliberate and less personal. His speech flashed with lightning-like rapidity and convinced by its sincerity and its apt illustrations. Both speakers employed the paradox with telling effect and neither one wandered from the subject or went in chase of a rabbit."

He said that each had the tone, accent and modulated voice of the true orator; they never ranted and never employed stage tricks. "They would have made indifferent radio speakers. Never could they have imitated the overtrained school boy accent mouthing every third word for mere effect. They had deep convictions, their heart was in every word they spoke."

Winston provided a contemporary's view of Vance before a crowd. "Vance's sentences were generally short and pungent and each one of them was punctuated with loud hurrahs for Vance! . . . Merely to get a look at Vance, his droll, imperturbable, quizzical, leonine face and his scrubby mustache, as he gazed down on the crowd from some improvised stump, was to break out in laughter and applause—applause which he did not covet. Vance indeed was the only public man I ever knew who strove how not to shine.

"When Vance was present no one wished to utter a word. All were delighted to sit and listen for another from Vance."[32]

Vance, like Lincoln, understood instinctively that oratory should be pitched to the ordinary run of citizen. Herndon quoted Lincoln as telling him, "Billy, don't shoot too high—aim lower and the common people will understand you. They are the ones you want to reach—at least they are the ones you ought to reach. The educated and refined people will understand you any way. If you aim too high your ideas will go over the heads of the masses, and only hit those who need no hitting."[33]

Such was Vance's speaking philosophy. Like Lincoln he was plain and lucid and, like Lincoln, resorted to incident and analogy. He told a visitor from abroad, after a political rally in Charlotte: "On the stump you have to confine yourself to what every man with a ragged shirt and one suspender can understand." He had a rule that as quickly as he saw anyone in the audience whittling, shifting, inattentive, he would say, "But this reminds me of an anecdote." That alerted everyone. "The man brightens up at that and you gain ten minutes for the rest of your argument."[34]

One of the highly rated storytellers of Congress of a later generation was Tom Heflin of Alabama, who served in both houses. Governor Locke Craig (1913-1917) asked Winston which told the better story, Vance or Heflin.

"Locke," he answered, "which is greater, a lion or a mouse?" He added that Heflin told funny stories to amuse the crowd, while Vance's "drove home the point and carried the day."

He spoke of the relationship of the two governors: "Of the young man Aycock, Vance was very fond. He seemed to feel that the mantle would some day fall on the shoulders of this youthful Elisha."[35]

In the Senate period occurred many of Vance's lectures and the greatest of these was his "Scattered Nation," which sprang from his lifelong interest in the Scriptures and the friendship of Samuel Wittkowsky. This lecture, serious, containing no drollery, partly historical, partly a plea for tolerance and innate kindness, was traditionally supposed to have been delivered first in Baltimore. Selig Adler, who made a study of the address, sought enlightenment on the point in the Peabody Institute and Enoch Pratt Free libraries in Baltimore, and found no corroboration, but considered that because Vance's old regimental surgeon, Dr. Thomas J. Boykin of the 26th North Carolina, had settled there and Vance had Baltimore connections, the tradition was probably correct. While 1882 is at times given as the date of the composition, Adler found otherwise and judged it was written between 1868 and 1873. Originally intended as a document for Gentiles, it was delivered "an almost countless number of times before Gentile and Jewish audiences." The first reference to it discovered was in 1875 but it was then already well known.[36] The oration, a perfect unit, cannot be well condensed. Widely published in the press, it was republished in *Oratory in the South; Modern Eloquence; The Library of Southern Literature,* and in various bound editions. Vance's birthday is remembered each May 13 by the Asheville chapters of B'nai B'rith and the United Daughters of the Confederacy, who hold a joint program and place a wreath at the Vance monument.

Vance had other noted lectures which he delivered during Senate recesses and at the summer Chautauqua programs, which originated in the early 1870s and were in their full vigor during his speaking career.

Aside from his "The Duties of Defeat" and "The Scattered Nation," other of his well-known lectures included "The Humorous Side of Politics," "The Last Days of the War in North Carolina," and "The Demagogue." He spoke frequently on special occasions and each address showed great care in its preparation. He had a war talk lightly entitled "All About It," which he delivered to the General Assembly in Raleigh.

So assiduously did he study that he strained his eyesight and eventually lost the sight of an eye, which he had removed. William R. Cox, North Carolina Congressman, attributed the loss to his intensive study for the debates on the McKinley tariff bill.[37] Hard use probably was not the cause, but such was the belief in Zeb's case. The operation was followed by a period of weakened health, largely a nervous exhaustion. From his home Gombroon, near Black Mountain, he wrote to Dr. S. S. Satchwell of Burgaw: "For a long time I could carry nothing to my mouth with my spoon. But I am fast getting better. This morning I shaved myself very comfortably, and I work in my garden and walk up and down the hills with considerable ease."[38]

Before this break in his health, Vance was such a fine physical speciman that his photograph came to be used in the elementary geography published by Matthew F. Maury, the distinguished former naval hydrographer and meteorologist and author of *The Physical Geography of the Sea*, as an example of the Caucasian race. The method of selection was of interest. Professor R. R. Hunter, agent for the Maury Company, explained it. When the geography was being revised, the publishers appointed a committee to select a photograph which in its composite elements would best delineate the typical features of the Caucasian.

The committee selected 100 photographs from various parts of Europe and wrote photographers in this country asking them to submit photographs which they considered representative of the Caucasian race. The American photographers submitted 150 photographs. A striking coincidence was that six sent in pictures of Zeb Vance. The committee members studied the 250 photographs and one by one eliminated those which seemed least suitable. As they gradually discarded these, they finally had six photographs remaining. All were photographs of Vance! As Professor Hunter explained, the voice of the judges was unanimous. "His physiognomy embodied the best and strongest in the Anglo-Saxon, who is dominant among the Caucasians."[39]

The circumstance is noteworthy because here was a happy example of nature matching the inner and outer man. The qualities of a healthy ambition that expresses itself in industry, of moral courage and steady principle that can yet know tolerance, and of rollicking wit that spreads gaiety and acts as a cathartic to bitterness, were his as much as a firm, strong countenance exuding magnetism and a large, handsome body denoting physical power.

## Chapter Twenty-Nine

## Ease and Honors at the Close

Gombroon, a three-story Victorian mansion which Vance purchased and improved during the 1880s, was situated in the deep woods near a little stream called North Fork, eight miles north of Black Mountain and about twenty-two miles northeast of Asheville.

He paid Francis Marion Stevens $3,000 for 1,000 acres, a part of a large tract of undeveloped land Stevens had bought from the sale of ginseng he had gathered in the mountains.

While the house was being built the Vances would visit with the Stevens family frequently and watch the progress of the work. Stevens early in life had become a schoolteacher as well as ginseng hunter. He had been one of Zeb's classmates in the early grades, where, although he had been named for the South Carolina patriot Francis Marion, he picked up the nickname of "France." When a daughter was born to Stevens during the building of Gombroon, Zeb with his jesting proclivity came forward with a suggested name, Algeria, which was accepted as appropriate because the colony of Algeria was giving France a lot of trouble at the time. So it was that Mrs. Algeria Stevens McLean was named. She resides in Asheville at this writing and retains memories of Zeb Vance, and recalls her father's stories about his visits.

Her own memory of him was made vivid by an incident when she was a child. Playing in the yard with her brother, she noticed Senator Vance coming up the walk. He dropped something, looked for it, stooped and picked it up, then wiped it off. The children were curious. He showed it to them and to their amazement it was a glass eye, something they had never seen before.

He clapped it back into the eye socket and went into the house, leaving behind him an indelible memory.[1]

Zeb on those visits was an eager eater. "France" Stevens used to tell Algeria that the old barnyard rooster could sense Zeb's coming, and would crow loudly, upon which all the hens would scurry off into the woods and hide until he departed.

The fact was that Zeb customarily ate enormous quantities of food and never seemed to forget the old soldier days when rations were scant and had to be put down quickly for any chance at seconds. His favorite bread was salt rising and his top delicacy was pound cake—country pound cake, made in those days with a pound of fresh churned country butter, a pound of sugar, a pound of flour, and a dozen eggs beaten very light and fluffy and added last to the mixture, which caused the cake to rise without soda or baking powder. If this rich diet was not available, Zeb's choice for dessert probably was home-canned peaches, which seemed to hold an especial place in his affections.[2]

Zeb's heavy but discriminating appetite was noticed when he visited the William Davidsons, his relatives who lived along the Swannanoa River and had their home where Warren Wilson College now is situated, ten miles east of Asheville. The table was loaded with ham, chicken, mashed potatoes, pies and cakes, but Zeb glanced over the food with dissatisfaction.

"Where are the beans, William? Where are the beans?" he implored. "I'm hungry for cornfield beans!"

"I believe, Governor, there is a small pot of beans cooked in the kitchen," said William. With that, Zeb took his plate, stalked into the kitchen and returned with his plate heaped high with cornfield beans exuding the fragrance of bacon smoked with sassafras and hickory.

"I tell you, William," Zeb went on, "when mother goes to the new-ground and gathers cornfield beans in her checkered apron, and bark from the new-ground fence, there's nothing better ever cooked than when she breaks those beans, puts in a slab of bacon the size of my hand and hangs the pot on the crane. Then, William, she must fill the Dutch oven with muffin bread, put potatoes in the ashes to roast and bring fresh butter from the springhouse. Food like that will make a man out of any boy."[3]

The lumber for Gombroon was sawed at the nearby Walker mill and the brick that went into the construction was fired on the place. Bascomb Burnett, who was reared in the North Fork section and as a lad would walk the two miles to Gombroon, said that Vance brought two cabinet-makers from Baltimore to finish the interior. When the Vances were there Burnett would go over to sell blackberries and chickens, and Zeb would usually be found sitting on the big, semicircular front porch. "He would look at what I had to sell and would generally buy. He would usually pay ten cents for a gallon of blackberries and a quarter for a good sized frier." Once he told the boy to put the chickens in the lot; they were so small they would have to be eaten with a spoon.[4]

When he was not on the lecture platform, Zeb passed his closing days between Gombroon and Washington. He was community-minded, attended all the log rollings and church and neighborhood sociables; he was willing to make a few remarks whenever called on, and young Burnett observed that he always had something appropriate for the occasion. Each Sunday morning he attended a Baptist church which had the only services in the neighborhood. He set out a large orchard and a vineyard, maintained a small dairy and cooled the milk at the spring-house.

Above him to the north extended the lofty Craggies and beyond them the Black Mountain range he had known as a boy. About him, except for his clearings, was the dense forest of oak, maple, and pine. Once he wrote for a school reader a florid description of the beauty of the woods in autumn. The urge to use words was always with him. During the depression period of the early 1890s he tried to create work for his neighbors.

"He was kind to the common folks," recalled Burnett, "and had a big stone wall built just to provide employment. He paid eighty cents a day for ten hours of labor and that was considered good in those times."[5]

Each summer after 1890 he invited the survivors of his first company, the Rough and Ready Guards, to hold their reunion at Gombroon. In 1890 only four were able to attend. The old soldiers were passing. When Vance was first in the Senate a goodly number of former Confederates sat in the two houses. Eight former Confederate brigadier generals were in the Senate and thirteen in the House. The Senate had also four former colonels who had worn the gray, one captain and two privates; the House had nineteen colonels, two majors, seven captains, one lieutenant and fourteen privates.

This made seventy-one ex-Confederate soldiers in the Halls of Congress. Veterans of the old Confederate Congress were there—Garland of Arkansas, Ben Hill and Alexander H. Stephens of Georgia, Singleton of Mississippi, Vest of Missouri. Joe Brown, war governor of Georgia, and Reagan of Texas, the Confederate postmaster general, sat on the Democratic side. The South had no lack of spokesmen in the legislative branch of the reunited nation.[6]

Now, in 1894, a dozen years later, taps were sounding across the Southland. Many were dying impoverished. Dick Taylor, son of a President, had lost everything in the war and died well-near penniless, though his book, *Destruction and Reconstruction*, remains one of the most engaging written about the conflict. Samuel Cooper had died poor, as had Bragg and many others, including several of the war casualties— Whiting, Bishop Polk, and Stonewall Jackson. Zack Deas of Chickamauga fame had attacked Wall Street with the same spirit with which he had assailed Rosecrans's left flank at the Widow Glenn's and had accumulated a second fortune, but he had been called to the last muster in the early 1880s. Loring had come back with his Egyptian decorations to gain wealth in western mining ventures.

These were exceptions. None could have been more comfortable or fortunate than the old colonel of the 26th North Carolina at Gombroon, idolized by most of a state, admired by much of a nation. Already the stories were being told of how he had personally gone to sea and steered the blockade-runners through the Federal fleet. According to old soldier Thomas Y. Lytle of McDowell County, Vance was a man of action. "He even went out and ran through the enemy blockades himself, giving the Northern ships the slip every time." Thus is fame fed by admiration.[7]

Lighthearted, jovial, he could jest even about his impaired vision. To a caller he remarked, "With one eye out and the other closed, I have more vision than any five Republicans."[8]

Was his partisanship as blind as his missing eye? Perhaps not, though he generally seemed to think of the Republicans in terms of Holdenism and the state's wasted resources during the heartlessness of reconstruction. Yet he numbered leading Republicans among his good friends. Two of his Senate colleagues, John Sherman of Ohio and Lot M. Morrill of Maine, were still there. Morrill recalled when Vance arrived in the

House: "Young and brimful of humor, song and story, he was highly esteemed by the members of all parties."[9] And John Sherman: "We were thrown frequently into kindly association."[10]

Highly partisan, never intentionally bitter—that was Zeb's political motif. When he told a cutting tale about the opposition he usually told it with an irrepressible twinkle. He did not maintain a costly organization in his campaigns; about the only expense above his travel was his rule to give five dollars to every boy he met who had been named in his honor. Once he had to pass out twenty-five dollars in a single afternoon.[11]

Zeb's last illness, though he was just entering his sixties, was protracted. A diagnosis in the light of modern medical information would be difficult, but the beginning appeared to be a fall from a wagon at Black Mountain, followed by pain in the muscles of his face. Then the eye operation had come in 1889 (sometimes mistakenly dated 1891) in which the doctors felt it was necessary to take one eye in order to save the other. After a convalescence he took a trip to the British Isles, whose political history he knew so well, and continued on to France, Germany, Italy, and Egypt. He brought home some Egyptian corn, but found it would not grow well in Buncombe County. He was homesick while abroad and told his son Charlie that the trip made him a better American. To gain strength, which the European journey did not give to him, he visited Tampa, Jacksonville, St. Augustine, and Suwannee Springs, Florida. Finally in early 1894 he returned to watch the spring burst forth over Washington and resume his Senate seat, and to reminisce at night, sitting at his home on Massachusetts Avenue with his wife and his son Charlie. Then came the fatal stroke.

His funeral ceremonies in the Senate chamber, April 16, 1894, were conducted by an acquaintance out of the long ago past. When the *Ad-Vance* made its first hazardous dash through the Federal blockade off Wilmington, it will be recalled that the Reverend Moses D. Hoge of Richmond was on board, bringing in a consignment of Bibles from England for Lee's army. Now he read the scriptural selections, said the prayer and delivered the funeral address for the governor he had met on board the famous blockade-runner. Present were the Supreme Court justices and members of Senate and House. All arose when the British Ambassador Sir Julian Pauncefote entered. None in Washington was more distinguished than the able diplomat who had cemented friendly relations between the two countries during the Bering Sea fishery dispute and would do so again during the Venezuelan crisis. Then came President Cleveland to sit in the morocco armchair at the head of his cabinet in the front row.

The cortege moved from the Capitol to the railroad station and at 9 P.M. the body was started on the last journey to North Carolina. In the early dawn at Danville, Virginia, and the morning at Greensboro, large crowds were at the stations to watch it pass and pay their last respects to their dearly beloved Zeb. When the train approached Durham, the bells could be heard tolling from the large Durham Tobacco Works, an outgrowth of the Civil War. Northern soldiers had remembered the good tobacco they had found in Durham and after the war had written back for more of it, and thus a town grew at what had been a little station, and a local industry was awarded nationwide sales. Veterans crowded into the car at Durham to look on the strong face of their old comrade and governor.

At Raleigh at 9:30 A.M. the official Governor's Guard conducted the casket, drawn in a hearse by four black horses, to the capitol in which Zeb had labored so diligently for the lost cause. There, less than an hour later it was opened and the long line began to pass. "The expression was wonderfully life-like." The familiar face of the great leader, now loved by substantially all in the state, was exposed to view throughout the day. That evening the train started for Asheville.

On the trip westward from Raleigh, passing again through Durham and Greensboro, all stations along the route were thronged with mournful waiters. At Durham, Negroes with their melodious voices sang "Father, We Rest in Thy Love." At Greensboro the familiar 26th Regimental Johnny Reb Band of Salem was on hand to give their old colonel parting refrains of sacred music. Vance might have known they would be there to say farewell.

Zeb's colleague, Senator Matt Ransom, gave a picture to the Senate of the journey: "On the night of the 16th of April we took his casket from these walls. We bore it across the Potomac—through the bosom of Virginia, close by the grave of Washington, almost in sight of the tombs of Jefferson and Madison, over the James, over the North and South Roanoke, over the unknown border line of the sister States—to the sad heart of his mother State. The night was beautiful. The white stars shed their hallowed radiance upon earth and sky. The serenity was lovely. The whole heavens almost seemed a happy reunion of the constellations. With the first light of day, the people, singly, in groups, in companies, in crowds, in multitudes, met us everywhere along the way—both sexes—all ages—all races—all classes and conditions. Their sorrow was like the gathering clouds in morning, ready to drop every moment in showers.

"We carried him to the State house in Raleigh, the scene of his greatest trials and grandest triumphs; the heart of the state melted over her dead son. Her brightest jewel had been taken away! We left Raleigh in the evening, and passing over the Neuse, over the Yadkin, over the Catawba, up to the summits of the Blue Ridge, we placed . . . his noble dust on the brow of his own mountain, the mountain he loved so well. On that exalted spot the willow and cypress, emblems of sorrow and mourning, can not grow, but the bay and the laurel, the trees of fame, will there flourish and bloom in perpetual beauty and glory. There will his great spirit, like the eternal sentinel of liberty and truth, keep watch. . . ."[12]

That day it rained in Asheville while the host of organizations and crowds of friends, and the Rough and Ready Guards as a special escort, accompanied the body of Zeb Vance to its resting place. Ten thousand marched in the procession through the city draped in mourning. The Reverend R. F. Campbell, the Presbyterian pastor, conducted the final rites at the grave. While the funeral was being held, all over North Carolina, on that day and the next, memorial services were ordered. Everywhere was sung his favorite hymn, "Jesus Lover of My Soul."[13] His friend Dowd said, "No North Carolinian ever had such a funeral and it is doubtful if any citizen of any State, with the possible exception of Jefferson Davis, ever had a like funeral—such a universal going forth of the people."[14]

Tributes to his greatness came from all quarters. William H. S. Burgwyn, brother of the youthful colonel of the 26th who fell at Gettysburg, wrote from Eufaula, Alabama: "I can never forget that he was a good friend to my brother. . . . Never before, probably never again, will such an outpouring of the feelings—love, veneration and respect—take place on the death of a public man in North Carolina."[15] None ever has.

A letter which must have touched Zeb's family was written by Nat Steed of the War Department Printing Office, addressed to Mrs. Vance: "I have special reasons for loving the memory of Senator Vance. Coming to this city from my native North Carolina, where my people had lived for nearly two centuries, a penniless, friendless boy, Senator

Vance took me under the sheltering influence of his great name, secured for me employment, and proved himself the only friend I ever had. May the angels guard his tomb, and green be the turf above him."[16]

When the monuments came to be built the tributes were renewed in swelling volume. The monument of heroic size at the south of the state capitol—the only North Carolina monument to an individual erected at state expense—portrays most naturally his great power—his large head, grand shoulders, barrel-shaped chest. Vance stands with his hand on a book, the source of his strength. The quotations from his remarks are appropriately chosen: that on the right: "The subjection of every passion and prejudice . . . to the cooler sway of judgment and reason, when the common welfare is concerned, is the first victory to be won." On the left is the expression of his deep faith in those he served and loved: "If there be a people on earth given to sober second thought, amenable to reason and regardful of their plighted honor, I believe that . . . it is the people of North Carolina."

Who more fitting than his old secretary of the war years, Richard H. Battle, could have delivered the dedicatory address?

The little girl who unveiled the statue in Statuary Hall at the nation's Capitol, Dorothy Espy Pillow, was the granddaughter of his son David, the only one of Zeb's four sons who had children. Of the unveiling the *Confederate Veteran* said: "Few men are gifted as was Vance. An eloquent and brilliant orator, an able debater, a profound thinker, a man of great constructive ability, he stood high in the estimation of the country; but he was more loved and esteemed for his patriotism, his integrity and honesty, and his unswerving devotion to his people. . . ."[17]

The Asheville shaft which dominates the main square of the city was completed in March, 1898. In 1960, largely through the efforts of D. Hiden Ramsey, retired Asheville newspaper executive, the state, Buncombe County, and the city of Asheville appropriated funds and restored the Zeb Vance birthplace on Reems Creek, which is maintained as a North Carolina shrine and historic site visited by thousands annually. The restoration work was begun on May 14, 1960.

At the dedication of the Asheville shaft, of the Vance monument in Charlotte, May 20, 1898, and of the Vance monument in Raleigh, August 22, 1900, an interesting gavel was employed. It was made of a pine limb with a minie ball embedded in it, taken from Chickamauga battlefield, and first used at the laying of the cornerstone of the Jefferson Davis monument in Richmond, July 2, 1896. General John B. Gordon used it at reunions of the United Confederate Veterans and on the important occasion, May 30, 1901, when he presided at the laying of the cornerstone of the Nathan Bedford Forrest monument in Forrest Park, Memphis, Tennessee, erected to as great a soldier as Vance was a statesman.

Zeb Vance would have appreciated it had he known that it would be used also at the dedication of the North Carolina monument at Appomattox, on the spot where the all-North Carolina brigade of William Ruffin Cox, of General Bryan Grimes's Division, on April 9, 1865, made the last glorious charge of Lee's army. Again, it was used at Bethel, to unveil the marker where the North Carolinian Henry Lawson Wyatt was the first Southern soldier killed in battle in the war. "First at Bethel, Farthest at Gettysburg, and Last at Appomattox." None more than Zeb Vance would have liked to have that story of the state's performance so preserved.

At the Statuary Hall unveiling many spoke. The graceful phrasing of a Northerner stood out. Henry Cabot Lodge of Massachusetts came to Washington the year before Vance died and was impressed with the Southerner's charm: "He dwells with me now as one of the most vivid memories of my early days in the Senate and stands out a marked and gracious figure in my visions of the past."

"Time rolls by," said Abraham Lincoln in one of his court cases; "the heroes of '76 have passed away and are encamped on the other shore." So it came to be with the heroes of '61 to '65. The others would follow Vance, until in this generation all are gone. The greatest of the North Carolinians lies in Asheville's Riverside Cemetery among many others of note: the talented governor and orator Locke Craig; the well-remembered authors O. Henry and Thomas Wolfe; the soldier and statesman Thomas L. Clingman. Zeb's stone is simple, as are the others. The musical French Broad, the stream of his boyhood, ripples past through its mountains. Peace is here, and peace was what he sought.

Greatest of his monuments is not his stone, or the memorials in the North Carolina cities or in Washington, but the heritage of his struggle for the protection of individual rights against the ever-recurring menace of usurping government. As put into words by his successor in the governor's chair and in the United States Senate, Thomas J. Jarvis:

"Individual rights and the majesty of the civil law never had a warmer advocate or more steadfast friend in this country than this great tribune of the people. I doubt if there were many states in the Union or the Confederacy during the war in which the writ of *habeas corpus*, that great writ of the people's rights, could at all times be properly executed and obeyed . . .

"Governor Vance, although ardently supporting the Confederacy, stood by the writ, even in the face of the army itself, and upheld the majesty of the civil law. At no time in his whole public career was he ever known to consent to the surrender of or encroachment upon any of the individual rights of an American citizen, but he was ever ready with tongue and pen to defend them from any attack, no matter whence that attack came."[18]

In an age that witnesses in many lands the continual diminution of individual, and the growth of governmental, rights, of how many may that be said? But Zeb Vance was well grounded:

"He was truly a student of the science of government, of politics, of the history of the rise and progress of States, nations, and peoples, and the more he learned and knew the more ardently attached he became to republican America and her democratic institutions. . . . It was his glory to stand by the people in all their struggles. . . ."

Senator Jarvis made a final inspiring analogy. He recalled that in Zeb's home section many lofty peaks reach to the clouds, some three, four, five and six thousand feet, any one of which impresses the traveler with its grandeur.

"But there is one that towers high above them all. Mount Mitchell stands out boldly as the center of attraction, and it is to this that people always turn when they wish to gaze upon the perfection and consummation of great mountain scenery in all its magnificence and sublimity.

"So in North Carolina we have had great men, any one of whom was and is an honor to the State, and of whom our people have been and still are justly proud; but it is no disparagement to those to say that Zebulon Baird Vance was the Mount Mitchell of all our great men, and that in the affections and love of the people he towered above them all. As ages to come will not be able to mar the grandeur and greatness of Mount Mitchell, so they will not be able to efface from the hearts and minds of the people the name and memory of their beloved Vance."[19]

# NOTES

## CHAPTER ONE: THE SENATOR REFLECTS

1. The scene is reconstructed from the letter of Charles N. Vance to Clement Dowd. Clement Dowd, *Life of Zebulon B. Vance*. Charlotte, N. C., 1897. Pgs. 314-315. Vance lived at 1627 Massachusetts Avenue, in the block between Scott and Dupont Circles.

2. Vance was elected to the Senate four times, but on his first election by the state legislature in 1870 the Senate refused to seat him because his "disabilities" under the Fourteenth Amendment had not been lifted. When he was unable to have them removed he resigned. Again a candidate in 1872, he was defeated by a coalition in the legislature, but was elected in 1879, 1885, and 1891.

3. Tarboro, N. C., *Southerner,* Jan. 15, 1885, quotes the Chicago *Daily News. Vance Papers,* Clipping Book Pg. 2319. North Carolina Archives, Raleigh.

4. *Vance Papers,* North Carolina Archives. Undated and unidentified clipping. Clipping Book Pg. 2352.

5. *Ibid.*

6. Fayetteville *Observer* (no date), *Vance Papers,* Clipping Book Pg. 2317.

7. *Ibid.*

8. Raleigh, N. C., *State Chronicle,* Jan 23, 1885. *Vance Papers,* Clipping Book Pg. 2320.

9. *Ibid.*

10. As a senator, Brown was described by the North Carolina newspaper as an "eminently shrewd man of great force," but "selfish."

11. Raleigh *State Chronicle*, Jan. 23, 1885. *Vance Papers*, Clipping Book Pg. 2320.

12. *Ibid.* Of Ingalls the *Dictionary of American Biography* says, ". . . he could pour out a flood of vitriolic abuse and blasting party misrepresentation suggestive of John Randolph."

13. Glenn Tucker, *Front Rank,* Pg. 4. Stuart's fascination with Vance's oratory is dealt with in a later chapter.

14. Alfred Moore Waddell, post-Civil War Congressman from North Carolina, quoted Cox, Dowd's *Life of Vance*, Pg. 202.

15. Blaine had lived on the east side of Lafayette Park in the house formerly occupied by Secretary of State William H. Seward while serving in Lincoln's cabinet. There Seward was stabbed on the night of the assassination of Lincoln.

16. *Southern Historical Society Papers* (hereafter *S.H.S.P.*) Vol. 24— Pg. 303. Reprint of Philadelphia *Times* article of Oct. 10, 1896. The three other survivors were Northerners: George W. Jones, ante-bellum senator from Iowa, who died in 1896; James Harlan, of Iowa, who after Senate service entered Lincoln's cabinet and survived until 1899; and James Ware Bradbury of Maine, who died in 1901 at the age of ninety-nine.

17. Quoted in Tarboro, N. C., *Southerner,* Jan. 15, 1885. *Vance Papers,* Clipping Book Pg. 2319.

18. Undated clipping. *Vance Papers*, Clipping Book Pg. 2352.

19. *Memorial Addresses on the Life and Character of Zebulon Baird Vance in the Senate and House of Representatives.* Washington. 1895. Pg. 28.

20. *Ibid.*

21. Cleveland *Leader,* June 17, 1883. *Vance Papers*, Clipping Book Pg. 2312.

22. Raleigh *State Chronicle*, Jan. 23, 1885. *Vance Papers*, Clipping Book Pg. 2320.

23. North Carolina folklore story.

24. This story was still being related around the Capitol, in different forms, when this writer first went to Washington in 1919, as a newspaper correspondent for the old New York *World*, though Vance had been dead twenty-five years. The memory of him and his stories still hung over the Senate, where some members and newspaper correspondents remained who had served in his time.

25. The story was that of Bill and Jim, related later in this chapter.

26. *Vance Papers.* Undated and unidentified clipping. Clipping Book Pg. 2352.

27. *Vance Papers,* 1894. Letter Box 1.

28. A. M. Luckey to Vance, Jan. 28, 1894. *Vance Papers,* 1894. Letter Box 1.

29. Wilmington, N. C., *Messenger,* April 26, 1894. *Vance Papers,* Clipping Book Pg. 2345.

30. E. A. Bancroft, "The Loneliness of Genius." *Winning Orations of the Interstate Oratorical Contest,* Charles Edgar Prather, editor. Topeka, Kansas, 1909. Vol. I, Pg. 67. Of John C. Calhoun it was said, "Insects buzz about the lion's mane, but do not arouse him from his lair." B. A. Botkin, *A Treasury of Southern Folklore,* Pg. 260.

31. Dowd's *Life of Vance,* Pgs. 221-222.

32. Wilmington, N. C., *Messenger,* April 26, 1894. *Vance Papers,* Clipping Book Pg. 2345.

33. *Ibid.*

34. *Vance Papers,* Clipping Book Pg. 2352. Undated and unidentified clipping.

35. *Ibid.*

36. Folklore story told with variations in western North Carolina.

37. *The State,* Raleigh. March 2, 1963.

38. Bess Furman, *White House Profile,* Pg. 248. Indianapolis. 1951.

39. Charles Vance to Clement Dowd mentions Vance's mood. Dowd's *Life of Vance,* Pg. 314.

40. *S.H.S.P.* Vol. 24—Pg. 35 (1896).

41. The old roster placed the number of Confederate troops at 125,000. This figure was broken down, Lefler and Newsome, *The History of a Southern State,* Pg. 430, as 111,000 combat troops for offensive operations outside the state, all being volunteers except 19,000 conscripts; 10,000 reserves, and 4,000 home guards. Vance used the number 121,038 of all grades. *S.H.S.P.* Vol. 14—Pg. 508 (1886). The figure of 129,000 also is used as in *Confederate Veteran,* Vol. 20—Pg. 169 (1912). The state's military population was placed at 115,369. *Confederate Reveille,* Raleigh, 1898. Pg. 121. The number of North Carolina soldiers in the Union Army usually was placed at 3,156. *Battles and Leaders of the Civil War* (hereafter *Battles & Leaders*) Vol. II—Pg. 581. Because of the uncertainty about the number in the Confederate service, the North Carolina Confederate Centennial Commission instigated a new roster count under its editor Louis H. Manarin, to replace Moore's *Roster,* the longstanding authority. Research showed promptly that the old roster, Moore's, was about 54 per cent incorrect. In the 10th North Carolina regiment alone 1,045 names had been omitted. The recheck is not complete at this writing in early 1965, but it is estimated by the Commission staff that the total will be between 185,000 and 200,000 of all grades, in-

cluding up to 6,000 who served in the Union Army. The rechecking and the difficulties involved are described in *News Letter* issued by the Commission, Vol. 2, No. 5, in August, 1961.

42. Vance's review of Lee's army is described in a later chapter.

43. In an address delivered before the Southern Historical Society at White Sulphur Springs, W. Va., August 18, 1875, Vance gave a good summary of the state's contributions to the Confederacy. The address is published in *S.H.S.P.* Vol. 14—Pgs. 506-521 (1886).

44. Tucker, *High Tide at Gettysburg,* Pg. 149; *Front Rank,* Pg. 45. *S.H.S.P.* gives details on the loss of this regiment, Vol. 24—Pgs. 16-17, which indicate a loss as high as 90.2 per cent. A loss of 82 per cent is often erroneously stated as that of the 1st Minnesota on the second day at Gettysburg, and alleged to be the highest of any regiment in the battle. The loss of the 1st Minnesota was analyzed fully by this writer in a paper entitled "Hancock at Gettysburg" read August 1, 1961, before the Fourth Annual Civil War Study Group at Gettysburg College. It appears to have been about 66 per cent on July 2 and not above 75 per cent in the two days July 2 and 3. The difficulty in obtaining exact figures results from the uncertainty as to how many of the missing were killed or mortally wounded. But the loss suffered by the 26th North Carolina seems clearly the heaviest sustained by any regiment.

According to a calculation in the Charlotte *Observer,* April 29, 1956, if the percentage of deaths in World War II had been at the same rate as those of North Carolina soldiers in the War Between the States, the state would have suffered 130,000 deaths between 1941 and 1945, instead of the actual number of 7,500.

45. The case that the South lost because of an unwillingness to sacrifice democracy was ably presented by O. W. Blacknall, of Kittrell, North Carolina, in an article "Why the South Lost" in *Confederate Veteran* Vol. 25— Pg. 118 (1917). He said the South was willing to pay every price except one. "That price was liberty, the temporary subordination of law and personal rights to military necessity. The South could not bring herself to let liberty wait even until independence was won." This attractive theory was espoused by David Donald in a paper "Died of Democracy" delivered at Gettysburg College and published Pg. 77 in *Why the North Won the Civil War,* Baton Rouge, 1960, David Donald, Editor. Henry Steele Commager follows similar reasoning in "How the 'Lost Cause' Was Lost," New York *Times Magazine,* August 4, 1963, and attributes the foundation and destruction of the Confederacy to the same cause, state sovereignty. Many others have written along this line during the century since the war, unwilling to concede what Vance contended, that the South succumbed to tremendous odds of men and supplies arrayed against her; or what this writer believes to be the case, that the

states—with North Carolina as an example—fought more resolutely and maintained better discipline when free than they would have under a closely regimented Federal dictation. The specious theory that only dictatorships can win wars is not borne out by the many gallant successes of free societies in history, including that of the colonials in the war of 1775-1783.

46. Dowd's *Life of Vance*, 314.


## CHAPTER TWO: A SPARK IS STRUCK IN THE MOUNTAINS

1. Substantially all the information about the Vance-Carson duel is from the 3,600-word manuscript account of eyewitness Silas McDowell in the North Carolina Room, Pack Memorial Library, Asheville; and from John Preston Arthur's *Western North Carolina: A History (From 1734 to 1913)*, Pgs. 259-263. Raleigh. 1915. An excellent account of the duel, drawn largely from these sources, was contained in a special ninetieth-anniversary edition of the Asheville *Citizen-Times*, July 17, 1960.

2. Arthur's *Western North Carolina*, Pg. 328.

3. *Ibid.*

4. McDowell Ms. Pg. 4.

5. Glenn Tucker, *Poltroons and Patriots*, Vol. 1—Pg. 35.

6. McDowell Ms. Pg. 7.

7. *Ibid.* Pg. 8.

8. Details of the Spaight-Stanly duel are given in *The State*, Raleigh, Oct. 12, 1963.

9. Crockett visited at times at the Carson house, Pleasant Gardens, which has been developed as a McDowell County museum. Here Carson lived at the time of the duel.

10. Kemp Plummer Battle, *Memories of an Old-Time Tar Heel*, Pg. 90. Chapel Hill, 1945. Battle referred to the passing of the library to Zeb and said: "It doubtless contributed much to the formation of his clear and vigorous style of writing and speaking." The Reverend R. N. Price, later Vance's regimental chaplain, in a chapter he wrote for Dowd's *Life of Vance*, gave a similar view. Stephen B. Weeks's *Scrapbook*, North Carolina Historical Collection, Chapel Hill, cited by Franklin Ray Shirley, *Zebulon Vance, Tarheel Spokesman*, Pg. 3, gives some of the volumes as Livy, Tacitus, Cicero, as well as English classics, Swift, Addison, Scott, Byron, Milton and Shakespeare.

11. McDowell Ms. Pg. 12. The reference apparently is to one of Rachel Donelson Jackson's nieces. Carson died Nov. 2, 1838.

12. *Vance Papers*, Pack Library, Asheville. Dowd's *Life of Vance*, Pg. 9. Lou Rogers, *Tar Heel Women*, Pg. 86. Raleigh, 1949. Foster A. Sondley, *A History of Buncombe County, North Carolina*, Pg. 528. Calhoun often spent the summer months in the mountains of western North Carolina.

13. Charlotte *Observer,* April 16, 1894. *Vance Papers,* Clipping Book Pg. 2338. Calhoun's ability as a preceptor might be seen in William Henry Gist, governor of South Carolina (1858-1860) and father of the Confederate general, States Rights Gist. Calhoun was credited with tutoring the father. *Confederate Veteran,* Vol. 19—Pg. 278 (1911).

14. Charlotte *Observer,* April 16, 1894.

15. Dowd's *Life of Vance,* Pg. 12. The chapter in Dowd dealing with Zeb's boyhood was written by Vance's elder brother, Robert.

16. Dowd's *Life of Vance,* 12. Edward W. Phifer, "Certain Aspects of Medical Practice in Ante-Bellum Burke County," *North Carolina Historical Review,* Vol. 36. No. 1 (Jan. 1959) Pgs. 39-40. Phifer has both treatments in Morganton.

17. Asheville *Citizen-Times,* July 17, 1960.

18. Arthur's *Western North Carolina.* Pg. 98.

19. The birthplace has been restored and made a state historical site. Dedication ceremonies, attended by this writer, were held May 13, 1961, on the 131st anniversary of Vance's birth. The historic house is visited by large numbers annually.

20. Robert Vance in Dowd's *Life of Vance,* Pg. 3.

21. Captain David Vance, *Narrative of the Battle of King's Mountain.* (Pamphlet published by D. Schenck, Greensboro, N. C., 1891) Pg. 80.

22. Kemp P. Battle gives the pronunciation. *Memories,* Pg. 89.

23. Uncertainty exists about the origin of the town's first name. Foster A. Sondley, Asheville scholar and bibliophile of an earlier generation, held that the town was named after William Morrison, member of the Buncombe County Board of Commissioners. There was a belief that his vote fixed the location of the courthouse. Arthur's *Western North Carolina* tends to the Robert Morris origin. Dick Kaplan, "Buncombe County, When Created in 1792, Embraced Vast Territory," a lengthy feature article in the Asheville *Citizen-Times* ninetieth-anniversary issue, July 17, 1960, appeared to incline toward the "seemingly authentic tradition" recorded by John Preston Arthur.

24. Frontis W. Johnston, editor, Volume One, *The Papers of Zebulon Baird Vance,* Raleigh, 1963 (hereafter *Vance Papers,* Vol. I). Vance to Martha E. Weaver, Aug. 12, 1851. Pg. 4.

25. Marie Louise Pool, *In Buncombe County.* Chicago. 1898.

26. Lou Rogers, *Tar Heel Women,* Pg. 86, attributed Zeb's wit to her, as do many others, and Vance himself paid her a great tribute. She could read her Bible without spectacles when 75 years old.

27. *Vance Papers,* Vol. I—Pg. 1.

28. *Ibid.* Pg. 3.

29. Folktale among older Buncombe County residents.

30. Pool's *In Buncombe County,* Pgs. 219-220.

31. Robert B. Vance in Dowd's *Life of Vance,* Pg. 11.

32. *Ibid.* Pg. 10.

33. *Vance Papers*, Vol. I—Pg. 3.

34. *Vance Papers*, North Carolina Room, Pack Memorial Library, Asheville. R. W. K. Mallett, Asheville *Citizen-Times*, June 29, 1930. Arthur's *Western North Carolina*, Pg. 359. Arthur does not tell the story of the slab of bacon, nor does Marquis James, *Andrew Jackson The Border Captain*, in discussing the duel, Pg. 47. He says merely that Avery twitted Jackson over the use of Bacon. The slab of bacon story has had wide acceptance as a folklore tale. Edward W. Phifer, in his history of the Avery family, "Saga of a Burke County Family," gives the more conventional version that Jackson affronted Avery in court, then challenged him. *North Carolina Historical Review*, Vol. 39, No. 1 (Winter 1962), Pg. 13.

35. The Rev. R. N. Price in Dowd's *Life of Vance*, Pg. 136.

36. Kemp P. Battle, *Memories*, Pg. 89, related the experience of a German newcomer who stooped to sip the hot water gushing from the spring. The minute he had a mouthful he jumped and shouted to his companion, "Hitch the horses, Hans! Hell ish not two miles from this place."

37. Luelle M. Clark, "Mountain Hospitality Renowned Through the Years." Feature article in Asheville *Citizen-Times* special ninetieth-anniversary issue. July 17, 1960. The story of the development of the Hot Springs hotels is given.

38. Folklore story told to this writer in Hot Springs.

39. Vance's *Memorial Address on David B. Swain*, Pg. 3.

## CHAPTER THREE: ENLIVENING CHAPEL HILL

1. Repeated often when this writer was a newspaper correspondent at the White House during the Coolidge administration, when Morrow was an occasional caller.

2. Kemp P. Battle's chapter, "As a Student at the University," in Dowd's *Life of Vance*, Pg. 16. The ensuing quotations are from this account. Battle refers also to the meeting in *Memories*, Pgs. 89-90.

3. Kemp P. Battle in Dowd's *Life of Vance*, Pg. 17.

4. *Ibid.*

5. *Ibid.*

6. Kemp P. Battle's *History of Univ. of N. C.*, Vol. 1—Pg. 580. Dowd's *Life of Vance*, Pg. 22.

7. Wilson letter to Kemp P. Battle quoted in Dowd's *Life of Vance*, Pg. 22.

8. Illustrious public men of the nineteenth century who attended the university are listed in *S.H.S.P.* Vol. 24 (1896), Pg. 3. Of Pettigrew, Kemp P. Battle said in his *Memories*, Pg. 78: "I admired James Johnston Pettigrew,

afterward a general in Lee's army, without stint. He was, it still seems to me, the brightest man I have known in all my life. His mind flashed through the hardest problems without effort. He was unexcelled in everything he attempted."

9. John Bowen Hamilton, editor. "Diary of Thomas Miles Garrett at the University of North Carolina, 1849." *North Carolina Historical Review* Vol. 38, Nos. 1, 2, 3, and 4. Pg. 64.

10. Vance's references to Swain and the various quotations are from his *Life and Character of Hon. David L. Swain, Late President of the University of North Carolina.* A Memorial Oration by Governor Zebulon B. Vance. Delivered in Gerrard Hall on Commencement Day, June 7, 1877. Durham, N. C., 1878. (Pamphlet.) Vance mistakenly gives the name of Swain's mother as Lowrie. She named her son for her first husband, Cordelia Camp, *David Lowry Swain,* (Pamphlet) Pg. 8.

11. In his oration on Swain, Pgs. 13-14, Vance said: "I had the honor,— and I consider it both an honor and a happy fortune—to be on terms of confidential intimacy with him from my first entrance into the University until his death. . . . So affectionately was his interest in my welfare always manifested, that many people supposed we were relatives, and I have frequently been asked if such were not the fact. . . . Perhaps he was more thoroughly versed in biography than any other man who ever lived in America; certainly North Carolina never produced his equal in this respect."

12. Kemp P. Battle, *Memories,* Pg. 52.

13. *Ibid.* Pg. 84.

14. Zebulon B. Vance, *Sketches of North Carolina,* Pg. 55.

15. Vance, *Memorial Address on Swain,* Pg. 13.

16. Garrett Diary, *North Carolina Historical Review,* Vol. 38. No. 2 (April 1961), Pg. 254.

17. *Ibid.* Pg. 562. John Bowen Hamilton, editor of the diary, appended a letter by Dr. Mitchell dated February 8, 1825, not before published, which gives an impression of his character and views.

18. *Vance Papers,* North Carolina Archives. Clipping Book Pg. 2304. An unidentified correspondent writing to *Hale's Weekly,* Fayetteville, May 4, 1880, told of the meeting under the "Davie poplar."

19. *Ibid.*

20. *Ibid.*

21. Kemp P. Battle in Dowd's *Life of Vance,* Pgs. 18-19.

22. Margaret McMahan, "Zeb Vance. Genius with Energy." Fayetteville *Observer,* July 20, 1961. The article contains an account of the effort to haze Zeb. A group tied his big toes to a bedpost. He did not struggle but said he would like to tell them some mountain yarns, which he continued relating until broad daylight. The fascinated listeners cut him loose when one of the

stronger members declared threateningly that they could not haze Vance while he was present. His ready tongue and good spirits won him his freedom. The story and that of the "retail currency" are based on Robert B. Vance's account, Dowd's *Life of Vance,* Pgs. 14-15.

23. Kemp P. Battle in Dowd's *Life of Vance,* Pg. 21.

24. *Ibid.* Pg. 23.

25. *Ibid.*

26. *Ibid.* Pg. 24.

27. *Ibid.* Pg. 25.

28. This is merely an assumption, as "The A. S. Merrimon Journal, 1853-1854," edited by A. R. Newsome, *North Carolina Historical Review,* Vol. 8. No. 3 (July 1931), is filled with strictures against drinking in western North Carolina. He did not in December, 1853, rate Vance's talents as high. Biographical Sketch in *Vance Papers,* Vol. I—Pg. xxiii.

29. Hugh Talmage Lefler and Albert Ray Newsome, *The History of a Southern State North Carolina,* Pg. 339.

30. Dowd's *Life of Vance,* Pg. 20.

31. *Ibid.* Pgs. 26-27.

32. *Ibid.* Pg. 27.

33. *Ibid.*

34. Vance to his cousin Martha E. Weaver from Chapel Hill, Sept. 24, 1851. *Vance Papers,* Vol. I—Pg. 11.

35. Dowd's *Life of Vance,* Pg. 134.

36. *Ibid.*

37. *Vance Papers,* Vol. I—Pgs. 3-7.

38. *Ibid.* Pgs. 7-9.

39. *Ibid.* Pgs. 9-11.

40. *Ibid.* Pgs. 12-14.

41. *Ibid.* Charles McDowell to Vance, April 25, 1852. Pgs. 16-17.

42. *Ibid.* Pg. 8.

43. Address of Vice President Thomas R. Marshall, *Proceedings in Statuary Hall . . . upon the Unveiling, Presentation and Acceptance of the Statue of Zebulon Baird Vance,* etc. Washington, 1917. Pgs. 27-28. Charlotte *Observer* clipping of 1916. *Vance Papers,* Pack Library, Asheville.

44. Duff Gilfond, *The Rise of Saint Calvin,* Pg. 19. New York. 1932.

45. Dowd's *Life of Vance,* Pgs. 29-30.


## CHAPTER FOUR: SEARCHING FOR DR. MITCHELL'S BODY

1. *Vance Papers,* Vol. I—Pgs. 21-24.

2. *Ibid.* Pg. 23.

3. *Ibid.* Pg. 23n.

4. *Ibid.* Pgs. 17-20.

5. *Ibid.* Pg. 23.

6. Vance's "The Search for Professor Mitchell's Body," written for the Asheville *Spectator,* July 1857. Republished by the Asheville Citizen-Times Company in pamphlet *Mount Mitchell and Dr. Elisha Mitchell,* by Chas. A. Webb. Asheville, 1946. Hereafter cited as *Vance Account.* Pgs. 12-13.

7. *Vance Account,* Pg. 13. One of the events of the search was the slaying and eating of a fat heifer by Vance's order. The animal was seen grazing on a mountain slope and so hungry were some of the searchers that they did not wait until the meat was cooked. B. A. Botkin, *A Treasury of Southern Folklore,* Pg. 375. New York. 1949.

8. *Vance Account,* Pg. 14.

9. *Ibid.* Pg. 15. Vance made an error, followed by others, in saying Mitchell fell into Cattail Creek. Instead, it was one of the branches of Sugar Camp Creek, which empties into Caney, or Cane, River.

10. Asheville *Citizen-Times,* July 17, 1960.

11. *Vance Account,* Pgs. 15-16.

12. *Harper's Weekly Magazine,* Sept. 1880. Reprinted in Asheville *Citizen-Times,* July 17, 1960.

## CHAPTER FIVE: MOUNTAIN POLITICIAN AND CONGRESSMAN

1. Merrimon "Journal," *North Carolina Historical Review,* Vol. 8, No. 3. Pgs. 310-311.

2. *Ibid.* Pg. 311.

3. Richard H. Battle, *Ceremonies Attending the Unveiling of the Bronze Statue of Zeb B. Vance, in Capitol Square, Raleigh, N. C.,* etc. Aug. 22, 1900. Pg. 15. (Pamphlet)

4. *Ibid.* Battle called Vance's imposition on the jury the *gaudium certaminis.*

5. Robert B. Vance in Dowd's *Life of Vance,* Pg. 32.

6. *Ibid.* Richard H. Battle also tells this story, *Unveiling Address,* Pg. 15.

7. Glenn Tucker, *Chickamauga,* Pgs. 270-271.

8. Merrimon "Journal," *North Carolina Historical Review,* Vol. 8, No. 3. Pg. 310.

9. Asheville *Citizen,* Nov. 25, 1885. The writer of the letter to the editor signed it merely "Citizen."

10. *Ibid.*

11. Edward W. Phifer, "Saga of a Burke County Family," *North Carolina*

*Historical Review,* Vol. 39, Nos. 1, 2, and 3 (hereafter Phifer's "Saga"), Pgs. 306-307.

12. *Ibid.* Vance in a letter to his friend John Evans Brown, Aug. 22, 1859, used the spelling *Flemming,* which Frontis W. Johnston, editor, *Vance Papers,* Vol. I—Pg. 56, follows. That spelling is used by Kemp P. Battle, *Memories,* Pgs. 91-92. The spelling *Fleming,* used in the text, is that of Dr. Phifer, a student of Burke County history.

13. Phifer's "Saga," Pgs. 308-310, is the source of most of this account. Kemp P. Battle, *Memories,* Pg. 92. *Vance Papers,* Vol. I—Pg. 56n.

14. Phifer's "Saga," Pg. 312.

15. Asheville *Citizen.* Nov. 25, 1885.

16. Letter in Asheville *Citizen,* signed "Citizen." Nov. 25, 1885.

17. *Ibid.*

18. Richard H. Battle's *Unveiling Address.* Pgs. 17-18. Vance may have recalled this incident when, soon after he became governor, he would read in the Raleigh *Standard,* Oct. 15, 1862, the news story of Colonel Fletcher Webster's funeral.

19. Kemp P. Battle's Scrapbook, University of North Carolina. Cited by Franklin Ray Shirley, *Zebulon Vance, Tarheel Spokesman,* Pg. 12.

20. Quoted in Asheville *News,* May 4, 1854.

21. James Schouler, *History of the United States* (World's Best History Series. New York and London. 1898), Vol. 6—Pg. 244. Richard W. Thompson, *Recollections of Sixteen Presidents from Washington to Lincoln,* Vol. II, Pg. 335, says of Pierce: "His nature was kindly, and he was so generous-hearted that many of his political adversaries were embraced within the circle of his private associations—a fact of which I speak from personal experience."

22. Asheville *News,* Jan. 31, 1861. *Vance Papers,* North Carolina Archives, Clipping Book Pg. 2283.

23. North Carolina's larger legislative body was called traditionally the "House of Commons." It was appropriate because all freemen could vote for the delegates, whereas only the owner of fifty or more acres could vote for a state senator. Throughout the nineteenth century the name, House of Commons, was over the door of the chamber. *The State,* Raleigh. Dec. 5, 1964.

24. This and the following extracts are from the letter in *Vance Papers,* Vol. I—Pgs. 32-36.

25. Asheville *Citizen,* Nov. 25, 1885.

26. Gales and his newspaper career are described in Glenn Tucker, *Poltroons and Patriots,* Vol. II—Pgs. 508-509.

27. J. G. Randall, *Lincoln and the South,* Pg. 45. Baton Rouge. 1946.

28. End of quotation from letter to Caldwell, *Vance Papers,* Vol. I—Pg. 34.

29. Extract of speech, Dowd's *Life of Vance.* Pg. 42.

30. *Ibid.* Pgs. 42-43.

31. *Ibid.* Pgs. 50-52.

32. *Ibid.* Pgs. 35-36.

33. *Memorial Addresses on the Life and Character of Zebulon Baird Vance* (delivered in the Senate and House of Representatives). Washington. 1895. Sherman told of his acquaintance with Vance.

34 Lloyd Lewis, *Sherman: Fighting Prophet,* Pg. 29.

35. George Stimpson, *A Book About American Politics,* Pg. 492. New York. 1952.

36. *Vance Papers.* Vol. I—Pg. xxxvi.

37. *Ibid.* Pg. 40.

38. Adele Cutts was the daughter of a wealthy Rockingham County, N. C., planter. Douglas married her in North Carolina.

39. Richard W. Thompson, *Recollections of Sixteen Presidents,* Pg. 324. Polk made the offer in 1848 through the American minister and Spain rejected it. The matter of purchasing Cuba became heatedly discussed again after the Ostend Manifesto was drawn up October 18, 1854, by U. S. Ministers James Buchanan, John Y. Mason, and Pierre Soule, recommending the purchase or seizure of Cuba. Secretary of State William L. Marcy disavowed the document. Soule resigned in disgust, Buchanan became President. The maximum price discussed was $125,000,000. Schouler's *History of the United States,* Vol. VI —Pg. 313n. Agitation for the purchase of Cuba remained an issue during Vance's early Congressional service.

40. Robert Vance in Dowd's *Life of Vance,* Pgs. 33-34.

41. *Ibid.* Pg. 35.

42. *Ibid.* Pgs. 36-37.

43. The correspondence with all the details of the controversy is found in *Vance Papers,* Vol. I—Pgs. 42-60.

## CHAPTER SIX: DEFENDER OF THE UNION

1. Vance's letters are filled with this sentiment during his second term in the House, as may be seen from those quoted in this and the following chapter.

2. *Biographical Directory of the American Congress,* Pg. 1980. Washington. 1950. A fourth brother, William D. Washburn, served in the House and Senate from Minnesota after the war.

3. Schouler's *History of the United States,* Vol. 6—Pgs. 445-446; Edmund C. Wilson, *Patriotic Gore,* Pg. 373. Edwin Emerson, Jr., *A History of the Nineteenth Century Year by Year,* Vol. III—Pg. 1287. New York. 1902; Dowd's *Life of Vance,* Pg. 53; George B. Galloway, *History of the House of Representatives,* Pgs. 46-47. New York. 1961.

4. Dowd's *Life of Vance*. Pgs. 55-56.

5. *Ibid*. Pg. 58.

6. *Ibid*. Pgs. 58-60.

7. *Ibid*. Pg. 60.

8. Kemp P. Battle, *Memories*, Pg. 160.

9. The rejection was purely political and involved no question of character or fitness. It was based on Badger's opposition to the Democratic party doctrine that Congress had no power to legislate on slavery in the territories. *Vance Papers*, Vol. I—Pg. 33n.

10. The principal sources followed in this account of the Salisbury Whig convention are Richard H. Battle's *Unveiling Address*, Pg. 21, and the news story of the Fayetteville *Observer*, written by Edward Joseph Hale, son of the publisher, Edward Jones Hale. Kemp P. Battle, *Memories*, Pg. 160, described the meeting, and commented: "I was called on vociferously but I did not feel in the humor and silently dodged. . . . I concluded afterwards I was wrong in this."

11. Vance was of course well acquainted in Caldwell and Wilkes counties, both of which lie east of the mountains, but not a familiar character to the old-line Whigs: Graham, Rayner, Badger, Dockery, and other noted men of a passing era.

12. Dispatch of Edward Joseph Hale, who attended the rally.

13. This is variously quoted. The statement here is from Richard S. Battle, *Unveiling Address*, Pg. 21.

14. *Vance Statue Dedication in Statuary Hall, Washington*. Pg. 17.

15. Richard S. Battle, *Unveiling Address*, Pg. 22.

16. *Vance Papers*, Vol. I—Pgs. 66-68.

17. *Ibid*. Pgs. 68-71.

18. *Ibid*. Pgs. 65-66.

19. *Vance Papers*, Pack Library, Asheville. Clipping headed "Disunion Programme." 1861. (No day or month given.)

20. Asheville *News*, Jan. 31, 1861.

21. *Vance Papers*. Vol. I—Pgs. 71-73.

22. *Ibid*.

## CHAPTER SEVEN: ZEB AND HIS STATE ARE CROWDED OUT

1. The state's part in the Revolutionary War is well pictured in Mrs. J. A. Fore, "North Carolinians at Valley Forge," *Confederate Veteran*, Vol. 37 (1929)—Pg. 218.

2. Jackson's birthplace is the subject of a well-known controversy between North and South Carolina.

3. John B. Floyd was indicted in Washington for complicity in the embezzlement of public funds and the indictment was pending while he served as a Confederate general, but the case was never tried. He died before the end of the war, August 26, 1863. *Battles and Leaders,* Vol. I—Pg. 401. Ezra J. Warner, *Generals in Gray,* Pg. 90. Baton Rouge. 1949.

4. *Vance Papers,* Vol. I—Pgs. 74-78. Vance was severe with Buchanan who, though not a strong leader for difficult times, was not corrupt.

5. Slavery was heavy in the eastern counties engaged in growing cotton, rice, and tobacco and producing naval stores, and a tier of counties along the Virginia line engaged in growing tobacco.

6. Houston G. Jones, *Bedford Brown: State Rights Unionist,* is an excellent though compact study of an individual who had a deep influence on North Carolina attitudes before the war and kept much sentiment tied closely to the Union.

7. Douglas Reed, "Woodfin Opposed Secessional Policies in State Senate," Asheville *Citizen-Times* (Ninetieth-anniversary issue), July 17, 1960. This is an excellent article on Woodfin's attitude and addresses on secession. Merrimon "Journal," Pg. 305, speaks highly of him. George Stimpson, *Popular Questions Answered,* 164, discusses the origin of the phrase Lincoln used, "government of the people, by the people, for the people." Theodore Parker's version in his address in Boston May 29, 1850, was "a government of all the people, by all the people, for all the people." Lincoln merely dropped the three uses of the word *all.* Billy Herndon tells of giving the Parker address to Lincoln, who marked the foregoing expression with a pencil. Herndon's *Life of Lincoln* (Premier Civil War Classics edition), Pg. 321. Stimpson shows many prior uses of a like expression, going back to John Wyclif and ultimately to Cleon of Athens. Woodfin's use of the similar phrase that the Federal government was of, by and for the people was in his address to the North Carolina Senate in 1851. The address was printed by Seaton Gales and a copy is in the North Carolina Room, Pack Library, Asheville. Kemp P. Battle, *Memories,* Pg. 90 gives an interesting sketch of Woodfin, an influential factor in retarding secessionist sentiment in North Carolina prior to Lincoln's election.

8. Woodfin address to state senate. Asheville *Citizen-Times,* July 17, 1960.

9. *Vance Papers,* Vol. I—Pg. 77.

10. *Ibid.* Pgs. 77-78.

11. *Ibid.* Pg. 78.

12. *Ibid.*

13. *Ibid.* Pgs. 79-81.

14. *Ibid.* Pg. 81.

15. *Ibid.* Pg. 83.

16. *Ibid.* Pgs. 83-84.

17. *Ibid*. Pg. 74.

18. *Ibid*. Pgs. 90-91.

19. Charles Harris, "State Sovereignty—Forgotten Testimony" analyzes this question in *S.H.S.P.*, Vol 9—Pgs. 433-454. A. C. Avery, *S.H.S.P.*, Vol. 21—Pg. 111.

20. Glenn Tucker, *Front Rank*. A picture is given in the chapter "Answering the Call to Arms" of the North Carolina attitude at the time of secession. Dowd's *Life of Vance*, Pg. 442.

21. There is no evidence that Lincoln, Seward or anyone else in the Lincoln administration ever called Vance into consultation on means of holding North Carolina in the Union, which evidences a lack of either time or statesmanship at this critical period. None could look ahead to the war with certainty, of course, but holding North Carolina would probably have meant the difference between a short war and one long and ghastly.

22. Kemp P. Battle, *Memories*, Pg. 168.

23. *Ibid*. Pg. 169.

24. Dowd's *Life of Vance*, Pgs. 441-442.

25. Robert B. Vance in Dowd's *Life of Vance*, Pg. 62.

26. Walter Clark, *North Carolina Regiments*, Vol. II—Pg. 405.

## CHAPTER EIGHT: COLONEL OF THE TWENTY-SIXTH

1. *Vance Papers*, Pack Library, Asheville. Unidentified clipping, apparently the Raleigh *Standard* of July 17, 1861. The clipping is marked "Holden's paper" and reprinted probably in the Asheville *News*.

2. Reprinted in Charlotte *Observer*, April 29, 1956.

3. Lasting effects are attributed to Vance's oratorical powers. One commonly told tale relates to Yancey and Mitchell counties. These two mountain counties lie side by side with virtually everything of a physical and topographical nature in common. They possess kindred economic conditions, occupations, and family connections. But Mitchell is overwhelmingly Republican and Yancey "dependably" Democratic. The explanation often given is that Vance in his stumping campaign to keep the state in the Union spoke on the first day at Bakersville, which became the county seat of Mitchell County. His handsome appearance, magnificent oratorical ability and fervor for his cause carried his audience with him and almost to a man they agreed that North Carolina should remain in the Union. Zeb's next engagement was the following day in Burnsville, the seat of Yancey County. But while he was on the way to fill the engagement a messenger reached him from Marion with intelligence that Lincoln had called on the state for volunteers to fight the other Southern states. He shifted quickly and when he spoke in Burnsville he made such a

rousing speech for secession and the new Confederacy that the Yancey County men were convinced, turned against Lincoln and the Republicans, and have been mainly Democrats ever since. Thus two of Vance's speeches, delivered on successive days according to this tradition, have shaped the politics of two counties contrariwise for more than a century! Muriel Early Sheppard, *Cabins in the Laurel*. cited by Asheville *Citizen-Times*. July 7, 1960, tells the story of the divorcement of Mitchell from Yancey County.

4. Colonel James M. Ray statement, *Vance Papers*, Pack Library, Asheville. Newspaper clipping of interview.

5. *Vance Papers*, Vol. I—Pg. 93n.

6. *Ibid*. Pg. 92n.

7. George W. McCoy, "Buncombe Riflemen at Bethel, First Battle of War." Asheville *Citizen-Times* feature article, April 30, 1961.

8. Ray interview, *Vance Papers*, Pack Library, Asheville. Asheville *Citizen* clipping. (No date.)

9. Vance's recorded use of this term is told in a later chapter dealing with his review of General Lee's army. B. A. Botkin, *A Treasury of Southern Folklore*, in one version, Pg. 41, places the origin at Sharpsburg where the 6th North Carolina was alleged to have shouted for the 4th Texas to put tar on their heels. But Botkin found the term long in use prior to the Civil War, Pg. 40, and thinks it originated among workers at the tar kilns in the eastern North Carolina tar, pitch and turpentine industry. The North Carolina Department of Conservation and Development has used a Civil War origin but at another time dates the term back to the Revolutionary War, where it probably belongs. See pamphlet *Historic North Carolina*. At first used derisively, Vance gave it elevation. Most North Carolinians appear to like it as a folklore expression, others accept it, and some dislike it as being no longer applicable to a state that long since has grown away from tar and pitch as a leading industry and has become one of the busy manufacturing areas of the nation. The version in the text is from an interview with Colonel James M. Ray of Asheville, Asheville *Citizen* (no date) in *Vance Papers*, Pack Library, Asheville.

10. *Vance Papers*, Pack Library, Asheville. Alfred was the eldest of eleven children of Adolphus Baird, farmer and merchant of Marshall.

11. Henry Steele Commager, *The Blue and the Gray*, Pgs. 561-562. Indianapolis. 1950. Tucker, *High Tide at Gettysburg*, Pgs. 40-41. Robert B. Vance's reference is from one of his chapters in Dowd's *Life of Vance*, Pg. 63.

12. *Ibid*. Pg. 64.

13. Colonel Bennett, one of the best writers among the North Carolina veterans of the war, left an excellent sketch of the 14th North Carolina regiment in Clark's *N. C. Regiments*, Vol. I—Pgs. 706-732.

14. Colonel Bennett in Clark's *N. C. Regiments*, Vol. I—Pgs. 706f, said

Gudger's wound entitled him to discharge but he remained. After the war he was appointed by Governor Alfred M. Scales as commissioner to determine at what point on the Nolichucky River the line with Tennessee crossed. He and the Tennessee commissioner failed to agree and the line remains as originally run by Zeb Vance's grandfather's party in 1799.

15. Letter from Gudger to Rev. W. T. Atkin contained in one of Colonel Ray's interviews, Asheville *Citizen,* May 5, 1935.

16. Price chapter in Dowd's *Life of Vance,* Pg. 137.

17. *Confederate Veteran,* Vol. 31, No. 7—Pg. 266. The Holston Conference Female College was located in Asheville. Merrimon *Journal,* Pg. 324n. It later became the Asheville College for Women. Arthur's *Western North Carolina,* Pg. 429.

18. Clark's *N. C. Regiments,* Vol. I—Pg. 711.

19. Col. Ray Interview, Asheville *Citizen,* May 5, 1935.

20. *Ibid.* May 27, 1918.

21. *Vance Papers,* Vol. I—Pgs. 100-101.

22. *Ibid.*

23. *Ibid.* Pgs. 115-117.

24. *Ibid.* Pgs. 109-110.

25. Col. Ray interview, Asheville *Citizen,* May 27, 1918. In *Vance Papers,* Pack Library, Asheville.

26. Fort Macon as it stood in 1861 had been constructed in the period around 1827, having been suggested by President Monroe and Nathaniel Macon of North Carolina. Other forts in the coastal defense system projected and constructed at this time or slightly later were Forts Sumter, Caswell, Monroe, Columbus, and Pulaski. The North Carolina Confederate Centennial Commission (1961-1965) issued a short pamphlet by Jerome F. Morris, *The Brief Belligerence of Fort Macon.*

27. Clark's *N. C. Regts.,* Vol. II—Pgs. 303-423 gives a full account of the service of the 26th.

28. *Ibid.* Vol. II—Pg. 306.

29. Tucker, *High Tide at Gettysburg,* Pg. 148.

30. Clark's *N. C. Regts.,* Vol. II—Pg. 336.

31. These are the titles used on the book by Harry H. Hall published by the North Carolina Confederate Centennial Commission, 1963.

32. *New Yorker,* Feb. 3, 1962. *Regiment Band of the Twenty-Sixth North Carolina,* by Julius Leinbach, edited by Donald M. McCorkle, issued by the Moravian Music Foundation, Inc. (reprint from *Civil War History,* Vol. IV, No. III, 1958), gives the repertory of the band and an interesting account of its performance at Gettysburg.

33. Quoted from Samuel T. Mickey diary by Henry H. Hall, *A Johnny Reb Band from Salem,* Pg. 10.

34. Clark's *N. C. Regts.,* Vol. II—Pg. 399.

35. Hall's *Johnny Reb Band.* Pg. 14.

36. Dowd's *Life of Vance,* Pg. 129.

37. Stedman address, 64th Congress. *Vance Statue Unveiling in Statuary Hall.* Pgs. 71-72.

38. Kemp P. Battle, *Memories.* Pg. 98.

## CHAPTER NINE: NEW BERN—THE TEST OF COMBAT

1. This account of the battle is mainly based on Clark's *N. C. Regts.* Vol. II; *Official Records,* hereafter *O. R.:* Richard Iobst, *Battle of New Bern* (pamphlet of North Carolina Confederate Centennial Commission) ; *Battles and Leaders of the Civil War,* Vol. I—Pgs. 632-670; John G. Barrett, *The Civil War in North Carolina,* Pgs. 66-130, Chapel Hill, 1963; John S. C. Abbott, *The History of the Civil War in America,* Vol. I—Pgs. 314-335, and contemporary newspapers. Abbott's value is that he wrote while the war was in progress and reflects current attitudes.

2. One of the Federal soldiers killed in Foster's attack was Adjutant Frazer A. Stearns, son of the president of Amherst College. Abbott I—Pg. 332.

3. Vance report on New Bern *O. R.* Series I—Vol. 9, Pgs. 254-257.

4. Clark's *N. C. Regts.* Vol. II—Pg. 543.

5. Lieutenant William A. Graham was a son of the former governor, senator and cabinet member William A. Graham of Hillsboro, N. C.

6. Tucker, *High Tide at Gettysburg,* Pg. 141.

7. Clark's *N. C. Regts.* Vol. II—Pg. 405. Vance was generally credited with effecting the transfer in order to assure Burgwyn his deserved promotion and in this he was aided by Major General D. H. Hill. An obscure story relating to the transfer was published by the Asheville *Citizen* May 11, 1930, two days before the centennial of Vance's birth, an interview by Robert Louie Khutz with Thomas Y. Lytle of Marion, N. C., then 87 years old, who had served in Robert Ransom's Brigade. After Malvern Hill, according to Lytle, when Ransom was marching the hungry, thirsty, exhausted brigade back toward Richmond, they came to some springs "of the most thirst quenching water that had ever eased parched throats." Ransom, so as to give each man a chance to drink and fill his canteen, ordered that they take care and not muddy the water. Just then a thirsty soldier who had been in the rear and was hard of hearing rushed up and soused his bucket into the spring. The bucket brought up mud and vegetable matter and fouled the water. Ransom, according to Lytle, drew his sword and struck the soldier across the head.

"Right then and there," declared Lytle, "Vance swore he would get the 26th Regiment out of Ransom's Brigade. . . . Sometime later he managed to bring about an exchange of the 56th Regiment of another brigade for the 26th in Ransom's, for he was no longer a colonel under Robert Ransom but the Governor of North Carolina."

8. Tuscarora was then as now a small station on the North Carolina and Atlantic Railroad.

9. Susie S. Taylor, editor, *The Battle of New Bern and the Retreat to Kinston*. Bulletin of Western Carolina College, 1957—Pg. 12.

10. Clark's *N. C. Regts.*, Vol. II—Pg. 544.

11. *Vance Papers*, Vol. I—Pg. 127.

12. *Ibid*. Pg. 129.

13. Clark's *N. C. Regts.*, Vol. II—Pg. 326.

14. Edward Warren, *A Doctor's Experiences in Three Continents*, Pgs. 291ff.

15. Susie S. Taylor, *Battle of New Bern*, Pg. 9.

16. *Ibid*. Pgs. 10-11.

17. Lee gave careful study to all intelligence respecting the North Carolina situation before launching his Gettysburg campaign and felt reassured only when he learned that a Massachusetts regiment was going north for recruitment, which did not indicate aggressive measures at the moment on the North Carolina coast. Still, the campaign in Pennsylvania was a major risk.

18. *Battles and Leaders*, Vol. I—Pg. 640. G. Moxley Sorrel, *Recollections of a Confederate Staff Officer*, Pg. 37. Tucker, *High Tide at Gettysburg*, Pg. 7.

19. *Battles and Leaders*, Vol. I—Pg. 202.

20. Clark's *N. C. Regts.*, Vol. II—Pg. 308.

21. Asheville *News*, April 26, 1862.

22. *Vance Papers*, Vol. I—Pgs. 119-120.

23. *Ibid*. Pg. 133.

24. *Ibid*. Pg. 134.

25. *Ibid*. Pgs. 136-137.

26. The letter, Raleigh *Standard*, July 23, 1862, does not show the officer's name.

27. *Vance Papers*, Vol. I—Pgs. 138-139.

28. *Ibid*. Pg. 139.

29. *Ibid*. Pg. 142-145.

30. *Ibid*. Pg. 144. The Greensboro *Patriot* said: "We regret to learn that many obstacles have been thrown in the way of Vance raising his legion— that a very large number of companies desired to join his legion—but a deaf ear was given to their wishes and they were distributed elsewhere." Reprinted in Raleigh *Standard* June 28, 1862. The expression apparently is a quotation from the Salisbury *Watchman*. It evidences that sympathy was with Vance in his struggle to raise a legion.

31. Asheville *News*, May 15, June 12, and June 26, 1862.

32. *Vance Papers*, Vol. I—Pg. 131.

33. *Confederate Veteran*, Vol. III. No. 4 (1895)—Pg. 109.

34. Clark's *N. C. Regts.*, Vol. II—Pgs. 404-405.


### CHAPTER TEN: MALVERN HILL

1. *Battles and Leaders*, Vol. II   Pg. 391.

2. George B. McClellan, *McClellan's Own Story*, Pg. 436. New York. 1887.

3. *Battles and Leaders*, Vol. II—Pg. 403.

4. Abbott's *Civil War in America*, Vol. II—Pg. 109.

5. Ransom in Clark's *N. C. Regts.*, Vol. II—Pgs. 332-333.

6. *Battles and Leaders*, Vol. II—Pg. 394.

7. McClellan's *Own Story*, Pg. 437.

8. *Battles and Leaders*, Vol. II—Pg. 403.

9. Clark's *N. C. Regts.*, Vol. II—Pg. 329. Dowd's *Life of Vance*, Pg. 139.

10. Clark's *N. C. Regts.*, Vol. II—Pg. 405.

11. *Ibid.* Vol. II—Pg. 498.

12. Hall's *Johnny Reb Band*, Pg. 17n.

13. Abbott's *Civil War in America*, Vol. II—Pg. 110.

14. Warren, *A Doctor's Experiences in Three Continents*, Pg. 302.

15. *Ibid.* Pg. 305.

16. Abbott, *Civil War in America*, Vol. II—Pg. 110.

17. The story is cited by *Confederate Veteran*, Vol. 37—Pg. 37 as an indication of how history is confused by exaggeration.


### CHAPTER ELEVEN: GOVERNOR BY A LANDSLIDE

1. Graham appears never to have been more than a mild secessionist, made so by force of circumstance and loyalty to his home people. His great service had been much more on a national than local scale. He would have been out of place in such a driving job as governor in wartime and was the first to recognize it. The Raleigh *Standard*, May 14, 1862, announced that Graham declined to be considered.

2. *Vance Papers*, Vol. I—Pg. 148n.

3. *Ibid.* Pgs. 148-149.

4. Hale statement in Dowd's *Life of Vance*, Pgs. 181-182.

5. The Raleigh *Standard*, June 21, 1862, said Colonel Johnston "won his title among the pork and beans of the Commissary Department."

6. *Vance Papers*, Vol. I—Pg. 152.

7. *Vance Papers.* Vol. I. These newspaper quotations are given by the editor, Frontis W. Johnston, in a footnote. Pgs. 140-141.

8. *Ibid.*

9. Quotations in and statements by the Asheville *News,* June 26, July 3, and July 17, 1862.

10. J. G. de Roulhac Hamilton, *Reconstruction in North Carolina,* Pg. 41.

11. Asheville *News,* June 19, 1862. Vance's regimental chaplain, Rev. R. N. Price, told of an incident about the Asheville *News,* usually Vance's enemy. When Vance went to Asheville to make a speech friends told him to denounce the editor "in unmeasured terms." His reply was: "No, I will not do that. A year hence that man may be my friend and supporter." Price in Dowd's *Life of Vance,* Pg. 139. The prediction proved accurate.

12. Hamilton, *Reconstruction in North Carolina,* Pg. 42.

13. Asheville *News,* June 6, 1862.

14. Mrs. Jackson, nee Mary Anna Morrison, lived in Charlotte, N. C., while her husband was actively campaigning.

15. Asheville *News,* July 17, 1862.

16. Hamilton, *Reconstruction in North Carolina,* Pgs. 42-43. Another of Stanly's services was that he kept the name of North Carolina off the official Washington list of states where slave property was to be confiscated, thereby preserving a fiction that because of the Union government at New Bern the state was no longer in rebellion. The absence of North Carolina from the list came to be noted and was an issue used against Vance. The Lincoln government presumably thought, according to this contention, that Vance would lead the state back into the Union, when nothing could have been farther from his intentions.

17. Issue of July 15, 1862.

18. Issue of July 4, 1862.

19. Hamilton, *Reconstruction in North Carolina,* Pg. 43. *Vance Papers,* Vol. I gives the slightly different total of 52,833 for Vance and 20,174 for Johnston, the most sweeping margin in the state's history. Clark's *N. C. Regts.,* Vol. II—Pg. 303.

20. *Vance Papers,* Vol. I—Pg. 151.

21. Clark's *N. C. Regts.,* Vol. II—Pg. 334.

22. Greensboro *Patriot,* Aug. 20, 1862.

23. Asheville *News,* Aug. 21, 1862.

24. Norfolk, Va., *Landmark,* Jan. 20, 1885. Clipping in *Vance Papers,* Pack Library, Asheville.

25. Asheville *News,* Aug. 28, 1862.

26. Hall's *Johnny Reb Band,* Pgs. 20-21.

27. Issue of August 19, 1862. The sentiment followed the election but preceded the inauguration.

28. Issue of Sept. 16, 1862.

29. *Vance Papers,* Vol. I—Pgs. 152-155. Swain's letter made it clear that Vance was not the youngest man to be elected governor, to that time, as is sometimes stated. Recalling that Vance was thirty-two years old when elected, Swain, Pg. 152, said: "I was but a month short of that age, when elected Governor, 30 years ago." Swain served three terms when the term was for one year, and the election was by the state legislature. The popular election of the governor was established in North Carolina in 1836. John M. Mullen, *Facts to Know North Carolina,* Pg. 125. Lincolnton, N. C., 1937.

## CHAPTER TWELVE: GIRDING FOR THE LONG WAR

1. *Proceedings in Statuary Hall,* Washington (64th Congress), Pg. 25.

2. Richard H. Battle wrote an article on his intimate association with Vance in the Governor's Palace, from which these facts are mainly drawn. It was printed in Dowd's *Life of Vance,* Pgs. 163-170. Hereafter called Battle's article.

3. Battle's article in Dowd, Pg. 167.

4. *Ibid.*

5. Raleigh *Standard,* Nov. 5, 1862.

6. Battle's article in Dowd, Pg. 168.

7. *Ibid.*

8. *Ibid.* Pg. 169.

9. *Dictionary of American Biography.* Hereafter D.A.B.

10. James D. McIver, who served in the 26th regiment, told this story. Dowd's *Life of Vance,* Pgs. 192-193. At the memorial services held in Charlotte in April, 1894, after Vance's death, one of his former law partners (not identified in the Charlotte *Observer* comment) told of his interest in military affairs.

11. *Ibid.* Pg. 321.

12. Lefler and Newsome, *The History of a Southern State,* Pg. 298.

13. *S.H.S.P.,* Vol. 14 (1886)—Pg. 511.

14. *Ibid.*

15. A good discussion of North Carolina at the time of secession is in James H. Boykin, *North Carolina in 1861.* New York. 1961. The figures on the slave population are from Pg. 128.

16. *S.H.S.P.,* Vol. 27 (1899)—Pg. 384.

17. Dowd's *Life of Vance,* Pg. 40.

18. Raleigh *Standard,* Oct. 29, 1862.

19. *Ibid.*

20. *Ibid.*

21. Vance to Davis, Oct. 20, 1862, Letter Books, North Carolina Archives. Vol. I—Pg. 35.

22. Davis to Vance, Oct. 27, 1862, Letter Books, Vol. I—Pgs. 35-36.

23. Secretary of War Randolph told Vance that "very inconsiderable contracts for harness are made in North Carolina." Randolph to Vance, Nov. 7, 1862. Letter Books, Vol. I—Pg. 47.

24. QMG. Myers to Vance, Sept. 17 and Dec. 8, 1862. Letter Books, Vol. I—Pg. 28. David A. Barnes to Myers, Oct. 14, 1862, Pg. 26.

25. *S.H.S.P.,* Vol. 14 (1886)—Pg. 511.

26. Richard W. Griffin, "Reconstruction of the North Carolina Textile Industry, 1865-1885." *North Carolina Historical Review,* Vol. XLI, No. 1 (Winter 1964)—Pg. 40.

27. *Ibid.*

28. *Vance Papers,* Vol. I—Pgs. 303-304.

29. *Ibid.* Pgs. 426-427.

30. Raleigh *Standard,* July 16, 1862.

31. *Ibid.* Feb. 17, 1863.

32. Vance to Lee, Dec. 21, 1863. Letter Books, Vol. II—Pg. 30.

33. Letter Books, Vol. I—Pg. 6. Sept. 18, 1862.

34. *Ibid.*

35. *Vance Papers,* Vol. I—Pgs. 304-305.

36. The Asheville *News* published the proclamation Oct. 30, 1862.

37. *Ibid.*

38. Quoted in Asheville *News,* Nov. 6, 1862.

39. *Ibid.* Nov. 27, 1862.

40. Issue of April 15, 1863.

41. Reprinted in Raleigh *Standard,* April 15, 1863.

42. *S.H.S.P.,* Vol. 14 (1886)—Pg. 514.

43. *Ibid.*

44. Raleigh *Standard,* Dec. 9, 1862.

45. Vance to Seddon, Dec. 31, 1863. Letter Books, Vol. II—Pg. 41.

46. *S.H.S.P.,* Vol. 14 (1886)—Pg. 514.

47. Letter Books, Vol. I—Pgs. 21-22.

48. John Christopher Schwab, *The Confederate States of America,* Pg. 272.

49. *North Carolina Historical Review,* Vol. XLI (Winter 1864)—Pg. 34.

50. *S.H.S.P.,* Vol. 14 (1886)—Pg. 514.

51. Fred Kelly in *The State,* Raleigh, Sept. 28, 1963.

52. Ralph W. Donnelly has written an excellent account of this enterprise, "The Charlotte, North Carolina, Navy Yard, C.S.N." in *Civil War History,* Vol. 5. No. 1 (March 1959).

53. Burton H. Smith, "Carolina's Contribution to the Confederate Navy," *Confederate Veteran,* Vol. 38 (1930)—Pgs. 376-377.

54. Asheville *Citizen-Times*, July 17, 1960.

55. Raleigh *Standard*, May 17, 1863.

56. "University of North Carolina in the Civil War," *S.H.S.P.*, Vol. 24 (1896)—Pgs. lff. Alfred Hoyt Bill, *The Beleaguered City*, Pg. 13. New York. 1946.

57. Quoted in North Carolina *Whig* (Raleigh), Nov. 18, 1862. Used by Asheville *News*, Nov. 27, 1862.

58. Dowd's *Life of Vance*, Pg. 179.

59. Tucker, "Some Aspects of North Carolina's Participation in the Gettysburg Campaign," *North Carolina Historical Review*, Vol. 35, No. 2 (April 1958)—Pg. 23. Clark's *N. C. Regts.*, Vol. 5—Pg. xii.

60. *S.H.S.P.*, Vol. 14 (1886)—Pg. 506.

61. *Ibid.* Pg. 508.

62. *Ibid.* Pgs. 510-511.

63. Considerable opinion appears to exist that the voluntary restrictive measures of World War I, with the full force of community and national feeling behind them, were more effective than the harsher methods of World II. Certainly they made the average citizen feel himself to be a ready and contributing participant in the struggle and not one subjected to restraints often seemingly unnecessary but imposed rigorously on the theory that the public had to be kept aware of the existence of the war. The service of members of most families and the recurring casualty lists, as in 1861-1865, were ample notices of that.

64. Credit for much of the early organizational work in North Carolina, especially before Vance became governor, belongs to Brigadier General James G. Martin, a West Point graduate of Elizabeth City, who formed the regiments and equipped the early volunteers going from the state. He was known as "Old One Wing" because he had lost an arm at Churubusco in the Mexican War, and in later times as the "Forgotten Hero," because his work was mostly behind the lines and he never had distinguished battle action.

The *Standard* in its issue of November 19, 1862, tried to pin on him responsibility for the poor Confederate showing in the eastern counties: "General Martin is wanting in decision of character, intellect and daring," Holden inveighed. "The Cherry Run affair and recent events around Tarborough prove this. He possesses the confidence of neither the troops nor the people. We have no confidence in a general who says, 'go, boys,' instead of 'come, boys.' We regret to have to write this way but our duty to our country must be performed."

The editorial followed the Federal General Foster's raid in the Tarboro neighborhood in early November, a minor affair. Martin could not be held blamable. But Holden did bring out that Martin had been serving as Adjutant General of North Carolina and as a brigadier general in the Confederate Army, which he held to be illegal. Vance did not respond to Holden's attack, but Martin wanted an opportunity for line duty. The *Standard* was able to announce March 17, 1863, that Vance had appointed Col. Daniel G. Fowle to be Adjutant General, "with General Martin barred from two jobs by the court." Holden was no better pleased and described the Fowle appointment as "very bad." Martin requested field duty, served for a time under Lee at Petersburg, and in the final stages took command of western North Carolina forces. Fowle did not work harmoniously with Vance and resigned after a few months, but he had a distinguished legal and political career after the war and became governor of North Carolina in 1889.

General Martin at Waynesville, North Carolina, on May 10, 1865, led a Confederate force in the last action of the war east of the Mississippi. While hostilities were in progress word came up the mountains that Lee had surrendered.

## CHAPTER THIRTEEN: THE CRISES COME IN CLUSTERS

1. John Pool to Vance, Sept. 18, 1862. Letter Books, Vol. I—Pg. 12.
2. Vance to Smith, Sept. 28, 1862. Letter Books, Vol. I—Pg. 16.
3. *Ibid.* Capt. Davis to Vance, Oct. 6.
4. Issue of Oct. 15, 1862.
5. Davis to Vance, Oct. 17, 1862. Letter Books, Vol. I—Pgs. 31-32.
6. Raleigh *Standard*, Oct. 8, 1862, and June 7, 1862.
7. *Ibid.* Oct. 15, 1862.
8. *Ibid.*
9. *Ibid.* Nov. 12, 1862.
10. *Ibid.* Oct. 15, 1862.
11. Vance to Davis, Nov. 12, 1862. Letter Books, Vol. I—Pgs. 48-49.
12. Raleigh *Standard*, Nov. 12, 1862.
13. *Ibid.* March 8, 1862.
14. Worth report, Sept. 19, 1862. Letter Books, Vol. I—Pgs. 8-9.
15. Vance to Worth, Oct. 1, 1862. Letter Books, Vol. I—Pg. 15.
16. Worth to Vance, Oct. 7, 1862. Letter Books, Vol. I—Pg. 20.
17. Surgeon General S. P. Moore to Vance, Sept. 17, 1862. Letter Books, Vol. I—Pg. 11.
18. Raleigh *Standard*, Oct. 8, Oct. 15, Oct. 22, and Nov. 19, 1862.
19. Barnes to Worth, Letter Books, Vol. I.—Pg. 21.
20. Raleigh *Standard,* Oct. 29, 1862. Fred Kelly in *The State,* Raleigh, Sept. 28, 1963.
21. Vance Proclamation. Governor Brown of Georgia to Vance, Nov. 17, 1862. Vance to Brown, Nov. 22, 1862. Letter Books, Vol. I—Pgs. 75 and 79.
22. Vance's Wilmington, Kinston, and Goldsboro trip was reported in Raleigh *Standard*, Dec. 16, 1862.

23. Letter Books, Vol. I—Pg. 76.

24. Vance to Smith, Jan. 24, 1863. Letter Books, Vol. I—Pg. 96.

25. Hamilton, *Reconstruction in North Carolina*, Pg. 76.

26. Vance to Myers, Dec. 26, 1862. Letter Books, Vol. I—Pg. 75.

27. Schwab, *The Confederate States of America*, Pg. 267.

28. J. E. Jones, *A Rebel War Clerk's Diary*, entry of Dec. 27, 1864. Vol. II—Pg. 376.

29. Part of the cost of operating the saltworks at Wilmington and at Saltville, Virginia, was covered by a bond issue. Salt thus procured kept the home people alive. During the reconstruction period the Supreme Court of North Carolina delivered the peculiar opinion—"a singular decision," said a later chief justice, Walter Clark—voiding these bonds as having been "issued in aid of the Rebellion." Judge Clark had the better view that they were "issued in aid of the destitute and suffering women and children of the State." Clark's *N. C. Regts.*, Vol. V—Pg. x. But among those contemptuous of the law during the reconstruction were legislatures and courts.

30. *Vance Papers*, Vol. I—Pgs. 427-428.

31. Raleigh *Standard*, May 6, 1863, gives this example of the roll. Other citations followed.

32. Reprinted in Raleigh *Standard*, Oct. 22, 1862.

33. Warren, *A Doctor's Experiences,* etc., Pg. 308.

34. *Ibid*. Pg. 309.

35. *Ibid*.

36. *Vance Papers,* Vol. I—Pg. 229n.

37. Warren, *A Doctor's Experiences,* Pg. 313.

38. *Ibid*. Pgs. 310-312.

39. *Ibid*. Pg. 312.

40. Letter Books, Vol. I—Pgs. 36-37. Hamilton, *Reconstruction in North Carolina*, Pg. 87ff. *Vance Papers*, Vol. I—Pg. 272n. *Biographical Directory of the American Congress*, Pgs. 1853-1854.

41. Letter Books, Vol. I—Pgs. 37-38.

42. *Vance Papers,* Vol. I—Pgs. 391-393.

43. *Ibid*. Pg. 272n.

44. Testimonials to Hoke were so numerous as to identify him as perhaps the most outstanding general from North Carolina during the war. Said Captain Charles G. Elliott, Assistant Adjutant General: "Hoke, as a division commander, was the peer of any in the army. Conspicuous for his bravery, coolness, and good judgment, the youngest major general in the army, his rapid promotion from the grade of lieutenant was due to his gallant and meritorious conduct and *fitness to command*." Quoted by *S.H.S.P.* from Raleigh *State*, Nov. 6, 1895.

45. Letter Books, Vol. 1—Pg. 53.

46. *Ibid.* Pgs. 54 and 64.

47. *Ibid.* Pg. 133.

48. *Ibid.* Pg. 59.

49. *Ibid.* Pg. 135.

50. Coulter, *Confederate States of America*, Pgs. 270-271.

51. Kemp P. Battle, *Memories*, Pg. 91.

## CHAPTER FOURTEEN: SHARPSBURG WOUNDED

1. Report of North Carolina Sharpsburg Battlefield Commission, Clark's *N. C. Regts.*, Vol. 5—Pg. 590.

2. Warren's report to Vance, Oct. 11, 1862. Letter Books, Vol. II—Pg. 29. A full biographical sketch of Dr. Warren is in *Confederate Veteran*, Vol. 34 (1926)—Pgs. 172-173. A sketch is contained also in *Vance Papers,* Vol. I— Pg. 159n.

3. *Ibid.*

4. *Ibid.*

5. Raleigh *Standard*, Oct. 22, 1862.

6. Dated Richmond, Oct. 9, 1862. Raleigh *Standard*, Oct. 15, 1862.

7. *Ibid.* Oct. 8, 1862.

8. *Ibid.*

9. *Ibid.* Oct. 29, 1862. The story lingered to be told during World War I.

10. Reprinted by Raleigh *Standard*, Oct. 22, 1862.

11. *Ibid.*

12. *Vance Papers*, Vol. I—Pgs. 238-239.

13. Clark's *N. C. Regts.*, Vol. 5—Pg. 588.

14. *Battles and Leaders*, Vol. II—Pg. 603.

15. Raleigh *Standard*, Oct. 15, 1862.

16. Reprinted in Raleigh *Standard*, Oct. 15, 1862.

17. *Vance Papers*, Vol. I—Pg. 172.

18. Vance to Griffin, Sept. 18, 1862. Letter Books, Vol. I.

19. *Vance Papers*, Vol. I—Pgs. 368-371.

20. Raleigh *Standard*, Oct. 8, 1862.

## CHAPTER FIFTEEN: DOUGHTY RUNNERS OF THE BLOCKADE

1. Lefler and Newsome, *History of a Southern State*, Pg. 445.

2. Tucker, *Front Rank*, Pg. 18. A new history of the 6th North Carolina,

one of the state's most embattled regiments, which Colonel Charles F. Fisher commanded, is being published this year (1965) by the North Carolina Confederate Centennial Commission, Richard W. Iobst, author.

3. *Confederate Veteran*, Vol. 38 (1930)—Pg. 227.

4. Vance frankly credited Martin with the suggestion, though the inspector general was a part of his administration at the time and he might, in keeping with a latter-day political practice, have assumed title to the whole project. Nothing had come of the recommendation until he became governor and adopted it. Vance in *S.H.S.P.*, Vol. 14 (1886)—Pg. 521n. *Vance Papers*, Vol. I—Pg. 219n. Hamilton's *Reconstruction in North Carolina*, Pg. 73.

5. *Vance Papers*, Vol. I—Pg. 288n.

6. Warton J. Green article in Dowd's *Life of Vance*, Pg. 179.

7. Vance to Randolph, Nov. 1, 1862. Letter Books, Vol. I.

8. Oliver's activities are set out in his letter to James Sprunt, *Confederate Veteran*, Vol. III (1895), Nos. 9 and 12. The information here is from Vol. III, No. 12 (December)—Pg. 361.

9. Oliver recorded the items purchased by John White from the proceeds from sales of this cotton and the North Carolina bonds, in addition to the *Lord Clyde*. These do not represent the total of Vance's imports but were Oliver's report of White's purchases and the totals were large. Richard H. Battle, *Unveiling Address*, Pg. 28, gives his total of what the *Ad-Vance* carried. No over-all figures of what Vance imported, except the rough estimates he gathered after the war, seem to exist.

10. Maglenn's account, *S.H.S.P.*, Vol. 5 (1877)—Pgs. 335-340.

11. *Ibid.* Pg. 342.

12. Clark's *N. C. Regiments*, Vol. 5—Pg. 359.

13. In Raleigh, women were waiting to convert the cargo of cloth into uniforms, which at that time were urgently needed. Hamilton Cochran, *Blockade Runners of the Confederacy*, Pg. 173. Indianapolis. 1958.

14. Vance gave a full account of the incident in his letter of protest to Davis, July 6, 1863. Letter Books, Vol. I—Pgs. 317-318.

15. *Ibid.*

16. J. B. Jones, *A Rebel War Clerk's Diary*, Vol. I—Pg. 377.

17. Letter Books, Vol. II—Pgs. 317-320.

18. Thorburn's letter of resignation to Secretary of War Seddon gave no reason, but said: "Tho about to leave the Army of the Confederate States, I trust that it will be in my power to aid the government in their financial matters more than I have been able to serve them with my sword." He remained in Wilmington and became an agent for the Mercantile Trading Company of London. National Archives. Letter from Louis H. Manarin, editor for North Carolina Confederate Centennial Commission, to author.

19. Sprunt wrote an article "Running of the Blockade" for the Charlotte

*Observer* which was reprinted by the Richmond *Dispatch*, Aug. 2, 1896, and by the *S.H.S.P.*, Vol. 24 (1896)—Pgs. 175ff.

20. *Dictionary of American Naval Fighting Ships*, Vol. II, Pg. 492. Navy Department, 1963.

21. Kemp P. Battle's *Memories*, Pgs. 111-112.

22. Clark's *N. C. Regts.*, Vol. II—Pg. 631. *S.H.S.P.*, Vol. 24 (1896)— Pgs. 159-160.

23. Sprunt in *S.H.S.P.*, Vol. 24 (1896)—Pgs. 159-160.

24. *Ibid.*

25. Letter Books, Vol. II, Oct. 18, 1863.

26. Vance's address before Andrew Post, Grand Army of the Republic, Boston, Dec. 8, 1886, in Dowd's *Life of Vance*, Pgs. 430-462. His references to blockade-running were mainly Pgs. 454-455.

27. *S.H.S.P.*, Vol. 21 (1893)—Pg. 257.

28. President Davis made a report showing that between November 1 and December 6, 1864, forty-three ships had entered Wilmington or Charleston, the only two ports then available on the Atlantic. The capture of outward-bound vessels was small, for out of 11,796 bales of cotton shipped over a somewhat longer period, only 1,272 bales had been lost. The Confederate Treasury Department listed some of the imports during a period of about six weeks, as 8,632,000 pounds of meat; 1,507,000 pounds of lead; 1,933,000 pounds of saltpeter; 546,000 pairs of shoes; 316,000 pairs of blankets; 520,000 pounds of coffee; 69,000 rifles; 97 packages of revolvers; 2,639 packages of medicines, 43 cannon, and much else. While the Confederacy could have used much more of virtually all these items, manifestly blockade-running was a distinct aid to Lee's and other Southern armies. Clark's *N. C. Regts.*, Vol. V—Pg. 354.

29. John G. Barrett, *The Civil War in North Carolina*, Pg. 251. Chapel Hill. 1963.

30. Clark article in Dowd's *Life of Vance*, Pgs. 172-173.

31. Green article in Dowd's *Life of Vance*, Pgs. 179-180.

32. Asheville *Citizen*, May 27, 1918. Clipping in *Vance Papers*, Pack Library, Asheville.

33. Letter Book, Vol. I—Pgs. 325 and 353.

34. Vance to Hale, Feb. 11, 1864, *Hale Papers*, North Carolina Archives, Raleigh. Vance listed what supplies he had on hand at that date. "But I will stop blowing," he told Hale. Neither these nor the totals given by Oliver, Note 9 of this chapter, represent the total of Vance's military imports. Nor is it clear how much of the uniform material he had on hand at the end of the war was made-up, ready-for-wear clothing. Clark, *N. C. Regts.*, Vol. V— Pg. 471, gave the total imports on the *Ad-Vance* alone as 250,000 uniforms, 12,000 overcoats, 250,000 pairs of shoes and 50,000 blankets, plus such

other material as foodstuffs and medicines. Richard H. Battle uses the same figures for the *Ad-Vance*. The aggregate of the imports including those of Vance's other ships would be much larger. The totals used by Vance in his talks were rough estimates apparently for the single vessel.

35. Some of the privately owned blockade-runners netted profits huge enough to pay the cost of the ship in a single round-trip voyage, and some of the owners became millionaires. They had the risk of the cargo and many of the vessels were left stranded at Nassau at the end of the war. Sprunt counted thirty-five British blockade-runners in Nassau on March 11, 1865, after the fall of Fort Fisher, and placed their value at $15,000,000, "their occupation gone; their profits at an end." *S.H.S.P.*, Vol. 24 (1896)—Pg. 159. The ship captains received fabulous payment and the pilots often did. The pay in Charleston went as high as $5,000 in gold to a captain for a single trip. *S.H.S.P.*, Vol. 35 (1907)—Pg. 201.

36. *O. R.* Series I, Vol. 51—Pt. 2—Pgs. 828-829 and 837ff. Yates; *The Confederacy and Zeb Vance*, Pg. 76.

37. Letter Books, Vol. I—Pg. 51.

38. Letter Books, Vol. II—Pg. 385.

39. Maglenn in Clark's *N. C. Regts.*, Vol V—Pgs. 335-340. There was no basis for the news story in Richmond that the *Ad-Vance* had on board a supply of gold when captured. Letter Books, Vol. III—Pg. 1.

40. Called "Egypt coal" because it came from the Egypt mine on Deep River in Chatham County, North Carolina.

41. Vance and Stephen R. Mallory, Secretary of the Confederate Navy, engaged in a spirited controversy after the loss of the *Ad-Vance*, mainly about the seizure of coal, which Vance insisted had been taken by the *Tallahassee*, thus forcing the *Ad-Vance* to use North Carolina bituminous, which left the telltale smoke and resulted in her capture. Vance condemned the practice of using Wilmington, the open port for trade with Europe, for armed naval vessels, which would only cause the enemy to intensify efforts there. He contended: "It is no exaggeration to say that the *Ad-Vance* alone in solid benefits has been worth more than all the cruisers we have ever had afloat. Why it should be the policy of our Government to compel the State to quit the importation of Supplies for its common benefit, and thus pursue a course with our armed vessels so well calculated to crush all importations whatsoever is to me inexplicably strange!"

Pinkney forwarded a statement from J. A. Willard, Naval Coal Agent, declaring in effect that not a single lump of coal was taken from the *Ad-Vance* at the Wilmington station, nor any impressed to which that steamer had claim. This was the point at issue. The agent of the *Ad-Vance* contended the coal taken was what should have been available to the ship. The Naval Coal Agent, to the contrary, declared Vance's statement "had little foundation in fact." Vance replied with a blast declaring he had made his statement deliberately and on authority he regarded reliable. The agents for the runners had accumulated the coal and to the stock the *Ad-Vance* had contributed her part. When she came to sail, this heap, destined as well for her and others of the group, had been taken by the Navy Department. He sent a certificate showing how much coal was actually taken and declared Flag Officer Pinkney's argument that the *Ad-Vance* might not have got this coal— that others under the same agent might have got it first—was "a subterfuge more becoming a lawyer than a gallant, high-minded sailor as is his reputation." Vance with his supporting evidence established his case well, but the argument brought him into dispute with still another Confederate cabinet member, who supported the view that the Navy acted properly. Letter Books, Vol. II—Pgs. 637ff, and Vol. III—Pgs. 1ff.

Vance's role in blockade-running was remembered in World War II when the first of the "Liberty Ships" built at the Wilmington, N. C., shipyard was christened the *Zebulon B. Vance*. She was in the convoy of ships that carried the North African invading force.

## CHAPTER SIXTEEN:
## RECRUITMENT AND PROMOTION CONTROVERSIES

1. Vance address to Maryland Line, Feb. 23, 1885. Dowd's *Life of Vance*, Pgs. 463-493. Vance sums up the different classes of North Carolina troops, Pg. 491, his total of 124,000 being 3,000 in excess of the figure he used in addressing the Southern Historical Society at White Sulphur Springs, referred to in Chapter One.

2. O. R. Series 4—Vol. 3—Pg. 1101. Lefler and Newsome, *The History of a Southern State*, Pg. 430, use the figure 19,000 for North Carolina conscripts. Yates, *The Confederacy and Zeb Vance*, Pg. 35n, says practically one fourth of all conscripts enrolled were from North Carolina, and, Pg. 35, that the state expended $240,000 effectively in executing the Confederate laws. This is clearly an unprejudiced view.

3. Schwab, *History of Confederate States*, Pg. 193. Coulter, *The Confederate States of America*, Pgs. 314ff.

4. Alfred B. Moore, *Conscription and Conflict in the Confederacy*, Pg. 289.

5. Letter Books, Vol. I—Pg. 5.

6. Vance to Randolph, Sept. 11, 1862. Letter Books, Vol. I—Pg. 3.

7. *Confederate Veteran*, Vol. II (May 1894)—Pg. 143. French told the story in a talk to Confederate veterans, June 2, 1892, at Orlando, Fla.

8. *Ibid.*

9. Vance to Randolph, Oct. 10, 1862. Letter Books, Vol. I—Pg. 23.

10. Capt. McRae to Vance, Oct. 10, 1862. Letter Books, Vol. I—Pg. 30.

11. Vance to Mallett, Oct. 10, 1862. Letter Books, Vol. I—Pg. 18.

12. Vance to Davis, Oct. 25, 1862. *Vance Papers*, Vol. I—Pgs. 275-278.

13. Davis to Vance, Nov. 1. *Ibid*. Pgs. 295-296.

14. Because the copy of Avery's letter is missing, the officer Seddon commissioned is unidentified.

15. Cooper to Vance, June 29, 1864. Letter Books, Vol. II—Pgs. 532-533. Cooper contended that when the regiments were transferred to Confederate service they became subject to the general laws of the Confederacy regarding appointments. He said when the question was raised before it was not deemed expedient to stop the practice of appointments by the governor, but he did not concede to Vance the right and it now became necessary for the Confederacy to exercise the power. Vance's desire to make the appointments has by some been regarded as of political motivation, but it was more clearly an honorable and justifiable insistence that the state's capable officers not be pushed aside so that those of other states might be accommodated. In replying to Cooper, July 20, 1864, he held to his right, which had been acquiesced in by the War Department. *Ibid*. Vol. II—Pg. 537. The opinion of Attorney General Bragg followed.

16. Yates, *The Confederacy and Zeb Vance*, at times discerns a limited, state interest by Vance in his dealings with the Confederacy, but says, Pgs. 40-41, that the twenty-five North Carolina brigadier generals were a number disproportionately small, out of a total of 480, considering the size of the North Carolina contingent in the Confederate armies. This would seem an unbiased judgment. Several North Carolinians became generals after moving to other states. The writer of this book counts forty-five generals of all ranks born in North Carolina, including cases like Braxton Bragg, who had removed to Louisiana, and Lewis A. Armistead, to Virginia. The number does not include officers appointed from North Carolina, like D. H. Hill, but born in other states. Vance could have had no genuine opposition to native North Carolinians commanding North Carolina troops, though this would not affect the principle that each state should be given its fair consideration, where merit permitted, in the appointments.

17. J. E. Jones, *A Rebel War Clerk's Diary*, Vol. I—Pg. 63.

18. Vance to Seddon, Jan. 26, 1863. Letter Books, Vol. II—Pgs. 97-98.

19. For the story of the tax-in-kind see Coulter, *The Confederate States of America*, Pgs. 179-180.

20. Letter signed "Cato," from Pineville, N. C., in Raleigh *Standard*, July 29, 1863. On the furor over the appointment, Tucker, *High Tide at Gettysburg*, Pgs. 339-340.

21. Vance to Davis, July 6, 1863. Davis to Vance, July 18, 1863. Letter Books, Vol. II—Pgs. 335-336.

22. Issue of Aug. 12, 1863. The appointment had led to a series of indignant mass meetings over the state and newspaper denunciations.

23. Tucker, *Hancock the Superb*, Pg. 87. *S.H.S.P.*, Vol. 21 (1893)—Pg. 122.

24. *Vance Papers*, Vol. I—Pg. 441.

25. *Ibid.* Pgs. 356-357.

26. McRae to Vance, Nov. 4, 1863. Letter Books, Vol. I—Pgs. 62-63.

27. *Vance Papers*, Vol. I—Pg. 357n.

28. *Ibid.* Pg. 335.

29. *Ibid.* Pgs. 163-167.

30. *Ibid.* Pgs. 440-441. For the Garrett case see also *O. R.* Series I—Vol. 51—Pt. 2—Pgs. 830-833.

31. "Diary of Thomas Miles Garrett," edited by John Bowen Hamilton, *North Carolina Historical Review*, Vol. 38, No. 1 (1961)—Pg. 73.

32. *Vance Papers*, Vol. I—Pgs. 349-351.

33. *O. R.* Series I—Vol. 51—Pt. 2—Pgs. 830-833.

34. Clark's *N. C. Regts.* Vol. II—Pg. 168.

35. *O. R.* Series I—Vol. 51—Pt. 2—Pg. 844.

36. Clark's *N. C. Regts.*, Vol. V—Pg. xii.

37. Letter Books, Vol. I—Pg. 24. Warner's *Generals in Gray*, Pg. 14.

38. *Vance Papers*, Vol. I—Pgs. 247-248n. Warner's *Generals in Gray*. Pg. 17.

39. Dick quit the Democratic party over secession and in 1864 favored the peace movement. *Vance Papers*, Vol. I Pg. 419n.

40. Issue of June 3, 1863.

41. *O. R.* Series IV—Vol. 2—Pg. 189.

42. *O. R.* Series I—Vol. 51—Pt. 2—Pgs. 832-833.

43. *O. R.* Series I—Vol. 51—Pt. 2—Pgs. 844-845.

44. J. B. Jones, *A Rebel War Clerk's Diary*, Vol. I—Pg. 380.

45. Kemp P. Battle, *Memories*, Pg. 186. These pictures of Seddon may have been tinged by Jones's dislike of him as a boss and by the momentary circumstances of Battle's observation. Rembert W. Patrick, *Jefferson Davis and His Cabinet*, shows him as able to perform hard work over long hours. He survived the war fifteen years and died at the age of sixty-five. E. Merton Coulter considered that the ablest secretary of war of the Confederacy was "the gaunt and corpse like James A. Seddon." *Confederate States*, Pg. 381. However able Seddon may have been, the contrast with one of Vance's ruggedness was apparent.

46. Albert Burton Moore, *Conscription and Conflict in the Confederacy*, Pg. 95. New York. 1924. *O. R.* Series IV—Vol. 3—Pg. 868, cited on exaggeration of figures.

47. Dowd's *Life of Vance*, Pg. 79. J. B. Jones, *War Clerk's Diary* Vol. I—Pg. 292.

48. Moore, *Conscription and Conflict*, Pgs. 95-96, on the amended figures,

says North Carolina probably certified as many as Georgia, because Vance certified all persons engaged in making supplies for state troops.

49. Letcher to Vance, Jan. 27, 1862. Letter Books, Vol. I—Pg. 102.


## CHAPTER SEVENTEEN: NEEDED: A WAR CORRESPONDENT

1. Much postwar writing was focused on this North Carolina-Virginia controversy, to the extent that T. B. Kingsbury in *Our Living and Our Dead* (New Bern, N. C.), the weekly official publication of the North Carolina branch of the Southern Historical Society, Vol. III—Pg. 749, said: "Our nearest neighbors have uniformly either slighted or abused us. We have never known but one Virginia writer to do us justice. We refer to the poet-editor of the Norfolk *Landmark*, James Barron Hope." Hope had been well treated in North Carolina when he moved to Fayetteville after Norfolk had been occupied by Federal forces in 1862. He became one of the governor's good friends, for whom Vance after the war wrote a series of articles about North Carolina.

Judge Walter Clark, Samuel A. Ashe, and others undertook to establish North Carolina's war record, to the extent that Colyer Meriwether, editor of the publications of the Southern Historical Association, wrote in Vol. IX (Sept. 1905)—Pg. 341: "North Carolina and Virginia have had a number of friendly quarrels over the deeds of their respective soldiery in the Civil War. North Carolina has put on the binding of her recently published *History of North Carolina Regiments* (Walter Clark) the proud claim of 'First at Bethel, farthest to the front at Gettysburg and Chickamauga, last at Appomattox.' These claims have been questioned by Virginians." He went on to say that the History Committee of the Grand Camp, Confederate Veterans, Department of Virginia, had published a pamphlet in which North Carolina's claims were combated. The North Carolinians through Judge Walter Clark and others of the North Carolina Literary and Historical Society returned to the attack with *Five Points in the Record of North Carolina in the Great War of 1861-5.* In this North Carolina's original contentions were reiterated and supported with battle maps and plans.

Editor Meriwether said the discussion was conducted "on both sides with admirable spirit." Colonel Risden T. Bennett of the 14th North Carolina delivered an address at Newton, N. C., Aug. 20, 1904, sharply dissenting with the North Carolina claims of "First at Bethel, etc.," saying it was not in historical proportion. He thought the South had a homogeneous population which performed consistently. His was apparently a lone cry. Press exchanges characterized the discussion. The *Confederate Veteran* published, Vol. 12 (1904)—Pgs. 161-169, a lengthy official report of the History Committee of the Virginia Grand Camp, conceding that North Carolina obtained great fame in the war but stanchly supporting the Virginia contributions to the war effort. The North Carolina claim of "First at Bethel, etc." was severely challenged.

Still, North Carolina had made a good case. The issue never could be settled and it was perhaps natural and wholesome that the veterans of both states retained a pride in their state's achievements. But the discussion was not always so cordial as Editor Meriwether implied. That was evident when Comrade James M. Ray of the Zebulon Vance Camp, United Confederate Veterans, reported on the reunion held in Richmond in June, 1896. He asserted that preference was given to Virginia in everything: "In the parade Virginia seemed to have to have the post of honor; at the grand concert this same thing, the front and most desirable seats in many instances being filled by Richmond families, children and nurses predominating, and old veterans crowded back to the undesirable standing room. It was here that I lost my temper. . . ." He complained about exorbitant prices, $5 being charged for the rental of a horse that would not have sold for more than $10 or $15. Four old, heavy-footed draft horses were provided for the North Carolina general's staff. *Confederate Veteran,* Vol. V, No. 2 (Feb. 1897)—Pg. 85. Perhaps Colonel Ray's trouble was that he had not attended many conventions, but his letter evidenced that the feeling between veterans of the two states during the argumentative years was not invariably sympathetic.

2. The North Carolina contention is discussed in Tucker, "Some Aspects of North Carolina's Participation in the Gettysburg Campaign," *North Carolina Historical Review,* Vol. 35 (April 1958)—Pgs. 191ff.

3. Letter Books, Vol. II—Pg. 317.

4. *Ibid.*

5. Lee to Seddon, July 18, 1863. Letter Books, Vol. II—Pg. 340.

6. J. B. Jones, *A Rebel War Clerk's Diary,* Vol. I—Pg. 391.

7. Vance to Seddon, July 26, 1863. Letter Books, Vol. II—Pgs. 338-339.

8. *Ibid.*

9. Richmond *Enquirer,* July 23, 1863.

10. E. A. Pollard, *Southern History of the War,* Vol. II—Pg. 40. New York. 1866.

11. William Parker Snow, *Southern Generals, Their Lives and Campaigns,* Pg. 105. New York. 1866.

12. Clark's *N. C. Regts.* Vol. I—Pg. 506. Richmond newspaper accounts influenced early Southern history so strongly because they were about the only written source readily available. When the Southern records were gathered and sent to Washington after Lee's and Johnston's surrenders, access to them was denied even to the officers who had prepared them in the first instance. This blackout continued during the years when much of the early Southern histories, such as Pollard's and Snow's, were written. William Allan,

E. P. Alexander, Charles Marshall, Vance and even Lee (indirectly) made application to examine the official Southern Army records but were denied the opportunity. The reason advanced was that the papers might be used "to prosecute false claims against the government." (Statement of Adjutant General E. D. Townsend in the Washington *Post,* March 14, 1878.) Not until Rutherford B. Hayes became President in 1877 and George W. McCrary, Secretary of War, and after a Northern newspaper writer, Henry W. Holland of Boston, inveighed against the unfairness of the situation were the Southern war records opened to the scrutiny of all. On Sept. 26, 1878, the Reverend J. William Jones, secretary of the Southern Historical Society and editor of its *Papers,* was able to announce that the Southern records were available to Southern writers. *S.H.S.P.,* Vol. VI (1878)—Pg. 236.

13. Walter Clark, *North Carolina Troops in the Great War,* Pg. 20. (Pamphlet) Raleigh. 1901. Judge Clark summarized: "Maj. W. M. Robbins, who was for years one of the United States Battlefield Commissioners at Gettysburg, wrote an article, 'Longstreet's Assault at Gettysburg,' which is printed in Vol. 5, Clark's Regimental Histories, Pgs. 101-112, in which he states that it was 'Longstreet's Assault' and that Pickett commanded only the 3 brigades of his own division, and, further, that the correspondents of the press at Richmond were responsible for the slander upon the North Carolinians, Tennesseans, Alabamians, Mississippians, and Brockenbrough's Virginians, which composed the left wing. Indeed, Brockenbrough's Virginians were on the extreme left, and being fired into on their flank by the 8th Ohio Regiment, was the first brigade on the left to give way." On the right, Wilcox's and Lang's brigades having gone astray, Stannard's Vermont command, especially the 13th and 16th Vermont, was enabled to fire into the right flank of Kemper's command and break the force of their charge. Clark continued:

"All soldiers know that in that charge all the troops did well, and there is glory enough to go around. All that the North Carolinians, Tennesseans, Alabamians, Mississippians, and Brockenbrough's Virginians have sought to do is not to question in any particular the conduct of the 15 regiments under Pickett's command, but to refute the slander by certain correspondents of the Richmond press at that time, that the 25 regiments and 2 battalions on the left wing did not do their duty."

Even the recent national commission which conducted the observance of the centennial of the Civil War was inaccurately informed about Lee's attack on the third day at Gettysburg. It stated that "George Pickett's 15,000 men charged across an open field" against the Union center. Pickett commanded about 4,500 men. The North Carolina and other units acted under Longstreet and were assigned to him, not to Pickett, who commanded his own division. *The Civil War,* Pg. 24. (Pamphlet of U. S. Civil War Centennial

Commission, Washington. 1963.) Had Pickett commanded the other divisions in the attack there would have been no occasion for the long controversy and such literature as Walter Clark's pamphlet, *Pickett's Charge a Misnomer*. Certainly Vance was correct in his belief that history rarely catches up with an initial injustice or error.

14. Letter Books, Vol. II—Pg. 373.
15. Raleigh *Standard*, May 20, 1863.
16. *Ibid.* May 27, 1863.
17. *Ibid.*
18. Whitaker, *Reminiscences,* Pg. 44.
19. Alfred Hoyt Bill, *The Beleaguered City*, Pg. 244.
20. Raleigh *Standard*, March 3, 1863.
21. *S.H.S.P.*, Vol. 14 (1886)—Pg. 510.
22. *Vance Papers*, Vol. I—Pg. 369n. Frontis W. Johnston, editor, gives in his biographical footnote an interesting account of McSween's adventures.

## CHAPTER EIGHTEEN: GUARDIAN OF CIVIL RIGHTS

1. Figures from *Confederate Veteran*, Vol. 20 (1912)—Pgs. 275-276.
2. Vance address to Andrew Post, Grand Army of the Republic, Boston. Dec. 8, 1886. Dowd's *Life of Vance*, Pg. 453.
3. *Vance Papers*, Vol. I—Pg. 445n.
4. Seddon to Vance, Dec. 27, 1862. Letter Books, Vol. I—Pg. 86.
5. *Ibid.* Pg. 87.
6. Yates, *The Confederacy and Zeb Vance*, Pg. 53.
7. Seddon to Vance, Dec. 27, 1862. Letter Books, Vol. I—Pgs. 86-87.
8. Referred to in Seddon's letter. Pg. 87.
9. *Ibid.*
10. Vance to Seddon, Jan. 2, 1863. Letter Books, Vol. I—Pg. 79.
11. *Ibid.* Jan. 1, 1863. Pgs. 79 and 81.
12. Dowd's *Life of Vance*, Pg. 94.
13. Letter Books, Vol. I—Pgs. 47-48.
14. *Ibid.* Pg. 61.
15. The assertion was made during his campaign for governor in 1876 against Judge Thomas Settle, Jr., Dowd's *Life of Vance*, Pg. 145.
16. Asheville *News*, March 13, 1862. Schwab, *The Confederate States of America*, Pgs. 186-187.
17. Issue of Oct. 22, 1862.
18. Schwab, *The Confederate States of America*, Pg. 190.
19. Raleigh *Standard*, June 14, 1862. But Holden was docile under the Federal military rule fastened on North Carolina after the war, and rode along with it compatibly!

20. Letter Books, Vol. II—Pgs. 106-108.

21. *Ibid.*

22. Thompson, *Recollections*, Vol. II—Pg. 316.

23. *S.H.S.P.*, Vol. 20 (1892)—Pg. 371.

24. J. B. Jones, *A Rebel War Clerk's Diary*, Vol. I—Pg. 391.

25. Letter Books, Vol. II—Pgs. 138-142.

26. Vance to Davis, March 9, 1864. Letter Books, Vol. II—Pgs. 143-146.

27. *The State*, Raleigh, Sept. 28, 1863. *Vance Papers*, Vol. I—Pg. 331n.

28. Kemp P. Battle, *Memories*, Pg. 102.

29. Raleigh *Standard*, April 29, 1863, gives a full story of the Irvin case, reprinted from the Salem *Press*.

30. Letter Books, Vol. I—Pgs. 264-265.

31. Raleigh *Standard,* June 16, 1863. Schwab, *Confederate States,* Pg. 191. Yates, *The Confederacy and Zeb Vance*, Pgs. 54-55.

32. Charles Cist, *The Cincinnati Miscellaney.* Vol. I—Pg. 206. Cincinnati. 1845.

33. Annie V. Mann, "The Supreme Court of the Confederate States— Why Was One Never Organized?" *Confederate Veteran,* Vol. 38 (1930)— Pgs. 426-428. Coulter, *Confederate States*, Pgs. 28-29.

34. *Confederate Veteran,* Vol. 38 (1930) Pgs. 427-428.

35. *Ibid.* Pg. 427.

36. *Ibid.* Coulter's *Confederate States,* Pgs. 393-395.

37. Isaac Wheeler Avery, *History of the State of Georgia from 1850 to 1881,* Pg. 34. The Georgia dead in early 1863 were estimated by Avery at 9,504, ahead of any other state, though war had not yet materially touched her borders; Alabama second with 8,987; North Carolina third, 8,261. The heavy North Carolina losses in the Chancellorsville and Gettysburg campaigns probably placed the state ahead of or alongside Georgia in war fatalities. At Gettysburg, North Carolina had the heaviest toll, with 770 soldiers killed in action. Georgia was second with battle deaths of 434; Virginia third, 399. The Gettysburg figures are from Clark's *N. C. Regts.* Vol. II—Pg. xii. *North Carolina Historical Review*, Vol. 35, No. 2 (1958)— Pgs. 197 and 200.

38. J. B. Jones, *Diary*, Vol. I—Pg. 340.

39. *Address of Ex-Governor Z. B. Vance at Wake Forest College,* June 26, 1872. Pgs. 9 and 13.

40. N. Y. *Herald*, Oct. 20, 1863. Reprinted in Raleigh *Standard,* Nov. 4, 1863.

41. Lee statement to Senator Benjamin H. Hill of Georgia, *Library of Southern Literature*, Vol. 4—Pg. 2397, reprinted in Tucker, *High Tide at Gettysburg*, Pg. 52.

42. Raleigh *Standard*, Nov. 4, 1863.

43. *Ibid*. Sept. 9, 1863.

44. *Ibid*. Aug. 12, 1863. *Vance Papers*, Vol. I—Pg. 157n.

## CHAPTER NINETEEN: MASSACRE IN THE MOUNTAINS

1. Ella Reed Mathews, "Our Town in the War Between the States," Pgs. 4-5. North Carolina Collection, Pack Library, Asheville. The detachment included some of Stuart's banjo players, and the cavalrymen strummed and sang "Lorena" and "Tenting on the Old Camp Ground." This was the first time "Tenting, etc." had been heard in Asheville.

2. The term "Buffalo" was used mainly to identify Northern sympathizers in the eastern counties, but applied broadly to any North Carolinian who gave aid and comfort to the enemy. Conrad Alexander in Wilkes *Journal-Patriot* quoted in *The State*, Raleigh, May 9, 1964, on Bandit's Roost.

3. Thesis of Mattie Russell (1956), "William Holland Thomas, White Chief of the North Carolina Cherokees," Pg. 1. Loaned to Pack Library, Asheville.

4. Copied by Raleigh *Standard*, May 3, 1863.

5. Clark's *N. C. Regts.*, Vol. III—Pgs. 659-667.

6. Wilma Dykeman, *The French Broad*, Pg. 96. New York. 1955. Letter Books, Vol. I—Pg. 120.

7. *Ibid*. Pgs. 94 and 119-120.

8. Republished by Frank Moore, *The Civil War in Song and Story*, Pgs. 206-208. New York. 1889.

9. *Ibid*. Pg. 207.

10. *Ibid*.

11. *O. R.* Series I—Vol. 18—Pg. 893.

12. *The French Broad*, Pg. 98. Arthur's *Western North Carolina*, Pg. 603.

13. Letter Books, Vol. I—Pg. 100.

14. *O. R.* Series I—Vol. 18—Pg. 897.

15. *Ibid*. Pg. 898.

16. Barrett's *Civil War in North Carolina*, Pg. 198.

17. Issue of Nov. 4, 1863.

## CHAPTER TWENTY:
## VANCE'S PLAGUES: DESERTERS AND CAVALRYMEN

1. Lefler and Newsome, *History of a Southern State*, Pg. 431, says, "The percentage of desertion, North and South, was about 20, and North Caro-

lina was not out of line in this respect." Desertions were 23,000, of whom 8,000 returned. If net desertions were 15,000, as is here given, and the newly-arrived-at enrollment of 185,000 troops from the state is accepted, the percentage of desertion of North Carolina troops would be just over 8 per cent, a very low figure. *O. R.* Series I—Vol. 25—Pt. 2—Pgs. 814-815. Yates, *Confederacy and Zeb Vance*, Pg. 42.

2. Vance to Pearson, Dec. 26, 1863. Letter Books, Vol. II—Pg. 34.

3. Letter Books, Vol. I—Pgs. 110-111.

4. The correspondence appeared in the Wilmington, N. C., *Journal*, June 22, 1863.

5. Vance to Hale, Oct. 26, 1863. *Hale Papers*, N. C. Archives. Vance added that he was now in a position to assure clothing for North Carolina troops until January, 1865, except shoes and "blue hats." This was the day before he left for western North Carolina after the Federal raid on Warm Springs.

6. *O. R. Series* I—Vol. 18—Pg. 928.

7. Letter Books, Vol. II—Pgs. 556-558.

8. *Confederate Veteran,* Vol. 32, No. 12 (Dec. 1924)—Pg. 465.

9. *Ibid.* Vol. 3, No. 3 (March 1897)—Pg. 130.

10. *Ibid.*

11. *O. R.* Series I—Vol. 51—Pt. 2—Pg. 710.

12. *North Carolina Historical Review,* Vol. 41, No. 2 (Spring 1964)— Pg. 169.

13. Letter Books, Vol. I—Pg. 82.

14. *Ibid.* Vol. I—Pg. 137.

15. *Ibid.* Vol. I—Pg. 280.

16. *Ibid.* Vol. I—Pg. 337.

17. *Ibid.* Vol. I—Pg. 351.

18. Undoubtedly the most thorough discussion of desertion in North Carolina is that of Richard Bardolph, "Inconstant Rebels: Desertion of North Carolina Troops in the Civil War," in *The North Carolina Historical Review,* Vol. XLI, No. 2 (April 1964). Pg. 163ff.

19. *O. R.* Series I—Vol. 51—Pt. 2—Pg. 709.

20. Jenkins to Vance, Jan. 28, 1863. Letter Books, Vol. I—Pg. 121; Vance to Jenkins, Feb. 2, 1863. Pgs. 122-123.

21. Jones, *Rebel War Clerk's Diary,* Vol. I—Pg. 75.

22. Letter Books, Vol. I—Pg. 95.

23. *O. R.* Series I—Vol. 18—Pg. 895.

24. Raleigh *Standard,* June 10, 1863.

25. *O. R.* Series I—Vol. 18—Pg. 1026.

26. Letter Books, Vol. II—Pg. 29.

## CHAPTER TWENTY-ONE: LONG TRAIL FROM GETTYSBURG

1. Raleigh *Standard*, May 20, 1863.
2. *Ibid.* June 3, 1863.
3. *Ibid.*
4. Letter Books, Vol. I—Pg. 329.
5. *Ibid.* Vol. I—Pg. 336.
6. *Ibid.* Vol. I—Pgs. 333-335.
7. *Ibid.* Vol. I—Pg. 352.
8. *Ibid.* Vol. I—Pg. 353.
9. Raleigh *Standard,* July 29, 1863.
10. *Ibid.* Oct. 29, 1862.
11. Vance lecture to Grand Army post in Boston, Dec. 8, 1886. Dowd's *Life of Vance,* Pgs. 458-459.
12. Douglas LeTell Rights, "Salem in the War Between the States," *North Carolina Historical Review,* Vol. 27, No. 3 (July 1950)—Pg. 286.
13. Kemp P. Battle, *History of the University of North Carolina,* Vol. I—Pg. 729.
14. Vance Boston lecture, Dowd's *Life of Vance,* Pgs. 455-456.

## CHAPTER TWENTY-TWO: THE GOVERNOR CHEERS LEE'S ARMY

1. Warren, *A Doctor in Three Continents,* Pg. 313.
2. *Ibid.*
3. *Ibid.*
4. Felix Hickerson, *Echoes of Happy Valley,* quoted, Tucker, *Front Rank,* Pgs. 60-61.
5. Warren, *Doctor in Three Continents,* Pgs. 314-315.
6. *Ibid.* Pgs. 315-316.
7. *Ibid.* Pg. 316. The remark sounds a trifle excessive for the restrained General Lee, but his enthusiasm was clearly aroused and there is nothing to suggest that Warren exaggerated. In *Confederate Veteran,* Vol. 27, No. 5—Pg. 173, Capt. S. A. Ashe says Lee spoke "with enthusiasm."
8. The nickname originally was most generally used in two words, Tar Heels. The recent tendency has been to join the words into Tarheels. The origin of the term is discussed also in Chapter Eight and in Note 9 of that chapter. Jeb Stuart as well as Vance used it on this occasion. Warren, Pg. 316. Warren says that here Vance made the term "classic" when it had previously been applied in derision.

9. Warren's *Three Continents.* Pgs. 316-318.

10. *Ibid.* Pg. 318.

11. *Ibid.* Pg. 319.

12. Hale statement in Dowd's *Life of Vance,* Pgs. 183-184.

13. James H. Lane, "Glimpses of Army Life," *S.H.S.P.,* Vol. 18 (1890)—Pgs. 406-408.

14. *Ibid.*

15. Felix Hickerson, *Echoes of Happy Valley,* quoted, Tucker, *Front Rank,* Pg. 61.

16. J. G. de Roulhac Hamilton, "George Patterson, North Carolinian by Adoption," *North Carolina Historical Review,* Vol. 30 (April 1953)—Pgs. 191-192.

17. *Ibid.*

18. Charles M. Stedman address, *Statuary Hall Proceedings* (64th Congress), Pgs. 74-75.

19. Chalmers G. Davidson, *North Carolina Historical Review,* Vol. 40, No. 2—Pg. 219.

20. Clark's *N. C. Regts.,* Vol. I—Pgs. 720-721.

21. Dowd's *Life of Vance,* Pg. 120.

22. *Confederate Veteran,* Vol. 38, No. 4—Pg. 140.

23. Raleigh *News and Observer,* Jan. 7, 1891.

24. Dowd's *Life of Vance,* Pg. 90.

## CHAPTER TWENTY-THREE: VANCE AND HOLDEN AS ADVERSARIES

1. For details of the transfer of Longstreet's two divisions see Tucker, *Chickamauga,* Pgs. 91-96, 165-166 and 211-217.

2. Benning to Adjutant General Cooper, Sept. 28, 1863. Letter Books, Vol. II—Pg. 7.

3. Horace W. Raper, "William W. Holden and the Peace Movement in North Carolina," *North Carolina Historical Review,* Vol. 31, No. 4 (Oct. 1954)—Pgs. 503-505. Schwab, *Confederate States,* Pgs. 224-255. Barrett, *Civil War in North Carolina,* Pgs. 195-196. Yates, *The Confederacy and Zeb Vance,* Pg. 92. Tucker, *Chickamauga,* Pg. 96. Raleigh *Standard,* Oct. 14, 1863, and May 13, 1864.

4. Vance to Davis, Sept. 10, 1863 (Telegram)—Letter Books, Vol. I—Pg. 361.

5. *Ibid.* Pg. 363.

6. Tucker, *Chickamauga,* Pg. 96.

7. Letter Books, Vol. II—Pgs. 8-9.

8. Vance to Davis, Sept. 11, 1863. Letter Books, Vol. I—Pg. 364.

9. Copied by Raleigh *Progress* and *Standard,* Oct. 2, 1863.

10. Raleigh *Standard,* Oct. 2, 1863. *Hale Papers.* Vol. III, Feb. 4, 1864.

11. *Ibid.* Oct. 8, 1862, and June 3, 1863.

12. Schwab, *Confederate States.* Pg. 191.

13. Horace W. Raper, "William W. Holden and the Peace Movement in North Carolina," *North Carolina Historical Review,* Vol. 31, No. 4 (Oct. 1954)—Pgs. 502-503.

14. Letter Books, Vol. II—Pg. 40.

15. Tucker, *High Tide at Gettysburg.* Pg. 26.

16. Mary Boykin Chesnut, *A Diary from Dixie,* Pg. 348.

17. *O. R.* Series I—Vol. 51—Pt. 2—Pg. 810. Letter Books, Vol. II—Pg. 70.

18. Raper in *North Carolina Historical Review,* Vol. 31, No. 4—Pg. 510. About this time Hale was getting a letter addressed to "your valuable paper the 'Holden Killer,' " which declared: "You have as completely used up the Standard as haman was when it was maid known to him that he had to be hung on a gallows he had prepaired to hang another man." *Hale Papers,* North Carolina Archives, Vol. III. Dec. 5, 1863. Another correspondent used the term of being "gulled" by Holden, an old-time word that seemed applicable.

19. Jonathan Worth, biographical sketch by Frontis W. Johnston, editor, is in *Vance Papers,* Vol. I—Pg. 184. A biographical sketch of John Pool is on Pg. 198n.

20. Vance to William A. Graham, Jan. 1, 1864. Cited by Raper in *North Carolina Historical Review,* Vol. 31, No. 4—Pg. 508.

21. Raleigh *Progress,* June 7, 1864. Schwab, *Confederate States,* Pgs. 225-226.

22. Raper in *North Carolina Historical Review,* Vol. 31, No. 4—Pgs. 510-511. Hamilton's *Reconstruction in North Carolina,* Pg. 60.

23. Dowd's *Life of Vance,* Pg. 427.

24. Lefler and Newsome, *History of a Southern State,* Pg. 448.

25. Julius Leinbach, *Regiment Band of the Twenty-Sixth North Carolina,* edited by Donald M. McCorkle. Pamphlet reprint of article from *Civil War History,* Sept. 1958—Pgs. 233-234. Winston-Salem. 1958.

26. Hall's *Johnny Reb Band from Salem,* Pg. 78.

27. *Ibid.* Excerpt from Leinbach diary.

28. *Ibid.* Pgs. 79-80.

29. Holden was confident in the summer, saying the intelligence to him was of a "most cheering character." Raper in *North Carolina Historical Review,* Vol. 31—Pg. 513.

30. Yates, *The Confederacy and Zeb Vance*, Pg. 102, cites Wilmington, N. C., *Journal*, March 17, 1864.

31. Coulter, *Confederate States*, Pg. 535.

32. Dowd's *Life of Vance*, Pg. 196.

33. Vance's Boston Address, Dec. 8, 1886. Dowd's *Life of Vance*, Pg. 457.

34. Raper in *North Carolina Historical Review*, Vol. 31—Pgs. 512-513.

35. Rossiter Johnson, *A History of the War of Secession 1861-1865*, Pg. 490.

36. *Vance Papers*, Raleigh. Clipping Book Pg. 2287 (no date or place).

37. Quoted in Yates, *Confederacy and Zeb Vance*, Pgs. 106-107.

38. Letter Books, Vol. II—Pgs. 581-582.

39. *Ibid*. Pgs. 586-587.

40. *Ibid*. Pg. 615.

41. Wade Hampton in a statement in Dowd's *Life of Vance*, Pg. 187, attributes the remark to Vance and the incident as occurring during Vance's travels, which would seem to place the date before his third term as governor. J. P. Davidson, compiler of the Asheville City Directory of 1883, credits Vance with the exchange. *Vance Papers*, Pack Library, Asheville. Asheville *Times*, Sept. 4, 1927. The North Carolina Department of Conservation and Development in its pamphlet *North Carolina Historyland*, Raleigh, 1964, attributes the remark to Governor John M. Morehead (term 1841-1845). Governor J. H. Hammond of South Carolina was alleged to have threatened an invasion of North Carolina and the remark was presumably made to relieve the tension. This story has been handed down in the Morehead family. The Vance version seems better documented and more authentic. The remark sounds like a typical "Vanceism."

## CHAPTER TWENTY-FOUR: GRINDING UP THE SEED CORN

1. Mrs. John H. Anderson, "Junior Reserves at Bentonville," *Confederate Veteran*, Vol. 35, No. 10 (1937)—Pg. 367. Schwab, *Confederate States*, Pgs. 191 and 194.

2. William Franklin Elkins, "In the Junior Reserves," *Confederate Veteran*, Vol. 30 (1932)—Pg. 171.

3. *Confederate Veteran*, Vol. 38 (1940)—Pg. 475.

4. Clark, *North Carolina in the Great War*, Pg. 35.

5. Mrs. A. A. Campbell, "Boy Soldiers of the Confederacy," *Confederate Veteran*, Vol. 30 (1922)—Pg. 135. *S.H.S.P.*, Vol. 35 (1907)—Pg. 103.

6. Kemp P. Battle, *History of the University of North Carolina*, Vol. I—Pgs. 709, 725, 731, 786; Vol. II—Pg. 819. At the commencement exercises of 1911, Broadfoot spoke: "Confederate soldiers! The years have brought

vindication of your struggle. To your sons we leave your example, to your daughters we leave your memory, and to God we trust your spirit." The Junior Reserves were commanded by Colonel J. H. Nethercutt, and the three regiments of the brigade were commanded by Colonels Charles W. Broadfoot, John H. Anderson, and John W. Hinsdale, and a separate battalion by Major D. T. Millard. The youngest general officer in the Confederate Army was Brigadier General William P. Roberts, known as the "boy brigadier," of Gates County, North Carolina, who served under Lee. He was twenty-three years old when commissioned a general. Warner's *Generals in Gray*, Pgs. 258-259.

7. Vance address, "Last Days of the War in North Carolina," to Maryland Line, Feb. 23, 1885. Dowd's *Life of Vance*, Pgs. 465-466.

8. *Ibid*. Pg. 467.

9. *Confederate Veteran*. Vol. 37 (1939)—Pg. 376.

10. Cornelia Phillips Spencer, *The Last Ninety Days of the War in North Carolina*, Pg. 35. Dowd's *Life of Vance*, Pg. 471.

11. Vance address to Maryland Line, Dowd's *Life of Vance*, Pgs. 470-474.

12. *Ibid*. Pgs. 475-479.

13. Verbal comments in television interview with Henry Steele Commager during observance of Civil War Centennial.

14. Vance address to Maryland Line, Dowd's *Life of Vance*, Pg. 464.

15. Arthur's *Western North Carolina*, Pgs. 49 and 610. Georgia Lee Tatum, *Disloyalty in the Confederacy*, Pg. 135. Chapel Hill. 1934. *O. R.* Series I—Vol. 42—Pt. III—Pg. 1253.

16. Letter Books, Vol. II—Pg. 535.

17. *Ibid*. Pg. 601.

18. *S.H.S.P.*, Vol. 27 (1899)—Pg. 14.

19. *Ibid*. Vol. 23 (1895)—Pg. 58. Reprint from Charlotte *Observer*, Oct. 20, 1895.

20. *Confederate Veteran*, Vol. 30—Pg. 169.

21. *Ibid*.

22. Vance to "personal friend," in Spencer's *Last Ninety Days*, Pg. 27. Undoubtedly to President Swain at Chapel Hill.

23. *Ibid*.

24. James R. Randall, "General W. H. C. Whiting. A Chevalier of the Lost Cause." *S.H.S.P.*, Vol. 24 (1896)—Pgs. 274-277.

25. *Confederate Veteran*, Vol. 38—Pg. 229.

26. *Battles and Leaders*, Vol. IV—Pg. 657.

27. Warren's *Three Continents*, Pg. 320. *Confederate Veteran*, Vol. 40, No. 7—Pgs. 250-251.

28. *Ibid. S.H.S.P.*, Vol. 24 (1896)—Pg. 276. *Battles and Leaders*, Vol. IV—Pgs. 642-662. *Fort Fisher*, folder of North Carolina Department of Archives and History, no page numbers.

29. *S.H.S.P.*, Vol. 21—Pg. 290.

30. Alexander McClurg, "The Last Chance of the Confederacy" in *The Blue and the Gray,* Henry Steele Commager, editor, Pg. 1116.

31. Tucker, *Front Rank*, Pg. 75.

32. Capt. B. L. Ridley, Journal, in *Confederate Veteran,* Vol. 3, No. 2 (Feb. 1894)—Pg. 36. (Continues in later issues.)

33. Kemp P. Battle, *Memories,* Pg. 189.

34. Letter Books, Vol. II—Pg. 544.

35. *Ibid.* Vol. II—Pg. 606.

36. *Ibid.* Vol. II—Pg. 607.

37. Tucker, *Hancock the Superb,* Pg. 255.

38. Letter Books, Vol. II—Pg. 560, Aug. 27, 1864.

39. *Ibid.* Pg. 563.

40. *Confederate Veteran,* Vol. 37—Pg. 173.

## CHAPTER TWENTY-FIVE: SUNSET HOURS OF A LOST CAUSE

1. When Graham left the state legislature to go to the Confederate Senate in Richmond, late in the war, Vance wrote to his friend Edward Jones Hale, Fayetteville publisher: "The legislature is a very weak body at best and after Graham is taken out of it, a catfish without a head." *Hale Papers,* Vol. III—Feb. 4, 1864.

2. Graham to Swain, April 8, 1865. Spencer's *Last Ninety Days,* Pgs. 137-141. He said he found Vance surprised at his statement.

3. *Ibid.*

4. *Ibid.*

5. *Ibid.* Pg. 146.

6. *Ibid.* Pg. 143. Swain arrived at early dawn and found Vance up and working as usual by candlelight.

7. Vance's Maryland Line Address, Feb. 23, 1885. Dowd's *Life of Vance,* Pg. 483.

8. Hamilton's *Reconstruction in North Carolina,* Pg. 97. Spencer, *Last Ninety Days,* Pgs. 143-144. Warren, *Three Continents,* Pg. 334.

9. Spencer, *Last Ninety Days,* Pgs. 143 and 148. Lloyd Lewis, *Sherman: Fighting Prophet,* Pg. 530. New York. 1932. Lewis pointed out that Graham and Swain understood Johnston approved the commission, and the fact that Hardee aided it argued that Johnston concurred.

10. Hamilton, *Reconstruction in North Carolina,* Pg. 98. Spencer, *Last Ninety Days,* Pgs. 147-148.

11. *Ibid.* Pgs. 149-150. Lewis, *Sherman: Fighting Prophet,* Pgs. 530-531. Warren, an eyewitness, gave a full account of the meetings with Kilpatrick and Sherman. *Three Continents,* Pgs. 335-341.

12. Spencer, *Last Ninety Days,* Pg. 154.

13. *Ibid.* Pg. 155.

14. *Ibid.* Pg. 156. Kemp P. Battle, *History of the University of North Carolina,* Vol. I—Pg. 528.

15. Vance address to Maryland Line, Feb. 23, 1885. Dowd's *Life of Vance,* Pg. 484. Hoke was camped at Cary Station, west of Raleigh.

16. Spencer, *Last Ninety Days,* Pgs. 158-159.

17. *Ibid.* Pgs. 157-158.

18. *Ibid.* Pgs. 160-162. The site of the hanging was a vacant square where the Governor's Mansion now stands. The remains were later removed to Oakwood Cemetery in Raleigh.

19. *Ibid.* Pg. 163.

20. Whitaker's *Reminiscences,* Pg. 20.

21. Warren's *Three Continents,* Pg. 347.

22. Saunders's story is in *S.H.S.P.,* Vol. 32 (1904)—Pgs. 164-168.

23. Vance address to Maryland Line, Feb. 23, 1885. Dowd's *Life of Vance,* Pgs. 485-486. Davis occupied at night a private residence but the cabinet remained in the boxcar and the President spent most of his time there.

24. *Ibid.*

25. Saunders in *S.H.S.P.,* Vol. 32 (1904)—Pgs. 167-168.

26. Vance address to Maryland Line, Feb. 23, 1885. Dowd's *Life of Vance,* Pg. 488.

27. Spencer, *Last Ninety Days,* Pg. 182.

28. Vance address to Maryland Line, Feb. 23, 1885. Dowd's *Life of Vance,* Pgs. 489 and 493.

29. *Ibid.* Pg. 465.

30. *Ibid.* Pg. 490.

31. Ella Lonn, *Desertion During the Civil War,* Pg. 111. New York. 1928. *O. R.* Series I—Vol. 53—Pg. 292. Settle Speech at Jonesboro, Aug. 25, 1876. Dowd's *Life of Vance,* Pg. 149.

32. *Ibid.* Pg. 490. Lefler and Newsome, *History of a Southern State,* Pg. 431.

33. *Confederate Veteran,* Vol. II (1894)—Pg. 340.

## CHAPTER TWENTY-SIX: JOVIAL PRISONER AT THE OLD CAPITOL

1. Samuel P. Bates, *History of the Pennsylvania Volunteers* (Harrisburg, 1869-1871), Vol. 3—Pg. 242. Stanton's order of May 8, 1865, and other correspondence regarding Vance's arrest is in Dowd's *Life of Vance,* Pgs. 98-99.

2. Selig Adler in *Zebulon Vance and the "Scattered Nation"* (pamphlet

reprint from *The Journal of Southern History,* Vol. VII, No. 7, Aug. 1941) tells the story of Wittkowsky's service to and relations with Vance. Wittkowsky's own account, from an address before the Historical Society of Charlotte, is in Dowd's *Life of Vance,* Pgs. 96-97.

3. Vance wrote from Charlotte Oct. 13, 1868, three years after his release, when he read Kilpatrick's statement. His letter is in Dowd's *Life of Vance,* Pg. 101.

4. Adler's *Vance and "Scattered Nation,"* Pgs. 358-359. The Asheville *Citizen-Times,* March 1, 1964, explains that the demand for ginseng has been high ever since the French botanists visited western North Carolina in 1795 and showed the inhabitants how to prepare ginseng for shipment and sale in China.

5. Kemp P. Battle, *Memories,* Pg. 196.

6. Cox article in Dowd's *Life of Vance,* Pg. 174.

7. Tucker, *Poltroons and Patriots,* Vol. II—Pgs. 593 and 742.

8. Mary Clemmer Ames, *Ten Years in Washington,* Pgs. 578-580.

9. Cox article in Dowd's *Life of Vance,* Pg. 196.

10. Mary Clemmer Ames, *Ten Years,* etc., Pg. 556.

11. Kemp P. Battle, *Memories,* Pg. 196.

12. *Vance Papers,* Pack Library, Asheville, Clipping file—Asheville *Citizen,* Oct. 15, 1933. Vance's close friend and adviser William A. Graham had served in the cabinet with Corwin under President Fillmore. Richard H. Battle, *Unveiling Address,* Pg. 36, tells of the Stevens visit.

13. Dowd's *Life of Vance,* Pgs. 97-98.

14. Kemp P. Battle, *Memories,* Pg. 196.

15. Junius Henri Browne, *Four Years in Secessia,* Pg. 238. Hartford. 1865.

16. *Ibid.* Pgs. 316, 317.

17. Ina W. Van Noppen, "The Significance of Stoneman's Last Raid," *North Carolina Historical Review,* Vol. 38—Pgs. 341ff describes the prison and quotes prisoners about the food and the boy guards.

18. Browne, *Four Years in Secessia,* Pg. 332. Capt. S. A. Ashe, North Carolina historian, "Salisbury Prisoners," *Confederate Veteran,* Vol. VI (1898)—Pg. 173, accepted Browne's explanation and said friends of the prisoners "raised such a howl that Stanton had to relent." Another explanation is that Stanton believed the unserviceable prisoners at the late stage of the war would be more hindrance than help to the South.

19. Ashe in *Confederate Veteran,* Vol. VI—Pg. 173.

20. Van Noppen in *North Carolina Historical Review,* Vol. 38—Pg. 348.

21. *Confederate Veteran,* Vol. VI—Pg. 173.

22. *Ibid.*

23. Warren, *Three Continents,* Pgs. 330-331.

24. Vance Address to Maryland Line, Feb. 23, 1885. Dowd's *Life of Vance*, Pgs. 491-492.

25. Houston G. Jones Ms., "The Public Archives of North Carolina, 1663-1903," contains the story of the records from which this account is largely drawn.

26. Spencer's *Last Ninety Days*, Pg. 23.

27. Letter Books, Vol. II—Pg. 256.

28. Letter Books, Vol. III—Pgs. 45-46.

29. *Ibid*. Pgs. 55-56.

30. Spencer, *Last Ninety Days*, Pgs. 21-22.

31. Letter Books, Vol. II—Pg. 343.

32. Memorial Addresses, 53rd Congress. Address of Senator Joseph Clay Stiles Blackburn of Kentucky, Pg. 59.

33. *Ibid*. Pg. 60.

34. *Vance Statue Proceedings in Statuary Hall*. 64th Congress. Stedman Address, Pg. 76.

35. Kemp P. Battle, *Memories*, Pg. 195.

36. Lefler and Newsome, *History of a Southern State*, Pgs. 453-456.

37. Jonathan Truman Dorris, "Pardoning North Carolinians," *North Carolina Historical Review*, Vol. 23, No. 3 (July 1946)—Pgs. 379-381.

38. Vance to John Evans Brown, Sidney, New South Wales. Copy in *Vance Papers*, Pack Library, Asheville.

39. Spencer, *Last Ninety Days*, Pgs. 214-215.

40. John Evans Brown Letter, Pack Library, Asheville.

41. Spencer, *Last Ninety Days*, Pgs. 215-216.

42. John Evans Brown Letter, Pack Library, Asheville.

## CHAPTER TWENTY-SEVEN: LAWYER, LECTURER, CAMPAIGNER

1. Asheville *Citizen-Times*, May 9, 1954.

2. Kemp P. Battle, *History of the University of North Carolina*, Vol. I—Pg. 753.

3. *Ibid*. Shirley, *Tarheel Spokesman*, Pg. 62.

4. Vance Address, "The Duties of Defeat." Dowd's *Life of Vance*, Pg. 401.

5. Vance's Memorial Oration on Swain, Pgs. 19-20.

6. Kemp P. Battle, *History of the University of North Carolina*, Pgs. 95-97.

7. "The City of Charlotte," *Confederate Veteran*, Vol. 37 (1929)—Pgs. 166-167.

8. David Macrae, *The Americans at Home*, Pg. 226. New York. 1952.

9. *Ibid*. Pg. 226n.

10. *Ibid.* Pg. 227.

11. *Ibid.* Pgs. 227-228.

12. Tom Dula's story is taken mainly from W. C. Burton's series of articles in the Greensboro *Daily News* in February, 1959; article by Harry Gatton in same newspaper after research into Dula's military record; Nancy Alexander, *Tom Dooley,* Lenoir, N. C., 1959; Johnson J. Hayes, *The Land of Wilkes,* Wilkesboro, N. C., 1962 (History of Wilkes County) ; Asheville *Citizen,* December 4, 1958. The "Ballad of Tom Dula" became a popular song at about that time.

13. Hayes, *Land of Wilkes,* Pg. 177, gives the ballad, which appears in a different form in Alan Lomax, *The Folk Songs of North Carolina,* Pg. 269.

14. Whitaker's *Reminiscences,* Pgs. 207-208.

15. *Ibid.* Pg. 207.

16. Asheville *Citizen-Times,* May 9, 1954.

17. Whitaker's *Reminiscences,* Pgs. 205-206.

18. Asheville *Citizen-Times,* May 9, 1954.

19. *Ibid.* When Vance had as his law partner Clement Dowd, who became his biographer, persons would come to the law office on municipal business, and sometimes would speak with a thick Southern accent. Once when Vance was talking with Colonel J. L. Morehead a man put his head in the door.

"Is the ma're in?" he inquired.

"No," said Vance, "the *mare* is not in, but here is the *old hoss.* What can I do for you?" Dowd's *Life of Vance,* Pg. 116.

The saying around Charlotte was that the court crier, when Vance was telling a story to illustrate a case, would call out, "Silence in the courtroom." Then, without even closing his mouth, he would emit a shout of laughter into which all in the room joined.

When Zeb visited his sister she complained of her health and moaned to him, "I have no constitution at all." Far from eliciting sympathy, she got this reply: "Just living by the by-laws, aren't you!" Asheville *Citizen,* June 29, 1930.

20. Tucker, *North Carolina Historical Review,* Vol. 35, No. 2 (April 1958)—Pg. 196.

21. Publisher Hope's comment on Pgs. viii-ix of pamphlet: Vance, *Sketches of North Carolina.*

22. *North Carolina Historyland,* Raleigh, 1964, pictures the group of three Presidents claimed by North Carolina. Pg. 37.

23. Vance, *Sketches of North Carolina,* Pg. 102.

24. Clipping in *Vance Papers,* Clipping Book, Raleigh. Only date given is 1886.

25. *The State,* Raleigh, Nov. 23, 1963.

26. *Ibid.*

27. Issue of Sept. 17, 1868. "Cowan of Wilmington" probably was Robert Cowan, railroad president, lawyer, and political figure.

28. The Milton *Chronicle* completed the account here, but with apparent reluctance.

29. *The State*, Raleigh, Nov. 23, 1963. Lefler and Newsome, *History of a Southern State*, Pgs. 469-470.

30. *Ibid.* Pgs. 466-469. *The State*, Raleigh, Nov. 23, 1963. *Vance Papers*, Raleigh, Clipping Book Pgs. 2301 and 2302.

31. James Schouler, *United States*, Vol. VIII—Pg. 81.

32. Kemp P. Battle, *History of the University of North Carolina*, Vol. II—Pgs. 135 and 144.

33. *Ibid.* Vol. II—Pg. 346.

34. *Ibid.*

## CHAPTER TWENTY-EIGHT: GOVERNOR AGAIN AND SENATOR

1. Hamilton, *Reconstruction in North Carolina*, says: "Judge Settle was a very magnetic man, an eloquent speaker, and a powerful debater. . . ."

2. Dowd's *Life of Vance*, Pg. 146. Kemp P. Battle, *History of the University of North Carolina*, Vol. I—Pg. 415.

3. Dowd's *Life of Vance*, Pgs. 144-145.

4. *Ibid.* Pg. 146.

5. *Vance Papers*, Raleigh. Clipping Book Pg. 2351. No date.

6. Dowd's *Life of Vance*, Pg. 161.

7. Raleigh *Sentinel* story in Dowd's *Life of Vance*, Pg. 147.

8. *Ibid.*

9. *Ibid.* Pg. 150.

10. *Ibid.*

11. A present-day view of Vance's oratory is Hal Tribble's, Asheville *Citizen-Times*, May 26, 1963:

"Vance had a way with words that may seem dated to a generation more accustomed to the clinical phrases of the modern speech-writers. He was, by turns, mellifluous, demagogic, entertaining, vindictive. He relied heavily on humor that often embodied vulgarity. But the audiences of his era laughed at his jokes, marvelled over his rhetoric, thrilled to his passionate appeals, and went to the polls in a proper mood on election day."

Hamilton (Vance's contemporary), in *Reconstruction in North Carolina*, Pg. 650, quotes an earlier viewpoint:

"His style of address was unique and never to be forgotten. I pass by the inimitable humor which lightened up his speeches. While to the heedless this was the distinguishing feature of Vance's oratory, it was indeed the merest incident of his public addresses. His arguments were ponderous, distinguished for originality of proposition and power of statement. He was a thinker, a logician, and while no thought escaped his tongue that had not already been subjected to the crucible of reason, no faulty argument could be advanced by an opponent and its weakness escape detection by him. His alertness was amazing; his readiness will ever remain a proverb in the State. He was never taken unawares; never found without an answer, and it a sufficient one. He was capable of the loftiest eloquence, and adorned with handsomest decorations whatever subject he chose to."

12. Dowd's *Life of Vance*, Pg. 150.

13. Issue of April 14, 1894.

14. *Confederate Veteran*, Vol. 30 (1922)—Pg. 165.

15. Shirley, *Tarheel Spokesman*, Pgs. 84-85. "Commorant" was a pet but unorthodox word of Vance's. He spelled it also "comorant," probably meaning cormorant.

16. Frenise A. Logan, "Legal Status of Public School Education for Negroes in North Carolina, 1877-1894." *North Carolina Historical Review*, Vol. 32 (July 1955)—Pgs. 346-347.

17. Lefler and Newsome, *History of a Southern State*, Pgs. 501-502.

18. Shirley, *Tarheel Spokesman*, Pgs. 86-87.

19. Frenise A. Logan, "The Movement of Negroes from North Carolina," *North Carolina Historical Review*, Vol. 33 (Jan. 1956)—Pg. 46. Cites Greensboro *Patriot*, March 21, 1877.

20. Samuel Thomas Peace, *Zeb's Black Baby, Vance County, North Carolina*. Henderson, N. C. 1955.

21. Lefler and Newsome, *History of a Southern State*, Pg. 518. *Biographical Directory of the American Congress* (1950 issue), Pg. 970.

22. Selig Adler, *Vance and the "Scattered Nation,"* Pg. 368. Dowd's *Life of Vance*, Pgs. 212-216, 218-219. Vance remarked laughingly: "I have tried Rum and Rebellion and have decided it was up to me to add Romanism." Doug Reed in Asheville *Citizen-Times*, July 17, 1960.

23. Vance related this story himself to Francis Stevens, his Buncombe County neighbor. Algeria Stevens McLean memorandum to author.

24. Fayetteville *Observer*, July 24, 1884. Reprint from Richmond *State*, *Vance Papers*, Raleigh. Clipping Book Pg. 2315. The story of the Chesapeake Bay trip was told by Vance to "France" Stevens, his Buncombe County neighbor. Memorandum from a member of the Stevens family to author.

25. *Vance Papers*, Raleigh. Clipping Book Pg. 2317.

26. Dowd's *Life of Vance*, Pg. 225. *North Carolina Historical Review*, Vol. 30—Pg. 184.

27. *Ibid*. Pgs. 238-239.

28. *Ibid.* Pg. 239.

29. *Vance Papers.* Raleigh. Letter Box, 1894. Someone mailed the undated clipping to Vance and it is in his papers.

30. *Vance Papers,* Raleigh. Clipping Book Pg. 2299.

31. Oliver H. Orr, Jr., *Charles Brantley Aycock.* Chapel Hill. 1961. Pg. 61 cites Fayetteville *Observer,* July 10, 1890.

32. Winston, University Day Oration, *Vance and Aycock,* Pgs. 3-7. (Pamphlet)

33. Herndon's *Life of Lincoln,* Pg. 270.

34. Macrae, *The Americans at Home,* Pg. 228.

35. Winston, *Vance and Aycock,* Pg. 8.

36. Adler, *Vance and "Scattered Nation,"* Pg. 370n.

37. Cox article in Dowd's *Life of Vance,* Pgs. 175-176. Dowd tells of the operation on Pg. 313.

38. Letter of July 1, 1889, in Wilmington, N. C., *Messenger* (no date), *Vance Papers,* Asheville.

39. This article, unidentified, is pasted inside the copy of Dowd's *Life of Vance* formerly owned by the Rev. R. F. Campbell, who delivered the Vance funeral oration in Asheville. The signature in the book is dated June, 1897.

## CHAPTER TWENTY-NINE: EASE AND HONORS AT THE CLOSE

1. Algeria Stevens McLean, memorandum to author.

Gombroon is a white, semitransparent Persian ware, the name derived from the port of Gombrun on the Persian Gulf. Vance looked on the name as meaning "Heart's Desire." Fred M. Burnett, *This Was My Valley,* Pg. 88, traces Vance's use to Thomas DeQuincey's *Autobiography,* when as a youth DeQuincey set up in fancy a little kingdom of that name.

2. Algeria Stevens McLean, memorandum.

3. Mrs. Sam Stokes's letter in Asheville *Citizen,* May 16, 1954.

4. Eugene Byrd interview with Bascomb Burnett, Asheville *Citizen-Times,* Aug. 7, 1949.

5. *Ibid.*

6. *S.H.S.P.,* Vol. 10 (1882)—Pg. 284.

7. Interview in Asheville *Citizen,* May 11, 1930.

8. Watertown, N. Y., *Times,* July 15, 1888, in *Vance Papers,* Raleigh. Clipping Book Pg. 2352.

9. Morrill Address in Dowd's *Life of Vance,* Pg. 343.

10. *Ibid.* Sherman Address, Pg. 345.

11. William R. Cox article in Dowd's *Life of Vance,* Pg. 175. Horses and dogs were named after Vance as well.

12. Address of Senator Ransom, Senate Memorial, 53rd Congress. Pgs. 37-38.

13. Charlotte *Observer,* April 29, 1894. Dowd's *Life of Vance,* Pg. 323.

14. *Ibid.* Pg. 320.

15. Letter in *Vance Papers,* Raleigh. Letter Box, 1894. Dated May 9, 1894.

16. *Ibid.* Dated May 1, 1894.

17. *Confederate Veteran,* Vol. 24 (1916)—Pg. 442.

18. *Statuary Hall Proceedings,* June 22, 1916. Pg. 47.

19. Memorial Addresses in Senate, Address by Senator Jarvis, Pgs. 84-87.

Vance was survived by his widow and four sons. Charles Noel Vance, the eldest son, born March 27, 1856, was familiarly known in the Asheville neighborhood as Charlie and was regarded as the most popular of the children, possibly because he worked as his father's secretary and had opportunity to become imbued with the senator's buoyant, democratic spirit. After leaving Washington he lived in Black Mountain, fourteen miles east of Asheville. David Mitchell Vance, the second son to survive him, born December 8, 1857, whose middle name honored Zeb's old professor, became a newspaperman, worked on the old New York *Sun* and later on the New Orleans *Times-Picayune.* He was the only son to have children.

Zebulon B. Vance, Jr., the third son, born in 1860 while his father was in Congress, became a regular army officer, but by the unusual route of attending the Naval Academy at Annapolis. He was graduated in 1883, but soon transferred to the army and became a second lieutenant in 1884. He was graduated from the infantry and cavalry schools in 1887 and served through the Spanish-American War, being a captain in the 10th and 11th regiments. When not on active service he made his home in Black Mountain.

Thomas M. Vance, the fourth son, followed his father into the law, settled in Lenoir, North Carolina, and was elected mayor of that city in April, 1885. He moved to the state of Washington, where he became attorney general. He was born September 6, 1862.

*Acknowledgments*

*and Bibliographical Note*

This book has resulted largely from the suggestions of three North Carolina newspaper acquaintances: D. Hiden Ramsey, retired Asheville publisher; Josh L. Horne, publisher of the Rocky Mount *Evening Telegram*; and the late Ernest B. Hunter, former managing editor of the Charlotte *Observer*. They and many others felt that Vance had been neglected both in nineteenth-century Civil War literature and in the vast outpouring of books attending the Civil War centennial observance of 1961-1965.

My interest in Vance was kindled some decades ago when my reading about the battle of Gettysburg was a zealous hobby. Zeb Vance was not in the battle, but his presence was felt there in the startling sacrifices of his old regiment, the 26th North Carolina. Later, when I was engaged in the research and writing of *High Tide at Gettysburg*, I resolved to study further two extraordinary men who figured directly or indirectly in that battle: the magnetic Federal Major General Winfield Scott Hancock, the mainstay of the Union Army, and Zeb Vance, who, though far removed, left his imprint on that blood-soaked field. *Hancock the Superb* was published in 1960. The wish is now fulfilled with this publication of *Zeb Vance: Champion of Personal Freedom*.

Books about Vance have been of limited scope or have had a specialized focus. His former law partner, Clement Dowd, wrote and assembled in the 1890s his *Life of Zebulon B. Vance* (Charlotte, 1897), much of which is a

537

symposium, and little of which deals with Vance's extraordinary Civil War service.

In 1958 Richard E. Yates's relatively brief but well-researched monograph, *The Confederacy and Zeb Vance*, was published in the Confederate Centennial Studies, William Stanley Hoole, editor-in-chief, Tuscaloosa, Alabama. Only 450 copies were printed, after which the type was destroyed. In 1962 Franklin Ray Shirley, professor of speech and drama at Wake Forest College, published another relatively brief study, dealing with Vance as a public speaker (*Zebulon Vance, Tarheel Spokesman*. Charlotte. 1962).

Vance's papers, consisting of many volumes and boxes of manuscripts, are possessed mainly by the North Carolina Department of Archives and History. The work of editing and publishing them, which will occupy many years, is in progress. Volume I, under the editorship of Frontis W. Johnston, who prefixed a brief biography, was published in 1963. Other Vance papers and clippings are possessed by the North Carolina Collection, Pack Memorial Library, Asheville. Still other papers and letters are in private hands.

Since there are several groups of papers, they are distinguished in the Notes of this book. Those already published by the State Department of Archives and History are called *Vance Papers*, Vol. I. Four or five later volumes are projected. Those in Asheville are called *Vance Papers*, Pack Library, Asheville. The unedited letters and papers in Raleigh are called *Vance Papers* with a letter-box designation or with the explanation, Raleigh. In addition, Vance's Letter Books, perhaps the leading source material for this book, three ponderous volumes, are designated Letter Books with the volume and page numbers cited.

So many persons in North Carolina and elsewhere have assisted me in gathering material about Zeb Vance that it is not feasible to mention all of them. I thank especially Houston G. Jones, State Archivist of North Carolina, Raleigh, and his staff for much help with the Vance correspondence and contemporary newspaper files; Myra Champion, Librarian, North Carolina Collection, Pack Memorial Library, Asheville, for similar assistance; D. Hiden Ramsey for the loan of material, for many informed opinions, and for manuscript suggestions; Bill Sharpe, editor of *The State*, Raleigh, whose magazine has been a mine of North Carolina anecdotes; Ray D. Smith, Chicago, and his secretary, Helen Reynolds, for an index of the references to Vance and other topics in the *Confederate Veteran* magazine; Col. Paul A. Rockwell of Asheville for the loan of letters and books; General and Mrs. Stanley L. Scott, Alexandria, Virginia; Dr. Christopher Crittenden, Director of the North Carolina Department of Archives and History, Raleigh, and his staff; Jerrold Orne, Librarian, University of North Carolina Libraries, Chapel Hill; Robert C. Tucker, Librarian, Furman University, Greenville, South Carolina; Margaret Ligon, Chief Librarian, Pack Memorial Library,

Asheville; Margaret McMahan, Fayetteville, North Carolina; Albert McLean, Asheville; Elizabeth Ulrich, Chief Reference Librarian, Pennsylvania State Library, Harrisburg; William H. Stauffer, Richmond, Virginia; Mary Seagle, Librarian, and Mrs. Emily Keeling, Hendersonville, North Carolina, Public Library, for obtaining books on interlibrary loan; Richard B. Wynne, Executive Editor, Asheville *Citizen;* Major General J. E. Sloan, Retired, Weaverville, North Carolina.

I am indebted to many with whom I discussed the career of Zeb Vance, who gave their evaluations of his service to the Confederacy and to the Union before and after the war. Finally, my sincere thanks are expressed to Richard W. Iobst, one of the able young students of North Carolina history, a writer and speaker for the North Carolina Confederate Centennial Commission, and a candidate at this writing for his doctor's degree at Chapel Hill; and to Elizabeth W. Wilborn, for many years Editorial Associate of the North Carolina *Historical Review*, a thorough student of North Caroliniana, for reading the manuscript of this book and making suggestions of value. They are not to be held accountable for the facts and opinions contained or for the manner of presentation.

As with my other books, I am indebted to my wife, Dorothy Thomas Tucker, for her interest in the career of Vance, her devoted assistance during the long research that went into the work, her perusal of newspaper files, and for reading the manuscript and proofs and offering many pertinent comments.

*Glenn Tucker*

*Route 1,*
*Flat Rock, North Carolina*
*February, 1965*

☆☆☆☆☆☆☆☆☆☆☆☆☆☆☆☆☆

# Bibliography

☆☆☆☆☆☆☆☆☆☆☆☆☆☆☆☆☆

ABBOTT, JOHN S.C. *The History of the Civil War in America.* 2 vols. New York. 1863 and 1866. (Contemporary writing from Northern viewpoint which gives the immediacy and partisanship of newspaper accounts.)

ADLER, SELIG. *Zebulon B. Vance and the "Scattered Nation."* Pamphlet reprinted from *The Journal of Southern History.* Vol. 7, No. 3, August 1941.

ALEXANDER, NANCY. *Tom Dooley.* Lenoir, N.C. 1959.

*American Almanac and Repository of Useful Knowledge.* 1860. Boston. 1860.

AMES, MARY CLEMMER. *Ten Years in Washington.* Hartford. 1874.

ANDERSON, MRS. JOHN H. "Junior Reserves at Bentonville." *Confederate Veteran.* Vol. 35, 1927.

"Literary Women of the Sixties in North Carolina." *Confederate Veteran.* Vol. 37, 1929.

ARTHUR, JOHN PRESTON. *Western North Carolina: A History.* Raleigh. 1914.

ASHE, SAMUEL A., Editor, *Biographical History of North Carolina.* 8 vols. Greensboro. 1907.

"Fort Fisher." *Confederate Veteran.* Vol. 40, 1932.

*History of North Carolina.* Raleigh. 1925.

"North Carolina in the War Between the States." *Confederate Veteran.* Vol. 37, 1929.

"Salisbury Prisoners." *Confederate Veteran.* Vol. 6, 1898.

Asheville *Citizen*

Asheville *Citizen-Times*

Asheville *News*

Asheville *Times*

AVERY, ISAAC WHEELER. *History of the State of Georgia from 1850 to 1881.* New York. 1881.

BARDOLPH, RICHARD. "Inconstant Rebels: Desertion of North Carolina Troops in the Civil War." *North Carolina Historical Review,* Vol. XLI, No. 2 (April 1964).

BARRETT, JOHN G. *The Civil War in North Carolina.* Chapel Hill. 1963. *North Carolina as a Civil War Battleground.* Raleigh. 1960.

BATTLE, KEMP B. *History of the University of North Carolina.* 2 vols. Raleigh. 1907.
    *Memories of an Old-Time Tar Heel.* (Edited by his son, William James Battle) Chapel Hill. 1945.

BATTLE, RICHARD H. *The Ceremonies Attending the Unveiling of the Bronze Statue of Zeb B. Vance, LL.D. in Capitol Square, Raleigh, N.C.,* etc. August 22, 1900. Raleigh, N.C. 1900.

BAXLEY, DR. HAUGHTON. "Surgeons of the Confederacy. Dr. Edward Warren of North Carolina." *Confederate Veteran.* Vol. 34, 1926.

BILL, ALFRED HOYT. *The Beleaguered City Richmond,* 1861-1865. New York. 1946.

*Biographical Directory of the American Congress.* Washington. 1950.

BLACKNELL, D. W. "Why the South Lost." *Confederate Veteran.* Vol. 25, No. 3, March 1917.

BOTKIN, B. A. *A Treasury of Southern Folklore.* New York. 1949.

BOWEN, COL. S. M. and IRWIN, LT. COL. R. B. *Sherman and His Campaigns: A Military Biography.* New York. 1865.

BOWERS, CLAUDE G. *The Tragic Era: The Revolution after Lincoln.* Cambridge. 1929.

BOYKIN, JAMES H. *North Carolina in 1861.* New York. 1961.

BRIDGES, HAL. *Lee's Maverick General Daniel Harvey Hill.* New York. 1961.

BROWNE, JUNIUS HENRI. *Four Years in Secessia.* Hartford. 1865.

BRYAN, T. CONN. *Confederate Georgia.* Athens, Ga. 1953.

BURNETT, FRED M. *This Was My Valley.* Ridgecrest, N.C. 1960.

BURTON, W. C. "Professor Burton's Class." Greensboro *Daily News* articles on Tom Dula case. February 1959.

BUTLER, BENJAMIN F. *Butler's Book.* Boston. 1892.

Calhoun. *Speeches and Life of John C. Calhoun* 1811-1843. (No author.) New York. 1843.

CALLAHAN, JAMES MORTON. *The Diplomatic History of the Southern Confederacy.* Baltimore. 1901.

CAMP, CORDELIA. *David Lowry Swain, Governor and University President.* (Pamphlet) Asheville. 1963.

CAMPBELL, MRS. A. A. "Boy Soldiers of the Confederacy." *Confederate Veteran.* Vol. 30. 1922.

Charlotte *Observer*

CHESNUT, MARY BOYKIN. *A Diary from Dixie.* New York. 1905.

"City of Charlotte, The." *Confederate Veteran.* Vol. 37, 1929.

CLARK, CHIEF JUSTICE WALTER. *North Carolina Troops in the Great War. 1861-1865.* Raleigh. 1901.

   Editor. *Histories of the Several Regiments and Battalions from North Carolina in the Great War 1861-1865.* 5 vols. Raleigh. 1901.

Clingman. "The Career of T. L. Clingman." (No author.) *Southern Historical Society Papers.* Vol. 24. 1896.

COCHRAN, HAMILTON. *Blockade Runners of the Confederacy.* Indianapolis. 1958.

*Collier's Encyclopaedia*

COMMAGER, HENRY STEELE. "How the 'Lost Cause' Was Lost." *New York Times Magazine,* Aug. 4, 1963.

   Editor. *The Blue and the Gray.* Indianapolis. 1950.

*Confederate Veteran,* Nashville

COULTER, E. MERTON. *The Confederate States of America 1861-1865.* Baton Rouge. 1950.

   *The South During Reconstruction 1865-1877.* Baton Rouge. 1947.

CRABTREE, BETH G. *"Zebulon B. Vance" A United States Liberty Ship.* Raleigh. 1956.

Daughters of the Confederacy, Pamlico Chapter. *Confederate Reveille.* Memorial Edition. Washington, D.C. 1898.

*Dictionary of American Biography*

DELANEY, NORMAN C. "Charles Henry Foster and the Unionists of Eastern North Carolina." *North Carolina Historical Review.* Vol. 37. 1960.

DONALD, DAVID, Editor. *Why the North Won the Civil War.* Baton Rouge. 1960.

DONNELLEY, RALPH W. "The Charlotte, North Carolina, Navy Yard. C.S.N." *Civil War History.* Vol. 5, No. 1. March 1959.

DORRIS, JONATHAN TRUMAN. "Pardoning North Carolinians." *North Carolina Historical Review* Vol. 23, No. 3. July 1946.

DOWD, CLEMENT. *Life of Zebulon B. Vance.* Charlotte. 1897.

DYKEMAN, WILMA. *The French Broad.* (Rivers of America series) New York. 1955.

ELKINS, WILLIAM FRANKLIN. "In the Junior Reserves." *Confederate Veteran.* Vol. 30. 1932.

EMERSON, EDWIN, JR. *A History of the Nineteenth Century Year by Year.* 3 vols. New York. 1902.

*Encyclopaedia Britannica*

Fayetteville *Observer*

FORE, MRS. J. A. "North Carolinians at Valley Forge." *Confederate Veteran.* Vol. 37. 1929.

*Fort Fisher State Historic Site.* (No author.) North Carolina Department of Archives and History. Pamphlet.

FRENCH, SAMUEL GIBBS. *Two Wars.* Nashville. 1901.

FURMAN, BESS. *White House Profile.* Indianapolis. 1951.

GALLOWAY, GEORGE B. *History of the House of Representatives.* New York. 1961.

GILFOND, DUFF. *The Rise of St. Calvin.* New York. 1932.

GOLDEN, HARRY L. "The Jewish People of North Carolina." *North Carolina Historical Review.* Vol. 32. April 1955.

Greensboro *Daily News*

Greensboro *Patriot*

HALE, EDWARD JONES. *Papers.* 3 vols. North Carolina Archives.

HALL, HARRY H. *A Johnny Reb Band from Salem: The Pride of Tarheelia.* Raleigh. 1963.

HAMILTON, JOHN BOWEN. "Diary of Thomas Miles Garrett at the University of North Carolina, 1849." *North Carolina Historical Review.* Vol. 38. 1961 (in three parts).

HAMILTON, JOSEPH G. DE ROULHAC. *Reconstruction in North Carolina.* New York. 1914.

"George Patterson, North Carolinian by Adoption," *North Carolina Historical Review.* Vol. 30. April 1953.

HARRIS, CHARLES. "State Sovereignty—Forgotten Testimony." *Southern Historical Society Papers.* Vol. 9. 1881.

HASSLER, WARREN W., JR. *General George B. McClellan: Shield of the Union.* Baton Rouge. 1957.

HAW, JOSEPH R. "The Last of C. S. Ordnance Department." *Confederate Veteran.* Vol. 34. 1926.

HAYES, JOHNSON J. *The Land of Wilkes.* Wilkesboro, N. C. 1962.

HERNDON, WILLIAM H. *Herndon's Life of Lincoln,* Paul M. Angle, editor. (Premier Civil War Classics) Greenwich, Conn. 1961.

HICKERSON, THOMAS FELIX. *Echoes of Happy Valley.* Chapel Hill. 1962.

HILL, D. H., JR. *North Carolina,* Vol. 4 in *Confederate Military History.* Atlanta. 1899.

HOLDEN, W. W. *Memoirs of W. W. Holden.* 2 vols. Durham. 1911.

HOOLE, WILLIAM STANLEY, Editor-in-Chief. Confederate Centennial Series. *The Confederacy and Zeb Vance,* by Richard E. Yates, Tuscaloosa, Ala. 1958.

HOUGHTON, WALTER R. *Conspectus of the History of Political Parties.* Indianapolis. 1880.

HOWELL, GERTRUDE JENKINS. "What Fort Fisher Meant to the Confederacy." *Confederate Veteran.* Vol. 38, 1930.

IOBST, RICHARD. *Battle of New Bern.* Raleigh. Pamphlet (no date).

JAMES, MARQUIS. *Andrew Jackson The Border Captain.* Indianapolis. 1933.

JOHNSON, ROBERT UNDERWOOD, AND RUEL, CLARENCE CLOUGH. *Battles and Leaders of the Civil War.* 4 vols. New York. 1884.

JOHNSON, ROSSITER. *A History of the War of Secession 1861-1865.* New York. 1910.

JOHNSTON, FRONTIS W., editor. *The Papers of Zebulon Baird Vance.* Vol. I. Raleigh. 1963.

JONES, HOUSTON G. *Bedford Brown: State Rights Unionist.* Carrollton, Georgia. 1955
"The Public Archives of North Carolina, 1663-1903" (Thesis).

JONES, J. B. *A Rebel War Clerk's Diary.* 2 vols. Philadelphia. 1866. Later edition, Howard Swiggett, editor. 2 vols. New York. 1935.

KEPHART, HORACE. *Our Southern Highlanders.* New York. 1922.

KINGSBURY, T. B. "North Carolina at Gettysburg," *Our Living and Our Dead,* Vol. I—p. 193. Raleigh. 1874.

KLEMENT, FRANK L. *The Copperheads in the Middle West.* Chicago. 1960.

LAMB, WILLIAM. "Fort Fisher." *Southern Historical Society Papers.* Vol. 21. 1893.

LANE, JAMES H. "History of Lane's North Carolina Brigade," *Southern Historical Society Papers.* Vols. 7 to 10.
"Glimpses of Army Life," *Southern Historical Society Papers.* Vol. 18.

LEFLER, HUGH TALMAGE, AND NEWSOME, ALBERT RAY. *The History of a Southern State North Carolina.* Chapel Hill. 1963.

LEINBACH, JULIUS. *Regiment Band of the Twenty-Sixth North Carolina.* Donald M. McCorkle, editor. Pamphlet reprint from *Civil War History.* Vol. IV, No. 3, Sept. 1958.

LEWIS, LLOYD. *Sherman: Fighting Prophet.* New York. 1932.

LOGAN, FRENISE A. "Legal Status of Public School Education for Negroes in North Carolina, 1877-1894." *North Carolina Historical Review.* Vol. 32, July 1955.
"The Movement of Negroes from North Carolina." *North Carolina Historical Review.* Vol. 33, Jan. 1956.

LONN, ELLA. *Desertion During the Civil War.* New York. 1928.

LUVAAS, JAY. "Johnston's Last Stand—Bentonville." *North Carolina Historical Review.* Vol. 33. July 1956.

MACRAE, DAVID. *The Americans at Home.* E. P. Dutton & Co., Inc. New York. 1952. (Published originally in 1871, present edition is first published in America.)

MCCLELLAN, GEORGE B. *McClellan's Own Story.* New York. 1887.

MCDOWELL MS. The Vance-Carson duel. Pack Library, Asheville.

MCMAHAN, MARGARET. "Zeb Vance. Genius with Energy." Feature article Fayetteville, N. C. *Observer*, July 30, 1961.

MANN, ANNIE V. "The Supreme Court of the Confederate States—Why Was One Never Organized?" *Confederate Veteran*. Vol. 38. 1930.

MATHEWS, MRS. ELLA REED. "Our Town in the War Between the States." Asheville. 1944. *Vance Papers*, N. C. Collection, Pack Library, Asheville, N. C.

*Memorial Addresses on the Life and Character of Zebulon Baird Vance* (Fifty-third Congress, Third Session). Washington. 1895.

MERRIMON, A. S. "The A. S. Merrimon Journal, 1853-1854." A. R. Newsome, editor. *North Carolina Historical Review*. Vol. 8, No. 3. July 1931.

MOORE, ALFRED B. *Conscription and Conflict in the Confederacy*. New York. 1924.

MOORE, FRANK. *The Civil War in Song and Story*. New York. 1889.

MOORE, JOHN W. *Roster of North Carolina Troops*. 4 vols. Raleigh. 1882.

MORRIS, JEROME F. *The Brief Belligerence of Fort Macon*. Raleigh. Pamphlet (no date).

MULLEN, JOHN M. *Facts to Know North Carolina*. Lincolnton, N. C. 1937.

Navy Department. *American Naval Fighting Ships*. Vol. II. Washington. 1963.

*New Yorker*. Magazine. Issue of February 3, 1962.

North Carolina Confederate Centennial Commission. News Letter Vols. 1-5.

*North Carolina Historyland*. Pamphlet of Department of Conservation and Development. Raleigh. 1964.

*Official Records of the Union and Confederate Armies*. Washington. 1882-1900.

"Official Report of the History Committee of the Grand Camp, C. V. Department of Virginia." *Confederate Veteran*. Vol. 12. 1904.

OLIVER, WILLIAM H. "Blockade Running from Wilmington." *Confederate Veteran*. Vol. 3, No. 12. Dec. 1895.

ORR, OLIVER H., JR. *Charles Brantley Aycock*. Chapel Hill. 1961.

OWSLEY, FRANK LAWRENCE. *State Rights in the Confederacy*. Chicago. 1925.

PATRICK, REMBERT W. *Jefferson Davis and his Cabinet*. Baton Rouge. 1944.

PEACE, SAMUEL THOMAS. *Zeb's Black Baby. Vance County, North Carolina*. Henderson, N. C. 1955.

PHIFER, EDWARD W. "Certain Aspects of Medical Practice in Ante-Bellum Burke County." *North Carolina Historical Review*. Vol. 36, No. 1. January 1959.

"Saga of a Burke County Family." *North Carolina Historical Review*. Vol. 39, Nos. 1, 2 and 3. 1962.

POLLARD, E. A. *Southern History of the War*. New York. 1866.

POOL, MARIE LOUISE. *In Buncombe County*. Chicago. 1898.

Raleigh *News and Observer*

Raleigh *Register*

Raleigh *Standard*

Raleigh *State Chronicle*

RAMSDELL, CHARLES W. "The Control of Manufacturing by the Confederate Government." *Mississippi Valley Historical Review*. Vol. 8, No. 3. December 1921.

RANDALL, J. G. *Lincoln and the South*. Baton Rouge. 1946.

RANDALL, JAMES R. "General W. H. C. Whiting. A Chevalier of the Lost Cause." *Southern Historical Society Papers*. Vol. 24. 1896.

RAPER, HORACE W., "William W. Holden and the Peace Movement in North Carolina." *North Carolina Historical Review*. Vol. 31. October 1954.

RIDLEY, CAPT. B. L. "Notes from His Journal, or, The Last Battles of the War. Murfreesboro." *Confederate Veteran*. Vol. 3. 1895.

RIGHTS, DOUGLAS LETELL. "Salem in the War Between the States." *North Carolina Historical Review*. Vol. 27, No. 3. July 1950.

ROBERTS, A. SELLOW. "The Peace Movement in North Carolina." *Mississippi Valley Historical Review*. Vol. 11, No. 2. June 1924.

ROGERS, LOU. *Tar Heel Women*. Raleigh. 1949.

ROSEBOOM, EUGENE H. *A History of Presidential Elections*. New York. 1957.

RUSSELL, MATTIE. "William Holland Thomas, White Chief of the North Carolina Cherokees." (Thesis in Graduate School of Arts and Sciences, Duke University.) 1956.

SAUNDERS, W. J. "Governor Z. B. Vance. Story of the Last Days of the Confederacy in North Carolina." *Southern Historical Society Papers*. Vol. 32. 1904.

SCHOULER, JAMES. *History of the United States*. (World's Best Histories series) 9 vols. New York. 1898-1904.

SCHWAB, JOHN CHRISTOPHER. *The Confederate States of America*. New York. 1901.

SHIRLEY, FRANKLIN RAY. *Zebulon Vance, Tarheel Spokesman*. Charlotte. 1962.

SMITH, BURTON H. "Carolina's Contributions to the Confederate Navy." *Confederate Veteran*. Vol. 38. 1930.

SNOW, WILLIAM PARKER. *Southern Generals, Their Lives and Campaigns*. New York. 1866.

SONDLEY, F. A. *A History of Buncombe County, North Carolina*. Asheville. 1930.

SORRELL, G. MOXLEY. *Recollections of a Confederate Staff Officer*. New York. 1905.

*Southern Historical Society Papers*. Richmond.

SPENCER, CORNELIA PHILLIPS. *The Last Ninety Days of the War in North Carolina.* New York. 1866.

SPRUNT, JAMES. "Running of the Blockade." *Southern Historical Society Papers.* Vol. 24. 1896.

*The State* (Magazine). Raleigh.

STIMPSON, GEORGE. *A Book About American Politics.* New York. 1952.

*A Book About a Thousand Things.* New York. 1946.

*Popular Questions Answered.* New York. 1930.

STRODE, HUDSON. *Jefferson Davis Tragic Hero The Last Twenty-five Years 1864-1889.* New York. 1964.

TATUM, GEORGIA LEE. *Disloyalty in the Confederacy.* Chapel Hill. 1934.

TAYLOR, SUSIE S., editor. *The Battle of New Bern and the Retreat to Kinston.* (Western Carolina Faculty Studies Bulletin) Cullowhee, N. C. 1957.

THOMPSON, RICHARD W. *Recollections of Sixteen Presidents from Washington to Lincoln.* 2 vols. Indianapolis. 1894.

TUCKER, GLENN. *Chickamauga.* Indianapolis. 1961.

*Front Rank.* Raleigh, 1962.

*Hancock the Superb.* Indianapolis. 1960.

*High Tide at Gettysburg.* Indianapolis. 1958.

*Poltroons and Patriots.* 2 vols. Indianapolis. 1954.

"Some Aspects of North Carolina's Participation in the Gettysburg Campaign." *North Carolina Historical Review.* Vol. 35, No. 2. April 1958.

*Unveiling of Statue of Zebulon Baird Vance* (erected in Statuary Hall of the United States Capitol by the State of North Carolina). Washington. 1917.

VANCE, DAVID. *Narrative of the Battle of King's Mountain.* Greensboro. 1891.

VANCE, ZEBULON B. *Sketches of North Carolina.* Norfolk. 1875.

Letter Books. 1862-1865.

*Papers.* North Carolina Room, Pack Memorial Library, Asheville.

*Papers.* Department of Archives and History. (Systematized by years, but consisting of a mass of correspondence yet to be edited, dealing mainly with his postwar career. Several future volumes of Vance papers are projected.)

*Papers.* Vol. I. Frontis W. Johnston, editor. Raleigh. 1963.

*Life and Character of Hon. David L. Swain.* Durham. 1878.

*The Duties of Defeat.* New York. 1866.

Clipping Book, *Vance Papers.* North Carolina Archives. Raleigh.

Address Before Southern Historical Society, at White Sulphur Springs, West Virginia, August 18, 1875. *Southern Historical Society Papers.* Vol. 14. 1886.

Conditions After the War. (Letter to John Evans Brown of Sidney, New South Wales.) *Confederate Veteran.* Vol. 39. 1931.

*Vance Papers,* Pack Library, Asheville.

"Autumn in the Swannanoa Valley." Excerpt from *Johnson's First Reader,* by Blanche Wynne Johnson. N. C. Collection, Pack Library, Asheville.

Address at Wake Forest College. June 26, 1872.

VAN NOPPEN, INA W. "The Significance of Stoneman's Last Raid." (4 parts) *North Carolina Historical Review.* Vol. 38. 1961.

WARNER, EZRA J. *Generals in Gray.* Baton Rouge. 1949.

*Generals in Blue.* Baton Rouge. 1964.

WARREN, EDWARD. *A Doctor's Experiences in Three Continents.* Baltimore. 1885.

WEBB, CHARLES A. *Mount Mitchell and Dr. Elisha Mitchell.* Asheville. 1946. Pamphlet.

WHITAKER, R. H. *Whitaker's Reminiscences. Incidents and Anecdotes.* Raleigh. 1905.

WILTSE, JOHN C. *John C. Calhoun.* Indianapolis. 1944.

*John C. Calhoun* (3 vols.) *Nationalist, Nullifier, Sectionalist.* Indianapolis. 1951.

WINSTON, ROBERT WATSON. *Vance and Aycock.* Pamphlet of address of acceptance of joint tablet memorializing Zebulon B. Vance and Charles B. Aycock. Chapel Hill. 1941.

YATES, RICHARD E. *The Confederacy and Zeb Vance.* Tuscaloosa. 1958.

# INDEX